Advances in Boundary Value Problems for Fractional Differential Equations

Editor

Rodica Luca

MDPI • Basel • Beijing • Wuhan • Barcelona • Belgrade • Manchester • Tokyo • Cluj • Tianjin

Editor
Rodica Luca
Department of Mathematics
"Gheorghe Asachi" Technical
University of Iasi
Iasi
Romania

Editorial Office
MDPI
St. Alban-Anlage 66
4052 Basel, Switzerland

This is a reprint of articles from the Special Issue published online in the open access journal *Fractal and Fractional* (ISSN 2504-3110) (available at: www.mdpi.com/journal/fractalfract/special_issues/BVP_FDE).

For citation purposes, cite each article independently as indicated on the article page online and as indicated below:

LastName, A.A.; LastName, B.B.; LastName, C.C. Article Title. *Journal Name* **Year**, *Volume Number*, Page Range.

ISBN 978-3-0365-7799-9 (Hbk)
ISBN 978-3-0365-7798-2 (PDF)

Contents

About the Editor vii

Rodica Luca
Advances in Boundary Value Problems for Fractional Differential Equations
Reprinted from: *Fractal Fract.* **2023**, *7*, 406, doi:10.3390/fractalfract7050406 1

Vladimir E. Fedorov, Marina V. Plekhanova and Elizaveta M. Izhberdeeva
Analytic Resolving Families forEquations with the Dzhrbashyan–Nersesyan Fractional Derivative
Reprinted from: *Fractal Fract.* **2022**, *6*, 541, doi:10.3390/fractalfract6100541 9

Ymnah Alruwaily, Bashir Ahmad, Sotiris K. Ntouyas and Ahmed S. M. Alzaidi
Existence Results for Coupled Nonlinear Sequential Fractional Differential Equations with Coupled Riemann–Stieltjes Integro-Multipoint Boundary Conditions
Reprinted from: *Fractal Fract.* **2022**, *6*, 123, doi:10.3390/fractalfract6020123 25

Shahram Rezapour, Mohammed Said Souid, Sina Etemad, Zoubida Bouazza, Sotiris K. Ntouyas and Suphawat Asawasamrit et al.
Mawhin's Continuation Technique for a Nonlinear BVP of Variable Order at Resonance via Piecewise Constant Functions
Reprinted from: *Fractal Fract.* **2021**, *5*, 216, doi:10.3390/fractalfract5040216 41

Yizhe Feng and Zhanbing Bai
Solvability of Some Nonlocal Fractional Boundary Value Problems at Resonance in R^n
Reprinted from: *Fractal Fract.* **2022**, *6*, 25, doi:10.3390/fractalfract6010025 55

Jun-Sheng Duan, Li-Xia Jing and Ming Li
The Mixed Boundary Value Problems and Chebyshev Collocation Method for Caputo-Type Fractional Ordinary Differential Equations
Reprinted from: *Fractal Fract.* **2022**, *6*, 148, doi:10.3390/fractalfract6030148 71

Alexandru Tudorache and Rodica Luca
Positive Solutions of a Singular Fractional Boundary Value Problem with r-Laplacian Operators
Reprinted from: *Fractal Fract.* **2021**, *6*, 18, doi:10.3390/fractalfract6010018 83

Alexandru Tudorache and Rodica Luca
Systems of Riemann–Liouville Fractional Differential Equations with ρ-Laplacian Operators and Nonlocal Coupled Boundary Conditions
Reprinted from: *Fractal Fract.* **2022**, *6*, 610, doi:10.3390/fractalfract6100610 103

Johnny Henderson, Rodica Luca and Alexandru Tudorache
On a System of Riemann–Liouville Fractional Boundary Value Problems with ϱ-Laplacian Operators and Positive Parameters
Reprinted from: *Fractal Fract.* **2022**, *6*, 299, doi:10.3390/fractalfract6060299 123

Dongping Li, Yankai Li and Fangqi Chen
Study on Infinitely Many Solutions for a Class of Fredholm Fractional Integro-Differential System
Reprinted from: *Fractal Fract.* **2022**, *6*, 467, doi:10.3390/fractalfract6090467 139

Yue Liang
Existence and Approximate Controllability of Mild Solutions for Fractional Evolution Systems of Sobolev-Type
Reprinted from: *Fractal Fract.* **2022**, *6*, 56, doi:10.3390/fractalfract6020056 151

About the Editor

Rodica Luca

Rodica Luca is a Full Professor of Mathematics at the "Gheorghe Asachi" Technical University of Iasi, Romania. She received her PhD in Mathematics from the "Alexandru Ioan Cuza" University of Iasi in 1996 and her Habilitation Certificate in Mathematics from the School of Advanced Studies of the Romanian Academy in Bucharest in 2017. She has published five monographs and more than 180 papers. Her research interests are boundary value problems for nonlinear ordinary differential equations, finite difference equations, fractional differential equations and systems, and initial-boundary value problems for nonlinear hyperbolic systems.

fractal and fractional

MDPI

Editorial

Advances in Boundary Value Problems for Fractional Differential Equations

Rodica Luca

Department of Mathematics, Gh. Asachi Technical University, 700506 Iasi, Romania; rluca@math.tuiasi.ro

Citation: Luca, R. Advances in Boundary Value Problems for Fractional Differential Equations. *Fractal Fract.* **2023**, *7*, 406. https://doi.org/10.3390/fractalfract7050406

Received: 14 May 2023
Accepted: 15 May 2023
Published: 17 May 2023

Fractional-order differential and integral operators and fractional differential equations have extensive applications in the mathematical modelling of real-world phenomena which occur in scientific and engineering disciplines such as physics, chemistry, biophysics, biology, medical sciences, financial economics, ecology, bioengineering, control theory, signal and image processing, aerodynamics, transport dynamics, thermodynamics, viscoelasticity, hydrology, statistical mechanics, electromagnetics, astrophysics, cosmology, and rheology. Fractional differential equations are also regarded as a better tool for the description of hereditary properties of various materials and processes than the corresponding integer-order differential equations. The Special Issue "Advances in Boundary Value Problems for Fractional Differential Equations" covers aspects of the recent developments in the theory and applications of fractional differential equations, inclusions, inequalities, and systems of fractional differential equations with Riemann–Liouville derivatives, Caputo derivatives, or other generalized fractional derivatives subject to various boundary conditions. In the papers published in this Special Issue, the authors study the existence, uniqueness, multiplicity, and nonexistence of classical or mild solutions, the approximation of solutions, and the approximate controllability of mild solutions for diverse models. I will present these papers in the following, grouped according to their subject.

1. Equations and Systems of Equations with Sequential Fractional Derivatives

In paper [1], the authors investigate the differential equation

$$D^{\sigma_n}z(t) = \mathcal{A}z(t) + f(t), \ \ t \in (0,T], \tag{1}$$

with the initial conditions

$$D^{\sigma_k}z(0) = z_k, \ \ k = 0,1,\ldots,n-1, \tag{2}$$

where the operator $\mathcal{A} : D_{\mathcal{A}} \subset \mathcal{Z} \to \mathcal{Z}$ is linear and closed with its domain $D_{\mathcal{A}}$ (a dense set), $\mathcal{Z}$ is a Banach space, $f : [0,T] \to \mathcal{Z}$ is a given function, and D^{σ_k}, $k = 0,1,\ldots,n$ are the Dzhrbashyan–Nersesyan fractional derivatives. For the set of numbers $\{\alpha_k\}_0^n$, with $\alpha_k \in (0,1]$, $k = 0,1,\ldots,n$, they introduced the numbers $\sigma_k = \sum_{j=0}^{k} \alpha_j - 1$, $k = 0,1,\ldots,n$, with the condition $\sigma_n > 0$. The fractional derivatives D^{σ_k}, $k = 0,1,\ldots,n$ are given by $D^{\sigma_0}z(t) = D_t^{\alpha_0 - 1}z(t)$, $D^{\sigma_k}z(t) = D_t^{\alpha_k - 1}D_t^{\alpha_{k-1}}D_t^{\alpha_{k-2}}\ldots D_t^{\alpha_0}z(t)$, for $k = 1,2,\ldots,n$, where D_t^{β} is the Riemann–Liouville integral for $\beta \le 0$ and the Riemann–Liouville derivative for $\beta > 0$. The Dzhrbashyan–Nersesyan fractional derivative D^{σ_n} is a generalization of the Riemann–Liouville and Caputo fractional derivatives. The authors prove firstly the existence and uniqueness of the k-resolving families of operators (for $k = 0,\ldots,n-1$) for the homogeneous equation $D^{\sigma_n}z(t) = \mathcal{A}z(t)$, and then they give a criterion for the existence and uniqueness of analytic k-resolving families, namely $\mathcal{A}$ belongs to a class of operators denoted by $\mathcal{A}_{\{\alpha_k\}}(\theta_0, a_0)$. Different properties of the resolving families are also studied, and a perturbation theorem for operators from $\mathcal{A}_{\{\alpha_k\}}(\theta_0, a_0)$ is presented. Then, the authors prove the existence and uniqueness of a solution for problem (1),(2), where f is continuous in the graph norm of $\mathcal{A}$ or it is a Hölderian function. As an application, they show the existence of a unique solution for an initial boundary value problem to a fractional linearized model of viscoelastic Oldroyd fluid dynamics.

Paper [2] deals with a nonlinear coupled system of sequential fractional differential equations

$$\begin{cases} ({}^cD^{q+1} + {}^cD^q)\mathrm{x}(t) = \mathrm{f}(t,\mathrm{x}(t),\mathrm{y}(t)), \ t \in [0,1], \\ ({}^cD^{p+1} + {}^cD^p)\mathrm{y}(t) = \mathrm{g}(t,\mathrm{x}(t),\mathrm{y}(t)), \ t \in [0,1], \end{cases} \tag{3}$$

supplemented with the coupled multipoint and Riemann–Stieltjes integral boundary conditions

$$\begin{cases} \mathrm{x}(0) = 0, \ \mathrm{x}'(0) = 0, \ \mathrm{x}'(1) = 0, \\ \mathrm{x}(1) = k\int_0^\rho \mathrm{y}(s)\,d\mathcal{A}(s) + \sum_{i=1}^{n-2} \alpha_i \mathrm{y}(\sigma_i) + k_1 \int_\nu^1 \mathrm{y}(s)\,d\mathcal{A}(s), \\ \mathrm{y}(0) = 0, \ \mathrm{y}'(0) = 0, \ \mathrm{y}'(1) = 0, \\ \mathrm{y}(1) = h\int_0^\rho \mathrm{x}(s)\,d\mathcal{A}(s) + \sum_{i=1}^{n-2} \beta_i \mathrm{x}(\sigma_i) + h_1 \int_\nu^1 \mathrm{x}(s)\,d\mathcal{A}(s), \end{cases} \tag{4}$$

where $p, q \in (2,3]$, ${}^cD^\kappa$ denotes the Caputo fractional derivative of order $\kappa \in \{q,p\}$, $0 < \rho < \sigma_i < \nu < 1$, $\mathrm{f}, \mathrm{g} : [0,1] \times \mathbb{R} \times \mathbb{R} \to \mathbb{R}$ are continuous functions, $k, h, k_1, h_1, \alpha_i, \beta_i \in \mathbb{R}$, for $i = 1, 2, \ldots, n-2$, and $\mathcal{A}$ is a function of bounded variation. The word sequential is used in the sense that the operator ${}^cD^{q+1} + {}^cD^q$ can be written as the composition of operators ${}^cD^q$ and $D + I$, where D is the usual differential operator and I is the identity operator. Under some assumptions of the data of the problem, the authors prove the existence and uniqueness of solutions for problem (3),(4) by applying the Leray–Schauder alternative and the Banach contraction mapping principle.

2. Resonance Problems for Caputo Fractional Differential Equations

Paper [3] is concerned with the nonlinear boundary value problem for a fractional differential equation of variable order at resonance

$$\begin{cases} {}^cD_{0+}^{\mathrm{u}(t)}\mathrm{x}(t) = \mathrm{g}(t,\mathrm{x}(t)), \ t \in [0,T], \\ \mathrm{x}(0) = \mathrm{x}(T), \end{cases} \tag{5}$$

where ${}^cD_{0+}^{\mathrm{u}(t)}$ is the Caputo derivative of variable order $\mathrm{u}(t)$ with $\mathrm{u} : [0,T] \to (0,1]$ and $\mathrm{g} : [0,T] \times \mathbb{R} \to \mathbb{R}$ is a continuous function. This problem is at resonance, that is, the corresponding linear homogeneous boundary value problem has non-trivial solutions. The authors transform firstly problem (5) to an equivalent standard boundary value problem at resonance with a fractional derivative of constant order by using some generalized intervals and piece-wise constant functions. Then, by applying Mawhin's continuation theorem, they demonstrate the existence of at least one solution to (5).

In paper [4], the authors study the fractional differential equation in space $\mathbb{R}^n$

$${}^cD_{0+}^\alpha \mathrm{u}(t) = \mathrm{f}(t, \mathrm{u}(t), {}^cD_{0+}^{\alpha-1}\mathrm{u}), \ t \in (0,1), \tag{6}$$

subject to the boundary conditions

$$\mathrm{u}(0) = \mathcal{B}\mathrm{u}(\xi), \ \mathrm{u}(1) = \mathcal{C}\mathrm{u}(\eta), \tag{7}$$

where ${}^cD_{0+}^k$ denotes the Caputo fractional derivative of order $k \in \{\alpha, \alpha-1\}$, $\xi, \eta \in (0,1)$, $\alpha \in (1,2]$, $\mathrm{f} : [0,1] \times \mathbb{R}^{2n} \to \mathbb{R}^n$ satisfies Carathéodory conditions, and $\mathcal{B}, \mathcal{C}$ are n-order nonzero square matrices. They prove the existence of solutions of problem (6),(7) by using Mawhin coincidence degree theory.

3. Approximations of Solutions for Caputo Fractional Differential Equations

Paper [5] is devoted to the Caputo fractional differential equation with variable coefficients

$$D_x^{\lambda}\mathrm{u}(x) + c_1(x)\mathrm{u}'(x) + c_0(x)\mathrm{u}(x) = \mathrm{g}(x), \;\; 0 < x < 1, \tag{8}$$

with the boundary conditions

$$p_0\mathrm{u}(0) - q_0\mathrm{u}'(0) = b_0, \;\; p_1\mathrm{u}(1) + q_1\mathrm{u}'(1) = b_1, \tag{9}$$

where $\lambda \in (1,2]$, D_x^{λ} is the Caputo fractional derivative of order λ, c_1, c_0, and g are continuous functions, $p_0, p_1, q_0, q_1 \geq 0$, and $p_0p_1 + p_0q_1 + q_0p_1 \neq 0$. By using the shifted Chebyshev polynomials of the first kind and the collocation method, the authors present approximate solutions to problem (8),(9).

4. Systems of Fractional Differential Equations with p-Laplacian Operators

In paper [6], the authors investigate the system of fractional differential equations with r_1-Laplacian and r_2-Laplacian operators

$$\begin{cases} D_{0+}^{\gamma_1}\left(\varphi_{r_1}\left(D_{0+}^{\delta_1}\mathrm{u}(t)\right)\right) = \mathrm{f}(t,\mathrm{u}(t),\mathrm{v}(t),I_{0+}^{\sigma_1}\mathrm{u}(t),I_{0+}^{\sigma_2}\mathrm{v}(t)), \;\; t \in (0,1), \\ D_{0+}^{\gamma_2}\left(\varphi_{r_2}\left(D_{0+}^{\delta_2}\mathrm{v}(t)\right)\right) = \mathrm{g}(t,\mathrm{u}(t),\mathrm{v}(t),I_{0+}^{\varsigma_1}\mathrm{u}(t),I_{0+}^{\varsigma_2}\mathrm{v}(t)), \;\; t \in (0,1), \end{cases} \tag{10}$$

supplemented with the uncoupled nonlocal boundary conditions

$$\begin{cases} \mathrm{u}^{(i)}(0) = 0, \; i = 0,\ldots,p-2, \;\; D_{0+}^{\delta_1}\mathrm{u}(0) = 0, \\ \varphi_{r_1}(D_{0+}^{\delta_1}\mathrm{u}(1)) = \int_0^1 \varphi_{r_1}(D_{0+}^{\delta_1}\mathrm{u}(\tau))\,d\mathcal{H}_0(\tau), \;\; D_{0+}^{\alpha_0}\mathrm{u}(1) = \sum_{k=1}^{n}\int_0^1 D_{0+}^{\alpha_k}\mathrm{u}(\tau)\,d\mathcal{H}_k(\tau), \\ \mathrm{v}^{(j)}(0) = 0, \; j = 0,\ldots,q-2, \;\; D_{0+}^{\delta_2}\mathrm{v}(0) = 0, \\ \varphi_{r_2}(D_{0+}^{\delta_2}\mathrm{v}(1)) = \int_0^1 \varphi_{r_2}(D_{0+}^{\delta_2}\mathrm{v}(\tau))\,d\mathcal{K}_0(\tau), \;\; D_{0+}^{\beta_0}\mathrm{v}(1) = \sum_{k=1}^{m}\int_0^1 D_{0+}^{\beta_k}\mathrm{v}(\tau)\,d\mathcal{K}_k(\tau), \end{cases} \tag{11}$$

where $\gamma_1, \gamma_2 \in (1,2]$, $p,q \in \mathbb{N}$, $p,q \geq 3$, $\delta_1 \in (p-1,p]$, $\delta_2 \in (q-1,q]$, $n,m \in \mathbb{N}$, $\sigma_1, \varsigma_1, \sigma_2, \varsigma_2 > 0$, $\alpha_i \in \mathbb{R}$, $i = 0,\ldots,n$, $0 \leq \alpha_1 < \alpha_2 < \ldots < \alpha_n \leq \alpha_0 < \delta_1 - 1$, $\alpha_0 \geq 1$, $\beta_j \in \mathbb{R}$, $j = 0,\ldots,m$, $0 \leq \beta_1 < \beta_2 < \ldots < \beta_m \leq \beta_0 < \delta_2 - 1$, $\beta_0 \geq 1$, $\varphi_{r_k}(\tau) = |\tau|^{r_k-2}\tau$, $r_k > 1$, $k = 1,2$, the functions $\mathrm{f},\mathrm{g} : (0,1) \times \mathbb{R}_+^4 \to \mathbb{R}_+$ are continuous, singular at $t = 0$ and/or $t = 1$, ($\mathbb{R}_+ = [0,\infty)$), $I_{0+}^{\varkappa}$ is the Riemann–Liouville fractional integral of order $\varkappa$ (for $\varkappa = \sigma_1, \varsigma_1, \sigma_2, \varsigma_2$), $D_{0+}^{\varkappa}$ is the Riemann–Liouville fractional derivative of order $\varkappa$ (for $\varkappa = \gamma_1, \gamma_2, \delta_1, \delta_2, \alpha_0, \ldots, \alpha_n, \beta_0, \ldots, \beta_m$), and the integrals from the boundary conditions (11) are Riemann–Stieltjes integrals with $\mathcal{H}_i : [0,1] \to \mathbb{R}$, $i = 0,\ldots,n$ and $\mathcal{K}_j : [0,1] \to \mathbb{R}$, $j = 0,\ldots,m$ functions of bounded variation. By using the Guo–Krasnoselskii fixed point theorem of cone expansion and norm-type compression, they prove the existence and multiplicity of positive solutions for problem (10),(11).

Paper [7] is focused on the system of fractional differential equations (10) subject to the nonlocal coupled boundary conditions

$$\begin{cases} \mathrm{u}^{(i)}(0) = 0, \; i = 0,\ldots,p-2, \;\; D_{0+}^{\delta_1}\mathrm{u}(0) = 0, \\ \varphi_{r_1}(D_{0+}^{\delta_1}\mathrm{u}(1)) = \int_0^1 \varphi_{r_1}(D_{0+}^{\delta_1}\mathrm{u}(\tau))\,d\mathcal{H}_0(\tau), \;\; D_{0+}^{\alpha_0}\mathrm{u}(1) = \sum_{i=1}^{n}\int_0^1 D_{0+}^{\alpha_i}\mathrm{v}(\tau)\,d\mathcal{H}_i(\tau), \\ \mathrm{v}^{(j)}(0) = 0, \; j = 0,\ldots,q-2, \;\; D_{0+}^{\delta_2}\mathrm{v}(0) = 0, \\ \varphi_{r_2}(D_{0+}^{\delta_2}\mathrm{v}(1)) = \int_0^1 \varphi_{r_2}(D_{0+}^{\delta_2}\mathrm{v}(\tau))\,d\mathcal{K}_0(\tau), \;\; D_{0+}^{\beta_0}\mathrm{v}(1) = \sum_{j=1}^{m}\int_0^1 D_{0+}^{\beta_j}\mathrm{u}(\tau)\,d\mathcal{K}_j(\tau), \end{cases} \tag{12}$$

where $\alpha_i \in \mathbb{R}$, $i = 0,\ldots,n$, $0 \leq \alpha_1 < \alpha_2 < \ldots < \alpha_n \leq \beta_0 < \delta_2 - 1$, $\beta_0 \geq 1$, $\beta_j \in \mathbb{R}$, $j = 0,\ldots,m$, $0 \leq \beta_1 < \beta_2 < \ldots < \beta_m \leq \alpha_0 < \delta_1 - 1$, $\alpha_0 \geq 1$. The authors present existence and multiplicity results for the positive solutions of problem (10),(12) by applying the Guo–Krasnoselskii fixed point theorem.

Paper [8] deals with a system of fractional differential equations with ϱ_1-Laplacian and ϱ_2-Laplacian operators

$$\begin{cases} D_{0+}^{\gamma_1}(\varphi_{\varrho_1}(D_{0+}^{\delta_1}u(t))) + a(t)f(v(t)) = 0, \ t \in (0,1), \\ D_{0+}^{\gamma_2}(\varphi_{\varrho_2}(D_{0+}^{\delta_2}v(t))) + b(t)g(u(t)) = 0, \ t \in (0,1), \end{cases} \tag{13}$$

with the coupled nonlocal boundary conditions

$$\begin{cases} u^{(i)}(0) = 0, \ i = 0,\ldots,p-2; \ D_{0+}^{\delta_1}u(0) = 0, \ D_{0+}^{\alpha_0}u(1) = \sum_{i=1}^{n}\int_0^1 D_{0+}^{\alpha_i}v(\tau)\, d\mathcal{H}_i(\tau) + c_0, \\ v^{(j)}(0) = 0, \ j = 0,\ldots,q-2; \ D_{0+}^{\delta_2}v(0) = 0, \ D_{0+}^{\beta_0}v(1) = \sum_{j=1}^{m}\int_0^1 D_{0+}^{\beta_j}u(\tau)\, d\mathcal{K}_j(\tau) + d_0, \end{cases} \tag{14}$$

where $\gamma_1, \gamma_2 \in (0,1]$, $p, q \in \mathbb{N}$, $p, q \geq 3$, $\delta_1 \in (p-1,p]$, $\delta_2 \in (q-1,q]$, $n, m \in \mathbb{N}$, $\alpha_i \in \mathbb{R}$ for all $i = 0,1,\ldots,n$, $0 \leq \alpha_1 < \alpha_2 < \ldots < \alpha_n \leq \beta_0 < \delta_2 - 1$, $\beta_0 \geq 1$, $\beta_j \in \mathbb{R}$ for all $j = 0,1,\ldots,m$, $0 \leq \beta_1 < \beta_2 < \ldots < \beta_m \leq \alpha_0 < \delta_1 - 1$, $\alpha_0 \geq 1$, the functions $f, g : \mathbb{R}_+ \to \mathbb{R}_+$ and $a, b : [0,1] \to \mathbb{R}_+$ are continuous, c_0 and d_0 are positive parameters, $\varrho_1, \varrho_2 > 1$, $\varphi_{\varrho_i}(\zeta) = |\zeta|^{\varrho_i - 2}\zeta$, $i = 1,2$, the functions $\mathcal{H}_j$, $j = 1,\ldots,n$ and $\mathcal{K}_i$, $i = 1,\ldots,m$ have bounded variation, and D_{0+}^{κ} denotes the Riemann–Liouville derivative of order κ (for $\kappa = \gamma_1, \gamma_2, \delta_1, \delta_2, \alpha_i$ for $i = 0,1,\ldots,n$, β_j for $j = 0,1,\ldots,m$). The authors give sufficient conditions for the functions f and g, and intervals for the parameters c_0 and d_0 such that problem (13),(14) have at least one positive solution or they have no positive solutions. They apply the Schauder fixed point theorem in the proof of the main existence result.

In paper [9], the authors study a system of nonlinear Fredholm fractional integro-differential equations with p-Laplacian operator

$$\begin{cases} {}_tD_T^{\gamma_j}(\mathrm{k}_j(t)\phi_p({}_0^cD_t^{\gamma_j}\mathrm{z}_j(t))) + \mathrm{l}_j(t)\phi_p(\mathrm{z}_j(t)) \\ \quad = \lambda \mathrm{f}_{\mathrm{z}_j}(t, \mathrm{z}_1(t),\ldots,\mathrm{z}_m(t)) + \int_0^T \mathrm{g}_j(t,s)\phi_p(\mathrm{z}_j(s))\, ds, \ t \in [0,T], \ j = 1,2,\ldots,m, \\ \mathrm{z}_j(t) = \int_0^T \mathrm{g}_j(t,s)\phi_p(\mathrm{z}_j(s))\, ds, \ t \in [0,T], \ j = 1,2,\ldots,m, \end{cases} \tag{15}$$

supplemented with the Sturm–Liouville boundary conditions

$$\begin{cases} c_j\mathrm{k}_j(0)\phi_p(\mathrm{z}_j(0)) - c_j' \, {}_tD_T^{\gamma_j - 1}(\mathrm{k}_j(0)\phi_p({}_0^cD_t^{\gamma_j}\mathrm{z}_j(0))) = 0, \ j = 1,2,\ldots,m, \\ d_j\mathrm{k}_j(T)\phi_p(\mathrm{z}_j(T)) + d_j' \, {}_tD_T^{\gamma_j - 1}(\mathrm{k}_j(T)\phi_p({}_0^cD_t^{\gamma_j}\mathrm{z}_j(T))) = 0, \ j = 1,2,\ldots,m, \end{cases} \tag{16}$$

where λ is a positive parameter, $\mathrm{k}_i, \mathrm{l}_i \in L^\infty[0,T]$ with $\operatorname{ess\,inf}_{[0,T]}\mathrm{k}_i(t) > 0$ and $\operatorname{ess\,inf}_{[0,T]}\mathrm{l}_i(t) \geq 0$, c_i, d_i, c_i', d_i', $i = 1,2,\ldots,m$, are positive constants, $p \in (1,\infty)$, $\phi_p(s) = |s|^{p-2}s$, $(s \neq 0)$, $\phi_p(0) = 0$, the functions $\mathrm{f} : [0,T] \times \mathbb{R}^m \to \mathbb{R}$ and $\mathrm{g}_i : [0,T] \times [0,T] \to \mathbb{R}$, $i = 1,\ldots,m$ satisfy some conditions, and ${}_0^cD_t^{\gamma_j}$ and ${}_tD_T^{\gamma_j}$ denote the left Caputo fractional derivative and the right Riemann–Liouville fractional derivative of order γ_j, respectively. By using the critical point theory, they prove the existence of infinitely many solutions of problem (15),(16).

5. Approximate Controllability for Fractional Differential Equations in Banach Spaces

Paper [10] is concerned with the fractional evolution equation of Sobolev type in the Hilbert space X, with a control and a nonlocal condition

$$\begin{cases} {}^LD_t^{\alpha}(\mathcal{E}\mathrm{x}(t)) = \mathcal{A}\mathrm{x}(t) + \mathrm{f}(t,\mathrm{x}(t)) + \mathcal{B}\mathrm{u}(t), \ t \in (0,b], \\ I_t^{1-\alpha}(\mathcal{E}\mathrm{x}(t))|_{t=0} + \mathrm{g}(\mathrm{x}) = x_0, \end{cases} \tag{17}$$

where $\alpha \in (0,1)$, $\mathcal{A} : D(\mathcal{A}) \subset X \to X$ and $\mathcal{E} : D(\mathcal{E}) \subset X \to X$ are linear operators, $\mathcal{B} : U \to X$ is a linear bounded operator, U is another Hilbert space, the control function $\mathrm{u} \in L^p([0,b], U)$ for $p\alpha > 1$, $x_0 \in X$, the functions f and g satisfy some assumptions, $I_t^{1-\alpha}$ is the Riemann–Liouville fractional integral operator of order $1-\alpha$, and ${}^L D_t^\alpha$ denotes the Riemann–Liouville fractional derivative of order α. By using the Schauder fixed point theorem and operator semigroup theory, the authors prove firstly the existence of mild solutions for problem (17) without the compactness of the operator semigroup. Then, they show that if the corresponding linear problem is approximately controllable on $[0,b]$, then problem (17) is also approximately controllable on $[0,b]$. An example with an initial boundary value problem for a partial differential equation with Riemann–Liouville fractional derivatives is finally presented.

Paper [11] is devoted to the fractional differential evolution equation in the Banach space X with a finite delay and a control

$$ {}^{c}\mathcal{D}^{\beta}\mathrm{x}(t) = \mathcal{A}\mathrm{x}(t) + \mathrm{f}(t,\mathrm{x}_t) + \mathcal{B}\mathrm{u}(t), \quad t \in [0,a], \tag{18} $$

subject to the initial date

$$ \mathrm{x}(t) = \phi(t), \quad t \in [-b,0], \tag{19} $$

or to the nonlocal condition with a parameter

$$ \mathrm{x}(t) + \lambda \mathrm{g}_t(\mathrm{x}) = \phi(t), \quad t \in [-b,0], \tag{20} $$

where $\mathcal{A} : \mathcal{D} \subset X \to X$ is a closed linear unbounded operator on X, where its domain $\mathcal{D}$ is a dense set; u is the control function; $\mathcal{B} : L^2([0,a];U) \to L^2([0,a];\mathcal{D})$ is a linear bounded operator, where U is another Banach space; $\phi \in L^1([-b,0];X)$, x_t denotes the history of the state function defined by $\mathrm{x}_t(\theta) = \{\mathrm{x}(t+\theta)$, if $t+\theta \geq 0$; $\phi(t+\theta)$, if $t+\theta \leq 0\}$ for $\theta \in [-b,0]$; λ is a parameter; $\mathrm{g}_t : C([-b,a];X) \to X$ is a given function satisfying some assumptions; and ${}^{c}\mathcal{D}^{\beta}$ is the Caputo fractional derivative of order β, with $\beta \in (1/2, 1]$. Under the assumption that $\mathcal{A}$ is the infinitesimal generator of a differentiable resolvent operator, the authors prove the existence and uniqueness of mild solutions for problems (18),(19) and (18),(20) by utilizing the Banach contraction mapping principle. Then, based on the iterative method, they give sufficient conditions for the approximate controllability of (18),(19) and (18),(20). As an application, an example of a Caputo fractional partial differential equation with delay in the space $X = L^2([0,\pi])$ is finally addressed.

6. Fractional Differential Inclusions and Inequalities

In paper [12], the authors investigate the neutral impulsive semi-linear fractional differential inclusion with delay and initial date

$$ \begin{cases} {}^{c}\mathcal{D}^{\alpha}_{0,t}[\mathrm{x}(t) - \mathrm{h}(t,\varkappa(t)\mathrm{x})] \in \mathcal{A}\mathrm{x}(t) + \mathcal{F}(t,\varkappa(t)\mathrm{x}), & \text{a.e. } t \in [0,b] \setminus \{t_1,\ldots,t_m\}, \\ I_i\mathrm{x}(t_i^-) = \mathrm{x}(t_i^-) - \mathrm{x}(t_i^+), \quad i = 1,\ldots,m, \\ \mathrm{x}(t) = \psi(t), \quad t \in [-r,0], \end{cases} \tag{21} $$

where $\alpha \in (0,1)$, $0 = t_0 < t_1 < \ldots < t_m < t_{m+1} = b$, $r > 0$, the operator $\mathcal{A}$ is the infinitesimal generator of the non-compact semigroup $\mathcal{T} = \{Y(t),\ t \geq 0\}$ on the Banach space E, and $\mathcal{F} : [0,b] \times \Theta \to 2^E \setminus \{\phi\}$ is a multifunction. Here, $\mathrm{h} : [0,b] \times \Theta \to E$, $I_i : E \to E$, $i = 1,\ldots,m$, $\psi \in \Theta$, and for every $t \in [0,b]$, the function $\varkappa(t) : \mathcal{H} \to \Theta$ is defined by $(\varkappa(t)\mathrm{x})(\theta) = \mathrm{x}(t+\theta)$ for $\theta \in [-r,0]$. ${}^{c}\mathcal{D}^{\alpha}_{0,t}$ denotes the Caputo fractional derivative of order α and the spaces Θ and $\mathcal{H}$ are defined in the paper. They show that the set of mild solutions to problem (21) is nonempty, compact, and an R_δ-set in a complete metric space H.

Paper [13] is focused on the Hilfer fractional neutral integro-differential inclusion with initial date

$$\begin{cases} D_{0+}^{k,\epsilon}[y(t) - \mathcal{N}(t, y(t))] \in \mathcal{A}y(t) + \mathcal{G}\left(t, y(t), \int_0^t e(t,s,y(s))\, ds\right), \ t \in (0,d], \\ I_{0+}^{(1-k)(1-\epsilon)} y(0) = y_0, \end{cases} \tag{22}$$

where $D_{0+}^{k,\epsilon}$ denotes the Hilfer fractional derivative of order k and type ϵ, with $k \in (0,1)$ and $\epsilon \in [0,1]$, $I_{0+}^{(1-k)(1-\epsilon)}$ is the Riemann–Liouville fractional integral of order $(1-k)(1-\epsilon)$, and $\mathcal{A}$ is an almost sectorial operator of the analytic semigroup $\{\mathcal{T}(t),\ t \geq 0\}$ on the Banach space Y. Here, $\mathcal{G} : [0,d] \times Y \times Y \to 2^Y \setminus \{\phi\}$ is a nonempty, bounded, closed, convex multivalued map and $\mathcal{N} : [0,d] \times Y \to Y$ and $e : [0,d] \times [0,d] \times Y \to Y$ are appropriate functions. By using the Martelli fixed point theorem, the authors prove the existence of mild solutions to problem (22).

In paper [14], the authors study the damped wave inequality

$$\frac{\partial^2 u}{\partial t^2} - \frac{\partial^2 u}{\partial x^2} + \frac{\partial u}{\partial t} \geq x^{\sigma}|u|^p, \ t > 0, \ x \in (0,L), \tag{23}$$

subject to initial boundary conditions

$$\begin{cases} (u(t,0), u(t,L)) = (f(t), g(t)), \ t > 0, \\ \left(u(0,x), \frac{\partial u}{\partial t}(0,x)\right) = (u_0(x), u_1(x)), \ x \in (0,L), \end{cases} \tag{24}$$

where $L > 0$, $\sigma \in \mathbb{R}$, $p > 1$, $f \in L^1_{loc}([0,\infty))$, $g(t) = C_g t^{\gamma}$ with $C_g \geq 0$ and $\gamma > -1$, and u_0, $u_1 \in L^1([0,L])$. They also investigate the time-fractional damped wave inequality

$$\frac{\partial^{\alpha} u}{\partial t^{\alpha}} - \frac{\partial^2 u}{\partial x^2} + \frac{\partial^{\beta} u}{\partial t^{\beta}} \geq x^{\sigma}|u|^p, \ t > 0, \ x \in (0,L), \tag{25}$$

supplemented with the initial boundary conditions in (24), where $\alpha \in (1,2)$, $\beta \in (0,1)$, and $\frac{\partial^{\kappa}}{\partial t^{\kappa}}$ is the time Caputo fractional derivative of order κ, for $\kappa \in \{\alpha, \beta\}$. By using the test function method, the authors give sufficient conditions depending on the above data under which problems (23),(24) and (23),(25) admit no global weak solutions.

7. Fractional q-Difference Equations and Systems

Paper [15] deals with the fractional q-difference equation in a Banach space E, with nonlinear integral conditions

$$\begin{cases} ({}^cD_q^{\alpha} y)(t) = f(t, y(t)), \ \text{a.e. } t \in [0,T], \\ y(0) - y'(0) = \int_0^T g(s, y(s))\, ds, \\ y(T) + y'(T) = \int_0^T h(s, y(s))\, ds, \end{cases} \tag{26}$$

where $T > 0$, $q \in (0,1)$, ${}^cD_q^{\alpha}$ denotes the Caputo fractional q-derivative of order α, with $\alpha \in (1,2]$, and $f, g, h : [0,T] \times E \to E$ are given functions satisfying some assumptions. By using the measures of noncompactness technique and the Mönch fixed point theorem, the authors prove the existence of solutions to problem (26).

Paper [16] is concerned with the system of nonlinear fractional q-difference equations

$$\begin{cases} (D_q^{\alpha} u)(t) + P(t, u(t), v(t), I_q^{\omega_1} u(t), I_q^{\delta_1} v(t)) = 0, \ t \in (0,1), \\ (D_q^{\beta} v)(t) + Q(t, u(t), v(t), I_q^{\omega_2} u(t), I_q^{\delta_2} v(t)) = 0, \ t \in (0,1), \end{cases} \tag{27}$$

subject to the coupled nonlocal boundary conditions

$$\begin{cases} u(0) = D_q u(0) = \ldots = D_q^{n-2} u(0) = 0, \ D_q^{\zeta_0} u(1) = \int_0^1 D_q^{\zeta} v(t)\, d_q \mathcal{H}(t), \\ v(0) = D_q v(0) = \ldots = D_q^{m-2} v(0) = 0, \ D_q^{\xi_0} v(1) = \int_0^1 D_q^{\xi} u(t)\, d_q \mathcal{K}(t), \end{cases} \tag{28}$$

where $q \in (0,1)$, $\alpha, \beta \in \mathbb{R}$, $\alpha \in (n-1, n]$, $\beta \in (m-1, m]$, $n, m \in \mathbb{N}$, $n, m \geq 2$, $\omega_1, \delta_1, \omega_2, \delta_2 > 0$, $\zeta \in [0, \beta - 1)$, $\xi \in [0, \alpha - 1)$, $\zeta_0 \in [0, \alpha - 1)$, $\xi_0 \in [0, \beta - 1)$. Here, D_q^{κ} denotes the Riemann–Liouville q-derivative of order κ for $\kappa \in \{\alpha, \beta, \zeta_0, \zeta, \xi_0, \xi\}$, I_q^k is the Riemann–Liouville q-integral of order k for $k \in \{\omega_1, \delta_1, \omega_2, \delta_2\}$, P and Q are nonlinear functions, and the integrals from conditions (28) are Riemann–Stieltjes integrals with $\mathcal{H}$, $\mathcal{K}$ functions of bounded variation. By applying varied fixed point theorems, the authors obtain existence and uniqueness results for the solutions of problem (27),(28).

Finally, I would like to thank all the authors for submitting papers to this Special Issue, and hope that their results will be useful to other researchers working in the field of fractional differential equations.

Funding: This research received no external funding.

Conflicts of Interest: The author declares no conflict of interest.

References

1. Fedorov, V.E.; Plehanova, M.V.; Izhberdeeva, E.M. Analytic resolving families for equations with the Dzhrbashyan-Nersesyan fractional derivative. *Fractal Fract.* **2022**, *6*, 541. [CrossRef]
2. Alruwaily, Y.; Ahmad, B.; Ntouyas, S.K.; Alzaidi, A.S.M. Existence results for coupled nonlinear sequential fractional differential equations with coupled Riemann-Stieltjes integro-multipoint boundary conditions. *Fractal Fract.* **2022**, *6*, 123. [CrossRef]
3. Rezapour, S.; Souid, M.S.; Etemad, S.; Bouazza, Z.; Ntouyas, S.K.; Asawasamrit, S.; Tariboon, J. Mawhin's continuation technique for a nonlinear BVP of variable order at resonance via piecewise constant functions. *Fractal Fract.* **2021**, *5*, 216. [CrossRef]
4. Feng, Y.; Bai, Z. Solvability of some nonlocal fractional boundary value problems at resonance in $\mathbb{R}^n$. *Fractal Fract.* **2022**, *6*, 25. [CrossRef]
5. Duan, J.; Jiang, L.; Li, M. The mixed boundary value problems and Chebyshev collocation method for Caputo-type fractional ordinary differential equations. *Fractal Fract.* **2022**, *6*, 148. [CrossRef]
6. Tudorache, A.; Luca, R. Positive solutions of a singular fractional boundary value problem with r-Laplacian operators. *Fractal Fract.* **2022**, *6*, 18. [CrossRef]
7. Tudorache, A.; Luca, R. Systems of Riemann–Liouville fractional differential equations with ρ-Laplacian operators and nonlocal coupled boundary conditions. *Fractal Fract.* **2022**, *6*, 610. [CrossRef]
8. Henderson, J.; Luca, R.; Tudorache, A. On a system of Riemann–Liouville fractional boundary value problems with ϱ-Laplacian operators and positive parameters. *Fractal Fract.* **2022**, *6*, 299. [CrossRef]
9. Li, D.; Li, Y.; Chen, F. Study on infinitely many solutions for a class of Fredholm fractional integro-differential system. *Fractal Fract.* **2022**, *6*, 467. [CrossRef]
10. Liang, Y. Existence and approximate controllability of mild solutions for fractional evolution systems of Sobolev-type. *Fractal Fract.* **2022**, *6*, 56. [CrossRef]
11. Zhao, D.; Liu, Y. New discussion on approximate controllability for semilinear fractional evolution systems with finite delay effects in Banach spaces via differentiable resolvent operators. *Fractal Fract.* **2022**, *6*, 424. [CrossRef]
12. Alsheekhhussain, Z.; Ibrahim, A.G.; Ali, A. Topological structure of the solution sets for impulsive fractional neutral differential inclusions with delay and generated by a non-compact demi group. *Fractal Fract.* **2022**, *6*, 188. [CrossRef]
13. Bose, C.S.V.; Udhayakumar, R. Existence of mild solutions for Hilfer fractional neutral integro-differential inclusions via almost sectorial operators. *Fractal Fract.* **2022**, *6*, 532. [CrossRef]
14. Sultan, A.B.; Jleli, M.; Samet, B. Nonexistence of global solutions to time-fractional damped wave inequalities in bounded domains with a singular potential on the boundary. *Fractal Fract.* **2021**, *5*, 258. [CrossRef]
15. Allouch, N.; Graef, J.R.; Hamani, S. Boundary value problem for fractional q-difference equations with integral conditions in Banach spaces. *Fractal Fract.* **2022**, *6*, 237. [CrossRef]
16. Yu, C.; Wang, S.; Wang, J.; Li, J. Solvability criterion for fractional q-integro-difference system with Riemann-Stieltjes integrals conditions. *Fractal Fract.* **2022**, *6*, 554. [CrossRef]

fractal and fractional

MDPI

Article

Analytic Resolving Families for Equations with the Dzhrbashyan–Nersesyan Fractional Derivative

Vladimir E. Fedorov [1,*], **Marina V. Plekhanova** [1,2] and **Elizaveta M. Izhberdeeva** [1]

[1] Mathematical Analysis Department, Chelyabinsk State University, 129, Kashirin Brothers St., Chelyabinsk 454001, Russia
[2] Computational Mechanics Department, South Ural State University, 76, Lenin Av., Chelyabinsk 454080, Russia
* Correspondence: kar@csu.ru; Tel.: +7-351-799-7106

Abstract: In this paper, a criterion for generating an analytic family of operators, which resolves a linear equation solved with respect to the Dzhrbashyan–Nersesyan fractional derivative, via a linear closed operator is obtained. The properties of the resolving families are investigated and applied to prove the existence of a unique solution for the corresponding initial value problem of the inhomogeneous equation with the Dzhrbashyan–Nersesyan fractional derivative. A solution is presented explicitly using resolving families of operators. A theorem on perturbations of operators from the found class of generators of resolving families is proved. The obtained results are used for a study of an initial-boundary value problem to a model of the viscoelastic Oldroyd fluid dynamics. Thus, the Dzhrbashyan–Nersesyan initial value problem is investigated in the essentially infinite-dimensional case. The use of the proved abstract results to study initial-boundary value problems for a system of partial differential equations is demonstrated.

Keywords: fractional Dzhrbashyan–Nersesyan derivative; differential equation with fractional derivatives; resolving family of operators; perturbation theorem; initial value problem; initial-boundary value problem; viscoelastic Oldroyd fluid

MSC: 34G10; 35R11; 34A08

Citation: Fedorov, V.E.; Plekhanova, M.V.; Izhberdeeva, E.M. Analytic Resolving Families for Equations with the Dzhrbashyan–Nersesyan Fractional Derivative. *Fractal Fract.* **2022**, *6*, 541. https://doi.org/10.3390/fractalfract6100541

Academic Editor: Carlo Cattani

Received: 2 August 2022
Accepted: 22 September 2022
Published: 25 September 2022

1. Introduction

Consider the differential equation

$$D^{\sigma_n} z(t) = Az(t) + f(t), \quad t \in (0, T], \tag{1}$$

where A is a linear closed operator, which has a dense domain D_A in a Banach space $\mathcal{Z}$, $T > 0$, $f : [0, T] \to \mathcal{Z}$ is a given function. Let D_t^β be the Riemann–Liouville integral for $\beta \leq 0$ and the Riemann–Liouville derivative for $\beta > 0$. Here $D^{\sigma_n} z := D_t^{\alpha_n - 1} D_t^{\alpha_{n-1}} D_t^{\alpha_{n-2}} \ldots D_t^{\alpha_0} z(t)$, where $\alpha_k \in (0, 1]$, is the Dzhrbashyan–Nersesyan fractional derivative [1]. Note that this derivative includes as partial cases the Gerasimov–Caputo ($\alpha_k = 1$, $k = 0, 1, \ldots, n-1$, $\alpha_n = \alpha - n + 1$) and the Riemann–Liouville ($\alpha_0 = \alpha - n + 1$, $\alpha_k = 1$, $k = 1, 2, \ldots, n$) fractional derivatives of an order α from $(n - 1, n]$.

In recent decades, fractional-order equations have been actively used in modeling various complex systems and processes in physics, chemistry, social sciences, and humanities [2–6]. We note recent works [7–12], combining theoretical studies in various fields of fractional integro-differential calculus and their use in real-world modeling problems, particularly when modeling biological processes in virology, which is especially important at present. Readers should also note the works [13,14], which consider some applied problems with the Dzhrbashyan–Nersesyan fractional derivative.

The initial value problem

$$D^{\sigma_k}z(0) = z_k, \quad k = 0,1,\ldots,n-1, \tag{2}$$

with

$$D^{\sigma_0}z(t) := D_t^{\alpha_0 - 1}z(t), \quad D^{\sigma_k}z(t) := D_t^{\alpha_k - 1}D_t^{\alpha_{k-1}}D_t^{\alpha_{k-2}}\ldots D_t^{\alpha_0}z(t), \quad k = 1,2,\ldots,n,$$

for Equation (1) in the scalar case ($\mathcal{Z} = \mathbb{R}$, $A \in \mathbb{R}$) is studied by M.M. Dzrbashyan, A.B. Nersesyan in [1]. The unique solvability theorem for such a problem with $\mathcal{Z} = \mathbb{R}^n$ and a matrix A was obtained in [15]. Various equations with partial derivatives of Dzhrbashyan and Nersesyan were studied in papers [16–21]. Problem (1), (2) with a linear continuous operator $A \in \mathcal{L}(\mathcal{Z})$ in an arbitrary Banach space $\mathcal{Z}$ was researched in [22] considering the methods used to resolve families of operators; see [23].

The results obtained in this work generalize the corresponding results of the theory of analytic semigroups of operators solving first-order equations in Banach spaces [24,25]. We also note the works in which the theory of analytical resolving families is constructed for evolutionary integral equations [26], equations with a Gerasimov–Caputo [27] or Riemann–Liouville [28] derivative, fractional multi-term linear differential equations in Banach spaces [29], and equations with various distributed fractional derivatives [30–34].

After the Introduction and Preliminaries, in the second section of the present work, the notion of a k-resolving family for homogeneous Equation (1), i.e., with $f \equiv 0$, $k = 0,1,\ldots,n-1$, is introduced. In the third section, it is shown that the existence of k-resolving families, $k = 1,2,\ldots,n-1$, follows from the existence of a zero-resolving family. In the fourth section, a criterion of the existence of a zero-resolving family of operators to the homogeneous Equation (1) is found in terms of conditions for a linear closed operator A. The class of operators which satisfy these conditions is denoted as $\mathcal{A}_{\{\alpha_k\}}(\theta_0, a_0)$. Various properties of the resolving families are investigated, and a perturbation theorem for operators from $\mathcal{A}_{\{\alpha_k\}}(\theta_0, a_0)$ is proved in the fifth section. For problem (1), (2) with a function f, which is continuous in the graph norm of A or Hölderian, the existence of a unique solution is obtained in the sixth section. In the last section, this result is used to prove the theorem on a unique solution existence for an initial-boundary value problem to a fractional linearized model of the viscoelastic Oldroyd fluid dynamics.

The theoretical significance of the obtained results lies in the fact that they give a correct statement of an initial problem and conditions for its unique solvability for equations with the Dzhrbashyan–Nersesian fractional derivative and with an unbounded linear operator at the unknown function. The unboundedness of the operator in the equation makes it possible to reduce initial-boundary value problems to various equations and systems of partial differential equations in problems of this type.

2. Preliminaries

Let $\mathcal{Z}$ be a Banach space. For the function $z : \mathbb{R}_+ \to \mathcal{Z}$, the Riemann–Liouville fractional integral of an order $\beta > 0$ has the form

$$J_t^{\beta}z(t) := \int_0^t \frac{(t-s)^{\beta-1}}{\Gamma(\beta)} z(s)ds, \quad t > 0.$$

For the function z, the Riemann–Liouville fractional derivative of an order $\alpha \in (m-1, m]$, where $m \in \mathbb{N}$ is defined as $D_t^{\alpha}z(t) := D_t^m J_t^{m-\alpha}z(t)$, $D_t^m := \frac{d^m}{dt^m}$. Further, we use the notation $D_t^{-\alpha} := J_t^{\alpha}$ for $\alpha > 0$; $D_t^0 = J_t^0$ is the identical operator.

Let $\{\alpha_k\}_0^n$ be a set of numbers $\alpha_k \in (0,1]$, $k = 0,1,\ldots,n \in \mathbb{N}$. We will use the denotations $\sigma_k := \sum\limits_{j=0}^{k} \alpha_j - 1$, $k = 0,1,\ldots,n$, hence $\sigma_k \in (-1, k-1]$. Further, we will assume that $\sigma_n > 0$. Define the Dzhrbashyan–Nersesyan fractional derivatives, which correspond to the sequence $\{\alpha_k\}_0^n$, by relations

$$D^{\sigma_0}z(t) := D_t^{\alpha_0-1}z(t), \tag{3}$$

$$D^{\sigma_k}z(t) := D_t^{\alpha_k-1}D_t^{\alpha_{k-1}}D_t^{\alpha_{k-2}}\dots D_t^{\alpha_0}z(t), \quad k=1,2,\dots,n. \tag{4}$$

Example 1. *Take* $\alpha \in (n-1,n]$, $\alpha_0 = \alpha - n + 1 \in (0,1]$, $\alpha_k = 1$, $k = 1,2,\dots,n$, *then* $D^{\sigma_0}z(t) := D_t^{\alpha-n}z(t) := J_t^{n-\alpha}z(t)$, $D^{\sigma_k}z(t) := D_t^{k-1}D_t^{\alpha-n+1}z(t) = D_t^kJ_t^{n-\alpha}z(t) := D_t^{k-n+\alpha}z(t)$, $k = 1,2,\dots,n$, *are the Riemann–Liouville fractional derivatives. In particular,* $D^{\sigma_n}z(t) = D_t^nJ_t^{n-\alpha}z(t) := D_t^{\alpha}z(t)$.

Example 2. *If* $\alpha \in (n-1,n]$, $\alpha_k = 1$, $k = 0,1,\dots,n-1$, $\alpha_n = \alpha - n + 1$, *then* $D^{\sigma_k}z(t) := D_t^kz(t)$, $k = 0,1,\dots,n-1$, $D^{\sigma_n}z(t) := D_t^{\alpha-n}D_t^nz(t) := J_t^{n-\alpha}D_t^nz(t) := {}^CD_t^{\alpha}$ *is the Gerasimov–Caputo fractional derivative.*

Example 3. *In [23], it is shown that the compositions of the Gerasimov–Caputo and the Riemann–Liouville fractional derivatives* $D_t^{\alpha}D_t^{\beta}$, $D_t^{\alpha}\,{}^CD_t^{\beta}$, ${}^CD_t^{\alpha}D_t^{\beta}$, ${}^CD_t^{\alpha}\,{}^CD_t^{\beta}$ *may be presented as Dzhrbashyan–Nersesyan fractional derivatives* D^{σ_n} *for some sequences* $\{\sigma_0,\sigma_1,\dots,\sigma_n\}$.

Let $\alpha \in (m-1,m]$, $m \in \mathbb{N}$. Then, for a function $z : \mathbb{R}_+ \to \mathcal{Z}$, we use $\widehat{z}$ to denote the Laplace transform, and for too-large expressions for z as Lap$[z]$. In [22], it is proved that

$$\widehat{D^{\sigma_n}z}(\lambda) = \lambda^{\sigma_n}\widehat{z}(\lambda) - \sum_{k=0}^{n-1}\lambda^{\sigma_n-\sigma_k-1}D^{\sigma_k}z(0). \tag{5}$$

$\mathcal{L}(\mathcal{Z})$ denotes the Banach space of all linear continuous operators on a Banach space $\mathcal{Z}$; $\mathcal{Cl}(\mathcal{Z})$ denotes the set of all linear closed operators, which are densely defined in $\mathcal{Z}$ and act into $\mathcal{Z}$. For an operator $A \in \mathcal{Cl}(\mathcal{Z})$, its domain D_A is endowed by the norm $\|\cdot\|_{D_A} := \|\cdot\|_{\mathcal{Z}} + \|A\cdot\|_{\mathcal{Z}}$, which is a Banach space due to the closedness of A.

Consider the initial value problem

$$D^{\sigma_k}z(0) = z_k, \quad k = 0,1,\dots,n-1. \tag{6}$$

to the linear homogeneous equation

$$D^{\sigma_n}z(t) = Az(t), \quad t > 0, \tag{7}$$

where $A \in \mathcal{Cl}(\mathcal{Z})$, D^{σ_n} is the Dzhrbashyan–Nersesyan fractional derivative, associated with a set of real numbers $\{\alpha_k\}_0^n$, $0 < \alpha_k \le 1$, $k = 0,1,\dots,n \in \mathbb{N}$, by (3), (4), $\sigma_n > 0$.

A solution to problem (6), (7) is a function $z \in C(\mathbb{R}_+; D_A)$, such that $D_t^{\sigma_k}z \in C(\overline{\mathbb{R}}_+;\mathcal{Z})$, $k = 0,1,\dots,n-1$, $D_t^{\sigma_n}z \in C(\mathbb{R}_+;\mathcal{Z})$, (7) holds for all $t \in \mathbb{R}_+$ and conditions (6) are valid. Hereafter, $\overline{\mathbb{R}}_+ := \mathbb{R}_+ \cup \{0\}$.

Denote $S_{\theta,a} := \{\lambda \in \mathbb{C} : |\arg(\lambda - a)| < \theta, \lambda \neq a\}$, $\theta \in [\pi/2,\pi]$, $a \in \mathbb{R}$, $\Sigma_\psi := \{t \in \mathbb{C} : |\arg t| < \psi, t \neq 0\}$ for $\psi \in (0,\pi/2]$ and formulate an assertion that is important for further considerations.

Theorem 1 ([34])**.** *Let* $\theta_0 \in (\pi/2,\pi]$, $a \in \mathbb{R}$, $\beta \in [0,1)$, $\mathcal{X}$ *be a Banach space,* $H : (a,\infty) \to \mathcal{X}$. *Then, the next statements are equivalent.*

(i) *There exists an analytic function* $F : \Sigma_{\theta_0-\pi/2} \to \mathcal{X}$. *For every* $\theta \in (\pi/2,\theta_0)$, *there exists such a* $C(\theta) > 0$ *that the inequality* $\|F(t)\|_{\mathcal{X}} \le C(\theta)|t|^{-\beta}e^{a\mathrm{Re}\,t}$ *is satisfied for all* $t \in \Sigma_{\theta-\pi/2}$; *for* $\lambda > a$ $\widehat{F}(\lambda) = H(\lambda)$.

(ii) *H is analytically extendable on* $S_{\theta_0,a}$*; for every* $\theta \in (\pi/2, \theta_0)$ *there exists* $K(\theta) > 0$*, such that for all* $\lambda \in S_{\theta,a}$

$$\|H(\lambda)\|_{\mathcal{X}} \le \frac{K(\theta)}{|\lambda - a|^{1-\beta}}.$$

3. *k*-Resolving Families of Operators

Definition 1. *A set of linear bounded operators* $\{S_l(t) \in \mathcal{L}(\mathcal{Z}) : t > 0\}$ *is called k-resolving family,* $k \in \{0, 1, \ldots, n-1\}$*, for Equation (7), if it satisfies the next conditions:*

(i) $S_k(t)$ *is a strongly continuous family at* $t > 0$*;*

(ii) $S_k(t)[D_A] \subset D_A$*, for all* $x \in D_A$*,* $t > 0$ $S_k(t)Ax = AS_k(t)x$*;*

(iii) *For every* $z_k \in D_A$ $S_k(t)z_k$ *is a solution of initial value problem* $D^{\sigma_k}z(0) = z_k$*,* $D^{\sigma_l}z(0) = 0$*,* $l \in \{0, \ldots, n-1\} \setminus \{k\}$ *to Equation (7).*

Let $\rho(A) := \{\lambda \in \mathbb{C} : R_\lambda(A) := (\lambda I - A)^{-1} \in \mathcal{L}(\mathcal{Z})\}$ be the resolvent set of operator A.

Proposition 1. *Let* $\alpha_l \in (0, 1]$*,* $l = 0, 1, \ldots, n$*,* $\sigma_n > 0$*. For* $k \in \{0, 1, \ldots, m-1\}$ *there exists a k-resolving family of operators* $\{S_k(t) \in \mathcal{L}(\mathcal{Z}) : t > 0\}$ *for Equation (7), such that at some* $K > 0$*,* $a \in \mathbb{R}$*,* $\beta \in [0, 1)$ $\|S_k(t)\|_{\mathcal{L}(\mathcal{Z})} \le Ke^{at}t^{-\beta}$ *for all* $t > 0$*. Then,* $\lambda^{\sigma_n} \in \rho(A)$ *for* $\mathrm{Re}\lambda > a$*,*

$$\widehat{S}_k(\lambda) = \lambda^{\sigma_n - \sigma_k - 1} R_{\lambda^{\sigma_n}}(A) \tag{8}$$

and a k-resolving family of operators for Equation (7) is unique.

Proof. Due to identity (5) and Definition 1 for arbitrary $z_k \in D_A$, $\mathrm{Re}\lambda > a$ $\lambda^{\sigma_n}\widehat{S}_k(\lambda)z_k - \lambda^{\sigma_n - \sigma_k - 1}z_k = A\widehat{S}_k(\lambda)z_k = \widehat{S}_k(\lambda)Az_k$. Therefore, the operator $\lambda^{\sigma_n}I - A : D_A \to \mathcal{Z}$ is invertible and equality (8) holds. Since $\widehat{S}_k(\lambda) \in \mathcal{L}(\mathcal{Z})$ for $\mathrm{Re}\lambda > a$, we have $\lambda^{\sigma_n} \in \rho(A)$. Due to equality (8) from the uniqueness of the inverse Laplace transform, we see the uniqueness of a *k*-resolving family for Equation (7). □

Proposition 2. *Let* $\alpha_k \in (0, 1]$*,* $k = 0, 1, \ldots, n$*,* $\sigma_n > 0$*. There exists a 0-resolving family* $\{S_0(t) \in \mathcal{L}(\mathcal{Z}) : t > 0\}$ *for (7), such that at some* $K > 0$*,* $a \in \mathbb{R}$ $\|S_0(t)\|_{\mathcal{L}(\mathcal{Z})} \le Ke^{at}t^{\sigma_0}$ *for all* $t > 0$*. Then, for every* $k = 0, 1, \ldots, n-1$*, there exists a unique k-resolving family* $\{S_k(t) \in \mathcal{L}(\mathcal{Z}) : t > 0\}$*. Moreover,* $S_k(t) \equiv J_t^{\sigma_k - \sigma_0}S_0(t)$ *and* $\|S_k(t)\|_{\mathcal{L}(\mathcal{Z})} \le K_1e^{at}t^{\sigma_k}$ *at some* $K_1 > 0$ *for all* $t > 0$*,* $k = 1, 2, \ldots, n-1$*.*

Proof. Since every $z_0 \in D_A \setminus \{0\}$ $J^{1-\alpha_0}S_0(t)z_0$ has a nonzero limit z_0 as $t \to 0+$, due to ([29], Lemma 1) $S_0(t)z_0 = t^{\alpha_0 - 1}z_0/\Gamma(\alpha_0) + o(t^{\alpha_0 - 1})$ as $t \to 0+$. Therefore, for every $z_0 \in \mathcal{Z}$, $T > 0$ $S_0(t)z_0 \in L_1(0, T; \mathcal{Z})$ and there are Riemann–Liouville fractional integrals for this function.

Define for $k = 1, 2, \ldots, n-1$ the families $\{S_k(t) := J_t^{\sigma_k - \sigma_0}S_0(t) \in \mathcal{L}(\mathcal{Z}) : t > 0\}$. By this construction, it satisfies condition (i) in the Definition 1. For $x \in D_A$, $t > 0$

$$J_t^{\sigma_k - \sigma_0}S_0(t)Ax = \int_0^t \frac{(t-s)^{\sigma_k - \sigma_0 - 1}}{\Gamma(\sigma_k - \sigma_0)}S_0(s)Axds = AJ_t^{\sigma_k - \sigma_0}S_0(t)x,$$

since $\{S_0(t) \in \mathcal{L}(\mathcal{Z}) : t > 0\}$ satisfies condition (ii) in Definition 1 and the operator A is closed. So, condition (ii) holds for $\{S_k(t) \in \mathcal{L}(\mathcal{Z}) : t > 0\}$, where $k = 1, 2, \ldots, n-1$.

Further, we have

$$\|S_k(t)\|_{\mathcal{L}(\mathcal{Z})} \le K\int_0^t \frac{(t-s)^{\sigma_k - \sigma_0 - 1}}{\Gamma(\sigma_k - \sigma_0)}s^{\sigma_0}e^{as}ds \le \frac{Ke^{at}t^{\sigma_k}\Gamma(\sigma_0 + 1)}{\Gamma(\sigma_k + 1)} = K_1e^{at}t^{\sigma_k}, \quad t > 0.$$

For $z_k \in D_A$, multiply the equality $\lambda^{\sigma_n}\widehat{S}_0(\lambda)z_k - \lambda^{\sigma_n-\sigma_0-1}z_k = A\widehat{S}_0(\lambda)z_k$, which follows from point (iii) of Definition 1 for $k=0$ after the Laplace transform action, by $\lambda^{\sigma_0-\sigma_k}$ and obtain the equality $\lambda^{\sigma_n}\widehat{J_t^{\sigma_k-\sigma_0}S_0}(\lambda)z_k - \lambda^{\sigma_n-\sigma_k-1}z_k = A\widehat{J_t^{\sigma_k-\sigma_0}S_0}(\lambda)z_k$, i.e., $\lambda^{\sigma_n}\widehat{S}_k(\lambda)z_k - \lambda^{\sigma_n-\sigma_k-1}z_k = A\widehat{S}_k(\lambda)z_k$, which means that $\{S_k(t) \in \mathcal{L}(\mathcal{Z}) : t > 0\}$ is a k-resolving family for Equation (7) due to the uniqueness of the inverse Laplace transform. Hence equality (8) is valid and a k-resolving family of Equation (7) is unique by Proposition 1. □

Remark 1. *The parameter σ_0 in the formulation of Proposition 2 defines the power singularity of the family $\{S_0(t) \in \mathcal{L}(\mathcal{Z}) : t > 0\}$ at zero. At the beginning of the proof of Proposition 2, it was shown that we have two possibilities only: the singularity at zero has a power of $\sigma_0 := \alpha_0 - 1 < 0$, or a singularity is absent in the case $\alpha_0 = 1$. Due to Proposition 2, the k-resolving family $\{S_k(t) \in \mathcal{L}(\mathcal{Z}) : t > 0\}$ has the singularity of the power $\sigma_k < 0$, or it is absent at zero, if $\sigma_k \geq 0$.*

Theorem 2. *Let $\alpha_l \in (0,1]$, $l = 0,1,\dots,n$, $\sigma_n > 0$, there exist a k-resolving family of operators $\{S_k(t) \in \mathcal{L}(\mathcal{Z}) : t > 0\}$ of (7) for some $k \in \{0,1,\dots,n-1\}$, such that $\|S_k(t)\|_{\mathcal{L}(\mathcal{Z})} \leq Ke^{at}t^{\sigma_k}$ at some $K > 0$, $a \in \mathbb{R}$ for all $t > 0$. Then, there exists a limit $\lim\limits_{t\to 0+} D^{\sigma_k}S_k(t) = I$ in the norm of the space $\mathcal{L}(\mathcal{Z})$, if and only if $A \in \mathcal{L}(\mathcal{Z})$.*

Proof. Note that $\widehat{D^{\sigma_k}S_k} = \lambda^{\sigma_k}\widehat{S}_k = \lambda^{\sigma_n-1}(\lambda^{\sigma_n}I - A)^{-1}$ due to (5), Definition 1 and Proposition 1. Hence for $z_k \in D_A$, $b > a$

$$D^{\sigma_k}S_k(t)z_k = \int\limits_{b-i\infty}^{b+i\infty} \lambda^{\sigma_n-1}R_{\lambda^{\sigma_n}}(A)e^{\lambda t}z_k d\lambda = z_k + \int\limits_{b-i\infty}^{b+i\infty} \lambda^{-1}R_{\lambda^{\sigma_n}}(A)e^{\lambda t}Az_k d\lambda. \tag{9}$$

Since, for large enough $|\lambda|$

$$\|\lambda^{-1}R_{\lambda^{\sigma_n}}(A)\|_{\mathcal{L}(\mathcal{Z})} \leq \frac{C_1}{|\lambda|^{\sigma_n-\sigma_0+\alpha_0}} = \frac{C_1}{|\lambda|^{\sigma_n+1}},$$

we have $\|D^{\sigma_k}S_k(t)z_k\|_{\mathcal{Z}} \leq K_1e^{bt}$.

For $\mathrm{Re}\lambda > b$

$$\int\limits_0^\infty e^{-\lambda t}(D^{\sigma_k}S_k(t) - I)dt = \lambda^{\sigma_n-1}R_{\lambda^{\sigma_n}}(A) - \lambda^{-1}I.$$

Assume that $\eta(t) := \|D^{\sigma_k}S_k(t) - I\|_{\mathcal{L}(\mathcal{Z})}$ is a continuous function on $[0,1]$ and $\eta(0) = 0$. For arbitrary $\varepsilon > 0$, take $\delta > 0$, such that for all $t \in [0,\delta]$ $\eta(t) \leq \varepsilon$; therefore, due to the inequality $\eta(t) \leq K_1e^{bt} + 1$ for $t \geq 0$, we have

$$\left\|\lambda^{\sigma_n-1}R_{\lambda^{\sigma_n}}(A) - \lambda^{-1}I\right\|_{\mathcal{L}(\mathcal{Z})} \leq \int\limits_0^\delta e^{-\lambda t}\eta(t)dt + \int\limits_\delta^\infty e^{-\lambda t}\eta(t)dt \leq \frac{\varepsilon}{\lambda} + o\left(\frac{1}{\lambda}\right)$$

as $\mathrm{Re}\lambda \to +\infty$. Hence, for large enough $\mathrm{Re}\lambda > 0$ $\left\|\lambda^{\sigma_n-1}R_{\lambda^{\sigma_n}}(A) - \lambda^{-1}I\right\|_{\mathcal{L}(\mathcal{Z})} < 1$. Consequently, $R_{\lambda^{\sigma_n}}(A)$ is a continuously invertible operator, so $A \in \mathcal{L}(\mathcal{Z})$.

Let $A \in \mathcal{L}(\mathcal{Z})$, $R > \|A\|_{\mathcal{L}(\mathcal{Z})}^{1/\sigma_n}$, $\Gamma_{1,R} := \{Re^{i\varphi} : \varphi \in (-\pi,\pi)\}$, $\Gamma_{2,R} := \{re^{i\pi} : r \in [R,\infty)\}$, $\Gamma_{3,R} := \{re^{-i\pi} : r \in [R,\infty)\}$, $\Gamma_R := \Gamma_{1,R} \cup \Gamma_{2,R} \cup \Gamma_{3,R}$. Due to equality (9), we obtain for $t > 0$

$$D^{\sigma_k}S_k(t) = I + \frac{1}{2\pi i}\int\limits_{\Gamma_R} \lambda^{-1}R_{\lambda^{\sigma_n}}(A)Ae^{\lambda t}d\lambda = I + \frac{1}{2\pi i}\int\limits_{\Gamma_R} \frac{1}{\lambda}\sum_{l=1}^{\infty}\frac{A^le^{\lambda t}d\lambda}{\lambda^{l\sigma_n}}.$$

Take $R = 1/t$ for small $t > 0$; then,

$$\|D^{\sigma_k} S_k(t) - I\|_{\mathcal{L}(\mathcal{Z})} \leq C_1 \sum_{k=1}^{3} \sum_{l=1}^{\infty} \int_{\Gamma_{k,R}} \frac{\|A\|^l_{\mathcal{L}(\mathcal{Z})} |d\lambda|}{|\lambda|^{l\sigma_n+1}} \leq \frac{C_2 t^{\sigma_n} \|A\|_{\mathcal{L}(\mathcal{Z})}}{1 - t^{\sigma_n} \|A\|_{\mathcal{L}(\mathcal{Z})}} \to 0$$

as $t \to 0+$. □

Remark 2. *An analogous result of Theorem 2 is well-known for resolving semigroups of operators for first-order equations (see, e.g., [35]). On resolving families of operators for equations, which are solved with respect to a Gerasimov–Caputo derivative, a similar theorem was obtained in work [27].*

4. Generation of Analytic k-Resolving Families

Let $k \in \{0, 1, \ldots, n-1\}$. A k-resolving family of operators is called *analytic*, if at some $\psi_0 \in (0, \pi/2]$ it has an analytic continuation to Σ_{ψ_0}. An analytic k-resolving family of operators $\{S_k(t) \in \mathcal{L}(\mathcal{Z}) : t > 0\}$ has a type (ψ_0, a_0, β) at some $\psi_0 \in (0, \pi/2]$, $a_0 \in \mathbb{R}$, $\beta \geq 0$, if, for arbitrary $\psi \in (0, \psi_0)$, $a > a_0$, there exists $C(\psi, a)$, such that the inequality $\|S_k(t)\|_{\mathcal{L}(\mathcal{Z})} \leq C(\psi, a) e^{a \mathrm{Re}\, t} |t|^{-\beta}$ is satisfied for all $t \in \Sigma_\psi$.

Remark 3. *From Proposition 2 and Remark 1 it follows that for a k-resolving family of operators $\{S_k(t) \in \mathcal{L}(\mathcal{Z}) : t > 0\}$, we may have $\beta = -\sigma_k$, or $\beta = 0$.*

Definition 2. *An operator $A \in Cl(\mathcal{Z})$ belongs to the class $\mathcal{A}_{\{\alpha_k\}}(\theta_0, a_0)$, $\theta_0 \in (\pi/2, \pi)$, $a_0 \geq 0$, $\alpha_k \in (0, 1]$, $k = 0, 1, \ldots, n$, $\sigma_n > 0$, if:*

(i) *For all $\lambda \in S_{\theta_0, a_0}$ we have $\lambda^{\sigma_n} \in \rho(A)$;*

(ii) *For arbitrary $\theta \in (\pi/2, \theta_0)$, $a > a_0$, there exists a constant $K(\theta, a) > 0$, such that for every $\lambda \in S_{\theta,a}$*

$$\|R_{\lambda^{\sigma_n}}(A)\|_{\mathcal{L}(\mathcal{Z})} \leq \frac{K(\theta, a)}{|\lambda - a|^{\alpha_0} |\lambda|^{\sigma_n - \sigma_0 - 1}}.$$

If $A \in \mathcal{A}_{\{\alpha_k\}}(\theta_0, a_0)$, the operators

$$Z_k(t) = \frac{1}{2\pi i} \int_{\gamma} \lambda^{\sigma_n - \sigma_k - 1} R_{\lambda^{\sigma_n}}(A) e^{\lambda t} d\lambda, \quad t > 0,\ k = 0, 1, \ldots, n-1,$$

are defined, where $\Gamma := \Gamma_+ \cup \Gamma_- \cup \Gamma_0$, $\Gamma_\pm := \{\lambda \in \mathbb{C} : \lambda = a + re^{\pm i\theta}, r \in (\delta, \infty)\}$, $\Gamma_0 := \{\lambda \in \mathbb{C} : \lambda = a + \delta e^{i\varphi}, \varphi \in (-\theta, \theta)\}$, $\theta \in (\pi/2, \theta_0)$, $a > a_0$, $\delta > 0$.

Theorem 3. *Let $\alpha_k \in (0, 1]$, $k = 0, 1, \ldots, n$, $\alpha_0 + \alpha_n > 0$, $\theta_0 \in (\pi/2, \pi]$, $a_0 \geq 0$.*

(i) *If there exists an analytic 0-resolving family of operators of the type $(\theta_0 - \pi/2, a_0, -\sigma_0)$ for (7), then $A \in \mathcal{A}_{\{\alpha_k\}}(\theta_0, a_0)$.*

(ii) *If $A \in \mathcal{A}_{\{\alpha_k\}}(\theta_0, a_0)$, then for every $k = 0, 1, \ldots, n-1$ there exists a unique analytic k-resolving family of operators $\{S_k(t) \in \mathcal{L}(\mathcal{Z}) : t > 0\}$ of the type $(\theta_0 - \pi/2, a_0, \max\{-\sigma_k, 0\})$ for (7). Moreover, for $t > 0$, $k = 0, 1, \ldots, n-1$ $S_k(t) \equiv Z_k(t) \equiv J_t^{\sigma_k - \sigma_0} Z_0(t)$.*

Proof. Choose $R > \delta$,

$$\Gamma_R := \bigcup_{k=1}^{4} \Gamma_{k,R}, \quad \Gamma_{1,R} := \Gamma_0, \quad \Gamma_{2,R} := \{\lambda \in \mathbb{C} : \lambda = a + Re^{i\varphi}, \varphi \in (-\theta, \theta)\},$$

$$\Gamma_{3,R} := \{\lambda \in \mathbb{C} : \lambda = a + re^{i\theta}, r \in [\delta, R]\}, \quad \Gamma_{4,R} := \{\lambda \in \mathbb{C} : \lambda = a + re^{-i\theta}, r \in [\delta, R]\},$$

Γ_R is the positively oriented closed loop,

$$\Gamma_{5,R} := \{\lambda \in \mathbb{C} : \lambda = a + re^{i\theta}, r \in [R, \infty)\}, \quad \Gamma_{6,R} := \{\lambda \in \mathbb{C} : \lambda = a + re^{-i\theta}, r \in [R, \infty)\},$$

then $\Gamma = \Gamma_{5,R} \cup \Gamma_{6,R} \cup \Gamma_R \setminus \Gamma_{2,R}$.

If $A \in \mathcal{A}_{\{\alpha_k\}}(\theta_0, a_0)$, then following Theorem 1 with $\mathcal{X} = \mathcal{L}(\mathcal{Z})$, the operators family $\{Z_0(t) \in \mathcal{L}(\mathcal{Z}) : t > 0\}$ is analytic of the type $(\theta_0 - \pi/2, a_0, -\sigma_0)$, it implies point (i) of Definition 1, and point (ii) of this definition is evidently fulfilled.

For any $\theta \in (\pi/2, \theta_0)$, $a > a_0$, we have such a $K(\theta, a) > 0$, that for every $\lambda \in S_{\theta,a}$

$$\left\|\lambda^{\sigma_n-\sigma_k-1}R_{\lambda^{\sigma_n}}(A)\right\|_{\mathcal{L}(\mathcal{Z})} \leq C\left\|\lambda^{\sigma_n-\sigma_0-1}R_{\lambda^{\sigma_n}}(A)\right\|_{\mathcal{L}(\mathcal{Z})} \leq \frac{CK(\theta,a)}{|\lambda-a|^{\alpha_0}}.$$

So, for $k = 0, 1, \dots, n-1$, $\mathrm{Re}\lambda > a_0$ there exists the Laplace transforms $\widehat{Z}_k(\lambda) = \lambda^{\sigma_n-\sigma_k-1}R_{\lambda^{\sigma_n}}(A)$, $\widehat{J_t^{\beta}Z_k}(\lambda) = \lambda^{\sigma_n-\sigma_k-1-\beta}R_{\lambda^{\sigma_n}}(A)$, $\beta > 0$, therefore, $Z_k(t) = J_t^{\sigma_k-\sigma_0}Z_0(t)$.

For $z_0 \in D_A$

$$D_t^{\alpha_0-1}Z_0(t)z_0 = \frac{1}{2\pi i}\int_{\Gamma}\lambda^{\sigma_n-1}R_{\lambda^{\sigma_n}}(A)e^{\lambda t}z_0 d\lambda =$$

$$= \frac{1}{2\pi i}\int_{\Gamma}\frac{e^{\lambda t}}{\lambda}z_0 d\lambda + \frac{1}{2\pi i}\int_{\Gamma}\lambda^{-1}R_{\lambda^{\sigma_n}}(A)e^{\lambda t}Az_0 d\lambda = z_0 + \frac{1}{2\pi i}\int_{\Gamma}\lambda^{-1}R_{\lambda^{\sigma_n}}(A)e^{\lambda t}Az_0 d\lambda.$$

If $t \in [0,1]$, $\lambda \in \Gamma \setminus \{\mu \in \mathbb{C} : |\mu| \leq 2a\}$, then

$$\left\|\lambda^{-1}R_{\lambda^{\sigma_n}}(A)e^{\lambda t}Az_0\right\|_{\mathcal{Z}} \leq \frac{e^{a+\delta}K(\theta,a)\|Az_0\|_{\mathcal{Z}}}{|\lambda-a|^{\alpha_0}|\lambda|^{\sigma_n-\sigma_0}} \leq \frac{C_1}{|\lambda|^{\sigma_n+1}}.$$

Hence,

$$\frac{1}{2\pi i}\int_{\Gamma}\lambda^{-1}R_{\lambda^{\sigma_n}}(A)e^{\lambda t}Az_0 d\lambda =$$

$$= \lim_{R\to\infty}\frac{1}{2\pi i}\left(\int_{\Gamma_R} - \int_{\Gamma_{2,R}} + \int_{\Gamma_{5,R}} + \int_{\Gamma_{6,R}}\right)\lambda^{-1}R_{\lambda^{\sigma_n}}(A)e^{\lambda t}Az_0 d\lambda = 0,$$

since by the Cauchy theorem

$$\int_{\Gamma_R}\lambda^{-1}R_{\lambda^{\sigma_n}}(A)e^{\lambda t}Az_0 d\lambda = 0, \quad \left\|\int_{\Gamma_{s,R}}\lambda^{-1}R_{\lambda^{\sigma_n}}(A)e^{\lambda t}Az_0 d\lambda\right\|_{\mathcal{Z}} \leq \frac{C_2}{R^{\sigma_n}} \to 0$$

as $R \to \infty$ for $s = 2, 5, 6$.

At the same time, due equality (5)

$$\mathrm{Lap}[D^{\sigma_1}Z_0(\cdot)z_0](\lambda) = \lambda^{\sigma_n-\sigma_0-1+\sigma_1}R_{\lambda^{\sigma_n}}(A)z_0 - \lambda^{\sigma_1-\sigma_0-1}z_0 = \lambda^{\alpha_1-1}R_{\lambda^{\sigma_n}}(A)Az_0,$$

for $\lambda \in \Gamma \setminus \{\mu \in \mathbb{C} : |\mu| \leq 2a\}$

$$\|\lambda^{\alpha_1-1}R_{\lambda^{\sigma_n}}(A)Az_0\|_{\mathcal{Z}} \leq \frac{C_3}{|\lambda|^{\sigma_n-\sigma_0+\alpha_0-\alpha_1}} = \frac{C_3}{|\lambda|^{\alpha_0+\alpha_2+\alpha_3+\dots+\alpha_n}},$$

$\alpha_0 + \alpha_2 + \alpha_3 + \dots + \alpha_n > \alpha_0 + \alpha_n > 1$, hence $D^{\sigma_1}Z_0(0)z_0 = 0$. Further, for every $k = 2, 3, \dots, n-1$

$$\mathrm{Lap}[D^{\sigma_k}Z_0(\cdot)z_0](\lambda) = \lambda^{\sigma_n-\sigma_0-1+\sigma_k}R_{\lambda^{\sigma_n}}(A)z_0 - \lambda^{\sigma_k-\sigma_0-1}z_0 = \lambda^{\sigma_k-\sigma_0-1}R_{\lambda^{\sigma_n}}(A)Az_0,$$

for $\lambda \in \Gamma \setminus \{\mu \in \mathbb{C} : |\mu| \leq 2a\}$

$$\|\lambda^{\sigma_k-\sigma_0-1}R_{\lambda^{\sigma_n}}(A)Az_0\|_{\mathcal{Z}} \leq \frac{C_3}{|\lambda|^{\sigma_n-\sigma_k+\alpha_0}} = \frac{C_3}{|\lambda|^{\alpha_0+\alpha_{k+1}+\alpha_{k+2}+\dots+\alpha_n}},$$

thus, $D^{\sigma_k} Z_0(0) z_0 = 0$. Finally,

$$\mathrm{Lap}[D^{\sigma_n} Z_0(\cdot) z_0](\lambda) = \lambda^{\sigma_n - \sigma_0 - 1 + \sigma_n} R_{\lambda^{\sigma_n}}(A) z_0 - \lambda^{\sigma_n - \sigma_0 - 1} z_0 = A \lambda^{\sigma_n - \sigma_0 - 1} R_{\lambda^{\sigma_n}}(A) z_0.$$

Acting on the inverse Laplace transform, we get the equality $D^{\sigma_n} Z_0(t) z_0 = A Z_0(t) z_0$, so $\{Z_0(t) \in \mathcal{L}(\mathcal{Z}) : t > 0\}$ is a zero-resolving family of operators for Equation (7). Then, by Proposition 2 for every $k = 1, 2, \ldots, n-1$, there exists a k-resolving family of operators, which coincide with operators $J_t^{\sigma_k - \sigma_0} Z_0(t) = Z_k(t)$. Every such family is analytic with the type $(\theta_0 - \pi/2, a_0, \max\{-\sigma_k, 0\})$; see the proof of Proposition 2 and Remark 3.

If there exists a zero-resolving family with the type $(\theta_0 - \pi/2, a_0, -\sigma_0)$, equality (8) at $k = 0$ and Theorem 1 with $\mathcal{X} = \mathcal{L}(\mathcal{Z})$ implies that $A \in \mathcal{A}_{\{\alpha_k\}}(\theta_0, a_0)$. □

Remark 4. *Note that $\sigma_n > 0$, if $\alpha_0 + \alpha_n > 1$.*

Remark 5. *An analogous for Theorem 3 result on the first-order equations is called the Solomyak–Yosida theorem on generation of analytic semigroups of operators [24,25]. Previously, similar results were obtained for evolutionary integral equations [26], differential equations with a Gerasimov–Caputo fractional derivative [27], with a Riemann–Liouville derivative [28], for multi-term linear fractional differential equations in Banach spaces [29], and equations with distributed fractional derivatives [30,31,33,34].*

Corollary 1. *Let $A \in \mathcal{A}_{\{\alpha_k\}}(\theta_0, a_0)$, $\alpha_k \in (0,1]$, $k = 0, 1, \ldots, n$, $\alpha_0 + \alpha_n > 0$, $\theta_0 \in (\pi/2, \pi]$, $a_0 \geq 0$. Then, for any $z_0, z_1, \ldots, z_{n-1} \in D_A$ problem (6), (7) has a unique solution, and it has the form*

$$z(t) = \sum_{k=0}^{n-1} Z_k(t) z_k.$$

The solution is analytic in $\Sigma_{\theta_0 - \pi/2}$.

Proof. After Theorem 3, we need to prove the uniqueness of a solution only. If problem (6), (7) has two solutions y_1, y_2, then the difference $y = y_1 - y_2$ is a solution of (7) with the initial conditions $D^{\sigma_k} y(0) = 0$, $k = 0, 1, \ldots, n-1$. Redefine y on (T, ∞) for any $T > 0$ as a zero function. The got function y_T satisfies equality (7) at $t > 0$ without the point T. Using the Laplace transform obtained from Equation (7) and zero initial conditions, the equality $\lambda^{\sigma_n} \widehat{y}_T(\lambda) = A \widehat{y}_T(\lambda)$. Since $A \in \mathcal{A}_{\{\alpha_k\}}(\theta_0, a_0)$, we have $\widehat{y}_T(\lambda) \equiv 0$ for $\lambda \in S_{\theta_0, a_0}$. Therefore, $y_T \equiv 0$ for arbitrary $T > 0$, hence $y \equiv 0$ on $\mathbb{R}_+$ and a solution of problem (6), (7) is unique. □

Remark 6. *For $A \in \mathcal{L}(\mathcal{Z})$ the k-resolving operators of Equation (7) have the form (see [22])*

$$Z_k(t) = t^{\sigma_k} E_{\sigma_n, \sigma_k + 1}(t^{\sigma_n} A), \quad t \in S_{\pi,0}, \quad k = 0, 1, \ldots, n-1.$$

Here, according to $E_{\beta,\gamma}$ the Mittag–Leffler function is denoted. Indeed, decomposing the resolvent $R_{\sigma_n}(A)$ in the series for large enough $|\lambda|$ and using the Hankel integral, we obtain these equalities.

Theorem 4. *Let $A \in \mathcal{A}_{\{\alpha_k\}}(\theta_0, a_0)$, $\alpha_k \in (0,1]$, $k = 0, 1, \ldots, n$, $\alpha_0 + \alpha_n > 0$, $\sigma_n \geq 2$, $\theta_0 \in (\pi/2, \pi]$, $a_0 \geq 0$. Then $A \in \mathcal{L}(\mathcal{Z})$.*

Proof. For some $\nu_0 \in \mathbb{C}$, such that $|\nu_0| \geq R^{\sigma_n}$, take $\lambda_0 = \nu_0^{1/\sigma_n}$, hence $|\lambda_0| \geq R$, $\arg \lambda_0 = \arg \nu_0 / \sigma_n \in [-\pi/2, \pi/2]$, since $\sigma_n \geq 2$. Then, $\lambda_0 \in S_{\theta_0, a_0}$ for sufficiently large $R > 0$. Therefore, $\{\nu \in \mathbb{C} : |\nu| \geq R^{\sigma_n}\} \subset [S_{\theta_0, a_0}]^{\sigma_n} \subset \rho(A)$, since $A \in \mathcal{A}_{\{\alpha_k\}}(\theta_0, a_0)$. Here, we use the principal branch of the power function.

So, for $|\nu| \geq R^{\sigma_n}$, where $\nu = \lambda^{\sigma_n}$,

$$\|\nu R_\nu(A)\|_{\mathcal{L}(\mathcal{Z})} \leq \frac{K(\theta,a)|\lambda|^{\sigma_0+1}}{|\lambda - a|^{\alpha_0}} \leq C$$

and by Lemma 5.2 [36] the operator A is bounded. □

Remark 7. *For strongly continuous resolving families of the equation with a Gerasimov–Caputo derivative, such a result was proved in [27].*

5. Inhomogeneous Equation

Let $f \in C([0,T];\mathcal{Z})$. Consider the equation

$$D^{\sigma_n} z(t) = Az(t) + f(t), \quad t \in (0,T]. \tag{10}$$

A solution of the initial value problem

$$D^{\sigma_k} z(0) = z_k, \quad k = 0,1,\ldots,n-1, \tag{11}$$

to Equation (10) is a function $z \in C((0,T];D_A)$, such that $D^{\sigma_k} z \in C([0,T];\mathcal{Z})$, $k = 0,1,\ldots,n-1$, $D^{\sigma_n} z \in C((0,T];\mathcal{Z})$, for all $t \in (0,T]$ equality (10) is fulfilled and conditions (11) are valid.

Denote

$$Z(t) = \frac{1}{2\pi i}\int_\Gamma R_{\lambda^{\sigma_n}}(A)e^{\lambda t}d\lambda, \quad Y_\beta(t) = \frac{1}{2\pi i}\int_\Gamma \lambda^\beta R_{\lambda^{\sigma_n}}(A)e^{\lambda t}d\lambda, \quad \beta \in \mathbb{R}.$$

Lemma 1. *Let $A \in \mathcal{A}_{\{\alpha_k\}}(\theta_0,a_0)$, $\alpha_k \in (0,1]$, $k = 0,1,\ldots,n$, $\alpha_0 + \alpha_n > 0$, $\theta_0 \in (\pi/2,\pi]$, $a_0 \geq 0$, $f \in C([0,T];D_A)$. Then,*

$$z_f(t) = \int_0^t Z(t-s)f(s)ds \tag{12}$$

is a unique solution for the initial value problem

$$D^{\sigma_k} z(0) = 0, \quad k = 0,1,\ldots,n-1, \tag{13}$$

to (10).

Proof. Since $A \in \mathcal{A}_{\{\alpha_k\}}(\theta_0,a_0)$, for sufficiently large $|\lambda|$ $\|R_{\lambda^{\sigma_n}}(A)\|_{\mathcal{L}(\mathcal{Z})} \leq C|\lambda|^{-\sigma_n}$, hence for $\mathrm{Re}\lambda > a_0$ $\widehat{Z}(\lambda) = R_{\lambda^{\sigma_n}}(A)$, $\widehat{D^{\sigma_0}Z}(\lambda) = \lambda^{\sigma_0}R_{\lambda^{\sigma_n}}(A)$, $\|Z(t)\|_{\mathcal{L}(\mathcal{Z})} \leq Ct^{\sigma_n-1}$, $\|D^{\sigma_0}Z(t)\|_{\mathcal{L}(\mathcal{Z})} \leq Ct^{\sigma_n-\sigma_0-1}$ for $t \in (0,T]$. Analogously, $\|Y_\beta(t)\|_{\mathcal{L}(\mathcal{Z})} \leq Ct^{\sigma_n-\beta-1}$ for $t \in (0,T]$, $\beta \in \mathbb{R}$.

Further,

$$\|D^{\sigma_0}z_f(t)\|_{\mathcal{Z}} = \left\|\int_0^t Y_{\sigma_0}(t-s)f(s)ds\right\|_{\mathcal{Z}} \leq C\max_{s\in[0,T]}\|f(s)\|_{\mathcal{Z}}t^{\sigma_n-\sigma_0},$$

hence $D^{\sigma_0}z_f(0) = 0$. Define f by zero outside the segment $[0,T]$; then, $z_f = Z * f$, $\widehat{z}_f(\lambda) = \widehat{Z}(\lambda)\widehat{f}(\lambda) = R_{\lambda^{\sigma_n}}(A)\widehat{f}(\lambda)$, $\widehat{D^{\sigma_1}z_f}(\lambda) = \lambda^{\sigma_1}R_{\lambda^{\sigma_n}}(A)\widehat{f}(\lambda)$,

$$\|D^{\sigma_1}z_f(t)\|_{\mathcal{Z}} = \left\|\int_0^t Y_{\sigma_1}(t-s)f(s)ds\right\|_{\mathcal{Z}} \leq C\max_{s\in[0,T]}\|f(s)\|_{\mathcal{Z}}t^{\sigma_n-\sigma_1}, \quad t \in (0,T],$$

$D^{\sigma_1}z_f(0) = 0$. Repeating the analogous reasoning sequentially, we get $k = 2, 3, \dots, n-1$ $\widehat{D^{\sigma_k}z_f}(\lambda) = \lambda^{\sigma_k}R_{\lambda^{\sigma_n}}(A)\widehat{f}(\lambda)$, $\|D^{\sigma_k}z_f(t)\|_{\mathcal{L}(\mathcal{Z})} \le C \max\limits_{s\in[0,T]} \|f(s)\|_{\mathcal{Z}} t^{\sigma_n-\sigma_k}$ for $t \in (0, T]$, $D^{\sigma_k}z_f(0) = 0$, $\widehat{D^{\sigma_n}z_f}(\lambda) = \lambda^{\sigma_n}R_{\lambda^{\sigma_n}}(A)\widehat{f}(\lambda)$.

Since $f \in C([0, T]; D_A)$, we have

$$\widehat{Az_f}(\lambda) = \widehat{z}_{Af}(\lambda) = AR_{\lambda^{\sigma_n}}(A)\widehat{f}(\lambda) = \lambda^{\sigma_n}R_{\lambda^{\sigma_n}}(A)\widehat{f}(\lambda) - \widehat{f}(\lambda),$$

so, $Az_f(t) = D^{\sigma_n}z_f(t) - f(t)$ for all $t > 0$. Thus, the function z_f satisfies equality (10). The proof of a solution's uniqueness is the same as for the homogeneous equation. □

Let $C^\gamma([0, T]; \mathcal{Z})$ for some $\gamma \in (0, 1]$ be the set of all functions $f : [0, T] \to \mathcal{Z}$, satisfying the Hölder condition:

$$\exists C > 0 \quad \forall s, t \in [0, T] \quad \|f(s) - f(t)\|_{\mathcal{Z}} \le C|s - t|^\gamma.$$

Lemma 2. *Let* $A \in \mathcal{A}_{\{\alpha_k\}}(\theta_0, a_0)$, $\alpha_k \in (0, 1]$, $k = 0, 1, \dots, n$, $\alpha_0 + \alpha_n > 0$, $\theta_0 \in (\pi/2, \pi]$, $a_0 \ge 0$, $f \in C^\gamma([0, T]; \mathcal{Z})$, $\gamma \in (0, 1]$. *Then, problem* (10), (13) *has a unique solution; it has form* (12).

Proof. Since A is closed,

$$AZ(t) = \frac{1}{2\pi i}\int\limits_\Gamma AR_{\lambda^{\sigma_n}}(A)e^{\lambda t}d\lambda = \frac{1}{2\pi i}\int\limits_\Gamma \lambda^{\sigma_n}R_{\lambda^{\sigma_n}}(A)e^{\lambda t}d\lambda = Y_{\sigma_n}(t), \quad t > 0,$$

therefore, $\mathrm{im}Z(t) \subset D_A$, as $t \to 0+$ $\|AZ(t)\|_{\mathcal{L}(\mathcal{Z})} = O(t^{-1})$ (see the previous proof). Therefore, for all $t, s \in (0, T]$

$$\|AZ(t - s)(f(s) - f(t))\|_{\mathcal{Z}} \le C|t - s|^{\gamma-1}.$$

Then

$$\int\limits_0^t AZ(t - s)f(s)ds = \int\limits_0^t AZ(t - s)(f(s) - f(t))ds + \int\limits_0^t Y_{\sigma_n}(t - s)f(t)ds,$$

$$\int\limits_0^t Y_{\sigma_n}(t - s)f(t)ds = -\int\limits_0^t D^1_s Y_{\sigma_n-1}(t - s)f(t)ds = (Y_{\sigma_n-1}(t) - Y_{\sigma_n-1}(0))f(t).$$

Note that for any $x \in D_A$

$$Y_{\sigma_n-1}(t)x = x + \frac{1}{2\pi i}\int\limits_\Gamma \lambda^{-1}R_{\lambda^{\sigma_n}}(A)e^{\lambda t}Axd\lambda \to x, \quad t \to 0+,$$

since for large enough $|\lambda|$ $\|\lambda^{-1}R_{\lambda^{\sigma_n}}(A)Ax\|_{\mathcal{Z}} \le C\|Ax\|_{\mathcal{Z}}|\lambda|^{-\sigma_n-1}$. At the same time, for sufficiently large $|\lambda|$ $\|\lambda^{\sigma_n-1}R_{\lambda^{\sigma_n}}(A)\|_{\mathcal{L}(\mathcal{Z})} \le C|\lambda|^{-1}$; therefore, the family $\{Y_{\sigma_n-1}(t) \in \mathcal{L}(\mathcal{Z}) : t > 0\}$ is bounded uniformly. Since D_A is dense in $\mathcal{Z}$, for every $x \in \mathcal{Z}$ $\lim\limits_{t\to 0+} Y_{\sigma_n-1}(t)x = x$.

Thus,

$$\left\|\int\limits_0^t AZ(t - s)f(s)ds\right\|_{\mathcal{Z}} \le C_1t^\gamma + \|Y_{\sigma_n-1}(t) - Y_{\sigma_n-1}(0)\|_{\mathcal{L}(\mathcal{Z})}\|f(t) - f(0)\|_{\mathcal{Z}} +$$
$$+\|(Y_{\sigma_n-1}(t) - Y_{\sigma_n-1}(0))f(0)\|_{\mathcal{Z}} \le$$
$$\le C_1t^\gamma + C_2\|f(t) - f(0)\|_{\mathcal{Z}} + \|(Y_{\sigma_n-1}(t) - Y_{\sigma_n-1}(0))f(0)\|_{\mathcal{Z}} \to 0$$

as $t \to 0+$. Therefore, $z_f(t) \in D_A$, $z_f \in C([0,T]; D_A)$.

Other arguing is the same as in the proof of the previous lemma. □

Corollary 1, Lemma 1 and Lemma 2 imply the following result.

Theorem 5. *Let $A \in \mathcal{A}_{\{\alpha_k\}}(\theta_0, a_0)$, $\alpha_k \in (0,1]$, $k = 0,1,\dots,n$, $\alpha_0 + \alpha_n > 0$, $\theta_0 \in (\pi/2, \pi]$, $a_0 \geq 0$, $\gamma \in (0,1]$, $f \in C([0,T]; D_A) \cup C^\gamma([0,T]; \mathcal{Z})$. Then problem* (10), (11) *has a unique solution, it has the form*

$$z(t) = \sum_{k=0}^{n-1} Z_k(t) z_k + \int_0^t Z(t-s) f(s) ds.$$

6. Perturbation Theorem

Theorem 6. *Let $A \in \mathcal{A}_{\{\alpha_k\}}(\theta_0, a_0)$, $\alpha_k \in (0,1]$, $k = 0,1,\dots,n$, $\alpha_0 + \alpha_n > 0$, $\theta_0 \in (\pi/2, \pi]$, $a_0 \geq 0$, $B \in Cl(\mathcal{Z})$, for some $\beta, \gamma \geq 0$*

$$\|Bx\|_{\mathcal{Z}} \leq \beta \|Ax\|_{\mathcal{Z}} + \gamma \|x\|_{\mathcal{Z}}, \quad x \in D_A \subset D_B, \tag{14}$$

there exists $q \in (0,1)$, such that $\beta(1 + K(\theta, a)) < q$ for all $\theta \in (\pi/2, \theta_0)$, $a > a_0$. Then, $A + B \in \mathcal{A}_{\{\alpha_k\}}(\theta_0, a_1)$ for sufficiently large $a_1 > a_0$.

Proof. Choose $l > \sin^{-1}\theta_0$, $\lambda \in S_{\theta,la} \subset S_{\theta,a}$ for some $\theta \in (\pi/2, \theta_0)$, $a > a_0$, then from (14), it follows that

$$\|BR_{\lambda^{\sigma_n}}(A)\|_{\mathcal{L}(\mathcal{Z})} \leq \beta \|AR_{\lambda^{\sigma_n}}(A)\|_{\mathcal{L}(\mathcal{Z})} + \gamma \|R_{\lambda^{\sigma_n}}(A)\|_{\mathcal{L}(\mathcal{Z})} \leq$$

$$\leq \beta\left(1 + \frac{|\lambda|^{\sigma_0+1} K_A(\theta, a)}{|\lambda - a|^{\alpha_0}}\right) + \frac{\gamma K_A(\theta, a)}{|\lambda - a|^{\alpha_0} |\lambda|^{\sigma_n - \sigma_0 - 1}},$$

where $K_A(\theta, a)$ is the constant from Definition 2. Note that the value

$$\frac{|\lambda|^{\alpha_0}}{|\lambda - a|^{\alpha_0}} \leq \frac{1}{\left(1 - \frac{a}{|\lambda|}\right)^{\alpha_0}} \leq \frac{1}{\left(1 - \frac{1}{l \sin\theta_0}\right)^{\alpha_0}}$$

is close to one, for a sufficiently large number l

$$\frac{|\lambda|^{\alpha_0}}{|\lambda - a|^{\alpha_0} |\lambda|^{\sigma_n}} \leq \frac{1}{\left(1 - \frac{1}{l \sin\theta_0}\right)^{\alpha_0} (l a_0 \sin\theta_0)^{\sigma_n}}$$

is close to zero. So, for such a l, we have

$$\|BR_{\lambda^{\sigma_n}}(A)\|_{\mathcal{L}(\mathcal{Z})} \leq \beta\left(1 + \frac{K_A(\theta, a)}{\left(1 - \frac{1}{l \sin\theta_0}\right)^{\alpha_0}}\right) + \frac{\gamma K_A(\theta, a)}{\left(1 - \frac{1}{l \sin\theta_0}\right)^{\alpha_0} (l a_0 \sin\theta_0)^{\sigma_n}} \leq$$

$$\leq \beta(1 + K(\theta, a)) + \varepsilon \leq q < 1.$$

Therefore,

$$R_{\lambda^{\sigma_n}}(A + B) = R_{\lambda^{\sigma_n}}(A)(I - BR_{\lambda^{\sigma_n}}(A))^{-1} = R_{\lambda^{\sigma_n}}(A) \sum_{k=0}^{\infty} [BR_{\lambda^{\sigma_n}}(A)]^k,$$

$$\frac{|\lambda - la|}{|\lambda - a|} = \left|1 - \frac{(l-1)a}{\lambda - a}\right| \leq 1 + \frac{(l-1)a}{|\lambda - a|} < 1 + \frac{1}{\sin\theta_0},$$

$$\|R_{\lambda^{\sigma_n}}(A+B)\|_{\mathcal{L}(\mathcal{Z})} \leq \frac{K_A(\theta,a)}{(1-q)|\lambda-a|^{\alpha_0}|\lambda|^{\sigma_n-\sigma_0-1}} \leq \frac{K_A(\theta,a)\left(1+\frac{1}{\sin\theta_0}\right)^{\alpha_0}}{(1-q)|\lambda-la|^{\alpha_0}|\lambda|^{\sigma_n-\sigma_0-1}}.$$

So, $A+B \in \mathcal{A}_{\{\alpha_k\}}(\theta_0,a_1)$ with $a_1 = la_0$, for all $\theta \in (\pi/2,\theta_0)$, $a > a_1$

$$K_{A+B}(\theta,a) = \frac{K_A(\theta,a/l)}{1-q}\left(1+\frac{1}{\sin\theta_0}\right)^{\alpha_0}.$$

□

Remark 8. *For every $B \in \mathcal{L}(\mathcal{Z})$ condition,* (14) *is satisfied with $\beta = 0$, $\gamma = \|B\|_{\mathcal{L}(\mathcal{Z})}$.*

Remark 9. *Theorem 6 generalizes the similar theorem for generators of analytic semigroups of operators [37]. Note that there are also analogous results for generators of resolving families for equations with distributed fractional derivatives in [30].*

7. Application to a Model of a Viscoelastic Oldroyd Fluid

Let $\alpha_k \in (0,1]$, $k = 0,1,\ldots,n$, $\alpha_0 + \alpha_n > 1$, $\sigma_n \in (0,2)$, $\Omega \subset \mathbb{R}^d$ be a bounded region, which has a smooth boundary $\partial\Omega$. We consider a fractional linearized model of the viscoelastic Oldroyd fluid dynamics with the order $N = 1$ (see [38])

$$D^{\sigma_k}v(x,0) = v_k(x),\ D^{\sigma_k}w(x,0) = w_k(x),\ x \in \Omega,\ k = 0,1,\ldots,n-1, \tag{15}$$

$$v(x,t) = 0, \quad w(x,t) = 0, \quad (x,t) \in \partial\Omega \times (0,T], \tag{16}$$

$$D^{\sigma_n}v = \mu\Delta v + \Delta w - \nabla p + g, \quad (x,t) \in \Omega \times (0,T], \tag{17}$$

$$D^{\sigma_n}w = bv + cw + h, \quad (x,t) \in \Omega \times (0,T], \tag{18}$$

$$\nabla \cdot v = 0, \quad \nabla \cdot w = 0, \quad (x,t) \in \Omega \times (0,T]. \tag{19}$$

Here, $T > 0$, D^{σ_k}, $k = 0,1,\ldots,n$, are Dzhrbashyan–Nersesyan fractional derivatives with respect to time t, $x = (x_1,x_2,\ldots,x_d)$ are spatial variables, $v = (v_1,v_2,\ldots,v_d)$ is the fluid velocity vector, $w = (w_1,w_2,\ldots,w_d)$ is a function of memory for the velocity, which is defined by a Volterra integral with respect to t for v, $\nabla p = (p_{x_1},p_{x_2},\ldots,p_{x_d})$ is the pressure gradient of the fluid, Δ is the Laplace operator with respect to all the spatial variables, $\Delta v = (\Delta v_1,\Delta v_2,\ldots,\Delta v_d)$, $\Delta w = (\Delta w_1,\Delta w_2,\ldots,\Delta w_d)$, $\nabla \cdot v = v_{1x_1} + v_{2x_2} + \cdots + v_{dx_d}$, $\nabla \cdot w = w_{1x_1} + w_{2x_2} + \cdots + w_{dx_d}$. The constants $\mu, b, c \in \mathbb{R}$ and the functions $g, h : \Omega \times [0,T] \to \mathbb{R}^d$ are given.

Take $\mathbb{L}_2 := (L_2(\Omega))^d$, $\mathbb{H}^1 := (W_2^1(\Omega))^d$, $\mathbb{H}^2 := (W_2^2(\Omega))^d$. The closure of $\mathfrak{L} := \{u \in (C_0^\infty(\Omega))^d : \nabla \cdot u = 0\}$ in the norm of $\mathbb{L}_2$ will be denoted by $\mathbb{H}_\sigma$, and in the norm of the space $\mathbb{H}^1$ by $\mathbb{H}_\sigma^1$. We also denote $\mathbb{H}_\sigma^2 := \mathbb{H}_\sigma^1 \cap \mathbb{H}^2$, $\mathbb{H}_\pi$ is the orthogonal complement for $\mathbb{H}_\sigma$ in the Hilbert space $\mathbb{L}_2$, $\Sigma : \mathbb{L}_2 \to \mathbb{H}_\sigma$, $\Pi := I - \Sigma : \mathbb{L}_2 \to \mathbb{H}_\pi$ are the projectors.

The operator $B = \Sigma\Delta$, extended to a closed operator in the space $\mathbb{H}_\sigma$ with the domain $\mathbb{H}_\sigma^2$, has a real, negative, discrete spectrum with finite multiplicities of eigenvalues, condensed at $-\infty$ only [39]. Denote by $\{\lambda_k\}$ eigenvalues of B, numbered in non-increasing order, taking into account their multiplicities. Then, $\{\varphi_k\}$ will be used to denote the orthonormal system of eigenfunctions, which forms a basis in $\mathbb{H}_\sigma$ [39].

In order for Equation (19) to be fulfilled, take $\mathcal{Z} = \mathbb{H}_\sigma \times \mathbb{H}_\sigma$ and define in $\mathcal{Z}$ an operator

$$A = \begin{pmatrix} \mu B & B \\ bI & cI \end{pmatrix} \in \mathcal{C}l(\mathcal{Z}), \quad D_A = \mathbb{H}_\sigma^2 \times \mathbb{H}_\sigma^2. \tag{20}$$

Theorem 7. *Let $\alpha_k \in (0,1]$, $k = 0,1,\ldots,n$, $\sigma_n \in [1,2)$, $\mu > 0$, $b, c \in \mathbb{R}$, $\mathcal{Z} = \mathbb{H}_\sigma \times \mathbb{H}_\sigma$, the operator A be defined by* (20)*. Then, for some $\theta_0 \in (\pi/2,\pi)$, $a_0 > 0$ $A \in \mathcal{A}_{\{\alpha_k\}}(\theta_0,a_0)$.*

Proof. Let $\theta_0 \in (\pi/2, \pi)$, $\theta \in (\pi/2, \theta_0)$, $a_0 > 0$, $a > a_0$, then for $\lambda \in S_{\theta,a}$

$$\frac{|\lambda - a|}{|\lambda|} \leq 1 + \frac{a}{|\lambda|} \leq 1 + \frac{1}{\sin\theta_0},$$

so,

$$\frac{1}{|\lambda|^{\sigma_n}} = \frac{|\lambda - a|^{\alpha_0}}{|\lambda|^{\alpha_0}} \frac{1}{|\lambda - a|^{\alpha_0}|\lambda|^{\sigma_n - \alpha_0}} \leq \frac{\left(1 + \frac{1}{\sin\theta_0}\right)^{\alpha_0}}{|\lambda - a|^{\alpha_0}|\lambda|^{\sigma_n - \sigma_0 - 1}}$$

and instead of estimates of the form $\|R_{\lambda^{\sigma_n}}(A)\|_{\mathcal{L}(\mathcal{Z})} \leq \frac{K}{|\lambda - a|^{\alpha_0}|\lambda|^{\sigma_n - \sigma_0 - 1}}$, it will be enough to get inequalities $\|R_{\lambda^{\sigma_n}}(A)\|_{\mathcal{L}(\mathcal{Z})} \leq \frac{K}{|\lambda|^{\sigma_n}}$.

Take $\theta_0 \in (\pi/2, \pi/\sigma_n)$, $a_0 = (l|c|)^{1/\sigma_n}$, where $l > 1$ is sufficiently large, then for $\lambda \in S_{\theta_0,a_0}$

$$\lambda^{\sigma_n} I - A = \sum_{k=1}^{\infty} \begin{pmatrix} \lambda^{\sigma_n} - \mu\lambda_k & -\lambda_k \\ -b & \lambda^{\sigma_n} - c \end{pmatrix} \langle \cdot, \varphi_k \rangle \varphi_k,$$

$$(\lambda^{\sigma_n} I - A)^{-1} = \sum_{k=1}^{\infty} \begin{pmatrix} \frac{\lambda^{\sigma_n} - c}{(\lambda^{\sigma_n} - c)(\lambda^{\sigma_n} - \mu\lambda_k) - b\lambda_k} & \frac{\lambda_k}{(\lambda^{\sigma_n} - c)(\lambda^{\sigma_n} - \mu\lambda_k) - b\lambda_k} \\ \frac{b}{(\lambda^{\sigma_n} - c)(\lambda^{\sigma_n} - \mu\lambda_k) - b\lambda_k} & \frac{\lambda^{\sigma_n} - \mu\lambda_k}{(\lambda^{\sigma_n} - c)(\lambda^{\sigma_n} - \mu\lambda_k) - b\lambda_k} \end{pmatrix} \langle \cdot, \varphi_k \rangle \varphi_k.$$

Since $\lambda^{\sigma_n} \in S_{\theta_0\sigma_n, l|c|}$ for $\lambda \in S_{\theta_0,a_0}$, we have $|\lambda^{\sigma_n} - c| \geq (l-1)|c|\sin(\pi - \theta_0\sigma_n)$, for sufficiently large l, the value $|b(\lambda^{\sigma_n} - c)^{-1}|$ is small enough and

$$\arg\left(\mu + \frac{b}{\lambda^{\sigma_n} - c}\right) < \frac{1}{2}(\pi - \theta_0\sigma_n).$$

Fix l, $a_0 = (l|c|)^{1/\sigma_n}$; then, for $\lambda \in S_{\theta_0,a_0}$, we have $\lambda^{\sigma_n} \in S_{\theta_0\sigma_n, l|c|} \subset S_{\theta_0\sigma_n, 0}$ and

$$\left|\frac{\lambda^{\sigma_n} - c}{(\lambda^{\sigma_n} - c)(\lambda^{\sigma_n} - \mu\lambda_k) - b\lambda_k}\right| = \frac{1}{\left|\lambda^{\sigma_n} - \lambda_k\left(\mu + \frac{b}{\lambda^{\sigma_n} - c}\right)\right|} \leq \frac{1}{|\lambda|^{\sigma_n}\sin\frac{\pi - \theta_0\sigma_n}{2}},$$

$$\left|\frac{\lambda_k}{(\lambda^{\sigma_n} - c)(\lambda^{\sigma_n} - \mu\lambda_k) - b\lambda_k}\right| = \frac{1}{\left|(\lambda^{\sigma_n} - c)\left(\frac{\lambda^{\sigma_n}}{\lambda_k} - \mu\right) - b\right|} \leq$$

$$\leq \frac{1}{|\lambda|^{\sigma_n}\sin(\pi - \theta_0\sigma_n)\inf\limits_{k\in\mathbb{N},\lambda\in S_{\theta_0,a_0}}\left|\frac{\lambda^{\sigma_n}}{\lambda_k} - \mu\right| - b} \leq$$

$$\leq \frac{2}{|\lambda|^{\sigma_n}\sin(\pi - \theta_0\sigma_n)\inf\limits_{k\in\mathbb{N},\lambda\in S_{\theta_0,a_0}}\left|\frac{\lambda^{\sigma_n}}{\lambda_k} - \mu\right|},$$

if we take l, such that

$$|b| < \frac{l|c|}{2}\sin^{\sigma_n}\theta_0\sin(\pi - \theta_0\sigma_n)\inf_{k\in\mathbb{N},\lambda\in S_{\theta_0,a_0}}\left|\frac{\lambda^{\sigma_n}}{\lambda_k} - \mu\right| \leq$$

$$\leq \frac{|\lambda|^{\sigma_n}}{2}\sin(\pi - \theta_0\sigma_n)\inf_{k\in\mathbb{N},\lambda\in S_{\theta_0,a_0}}\left|\frac{\lambda^{\sigma_n}}{\lambda_k} - \mu\right|.$$

Further, for large $k \in \mathbb{N}$

$$\left|\frac{b}{(\lambda^{\sigma_n} - c)(\lambda^{\sigma_n} - \mu\lambda_k) - b\lambda_k}\right| \leq$$

$$\leq \frac{|b|}{\left|\left(\lambda^{\sigma_n} - \frac{c+\mu\lambda_k+\sqrt{\frac{(c-\mu\lambda_k)^2-4b\lambda_k}{2}}}{2}\right)\left(\lambda^{\sigma_n} - \frac{c+\mu\lambda_k-\sqrt{\frac{(c-\mu\lambda_k)^2-4b\lambda_k}{2}}}{2}\right)\right|} \leq$$

$$\leq \frac{|b|}{|\lambda|^{2\sigma_n}\sin^2(\pi-\theta_0\sigma_n)} \leq \frac{|b|(l|c|)^{-1}\sin^{-\sigma_n}\theta_0}{|\lambda|^{\sigma_n}\sin^2(\pi-\theta_0\sigma_n)},$$

$$\left|\frac{\lambda^{\sigma_n}-\mu\lambda_k}{(\lambda^{\sigma_n}-c)(\lambda^{\sigma_n}-\mu\lambda_k)-b\lambda_k}\right| \leq \frac{1}{\left|\lambda^{\sigma_n}-c-\frac{b\lambda_k}{\lambda^{\sigma_n}-\mu\lambda_k}\right|} \leq \frac{2}{|\lambda|^{\sigma_n}}$$

for sufficiently large l, since

$$\sup_{k\in\mathbb{N},\lambda\in S_{a_0,\theta_0}}\left|c+\frac{b\lambda_k}{\lambda^{\sigma_n}-\mu\lambda_k}\right| < \infty.$$

Thus, $A \in \mathcal{A}_{\{\alpha_k\}}(\theta_0, a_0)$ with $\theta_0 \in (\pi/2, \pi/\sigma_n)$, $a_0 = (l|c|)^{1/\sigma_n}$ with a chosen sufficiently large $l > 1$. □

Theorem 8. *Let* $\alpha_k \in (0,1]$, $k = 0,1,\ldots,n$, $\alpha_0 + \alpha_n > 1$, $\sigma_n \in [1,2)$, $\Sigma g, h \in C([0,T];\mathbb{H}_\sigma^2) \cup C^\gamma([0,T];\mathbb{H}_\sigma)$, $\gamma \in (0,1]$. *Then, problem* (15)–(19) *has a unique solution.*

Proof. Problem (15)–(19) is represented as abstract problem (10), (11) due to the above choice of $\mathcal{Z}$ and A. Since we find the vector functions $v(\cdot,t)$ and $w(\cdot,t)$ with the values in $\mathbb{H}_\sigma$ for every $t \in (0,T]$, instead of Equation (17), we consider its projection on $\mathbb{H}_\sigma$

$$D^{\sigma_n}v = \mu Bv + Bw + \Sigma g, \quad (x,t) \in \Omega \times (0,T],$$

In this case, the projection of Equation (18) on $\mathbb{H}_\sigma$ has the form

$$D^{\sigma_n}w = bv + cw + \Sigma h, \quad (x,t) \in \Omega \times (0,T],$$

hence, $\Pi h \equiv 0$. Theorem 7 and Theorem 5 imply the required statement. □

Remark 10. *If we found* $v(x,t)$ *and* $w(x,t)$, *we obtain the pressure gradient using the formula* $\nabla p(\cdot,t) = \mu\Pi\Delta v(\cdot,t) + \Pi\Delta w(\cdot,t) + \Pi f(\cdot,t)$ *from the projection of Equation* (17) *on the subspace* $\mathbb{H}_\pi$.

8. Conclusions

On the one hand, the results obtained will become the basis for the study of various classes of semilinear and quasilinear equations with the Dzhrbashyan–Nersesyan derivative. It is supposed to consider cases when the nonlinearity in the equation is continuous in the norm of the graph of the operator A and when it is Hölderian. In addition, there are plans to investigate similar equations with a degenerate linear operator at the Dzhrbashyan–Nersesyan derivative, linear, semi-linear and quasilinear. On the other hand, abstract results will be used to study various initial-boundary value problems for partial differential equations and their systems encountered in applications.

Author Contributions: Conceptualization, V.E.F. and M.V.P.; methodology, V.E.F.; software, E.M.I.; validation, E.M.I. and M.V.P.; formal analysis, E.M.I. and M.V.P.; investigation, E.M.I. and V.E.F.; resources, E.M.I.; data curation, E.M.I.; writing—original draft preparation, E.M.I. and M.V.P.; writing—review and editing, V.E.F. and M.V.P.; visualization, E.M.I.; supervision, V.E.F. and M.V.P.; project administration, V.E.F.; funding acquisition, V.E.F. All authors have read and agreed to the published version of the manuscript.

Funding: This research was funded by the Russian Science Foundation, grant number 22-21-20095.

Data Availability Statement: Not applicable.

Conflicts of Interest: The funders had no role in the design of the study; in the collection, analyses, or interpretation of data; in the writing of the manuscript, or in the decision to publish the results.

References

1. Dzhrbashyan, M.M.; Nersesyan, A.B. Fractional derivatives and the Cauchy problem for differential equations of fractional order. *Izv. Akad. Nauk Armyanskoy SSR Mat.* **1968**, *3*, 3–28. (In Russian) [CrossRef]
2. Samko, S.G.; Kilbas, A.A.; Marichev, O.I. *Fractional Integrals and Derivatives. Theory and Applications*; Gordon and Breach Science Publishers: Philadelphia, PA, USA, 1993.
3. Podlubny, I. *Fractional Differential Equations*; Academic Press: Boston, MA, USA, 1999.
4. Nakhushev, A.M. *Fractional Calculus ant Its Applications*; Fizmatlit: Moscow, Russia, 2003. (In Russian)
5. Kilbas, A.A.; Srivastava, H.M.; Trujillo, J.J. *Theory and Applications of Fractional Differential Equations*; Elsevier Science Publishing: Amsterdam, The Netherlands; Boston, MA, USA; Heidelberg, Germany, 2006.
6. Tarasov, V.E. *Fractional Dynamics: Applications of Fractional Calculus to Dynamics of Particles, Fields and Media*; Springer: New York, NY, USA, 2011.
7. Khan, H.; Alzabut, J.; Shah, A.; Etemad S.; Rezapour, S.; Park, C. A study on the fractal-fractional tobacco smoking model. *AIMS Math.* **2022**, *7*, 13887–13909. [CrossRef]
8. Mohammadi, H.; Kumar, S.; Rezapour, S.; Etemad, S. A theoretical study of the Caputo—Fabrizio fractional modeling for hearing loss due to Mumps virus with optimal control. *Chaos Solitons Fractals* **2021**, *144*, 110668. [CrossRef]
9. Mohammadi, H.; Rezapour, S.; Etemad, S. On a hybrid fractional Caputo—Hadamard boundary value problem with hybrid Hadamard integral boundary value conditions. *Adv. Differ. Equ.* **2020**, *2020*, 455. [CrossRef]
10. Najafi, H.; Etemad, S.; Patanarapeelert, N.; Asamoah, J.K.K.; Rezapour, S.; Sitthiwirattham, T. A study on dynamics of $CD4^{+}$ T-cells under the effect of HIV-1 infection based on a mathematical fractal-fractional model via the Adams—Bashforth scheme and Newton polynomials. *Mathematics* **2022**, *10*, 1366. [CrossRef]
11. Rezapour, S.; Etemad, S.; Mohammadi, H. A mathematical analysis of a system of Caputo—Fabrizio fractional differential equations for the anthrax disease model in animals. *Adv. Differ. Equ.* **2020**, *2020*, 481. [CrossRef]
12. Fu, L.; Zhang, Z.; Yang, H. Fractional model of blood flow and rogue waves in arterial vessels. *Mathematical Methods in the Applied Sciences*; John Wiley and Sons, Inc.: Hoboken, NJ, USA, 2022. [CrossRef]
13. Losanova, F.M.; Kenetova, R.O. Nonlocal problem for generalized Mckendrick—Von Foerster equation with Caputo operator. *Nonlinear World* **2018**, *16*, 49–53. (In Russian)
14. Berezgova, R.Z. A priori estimate for the solution of a nonlocal boundary value problem for the Mckendrick—Von Foerster equation of fractional order. *Dokl. Adyg. (Cherkesskoy) Mezhdunarodnoy Akad.* **2020**, *20*, 9–14. (In Russian)
15. Mamchuev, M.O. Cauchy problem for a linear system of ordinary differential equations of the fractional order. *Mathematics* **2020**, *8*, 1475. [CrossRef]
16. Pskhu, A.V. The fundamental solution of a diffusion-wave equation of fractional order. *Izv. Math.* **2009**, *73*, 351–392. [CrossRef]
17. Pskhu, A.V. Fractional diffusion equation with discretely distributed differentiation operator. *Sib. Electron. Math. Rep.* **2016**, *13*, 1078–1098.
18. Pskhu, A.V. Boundary value problem for a first-order partial differential equation with a fractional discretely distributed differentiation operator. *Differ. Equ.* **2016**, *52*, 1610–1623. [CrossRef]
19. Pskhu, A.V. Stabilization of solutions to the Cauchy problem for fractional diffusion-wave equation. *J. Math. Sci.* **2020**, *250*, 800–810. [CrossRef]
20. Bogatyreva, F.T. On representation of a solution for first-order partial differential equation with Dzhrbashyan—Nersesyan operator of fractional differentiation. *Dokl. Adyg. (Cherkesskoy) Mezhdunarodnoy Akad. Nauk* **2020**, *20*, 6–11. (In Russian) [CrossRef]
21. Bogatyreva, F.T. Boundary value problems for first order partial differential equation with the Dzhrbashyan—Nersesyan operators. *Chelyabinsk Phys. Math. J.* **2021**, *6*, 403–416.
22. Fedorov, V.E.; Plekhanova, M.V.; Izhberdeeva, E.M. Initial value problems of linear equations with the Dzhrbashyan—Nersesyan derivative in Banach spaces. *Symmetry* **2021**, *13*, 1058. [CrossRef]
23. Volkova, A.R.; Izhberdeeva, E.M.; Fedorov, V.E. Initial value problems for equations with a composition of fractional derivatives. *Chelyabinsk Phys. Math.* **2021**, *6*, 269–277. [CrossRef]
24. Solomyak, M.Z. Application of semigroup theory to the study of differential equations in Banach spaces. *Dokl. Akad. Nauk SSSR* **1958**, *122*, 766–769.
25. Yosida, K. *Functional Analysis*; Springer: Berlin/Heidelberg, Germany; New York, NY, USA, 1965.
26. Prüss, J. *Evolutionary Integral Equations and Applications*; Springer: Basel, Switzerland, 1993.
27. Bajlekova, E.G. Fractional Evolution Equations in Banach Spaces. Ph.D. Thesis, Eindhoven University of Technology, Eindhoven, The Netherlands, 2001.
28. Fedorov, V.E.; Avilovich, A.S. A Cauchy type problem for a degenerate equation with the Riemann—Liouville derivative in the sectorial case. *Sib. Math. J.* **2019**, *60*, 359–372. [CrossRef]

29. Fedorov, V.E.; Du, W.-S.; Turov, M.M. On the unique solvability of incomplete Cauchy type problems for a class of multi-term equations with the Riemann—Liouville derivatives. *Symmetry* **2022**, *14*, 75. [CrossRef]
30. Fedorov, V.E. Generators of analytic resolving families for distributed order equations and perturbations. *Mathematics* **2020**, *8*, 1306. [CrossRef]
31. Fedorov, V.E.; Filin, N.V. Linear equations with discretely distributed fractional derivative in Banach spaces. *Tr. Inst. Mat. Mekhaniki UrO RAN* **2021**, *27*, 264–280.
32. Fedorov, V.E.; Filin, N.V. On strongly continuous resolving families of operators for fractional distributed order equations. *Fractal Fract.* **2021**, *5*, 20. [CrossRef]
33. Fedorov, V.E. On generation of family of resolving operators for a distributed order equation analytic in sector. *J. Math. Sci.* **2022**, *260*, 75–86. [CrossRef]
34. Fedorov, V.E.; Du, W.-S.; Kostic, M.; Abdrakhmanova, A.A. Analytic resolving families for equations with distributed Riemann—Liouville derivatives. *Mathematics* **2022**, *10*, 681. [CrossRef]
35. Pazy, A. *Semigroups and Linear Operators and Applications to Partial Differential Equations*; Springer: New York, NY, USA, 1983.
36. Goldstein, J.A. Semigroups and second-order differential equations. *J. Funct. Anal.* **1969**, *4*, 50–70. [CrossRef]
37. Kato, K. *Perturbation Theory for Linear Operators*; Springer: Berlin/Heidelberg, Germany, 1966.
38. Oskolkov, A.P. Initial-boundary value problems for equations of motion of Kelvin—Voight fluids and Oldroyd fluids. *Proc. Steklov Inst. Math.* **1989**, *179*, 137–182.
39. Ladyzhenskaya, O.A. *The Mathematical Theory of Viscous Incompressible Flow*; Gordon and Breach Science Publishers: New York, NY, USA, 1969.

fractal and fractional

MDPI

Article

Existence Results for Coupled Nonlinear Sequential Fractional Differential Equations with Coupled Riemann–Stieltjes Integro-Multipoint Boundary Conditions

Ymnah Alruwaily [1], Bashir Ahmad [2,*], Sotiris K. Ntouyas [3] and Ahmed S. M. Alzaidi [4,*]

[1] Department of Mathematics, College of Science, Jouf University, P.O. Box 2014, Sakaka 72388, Saudi Arabia; ymnah@ju.edu.sa
[2] Department of Mathematics, Faculty of Science, King Abdulaziz University, P.O. Box 80203, Jeddah 21589, Saudi Arabia
[3] Department of Mathematics, University of Ioannina, 451 10 Ioannina, Greece; sntouyas@uoi.gr
[4] Department of Mathematics and Statistics, College of Science, Taif University, P.O. Box 11099, Taif 21944, Saudi Arabia
* Correspondence: bahmad@kau.edu.sa (B.A.); azaidi@tu.edu.sa (A.S.M.A.)

Abstract: This paper is concerned with the existence of solutions for a fully coupled Riemann–Stieltjes, integro-multipoint, boundary value problem of Caputo-type sequential fractional differential equations. The given system is studied with the aid of the Leray–Schauder alternative and contraction mapping principle. A numerical example illustrating the abstract results is also presented.

Keywords: sequential fractional differential equations; Caputo fractional derivative; Riemann–Stieltjes integro-multipoint boundary conditions; existence and uniqueness; fixed point

Citation: Alruwaily, Y.; Ahmad, B.; Ntouyas, S.K.; Alzaidi, A.S.M. Existence Results for Coupled Nonlinear Sequential Fractional Differential Equations with Coupled Riemann–Stieltjes Integro-Multipoint Boundary Conditions. *Fractal Fract.* **2022**, *6*, 123. https://doi.org/10.3390/fractalfract6020123

Academic Editor: Maria Rosaria Lancia

Received: 8 January 2022
Accepted: 16 February 2022
Published: 20 February 2022

1. Introduction

Coupled systems of fractional-order differential equations appear in the mathematical models of several real-world problems. Examples include chaos and fractional dynamics [1], bio-engineering [2], ecology [3], financial economics [4], etc. The topic of fractional differential systems, complemented by different kinds of boundary conditions, has been one a popular and important area of scientific investigation. Many researchers have contributed to the development of this subject by publishing numerous articles, Special Issues, etc. The modern methods of functional analysis areof great support in achieving existence and uniqueness results for these problems [5,6]. For some recent works on fractional or sequential fractional differential equations with nonlocal integral boundary conditions, we refer the reader to a series of papers [7–13].

In the article of [14], the authors investigated the solvability of an initial value problem involving a sequential fractional differential equation by means of fixed-point theorems in partially ordered sets. In [15], the existence and uniqueness results for a periodic boundary value problem of nonlinear sequential fractional differential equations were obtained by the method of upper and lower solutions, together with the monotone iterative technique.

Now, we briefly describe some recent works on sequential fractional-order coupled systems equipped with coupled boundary conditions. A fully coupled two-parameter system of sequential fractional integro-differential equations with nonlocal integro-multipoint boundary conditions was studied in [16]. The authors discussed the existence and uniqueness of solutions for a system of Hilfer–Hadamard sequential fractional differential equations with two-point boundary conditions in [17]. The sequential hybrid inclusion boundary value problem with three-point integro-derivative boundary conditions was investigated by using the analytic methods relying on α-ψ-contractive mappings, endpoints, and the fixed points of the product operators in [18]. The authors studied the existence and uniqueness of solutions for an initial value problem of coupled sequential fractional differential equations in [19]. The existence results for a nonlocal coupled system of sequential fractional differential equations involving ψ-Hilfer fractional derivatives were presented in [20].

The objective of the present work is to develop the existence theory for a new class of nonlinear coupled systems of sequential fractional differential equations supplemented with coupled, non-conjugate, Riemann–Stieltjes, integro-multipoint boundary conditions. In precise terms, we investigate the following system:

$$\begin{cases} ({}^cD^{q+1} + {}^cD^{q})\mathcal{X}(t) = \mathfrak{f}(t, \mathcal{X}(t), \mathcal{Y}(t)), \ 2 < q \leq 3, \ t \in [0,1], \\ ({}^cD^{p+1} + {}^cD^{p})\mathcal{Y}(t) = \mathfrak{g}(t, \mathcal{X}(t), \mathcal{Y}(t)), \ 2 < p \leq 3, \ t \in [0,1], \end{cases} \tag{1}$$

subject to the coupled boundary conditions:

$$\begin{cases} \mathcal{X}(0) = 0, \ \mathcal{X}'(0) = 0, \ \mathcal{X}'(1) = 0, \ \mathcal{X}(1) = k \int_0^{\rho} \mathcal{Y}(s)dA(s) + \sum\limits_{i=1}^{n-2} \alpha_i \mathcal{Y}(\sigma_i) + k_1 \int_{\nu}^{1} \mathcal{Y}(s)dA(s), \\ \mathcal{Y}(0) = 0, \ \mathcal{Y}'(0) = 0, \ \mathcal{Y}'(1) = 0, \ \mathcal{Y}(1) = h \int_0^{\rho} \mathcal{X}(s)dA(s) + \sum\limits_{i=1}^{n-2} \beta_i \mathcal{X}(\sigma_i) + h_1 \int_{\nu}^{1} \mathcal{X}(s)dA(s), \end{cases} \tag{2}$$

where ${}^cD^{\xi}$ denotes the Caputo fractional derivative of order $\xi \in \{q, p\}, 0 < \rho < \sigma_i < \nu < 1$, $\mathfrak{f}, \mathfrak{g} : [0,1] \times \mathbb{R} \times \mathbb{R} \to \mathbb{R}$ are given continuous functions, $k, k_1, h, h_1, \alpha_i, \ \beta_i \in \mathbb{R}$, i=1,2,$\cdots$, $n-2$ and A is a function of bounded variation.

Riemann–Stieltjes boundary conditions are quite general, since they include multipoint and integral boundary conditions as special cases [21]. The Riemann–Stieltjes integral is a generalization of the Riemann integral due to the Dutch astronomer T. J. Stieltjes and has potential applications in probability theory [22]. In addition, the Riemann–Stieltjes integral of the random variable with respect to its distribution function interprets the expected value of random variable [23]. Moreover, the boundary conditions (2) have useful applications in diffraction-free and self-healing optoelectronic devices. For more details, see [7].

The main emphasis in the present work is to investigate the existence criteria for the solutions to a coupled system of nonlinear sequential fractional differential equations equipped with multipoint Riemann–Stieltjes integral-type boundary conditions. Here, one can see that the coupled boundary conditions relate the value of the unknown function $\mathcal{X}(t)$ ($\mathcal{Y}(t)$) at $t = 1$ with the distributions of the unknown function $\mathcal{Y}(t)$ ($\mathcal{X}(t)$) on the segments $[0, \rho]$ and $[\nu, 1]$ in the sense of Riemann–Stieltjes integrals, together with the sum of its discrete values at $\sigma_i, i = 1, 2, \cdots, n-2$. The present study is novel in the given configuration and enriches the literature on boundary value problems of sequential fractional differential equations.

Concerning our strategy when studying the problem (1)–(2), we use the fixed-point approach, which is based on the idea of converting the given problem into a fixed-point problem, followed by the application of appropriate fixed-point theorems to show the existence of the fixed points for the operator involved in the problem at hand. We make use of the Leray–Schauder alternative to show the existence of a solution to the given problem, while the uniqueness result for the given problem is derived with the aid of the contraction mapping principle due to Banach.

The rest of this paper is organized as follows. In Section 2, we present some basic definitions of fractional calculus and prove an auxiliary lemma concerning the linear variant of the problem (1)–(2), helping to convert it into a fixed-point problem. Section 3 establishes the existence and uniqueness results for the given problem, whereas Section 4 contains an example illustrating the main results. The paper ends with a discussion in Section 5, where some special cases and possible future works are indicated.

2. Preliminary Material

First, we outline some basic concepts of fractional calculus [24].

Definition 1. *The Riemann–Liouville fractional integral of order $\vartheta \in \mathbb{R}$ $(\vartheta > 0)$ for a locally integrable, real-valued function U on $-\infty \leq a < z < b \leq +\infty$, denoted by $I_a^\vartheta U(z)$, is defined by*

$$I_a^\vartheta U(z) = \frac{1}{\Gamma(\vartheta)} \int_a^z (z-s)^{\vartheta-1} U(s) ds.$$

Here, $\Gamma(\cdot)$ is the familiar Gamma function.

Definition 2. *The Caputo derivative of fractional order ϑ for an $(r-1)$-times absolutely continuous function $U : [a,\infty) \longrightarrow \mathbb{R}$ is defined as*

$${}^cD^\vartheta U(z) = \frac{1}{\Gamma(r-\vartheta)} \int_a^z (z-s)^{r-\vartheta-1} U^{(r)}(s) ds, \; r-1 < \vartheta < r, \; r = [\vartheta]+1,$$

where $[\vartheta]$ denotes the integer part of the real number ϑ.

Lemma 1. *The general solution of the fractional differential equation ${}^cD^\vartheta \mathcal{X}(z) = 0$, $r-1 < \vartheta < r$, $z \in [a,b]$, is*

$$\mathcal{X}(z) = \varrho_0 + \varrho_1(z-a) + \varrho_2(z-a)^2 + \cdots + \varrho_{r-1}(z-a)^{r-1},$$

where $\varrho_i \in \mathbb{R}$, $i = 0,1,\cdots,r-1$. Furthermore,

$$I^\vartheta\, {}^cD^\vartheta \mathcal{X}(z) = \mathcal{X}(z) + \sum_{i=0}^{r-1} \varrho_i (z-a)^i.$$

Lemma 2. *Let $\psi, \phi \in (C[0,1],\mathbb{R})$ and $\Delta \neq 0$. Then the unique solution of the linear system of fractional differential*

$$\begin{cases} ({}^cD^{q+1} + {}^c D^q)\mathcal{X}(t) = \psi(t), & 2 < q \leq 3, \; t \in [0,1], \\ ({}^cD^{p+1} + {}^c D^p)\mathcal{Y}(t) = \phi(t), & 2 < p \leq 3, \; t \in [0,1], \end{cases} \tag{3}$$

supplemented with the boundary conditions (2), can be expressed in the following formulas:

$$\mathcal{X}(t) = \int_0^t e^{-(t-s)} I_{0^+}^q \psi(s) ds + \sum_{i=1}^4 \mathcal{Q}_i(t)\mathcal{E}_i, \; i = 1,2,3,4, \tag{4}$$

$$\mathcal{Y}(t) = \int_0^t e^{-(t-s)} I_{0^+}^p \phi(s) ds + \sum_{j=1}^4 \mathcal{P}_j(t)\mathcal{E}_j, \; j = 1,2,3,4, \tag{5}$$

where

$$\begin{aligned}
\mathcal{E}_1 &= \int_0^1 e^{-(1-s)} I_{0^+}^q \psi(s) ds - I_{0^+}^q \psi(1), \\
\mathcal{E}_2 &= \int_0^1 e^{-(1-s)} I_{0^+}^p \phi(s) ds - I_{0^+}^p \phi(1), \\
\mathcal{E}_3 &= k \int_0^\rho \Big(\int_0^s e^{-(s-z)} I_{0^+}^p \phi(z) dz \Big) dA(s) + \sum_{i=1}^{n-2} \alpha_i \int_0^{\sigma_i} e^{-(\sigma_i - s)} I_{0^+}^p \phi(s) ds \\
&\quad + k_1 \int_\nu^1 \Big(\int_0^s e^{-(s-z)} I_{0^+}^p \phi(z) dz \Big) dA(s) - \int_0^1 e^{-(1-s)} I_{0^+}^q \psi(s) ds \\
\mathcal{E}_4 &= h \int_0^\rho \Big(\int_0^s e^{-(s-z)} I_{0^+}^q \psi(z) dz \Big) dA(s) + \sum_{i=1}^{n-2} \beta_i \int_0^{\sigma_i} e^{-(\sigma_i - s)} I_{0^+}^q \psi(s) ds
\end{aligned}$$

$$+h_1\int_{\nu}^{1}\Big(\int_0^s e^{-(s-z)}I_{0^+}^{q}\psi(z)dz\Big)dA(s)-\int_0^1 e^{-(1-s)}I_{0^+}^{p}\phi(s)ds, \tag{6}$$

$$\begin{aligned}\mathcal{Q}_i(t) &= (e^{-t}+t-1)\lambda_i+(-2e^{-t}+t^2-2t+2)\nu_i,\ i=1,2,3,4,\\ \mathcal{P}_j(t) &= (e^{-t}+t-1)\rho_j+(-2e^{-t}+t^2-2t+2)\omega_j,\ j=1,2,3,4,\end{aligned} \tag{7}$$

$$\nu_1 = \frac{e+(1-e)\lambda_1}{2},\ \nu_2=\frac{(1-e)\lambda_2}{2},\ \nu_3=\frac{(1-e)\lambda_3}{2},\ \nu_4=\frac{(1-e)\lambda_4}{2}, \tag{8}$$

$$\omega_1 = \frac{(1-e)\rho_1}{2},\ \omega_2=\frac{e+(1-e)\rho_2}{2},\ \omega_3=\frac{(1-e)\rho_3}{2},\ \omega_4=\frac{(1-e)\rho_4}{2}, \tag{9}$$

$$\lambda_1 = \frac{(2-e)\gamma_1-A_4\gamma_2 e}{2\Delta},\ \lambda_2=\frac{A_2\gamma_1 e-(2-e)\gamma_2}{2\Delta},\ \lambda_3=\frac{\gamma_1}{\Delta},\ \lambda_4=\frac{-\gamma_2}{\Delta}, \tag{10}$$

$$\rho_1 = \frac{A_4\gamma_1 e-(2-e)\gamma_3}{2\Delta},\ \rho_2=\frac{(2-e)\gamma_1-A_2\gamma_3 e}{2\Delta},\ \rho_3=\frac{-\gamma_3}{\Delta},\ \rho_4=\frac{\gamma_1}{\Delta}, \tag{11}$$

$$\Delta=\gamma_1^2-\gamma_2\gamma_3,\ \gamma_1=\frac{3-e}{2},\ \gamma_2=-A_1-A_2\frac{(1-e)}{2},\ \gamma_3=-A_3-A_4\frac{(1-e)}{2}, \tag{12}$$

$$\begin{aligned}A_1 &= k\int_0^{\rho}(e^{-s}+s-1)dA(s)+\sum_{i=1}^{n-2}\alpha_i(e^{-\sigma_i}+\sigma_i-1)+k_1\int_{\nu}^{1}(e^{-s}+s-1)dA(s),\\ A_2 &= k\int_0^{\rho}(-2e^{-s}+s^2-2s+2)dA(s)+\sum_{i=1}^{n-2}\alpha_i(-2e^{-\sigma_i}+\sigma_i^2-2\sigma_i+2)\\ &\quad +k_1\int_{\nu}^{1}(-2e^{-s}+s^2-2s+2)dA(s),\\ A_3 &= h\int_0^{\rho}(e^{-s}+s-1)dA(s)+\sum_{i=1}^{n-2}\beta_i(e^{-\sigma_i}+\sigma_i-1)+h_1\int_{\nu}^{1}(e^{-s}+s-1)dA(s),\\ A_4 &= h\int_0^{\rho}(-2e^{-s}+s^2-2s+2)dA(s)+\sum_{i=1}^{n-2}\beta_i(-2e^{-\sigma_i}+\sigma_i^2-2\sigma_i+2)\\ &\quad +h_1\int_{\nu}^{1}(-2e^{-s}+s^2-2s+2)dA(s).\end{aligned} \tag{13}$$

Proof. Rewriting the first equation in (3) as ${}^{c}D^{q}(D+1)\mathcal{X}(t)=\psi(t)$ and then applying the integral operator $I_{0^+}^{q}$ to it, we obtain

$$\begin{aligned}\mathcal{X}(t) &= (-e^{-t}+1)c_1+(e^{-t}+t-1)c_2+(-2e^{-t}+t^2-2t+2)c_3+e^{-t}c_4\\ &\quad +\int_0^t e^{-(t-s)}I_{0^+}^{q}\psi(s)ds,\end{aligned} \tag{14}$$

where $c_i\in\mathbb{R},\ i=1,2,3,4$ are unknown arbitrary constants. In a similar manner, applying the integral operator $I_{0^+}^{p}$ to the second equation in (3), we get

$$\begin{aligned}\mathcal{Y}(t) &= (-e^{-t}+1)b_1+(e^{-t}+t-1)b_2+(-2e^{-t}+t^2-2t+2)b_3+e^{-t}b_4\\ &\quad +\int_0^t e^{-(t-s)}I_{0^+}^{p}\phi(s)ds,\end{aligned} \tag{15}$$

where $b_i\in\mathbb{R},\ i=1,2,3,4$ are unknown arbitrary constants. From (14) and (15), we have

$$\begin{aligned}\mathcal{X}'(t) &= e^{-t}c_1+(-e^{-t}+1)c_2+(2e^{-t}+2t-2)c_3-e^{-t}c_4\\ &\quad -\int_0^t e^{-(t-s)}I_{0^+}^{q}\psi(s)ds+I_{0^+}^{q}\psi(t),\end{aligned} \tag{16}$$

$$\mathcal{Y}'(t) = e^{-t}b_1 + (-e^{-t}+1)b_2 + (2e^{-t}+2t-2)b_3 - e^{-t}b_4 - \int_0^t e^{-(t-s)} I_{0+}^p \phi(s)ds + I_{0+}^p \phi(t). \quad (17)$$

Using the conditions $\mathcal{X}(0) = 0, \mathcal{Y}(0) = 0, \mathcal{X}'(0) = 0, \mathcal{Y}'(0) = 0$ in Equations (14)–(17), we obtain $c_1 = c_4 = 0$ and $b_1 = b_4 = 0$. Then (14)–(17) become

$$\mathcal{X}(t) = (e^{-t}+t-1)c_2 + (-2e^{-t}+t^2-2t+2)c_3 + \int_0^t e^{-(t-s)} I_{0+}^q \psi(s)ds, \quad (18)$$

$$\mathcal{X}'(t) = (-e^{-t}+1)c_2 + (2e^{-t}+2t-2)c_3 - \int_0^t e^{-(t-s)} I_{0+}^q \psi(s)ds + I_{0+}^q \psi(t), \quad (19)$$

$$\mathcal{Y}(t) = (e^{-t}+t-1)b_2 + (-2e^{-t}+t^2-2t+2)b_3 + \int_0^t e^{-(t-s)} I_{0+}^p \phi(s)ds, \quad (20)$$

$$\mathcal{Y}'(t) = (-e^{-t}+1)b_2 + (2e^{-t}+2t-2)b_3 - \int_0^t e^{-(t-s)} I_{0+}^p \phi(s)ds + I_{0+}^p \phi(t). \quad (21)$$

Using (18)–(21) in the rest of the boundary conditions given by (2), together with notation (13), yields

$$(-e^{-1}+1)c_2 + 2e^{-1}c_3 = \mathcal{E}_1, \quad (22)$$

$$(-e^{-1}+1)b_2 + 2e^{-1}b_3 = \mathcal{E}_2, \quad (23)$$

$$e^{-1}c_2 + (-2e^{-1}+1)c_3 - A_1b_2 - A_2b_3 = \mathcal{E}_3, \quad (24)$$

$$e^{-1}b_2 + (-2e^{-1}+1)b_3 - A_3c_2 - A_4c_3 = \mathcal{E}_4, \quad (25)$$

where $A_i,\ i = 1,2,3,4$ are given by (13) and $\mathcal{E}_i,\ i = 1,2,3,4$ are defined by (6). Inserting the values of c_3 and b_3 from (22) and (23) into (24) and (25), we obtain

$$\gamma_1 c_2 + \gamma_2 b_2 = \frac{(2-e)}{2}\mathcal{E}_1 + \frac{A_2 e}{2}\mathcal{E}_2 + \mathcal{E}_3, \quad (26)$$

$$\gamma_3 c_2 + \gamma_1 b_2 = \frac{A_4 e}{2}\mathcal{E}_1 + \frac{(2-e)}{2}\mathcal{E}_2 + \mathcal{E}_4, \quad (27)$$

where $\gamma_i,\ i = 1,2,3$ are given by (12). Solving (26) and (27) for c_2 and b_2, we obtain

$$c_2 = \sum_{i=1}^{4} \lambda_i \mathcal{E}_i, \quad b_2 = \sum_{j=1}^{4} \rho_j \mathcal{E}_j,$$

where λ_i $(i = 1,2,3,4)$ and ρ_j $(j = 1,2,3,4)$ are given in (10) and (11), respectively. Substituting the values of c_2 and b_2 into (22) and (23) respectively, we find that

$$c_3 = \sum_{i=1}^{4} \nu_i \mathcal{E}_i, \quad b_3 = \sum_{j=1}^{4} \omega_j \mathcal{E}_j,$$

where $\nu_i, i = 1,2,3,4$, and $\omega_j,\ j = 1,2,3,4$ are given by (8) and (9) respectively. Inserting the values of c_2, c_3, b_2 and b_3 in (18) and (20), together with the notation (7), we obtain the solution (4) and (5). One can obtain the converse of this lemma by direct computation. This completes the proof. □

For computational convenience, we introduce the following lemma:

Lemma 3. *For $\psi,\ \phi \in C([0,1],\mathbb{R})$, we have*

(i) $\left| \int_0^t e^{-(t-s)} I_{0+}^q \psi(s)ds \right| \le \frac{1}{\Gamma(q+1)}(1-e^{-1})\|\psi\|,$

$$\left|\int_0^t e^{-(t-s)} I_{0+}^p \phi(s)ds\right| \leq \frac{1}{\Gamma(p+1)}(1-e^{-1})\|\phi\|.$$

(ii) $$\left|\int_0^1 e^{-(1-s)} I_{0+}^q \psi(s)ds\right| \leq \frac{1}{\Gamma(q+1)}(1-e^{-1})\|\psi\|,$$

$$\left|\int_0^1 e^{-(1-s)} I_{0+}^p \phi(s)ds\right| \leq \frac{1}{\Gamma(p+1)}(1-e^{-1})\|\phi\|.$$

(iii) $$\left|\sum_{i=1}^{n-2} \alpha_i \int_0^{\sigma_i} e^{-(\sigma_i-s)} I_{0+}^p \phi(s)ds\right| \leq \frac{1}{\Gamma(p+1)} \sum_{i=1}^{n-2} |\alpha_i|\sigma_i^p(1-e^{-\sigma_i})\|\phi\|,$$

$$\left|\sum_{i=1}^{n-2} \beta_i \int_0^{\sigma_i} e^{-(\sigma_i-s)} I_{0+}^q \psi(s)ds\right| \leq \frac{1}{\Gamma(q+1)} \sum_{i=1}^{n-2} |\beta_i|\sigma_i^q(1-e^{-\sigma_i})\|\psi\|.$$

(iv) $$\left|\int_0^\rho \Big(\int_0^s e^{-(s-z)} I_{0+}^p \phi(z)dz\Big)dA(s)\right| \leq \Big[\int_0^\rho \frac{s^p}{\Gamma(p+1)}(1-e^{-s})dA(s)\Big]\|\phi\|,$$

$$\left|\int_0^\rho \Big(\int_0^s e^{-(s-z)} I_{0+}^q \psi(z)dz\Big)dA(s)\right| \leq \Big[\int_0^\rho \frac{s^q}{\Gamma(q+1)}(1-e^{-s})dA(s)\Big]\|\psi\|.$$

(v) $$\left|\int_\nu^1 \Big(\int_0^s e^{-(s-z)} I_{0+}^p \phi(z)dz\Big)dA(s)\right| \leq \Big[\int_\nu^1 \frac{s^p}{\Gamma(p+1)}(1-e^{-s})dA(s)\Big]\|\phi\|,$$

$$\left|\int_\nu^1 \Big(\int_0^s e^{-(s-z)} I_{0+}^q \psi(z)dz\Big)dA(s)\right| \leq \Big[\int_\nu^1 \frac{s^q}{\Gamma(q+1)}(1-e^{-s})dA(s)\Big]\|\psi\|.$$

Proof. To prove (i), we have

$$\begin{aligned}\left|\int_0^t e^{-(t-s)} I_{0+}^q \psi(s)ds\right| &= \left|\int_0^t e^{-(t-s)}\Big(\int_0^s \frac{(s-z)^{q-1}}{\Gamma(q)}\psi(z)dz\Big)ds\right| \\ &\leq \frac{t^q}{\Gamma(q+1)}(1-e^{-t})\|\psi\| \\ &\leq \frac{1}{\Gamma(q+1)}(1-e^{-1})\|\psi\|.\end{aligned}$$

The other cases are similar. Therefore, we omit the details. □

3. Main Results

Let $(\mathfrak{X}, \|\cdot\|)$ be a Banach space equipped with the norm $\|\mathcal{X}\| = \sup\{|\mathcal{X}(t)|, t \in [0,1]\}$, where $\mathfrak{X} = \{\mathcal{X}(t)|\mathcal{X}(t) \in (C[0,1],\mathbb{R})\}$. Then $(\mathfrak{X}\times\mathfrak{X}, \|(\cdot,\cdot)\|)$ is also a Banach space endowed with norm $\|(\mathcal{X},\mathcal{Y})\| = \|\mathcal{X}\| + \|\mathcal{Y}\|, \mathcal{X},\mathcal{Y} \in \mathfrak{X}$.

By Lemma 2, we introduce an operator $T : \mathfrak{X}\times\mathfrak{X} \to \mathfrak{X}\times\mathfrak{X}$ defined by

$$T(\mathcal{X},\mathcal{Y})(t) = \begin{pmatrix} T_1(\mathcal{X},\mathcal{Y})(t) \\ T_2(\mathcal{X},\mathcal{Y})(t) \end{pmatrix}, \tag{28}$$

where

$$\begin{aligned}T_1(\mathcal{X},\mathcal{Y})(t) &= \int_0^t e^{-(t-s)} I_{0+}^q \mathfrak{f}(s,\mathcal{X}(s),\mathcal{Y}(s))ds \\ &+\mathcal{Q}_1(t)\Big[\int_0^1 e^{-(1-s)} I_{0+}^q \mathfrak{f}(s,\mathcal{X}(s),\mathcal{Y}(s))ds - I_{0+}^q \mathfrak{f}(s,\mathcal{X}(s),\mathcal{Y}(s))(1)\Big] \\ &+ \mathcal{Q}_2(t)\Big[\int_0^1 e^{-(1-s)} I_{0+}^p \mathfrak{g}(s,\mathcal{X}(s),\mathcal{Y}(s))ds - I_{0+}^p \mathfrak{g}(s,\mathcal{X}(s),\mathcal{Y}(s))(1)\Big]\end{aligned}$$

$$
\begin{aligned}
& + \mathcal{Q}_3(t)\Big[k\int_0^{\rho}\Big(\int_0^{s} e^{-(s-z)} I_{0^+}^{p}\mathfrak{g}(z,\mathcal{X}(z),\mathcal{Y}(z))dz\Big)dA(s) \\
& + \sum_{i=1}^{n-2}\alpha_i\int_0^{\sigma_i} e^{-(\sigma_i-s)} I_{0^+}^{p}\mathfrak{g}(s,\mathcal{X}(s),\mathcal{Y}(s))ds \\
& + k_1\int_{\nu}^{1}\Big(\int_0^{s} e^{-(s-z)} I_{0^+}^{p}\mathfrak{g}(z,\mathcal{X}(z),\mathcal{Y}(z))dz\Big)dA(s) \\
& - \int_0^{1} e^{-(1-s)} I_{0^+}^{q}\mathfrak{f}(s,\mathcal{X}(s),\mathcal{Y}(s))ds\Big] \\
& + \mathcal{Q}_4(t)\Big[h\int_0^{\rho}\Big(\int_0^{s} e^{-(s-z)} I_{0^+}^{q}\mathfrak{f}(z,\mathcal{X}(z),\mathcal{Y}(z))dz\Big)dA(s) \\
& + \sum_{i=1}^{n-2}\beta_i\int_0^{\sigma_i} e^{-(\sigma_i-s)} I_{0^+}^{q}\mathfrak{f}(s,\mathcal{X}(s),\mathcal{Y}(s))ds \\
& + h_1\int_{\nu}^{1}\Big(\int_0^{s} e^{-(s-z)} I_{0^+}^{q}\mathfrak{f}(z,\mathcal{X}(z),\mathcal{Y}(z))dz\Big)dA(s) \\
& - \int_0^{1} e^{-(1-s)} I_{0^+}^{p}\mathfrak{g}(s,\mathcal{X}(s),\mathcal{Y}(s))ds\Big],
\end{aligned}
\tag{29}
$$

$$
\begin{aligned}
T_2(\mathcal{X},\mathcal{Y})(t) = & \int_0^{t} e^{-(t-s)} I_{0^+}^{p}\mathfrak{g}(s,\mathcal{X}(s),\mathcal{Y}(s))ds \\
& + \mathcal{P}_1(t)\Big[\int_0^{1} e^{-(1-s)} I_{0^+}^{q}\mathfrak{f}(s,\mathcal{X}(s),\mathcal{Y}(s))ds - I_{0^+}^{q}\mathfrak{f}(s,\mathcal{X}(s),\mathcal{Y}(s))(1)\Big] \\
& + \mathcal{P}_2(t)\Big[\int_0^{1} e^{-(1-s)} I_{0^+}^{p}\mathfrak{g}(s,\mathcal{X}(s),\mathcal{Y}(s))ds - I_{0^+}^{p}\mathfrak{g}(s,\mathcal{X}(s),\mathcal{Y}(s))(1)\Big] \\
& + \mathcal{P}_3(t)\Big[k\int_0^{\rho}\Big(\int_0^{s} e^{-(s-z)} I_{0^+}^{p}\mathfrak{g}(z,\mathcal{X}(z),\mathcal{Y}(z))dz\Big)dA(s) \\
& + \sum_{i=1}^{n-2}\alpha_i\int_0^{\sigma_i} e^{-(\sigma_i-s)} I_{0^+}^{p}g(s,\mathcal{X}(s),\mathcal{Y}(s))ds \\
& + k_1\int_{\nu}^{1}\Big(\int_0^{s} e^{-(s-z)} I_{0^+}^{p}\mathfrak{g}(z,\mathcal{X}(z),\mathcal{Y}(z))dz\Big)dA(s) \\
& - \int_0^{1} e^{-(1-s)} I_{0^+}^{q}\mathfrak{f}(s,\mathcal{X}(s),\mathcal{Y}(s))ds\Big] \\
& + \mathcal{P}_4(t)\Big[h\int_0^{\rho}\Big(\int_0^{s} e^{-(s-z)} I_{0^+}^{q}\mathfrak{f}(z,\mathcal{X}(z),\mathcal{Y}(z))dz\Big)dA(s) \\
& + \sum_{i=1}^{n-2}\beta_i\int_0^{\sigma_i} e^{-(\sigma_i-s)} I_{0^+}^{q}\mathfrak{f}(s,\mathcal{X}(s),\mathcal{Y}(s))ds \\
& + h_1\int_{\nu}^{1}\Big(\int_0^{s} e^{-(s-z)} I_{0^+}^{q}\mathfrak{f}(z,\mathcal{X}(z),\mathcal{Y}(z))dz\Big)dA(s) \\
& - \int_0^{1} e^{-(1-s)} I_{0^+}^{p}\mathfrak{g}(s,\mathcal{X}(s),\mathcal{Y}(s))ds\Big],
\end{aligned}
\tag{30}
$$

where $\mathcal{Q}_i(t),\ i=1,2,3,4$ and $\mathcal{P}_j(t),\ j=1,2,3,4$ are given in (7).

In the forthcoming analysis, we assume that $\mathfrak{f},\mathfrak{g}:[0,1]\times\mathbb{R}\times\mathbb{R}\to\mathbb{R}$ are continuous functions satisfying the following conditions:

($\mathcal{F}_1$) There are real constants $\eta_i,\zeta_i\geq 0, i=1,2,\ \eta_0,\zeta_0>0$ such that

$$|\mathfrak{f}(t,\mathcal{X},\mathcal{Y})|\leq \eta_0+\eta_1|\mathcal{X}|+\eta_2|\mathcal{Y}|,$$

$$|\mathfrak{g}(t,\mathcal{X},\mathcal{Y})|\leq \zeta_0+\zeta_1|\mathcal{X}|+\zeta_2|\mathcal{Y}|,$$

$\forall t\in[0,1],\mathcal{X},\mathcal{Y}\in\mathbb{R}$.

($\mathcal{F}_2$) There are positive real constants L_1 and L_2, such that

$$|\mathfrak{f}(t,\mathcal{X}_1,\mathcal{Y}_1) - \mathfrak{f}(t,\mathcal{X}_2,\mathcal{Y}_2)| \leq L_1(|\mathcal{X}_1 - \mathcal{X}_2| + |\mathcal{Y}_1 - \mathcal{Y}_2|),$$

$$|\mathfrak{g}(t,\mathcal{X}_1,\mathcal{Y}_1) - \mathfrak{g}(t,\mathcal{X}_2,\mathcal{Y}_2)| \leq L_2(|\mathcal{X}_1 - \mathcal{X}_2| + |\mathcal{Y}_1 - \mathcal{Y}_2|),$$

$\forall t \in [0,1], \mathcal{X}_1, \mathcal{X}_2, \mathcal{Y}_1, \mathcal{Y}_2 \in \mathbb{R}$;

In the sequel, we use the notation:

$$\Theta = \Lambda_1 L_1 + \Lambda_2 L_2, \ \ \overline{\Theta} = \overline{\Lambda}_1 L_1 + \overline{\Lambda}_2 L_2, \tag{31}$$

$$\mathcal{M} = \Lambda_1 \mathcal{N}_1 + \Lambda_2 \mathcal{N}_2, \ \ \overline{\mathcal{M}} = \overline{\Lambda}_1 \mathcal{N}_1 + \overline{\Lambda}_2 \mathcal{N}_2, \tag{32}$$

$$\begin{aligned}
\Lambda_1 &= \frac{1}{\Gamma(q+1)}\Big\{(1-e^{-1}) + (2-e^{-1})\widetilde{\mathcal{Q}}_1 + (1-e^{-1})\widetilde{\mathcal{Q}}_3 + \widetilde{\mathcal{Q}}_4\Big[|h|\int_0^\rho s^q(1-e^{-s})dA(s) \\
&\quad + \sum_{i=1}^{n-2}|\beta_i|\sigma_i^q(1-e^{-\sigma_i}) + |h_1|\int_\nu^1 s^q(1-e^{-s})dA(s)\Big]\Big\}, \\
\Lambda_2 &= \frac{1}{\Gamma(p+1)}\Big\{(2-e^{-1})\widetilde{\mathcal{Q}}_2 + \widetilde{\mathcal{Q}}_3\Big[|k|\int_0^\rho s^p(1-e^{-s})dA(s) \\
&\quad + \sum_{i=1}^{n-2}|\alpha_i|\sigma_i^p(1-e^{-\sigma_i}) + |k_1|\int_\nu^1 s^p(1-e^{-s})dA(s)\Big] + (1-e^{-1})\widetilde{\mathcal{Q}}_4\Big\},
\end{aligned} \tag{33}$$

$$\begin{aligned}
\overline{\Lambda}_1 &= \frac{1}{\Gamma(q+1)}\Big\{(2-e^{-1})\widetilde{\mathcal{P}}_1 + (1-e^{-1})\widetilde{\mathcal{P}}_3 + \widetilde{\mathcal{P}}_4\Big[|h|\int_0^\rho s^q(1-e^{-s})dA(s) \\
&\quad + \sum_{i=1}^{n-2}|\beta_i|\sigma_i^q(1-e^{-\sigma_i}) + |h_1|\int_\nu^1 s^q(1-e^{-s})dA(s)\Big]\Big\}, \\
\overline{\Lambda}_2 &= \frac{1}{\Gamma(p+1)}\Big\{(1-e^{-1}) + (2-e^{-1})\widetilde{\mathcal{P}}_2 + \widetilde{\mathcal{P}}_3\Big[|k|\int_0^\rho s^p(1-e^{-s})dA(s) \\
&\quad + \sum_{i=1}^{n-2}|\alpha_i|\sigma_i^p(1-e^{-\sigma_i}) + |k_1|\int_\nu^1 s^p(1-e^{-s})dA(s)\Big] + (1-e^{-1})\widetilde{\mathcal{P}}_4\Big\},
\end{aligned} \tag{34}$$

$$\mathcal{N}_1 = \sup_{t\in[0,1]}|\mathfrak{f}(t,0,0)| < \infty, \ \mathcal{N}_2 = \sup_{t\in[0,1]}|\mathfrak{g}(t,0,0,)| < \infty, \tag{35}$$

where $\widetilde{\mathcal{Q}}_i = \sup_{t\in[0,1]}|\mathcal{Q}_i(t)|$, $i = 1,2,3,4$ and $\widetilde{\mathcal{P}}_j = \sup_{t\in[0,1]}|\mathcal{P}_j(t)|$, $j = 1,2,3,4$,

$$\begin{aligned}
\Omega_0 &= (\Lambda_1 + \overline{\Lambda}_1)\eta_0 + (\Lambda_2 + \overline{\Lambda}_2)\zeta_0, \\
\Omega_1 &= (\Lambda_1 + \overline{\Lambda}_1)\eta_1 + (\Lambda_2 + \overline{\Lambda}_2)\zeta_1, \\
\Omega_2 &= (\Lambda_1 + \overline{\Lambda}_1)\eta_2 + (\Lambda_2 + \overline{\Lambda}_2)\zeta_2,
\end{aligned} \tag{36}$$

and

$$\Omega = \max\{\Omega_1, \Omega_2\}. \tag{37}$$

The following result shows the existence of a solution for the coupled system (1)–(2) and is based on the Leray–Schauder alternative [6].

Theorem 1. *Assume that the condition* $(\mathcal{F}_1)$ *holds and* $\Omega < 1$, *where* Ω *is given by (37). Then, the problem (1) and (2) has at least one solution on* $[0,1]$.

Proof. In the first step, it will be shown that the operator $T : \mathfrak{X} \times \mathfrak{X} \to \mathfrak{X} \times \mathfrak{X}$ is completely continuous. Note that the operator T is continuous in view of the continuity of the functions $\mathfrak{f}$ and $\mathfrak{g}$. Let $\mathcal{V} \subset \mathfrak{X} \times \mathfrak{X}$ be bounded. Then, we can find positive constants M_1 and M_2 such that $|\mathfrak{f}(t, \mathcal{X}(t), \mathcal{Y}(t))| \leq M_1$ and $|\mathfrak{g}(t, \mathcal{X}(t), \mathcal{Y}(t))| \leq M_2$, $\forall(\mathcal{X}, \mathcal{Y}) \in \mathcal{V}$. Therefore, for any $(\mathcal{X}, \mathcal{X}) \in \mathcal{V}$, we have

$$
\begin{aligned}
|T_1(\mathcal{X},\mathcal{Y})(t)| \leq\; & \int_0^t e^{-(t-s)} I_{0+}^q |\mathfrak{f}(s,\mathcal{X}(s),\mathcal{Y}(s))| ds \\
& + |\mathcal{Q}_1(t)| \Big[\int_0^1 e^{-(1-s)} I_{0+}^q |\mathfrak{f}(s,\mathcal{X}(s),\mathcal{Y}(s))| ds + I_{0+}^q |\mathfrak{f}(s,\mathcal{X}(s),\mathcal{Y}(s))|(1) \Big] \\
& + |\mathcal{Q}_2(t)| \Big[\int_0^1 e^{-(1-s)} I_{0+}^p |\mathfrak{g}(s,\mathcal{X}(s),\mathcal{Y}(s))| ds + I_{0+}^p |\mathfrak{g}(s,\mathcal{X}(s),\mathcal{Y}(s))|(1) \Big] \\
& + |\mathcal{Q}_3(t)| \Big[|k| \int_0^\rho \Big(\int_0^s e^{-(s-z)} I_{0+}^p |\mathfrak{g}(z,\mathcal{X}(z),\mathcal{Y}(z))| dz \Big) dA(s) \\
& + \sum_{i=1}^{n-2} |\alpha_i| \int_0^{\sigma_i} e^{-(\sigma_i - s)} I_{0+}^p |\mathfrak{g}(s,\mathcal{X}(s),\mathcal{Y}(s))| ds \\
& + |k_1| \int_\nu^1 \Big(\int_0^s e^{-(s-z)} I_{0+}^p |\mathfrak{g}(z,\mathcal{X}(z),\mathcal{Y}(z))| dz \Big) dA(s) \\
& + \int_0^1 e^{-(1-s)} I_{0+}^q |\mathfrak{f}(s,\mathcal{X}(s),\mathcal{Y}(s))| ds \Big] \\
& + |\mathcal{Q}_4(t)| \Big[|h| \int_0^\rho \Big(\int_0^s e^{-(s-z)} I_{0+}^q |\mathfrak{f}(z,\mathcal{X}(z),\mathcal{Y}(z))| dz \Big) dA(s) \\
& + \sum_{i=1}^{n-2} |\beta_i| \int_0^{\sigma_i} e^{-(\sigma_i - s)} I_{0+}^q |\mathfrak{f}(s,\mathcal{X}(s),\mathcal{Y}(s))| ds \\
& + |h_1| \int_\nu^1 \Big(\int_0^s e^{-(s-z)} I_{0+}^q |\mathfrak{f}(z,\mathcal{X}(z),\mathcal{Y}(z))| dz \Big) dA(s) \\
& + \int_0^1 e^{-(1-s)} I_{0+}^p |\mathfrak{g}(s,\mathcal{X}(s),\mathcal{Y}(s))| ds \Big] \\
\leq\; & M_1 \frac{1}{\Gamma(q+1)}(1-e^{-1}) + \widetilde{\mathcal{Q}}_1 \Big[M_1 \frac{1}{\Gamma(q+1)}(1-e^{-1}) + M_1 \frac{1}{\Gamma(q+1)} \Big] \\
& + \widetilde{\mathcal{Q}}_2 \Big[M_2 \frac{1}{\Gamma(p+1)}(1-e^{-1}) + M_2 \frac{1}{\Gamma(p+1)} \Big] \\
& + \widetilde{\mathcal{Q}}_3 \Big[|k| M_2 \int_0^\rho \frac{s^p}{\Gamma(p+1)}(1-e^{-s}) dA(s) \\
& + M_2 \sum_{i=1}^{n-2} |\alpha_i| \frac{1}{\Gamma(p+1)} \sigma_i^p (1-e^{-\sigma_i}) \\
& + M_2 |k_1| \int_\nu^1 \frac{s^p}{\Gamma(p+1)}(1-e^{-s}) dA(s) + M_1 \frac{1}{\Gamma(q+1)}(1-e^{-1}) \Big] \\
& + \widetilde{\mathcal{Q}}_4 \Big[M_1 |h| \int_0^\rho \frac{s^q}{\Gamma(q+1)}(1-e^{-s}) dA(s) + M_1 \sum_{i=1}^{n-2} |\beta_i| \sigma_i^q (1-e^{-\sigma_i}) \\
& + M_1 |h_1| \int_\nu^1 \frac{s^p}{\Gamma(p+1)}(1-e^{-s}) dA(s) + M_2 \frac{1}{\Gamma(p+1)}(1-e^{-1}) \Big] \\
\leq\; & \frac{M_1}{\Gamma(q+1)} \Big\{ (1-e^{-1}) + (2-e^{-1})\widetilde{\mathcal{Q}}_1 + (1-e^{-1})\widetilde{\mathcal{Q}}_3 \\
& + \widetilde{\mathcal{Q}}_4 \Big[|h| \int_0^\rho s^q (1-e^{-s}) dA(s) + \sum_{i=1}^{n-2} |\beta_i| \sigma_i^q (1-e^{-\sigma_i})
\end{aligned}
$$

$$
\begin{aligned}
&+|h_1|\int_\nu^1 s^q(1-e^{-s})dA(s)\Big]\Big\} + \frac{M_2}{\Gamma(p+1)}\Big\{(2-e^{-1})\widetilde{\mathcal{Q}}_2 \\
&+\widetilde{\mathcal{Q}}_3\Big[|k|\int_0^\rho s^p(1-e^{-s})dA(s) + \sum_{i=1}^{n-2}|\alpha_i|\sigma_i^p(1-e^{-\sigma_i}) \\
&+|k_1|\int_\nu^1 s^p(1-e^{-s})dA(s)\Big] + (1-e^{-1})\widetilde{\mathcal{Q}}_4\Big\} \\
= \;& \Lambda_1 M_1 + \Lambda_2 M_2.
\end{aligned}
$$

Thus,

$$
\|T_1(\mathcal{X},\mathcal{Y})\| \leq \Lambda_1 M_1 + \Lambda_2 M_2. \tag{38}
$$

Similarly, we have

$$
\|T_2(\mathcal{X},\mathcal{Y})\| \leq \overline{\Lambda}_1 M_1 + \overline{\Lambda}_2 M_2. \tag{39}
$$

Hence, (38) and (39) imply that the operator T uniformly bounded.

Now, we establish that the operator T is equicontinuous. For $t_1, t_2 \in [0,1]$ with $t_1 < t_2$, we obtain

$$
\begin{aligned}
&\Big|T_1(\mathcal{X},\mathcal{Y})(t_2) - T_1(\mathcal{X},\mathcal{Y})(t_1)\Big| \\
\leq\;& \Big|\int_0^{t_1}[e^{-(t_2-s)} - e^{-(t_1-s)}]I_{0+}^q \mathfrak{f}(s,\mathcal{X}(s),\mathcal{Y}(s))ds\Big| + \Big|\int_{t_1}^{t_2} e^{-(t_2-s)} I_{0+}^q \mathfrak{f}(s,\mathcal{X}(s),\mathcal{Y}(s))ds\Big| \\
&+\Big|\mathcal{Q}_1(t_2) - \mathcal{Q}_1(t_1)\Big|\Big[\Big|\int_0^1 e^{-(1-s)} I_{0+}^q \mathfrak{f}(s,\mathcal{X}(s),\mathcal{Y}(s))ds\Big| + \Big|I_{0+}^q \mathfrak{f}(s,\mathcal{X}(s),\mathcal{Y}(s))(1)\Big|\Big] \\
&+\Big|\mathcal{Q}_2(t_2) - \mathcal{Q}_2(t_1)\Big|\Big[\Big|\int_0^1 e^{-(1-s)} I_{0+}^p \mathfrak{g}(s,\mathcal{X}(s),\mathcal{Y}(s))ds\Big| + \Big|I_{0+}^p \mathfrak{g}(s,\mathcal{X}(s),\mathcal{Y}(s))(1)\Big|\Big] \\
&+\Big|\mathcal{Q}_3(t_2) - \mathcal{Q}_3(t_1)\Big|\Big[|k|\Big|\int_0^\rho\Big(\int_0^s e^{-(s-z)} I_{0+}^p \mathfrak{g}(z,\mathcal{X}(z),\mathcal{Y}(z))dz\Big)dA(s)\Big| \\
&+\sum_{i=1}^{n-2}|\alpha_i|\Big|\int_0^{\sigma_i} e^{-(\sigma_i-s)} I_{0+}^p \mathfrak{g}(s,\mathcal{X}(s),\mathcal{Y}(s))ds\Big| \\
&+|k_1|\Big|\int_\nu^1\Big(\int_0^s e^{-(s-z)} I_{0+}^p \mathfrak{g}(z,\mathcal{X}(z),\mathcal{Y}(z))dz\Big)dA(s)\Big| \\
&+\Big|\int_0^1 e^{-(1-s)} I_{0+}^q \mathfrak{f}(s,\mathcal{X}(s),\mathcal{Y}(s))ds\Big|\Big] \\
&+\Big|\mathcal{Q}_4(t_2) - \mathcal{Q}_4(t_1)\Big|\Big[|h|\Big|\int_0^\rho\Big(\int_0^s e^{-(s-z)} I_{0+}^q \mathfrak{f}(z,\mathcal{X}(z),\mathcal{Y}(z))dz\Big)dA(s)\Big| \\
&+\sum_{i=1}^{n-2}|\beta_i|\Big|\int_0^{\sigma_i} e^{-(\sigma_i-s)} I_{0+}^q \mathfrak{f}(s,\mathcal{X}(s),\mathcal{Y}(s))ds\Big| \\
&+|h_1|\Big|\int_\nu^1\Big(\int_0^s e^{-(s-z)} I_{0+}^q \mathfrak{f}(z,\mathcal{X}(z),\mathcal{Y}(z))dz\Big)dA(s)\Big| \\
&+\Big|\int_0^1 e^{-(1-s)} I_{0+}^p \mathfrak{g}(s,\mathcal{X}(s),\mathcal{Y}(s))ds\Big|\Big] \\
\leq\;& \frac{M_1}{\Gamma(q+1)}\Big[t_1^q\Big(e^{-(t_2-t_1)} - 1 - e^{-t_2} + e^{-t_1}\Big) + t_2^q\Big(1 - e^{-(t_2-t_1)}\Big)\Big]
\end{aligned}
$$

$$+\frac{M_1}{\Gamma(q+1)}\Bigg\{(2-e^{-1})\Big|\mathcal{Q}_1(t_2)-\mathcal{Q}_1(t_1)\Big|+(1-e^{-1})\Big|\mathcal{Q}_3(t_2)-\mathcal{Q}_3(t_1)\Big|$$
$$+\Big|\mathcal{Q}_4(t_2)-\mathcal{Q}_4(t_1)\Big|\Big[|h|\Big|\int_0^\rho s^q(1-e^{-s})dA(s)\Big|$$
$$+\Big|\sum_{i=1}^{n-2}\beta_i\sigma_i^q(1-e^{-\sigma_i})\Big|+|h_1|\Big|\int_\nu^1 s^q(1-e^{-s})dA(s)\Big|\Big]\Bigg\}$$
$$+\frac{M_2}{\Gamma(p+1)}\Big\{(2-e^{-1})\Big|\mathcal{Q}_2(t_2)-\mathcal{Q}_2(t_1)\Big|$$
$$+\Big|\mathcal{Q}_3(t_2)-\mathcal{Q}_3(t_1)\Big|\Big[|k|\Big|\int_0^\rho s^p(1-e^{-s})dA(s)\Big|$$
$$+\Big|\sum_{i=1}^{n-2}\alpha_i\sigma_i^p(1-e^{-\sigma_i})\Big|+|k_1|\Big|\int_\nu^1 s^p(1-e^{-s})dA(s)\Big|\Big]+(1-e^{-1})\Big|\mathcal{Q}_4(t_2)-\mathcal{Q}_4(t_1)\Big|\Big\},$$

and

$$\Big|T_2(\mathcal{X},\mathcal{Y})(t_2)-T_2(\mathcal{X},\mathcal{Y})(t_1)\Big|$$
$$\leq \frac{M_2}{\Gamma(p+1)}\Big[t_1^p\Big(e^{-(t_2-t_1)}-1-e^{-t_2}+e^{-t_1}\Big)+t_2^p\Big(1-e^{-(t_2-t_1)}\Big)\Big]$$
$$+\frac{M_1}{\Gamma(q+1)}\Bigg\{(2-e^{-1})\Big|\mathcal{P}_1(t_2)-\mathcal{P}_1(t_1)\Big|+(1-e^{-1})\Big|\mathcal{P}_3(t_2)-\mathcal{P}_3(t_1)\Big|$$
$$+\Big|\mathcal{P}_4(t_2)-\mathcal{P}_4(t_1)\Big|\Big[|h|\Big|\int_0^\rho s^q(1-e^{-s})dA(s)\Big|$$
$$+\Big|\sum_{i=1}^{n-2}\beta_i\sigma_i^q(1-e^{-\sigma_i})\Big|+|h_1|\Big|\int_\nu^1 s^q(1-e^{-s})dA(s)\Big|\Big]\Bigg\}$$
$$+\frac{M_2}{\Gamma(p+1)}\Big\{(2-e^{-1})\Big|\mathcal{P}_2(t_2)-\mathcal{P}_2(t_1)\Big|$$
$$+\Big|\mathcal{P}_3(t_2)-\mathcal{P}_3(t_1)\Big|\Big[|k|\Big|\int_0^\rho s^p(1-e^{-s})dA(s)\Big|$$
$$+\Big|\sum_{i=1}^{n-2}\alpha_i\sigma_i^p(1-e^{-\sigma_i})\Big|+|k_1|\Big|\int_\nu^1 s^p(1-e^{-s})dA(s)\Big|\Big]+(1-e^{-1})\Big|\mathcal{P}_4(t_2)-\mathcal{P}_4(t_1)\Big|\Big\}.$$

Clearly, $|T_1(\mathcal{X},\mathcal{Y})(t_2)-T_1(\mathcal{X},\mathcal{Y})(t_1)|\to 0$ and $|T_2(\mathcal{X},\mathcal{Y})(t_2)-T_2(\mathcal{X},\mathcal{Y})(t_1)|\to 0$ as $t_2\to t_1$ independent of $(\mathcal{X},\mathcal{Y})\in\mathcal{V}$. In consequence, the operator $T(\mathcal{X},\mathcal{Y})$ is equicontinuous. Hence, it follows, according to Arzelá-Ascoli theorem, that $T(\mathcal{X},\mathcal{Y})$ is completely continuous.

In the second step, we consider a set

$$\mathcal{U}=\{(\mathcal{X},\mathcal{Y})\in\mathfrak{X}\times\mathfrak{X}|(\mathcal{X},\mathcal{Y})=\sigma T(\mathcal{X},\mathcal{Y}),0<\sigma<1\}$$

and show that it is bounded. Let $(\mathcal{X},\mathcal{Y})\in\mathcal{U}$, then $(\mathcal{X},\mathcal{Y})=\sigma T(\mathcal{X},\mathcal{Y})$ and for any $t\in[0,1]$, we have

$$\mathcal{X}(t)=\sigma T_1(\mathcal{X},\mathcal{Y})(t),\ \mathcal{Y}(t)=\sigma T_2(\mathcal{X},\mathcal{Y})(t).$$

In consequence, we have

$$|\mathcal{X}(t)|\leq\Lambda_1(\eta_0+\eta_1|\mathcal{X}|+\eta_2|\mathcal{Y}|)+\Lambda_2(\zeta_0+\zeta_1|\mathcal{X}|+\zeta_2|\mathcal{Y}|),$$

which leads to

$$\|\mathcal{X}\|\leq\Lambda_1(\eta_0+\eta_1\|\mathcal{X}\|+\eta_2\|\mathcal{Y}\|)+\Lambda_2(\zeta_0+\zeta_1\|\mathcal{X}\|+\zeta_2\|\mathcal{Y}\|). \tag{40}$$

Likewise, one can obtain that

$$\|\mathcal{Y}\| \leq \overline{\Lambda}_1(\eta_0 + \eta_1\|\mathcal{X}\| + \eta_2\|\mathcal{Y}\|) + \overline{\Lambda}_2(\zeta_0 + \zeta_1\|\mathcal{X}\| + \zeta_2\|\mathcal{Y}\|). \tag{41}$$

From (40) and (41), together with notations (36) and (37), we obtain

$$\begin{aligned}\|\mathcal{X}\| + \|\mathcal{Y}\| \leq & \left[(\Lambda_1 + \overline{\Lambda}_1)\eta_0 + (\Lambda_2 + \overline{\Lambda}_2)\zeta_0\right] + \left[(\Lambda_1 + \overline{\Lambda}_1)\eta_1 + (\Lambda_2 + \overline{\Lambda}_2)\zeta_1\right]\|\mathcal{X}\| \\ & + \left[(\Lambda_1 + \overline{\Lambda}_1)\eta_2 + (\Lambda_2 + \overline{\Lambda}_2)\zeta_2\right]\|\mathcal{Y}\|,\end{aligned}$$

which implies that

$$\|(\mathcal{X},\mathcal{Y})\| \leq \Omega_0 + \max\{\Omega_1 + \Omega_2\}\|(\mathcal{X},\mathcal{Y})\| \leq \Omega_0 + \Omega\|(\mathcal{X},\mathcal{Y})\|.$$

Thus

$$\|(\mathcal{X},\mathcal{Y})\| \leq \frac{\Omega_0}{1-\Omega},$$

which shows that $\mathcal{U}$ is bounded. In view of the foregoing steps, we deduce that the hypothesis of the Leray–Schauder alternative [6] is satisfied; hence, its conclusion implies that the operator T has at least one fixed point. Thus, there is at least one solution to the problem (1) and (2) on $[0,1]$. □

Our next result deals with the uniqueness of solutions for the problem (1) and (2) and relies on Banach's fixed point theorem.

Theorem 2. *Let the condition* $(\mathcal{F}_2)$ *hold, and that*

$$\Theta + \overline{\Theta} < 1, \tag{42}$$

where Θ *and* $\overline{\Theta}$ *are given in (31). Then, there is a unique solution to the problem (1) and (2) on* $[0,1]$.

Proof. Let us first establish that $T\mathcal{U}_\varepsilon \subset \mathcal{U}_\varepsilon$, where the operator T is given by (28) and

$$\mathcal{U}_\varepsilon = \{(\mathcal{X},\mathcal{Y}) \in \mathfrak{X} \times \mathfrak{X} : \|(\mathcal{X},\mathcal{Y})\| \leq \varepsilon\},$$

with $\varepsilon > \dfrac{\mathcal{M} + \overline{\mathcal{M}}}{1-(\Theta + \overline{\Theta})}$, $\Theta, \overline{\Theta}$ and $\mathcal{M}, \overline{\mathcal{M}}$ are respectively given by (31) and (32). By the assumption $(\mathcal{F}_2)$ and (35), for $(\mathcal{X},\mathcal{Y}) \in \mathcal{U}_\varepsilon$, $t \in [0,1]$, we have

$$\begin{aligned}|\mathfrak{f}(t,\mathcal{X}(t),\mathcal{Y}(t))| &\leq |\mathfrak{f}(t,\mathcal{X}(t),\mathcal{Y}(t)) - \mathfrak{f}(t,0,0)| + |\mathfrak{f}(t,0,0)| \\ &\leq L_1(|\mathcal{X}(t)| + |\mathcal{Y}(t)|) + \mathcal{N}_1 \leq L_1(\|\mathcal{X}\| + \|\mathcal{Y}\|) + \mathcal{N}_1 \leq L_1\varepsilon + \mathcal{N}_1.\end{aligned}$$

Similarly, one can show that $|\mathfrak{g}(t,\mathcal{X}(t),\mathcal{Y}(t))| \leq L_2\varepsilon + \mathcal{N}_2$. Taking into account (31) and (32), we obtain

$$|T_1(\mathcal{X},\mathcal{Y})(t)| \leq (\Lambda_1 L_1 + \Lambda_2 L_2)\varepsilon + (\Lambda_1\mathcal{N}_1 + \Lambda_2\mathcal{N}_2) = \Theta\varepsilon + \mathcal{M},$$

which yields

$$\|T_1(\mathcal{X},\mathcal{Y})\| \leq \Theta\varepsilon + \mathcal{M}. \tag{43}$$

In a similar manner, we obtain

$$\|T_2(\mathcal{X},\mathcal{Y})\| \leq \overline{\Theta}\varepsilon + \overline{\mathcal{M}}. \tag{44}$$

It then follows from (43) and (44) that

$$\|T(\mathcal{X},\mathcal{Y})\| \leq (\Theta\varepsilon + \mathcal{M}) + (\overline{\Theta}\varepsilon + \overline{\mathcal{M}}) = (\Theta + \overline{\Theta})\varepsilon + (\mathcal{M} + \overline{\mathcal{M}}) \leq \varepsilon.$$

Consequently, $T\mathcal{U}_\varepsilon \subset \mathcal{U}_\varepsilon$. Next, we show that the operator T is a contraction. Using conditions $(\mathcal{F}_2)$ and (31), we get

$$\begin{aligned}
& \|T_1(\mathcal{X}_1,\mathcal{Y}_1) - T_1(\mathcal{X}_2,\mathcal{Y}_2)\| \\
= & \sup_{t\in[0,1]} |T_1(\mathcal{X}_1,\mathcal{Y}_1)(t) - T_1(\mathcal{X}_2,\mathcal{Y}_2)(t)| \\
\leq & \sup_{t\in[0,1]} \bigg\{ \int_0^t e^{-(t-s)} \Big| I_{0^+}^q \mathfrak{f}(s,\mathcal{X}_1(s),\mathcal{Y}_1(s)) - I_{0^+}^q \mathfrak{f}(s,\mathcal{X}_2(s),\mathcal{Y}_2(s)) \Big| ds \\
& + |\mathcal{Q}_1(t)| \Big[\int_0^1 e^{-(1-s)} \Big| I_{0^+}^q \mathfrak{f}(s,\mathcal{X}_1(s),\mathcal{Y}_1(s)) - I_{0^+}^q \mathfrak{f}(s,\mathcal{X}_2(s),\mathcal{Y}_2(s)) \Big| ds \\
& + \Big| I_{0^+}^q \mathfrak{f}(s,\mathcal{X}_1(s),\mathcal{Y}_1(s)) - I_{0^+}^q \mathfrak{f}(s,\mathcal{X}_2(s),\mathcal{Y}_2(s)) \Big| (1) \Big] \\
& + |\mathcal{Q}_2(t)| \Big[\int_0^1 e^{-(1-s)} \Big| I_{0^+}^p \mathfrak{g}(s,\mathcal{X}_1(s),\mathcal{Y}_1(s)) - I_{0^+}^p \mathfrak{g}(s,\mathcal{X}_2(s),\mathcal{Y}_2(s)) \Big| ds \\
& + \Big| I_{0^+}^p \mathfrak{g}(s,\mathcal{X}_1(s),\mathcal{Y}_1(s)) - I_{0^+}^p \mathfrak{g}(s,\mathcal{X}_2(s),\mathcal{Y}_2(s)) \Big| (1) \Big] \\
& + |\mathcal{Q}_3(t)| \Big[|k| \int_0^\rho \Big(\int_0^s e^{-(s-z)} \Big| I_{0^+}^p \mathfrak{g}(z,\mathcal{X}_1(z),\mathcal{Y}_1(z)) - I_{0^+}^p \mathfrak{g}(z,\mathcal{X}_2(z),\mathcal{Y}_2(z)) \Big| dz \Big) dA(s) \\
& + \sum_{i=1}^{n-2} |\alpha_i| \int_0^{\sigma_i} e^{-(\sigma_i-s)} \Big| I_{0^+}^p \mathfrak{g}(s,\mathcal{X}_1(s),\mathcal{Y}_1(s)) - I_{0^+}^p \mathfrak{g}(s,\mathcal{X}_2(s),\mathcal{Y}_2(s)) \Big| ds \\
& + |k_1| \int_\nu^1 \Big(\int_0^s e^{-(s-z)} \Big| I_{0^+}^p \mathfrak{g}(z,\mathcal{X}_1(z),\mathcal{Y}_1(z)) - I_{0^+}^p \mathfrak{g}(z,\mathcal{X}_2(z),\mathcal{Y}_2(z)) \Big| dz \Big) dA(s) \\
& + \int_0^1 e^{-(1-s)} \Big| I_{0^+}^q \mathfrak{f}(s,\mathcal{X}_1(s),\mathcal{Y}_1(s)) - I_{0^+}^q \mathfrak{f}(s,\mathcal{X}_2(s),\mathcal{Y}_2(s)) \Big| ds \Big] \\
& + |\mathcal{Q}_4(t)| \Big[|h| \int_0^\rho \Big(\int_0^s e^{-(s-z)} \Big| I_{0^+}^q \mathfrak{f}(z,\mathcal{X}_1(z),\mathcal{Y}_1(z)) - I_{0^+}^q \mathfrak{f}(z,\mathcal{X}_2(z),\mathcal{Y}_2(z)) \Big| dz \Big) dA(s) \\
& + \sum_{i=1}^{n-2} |\beta_i| \int_0^{\sigma_i} e^{-(\sigma_i-s)} \Big| I_{0^+}^q \mathfrak{f}(s,\mathcal{X}_1(s),\mathcal{Y}_1(s)) - I_{0^+}^q \mathfrak{f}(s,\mathcal{X}_2(s),\mathcal{Y}_2(s)) \Big| ds \\
& + |h_1| \int_\nu^1 \Big(\int_0^s e^{-(s-z)} \Big| I_{0^+}^q \mathfrak{f}(z,\mathcal{X}_1(z),\mathcal{Y}_1(z)) - I_{0^+}^q \mathfrak{f}(z,\mathcal{X}_2(z),\mathcal{Y}_2(z)) \Big| dz \Big) dA(s) \\
& + \int_0^1 e^{-(1-s)} \Big| I_{0^+}^p \mathfrak{g}(s,\mathcal{X}_1(s),\mathcal{Y}_1(s)) - I_{0^+}^p \mathfrak{g}(s,\mathcal{X}_2(s),\mathcal{Y}_2(s)) \Big| ds \Big] \bigg\} \\
\leq & \Lambda_1 L_1 \Big(\|\mathcal{X}_1 - \mathcal{X}_2\| + \|\mathcal{Y}_1 - \mathcal{Y}_2\| \Big) + \Lambda_2 L_2 \Big(\|\mathcal{X}_1 - \mathcal{X}_2\| + \|\mathcal{Y}_1 - \mathcal{Y}_2\| \Big) \\
= & \Big(\Lambda_1 L_1 + \Lambda_2 L_2 \Big) \Big(\|\mathcal{X}_1 - \mathcal{X}_2\| + \|\mathcal{Y}_1 - \mathcal{Y}_2\| \Big) \\
= & \Theta \Big(\|\mathcal{X}_1 - \mathcal{X}_2\| + \|\mathcal{Y}_1 - \mathcal{Y}_2\| \Big).
\end{aligned}$$

Similarly, we can find that

$$\begin{aligned}
\|T_2(\mathcal{X}_1,\mathcal{Y}_1) - T_2(\mathcal{X}_2,\mathcal{Y}_2)\| & = \sup_{t\in[0,1]} |T_2(\mathcal{X}_1,\mathcal{Y}_1)(t) - T_2(\mathcal{X}_2,\mathcal{Y}_2)(t)| \\
& \leq \Big(\overline{\Lambda}_1 L_1 + \overline{\Lambda}_2 L_2 \Big) \Big(\|\mathcal{X}_1 - \mathcal{X}_2\| + \|\mathcal{Y}_1 - \mathcal{Y}_2\| \Big) \\
& = \overline{\Theta} \Big(\|\mathcal{X}_1 - \mathcal{X}_2\| + \|\mathcal{Y}_1 - \mathcal{Y}_2\| \Big).
\end{aligned}$$

Hence we obtain

$$\|T(\mathcal{X}_1,\mathcal{Y}_1) - T(\mathcal{X}_2,\mathcal{Y}_2))\| \leq (\Theta + \overline{\Theta})(\|\mathcal{X}_1 - \mathcal{X}_2\| + \|\mathcal{Y}_1 - \mathcal{Y}_2\|),$$

which, in view of the condition (42), shows that T is a contraction. Thus, the conclusion of Banach's fixed-point theorem applies and, hence, the problem (1) and (2) has a unique solution on $[0,1]$. The proof is finished. □

4. An Example

Example 1. *Consider a coupled system of fractional differential equations*

$$\begin{cases} ({}^cD^{26/7} +^c D^{19/7})\mathcal{X}(t) = \dfrac{135\mathcal{X}(t)}{225+t} + \dfrac{3\sin\mathcal{Y}(t)}{13+t^2} + \dfrac{3}{13\sqrt{9+t^2}}, \\ ({}^cD^{17/5} +^c D^{12/5})\mathcal{Y}(t) = \dfrac{\sqrt{16-t^2}}{\pi(40+t)}\sin(2\pi\mathcal{X}(t)) + \dfrac{24|\tan^{-1}\mathcal{Y}(t)|}{\pi(t^2+120)} + \dfrac{\ln 5}{2}, \quad t\in[0,1], \end{cases} \tag{45}$$

equipped with the coupled boundary conditions

$$\begin{cases} \mathcal{X}(0)=0,\ \mathcal{X}'(0)=0,\ \mathcal{X}'(1)=0,\ \mathcal{X}(1)=k\displaystyle\int_0^\rho \mathcal{Y}(s)dA(s)+\sum_{i=1}^{3}\alpha_i\mathcal{Y}(\sigma_i)+k_1\int_\nu^1 \mathcal{Y}(s)dA(s), \\ \mathcal{Y}(0)=0,\ \mathcal{Y}'(0)=0,\ \mathcal{Y}'(1)=0,\ \mathcal{Y}(1)=h\displaystyle\int_0^\rho \mathcal{X}(s)dA(s)+\sum_{i=1}^{3}\beta_i\mathcal{X}(\sigma_i)+h_1\int_\nu^1 \mathcal{X}(s)dA(s). \end{cases} \tag{46}$$

Here $q=19/7$, $p=12/5$, $k=3/16$, $k_1=2/175$, $h=5/88$, $h_1=3/104$, $A(s)=1+\frac{s^{r+1}}{r+1}$, $r\in\mathbb{N}$, $\rho=2/7$, $\nu=6/7$, $\sigma_1=3/7$, $\sigma_2=4/7$, $\sigma_3=5/7$, $\alpha_1=1/10$, $\alpha_2=1/414$, $\alpha_3=3/313$, $\beta_1=1/3$, $\beta_2=1/41$, $\beta_3=7/121$. *Clearly*

$$\begin{aligned} |\mathfrak{f}(t,\mathcal{X}(t),\mathcal{Y}(t))| &\le \frac{1}{13}+\frac{3}{5}\|\mathcal{X}\|+\frac{3}{13}\|\mathcal{Y}\|, \\ |\mathfrak{g}(t,\mathcal{X}(t),\mathcal{Y}(t))| &\le \frac{\ln 5}{2}+\frac{1}{5}\|\mathcal{X}\|+\frac{1}{10}\|\mathcal{Y}\|, \end{aligned}$$

and hence $\eta_0=1/13$, $\eta_1=3/5$, $\eta_2=3/13$, $\zeta_0=(\ln 5)/2$, $\zeta_1=1/5$, $\zeta_2=1/10$. *Using (36) and (37) with the given data and* $r=2$, *we find that* $\Omega_1\simeq 0.331501$, $\Omega_2\simeq 0.138843$ *and* $\Omega=\max\{\Omega_1,\Omega_2\}\simeq 0.331501<1$. *Therefore, by Theorem 1, the problem (45) and (46) has at least one solution on* $[0,1]$.

To explain Theorem 2, we consider the following system of sequential fractional differential equations supplemented with the boundary conditions (46):

$$\begin{cases} ({}^cD^{26/7} +^c D^{19/7})\mathcal{X}(t) = \dfrac{3e^{-t}}{\sqrt{(t^4+25)}}\dfrac{|\mathcal{X}(t)|}{(1+|\mathcal{X}(t)|)} + \dfrac{18}{(t^2+30)}\sin(\mathcal{Y}(t)) + \dfrac{9}{2\sqrt{5+t}}, \\ ({}^cD^{17/5} +^c D^{12/5})\mathcal{Y}(t) = \dfrac{1}{(t+10)}\tan^{-1}\mathcal{X}(t) + \dfrac{e^{-t}}{10}\dfrac{|\mathcal{Y}(t)|^3}{(1+|\mathcal{Y}(t)|^3)} + \dfrac{\cos(t+1)}{(9+t)}, \end{cases} \tag{47}$$

$t\in[0,1]$. *It is easy to check whether* $|\mathfrak{f}(t,\mathcal{X}_1,\mathcal{Y}_1)-\mathfrak{f}(t,\mathcal{X}_2,\mathcal{Y}_2)|\le L_1(\|\mathcal{X}_1-\mathcal{X}_2\|+\|\mathcal{Y}_1-\mathcal{Y}_2\|)$ *with* $L_1=3/5$ *and* $|\mathfrak{g}(t,\mathcal{X}_1,\mathcal{Y}_1)-\mathfrak{g}(t,\mathcal{X}_2,\mathcal{Y}_2)|\le L_2(\|\mathcal{X}_1-\mathcal{X}_2\|+\|\mathcal{Y}_1-\mathcal{Y}_2\|)$ *with* $L_2=1/10$. *Additionally,* $\Theta+\overline{\Theta}\simeq 0.282351<1$. *Therefore, the hypothesis of Theorem 2 is satisfied. Hence, by the conclusion of Theorem 2, there is a unique solution to the system (47) equipped with the boundary conditions (46) on* $[0,1]$.

5. Discussion

We have presented the criteria ensuring the existence and uniqueness of solutions for a coupled system of higher-order sequential Caputo fractional differential equations complemented with Riemann–Stieltjes integro-multipoint boundary conditions on the interval $[0,1]$. A characteristic of the method employed in the present study is its generality, as it can be applied to a variety of boundary value problems. As a special case, our results become associated with multipoint boundary conditions:

$$\begin{cases} \mathcal{X}(0)=0,\ \mathcal{X}'(0)=0,\ \mathcal{X}'(1)=0,\ \mathcal{X}(1)=\sum_{i=1}^{n-2}\alpha_i\mathcal{Y}(\sigma_i), \\ \mathcal{Y}(0)=0,\ \mathcal{Y}'(0)=0,\ \mathcal{Y}'(1)=0,\ \mathcal{Y}(1)=\sum_{i=1}^{n-2}\beta_i\mathcal{X}(\sigma_i), \end{cases} \tag{48}$$

if we take $k = k_1 = h = h_1 = 0$ in (2). In this case, the corresponding operators take the form:

$$\begin{aligned} \widehat{T}_1(\mathcal{X},\mathcal{Y})(t) &= \int_0^t e^{-(t-s)} I_{0^+}^q \mathfrak{f}(s,\mathcal{X}(s),\mathcal{Y}(s))ds \\ &+\mathcal{Q}_1(t)\Big[\int_0^1 e^{-(1-s)} I_{0^+}^q \mathfrak{f}(s,\mathcal{X}(s),\mathcal{Y}(s))ds - I_{0^+}^q \mathfrak{f}(s,\mathcal{X}(s),\mathcal{Y}(s))(1)\Big] \\ &+ \mathcal{Q}_2(t)\Big[\int_0^1 e^{-(1-s)} I_{0^+}^p \mathfrak{g}(s,\mathcal{X}(s),\mathcal{Y}(s))ds - I_{0^+}^p \mathfrak{g}(s,\mathcal{X}(s),\mathcal{Y}(s))(1)\Big] \\ &+ \mathcal{Q}_3(t)\Big[\sum_{i=1}^{n-2}\alpha_i\int_0^{\sigma_i} e^{-(\sigma_i-s)} I_{0^+}^p \mathfrak{g}(s,\mathcal{X}(s),\mathcal{Y}(s))ds \\ &- \int_0^1 e^{-(1-s)} I_{0^+}^q \mathfrak{f}(s,\mathcal{X}(s),\mathcal{Y}(s))ds\Big] \\ &+ \mathcal{Q}_4(t)\Big[\sum_{i=1}^{n-2}\beta_i\int_0^{\sigma_i} e^{-(\sigma_i-s)} I_{0^+}^q \mathfrak{f}(s,\mathcal{X}(s),\mathcal{Y}(s))ds \\ &- \int_0^1 e^{-(1-s)} I_{0^+}^p \mathfrak{g}(s,\mathcal{X}(s),\mathcal{Y}(s))ds\Big], \end{aligned}$$

$$\begin{aligned} \widehat{T}_2(\mathcal{X},\mathcal{Y})(t) &= \int_0^t e^{-(t-s)} I_{0^+}^p \mathfrak{g}(s,\mathcal{X}(s),\mathcal{Y}(s))ds \\ &+\mathcal{P}_1(t)\Big[\int_0^1 e^{-(1-s)} I_{0^+}^q \mathfrak{f}(s,\mathcal{X}(s),\mathcal{Y}(s))ds - I_{0^+}^q \mathfrak{f}(s,\mathcal{X}(s),\mathcal{Y}(s))(1)\Big] \\ &+ \mathcal{P}_2(t)\Big[\int_0^1 e^{-(1-s)} I_{0^+}^p \mathfrak{g}(s,\mathcal{X}(s),\mathcal{Y}(s))ds - I_{0^+}^p \mathfrak{g}(s,\mathcal{X}(s),\mathcal{Y}(s))(1)\Big] \\ &+ \mathcal{P}_3(t)\Big[\sum_{i=1}^{n-2}\alpha_i\int_0^{\sigma_i} e^{-(\sigma_i-s)} I_{0^+}^p \mathfrak{g}(s,\mathcal{X}(s),\mathcal{Y}(s))ds \\ &- \int_0^1 e^{-(1-s)} I_{0^+}^q \mathfrak{f}(s,\mathcal{X}(s),\mathcal{Y}(s))ds\Big] \\ &+ \mathcal{P}_4(t)\Big[\sum_{i=1}^{n-2}\beta_i\int_0^{\sigma_i} e^{-(\sigma_i-s)} I_{0^+}^q \mathfrak{f}(s,\mathcal{X}(s),\mathcal{Y}(s))ds \\ &- \int_0^1 e^{-(1-s)} I_{0^+}^p \mathfrak{g}(s,\mathcal{X}(s),\mathcal{Y}(s))ds\Big]. \end{aligned}$$

In future, we plan to develop the existence theory for the multivalued analogue of the problem (1) and (2). Moreover, the boundary value problem considered in this paper can be studied for other kinds of derivatives, such as Hadamard, Caputo–Hadamard, Hilfer, Hilfer–Hadamard, etc.

Author Contributions: Conceptualization, Y.A., B.A. and S.K.N.; methodology, Y.A., B.A., S.K.N. and A.S.M.A.; validation, Y.A., B.A., S.K.N. and A.S.M.A.; formal analysis, Y.A., B.A., S.K.N. and A.S.M.A.; writing—original draft preparation, Y.A., B.A., S.K.N. and A.S.M.A.; funding acquisition, A.S.M.A. All authors have read and agreed to the published version of the manuscript.

Funding: Taif University Researchers Supporting Project number (TURSP-2020/303), Taif University, Taif, Saudi Arabia.

Acknowledgments: Taif University Researchers Supporting Project number (TURSP-2020/303), Taif University, Taif, Saudi Arabia. The authors thank the reviewers for their constructive remarks on their work.

Conflicts of Interest: The authors declare no conflict of interest.

References

1. Zaslavsky, G.M. *Hamiltonian Chaos and Fractional Dynamics*; Oxford University Press: Oxford, UK, 2005.
2. Magin, R.L. *Fractional Calculus in Bioengineering*; Begell House Publishers: Danbury, CT, USA, 2006.
3. Javidi, M.; Ahmad, B. Dynamic analysis of time fractional order phytoplankton-toxic phytoplankton–zooplankton system. *Ecol. Model.* **2015**, *318*, 8–18. [CrossRef]
4. Fallahgoul, H.A.; Focardi, S.M.; Fabozzi, F.J. *Fractional Calculus and Fractional Processes with Applications to Financial Economics. Theory and Application*; Elsevier/Academic Press: London, UK, 2017.
5. Granas, A.; Dugundji, J. *Fixed Point Theory*; Springer: New York, NY, USA, 2005.
6. Smart, D.R. *Fixed Point Theorems*; Cambridge University Press: Cambridge, UK, 1980.
7. Ahmad, B.; Alruwaily, Y.; Ntouyas, S.K.; Alsaedi, A. Existence and stability results for a fractional order differential equation with non-conjugate Riemann–Stieltjes integro-multipoint boundary conditions. *Mathematics* **2019**, *7*, 249. [CrossRef]
8. Henderson, J.; Luca, R.; Tudorache, A. On a system of fractional differential equations with coupled integral boundary conditions. *Fract. Calc. Appl. Anal.* **2015**, *18*, 361–386. [CrossRef]
9. Sabatier, J.; Agrawal, O.P.; Machado, J.A.T. (Eds.) *Advances in Fractional Calculus: Theoretical Developments and Applications in Physics and Engineering*; Springer: Dordrecht, The Netherlands, 2007.
10. Tariboon, J.; Ntouyas, S.K.; Asawasamrit, S.; Promsakon, C. Positive solutions for Hadamard differential systems with fractional integral conditions on an unbounded domain. *Open Math.* **2017**, *15*, 645–666.
11. Lin, L.; Liu, Y.; Zhao, D. Study on implicit-type fractional coupled system with integral boundary conditions. *Mathematics* **2021**, *9*, 300. [CrossRef]
12. Ahmad, B.; Alghanmi, M.; Alsaedi, A.; Nieto, J.J. Existence and uniqueness results for a nonlinear coupled system involving Caputo fractional derivatives with a new kind of coupled boundary conditions. *Appl. Math. Lett.* **2021**, *116*, 107018. [CrossRef]
13. Lin, L.; Liu, Y.; Zhao, D. Controllability of impulsive ψ-Caputo fractional evolution equations with nonlocal conditions. *Mathematics* **2021**, *9*, 1358. [CrossRef]
14. Fazli, H.; Nieto, J.J.; Bahrami, F. On the existence and uniqueness results for nonlinear sequential fractional differential equations, *Appl. Comput. Math.* **2018**, *17*, 36–47.
15. Su, X.; Zhang, S.; Zhang, L. Periodic boundary value problem involving sequential fractional derivatives in Banach space. *AIMS Math.* **2020**, *5*, 7510–7530. [CrossRef]
16. Alsaedi, A.; Ahmad, B.; Aljoudi, S.; Ntouyas, S.K. A study of a fully coupled two-parameter system of sequential fractional integro-differential equations with nonlocal integro-multipoint boundary conditions. *Acta Math. Sci. Ser. B* **2019**, *39*, 927–944. [CrossRef]
17. Saengthong, W.; Thailert, E.; Ntouyas, S.K. Existence and uniqueness of solutions for system of Hilfer-Hadamard sequential fractional differential equations with two point boundary conditions. *Adv. Differ. Equ.* **2019**, *2019*, 525. [CrossRef]
18. Mohammadi, H.; Rezapour, S.; Etemad, S.; Baleanu, D. Two sequential fractional hybrid differential inclusions. *Adv. Differ. Equ.* **2020**, *2020*, 385. [CrossRef]
19. Baghani, H.; Alzabut, J.; Farokhi-Ostad, J.; Nieto, J.J. Existence and uniqueness of solutions for a coupled system of sequential fractional differential equations with initial conditions. *J. Pseudo-Differ. Oper. Appl.* **2020**, *11*, 1731–1741. [CrossRef]
20. Wongcharoen, A.; Ntouyas, S.K.; Wongsantisuk, P.; Tariboon, J. Existence results for a nonlocal coupled system of sequential fractional differential equations involving ψ-Hilfer fractional derivatives. *Adv. Math. Phys.* **2021**, *2021*, 5554619. [CrossRef]
21. Webb, J.R.L.; Infante, G. Positive solutions of nonlocal boundary value problems involving integral conditions. *Nonlinear Differ. Equ. Appl.* **2008**, *15*, 45–67. [CrossRef]
22. Ok, E.A. *Probability Theory with Economic Applications*; Lecture Notes; Economics Department, State University of New York-Oswego (SUNY): Oswego, NY, USA, 2014.
23. Anevski, D. *Riemann-Stieltjes Integrals*; Lecture Notes; Mathematical Sciences, Lund University: Lund, Sweden, 2012.
24. Kilbas, A.A.; Srivastava, H.M.; Trujillo, J.J. *Theory and Applications of Fractional Differential Equations*; North-Holland Mathematics Studies, 204; Elsevier Science B.V.: Amsterdam, The Netherlands, 2006; Volume 24.

fractal and fractional

Article

Mawhin's Continuation Technique for a Nonlinear BVP of Variable Order at Resonance via Piecewise Constant Functions

Shahram Rezapour [1,2,†], Mohammed Said Souid [3,†], Sina Etemad [1,†], Zoubida Bouazza [4,†], Sotiris K. Ntouyas [5,6,†], Suphawat Asawasamrit [7,†] and Jessada Tariboon [7,*,†]

1 Department of Mathematics, Azarbaijan Shahid Madani University, Tabriz 53751-71379, Iran; sh.rezapour@azaruniv.ac.ir (S.R.); sina.etemad@azaruniv.ac.ir (S.E.)
2 Department of Medical Research, China Medical University Hospital, China Medical University, Taichung 40402, Taiwan
3 Department of Economic Sciences, University of Tiaret, Tiaret 14035, Algeria; souimed2008@yahoo.com
4 Laboratory of Mathematics, Djillali Liabes University, Sidi Bel-Abbès 22000, Algeria; bouazza3@yahoo.fr
5 Department of Mathematics, University of Ioannina, 451 10 Ioannina, Greece; sntouyas@uoi.gr
6 Nonlinear Analysis and Applied Mathematics (NAAM)-Research Group, Department of Mathematics, Faculty of Science, King Abdulaziz University, P.O. Box 80203, Jeddah 21589, Saudi Arabia
7 Intelligent and Nonlinear Dynamic Innovations Research Center, Department of Mathematics, Faculty of Applied Science, King Mongkut's University of Technology North Bangkok, Bangkok 10800, Thailand; suphawat.a@sci.kmutnb.ac.th
* Correspondence: jessada.t@sci.kmutnb.ac.th
† These authors contributed equally to this work.

Abstract: In this paper, we establish the existence of solutions to a nonlinear boundary value problem (BVP) of variable order at resonance. The main theorem in this study is proved with the help of generalized intervals and piecewise constant functions, in which we convert the mentioned Caputo BVP of fractional variable order to an equivalent standard Caputo BVP at resonance of constant order. In fact, to use the Mawhin's continuation technique, we have to transform the variable order BVP into a constant order BVP. We prove the existence of solutions based on the existing notions in the coincidence degree theory and Mawhin's continuation theorem (MCTH). Finally, an example is provided according to the given variable order BVP to show the correctness of results.

Keywords: piecewise constant function; Mawhin's continuation technique; variable order; resonance; existence

Citation: Rezapour, S.; Souid, M.S.; Etemad, S.; Bouazza, Z.; Ntouyas, S.K.; Asawasamrit, S.; Tariboon, J. Mawhin's Continuation Technique for a Nonlinear BVP of Variable Order at Resonance via Piecewise Constant Functions. *Fractal Fract.* **2021**, 5, 216. https://doi.org/10.3390/fractalfract5040216

Academic Editor: Rodica Luca

Received: 17 October 2021
Accepted: 10 November 2021
Published: 12 November 2021

1. Introduction

The initial idea of fractional calculus is taken from the powers of real or complex numbers in the order of differentiation and integration operators. In recent decades, fractional operators of variable order are appeared extensively in a vast domain of sciences including chaotic dynamical systems, fractal theory, rheology, signal processing, mathematical modeling, control theory, and biomedical applications. This range of applications is due to the fact that fractional derivatives provide a strong tool in the mathematics to describe the memory and hereditary properties of processes and various materials; see, for example [1–3].

Before the variable order systems, discussion of boundary value problems with fractional constant orders has attracted the attention of most researchers, and valuable findings have been established. Various researches have been conducted to study the behaviors of different fractional BVPs by means of some known methods such as fixed point theorems, numerical methods, monotone iterative methods, variational methods, and etc. [4–12].

Nevertheless, in addition to numerous published papers on fractional constant order problems, few studies on the existence theory have been done in relation to variable order problems [13–19]. Hence, investigation of this interesting and general topic makes all our findings worthy.

In 1970, Gaines and Mawhin [20] introduced the theory of coincidence degree for analysis of differential and functional equations. Mawhin has made important contributions since then, and the mentioned theory is also famous to the Mawhin's coincidence theory. Coincidence theory is considered as a powerful technique, especially with regard to questions about the existence of solutions for nonlinear differential equations. Mawhin's theory permits the use of a method based on the topological degree notion for some problems which can be written as an abstract operator equation of the form $\Theta x = Wx$, where Θ is a linear non-invertible operator and W is a nonlinear operator acting on a Banach space.

In 1972, Mawhin extended a technique to solve this operator equation in his famous paper [21]. He assumed that Θ is a Fredholm operator of index zero. Then, he developed a new theory of topological degree known as the degree of coincidence for (Θ, W), that is also known as Mawhin's coincidence degree theory in honor of him.

A given boundary value problem is said to be at resonance if the corresponding linear homogeneous BVP has a non-trivial solution. Many authors studied ordinary BVPs at resonance using Mawhin's coincidence degree theory; we can cite some works done by Feng and Webb [22], Guezane-Lakoud and Frioui [23], Mawhin and Ward [24], Infante [25], and references therein.

Based on the aforementioned technique in relation to Mawhin's method, in this paper, we shall investigate a nonlinear boundary value problem of variable order at resonance which takes the form as follows

$$\begin{cases} {}^{c}D_{0^+}^{u(t)}\phi(t) = g(t, \phi(t)), \ t \in A, \\ \phi(0) = \phi(T), \end{cases} \tag{1}$$

where $A = [0, T]$, $T \in (0, \infty)$, the function $u(t) : A \to (0, 1]$ is the order of the existing derivative in the above boundary problem, ${}^{c}D_{0^+}^{u(t)}$ is the variable order Caputo derivative, and also $g \in C(A \times \mathbb{R}, \mathbb{R})$.

The important aim of this research is to investigate some qualitative properties of solutions of the given Caputo boundary value problem of variable order (1). The main novelty of this paper is that we use the Mawhin's continuation technique for the first time for proving the existence of solutions of a Caputo boundary value problem at resonance equipped with variable order. Most papers apply this technique on the constant order systems, while we here try to derive the necessary conditions on a variable order system. In comparison to variable order partial systems, a linear analogue of this problem can be observed in the framework of partial differential equation [26] and this shows another version of such problems and specify our main contribution in this work. It is notable for young researchers that they can implement and investigate this methods and techniques on hidden-memory variable-order fractional problems introduced in [27,28] in the future.

The structure of the paper is organized as follows: Initially, some auxiliary definitions and remarks are collected for recalling the required notions in Section 2. Further, in Section 3, based on coincidence degree theory, a partition of the given interval A is applied, and by defining the relevant piecewise constant functions, the existence results are derived for an equivalent constant-order BVP at resonance and accordingly, for the given Caputo BVP of variable order (1). This proof is completed in some steps. In Section 4, we give an example to illustrate the theoretical existence theorems. The paper is completed with conclusions in Section 5.

2. Auxiliary Concepts

At first, some needed concepts about our study are collected from different sources. Here, the Banach space $C(A, \mathbb{R})$ consisting of continuous functions like $\phi : A \to \mathbb{R}$ is equipped with the sup-norm $\|\phi\| = \sup\{|\phi(t)| : t \in A\}$.

Definition 1 ([29,30]). *The Riemann-Liouville fractional integral (RLFI) of variable order $u(t)$ for the function ϕ is defined by*

$$I_{0^+}^{u(t)}\phi(t) = \frac{1}{\Gamma(u(t))}\int_0^t (t-s)^{u(t)-1}\phi(s)ds, \; t \in A, \tag{2}$$

where $\Gamma(z) = \int_0^\infty x^{z-1}e^{-x}dx$, and the left Caputo fractional derivative (CFD) of variable order $u(t)$ for $\phi(t)$ is defined by

$${}^{c}D_{0^+}^{u(t)}\phi(t) = \frac{1}{1-\Gamma(u(t))}\int_0^t (t-s)^{-u(t)}\phi'(s)ds, \; t \in A. \tag{3}$$

Remark 1. *Notice that in* (2)*, we have specified the variable order as the function $u : A \to (0,1]$, while for defining RLFI, we can consider it as a function with extended values like $u : A \to (0,\infty)$.*

Remark 2 ([30]). *When we define the variable order u as a constant-valued function in both* (2) *and* (3)*, then the variable order RLFI and CFD operators are the same as the usual RLFI and CFD operators, respectively.*

Remark 3 ([29]). *As we know, the semigroup property is satisfied for the standard RLFI operators equipped with constant order, while it is not valid for extended case of variable orders $\beta_1(t)$ and $\beta_2(t)$. In other words, $I_{0^+}^{\beta_1(t)}(\,I_{0^+}^{\beta_2(t)})\phi(t) \neq I_{0^+}^{\beta_1(t)+\beta_2(t)}\phi(t)$.*

To see this problem, we give the following example.

Example 1. *Let $A = [0,3]$ and $\phi(t) \equiv 1$, $\forall t \in A$. The variable orders of RLFI operator can be taken as: $\beta_1(t) = \frac{t}{2}$ and $\beta_2(t) = \begin{cases} 1, \; t \in [0,1] \\ 2, \; t \in \; [1,3] \end{cases}$.*

Then for all $t \in A$, and according to Definition (2)*, we compute*

$$\begin{aligned} I_{0^+}^{\beta_1(t)}\left(I_{0^+}^{\beta_2(t)}\phi(t)\right) &= \int_0^t \frac{(t-s)^{\beta_1(t)-1}}{\Gamma(\beta_1(t))}\int_0^s \frac{(s-\tau)^{\beta_2(s)-1}}{\Gamma(\beta_2(s))}\phi(\tau)d\tau ds \\ &= \int_0^t \frac{(t-s)^{\beta_1(t)-1}}{\Gamma(u(t))}[\int_0^1 \frac{(s-\tau)^0}{\Gamma(1)}d\tau + \int_1^s \frac{(s-\tau)}{\Gamma(2)}d\tau]ds \\ &= \int_0^t \frac{(t-s)^{\beta_1(t)-1}}{\Gamma(\beta_1(t))}[\frac{s^2}{2} - s + \frac{3}{2}]ds, \end{aligned}$$

and

$$I_{0^+}^{\beta_1(t)+\beta_2(t)}\phi(t) = \int_0^t \frac{(t-s)^{\beta_1(t)+\beta_2(t)-1}}{\Gamma(beta_1(t)+\beta_2(t))}\phi(s)ds.$$

For $t = 2$, it becomes

$$\begin{aligned} I_{0^+}^{\beta_1(t)}\left(I_{0^+}^{\beta_2(t)}\phi(t)\right)|_{t=2} &= \int_0^2 \frac{(2-s)^0}{\Gamma(1)}[\frac{s^2}{2} - s + \frac{3}{2}]ds \\ &= \int_0^2 (\frac{s^2}{2} - s + \frac{3}{2})ds \\ &= \frac{7}{3}, \end{aligned}$$

and

$$
\begin{aligned}
I_{0^+}^{\beta_1(t)+\beta_2(t)}\phi(t)|_{t=2} &= \int_0^2 \frac{(2-s)^{\beta_1(t)+\beta_2(t)-1}}{\Gamma(\beta_1(t)+\beta_2(t))}\phi(s)ds \\
&= \int_0^1 \frac{(2-s)^1}{\Gamma(2)}ds + \int_1^2 \frac{(2-s)^2}{\Gamma(3)}ds \\
&= \frac{3}{2}+\frac{1}{6} \\
&= \frac{5}{3}.
\end{aligned}
$$

Hence, it is simply seen that the mentioned property is not correct for the generalized RLFI operators with respect to variable orders.

The following expansion is key for our argument.

Lemma 1 ([31])**.** *Let $a_1, \alpha_1 > 0$ and $n = 1 + [\alpha_1]$. Then*

$$I_{a_1^+}^{\alpha_1}({}^cD_{a_1^+}^{\alpha_1}\phi(t)) = \phi(t) - \sum_{k=0}^{n-1} \frac{\phi^{(k)}(a_1)}{k!}t^k.$$

Lemma 2 ([32])**.** *Let $\alpha_1,\ \alpha_2 > 0$, $\phi, {}^c D_{a_1^+}^{\alpha_1}\phi \in L^1(a_1, a_2)$. Then, the differential equation*

$${}^cD_{a_1^+}^{\alpha_1}\phi(t) = 0,$$

has unique solution

$$\phi(t) = r_0 + r_1(t-a_1) + r_2(t-a_1)^2 + \ldots + r_{n-1}(t-a_1)^{n-1},$$

and we have

$$I_{a_1^+}^{\alpha_1}({}^cD_{a_1^+}^{\alpha_1})\phi(t) = \phi(t) + r_0 + r_1(t-a_1) + r_2(t-a_1)^2 + \ldots + r_{n-1}(t-a_1)^{n-1},$$

such that $n-1 < \alpha_1 \le n$, $r_j \in \mathbb{R}$, $j = 1, 2, \ldots, n$.

Furthermore, we have

$${}^cD_{a_1^+}^{\alpha_1}(I_{a_1^+}^{\alpha_1})\phi(t) = \phi(t),$$

and

$$I_{a_1^+}^{\alpha_1}(I_{a_1^+}^{\alpha_2})\phi(t) = I_{a_1^+}^{\alpha_2}(I_{a_1^+}^{\alpha_1})\phi(t) = I_{a_1^+}^{\alpha_1+\alpha_2}\phi(t).$$

We recall some properties of variable order RLFI operator formulated by (2) which will be used in the sequel.

Lemma 3 ([33])**.** *If $u : A \to (0,1]$ has the continuity property, then for*

$$h \in C_\delta(A,\mathbb{R}) = \{h(t) \in C(A,\mathbb{R}),\ t^\delta h(t) \in C(A,\mathbb{R})\},\ 0 \le \delta \le 1,$$

the integral $I_{0^+}^{u(t)}h(t)$ admits a finite value for all $t \in A$.

Lemma 4 ([33])**.** *Assume that $u : A \to (0,1]$ has the continuity property. Then*

$$I_{0^+}^{u(t)}h(t) \in C(A,\mathbb{R}) \text{ for } h \in C(A,\mathbb{R}).$$

Definition 2 ([34,35]). *An interval $J \subseteq \mathbb{R}$ is termed as a generalized interval if I is either an interval, or $\{a_1\}$, or $\emptyset$. A finite set $\mathcal{F}$ is defined to be a partition of J if every $x \in J$ belongs to exactly one and one generalized interval $\mathbb{I}$ in $\mathcal{F}$. Finally, $w : J \to \mathbb{R}$ is piecewise constant w.r.t $\mathcal{F}$ as a partition of J, if for each $\mathbb{I} \in \mathcal{F}$, w is constant on $\mathbb{I}$.*

The next definitions and basic lemmas from coincidence degree theory are fundamental in the proof of theorems which we will establish them later.

Definition 3 ([20,36]). *Consider two normed spaces $\mathbb{S}_1$ and $\mathbb{S}_2$. A Fredholm operator of index zero is a linear operator like $\Theta : Dom(\Theta) \subset \mathbb{S}_1 \to \mathbb{S}_2$ satisfying:*

(a) $\mathbb{IMG}(\Theta) \subseteq \mathbb{S}_2$ *is closed;*
(b) $\dim \mathbb{KER}(\Theta) = \text{codim}\mathbb{IMG}(\Theta) < +\infty$.

In view of Definition 3, it is followed the existence of continuous projections $\Psi : \mathbb{S}_1 \to \mathbb{S}_1$ and $\Phi : \mathbb{S}_2 \to \mathbb{S}_2$ such that $\mathbb{IMG}(\Psi) = \mathbb{KER}(\Theta)$, $\mathbb{KER}(\Phi) = \mathbb{IMG}(\Theta)$, $\mathbb{S}_1 = \mathbb{KER}(\Theta) \oplus \mathbb{KER}(\Psi)$, and $\mathbb{S}_2 = \mathbb{IMG}(\Theta) \oplus \mathbb{IMG}(\Phi)$.

It is known that the restriction of Θ to $Dom(\Theta) \cap \mathbb{KER}(\Psi)$, which we shall represent by Θ_Ψ, will be an isomorphism onto its image [20,36].

Definition 4 ([20,36]). *Let Θ be a Fredholm operator of index zero and $\Omega \subseteq \mathbb{S}_1$ be bounded with $Dom(\Theta) \cap \Omega \neq \emptyset$. We say $W : \overline{\Omega} \to \mathbb{S}_2$ has the Θ-compactness property in $\overline{\Omega}$ whenever:*

(H1) $\Phi W : \overline{\Omega} \to \mathbb{S}_2$ *is continuous, and* $\Phi W(\overline{\Omega}) \subseteq \mathbb{S}_2$ *is bounded,*
(H2) $(\Theta_\Psi)^{-1}(I - \Phi)W : \overline{\Omega} \to \mathbb{S}_1$ *is completely continuous.*

The next theorem entitled *Mawhin's Continuation Theorem* is our main criterion in the present study which proves the existence of solution.

Theorem 1 ([37]). *Assume that $\mathbb{S}_1$ and $\mathbb{S}_2$ are two Banach spaces and $\Omega \subset \mathbb{S}_1$ is an open, bounded and symmetric set with $0 \in \Omega$. Also, assume that:*

(A1) the Fredholm operator $\Theta : Dom(\Theta) \subset \mathbb{S}_1 \to \mathbb{S}_2$ of index zero is such that

$$Dom(\Theta) \cap \overline{\Omega} \neq \emptyset,$$

(A2) the operator $W : \mathbb{S}_1 \to \mathbb{S}_2$ is Θ-compact on $\overline{\Omega}$,
(A3) $\forall\, x \in Dom(\Theta) \cap \partial\Omega$ and $\forall\, \lambda \in (0,1]$,

$$\Theta x - Wx \neq -\lambda(\Theta x + W(-x)),$$

where $\partial\Omega$ denotes the boundary of Ω w.r.t. $\mathbb{S}_1$.

Then the operator equation $\Theta x = Wx$ has at least one solution on $Dom(\Theta) \cap \overline{\Omega}$.

3. Existence of Solutions

To begin the desired analysis, we consider the following assumptions:

(AS1) Consider a sequence of finite many points $\{T_k\}_{k=0}^n$ so that $1 = T_0 < T_k < T_n = T$, $k \in \mathbb{N}_1^{n-1}$. For $k \in \mathbb{N}_1^n$, denote the subintervals A_k as $A_k := (T_{k-1}, T_k]$. Then $\mathcal{P} = \bigcup_{k=1}^n A_k$ is a partition of A.

(AS2) Let $g \in C(A_j \times \mathbb{R}, \mathbb{R})$ and there exists $\delta \in (0,1)$ such that $t^\delta g \in C(A_j \times \mathbb{R}, \mathbb{R})$ and there exists $K > 0$ with $K < \min\left\{1, \dfrac{\Gamma(u_j+1)}{(T_j - T_{j-1})^{u_j}}\right\}$ so that $t^\delta |g(t,\phi_1) - g(t,\phi_2)| \leq K|\phi_1 - \phi_2|$, for any $\phi_1, \phi_2 \in \mathbb{R}$ and $t \in A_j$.

For each $j \in \mathbb{N}_1^n$, the notation $E_j = C(A_j, \mathbb{R})$ denotes the Banach space of continuous functions $\phi : A_j \to \mathbb{R}$ with the sup-norm $\|\phi\|_{E_j} = \sup_{t \in A_j} |\phi(t)|$.

On the other side, consider the piecewise constant mapping $u(t) : A \to (0,1]$ w.r.t. $\mathcal{P}$, i.e.,

$$u(t) = \sum_{j=1}^{n} u_j I_j(t),$$

where $0 < u_j \leq 1$ are real numbers, and I_j denotes the indicator of A_j, $j \in \mathbb{N}_1^n$; that is, $I_j(t) = 1$ if $t \in A_j$ and $I_j(t) = 0$ otherwise. In this case, the left CFD of variable order $u(t)$ for $\phi(t) \in C(A, \mathbb{R})$, defined as (3), can be formulated as a sum of the left CFD operators of constant orders $u_k \in \mathbb{R}$ which takes the form

$$^{c}D_{0^+}^{u(t)}\phi(t) = \sum_{k=1}^{j-1} \int_{T_{k-1}}^{T_k} \frac{(t-s)^{-u_k}}{\Gamma(1-u_k)}\phi'(s)ds + \int_{T_{j-1}}^{t} \frac{(t-s)^{-u_j}}{\Gamma(1-u_j)}\phi'(s)ds. \tag{4}$$

Thus, the given Caputo BVP of variable order (1) can be reformulated for each $t \in A_j$, $j \in \mathbb{N}_1^n$ in the following structure

$$\sum_{k=1}^{j-1} \int_{T_{k-1}}^{T_k} \frac{(t-s)^{-u_k}}{\Gamma(1-u_k)}\phi'(s)ds + \int_{T_{j-1}}^{t} \frac{(t-s)^{-u_j}}{\Gamma(1-u_j)}\phi'(s)ds = g(t,\phi(t)). \tag{5}$$

Let the function $\tilde{\phi} \in E_j$ be so that $\tilde{\phi}(t) \equiv 0$ on $t \in [0, T_{j-1}]$ and it satisfies the above integral Equation (5). In such a situation, (5) is converted to the standard constant order fractional differential equation (FDE) as

$$^{c}D_{T_{j-1}^+}^{u_j}\tilde{\phi}(t) = g(t,\tilde{\phi}(t)), \;\; t \in A_j.$$

In accordance with above equation, for each $j \in \mathbb{N}_1^n$, we have the auxiliary FBVP equipped with Caputo constant order CFD operator

$$\begin{cases} ^{c}D_{T_{j-1}^+}^{u_j}\phi(t) = g(t,\phi(t)), \;\; t \in A_j, \\ \phi(T_{j-1}) = \phi(T_j). \end{cases} \tag{6}$$

A resonance problem is a boundary problem in which the corresponding homogeneous BVP has a non–trivial solution. Hence, we consider the homogeneous version of the given equivalent constant order FBVP (6) by

$$\begin{cases} ^{c}D_{T_{j-1}^+}^{u_j}\phi(t) = 0, \;\; t \in A_j, \\ \phi(T_{j-1}) = \phi(T_j). \end{cases} \tag{7}$$

By Lemma 2, the homogeneous constant order FBVP (7) has nontrivial solution $\phi(t) = c$ which converts the equivalent constant order FBVP (6) to a resonance FBVP.

As well as, on the given subintervals, let $\mathbb{S}_1 = \{\phi \in E_j : \phi(t) = I_{T_{j-1}^+}^{u_j} v(t) : v \in E_j, t \in A_j\}$ with the norm

$$\|\phi\|_{\mathbb{S}_1} = \|\phi\|_{E_j}.$$

The linear operator $\Theta : Dom(\Theta) \subseteq \mathbb{S}_1 \to E_j$ along with the operator $W : \mathbb{S}_1 \to E_j$ are defined as

$$\Theta[\phi(t)] := {}^{c}D_{T_{j-1}^+}^{u_j}\phi(t), \tag{8}$$

and

$$W[\phi(t)] := g(t,\phi(t)), \;\;\; t \in A_j, \tag{9}$$

where

$$Dom(\Theta) = \{\phi \in \mathbb{S}_1 : {}^{c}D_{T_{j-1}^+}^{u_j}\phi \in E_j \;\; \text{and} \;\; \phi(T_{j-1}) = \phi(T_j)\}.$$

Then the equivalent constant order resonance FBVP (6) can be reformulated by the equation $\Theta\phi = W\phi$.

The first theorem on the existence of solutions for the equivalent constant order resonance FBVP (6) is established in this position.

Theorem 2. *If the condition* (AS2) *holds, then the equivalent constant order resonance FBVP* (6) *has at least one solution.*

Proof. The proof will be followed in a sequence of claims.

Claim 1. We show that

$$\mathbb{KER}(\Theta) = \{c : c \in \mathbb{R}\},$$

and

$$\mathbb{IMG}(\Theta) = \Big\{\phi \in E_j : \int_{T_{j-1}}^{T_j} (T_j - s)^{u_j - 1}\phi(s)ds = 0\Big\}.$$

Let Θ (defined by (8)) be such that for $t \in A_j$ and by Lemma 2, the equation $\Theta[\phi(t)] = {}^cD^{u_j}_{T^+_{j-1}}\phi(t) = 0$ has the solution $\phi(t) = c,\ c \in \mathbb{R}$. Then

$$\mathbb{KER}(\Theta) = \{\phi(t) = c : c \in \mathbb{R}\}.$$

On the other hand, for $v \in \mathbb{IMG}(\Theta)$, there exits $\phi \in Dom(\Theta)$ such that $v = \Theta\phi \in E_j$. By Lemma 1, for any $t \in A_j$, we have

$$\phi(t) = \phi(T_{j-1}) + \frac{1}{\Gamma(u_j)}\int_{T_{j-1}}^{t} (t - s)^{u_j - 1}v(s)ds.$$

Since $\phi \in Dom(\Theta)$, v satisfies

$$\frac{1}{\Gamma(u_j)}\int_{T_{j-1}}^{T_j} (T_j - s)^{u_j - 1}v(s)ds = 0.$$

Also, assume that $v \in E_j$ satisfies

$$\int_{T_{j-1}}^{T_j} (T_j - s)^{u_j - 1}v(s)ds = 0.$$

Let $\phi(t) = I^{u_j}_{T^+_{j-1}}v(t)$. Then $v(t) = {}^cD^{u_j}_{T^+_{j-1}}\phi(t)$ and so $\phi \in Dom(\Theta)$. Hence, $v \in \mathbb{IMG}(\Theta)$, so

$$\mathbb{IMG}(\Theta) = \Big\{\phi \in \mathbb{S}_2 : \int_{T_{j-1}}^{T_j} (T_j - s)^{u_j - 1}\phi(s)ds = 0\Big\}.$$

Claim 2. Θ is a Fredholm operator of index zero.

The linear continuous projector operators $\Psi : \mathbb{S}_1 \to \mathbb{S}_1$ and $\Phi : E_j \to E_j$ can be considered by the following forms

$$\Psi\phi = \phi(T_{j-1}), \quad \Phi v(t) = \frac{u_j}{(T_j - T_{j-1})^{u_j}}\int_{T_{j-1}}^{T_j} (T_j - s)^{u_j - 1}v(s)ds.$$

Clearly, $\mathbb{IMG}(\Psi) = \mathbb{KER}(\Theta)$ and $\Psi^2 = \Psi$. It follows that for any $\phi \in \mathbb{S}_1$,

$$\phi = (\phi - \Psi\phi) + \Psi\phi,$$

i.e., $\mathbb{S}_1 = \mathbb{KER}(\Psi) + \mathbb{KER}(\Theta)$. A simple computation shows that $\mathbb{KER}(\Psi) \cap \mathbb{KER}(\Theta) = 0$. Therefore, $\mathbb{S}_1 = \mathbb{KER}(\Psi) \oplus \mathbb{KER}(\Theta)$. A similar argument shows that for every $v \in E_j$, $\Phi^2 v = \Phi v$ and $v = (v - \Phi(v)) + \Phi(v)$, where $(v - \Phi(v)) \in \mathbb{KER}(\Phi) = \mathbb{IMG}(\Theta)$.

From $\mathbb{IMG}(\Theta) = \mathbb{KER}(\Phi)$ and $\Phi^2 = \Phi$, we have

$$\mathbb{IMG}(\Phi) \cap \mathbb{IMG}(\Theta) = 0.$$

Then, $E_j = \mathbb{IMG}(\Theta) \oplus \mathbb{IMG}(\Phi)$.

In this case,

$$\dim(\mathbb{KER}(\Theta) = \dim \mathbb{IMG}(\Phi) = \mathrm{codim}\mathbb{IMG}(\Theta).$$

The obtained result shows that Θ is a Fredholm operator of index zero.

Claim 3. $\Theta_{\Psi}^{-1} = (\Theta|_{Dom(\Theta)\cap\mathbb{KER}(\Psi)})^{-1}$ (the inverse of $\Theta|_{Dom(\Theta)\cap\mathbb{KER}(\Psi)}$). Clearly, $\Theta_{\Psi}^{-1} : \mathbb{IMG}(\Theta) \to \mathbb{S}_1 \cap \mathbb{KER}(\Psi)$ satisfies

$$\Theta_{\Psi}^{-1}(v)(t) = I_{T_{j-1}^+}^{u_j} v(t).$$

Let $v \in \mathbb{IMG}(\Theta)$. Then

$$\Theta\Theta_{\Psi}^{-1}(v) = {}^cD_{T_{j-1}^+}^{u_j}(I_{T_{j-1}^+}^{u_j} v) = v. \tag{10}$$

Furthermore, for $\phi \in Dom(\Theta) \cap \mathbb{KER}(\Psi)$, we get

$$\Theta_{\Psi}^{-1}(\Theta(\phi(t))) = I_{T_{j-1}^+}^{u_j}({}^cD_{T_{j-1}^+}^{u_j}\phi(t)) = \phi(t) - \phi(T_{j-1}).$$

Since $\phi \in Dom(\Theta) \cap \mathbb{KER}(\Psi)$, we know that $\phi(T_{j-1}) = 0$. Thus

$$\Theta_{\Psi}^{-1}(\Theta(\phi(t))) = \phi(t). \tag{11}$$

Combining (10) and (11) shows that $\Theta_{\Psi^{-1}} = (\Theta|_{Dom(\Theta)\cap\mathbb{KER}(\Psi)})^{-1}$.

Claim 4. On every bounded and open set $\Omega \subset \mathbb{S}_1$, W is Θ-compact. Define $\Omega = \{\phi \in \mathbb{S}_1 : \|\phi\|_{\mathbb{S}_1} < M\}$ as a bounded and open set, where $M > 0$.

The proof of this claim will be done in three steps.

Step 1. ΦW is continuous.

This property for ΦW is derived due to the imposed conditions on the nonlinear function g and the Lebesgue dominated convergence criterion, immediately.

Step 2. $\Phi W(\overline{\Omega})$ is bounded.

Now, for each $\phi \in \overline{\Omega}$ and for all $t \in A_j$, we have

$$\begin{aligned}
|\Phi W(\phi)(t)| &\leq \frac{u_j}{(T_j - T_{j-1})^{u_j}} \int_{T_{j-1}}^{T_j} (T_j - s)^{u_j - 1} |g(s, \phi(s))| ds \\
&\leq \frac{u_j}{(T_j - T_{j-1})^{u_j}} \int_{T_{j-1}}^{T_j} (T_j - s)^{u_j - 1} |g(s, \phi(s)) - g(s, 0)| ds \\
&\quad + \frac{u_j}{(T_j - T_{j-1})^{u_j}} \int_{T_{j-1}}^{T_j} (T_j - s)^{u_j - 1} |g(s, 0)| ds \\
&\leq g^* + \frac{u_j}{(T_j - T_{j-1})^{u_j}} \int_{T_{j-1}}^{T_j} (T_j - s)^{u_j - 1} s^{-\delta} (K|\phi(s)|) ds \\
&\leq g^* + MKT_{j-1}^{-\delta},
\end{aligned}$$

by assuming $g^* = \sup_{t\in A_j} |g(t,0)|$. Thus,

$$\|\Phi W(\phi)\|_{E_j} \le g^* + MKT_{j-1}^{-\delta} := R > 0.$$

This shows that $\Phi W(\overline{\Omega}) \subseteq E_j$ is bounded.

Step 3. $\Theta_{\Psi}^{-1}(I-\Phi)W : \overline{\Omega} \to \mathbb{S}_1$ is completely continuous.

By considering the existing hypotheses in relation to Ascoli-Arzelà theorem, it is necessary that we prove two properties of the boundedness and equi-continuity for $\Theta_{\Psi}^{-1}(I-\Phi)W(\overline{\Omega}) \subset \mathbb{S}_1$. At first, for each $\phi \in \overline{\Omega}$ and for all $t \in A_j$, we have

$$\begin{aligned}
\Theta_{\Psi}^{-1}(I-\Phi)W\phi(t) &= \Theta_{\Psi}^{-1}(W\phi(t) - \Phi W\phi(t)) \\
&= I_{T_{j-1}^+}^{u_j}\Big[g(t,\phi(t)) - \frac{u_j}{(T_j-T_{j-1})_j^u}\int_{T_{j-1}}^{T_j}(T_j-s)^{u_j-1}g(s,\phi(s))\Big]ds \\
&= \frac{1}{\Gamma(u_j)}\int_{T_{j-1}}^{t}(t-s)^{u_j-1}g(s,\phi(s))ds \\
&\quad - \frac{t^{u_j}}{(T_j-T_{j-1})^{u_j}\Gamma(u_j)}\int_{T_{j-1}}^{T_j}(T_j-s)^{u_j-1}g(s,\phi(s))ds.
\end{aligned}$$

Further, for each $\phi \in \overline{\Omega}$ and for all $t \in A_j$, we get

$$\begin{aligned}
|\Theta_{\Psi}^{-1}(I-\Phi)W\phi(t)| &\le \frac{2}{\Gamma(u_j)}\int_{T_{j-1}}^{T_j}(T_j-s)^{u_j-1}|g(s,\phi(s)) - g(t,0)|ds \\
&\quad + \frac{2}{\Gamma(u_j)}\int_{T_{j-1}}^{T_j}(T_j-s)^{u_j-1}|g(t,0)|ds \\
&\le [g^* + MKT_{j-1}^{-\delta}]\frac{2(T_j-T_{j-1})^{u_j}}{\Gamma(u_j+1)} := B_1.
\end{aligned}$$

so

$$\|\Theta_{\Psi}^{-1}(I-\Phi)W\phi\|_{E_j} \le B_1,$$

which gives the uniform boundedness of $\Theta_{\Psi}^{-1}(I-\Phi)W(\overline{\Omega})$ in $\mathbb{S}_1$.

To prove the equi-continuity of $\Theta_{\Psi}^{-1}(I-\Phi)W(\overline{\Omega})$, notice that for $T_{j-1} \le t_1 \le t_2 \le T_j$ and $\phi \in \overline{\Omega}$, we get

$$\begin{aligned}
|\Theta_{\Psi}^{-1}(I-\Phi)W\phi(t_2) - \Theta_{\Psi}^{-1}(I-\Phi)W\phi(t_1)| &\le \frac{g^* + T_{j-1}^{-\delta}MK}{\Gamma(u_j)}\Big[\int_{t_1}^{t_2}(t_2-s)^{u_j-1}ds \\
&\quad + \int_{T_{j-1}}^{t_1}|(t_2-s)^{u_j-1} - (t_1-s)^{u_j-1}|ds\Big] + \Big[\frac{T_{j-1}^{-\delta}MK + g^*}{\Gamma(u_j+1)}\Big](t_2^{u_j} - t_1^{u_j}).
\end{aligned}$$

The right-hand side of above inequality tends to zero as $t_1 \to t_2$. Thus, $\Theta_{\Psi}^{-1}(I-\Phi)W(\overline{\Omega})$ is equicontinuous in $\mathbb{S}_1$. On the basis of the Ascoli-Arzelà theorem, $L_{\Psi}^{-1}(I-\Phi)W(\overline{\Omega})$ is relatively compact. In accordance with the steps 1 to 3, we can follow that W is Θ-compact in $\overline{\Omega}$.

Claim 5. There exists $\epsilon > 0$ (not depending on λ) so that if

$$\Theta(\phi) - W(\phi) = -\lambda[\Theta(\phi) + W(-\phi)], \quad \lambda \in (0,1], \tag{12}$$

then $\|\phi\|_{\mathbb{S}_1} \leq \epsilon$. By the condition (AS2) and for each $\phi \in \mathbb{S}_1$ satisfying (12), we get

$$\Theta(\phi) - W(\phi) = -\lambda\Theta(\phi) - \lambda W(-\phi).$$

So

$$\Theta(\phi) = \frac{1}{1+\lambda}W(\phi) - \frac{\lambda}{1+\lambda}W(-\phi). \tag{13}$$

By (13), and for all $t \in A_j$, we get

$$\phi(t) = \frac{1}{1+\lambda}\Theta_{\Psi}^{-1}W\phi(t) - \frac{\lambda}{1+\lambda}\Theta_{\Psi}^{-1}W(-\phi(t)),$$

and so we estimate

$$\begin{aligned}
|\phi(t)| \leq& \frac{1}{(1+\lambda)\Gamma(u_j)}\int_{T_{j-1}}^{t}(t-s)^{u_j-1}|g(s,\phi(s)) - g(s,0)|ds \\
&+ \frac{\lambda}{(1+\lambda)\Gamma(u_j)}\int_{T_{j-1}}^{t}(t-s)^{u_j-1}|g(s,-\phi(s)) - g(s,0)|ds \\
&+ \frac{g^*(T_j - T_{j-1})^{u_j}}{(1+\lambda)\Gamma(u_j+1)} + \frac{\lambda g^*(T_j - T_{j-1})^{u_j}}{(1+\lambda)\Gamma(u_j+1)} \\
\leq& \left(\frac{1}{1+\lambda} + \frac{\lambda}{1+\lambda}\right)\frac{T_{j-1}^{-\delta}(T_j - T_{j-1})^{u_j}}{\Gamma(u_j+1)}(K\|\phi\|_{E_j}) \\
&+ \left(\frac{1}{1+\lambda} + \frac{\lambda}{1+\lambda}\right)\frac{g^*(T_j - T_{j-1})^{u_j}}{\Gamma(u_j+1)} \\
=& \frac{KT_{j-1}^{-\delta}(T_j - T_{j-1})^{u_j}}{\Gamma(u_j+1)}\|\phi\|_{E_j} + \frac{g^*(T_j - T_{j-1})^{u_j}}{\Gamma(u_j+1)}.
\end{aligned}$$

Hence,

$$\|\phi\|_{E_j} \leq \left(g^* + KT_{j-1}^{-\delta}\|\phi\|_{E_j}\right)\frac{(T_j - T_{j-1})^{u_j}}{\Gamma(u_j+1)}, \tag{14}$$

and so

$$\|\phi\|_{\mathbb{S}_1} \leq \frac{g^*}{\frac{\Gamma(u_j+1)}{(T_j - T_{j-1})^{u_j}} - KT_{j-1}^{-\delta}} := \epsilon.$$

Claim 6. There exists a bounded and open set $\Omega \subset \mathbb{S}_1$ such that

$$\Theta(\phi) - W(\phi) \neq -\lambda[\Theta(\phi) + W(-\phi)],$$

for all $\phi \in \partial\Omega$ and all $\lambda \in (0,1]$.

By the condition (AS2) and Claim 5, there exits $\epsilon > 0$ (independent of λ) such that if ϕ solves

$$\Theta(\phi) - W(\phi) = -\lambda[\Theta(\phi) + W(-\phi)],\ \lambda \in (0,1],$$

then $\|\phi\|_{\mathbb{S}_1} \leq \epsilon$. Consequently, if

$$\Omega = \{\phi \in \mathbb{S}_1 : \|\phi\|_{\mathbb{S}_1} < B\}, \tag{15}$$

then from the condition (AS2), it is immediately obtained that the set Ω introduced by (15), is symmetric, $0 \in \Omega$, and $\mathbb{S}_1 \cap \overline{\Omega} = \overline{\Omega} \neq \emptyset$.

Furthermore, it is obtained that

$$\Theta(\phi) - W(\phi) \neq -\lambda[\Theta(\phi) - W(-\phi)],$$

for all $\phi \in \partial\Omega = \{\phi \in \mathbb{S}_1 : \|\phi\|_{\mathbb{S}_1} = B\}$ and for all $\lambda \in (0,1]$, where $B > \epsilon$. This together with Theorem 1 imply that the equivalent constant order resonance FBVP (6) has at least one solution, and this completes the proof. □

Now, we complete our deduction on the existence property for solutions of the given Caputo FBVP of variable order (1).

Theorem 3. *Let the conditions* (AS1) *and* (AS2) *be satisfied for all* $j \in \mathbb{N}_1^n$. *Then, the given Caputo FBVP of variable order* (1) *has at least a solution in* $C(A, \mathbb{R})$.

Proof. We know that for all $j \in \mathbb{N}_1^n$, and according to Theorem 2, the equivalent constant order resonance FBVP (6) has at least one solution $\widetilde{\phi}_j \in E_j$. For each $j \in \mathbb{N}_1^n$, and on the existing subintervals, define

$$\phi_j = \begin{cases} 0, & t \in [0, T_{j-1}], \\ \widetilde{\phi}_j, & t \in A_j. \end{cases}$$

In such a case, $\phi_j \in C([0, T_j], \mathbb{R})$ satisfies the integral equation (5) for $t \in A_j$, which means that $\phi_j(0) = 0, \phi_j(T_j) = \widetilde{\phi}_j(T_j) = 0$ and satisfies (5) for $t \in A_j, j \in \mathbb{N}_1^n$. Therefore, the piecewise function

$$\phi(t) = \begin{cases} \phi_1(t), & t \in A_1, \\ \phi_2(t), & t \in A_2, \\ \ldots\ldots\ldots\ldots\ldots \\ \phi_n(t), & t \in A_n = [0, T], \end{cases}$$

is a solution to the given Caputo FBVP of variable order (1) in $C(A, \mathbb{R})$. □

4. Example

Example 2. *Consider the following FBVP (based on the given Caputo FBVP of variable order* (1)*) as follows*

$$\begin{cases} {}^cD_{0^+}^{u(t)}\phi(t) = \dfrac{\sin\phi(t) - \phi(t)\cos t}{5\sqrt{1+t}}, & t \in A := [0,2], \\ \phi(0) = \phi(2). \end{cases} \tag{16}$$

Let

$$g(t,\phi) = \frac{\sin\phi - \phi\cos t}{5\sqrt{1+t}}, \ (t,\phi) \in [0,2] \times [0, +\infty),$$

and

$$u(t) = \begin{cases} \dfrac{7}{5}, & t \in A_1 := [0,1], \\ \dfrac{3}{2}, & t \in A_2 := [1,2]. \end{cases} \tag{17}$$

In this case,

$$\begin{aligned} t^{\frac{1}{2}}|g(t,\phi_1) - g_1(t,\phi_2)| &= \left| \frac{t^{\frac{1}{2}}(\sin\phi_1 - \phi_1\cos t)}{5\sqrt{1+t}} - \frac{t^{\frac{1}{2}}(\sin\phi_2 - \phi_2\cos t)}{5\sqrt{1+t}} \right| \\ &\leq \frac{1}{5}\sqrt{\frac{t}{1+t}}\Big(|\sin\phi_1 - \sin\phi_2| + |\cos t||\phi_1 - \phi_2|\Big) \\ &\leq \frac{2}{5}|\phi_1 - \phi_2|. \end{aligned}$$

By (17) *and* (6), *on every subintervals* A_1 *and* A_2, *two auxiliary constant order resonance FBVPs are considered as*

$$\begin{cases} {}^{c}D_{0^+}^{\frac{7}{5}}\phi(t) = \dfrac{\sin\phi(t) - \phi(t)\cos t}{5\sqrt{1+t}}, & t \in A_1, \\ \phi(0) = \phi(1), \end{cases} \tag{18}$$

and

$$\begin{cases} {}^{c}D_{1^+}^{\frac{3}{2}}\phi(t) = \dfrac{\sin\phi(t) - \phi(t)\cos t}{5\sqrt{1+t}}, & t \in A_2, \\ \phi(1) = \phi(2). \end{cases} \tag{19}$$

Evidently, the condition (AS2) *is satisfied for* $j = 1$ *with* $\delta = \frac{1}{2}$ *and* $K = \frac{2}{5}$, *and*

$$0 < K = \frac{2}{5} < \min\left\{1, \frac{\Gamma(u_j+1)}{(T_j - T_{j-1})^{u_j}}\right\} = \min\left\{1, \Gamma(\frac{12}{5})\right\} = 1.$$

According to Theorem 2, the constant order resonance FBVP (18) *has a solution like* $\widetilde{\phi}_1 \in E_1$. *Next, the condition* (AS2) *is also valid for* $j = 2$ *with* $\delta = \frac{1}{2}$ *and* $K = \frac{2}{5}$, *and*

$$0 < K = \frac{2}{5} < \min\left\{1, \frac{\Gamma(u_j+1)}{(T_j - T_{j-1})^{u_j}}\right\} = \min\left\{1, \Gamma(\frac{5}{2})\right\} = 1.$$

According to Theorem 2, the constant order resonance FBVP (19) *has a solution like* $\widetilde{\phi}_2 \in E_2$. *Then, by Theorem 3, the given Caputo FBVP of variable order* (16) *has a solution as*

$$\phi(t) = \begin{cases} \widetilde{\phi}_1(t), & t \in A_1, \\ \phi_2(t), & t \in A_2, \end{cases}$$

where

$$\phi_2(t) = \begin{cases} 0, & t \in A_1, \\ \widetilde{\phi}_2(t), & t \in A_2, \end{cases}$$

and this shows the correctness of our results.

5. Conclusions

In this paper, a theoretical study was done for the given Caputo BVP of variable order (1) at resonance. To conduct this research, we defined some generalized subintervals as a partition of the main interval, and then on each subinterval, the piecewise constant functions were defined. With the help of these notions, we converted the given variable-order system to a constant-order system at resonance. In this case, we implemented the conditions of the Mawhin's continuation theorem for proving the existence criterion for solutions of the corresponding BVP. Finally, an example was simulated numerically to show the correctness of our results. This technique on a variable-order BVP is new and determines the novelty of this work compared with other limited published papers in the form of variable orders. In relation to next studies, we aim to work on hidden-memory variable order systems and analyze the qualitative behaviors of their solutions such as existence, stability, and numerical solutions.

Author Contributions: Conceptualization, M.S.S. and Z.B.; Formal analysis, S.R., M.S.S., S.E., Z.B., S.K.N., S.A. and J.T.; Funding acquisition, J.T.; Methodology, S.R., M.S.S., S.E., Z.B., S.K.N. and S.A.; Software, S.E. All authors have read and agreed to the published version of the manuscript.

Funding: This research was funded by King Mongkut's University of Technology North Bangkok. Contract No. KMUTNB-62-KNOW-29.

Institutional Review Board Statement: Not applicable.

Informed Consent Statement: Not applicable.

Data Availability Statement: Data sharing not applicable to this article as no datasets were generated or analyzed during the current study.

Acknowledgments: The first and third authors would like to thank Azarbaijan Shahid Madani University.

Conflicts of Interest: The authors declare no conflict of interest.

Abbreviations

The following abbreviations are used in this manuscript:

BVP Boundary Value Problem

References

1. Gomez-Aguilar, J.F. Analytical and numerical solutions of a nonlinear alcoholism model via variable-order fractional differential equations. *Phys. A Stat. Mech. Its Appl.* **2018**, 494, 52–75. [CrossRef]
2. Almeida, R.; Tavares, D.; Torres, D.F.M. *The Variable-Order Fractional Calculus of Variations*; Springer: Cham, Switzerland, 2019.
3. Sun, H.G.; Chang, A.; Zhang, Y.; Chen, W. A review on variable-order fractional differential equations: Mathematical foundations, Physical models, numerical methods and applications. *Fract. Calc. Appl. Anal.* **2019**, *22*, 27–59. [CrossRef]
4. Abdeljawad, A.; Agarwal, R.P.; Karapinar, E.; Kumari, P.S. Solutions of the nonlinear integral equation and fractional differential equation using the technique of a fixed point with a numerical experiment in extended b-Metric Space. *Symmetry* **2019**, *11*, 686. [CrossRef]
5. Abbas, M.I.; Ragusa, M.A. On the hybrid fractional differential equations with fractional proportional derivatives of a function with respect to a certain function. *Symmetry* **2021**, *13*, 264. [CrossRef]
6. Boutiara, A.; Adjimi, N.; Benbachir, M.; Abdo, M.S. Analysis of a fractional boundary value problem involving Riesz-Caputo fractional derivative. *Adv. Theory Nonlinear Anal. Its Appl.* **2022**, *6*, 14–27.
7. Ntouyas, S.K.; Etemad, S.; Tariboon, J. Existence results for multi-term fractional differential inclusions. *Adv. Differ. Equ.* **2015**, *2015*, 140. [CrossRef]
8. Rezapour, S.; Ntouyas, S.K.; Iqbal, M.Q.; Hussain, A.; Etemad, S.; Tariboon, J. An analytical survey on the solutions of the generalized double-order φ-integrodifferential equation. *J. Funct. Spaces*, **2021**, *2021*, 6667757. [CrossRef]
9. Adiguzel, R.S.; Aksoy, U.; Karapinar, E.; Erhan, I.M. On the solution of a boundary value problem associated with a fractional differential equation. *Math. Methods Appl. Sci.* **2020**. [CrossRef]
10. Afshari, H.; Karapinar, E. A discussion on the existence of positive solutions of the boundary value problems via ψ-Hilfer fractional derivative on b-metric spaces. *Adv. Differ. Equ.* **2020**, *2020*, 616. [CrossRef]
11. Etemad, S.; Rezapour, S.; Samei, M.E. α-ψ-contractions and solutions of a q-fractional differential inclusion with three-point boundary value conditions via computational results. *Adv. Differ. Equ.* **2020**, *2020*, 218. [CrossRef]
12. Boutiara, A.; Etemad, S.; Hussain, A.; Rezapour, S. The generalized U-H and U-H stability and existence analysis of a coupled hybrid system of integro-differential IVPs involving φ-Caputo fractional operators. *Adv. Differ. Equ.* **2021**, *2021*, 95. [CrossRef]
13. Zhang, S.; Hu, L. The existence of solutions and generalized Lyapunov-type inequalities to boundary value problems of differential equations of variable order. *AIMS Math.* **2020**, *5*, 2923–2943. [CrossRef]
14. Sousa, J.V.d.C.; de Oliveira, E.C. Two new fractional derivatives of variable order with non-singular kernel and fractional differential equation. *Comput. Appl. Math.* **2018**, *37*, 5375–5394. [CrossRef]
15. Benkerrouche, A.; Souid, M.S.; Etemad, S.; Hakem, A.; Agarwal, P.; Rezapour, S.; Ntouyas, S.K.; Tariboon, J. Qualitative study on solutions of a Hadamard variable order boundary problem via the Ulam-Hyers-Rassias stability. *Fractal Fract.* **2021**, *5*, 108. [CrossRef]
16. Kaabar, M.K.A.; Refice, A.; Souid, M.S.; Martínez, F.; Etemad, S.; Siri, Z.; Rezapour, S. Existence and U-H-R stability of solutions to the implicit nonlinear FBVP in the variable order settings. *Mathematics* **2021**, *9*, 1693. [CrossRef]
17. Zhang, S.; Hu, L. Unique existence result of approximate solution to initial value problem for fractional differential equation of variable order involving the derivative arguments on the half-axis. *Mathematics* **2019**, *7*, 286. [CrossRef]
18. Zhang, S.; Li, S.; Hu, L. The existence and uniqueness result of solutions to initial value problems of nonlinear diffusion equations involving with the conformable variable derivative. *Revista de la Real Academia de Ciencias Exactas Físicas y Naturales Serie A Matemáticas* **2019**, *113*, 1601–1623. [CrossRef]
19. Bouazza, Z.; Etemad, S.; Souid, M.S.; Rezapour, S.; Martínez, F.; Kaabar, M.K.A. A study on the solutions of a multiterm FBVP of variable order. *J. Funct. Spaces* **2021**, *2021*, 9939147. [CrossRef]

20. Gaines, R.E.; Mawhin, J.L. *Coincidence Degree and Nonlinear Differential Equations*; Lecture Notes in Mathematics; Springer: Berlin/Heidelberg, Germany, 1977.
21. Mawhin, J. Topological degree and boundary value problems for nonlinear differential equations. In *Topological Methods for Ordinary Differential Equations*; Furi, M., Zecca, P., Eds.; Lecture Notes in Mathematics; Springer: Berlin/Heidelberg, Germany, 1993; Volume 1537.
22. Feng, W.; Webb, J.R.L. Solvability of three point boundary value problems at resonance. *Nonlinear Anal. Theory Methods Appl.* **1997**, *30*, 3227–3238. [CrossRef]
23. Guezane-Lakoud, A.; Frioui, A. Third order boundary value problem with integral condition at resonance. *Theory Appl. Math. Comput. Sci.* **2013**, *3*, 56–64.
24. Mawhin, J.; Ward, J.R., Jr. Periodic solutions of some forced Lienard differential equations at resonance. *Archiv. Math.* **1983**, *41*, 337–351. [CrossRef]
25. Infante, G.; Zima, M. Positive solutions of multi-point boundary value problems at resonance. *Nonlinear Anal. Theory Methods Appl.* **2008**, *69*, 2458–2465. [CrossRef]
26. Umarov, S.; Steinberg, S. Variable order differential equations with piecewise constant order-function and diffusion with changing modes. *Z. Anal. Ihre Anwendungen* **2009**, *28*, 431–450. [CrossRef]
27. Zheng, X.; Wang, H. A hidden-memory variable-order time-fractional optimal control model: Analysis and approximation. *SIAM J. Control Optim.* **2021**, *59*, 1851–1880. [CrossRef]
28. Lorenzo, C.F.; Hartley, T.T. Initialization, conceptualization, and application in the generalized (fractional) calculus. *Crit. Rev. Biomed. Eng.* **2007**, *35*, 447–553. [CrossRef] [PubMed]
29. Samko, S.G. Fractional integration and differentiation of variable order. *Anal. Math.* **1995**, *21*, 213–236. [CrossRef]
30. Samko, S.G.; Ross, B. Integration and differentiation to a variable fractional order. *Integral Transform. Spec. Funct.* **1993**, *1*, 277–300. [CrossRef]
31. Kilbas, A.A.; Srivastava, H.M.; Trujillo, J.J. *Theory and Applications of Fractional Differenatial Equations*; North-Holland Mathematics Studies, 204; Elsevier Science B.V.: Amsterdam, The Netherlands, 2006.
32. Podlubny, I. *Fractional Differential Equations*; Academic Press: San Diego, CA, USA, 1999; Volume 198
33. Zhang, S.; Sun, S.; Hu, L. Approximate solutions to initial value problem for differential equation of variable order. *J. Fract. Calc. Appl.* **2018**, *9*, 93–112.
34. An, J.; Chen, P. Uniqueness of solutions to initial value problem of fractional differential equations of variable-order. *Dyn. Syst. Appl.* **2019**, *28*, 607–623.
35. Zhang, S. The uniqueness result of solutions to initial value problems of differential equations of variable-order. *Revista de la Real Academia de Ciencias Exactas Físicas y Naturales Serie A Matemáticas* **2018**, *112*, 407–423. [CrossRef]
36. Mawhin, J. *Topological Degree Methods in Nonlinear Boundary Value Problems*; CBMS Regional Conference Series in Mathematics; American Mathematical Society: Providence, RI, USA, 1979; Volume 40.
37. O'Regan, D.; Cho, Y.J.; Chen, Y.Q. *Topological Degree Theory and Application*; Chapman and Hall/CRC: Boca Raton, FL, USA, 2006; Volume 10.

fractal and fractional

MDPI

Article

Solvability of Some Nonlocal Fractional Boundary Value Problems at Resonance in $\mathbb{R}^n$

Yizhe Feng † **and Zhanbing Bai** *,†

College of Mathematics and System Science, Shandong University of Science and Technology, Qingdao 266590, China; yzfeng2021@163.com

* Correspondence: zhanbingbai@163.com

† These authors contributed equally to this work.

Abstract: In this paper, the solvability of a system of nonlinear Caputo fractional differential equations at resonance is considered. The interesting point is that the state variable $x \in \mathbb{R}^n$ and the effect of the coefficient matrices matrices B and C of boundary value conditions on the solvability of the problem are systematically discussed. By using Mawhin coincidence degree theory, some sufficient conditions for the solvability of the problem are obtained.

Keywords: coincidence degree theory; four-point boundary value problem system; at resonance

Citation: Feng, Y.; Bai, Z. Solvability of Some Nonlocal Fractional Boundary Value Problems at Resonance in $\mathbb{R}^n$. *Fractal Fract.* **2022**, *6*, 25. https://doi.org/10.3390/fractalfract6010025

Academic Editor: Rodica Luca

Received: 12 December 2021
Accepted: 31 December 2021
Published: 1 January 2022

1. Introduction

In partial differential equations theory, multipoint boundary conditions are those which the solutions of multiple-parameter differential equations should satisfy. In recent decades, more and more mathematicians turned their attention to nonlinear boundary value problems (BVPs) in resonance cases and non-resonance cases. For some non-resonance cases, we recommend readers to [1–4], and for resonance cases to [5–12] and the references therein. In [8], Feng first obtained the existence of one solution of semilinear three-point BVPs at resonance by making use of the coincidence degree theory of Mawhin. Then, as an extension of [8], Ma [9] first developed the upper and lower solution method to obtain some multiplicity results. Motivated by [9], Bai [6] researched a four-point boundary value problem, and proved the existence and multiplicity results by making use of the method of upper and lower solutions established by the coincidence degree theorem. Subsequently, various boundary value conditions were studied.

V.A. Il'in and E.I. Moiseev in [1] studied Sturm–Liouville operator of the first kind of nonlocal boundary value problem, which originated from the famous work of A. V. Bitsadze and A. A. Samarskogo [3]: In the Euclidean n-dimensional space with orthogonal Cartesian coordinates $x_1, x_2, ..., x_n$, the elliptic linear differential equation on the $(n-1)$ -dimensional piecewise smooth Lyapunov surface is transformed into a nonlocal problem of an ordinary differential equation when solving a partial differential equation by the separation of variables method. When the state variable is n-dimensional, consideration of the general fractional model will naturally involve the model of the problem considered in this paper.

To our best knowledge, before P.D. Phung [13], almost all articles on resonance BVPs were focused on a single second-order equation with the dimension of Ker $L \in [0,2]$. For a second-order equation boundary value problem system with $x \in \mathbb{R}^n$, the dimension of Ker L will be between 0 and $2n$; it will not be as easy as dim Ker $L = 1$ to establish projections Q for matrices B and C with different properties. For the case of $n = 2$, Zhang in [12] considered a three-point BVP at resonance for nonlinear fractional differential equations:

$$\begin{cases} D_{0+}^{\alpha} u(t) = f(t, v(t), D_{0+}^{\beta-1} v(t)), & 0 < t < 1, \\ D_{0+}^{\beta} v(t) = g(t, u(t), D_{0+}^{\alpha-1} u(t)), & 0 < t < 1, \\ u(0) = v(0) = 0, \quad u(1) = \sigma_1 u(\eta_1), & v(1) = \sigma_2 v(\eta_2), \end{cases}$$

and obtained two existence results using the coincidence degree theory. In [13]. P.D. Phung first researched the following resonant three-point BVPs in $\mathbb{R}^n$:

$$\begin{cases} x''(t) = f(t,x,x'), & t \in (0,1), \\ x'(0) = \theta, & x(1) = Ax(\eta), \end{cases}$$

where θ is an n-order zero vector, the matrix A satisfies one of the following conditions:

$$\begin{cases} A^2 = I \text{ (stands for } n - \text{order identity matrix)}, \\ A^2 = A. \end{cases}$$

In [14], P.D. Phung removed the restriction on matrix A and studied the solvability of the same problem as in [13]. Then, P.D. Phung [15] used similar methods to study the following three-point boundary conditions in the fractional differential equations at resonance:

$$D^{\alpha}x(t) = f(t, x(t), D^{\alpha-1}x(t),$$
$$x(0) = \theta, \ D^{\alpha-1}x(1) = AD^{\alpha-1}x(\eta).$$

Recently, the solvability of integer or fractional differential equations with a wide range of boundary value conditions at resonance in $\mathbb{R}^n$ has been researched. We direct readers to [13–21] for details.

For nearly a decade, the resonant boundary value problem with n equations has been studied by an increasing number of mathematicians. However, we found that the following two problems have not been addressed. First, Zhang in [12] studied the resonance boundary value problem of two equations, but used the same boundary value conditions for different state variables u and v, so the study was similar to that of a single equation and could not be easily extended to the case of n dimensions. Therefore, in this study we consider the characterization of different constraints on different state variables, in other words, we introduce matrices to control the constraints on state variables so that the expression of the equation can be richer. However, other works [13–16,20,21] under the condition of zero boundary value (similar to $u(0) = 0$) studied n equations of the problem. Gupta in [10] proposed that many multi-point boundary value problems can be transformed into four-point boundary value problems under certain conditions, so studying four-point BVPs is more meaningful. The four-point boundary value condition does not contain zero boundary value, which makes the structure of irreversible operators and the construction of projection P and Q more complicated than that of three-point BVPs. Therefore, it is more meaningful to introduce a matrix to study four-point boundary value problems in mathematics.

Motivated by the above ideas, we consider the following fractional-order equations with a new boundary value condition in $\mathbb{R}^n$:

$$^{c}D^{\alpha}_{0+}u(t) = f(t, u(t), {}^{c}D^{\alpha-1}_{0+}u), \quad t \in (0,1), \tag{1}$$
$$u(0) = Bu(\xi), \quad u(1) = Cu(\eta), \tag{2}$$

where $0 < \eta, \xi < 1$, $1 < \alpha \leqslant 2$; B, C are two n-order nonzero square matrices, $^{c}D^{\alpha}_{0+}$ represents the Caputo differentiation, and $f : [0,1] \times \mathbb{R}^{2n} \to \mathbb{R}^n$ satisfies Carathéodory conditions. In this situation, Ker L may become a polynomial set with vector coefficients and the construction of projectors will be somewhat complex. We say $f : [0,1] \times \mathbb{R}^{2n} \to \mathbb{R}^n$ satisfies Carathéodory conditions, that is,

(A1) $f(\cdot, u, v)$ is measurable on [0,1] for all $(u,v) \in \mathbb{R}^n \times \mathbb{R}^n$.
(A2) $f(s, \cdot, \cdot)$ is continuous on $\mathbb{R}^n \times \mathbb{R}^n$, for a.e. $s \in [0,1]$.
(A3) The function $g_W(t) = \sup_{(u,v)\in\overline{W}} |f(s,u,v)|$ is Lebesgue integrable on $0 \leqslant s \leqslant 1$ for all compact set $W \subset \mathbb{R}^n \times \mathbb{R}^n$.

The problem in (1) and (2) is in resonance, meaning that the following linear homogeneous boundary value problem has nontrivial solutions:

$$ {}^{C}D_{0+}^{\alpha}u(t) = \theta, \quad 0 < t < 1, \tag{3} $$

$$ u(0) = Bu(\xi), \quad u(1) = Cu(\eta). \tag{4} $$

By (3), there is $u(t) = c_1 + c_2 t$, $c_1, c_2 \in \mathbb{R}^n$. Combining with (4), we can get the following equations:

$$ \begin{cases} (I - \eta C)c_1 + (I - C)c_2 = \theta, \\ -\xi Bc_1 + (I - B)c_2 = \theta. \end{cases} $$

Clearly, the resonance condition is

$$ \Delta = \begin{vmatrix} I - \eta C & I - C \\ -\xi B & I - B \end{vmatrix} = 0. $$

From the calculation formula of block matrix determinant, we can know that $\Delta = 0$ if and only if

$$ |(I - \eta C)(I - B) + \xi B(I - C)| = 0. \tag{5} $$

Condition (5) can be divided into three cases:
Case (1) $B \neq I, C \neq I, |(I - \eta C)(I - B) + \xi B(I - C)| = 0$;
Case (2) $B = I, |I - C| = 0$;
Case (3) $B \neq I, C = I, |I - B| = 0$.

The paper is organized as follows. In Section 2, we state several notations and definitions. In Sections 3 and 4, two main theorems (see Theorem 2 and 3) are established for the solvability of problem (1) and (2) under resonance cases (1) and (2), respectively. It is worth mentioning that, inspired by [14], in Section 4, we remove the restriction on the matrix C, and give the existence theorem of the solution of the problem only under the most basic resonance conditions (refer to *case* (2)).

2. Preliminaries

First, we recall some related definitions and lemmas of fractional calculus; we refer the readers to [22] for more properties.

Definition 1. *The α–order ($\alpha > 0$) Riemann–Liouville fractional integral of function u is defined as*

$$ I_{0+}^{\alpha}u(t) = \frac{1}{\Gamma(\alpha)} \int_0^t \frac{u(s)}{(t-s)^{1-\alpha}} ds, \tag{6} $$

and the right side of the equation is defined at $(0, \infty)$.

Definition 2. *The α–order ($\alpha > 0$) Caputo fractional derivative of function $u : R_+ \to R$ is defined as*

$$ {}^{C}D_{0+}^{\alpha}u(t) = I_{0+}^{n-\alpha}D^n u(t) = \frac{1}{\Gamma(n-a)} \int_0^t \frac{u^{(n)}(s)}{(t-s)^{1+\alpha-n}} ds \tag{7} $$

as long as the right side of the equation is defined at $(0, \infty)$.

Lemma 1 ([22]). *If $u \in C^{n-1}(0,1) \cap L[0,1]$, then the fractional differential equation*

$$ {}^{C}D_{0+}^{\alpha}u(t) = 0 \tag{8} $$

has a unique solution

$$ u(t) = \sum_{i=0}^{n-1} \frac{u^{(i)}(0)}{i!} t^k. \tag{9} $$

The following lemma is also very important for subsequent research.

Lemma 2 ([22]). *Let $\alpha > 0$ and $n-1 < \alpha \leqslant n$.*

(1) Let $\alpha > \theta > 0$ and u be a continuous function, then

$$^{C}D_{0+}^{\theta} I_{0+}^{\alpha} u(t) = I_{0+}^{\alpha-\theta} u. \tag{10}$$

(2) Let u be an absolute continuous function of $n-1$ times differentiable, then

$$I_{0+}^{\alpha}\, {}^{C}D_{0+}^{\alpha} u(t) = u(t) - \sum_{i=0}^{n-1} \frac{D^i u(0)}{i!} t^i. \tag{11}$$

Let X, Y be two Banach spaces, we call $L : \mathrm{dom}\, L \subset X \to Y$ a Fredholm mapping of index zero if

(E1) Im L is closed in Y and has codimension of finite dimension;
(E2) Tthe dimension of Ker L is equal to the codimension of Im L.

If L satisfies (E1) and (E2), then there will be two projectors $Q : Y \to Y, P : X \to X$ satisfies Ker Q = Im L, Im P = Ker L. Therefore, we can get the straight-sum decomposition: Y = Im $L \oplus$ Im Q, X = Ker $L \oplus$ Ker P. Here, by K_P we denote the inverse of $L|_{\mathrm{Ker}\, P \cap \mathrm{dom}\, L}$: Ker $P \cap \mathrm{dom}\, L \to$ Im L and by $K_{P,Q} := K_P(Id - Q)$ the generalized inverse of L.

We call N L-compact on $\overline{\Omega}$ (Ω is an open bounded subset of X with $\mathrm{dom}\, L \cap \Omega \neq \emptyset$, when it satisfies

(F1) $QN(\overline{\Omega})$ is bounded;
(F2) $K_P(Id - Q)N : \overline{\Omega} \to X$ is completely continuous.

Theorem 1 ([23]). *Let L be a Fredholm operator of index zero and $N(\overline{\Omega})$ be L-compact. Suppose the following conditions are satisfied:*

(i) $Lu \neq \lambda Nu$ for all $x \in \partial\Omega \cap (\mathrm{dom}\, L \setminus \mathrm{Ker}\, L)$ and $0 < \lambda < 1$;
(ii) $Nu \notin \mathrm{Im}\, L$ for all $x \in \partial\Omega \cap \mathrm{Ker}\, L$;
(iii) $\deg(\mathcal{J}QN|_{\overline{\Omega}\cap \mathrm{Ker}\, L}, \mathrm{Ker}\, L \cap \Omega, 0) \neq 0$, where $\mathcal{J} : \mathrm{Im}\, Q \to \mathrm{Ker}\, L$ is an isomorphism, and $Q : Y \to Y$ is a projection as above.

Then, the equation $Lu = Nu$ has at least one solution in $\mathrm{dom}\, L \cap \overline{\Omega}$.

By $\|u\| = max\{\|u\|_\infty, \|^{c}D_{0+}^{\alpha-1}u\|_\infty\}$ we denote the norm of space $X = C^1([0,1];\mathbb{R}^n)$, where $\|\cdot\|_\infty$ is the maximum norm. Additionally, by $\|y\|_1$ we denote the Lebesgue norm of $Y = L^1([0,1];\mathbb{R}^n)$. Set

$$X_1 := \{u : [0,1] \to \mathbb{R}^n \mid u \in C^2([0,1];\mathbb{R}^n)\}.$$

Then, define map $L : \mathrm{dom}\, L \to Y$ by setting

$$\mathrm{dom}\, L = \{u \in X_1 : u(0) = Bu(\xi),\ u(1) = Cu(\eta)\},$$

for $u \in \mathrm{dom}\, L$,

$$Lu := {}^{C}D_{0+}^{\alpha} u. \tag{12}$$

3. Existence Results for Case (1)

Now, we show the solvability of BVP (1), (2) when $B \neq I, C \neq I, |(I - \eta C)(I - B) + \xi B(I - C)| = 0$. Furthermore, suppose the matrices B, C satisfy the following conditions:

(H1) $I - B$ is reversible;
(H2) $(\eta C - I)\xi^{\alpha-1} - \eta^\alpha C + I$ is reversible;
(H3) $I - \eta C + \xi(I - C)(I - B)^{-1}B = \Theta$,

where Θ is an n-order zero matrix. From (12) we can know

$$\text{Ker } L = \{c_2 t + C_0 c_2,\ c_2 \in \mathbb{R}^n\},$$

where $C_0 = \xi(I-B)^{-1}B$, and from (H3) we have $(I-C)C_0 = (\eta C - I)$. Let

$$G(s) = \begin{cases} (\xi - s)^{\alpha-1}(I-C)(I-B)^{-1}B - (\eta - s)^{\alpha-1}C + (1-s)^{\alpha-1}I, & 0 \leqslant s \leqslant \xi; \\ -(\eta - s)^{\alpha-1}C + (1-s)^{\alpha-1}I, & \xi < s < \eta; \\ (1-s)^{\alpha-1}I, & \eta \leqslant s \leqslant 1, \end{cases}$$

then

$$\text{Im } L = \left\{ y \in Y \,\middle|\, \frac{1}{\Gamma(\alpha)} \int_0^1 G(s)y(s)ds = \theta \right\}.$$

Define a mapping $Q : Y \to Y$ as

$$Qy = \gamma \int_0^1 G(s)y(s)ds, \tag{13}$$

where

$$\gamma = \alpha\{(\eta C - I)\xi^{\alpha-1} - \eta^\alpha C + I\}^{-1}.$$

Lemma 3. *The operator L is a Fredholm operator with an index of zero.*

Proof. For $y \in Y$, $\forall t \in [0, 1]$

$$\begin{aligned} Q^2 y(t) &= \gamma \int_0^1 G(s)Qy(s)ds \\ &= \frac{\gamma}{\alpha}\{(\eta C - I)\xi^{\alpha-1} - \eta^\alpha C + I\}Qy(t) \\ &= Qy(t), \end{aligned}$$

so linear operator Q is a continuous projector. For $y \in \text{Im } L$, one has $Qy(t) = \theta$; this shows that $y \in \text{Ker } Q$. In fact, Im L = Ker Q.

Let $y \in Y$ and it is easy to verify $y - Qy \in \text{Im } L$. Thus, $Y = \text{Im } L + \text{Im } Q$. For every $y \in \text{Im } Q$ have the form $y = c, c \in \mathbb{R}^n$. At this time, if $y \in \text{Im } L$, then $y = \theta$. Hence, $Y = \text{Im } L \oplus \text{Im } Q$. Combine with codim Im L = dim Im Q = dim Ker L, so L satisfies (E1) and (E2), and the index of the Fredholm operator L is zero. □

Define another projector $P : X \to X$ by

$$Pu = u'(0)t + C_0 u'(0). \tag{14}$$

For $v \in \text{Ker } L$, one has

$$v(t) = c_2 t + C_0 c_2,\ c_2 \in \mathbb{R}^n,$$

and

$$Pv(t) = c_2 t + C_0 c_2 = v(t).$$

This shows that $v \in \text{Im } P$. Conversely, for every $v \in \text{Im } P$, there is $x \in X$ such that $v(t) = Px(t)$. Thus,

$$v(t) = Px(t) = x'(0)t + c_0 x'(0) \in \text{Ker} L. \tag{15}$$

Hence, Ker L = Im P. Clearly, $X = \text{Ker } P \oplus \text{Ker } L$. In fact, Ker $P \cap$ Ker $L = \{\theta\}$.

Define a mapping $K_P : \text{Im } L \to \text{Ker } P \cap \text{dom } L$ as

$$K_P y(t) = (I-B)^{-1}BI^\alpha_{0+}y(\xi) + I^\alpha_{0+}y(t),\ 0 \leqslant t \leqslant 1. \tag{16}$$

Lemma 4. *K_P is the inverse of the mapping $L|_{\text{Ker } P \cap \text{dom } L}$ and*

$$\|K_P y\| \leqslant D\|y\|_1, \tag{17}$$

where $D = 1 + \xi\|(I-B)^{-1}B\|_*$, $\|\cdot\|_*$ stand for the max-norm of matrices.

Proof. Let $y \in \text{Im } L$. It is clear that $K_P y(0) = BK_P y(\xi)$ and $K_P y(1) = CK_P y(\eta)$, such that $K_P y \in \text{dom } L$. Furthermore

$$PK_P y(t) = (K_P y)'(t)|_{t=0} t + c_0 (K_P y)'(t)|_{t=0} = \theta. \tag{18}$$

This shows that $K_P y \in \text{Ker } P$. So, the definition of K_P is reasonable.

For $u \in \text{Ker } P \cap \text{dom } L$, from (11), one has

$$\begin{aligned} K_P L u &= (I-B)^{-1} B I_{0+}^{\alpha}\, {}^c D_{0+}^{\alpha} u(\xi) + I_{0+}^{\alpha}\, {}^c D_{0+}^{\alpha} u(t) \\ &= (I-B)^{-1} B\Big[u(\xi) - u(0) - u'(0)\xi\Big] - I(u(0) - u(t) + u'(0)t) \\ &= u. \end{aligned}$$

Conversely, for $y \in \text{Im } L$, one has $LK_P y = y$. Thus, $K_P = (L|_{\text{dom } L \cap \text{Ker } P})^{-1}$.

Again, since

$$\begin{aligned} \|{}^c D_{0+}^{\alpha-1}(K_P y)(t)\|_\infty &= \|(I-B)^{-1} B I_{0+}^{1} y(\xi)\|_\infty + \|I_{0+}^{1} y(t)\|_\infty \\ &\leqslant (1 + \xi\|(I-B)^{-1}B\|_*)\|y(t)\|_1, \end{aligned}$$

combining with (16), one has

$$\|K_P y\|_\infty \leqslant \frac{D}{\Gamma(\alpha)}\|y\|_1.$$

Thus, we have $\|K_P y\| \leqslant D\|y\|_1$. □

Define an operator $N : X \to Y$ by

$$Nu(t) = f(t, u(t), {}^c D_{0+}^{\alpha-1} u(t)),\ 0 \leqslant t \leqslant 1. \tag{19}$$

Lemma 5. *N is L-compact.*

Proof. We divide the proof into two parts. The first part is bounded continuous. The second part is completely continuous. Indeed, for $f(t, u(t), {}^c D_{0+}^{\alpha-1} u(t))$, there exists a function $g_W(t) : R \to Y$ s.t. for every $u \in W \subset X$ and a.e. $0 \leqslant t \leqslant 1$

$$\|f(t, u, {}^c D_{0+}^{\alpha-1} u)\|_\infty \leqslant g_W. \tag{20}$$

Combining with (13), one has

$$\|Qy\|_1 \leqslant \|G(s)\|_* \|\gamma\|_* \|y\|_1, \tag{21}$$

where

$$\begin{aligned} \|\gamma\|_* &= \alpha\|\{(\eta C - I)\xi^{\alpha-1} - \eta^\alpha C + I\}^{-1}\|_*, \\ \|G(s)\|_* &= (1 + \|C\|_* + \|(I-C)(I-B)^{-1}B\|_*). \end{aligned}$$

Thus, $QN(\overline{W})$ is bounded. Obviously, $QN(W)$ is continuous.

For all $u \in W \subset X$, one has

$$\begin{aligned} K_{P,Q} Nu =& K_P(I-Q)Nu \\ =& (I-B)^{-1} B I_{0+}^{\alpha} Nu(\xi) + I_{0+}^{\alpha} Nu(t) - (I-B)^{-1} B I_{0+}^{\alpha} QNu(\xi) - I_{0+}^{\alpha} QNu(t) \\ =& (I-B)^{-1} B I_{0+}^{\alpha} Nu(\xi) + I_{0+}^{\alpha} Nu(t) \end{aligned}$$

$$-\frac{\gamma}{\Gamma(\alpha)}\left\{\xi^{\alpha}(Id-B)^{-1}B\int_0^1 G(s)Nu(s)ds+t^{\alpha}\int_0^1 G(s)Nu(s)ds\right\}. \quad (22)$$

$${}^cD_{0+}^{\alpha-1}K_{P,Q}Nu={}^cD_{0+}^{\alpha-1}K_P(Id-Q)Nu=I_{0+}^1Nx(t)-\gamma\Gamma(\alpha+1)t\int_0^1 G(s)Nu(s)ds. \quad (23)$$

Combining (20), (22), and (23), we have

$$\begin{aligned}|K_{P,Q}Nu(t)| \leqslant &(1+\|(I-B)^{-1}B\|_*)\|Nu\|_1\\ &+\frac{\|\gamma\|_*}{\Gamma(\alpha)}(1+\|(I-B)^{-1}B\|_*)\|G(s)\|_*\|Nu\|_1,\end{aligned}$$

$$\left|{}^cD_{0+}^{\alpha-1}K_{P,Q}Nu(t)\right| \leqslant (1+\Gamma(\alpha+1)\|\gamma\|_*\|G(s)\|_*)\|Nu\|_1.$$

That is, $K_{P,Q}Nu(W)$ is uniformly bounded in X. Now we only need to prove $K_{P,Q}Nu(W)$ is equicontinuous in X to end the proof of Lemma 5. For $0\leqslant t_1<t_2\leqslant 1$, one has

$$\begin{aligned}&|K_{P,Q}Nu(t_2)-K_{P,Q}Nu(t_1)|\\ &\leqslant \frac{1}{\Gamma(\alpha)}\left|\int_{t_1}^{t_2}(t_2-s)^{\alpha-1}Nu(s)ds+\int_0^{t_1}((t_2-s)^{\alpha-1}-(t_1-s)^{\alpha-1})Nu(s)ds\right|\\ &\quad+\frac{\gamma}{\alpha\Gamma(\alpha)}\|G(s)\|_*\|Nu\|_1|t_2^{\alpha}-t_1^{\alpha}|\\ &\leqslant \frac{1}{\Gamma(\alpha)}\left(\int_0^{t_1}(t_2-t_1)^{\alpha-1}g_W(s)ds+\int_{t_1}^{t_2}g_W(s)ds\right)\\ &\quad+\frac{\gamma}{\alpha\Gamma(\alpha)}\|G(s)\|_*\|g_W(t)\|_1|t_2^{\alpha}-t_1^{\alpha}|,\end{aligned}$$

and

$$\left|{}^cD_{0+}^{\alpha-1}K_{P,Q}Nu(t_2)-{}^cD_{0+}^{\alpha-1}K_{P,Q}Nu(t_1)\right| \leqslant \int_{t_1}^{t_2}g_W(s)ds+\gamma\|G(s)\|_*\|g_W(t)\|_1|t_2-t_1|.$$

Thus, $K_{P,Q}Nu(W)$ is equicontinuous in X. In summary, N is L-compact. □

We will use the following assumptions:

(M1) For all $t\in[0,1]$, $x,y\in\mathbb{R}^n$, there exist three functions $a_1,\ b_1,\ c\in Y$, s.t.

$$(1+\|c_0\|_*+D)(\|a_1\|_1+\|b_1\|_1)<1, \quad (24)$$

and

$$|f(t,x,y)|\leqslant a_1(t)|x|+b_1(t)|y|+c(t), \quad (25)$$

where D is the constant given in (17).

(M2) For $u\in \mathrm{dom}\, L$, if there exist $\sigma_1\in R_+$, s.t.

$$|{}^cD_{0+}^{\alpha-1}u(v)|>\sigma_1,\ \forall v\in[0,1],$$

then

$$\begin{aligned}&C\int_0^{\eta}(\eta-s)^{\alpha-1}f(v,u(v),{}^cD_{0+}^{\alpha-1}u(v))dv\\ &\qquad -I\int_0^1(1-s)^{\alpha-1}f(v,u(v)dv,{}^cD_{0+}^{\alpha-1}u(v))dv\in \mathrm{Im}\,(I-C).\end{aligned}$$

(M3) Let $q(t):=(tI+C_0),\ C_0=\xi(I-B)^{-1}B$, and

$$q(t)\tau=(q_1,\dots,q_n)^{\top},\ q_i\in\mathbb{R}.$$

If there exist $\sigma_2 \in R_+$, s.t. $\forall t \in [0,1]$,

$$|q_i| > \sigma_2, \ \forall \tau \in \mathbb{R}^n, \ i = 1, ..., n,$$

then either

$$\langle q(t)\tau, QN(q(t)\tau)\rangle \leqslant 0 \ or \ \langle q(t)\tau, QN(q(t)\tau)\rangle \geqslant 0, \tag{26}$$

$\langle \cdot, \cdot \rangle$ stands for the scalar product in $\mathbb{R}^n$.

Theorem 2. *If assumptions (M1)–(M3) are satisfied, then Problem* (1), (2) *has at least one solution in X.*

Proof. Set $\Omega_1 = \{x \in \text{ dom } L \setminus \text{Ker } L \ : \ Lx = \lambda Nx, \ 0 < \lambda < 1\}$. For $u \in \Omega_1$, one has $Nu \in \text{Im } L = \text{Ker } Q$. Thus,

$$\begin{aligned} C\int_0^{\eta}(\eta - s)^{\alpha-1} f(s, u(s), {}^cD_{0+}^{\alpha-1}u(s))ds - I\int_0^1 (1-s)^{\alpha-1} f(s, u(s), {}^cD_{0+}^{\alpha-1}u(s))ds \\ = (I-C)(I-B)^{-1}B\int_0^{\xi}(\xi - s)^{\alpha-1} f(s, u(s), {}^cD_{0+}^{\alpha-1}u(s))ds \in \text{Im } (I-C). \end{aligned}$$

From (M2), there exist $t_0 \in [0,1]$, s.t. $|{}^cD_{0+}^{\alpha-1}u(t_0)| \leqslant \sigma_1$, thus

$$|{}^cD_{0+}^{\alpha-1}u(0)| = \left|{}^cD_{0+}^{\alpha-1}u(t_0) - \int_0^{t_0} {}^cD_{0+}^{\alpha}u(s)ds\right| \leqslant \sigma_1 + \|{}^cD_{0+}^{\alpha}u(t)\|_1.$$

Furthermore

$$\|Pu(t)\| = \|u'(0)t + C_0u'(0)\| \leqslant (\|Nu\|_1 + \sigma_1)(1 + \|C_0\|_*). \tag{27}$$

Note that Id is the identity operator. Combining with (27), one has

$$\begin{aligned} \|u(t)\| &= \|Pu + (Id - P)u\| \\ &\leqslant \|Pu\| + \|K_PL(Id - P)u\| \\ &\leqslant (\|Nu\|_1 + \sigma_1)(1 + \|C_0\|_*) + D\|Nu\|_1 \\ &= (1 + \|C_0\|_* + D)\|Nu\|_1 + (1 + \|C_0\|_*)\sigma_1, \end{aligned} \tag{28}$$

where D was given in (16). Combining (19), (28), and (M1), we get

$$\begin{aligned} \|Nu\|_1 &\leqslant \int_0^1 |f(s, u(s), {}^cD_{0+}^{\alpha-1}u(s))|ds \\ &\leqslant \|a_1\|_1\|u\|_\infty + \|b_1\|_1\|{}^cD_{0+}^{\alpha-1}u\|_\infty + \|c\|_1 \\ &\leqslant (\|a_1\|_1 + \|b_1\|_1)\|u\| + \|c\|_1 \\ &\leqslant (\|a_1\|_1 + \|b_1\|_1)[(1 + \|C_0\|_* + D)\|Nu\|_1 + (1 + \|C_0\|_*)\sigma_1] + \|c\|_1. \end{aligned}$$

Therefore, it can be obtained that

$$\|Nu\|_1 \leqslant \frac{(\|a_1\|_1 + \|b_1\|_1)(1 + \|C_0\|_*)\sigma_1] + \|c\|_1}{1 - (1 + \|C_0\|_* + D)(\|a_1\|_1 + \|b_1\|_1)}. \tag{29}$$

From (29) and (28), one has

$$\sup_{u \in \Omega_1} \|u\| = \sup_{u \in \Omega_1} max\{\|u\|_\infty, \|{}^cD_{0+}^{\alpha-1}u\|_\infty\} < +\infty.$$

Hence Ω_1 is bounded in X.

Set $\Omega_2 = \{u \in \text{Ker } L \mid Nu \in \text{Im } L\}$. Assuming $u \in \Omega_2$, one has $u = c_2 t + C_0 c_2$, $c_2 \in \mathbb{R}^n$. Thus

$$C\int_0^\eta (\eta - s)^{\alpha-1} f(s, c_2 s + C_0 c_2, c_2) ds - I\int_0^1 (1-s)^{\alpha-1} f(s, c_2 s + C_0 c_2, c_2) ds$$
$$= (I - C)(I - B)^{-1} B \int_0^\xi (\xi - s)^{\alpha-1} f(s, c_2 s + C_0 c_2, c_2) ds \in \text{Im } (I - C).$$

Then, from assumption (M2), one has

$$\begin{aligned} \|u\| &= max\{\|u\|_\infty, \|^c D_{0+}^{\alpha-1} u\|_\infty\} \\ &= max\{\|c_2 t + C_0 c_2\|_\infty, \|c_2\|_\infty\} \\ &\leqslant max\{(1 + \|C_0\|_*)\sigma_1, \sigma_1\} \\ &\leqslant (1 + \|C_0\|_*)\sigma_1 < +\infty. \end{aligned}$$

Therefore, Ω_2 is a bounded subset.

Set $\Omega_3^{\pm} = \{u \in \text{Ker } L : \pm\lambda_1 u + (1 - \lambda_1) QNu = \theta,\ 0 \leqslant \lambda_1 \leqslant 1\}$. We divide the proof into the following two steps:

Step 1 : For $u = c_2 t + C_0 c_2 \in \Omega_3^+$, one has

$$\lambda_1(c_2 t + C_0 c_2) + (1 - \lambda_1) QN(c_2 t + C_0 c_2) = \theta.$$

Case 1 : If $\lambda_1 = 0$, then $QN(c_2 t + C_0 c_2) = \theta$, such that $N(c_2 t + C_0 c_2) \in \text{Ker } Q = \text{Im } L$. Thus we have $N(c_2 t + C_0 c_2) \in \Omega_2$, so $\|u\| \leqslant (1 + \|C_0\|_*)\sigma_1$.

Case 2 : If $\lambda_1 \in (0, 1]$, suppose $\|u\| > n\sigma_2$. Then, from (M3) obtain that

$$0 > -\lambda_1 |u|^2 = (1 - \lambda_1)\langle u, QNu\rangle \geqslant 0.$$

So, we have a contradiction. Thus $\|u\| \leqslant \sigma_2$.

Step 2 : For $u \in \Omega_3^-$, using same arguments as in Step 1 above, we can deduce that $\|u\| \leqslant \sigma_2$. Thus we can show that $\Omega_3^-, \Omega_3^+ \subset X$ are two bounded subsets.

Now, let $\Omega \subset Y$ and $\bigcup_{i=1}^3 \overline{\Omega_i} \subset \Omega$. According to the above arguments, we know that both conditions (i) and (ii) of Theorem 1 are satisfied. In order to prove (iii), we use isomorphic mapping $\mathcal{J}$ to construct the homotopy operator by

$$H(x(t), \lambda) = \pm\lambda x(t) + (1 - \lambda)\mathcal{J} QNx(t).$$

Hence

$$\begin{aligned} deg(\mathcal{J} QN|_{\text{Ker } L}, \Omega \cap \text{Ker } L, \theta) &= deg(H(\cdot, 0), \Omega \cap \text{Ker } L, \theta) \\ &= deg(\pm Id, \Omega \cap \text{Ker } L, \theta) \neq 0. \end{aligned}$$

Therefore, (iii) of Theorem 1 is satisfied. Theorem 2 is proved. □

4. Existence Results for Case (2)

Now, we show the solvability of BVP (1), (2) when $B = I$, $|I - C| = 0$. In this case, the boundary value condition degenerates to

$$x(0) = x(\xi), \quad x(1) = Cx(\eta). \tag{30}$$

Unlike Section 3, this section removes the restriction on matrix C and uses the generalized inverse to conduct research under the most basic resonance conditions, inspired by [14].

Now we study the BVP (1) and (30) using Theorem 1. We use the same notations as in Section 3. $L, N, \mathcal{J}$. In this case,

$$\text{dom } L = \{x \in X_1 : x \text{ satisfies } (30)\}.$$

Let $\mathcal{T} = I - C$ and $\mathcal{T}^+$ be the *Moore–Penrose pseudoinverse matrix* of $\mathcal{T}$. From [24] we can get the following conclusions, which are necessary for our subsequent research:
(I_1) $\mathcal{T}^+\mathcal{T}\mathcal{T}^+ = \mathcal{T}^+$;
(I_2) $\mathcal{T}\mathcal{T}^+\mathcal{T} = \mathcal{T}$;
(I_3) $\text{Im } \mathcal{T}^+\mathcal{T} = \text{Im } \mathcal{T}$;
(I_4) $\text{Im } (I - \mathcal{T}^+\mathcal{T}) = \text{Ker } \mathcal{T}$.
From (12), we have

$$\text{Ker } L = \{c_1^* \in \mathbb{R}^n : \mathcal{T}c_1^* = \theta\}.$$

Define a linear operator H^* by

$$H^*y(t) = \frac{\eta C - I}{\xi} I_{0+}^{\alpha} y(\xi) - C I_{0+}^{\alpha} y(\eta) + I_{0+}^{\alpha} y(1).$$

Then

$$\text{Im } L = \{y \in Y \mid H^*y(t) \in \text{Im } \mathcal{T}\}.$$

Define an operator $Q^* : Y \to Y$ as

$$Q^*y = \gamma^* H^* y(t), \tag{31}$$

where

$$\gamma^* = \frac{\xi\alpha\Gamma(\alpha)}{\eta\xi^{\alpha} - \xi^{\alpha} + \xi - \xi\eta^{\alpha}}(I - \mathcal{T}\mathcal{T}^+).$$

Then for $y \in Y$, we can get

$$\begin{aligned} Q^{*2}y &= \gamma^* H^* Q^* y \\ &= \frac{\xi\alpha\Gamma(\alpha)}{\eta\xi^{\alpha} - \xi^{\alpha} + \xi - \xi\eta^{\alpha}}(I - \mathcal{T}\mathcal{T}^+)\frac{(\eta C - I)\xi^{\alpha} + \xi I - \xi\eta^{\alpha} C}{\alpha\xi\Gamma(\alpha)} Q^* y \\ &= Q^* y. \end{aligned}$$

In fact

$$\begin{aligned} &(I - \mathcal{T}\mathcal{T}^+)(\eta C - I)\xi^{\alpha} + \xi I - \xi\eta^{\alpha} C \\ &\quad = (I - \mathcal{T}\mathcal{T}^+)\{\eta(C - I)\xi^{\alpha} + (\eta - 1)\xi^{\alpha} I + \eta^{\alpha}(I - C) + (1 - \eta^{\alpha})I)\} \\ &\quad = (\eta - 1)\xi^{\alpha} I + \xi(1 - \eta^{\alpha})(I - \mathcal{T}\mathcal{T}^+). \end{aligned}$$

By similar arguments to Lemma 2.5 in [14], we have that the index of the Fredholm operator L is zero.

Define an operator $P^* : X \to X$ as

$$P^*x(t) = (I - \mathcal{T}^+\mathcal{T})x(0). \tag{32}$$

If $v \in \text{Ker } L$, one has $v = c_1^*$, $c_1^* \in \mathbb{R}^n \cap \text{Ker}(\mathcal{T}) = \text{Im } (I - \mathcal{T}^+\mathcal{T})$, thus there exists $d_1^* \in \mathbb{R}^n$ suct that

$$c_1^* = (I - \mathcal{T}^+\mathcal{T})d_1^*.$$

So, $v \in \text{Im } P^*$. Conversely, if $v \in \text{Im } P^*$, from (I_2) we can know that $v \in \text{Ker } \mathcal{T}$. Again, since $\text{Ker } P^* \cap \text{Ker } L = \{\theta\}$, then $X = \text{Ker } P^* \oplus \text{Ker } L$.

Define a mapping $K_P^* : \text{Im } L \to \text{Ker } P^* \cap \text{dom } L$ as

$$K_P^* y(s) = \mathcal{T}^+ H^* y + I_{0+}^{\alpha} y(s) - \frac{s}{\xi} I_{0+}^{\alpha} y(\xi). \tag{33}$$

Through checking calculation, we can get $K_P^* y \in \text{dom } L$ and $K_P^* y \in \text{Ker } P^*$. Thus the definition of K_P^* is reasonable.

Letting $u \in \text{Ker } P^* \cap \text{dom } L$, one has

$$\begin{aligned}K_P^* Lu(t) &= \mathcal{T}^+ H^{*c} D_{0+}^{\alpha} u + I_{0+}^{\alpha}\, {}^c D_{0+}^{\alpha} u(t) - \frac{t}{\xi} I_{0+}^{\alpha}\, {}^c D_{0+}^{\alpha} u(\xi) \\ &= -\mathcal{T}^+(\eta C - I)u'(0)\xi - \mathcal{T}^+ C(u(0) + u'(0)\eta) + \mathcal{T}^+(u(0) + u'(0)) + u(t) - u(0) \\ &= -\mathcal{T}^+ C u'(0)\eta + \mathcal{T}^+ u'(0) + \mathcal{T}^+((\eta C - I))u'(0) - (I - \mathcal{T}^+\mathcal{T})u(0) + u(t) \\ &= u(t).\end{aligned}$$

Similarly, for $y \in \text{Im } L$, we have $LK_P^* y = y$. Then we can deduce that $K_P^* = (L|_{\text{dom } L \cap \text{Ker } P})^{-1}$.

Denote

$$D^* = 2 + \|\mathcal{T}^+\|_*((\eta + 1)\|C\|_* + 2). \tag{34}$$

By the similar proof process as in Lemma 4 and Lemma 5, we know that $\|K_P^* y\| \leqslant D^* \|y\|_1$, and $K_P^*(I - Q)N$ is completely continuous.

Now we give the following assumptions:

(M1*) For all $s \in [0,1]$, $u, v \in \mathbb{R}^n$, we have

$$|f(s,u,v)| \leqslant a|u| + b|v| + c, \tag{35}$$

where $a,\ b,\ c \in Y$ are three positive functions satisfying $(\|I - \mathcal{T}\mathcal{T}^+\|_* + D^*)(\|a\|_1 + \|b\|_1) < 1$, and D^* is the constant given in (34).

(M2*) For all $u \in \text{dom } L$, if

$$H^* f(s, u(t), {}^c D_{0+}^{\alpha-1} u(t)) \in \text{Im}(\mathcal{T}). \tag{36}$$

Then, there exist $\sigma_1^* \in R_+$ and $s_0 \in [0,1]$, s.t. $|u(s_0)| \leqslant \sigma_1^*$.

(M3*) There exist $\sigma_2^* \in R_+$, s.t. for every $\nu \in \mathbb{R}^n$ with $\nu = C\nu$ and $|\nu| > \sigma_2^*$, either

$$\langle \nu, Q^* N(\nu) \rangle \leqslant 0 \text{ or } \langle \nu, Q^* N(\nu) \rangle \geqslant 0, \tag{37}$$

where $\langle \cdot, \cdot \rangle$ stands for scalar product in $\mathbb{R}^n$.

Theorem 3. *If assumptions (M1*)–(M3*) are satisfied, BVP* (1) *and* (30) *has at least one solution in* X.

Proof. We use the same definitions of Ω_1, Ω_2, and Ω_3 as in Theorem 2.

For $x \in \Omega_1$, we have that $Nx \in \text{Im } L = \text{Ker } Q^*$. Similarly, we can show

$$H^* f(s, u(t), {}^c D_{0+}^{\alpha-1} u(t)) \in \text{Im}(\mathcal{T}).$$

In fact,

$$\begin{aligned}H^* f(s, u, {}^c D_{0+}^{\alpha-1} u) &= H^{*c} D_{0+}^{\alpha} u \\ &= (\eta C - I)u'(0) + Cu(\eta) + u(0) - Cu(0) + (I - C\eta)u'(0) - u(1) \\ &= \mathcal{T} u(0) \in \text{Im}(\mathcal{T}).\end{aligned}$$

Using assumption (M2*), we can deduce that

$$|u(0)| = \left| u(t_0) - \int_0^{t_0} {}^c D_{0+}^{\alpha-1} u(s) ds \right| \leqslant \sigma_1^* + \|{}^c D_{0+}^{\alpha-1} u\|_\infty,$$

and

$$|{}^c D_{0+}^{\alpha-1} u(t)| \leqslant \int_0^t |{}^c D_{0+}^{\alpha} u(s)| ds \leqslant \|Lu\|_1.$$

Then with the similar proof process in Theorem 2 we can know that

$$\|u(t)\| \leqslant (\|I-\mathcal{T}^{+}\mathcal{T}\|_{*}+D^{*})\|Nu\|_{1}+\sigma_{1}^{*}\|I-\mathcal{T}^{+}\mathcal{T}\|_{*}, \tag{38}$$

and

$$\|Nu\|_{1} \leqslant \frac{\sigma_{1}^{*}(\|a\|_{1}+\|b\|_{1})\|I-\mathcal{T}^{+}\mathcal{T}\|_{*}+\|c\|_{1}}{-(\|I-\mathcal{T}^{+}\mathcal{T}\|_{*}+D^{*})(\|a\|_{1}+\|b\|_{1})+1}. \tag{39}$$

Combining (38) and (39) we can deduce that

$$\sup_{x\in\Omega_1}\|u\| = \sup_{u\in\Omega_1} max\{\|u\|_{\infty}, \|^{c}D_{0+}^{\alpha-1}u\|_{\infty}\} < +\infty.$$

Hence Ω_1 is a bounded subset of X.

For $u \in \Omega_2$, one has $u = c_1^*$, $c_1^* \in \mathbb{R}^n$. Combining with $Nu \in \operatorname{Im} L$, we can get

$$H^{*}Nu \in \operatorname{Im}(\mathcal{T}).$$

From assumptions (M2*), we get

$$\|u\| = max\{\|u\|_{\infty}, \|^{c}D_{0+}^{\alpha-1}u\|_{\infty}\} = \|c\|_{\infty} = |u(t_0)| \leqslant \sigma_1^* < +\infty.$$

Such that Ω_2 is bounded in X.

In order to prove both Ω_3^- and Ω_3^+ are bounded, we also divide the proof process into two steps:

Step 1 : Assuming $u \in \Omega_3^-$, one has $u = c_1^*$, where $c_1^* \in \mathbb{R}^n \cap \operatorname{Ker}(\mathcal{T})$. Thus we have

$$-\lambda c_1^* + (1-\lambda)QN(c_1^*) = \theta.$$

Case 1 : If $\lambda = 0$, then $QN(c_1^*) = \theta$, such that $N(c_1^*) \in \operatorname{Ker} Q = \operatorname{Im} L$. Thus we have $Nx \in \Omega_2$, so $\|x\| \leqslant \sigma_1^*$.

Case 2 : If $\lambda \in (0,1]$, suppose $\|u\| > \sigma_2$. From (B3) we get

$$0 < \lambda|c_1^*|^2 = (1-\lambda)\langle c_1^*, QNc_1^*\rangle \leqslant 0.$$

Therefore, we have $\|u\| \leqslant \sigma_2^*$.

Step 2 : For $u \in \Omega_3^+$, through a similar proof process as in Step 1, we can deduce that $\|u\| \leqslant \sigma_2^*$.

Thus, Ω_3^- and Ω_3^+ are two bounded subsets in X.

Let the definitions of bounded open subset Ω and homotopy $H(u,\lambda)$ be the same as in Theorem 2. Then we can deduce that *(iii)* of Theorem 1 is also satisfied. By Theorem 1, Equations (1) and (30) must have a solution in $\operatorname{dom} L \cap \Omega$. □

5. Examples

In this section, we present two examples to illustrate our main results in Sections 3 and 4.

Example 1. Consider the following boundary value problem:

$$\begin{cases} {}^{C}D_{0+}^{\alpha}x(t) = f_1(t, x(t), y(t), {}^{C}D_{0+}^{\alpha-1}x(t), {}^{C}D_{0+}^{\alpha-1}y(t)), & t \in (0,1), \\ {}^{C}D_{0+}^{\alpha}y(t) = f_2(t, x(t), y(t), {}^{C}D_{0+}^{\alpha-1}x(t), {}^{C}D_{0+}^{\alpha-1}y(t)), & t \in (0,1), \\ x(0) = 5x(\frac{1}{4}),\ y(0) = 0, \\ x(1) = \frac{1}{2}x(\frac{3}{4}),\ y(1) = \frac{4}{3}y(\frac{3}{4}), \end{cases} \tag{40}$$

where $\alpha = \frac{3}{2}$, $f_i : [0,1] \times \mathbb{R}^4 \to \mathbb{R}$, $i = 1,2$, *are defined as*

$$f_1(t, x_1, x_2, y_1, y_2) = -\frac{x_1 + y_1}{40}, \tag{41}$$

$$f_2(t,x_1,x_2,y_1,y_2) = \frac{|x_2| + |y_2| + 1}{60}, \tag{42}$$

for all $t \in [0,1]$.

Clearly, $\xi = \frac{1}{4}$, $\eta = \frac{3}{4}$,

$$B = \begin{bmatrix} 5 & 0 \\ 0 & 0 \end{bmatrix}, C = \begin{bmatrix} \frac{1}{2} & 0 \\ 0 & \frac{4}{3} \end{bmatrix}, (I-C)(I-B)^{-1}B = \begin{bmatrix} -\frac{5}{8} & 0 \\ 0 & 0 \end{bmatrix}, C_0 = \begin{bmatrix} -\frac{5}{16} & 0 \\ 0 & 0 \end{bmatrix},$$

and $I - \eta C + \xi(I-C)(I-B)^{-1}B = \Theta$. Denote $u_1 = (x_1, x_2)$, $u_2 = (y_1, y_2) \in \mathbb{R}^2$, define function $f : [0,1] \times \mathbb{R}^2 \times \mathbb{R}^2 \to \mathbb{R}^2$

$$f(t,u_1,u_2) = (f_1(t,u_1,u_2), f_2(t,u_1,u_2))^\top, \ \forall t \in [0,1].$$

By (41), (42), and (43), f satisfies Carathéodory conditions.

Now we show that the other conditions of Theorem 3 hold. Choose positive integrable functions

$$a(t) = b(t) = c(t) = \frac{1}{40}.$$

Then we have

$$|f(t,u,v)| \leqslant a(t)|u| + b(t)|v| + c(t),$$

By some simple computation, we get

$$(1 + \|C_0\|_* + D)(\|a\|_1 + \|b\|_1) = \frac{25}{384} < 1.$$

Hence, (M1) is satisfied.

In order to check (M2), one has

$$f_2(t,u(t),^C D_{0+}^{\alpha-1}u(t)) > \frac{1}{60},$$

for all $u \in C^1([0,1];\mathbb{R}^2)$ and all $t \in [0,1]$. Letting $f_2(t,u(t),^C D_{0+}^{\alpha-1}u(t)) = f_2$ be a positive constant, we have

$$\begin{aligned} C &\int_0^\eta (\eta - s)^{\alpha-1} f(t,u(t),^C D_{0+}^{\alpha-1}u(t))dt \\ &- I\int_0^1 (1-s)^{\alpha-1} f(t,u(t),^C D_{0+}^{\alpha-1}u(t))dt = \begin{bmatrix} \frac{1}{2}f_1^* + f_2^* \\ \frac{260}{2911}f_2 \end{bmatrix}, \end{aligned}$$

where $f_1^* = I_{0+}^\alpha f_1(\eta)$, $f_2^* = I_{0+}^\alpha f_1(1)$. If $f_2 = \frac{1}{60}$, there is

$$\begin{aligned} C &\int_0^\eta (\eta - s)^{\alpha-1} f(t,u(t),^C D_{0+}^{\alpha-1}u(t))dt \\ &- I\int_0^1 (1-s)^{\alpha-1} f(t,u(t),^C D_{0+}^{\alpha-1}u(t))dt = \begin{bmatrix} \frac{1}{2}f_1^* + f_2^* \\ \frac{13}{8733} \end{bmatrix}. \end{aligned}$$

This shows that when $f_2(t,u(t),^C D_{0+}^{\alpha-1}u(t)) > f_2 = \frac{1}{60}$, one has

$$\begin{aligned} C &\int_0^\eta (\eta - s)^{\alpha-1} f(t,u(t),^C D_{0+}^{\alpha-1}u(t))dt \\ &- I\int_0^1 (1-s)^{\alpha-1} f(t,u(t),^C D_{0+}^{\alpha-1}u(t))dt \notin \mathrm{Im}((I-C)(I-B)^{-1}B), \end{aligned}$$

because $\mathrm{Im}((I-C)(I-B)^{-1}B) = \{(p,0)^\top : p \in \mathbb{R}\}$.

Finally, we check (M3). Let $q(t) = (tI + C_0)$. Denote $\tau = (\tau_1, \tau_2)^\top$. So

$$q(t)\tau = ((t + \frac{5}{16})\tau_1, t\tau_2)^\top$$

$$^CD_{0+}^{\alpha-1} q(t) = (\frac{2\tau_1\sqrt{t}}{\sqrt{\pi}}, \frac{2\tau_2\sqrt{t}}{\sqrt{\pi}})^\top.$$

Then there is

$$Nq(t)\tau = \left(-\frac{(t+\frac{5}{16})\tau_1}{40} - \frac{2\tau_1\sqrt{t}}{40\sqrt{\pi}}, \frac{t|\tau_2| + \frac{2\sqrt{t}}{\sqrt{\pi}}|\tau_2| + 1}{60} \right)^\top.$$

So

$$QN(q(t)\tau) = \alpha \begin{bmatrix} -\frac{31}{5234}\tau_1 \\ \frac{14}{34946}|\tau_2| + \frac{25}{181937} \end{bmatrix},$$

and

$$\langle q(t)\tau, QN(q(t)\tau) \rangle = \alpha(-\frac{31}{5234}\tau_1^2 + \frac{15}{34946}|\tau_2|\tau_2 + \frac{25}{181937}\tau_2) \leqslant 0.$$

In fact, if $\tau_2 \leqslant 0$, this is obviously true. If $\tau_2 > 0$, letting $|\tau_2| \geq 1$, one has $\tau_2^2 > \tau_2$. Again, since

$$\frac{15}{34946} > \frac{25}{181937}.$$

So, the formula above has no real root, which means $-\frac{31}{5234}\tau_1^2 + \frac{15}{34946}|\tau_2|\tau_2 + \frac{25}{181937}\tau_2 < 0$. Thus, by Theorem 2, BVP (40) has at least one solution.

Example 2. Consider the following boundary value problem:

$$\begin{cases} ^CD_{0+}^{\alpha}x(t) = f_1(t, x(t), y(t), {}^CD_{0+}^{\alpha-1}x(t), {}^CD_{0+}^{\alpha-1}y(t)), & t \in (0,1), \\ ^CD_{0+}^{\alpha}y(t) = f_2(t, x(t), y(t), {}^CD_{0+}^{\alpha-1}x(t), {}^CD_{0+}^{\alpha-1}y(t)), & t \in (0,1), \\ x(0) = x(\frac{1}{4}),\ y(0) = y(\frac{1}{4}), \\ x(1) = y(\frac{3}{4}),\ y(1) = y(\frac{3}{4}). \end{cases} \tag{43}$$

We use the same α, f, ξ, η, $a(t)$, $b(t)$, and $c(t)$ as in Example 1 and $f_i : [0,1] \times \mathbb{R}^4 \to \mathbb{R}, i = 1,2$ are defined as

$$f_1(t, x_1, x_2, y_1, y_2) = \frac{x_2 + y_2}{40}.$$

$$f_2(t, x_1, x_2, y_1, y_2) = \begin{cases} \frac{\sqrt{y_1^2+y_2^2}}{40}, & \text{if } |u_2| > 1; \\ f_1(t, x_1, x_2, y_1, y_2), & \text{otherwise.} \end{cases}$$

$$C = \begin{bmatrix} 0 & 1 \\ 0 & 1 \end{bmatrix}, \mathcal{T} = \begin{bmatrix} 1 & -1 \\ 0 & 0 \end{bmatrix}, \mathcal{T}^+ = \begin{bmatrix} \frac{1}{2} & 0 \\ -\frac{1}{2} & 0 \end{bmatrix}.$$

We can easily check that assumption (M1*) is satisfied. When $|u_2| > 1$, from the definition of f, one has $y_1^2 + y_2^2 > 1$ and $H^*f_2 > H^*\frac{1}{40} = \frac{51}{13571} > 0$. According to a similar proof process as Example 1, one has

$$H^*f(t, u(t), {}^CD_{0+}^{\alpha-1}u(t)) = \begin{bmatrix} H^*f_1 \\ H^*f_2 \end{bmatrix} \notin \mathrm{Im}(\mathcal{T}),$$

because $\mathrm{Im}(\mathcal{T}) = \{(p,0)^\top : p \in \mathbb{R}\}$. Finally, we check (M3*). Letting $\tau = (\tau_0, \tau_0)^\top \in \mathrm{Ker}(\mathcal{T})$, one has

$$N\tau = (f_1(t,\tau,\theta), f_2(t,\tau,\theta))^\top = \begin{cases} \left(\frac{\tau_0}{40}, 0\right)^\top, & \text{if } |u_2| > 1; \\ \left(\frac{\tau_0}{40}, \frac{\tau_0}{40}\right)^\top, & \text{otherwise.} \end{cases}$$

So

$$QN\tau = \gamma^* \begin{cases} \begin{bmatrix} \frac{\tau_0}{120} \\ 0 \end{bmatrix}, & \text{if } |u_2| > 1; \\ \begin{bmatrix} (7\tau_0)/480 - (3^{1/2}\tau_0)/160 \\ (7\tau_0)/480 - (3^{1/2}\tau_0)/160 \end{bmatrix}, & \text{otherwise,} \end{cases}$$

and

$$\langle \tau, QN\tau \rangle = \begin{cases} \frac{1}{120}\tau_0^2 c, & \text{if} |u_2| > 1; \\ \frac{7-3*3^{1/2}}{480}\tau_0^2 c, & \text{otherwise,} \end{cases}$$

where $c = \frac{\xi\alpha\Gamma(\alpha)}{\eta\xi^\alpha - \xi^\alpha + \xi - \xi\eta^\alpha} = \frac{5302\pi^{1/2}}{1594} > 0$. Thus, $\langle \tau, QN\tau \rangle > 0$, by Theorem 3, (43) has at least one solution.

6. Conclusions

This paper mainly studied a class of second-order nonlocal boundary value problem systems at resonance which state variable $x \in \mathbb{R}^n$, and gave two new theorems on the existence of solutions in different kernel spaces by using the Mawhin coincidence degree theorem.

In the future, we could consider studying resonance boundary value problems under less-restricted conditions or under more complicated boundary value conditions.

Author Contributions: Conceptualization, Y.F. and Z.B. All authors have read and agreed to the published version of the manuscript.

Funding: This research was funded by NSFC grant number 11571207 and Shandong Provincial Natural Science Foundation number ZR2021MA064 and the Taishan Scholar project.

Institutional Review Board Statement: Not applicable.

Informed Consent Statement: Not applicable.

Data Availability Statement: Not applicable.

Conflicts of Interest: The authors declare no conflict of interest.

References

1. Il'in, V.A.; Moiseev, E.I. Nonlocal boundary value problem of the first kind for a Sturm-Liuville operator in its differential and finite difference aspects. *Differ. Uravn.* **1987**, *23*, 803–810.
2. Il'in, V.A.; Moiseev, E.I. Nonlocal boundary value problem of the second kind for a Sturm-Liuville operator. *Differ. Uravn.* **1987**, *23*, 979–987.
3. Bitsadze, A.V.; Samarskogo, A.A. On some simplest generalizations of linear elliptic boundary value problems. *Rep. Acad. Sci.* **1969**, *185*, 739–740.
4. Gupta, C.P. A sharper condition for the solvability of a three-point second order boundary value problem. *J. Math. Anal. Appl.* **1997**, *205*, 579–586. [CrossRef]
5. Cui, Y.J. Solvability of second-order boundary-value problems at resonance involving integral conditions. *Electron. J. Differ. Equ.* **2012**, *45*, 1–9.
6. Bai, Z.B.; Li, W.G.; Ge, W.G. Existence and multiplicity of solutions for four-point boundary value problems at resonance. *Nonlinear Anal.* **2005**, *60*, 1151–1162. [CrossRef]
7. Kosmatov, N. A singular non-local problem at resonance. *J. Math. Anal. Appl.* **2005**, *394*, 425–431. [CrossRef]

8. Feng, W.; Webb, J.R.L. A singular non-local problem at resonance. *Nonlinear Anal.* **1997**, *30*, 3227–3238. [CrossRef]
9. Ma, R.Y. Multiplicity results for a three-point boundary value problem at resonance. *Nonlinear Anal.* **1997**, *53*, 777–789. [CrossRef]
10. Gupta, C.P. Existence theorems for a second order m-point boundary value problem at resonance. *Internat. J. Math. Math. Sci.* **1997**, *53*, 777–789.
11. Liu, B. Solvability of multi-point boundary value problem at resonance—Part IV. *Appl. Math. Comput.* **2003**, *143*, 275–299. [CrossRef]
12. Zhang, Y.H.; Bai, Z.B.; Feng, T.T. Existence results for a coupled system of nonlinear fractional three-point boundary value problems at resonance. *Comput. Math. Appl.* **2011**, *61*, 1032–1047. [CrossRef]
13. Phung, P.D.; Truong, L.X. On the existence of a three point boundary value problem at resonance in $\mathbb{R}^n$. *J. Math. Anal. Appl.* **2014**, *416*, 522–533. [CrossRef]
14. Phung, P.D.; Truong, L.X. Existence of solutions to three-point boundary-value problems at resonance. *Electron. J. Diff. Eqns.* **2016**, *115*, 1–13.
15. Phung, P.D.; Minh, H.B. Existence of solutions to fractional boundary value problems at resonance in Hilbert spaces. *Bound. Value Probl.* **2017**, *2017*, 105. [CrossRef]
16. Phung, P.D. Solvability of multipoint BVPs at resonance for various kernels. *J. Sci. Technol. Food.* **2020**, *20*, 3–16.
17. Jiang, W.H.; Yang, C.X. Existence of positive solutions for multi-point resonance systems of differential equations with boundary value conditions. *J. Hebei Univ. Sci. Tech.* **2016**, *37*, 340–348.
18. Mawhin, J.; Szymańska-Debowska, K. Convexity, topology and nonlinear differential systems with nonlocal boundary conditions: A survey. *Rend. Istit. Mat. Univ.* **2019**, *51*, 125–166.
19. Mawhin, J.; Szymańska-Debowska, K. Existence of solutions for fractional differential equations with three-point boundary conditions at resonance in $\mathbb{R}^n$. *Electron. J. Qual. Theory Differ.* **2014**, *68*, 1–18.
20. He, B.B. Existence of solutions to fractional differential equations with three-point boundary conditions at resonance with general conditions. *Fract. Calc. Appl.* **2018**, *9*, 120–136.
21. Zhou, H.C.; Ge, F.D.; Kou, C.H. Existence of solutions to fractional differential equations with multi-point boundary conditions at resonance in Hilbert spaces. *Electron. J. Differ. Equ.* **2016**, *61*, 1–16.
22. Kilbas, A.A.; Srivastava, H.M.; Trujillo, J.J. *Theory and Applications of Fractional Differential Equations*; North-Holland Mathematics Studies; Elsevier: Amsterdam, The Netherlands, 2006; Volume 204.
23. Mawhin, J. *Topological Degree Methods in Nonlinear Boundary Value Problems*, 1st ed.; American Mathematical Society: Providence, RI, USA, 1979.
24. Ben-Israel, A.; Greville, T.N.E. *Generalized Inverses: Theory and Applications*, 1st ed.; Springer: New York, NY, USA, 2003.

fractal and fractional

MDPI

Article

The Mixed Boundary Value Problems and Chebyshev Collocation Method for Caputo-Type Fractional Ordinary Differential Equations

Jun-Sheng Duan [1], Li-Xia Jing [1] and Ming Li [2,3,*]

[1] School of Sciences, Shanghai Institute of Technology, Shanghai 201418, China; duanjs@sit.edu.cn (J.-S.D.); 206181136@mail.sit.edu.cn (L.-X.J.)
[2] Ocean College, Zhejiang University, Zhejiang 310012, China
[3] Village 1, East China Normal University, Shanghai 200062, China
* Correspondence: mli@ee.ecnu.edu.cn or mli15@zju.edu.cn

Abstract: The boundary value problem (BVP) for the varying coefficient linear Caputo-type fractional differential equation subject to the mixed boundary conditions on the interval $0 \leq x \leq 1$ was considered. First, the BVP was converted into an equivalent differential–integral equation merging the boundary conditions. Then, the shifted Chebyshev polynomials and the collocation method were used to solve the differential–integral equation. Varying coefficients were also decomposed into the truncated shifted Chebyshev series such that calculations of integrals were only for polynomials and can be carried out exactly. Finally, numerical examples were examined and effectiveness of the proposed method was verified.

Keywords: fractional calculus; fractional differential equation; boundary value problem; Chebyshev polynomial; collocation method

Citation: Duan, J.-S.; Jing, L.-X.; Li, M. The Mixed Boundary Value Problems and Chebyshev Collocation Method for Caputo-Type Fractional Ordinary Differential Equations. *Fractal Fract.* **2022**, *6*, 148. https://doi.org/10.3390/fractalfract6030148

Academic Editor: Rodica Luca

Received: 11 February 2022
Accepted: 7 March 2022
Published: 9 March 2022

1. Introduction

In recent decades, the theory of fractional calculus has been attracting much attention partly due to its ability for describing memory and hereditary properties of various materials and processes [1–7]. Fractional calculus has been applied to different fields such as viscoelastic constitutive equations and related mechanical models [6–11], anomalous diffusion phenomena [4,6,12,13], hydrology [14], control and optimization theory [3,15], etc. It is worthwhile to mention that fractional calculus can be used to describe not only viscoelasticity, but also viscoinertia by different values of order [16,17]. The applications of fractional calculus lead to fractional differential equations (FDEs) in theory [2–5,18].

Let us recall some related definitions of fractional calculus used in this article. Let $f(x)$ be piecewise continuous on $(0, +\infty)$ and integrable on any finite subinterval of $(0, +\infty)$. Then, for $x > 0$, the Riemann–Liouville fractional integral of $f(x)$ is defined as

$$I_x^{\beta} f(x) = \int_0^x \frac{(x-\tau)^{\beta-1}}{\Gamma(\beta)} f(\tau) d\tau, \tag{1}$$

for $\beta > 0$, and $I_x^0 f(x) = f(x)$ for $\beta = 0$, where $\Gamma(\cdot)$ is the gamma function. The fractional integral satisfies the following equalities:

$$I_x^{\beta}\, I_x^{\nu} f(x) = I_x^{\beta+\nu} f(x),\ \beta \geq 0,\ \nu \geq 0, \tag{2}$$

$$I_x^{\nu} x^{\mu} = \frac{\Gamma(\mu+1)}{\Gamma(\mu+\nu+1)} x^{\mu+\nu},\ \nu \geq 0,\ \mu > -1. \tag{3}$$

Let α be a positive real number, $m-1<\alpha\leq m$, $m\in\mathbb{N}^+$, and $f^{(m)}(x)$ be piecewise continuous on $(0,+\infty)$ and integrable on any finite subinterval of $(0,+\infty)$. Then, the Caputo fractional derivative of $f(x)$ of order α is defined as

$$D_x^\alpha f(x)=I_x^{m-\alpha}f^{(m)}(x),\ m-1<\alpha\leq m. \tag{4}$$

For the power function x^μ, $\mu>0$, if $0\leq m-1<\alpha\leq m<\mu+1$, then we have

$$D_x^\alpha x^\mu = \frac{\Gamma(\mu+1)}{\Gamma(\mu-\alpha+1)}x^{\mu-\alpha},\ x>0. \tag{5}$$

The α-order integral of the α-order Caputo fractional derivative requires the knowledge of the initial values of the function and its integer-ordered derivatives,

$$I_x^\alpha\, D_x^\alpha f(x)=f(x)-\sum_{k=0}^{m-1}f^{(k)}(0)\frac{x^k}{k!},\ m-1<\alpha\leq m. \tag{6}$$

This property enables the Caputo fractional derivative to be conveniently applied and analyzed.

In the earlier monograph [1], the Grünwald definition and the Riemann–Liouville definition of fractional calculus were introduced, where numerical differentiation and integration were considered and semi-integration was introduced by a designed electrical circuit model and semi-differentiation was applied to diffusion problems. The Weyl fractional calculus was introduced in [2] beside the Grünwald definition and the Riemann–Liouville definition. In [3], FDEs and fractional-order system and controllers were considered, where the Caputo fractional derivative was introduced. The existence, uniqueness and analytical methods of solutions for FDEs were investigated in [4]. In [18], the Caputo-type fractional derivative and FDEs were emphasized. In [6], fractional viscoelastic models and fractional wave models in viscoelastic media were introduced. In [5], numerical methods and fractional variational principle were reviewed.

Damping, deformation, vibration and dissipation arising from viscoelastic material can be modeled by FDEs [3,4,6,7]. The method of variable separation for fractional partial differential equation describing anomalous diffusion [4,6,12,14] can lead to a boundary value problem (BVP) for a fractional ordinary differential equation (ODE) [19]. The theorem of existence and uniqueness of solutions for fractional ODEs was presented in [3,4,18,20]. Some analytical and numerical methods were proposed to solve FDEs, e.g., see [3–5,21–25]. BVPs for fractional ODEs were considered in [19,26–29] by using the Adomian decomposition method, wavelet method, the method of upper and lower solutions, orthogonal polynomial method, etc. However, a fractional BVP with varying coefficients and mixed boundary conditions has hardly been considered.

In this work, we consider the BVP for the varying coefficient linear Caputo fractional ODE

$$D_x^\lambda u(x)+c_1(x)u'(x)+c_0(x)u(x)=g(x),\ 0<x<1,\ 1<\lambda\leq 2, \tag{7}$$

Subject to the mixed boundary conditions

$$p_0u(0)-q_0u'(0)=b_0, \tag{8}$$
$$p_1u(1)+q_1u'(1)=b_1, \tag{9}$$

where the coefficients $c_1(x)$, $c_0(x)$, $g(x)$ are specified continuous functions, the boundary parameters satisfy $p_0,q_0,p_1,q_1\geq 0$ and $p_0p_1+p_0q_1+q_0p_1\neq 0$. In the next Section 2, some preliminaries about the shifted Chebyshev polynomials are presented. In Section 3, we first convert the BVP, (7)–(9), into an equivalent fractional differential–integral equation merging the boundary conditions, then introduce the collocation method using the shifted Chebyshev polynomials of the first kind to solve the fractional differential–integral equation.

Next, three numerical examples are solved by using the proposed method. Section 4 summarizes our conclusions.

2. The Shifted Chebyshev Polynomials of the First Kind

The Chebyshev polynomials of the first kind are defined by the formulae [30]

$$T_n(x) = \cos(n \arccos x),\ -1 \le x \le 1,\ n = 0, 1, \ldots. \tag{10}$$

They take on the explicit expressions as

$$T_0(x) = 1,\ T_n(x) = \frac{n}{2} \sum_{k=0}^{[n/2]} (-1)^k \frac{(n-k-1)!}{k!(n-2k)!} (2x)^{n-2k},\ n \ge 1. \tag{11}$$

It is well-known that the Chebyshev polynomials of the first kind are orthogonal on the interval $[-1,1]$ with the weight function $\rho(x) = \frac{1}{\sqrt{1-x^2}}$, and $T_n(x)$ has exactly n zeros within the interval $(-1,1)$: $\xi_i = \cos\left(\frac{2i+1}{2n}\pi\right)$, $i = 0, 1, \ldots, n-1$. The Chebyshev polynomials of the first kind satisfy the recurrence relation

$$T_0(x) = 1,\ T_1(x) = x,\ T_n(x) = 2xT_{n-1}(x) - T_{n-2}(x),\ n = 2, 3, \ldots. \tag{12}$$

It is well-known that if $f(x)$ is L_2 integrable on $[-1,1]$ with the weight function $\rho(x)$, then its Chebyshev series expansion is L_2 convergent with respect to its weight function $\rho(x)$. If $f(x)$ has better smoothness, then stronger convergence can be attained for its Chebyshev series. If the function $f(x)$ has $n+1$ continuous derivatives on $[-1,1]$, then $|f(x) - S_m f(x)| = O(m^{-n})$ for all $x \in [-1,1]$, where $S_m f(x)$ is the $(m+1)$-term truncation of the Chebyshev series expansion of $f(x)$. For more details for convergence, see [30].

In order to deal with the BVP on the interval $[0,1]$, we consider the shifted Chebyshev polynomials

$$T_n^*(x) = T_n(2x-1),\ x \in [0,1],\ n = 0, 1, \ldots. \tag{13}$$

They are orthogonal on the interval $[0,1]$ with the weight function $\rho^*(x) = \frac{1}{\sqrt{x-x^2}}$, and the zeros of $T_n^*(x)$ are $x_i = \frac{1}{2} + \frac{1}{2}\cos\left(\frac{2i+1}{2n}\pi\right)$, $i = 0, 1, \ldots, n-1$. As a complement to Equation (13), the shifted Chebyshev polynomials satisfy the relationship $T_n^*(x) = T_{2n}(\sqrt{x})$. So, the explicit expressions of the shifted Chebyshev polynomials are conveniently obtained:

$$T_0^*(x) = 1,\ T_n^*(x) = n \sum_{k=0}^{n} (-1)^k \frac{(2n-k-1)!}{k!(2n-2k)!} (4x)^{n-k},\ n \ge 1. \tag{14}$$

Finally, we mention the shifted Chebyshev polynomials of the second kind, which will also be used in the next section for the representation of solutions, $U_n^*(x) = U_n(2x-1)$, $0 \le x \le 1$, $n = 0, 1, \ldots$, where $U_n(x)$ is the Chebyshev polynomials of the second kind.

3. The Equivalent Fractional Differential-Integral Equation and Chebyshev Collocation Method

First, we derive an equivalent differential–integral equation to the BVP (7)–(9). Applying the integral operator $I_x^\lambda(\cdot)$ to both sides of Equation (7) and using Equation (6) yields

$$u(x) - u(0) - u'(0)x + I_x^\lambda(c_1(x)u'(x) + c_0(x)u(x)) = I_x^\lambda g(x). \tag{15}$$

Our aim is to solve for $u(0)$ and $u'(0)$ from the boundary conditions (8) and (9), and then obtain an equation about the solution $u(x)$ without any undetermined constants. Substituting $x = 1$ in Equation (15) yields

$$u(1) = u(0) + u'(0) - I_{x,1}^\lambda(c_1(x)u'(x) + c_0(x)u(x)) + I_{x,1}^\lambda g(x), \tag{16}$$

where the value of the fractional integral is defined for a general βth order integral of a function $v(x)$ at $x = \xi$ as

$$I_{x,\xi}^{\beta} v(x) = \int_0^{\xi} \frac{(\xi-\tau)^{\beta-1}}{\Gamma(\beta)} v(\tau) d\tau. \tag{17}$$

Calculating the first order derivative on the both sides of Equation (15) leads to

$$u'(x) - u'(0) + I_x^{\lambda-1}(c_1(x)u'(x) + c_0(x)u(x)) = I_x^{\lambda-1} g(x). \tag{18}$$

Substituting $x = 1$ yields

$$u'(1) = u'(0) - I_{x,1}^{\lambda-1}(c_1(x)u'(x) + c_0(x)u(x)) + I_{x,1}^{\lambda-1} g(x). \tag{19}$$

Substituting Equations (16) and (19) into Equation (9) yields

$$p_1 u(0) + (p_1 + q_1)u'(0) = b_1^*, \tag{20}$$

where

$$b_1^* = b_1 + p_1 I_{x,1}^{\lambda}(c_1(x)u'(x) + c_0(x)u(x)) - p_1 I_{x,1}^{\lambda} g(x) + q_1 I_{x,1}^{\lambda-1}(c_1(x)u'(x) + c_0(x)u(x)) - q_1 I_{x,1}^{\lambda-1} g(x). \tag{21}$$

Equations (8) and (20) constitute a system of algebraic equations about $u(0)$ and $u'(0)$. The coefficient determinant is

$$P = p_0 p_1 + p_0 q_1 + q_0 p_1, \tag{22}$$

which is positive by our assumptions. Thus, we can solve the system of algebraic Equations (8) and (20) and obtain

$$u(0) = \frac{(p_1+q_1)b_0}{P} + \frac{q_0 b_1^*}{P}, \tag{23}$$

$$u'(0) = -\frac{p_1 b_0}{P} + \frac{p_0 b_1^*}{P}. \tag{24}$$

Substituting Equations (23) and (24) into Equation (15), we obtain

$$u(x) - \frac{(p_1+q_1)b_0}{P} + \frac{p_1 b_0}{P}x - \frac{p_0 x + q_0}{P} b_1^* + I_x^{\lambda}(c_1(x)u'(x) + c_0(x)u(x)) = I_x^{\lambda} g(x). \tag{25}$$

Replacing b_1^* by using Equation (21) and reorganizing the equation yield

$$\begin{aligned} & u(x) - \frac{p_1(p_0 x + q_0)}{P} I_{x,1}^{\lambda}(c_1(x)u'(x) + c_0(x)u(x)) \\ & - \frac{q_1(p_0 x + q_0)}{P} I_{x,1}^{\lambda-1}(c_1(x)u'(x) + c_0(x)u(x)) + I_x^{\lambda}(c_1(x)u'(x) + c_0(x)u(x)) = h(x), \end{aligned} \tag{26}$$

where

$$h(x) = \frac{(p_1+q_1)b_0 - p_1 b_0 x}{P} + \frac{p_0 x + q_0}{P}\left(b_1 - p_1 I_{x,1}^{\lambda} g(x) - q_1 I_{x,1}^{\lambda-1} g(x)\right) + I_x^{\lambda} g(x), \tag{27}$$

Only involves the known boundary parameters and the known input function $g(x)$. Equation (26) is the equivalent differential–integral equation to the BVP (7)–(9). In the sequel, we seek for the solution to the differential-integral Equation (26).

We approximate the solution by an $(m+1)$-term truncation of the shifted Chebyshev series,

$$\varphi_m(x) = \sum_{n=0}^{m} a_n T_n^*(x), \tag{28}$$

where a_n, $n = 0, 1, \ldots, m$, are undetermined coefficients. Inserting $\varphi_m(x)$ into Equation (26), we obtain the linear equation about a_n, $n = 0, 1, \ldots, m$,

$$\begin{aligned}\sum_{n=0}^{m} a_n\Big(T_n^*(x) &- \frac{p_1(p_0x+q_0)}{P} I_{x,1}^{\lambda}\Big(c_1(x)T_n^{*\prime}(x) + c_0(x)T_n^*(x)\Big)\\ &- \frac{q_1(p_0x+q_0)}{P} I_{x,1}^{\lambda-1}\Big(c_1(x)T_n^{*\prime}(x) + c_0(x)T_n^*(x)\Big) + I_x^{\lambda}\Big(c_1(x)T_n^{*\prime}(x) + c_0(x)T_n^*(x)\Big)\Big) = h(x).\end{aligned} \tag{29}$$

We note that in Equation (29), $I_{x,1}^{\lambda}(c_1(x)T_n^{*\prime}(x) + c_0(x)T_n^*(x))$ and $I_{x,1}^{\lambda-1}$ $(c_1(x)T_n^{*\prime}(x) + c_0(x)T_n^*(x))$ are constants, represent the values of fractional integrals.

The collocation method may be applied to determine the coefficients a_n. The collocation points are taken as the zeroes of the $m+1$ degree shifted Chebyshev polynomial $T_{m+1}^*(x)$,

$$x_i = \frac{1}{2} + \frac{1}{2}\cos\left(\frac{2i+1}{2m+2}\pi\right),\ i = 0, 1, \ldots, m. \tag{30}$$

Thus, the collocation equation system is

$$\begin{aligned}\sum_{n=0}^{m} a_n\ \Big(T_n^*(x_i) &- \frac{p_1(p_0x_i+q_0)}{P} I_{x,1}^{\lambda}\Big(c_1(x)T_n^{*\prime}(x) + c_0(x)T_n^*(x)\Big)\\ &- \frac{q_1(p_0x_i+q_0)}{P} I_{x,1}^{\lambda-1}\Big(c_1(x)T_n^{*\prime}(x) + c_0(x)T_n^*(x)\Big)\\ &+ I_{x,x_i}^{\lambda}\Big(c_1(x)T_n^{*\prime}(x) + c_0(x)T_n^*(x)\Big)\Big) = h(x_i),\end{aligned} \tag{31}$$

where

$$h(x_i) = \frac{(p_1+q_1)b_0 - p_1b_0x_i}{P} + \frac{p_0x_i+q_0}{P}\Big(b_1 - p_1I_{x,1}^{\lambda}g(x) - q_1I_{x,1}^{\lambda-1}g(x)\Big) + I_{x,x_i}^{\lambda}g(x),\ i = 0, 1, \ldots, m. \tag{32}$$

The matrix form of the collocation equation system (31) is

$$W\vec{a} = \vec{h}, \tag{33}$$

where

$$\vec{a} = (a_0, a_1, \ldots, a_m)^T,\ \vec{h} = (h(x_0), h(x_1), \ldots, h(x_m))^T, \tag{34}$$

and the entries of the matrix W are

$$\begin{aligned} w_{ij} \;=\;& T_j^*(x_i) - \frac{p_1(p_0x_i+q_0)}{P} I_{x,1}^{\lambda}\Big(c_1(x)T_j^{*\prime}(x) + c_0(x)T_j^*(x)\Big)\\ &- \frac{q_1(p_0x_i+q_0)}{P} I_{x,1}^{\lambda-1}\Big(c_1(x)T_j^{*\prime}(x) + c_0(x)T_j^*(x)\Big) + I_{x,x_i}^{\lambda}\Big(c_1(x)T_j^{*\prime}(x) + c_0(x)T_j^*(x)\Big),\\ & i,j = 0, 1, \ldots, m.\end{aligned} \tag{35}$$

The solution of the linear algebraic equation system (31) or (33) gives the coefficients a_n in Equation (28).

For the Dirichlet boundary conditions $u(0) = b_0$, $u(1) = b_1$, the boundary parameters are simplified as $p_0 = p_1 = 1$ and $q_0 = q_1 = 0$, and thus Equation (31) degenerates to

$$\sum_{n=0}^{m} a_n\Big(T_n^*(x_i) - x_i I_{x,1}^{\lambda}\Big(c_1(x)T_n^{*\prime}(x) + c_0(x)T_n^*(x)\Big) + I_{x,x_i}^{\lambda}\Big(c_1(x)T_n^{*\prime}(x) + c_0(x)T_n^*(x)\Big)\Big) = h(x_i), \tag{36}$$

where $h(x_i) = b_0 + (b_1 - b_0)x_i - x_i I_{x,1}^{\lambda} g(x) + I_{x,x_i}^{\lambda} g(x)$, $i = 0, 1, \ldots, m$.

We remark that by the relationship of the first-kind and second-kind Chebyshev polynomials $T_n{}'(x) = nU_{n-1}(x)$, we have the relationship of the shifted Chebyshev polynomials of the two kinds

$$T_n^{*\prime}(x) = 2nU_{n-1}^*(x). \tag{37}$$

So, the derivative $T_n^{*\prime}(x)$ in Equations (31), (35) and (36) may be replaced by the second-kind Chebyshev polynomials.

The operators $I_{x,1}^{\lambda}(\cdot)$, $I_{x,1}^{\lambda-1}(\cdot)$ and $I_{x,x_i}^{\lambda}(\cdot)$ in Equations (31), (32) and (35) represent the values of fractional integrals of the known functions. Since the appearance of the varying coefficients $g(x)$ and $c_k(x)$, manual computations for these integrals are laborious in general. Here we approximate the varying coefficients again using their truncated shifted Chebyshev series as

$$g(x) = {\sum_{n=0}^{M}}' g_n T_n^*(x),\ c_k(x) = {\sum_{n=0}^{M}}' c_{k,n} T_n^*(x),\ k = 0, 1,\ 0 \le x \le 1, \tag{38}$$

where

$$g_n = \frac{2}{\pi}\int_0^1 \frac{1}{\sqrt{x - x^2}} g(x)T_n^*(x)dx,\ n = 0, 1, \ldots, M, \tag{39}$$

$$c_{k,n} = \frac{2}{\pi}\int_0^1 \frac{1}{\sqrt{x - x^2}} c_k(x)T_n^*(x)dx,\ k = 0, 1,\ n = 0, 1, \ldots, M, \tag{40}$$

and the superscript $'$ of $\sum$ denotes that the first term in the sum is halved. We note that there is no need of connections between the values of m and M in Equations (28) and (38). Utilizing the Gauss–Chebyshev quadrature formula we derive the numerical formulae for g_n and $c_{k,n}$ as

$$g_n = \frac{2}{M+1}\sum_{i=0}^{M} g(x_i)T_n^*(x_i),\ n = 0, 1, \ldots, M, \tag{41}$$

$$c_{k,n} = \frac{2}{M+1}\sum_{i=0}^{M} c_k(x_i)T_n^*(x_i),\ k = 0, 1,\ n = 0, 1, \ldots, M, \tag{42}$$

where x_i are the zeroes of the $M+1$ degree shifted Chebyshev polynomial $T_{M+1}^*(x)$,

$$x_i = \frac{1}{2} + \frac{1}{2}\cos\left(\frac{2i+1}{2M+2}\pi\right),\ i = 0, 1, \ldots, M. \tag{43}$$

Thus, making use of the decompositions in (38), the calculation of the integrals $I_{x,1}^{\lambda}(\cdot)$, $I_{x,1}^{\lambda-1}(\cdot)$ and $I_{x,x_i}^{\lambda}(\cdot)$ in Equations (31), (32) and (35) only involves integrals of polynomials, so can be carried out exactly.

In the following three examples, we take $M = 5$ in Equation (38) to truncate the decompositions of the coefficients $g(x)$ and $c_k(x)$ and to calculate the involved integrals $I_{x,1}^{\lambda}(\cdot)$, $I_{x,1}^{\lambda-1}(\cdot)$ and $I_{x,x_i}^{\lambda}(\cdot)$. Collocation equation systems are solved by using Mathematica command "LinearSolve". Figures of approximate analytical solutions and errors are generated by using Mathematica.

Example 1. *Consider the BVP for the linear FDE*

$$D_x^{1.5}u(x) - \frac{x\sin(x)}{3}u'(x) + \sin(x)u(x) = g(x),\ 0 < x < 1, \tag{44}$$
$$u'(0) = -1,\ u(1) = 1, \tag{45}$$

where $g(x) = \frac{3\sqrt{\pi}}{4} + \frac{8x^{1.5}}{\sqrt{\pi}} - \frac{2}{3}x\sin(x) + \frac{1}{2}x^{1.5}\sin(x)$.

The BVP has the exact solution $u^*(x) = -x + x^{1.5} + x^3$. The boundary parameters are $p_0 = 0, q_0 = -1, b_0 = -1, p_1 = 1, q_1 = 0, b_1 = 1$. The collocation equation system in (31) is

$$\sum_{n=0}^{m} a_n \left(T_n^*(x_i) - I_{x,1}^{1.5}\left(\frac{-x\sin(x)}{3}T_n^{*\prime}(x) + \sin(x)T_n^*(x)\right) + I_{x,x_i}^{1.5}\left(\frac{-x\sin(x)}{3}T_n^{*\prime}(x) + \sin(x)T_n^*(x)\right)\right) = h(x_i), \tag{46}$$

where $h(x_i) = 2 - x_i - I_{x,1}^{1.5}g(x) + I_{x,x_i}^{1.5}g(x),\ i = 0,1,\ldots,m$.

Take $m = 2,3,4$ and 5, respectively, the solution approximations $\varphi_m(x)$ are calculated as

$$\begin{aligned}
\varphi_2(x) &= 0.0175774 - 1.10039x + 2.05832x^2,\\
\varphi_3(x) &= -0.00586106 - 0.689478x + 0.925577x^2 + 0.768798x^3,\\
\varphi_4(x) &= -0.00288415 - 0.76024x + 1.24242x^2 + 0.293418x^3 + 0.22758x^4,\\
\varphi_5(x) &= -0.00167028 - 0.8038x + 1.54387x^2 - 0.47843x^3 + 1.05648x^4 - 0.316564x^5.
\end{aligned}$$

The error function and maximum error of the approximate solution $\varphi_m(x)$ are defined as

$$ER_m(x) = |\varphi_m(x) - u^*(x)| \text{ and } ME_m = \max_{0\le x\le 1} ER_m(x). \tag{47}$$

In Figure 1, the error functions $ER_m(x)$ for $m = 2,3,4,5$ are depicted, where at the $m+1$ collocation points of $\varphi_m(x)$, errors are zero. The maximum errors of the four approximate solutions are 0.028696, 0.005861, 0.002884, and 0.001670, respectively.

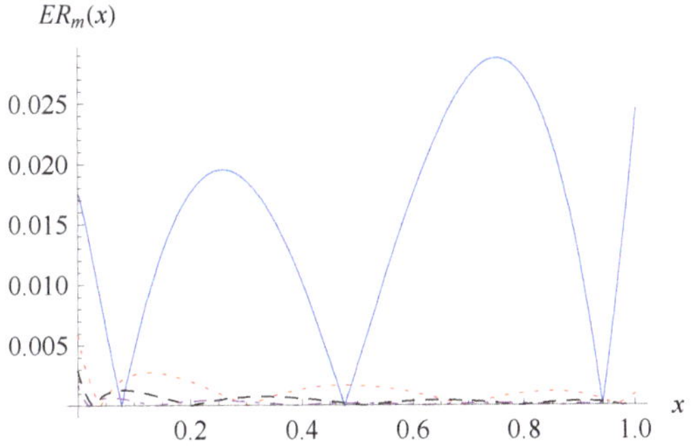

Figure 1. The error functions $ER_m(x)$ for $m = 2$ (solid line), $m = 3$ (dot line), $m = 4$ (dash line) and $m = 5$ (dot-dash line).

Example 2. *Consider the BVP for the linear FDE*

$$D_x^{\lambda}u(x) - u(x) = -4xe^x,\ 0 < x < 1,\ 1 < \lambda \le 2, \tag{48}$$
$$u(0) - u'(0) = -1,\ u(1) + u'(1) = -e. \tag{49}$$

If $\lambda = 2$, the BVP has the exact solution $u^*(x) = x(1-x)e^x$.

For this example, the coefficients and parameters are $c_1(x) = 0$, $c_0(x) = -1$, $g(x) = -4xe^x$, $p_0 = q_0 = p_1 = q_1 = 1$, $b_0 = -1$ and $b_1 = -e$. The collocation equation system in Equation (31) becomes

$$\sum_{n=0}^{m} a_n \Big(T_n^*(x_i) - \frac{x_i+1}{3} I_{x,1}^{\lambda}(-T_n^*(x)) - \frac{x_i+1}{3} I_{x,1}^{\lambda-1}(-T_n^*(x)) + I_{x,x_i}^{\lambda}(-T_n^*(x)) \Big) = h(x_i),$$

where $h(x_i) = \frac{x_i-2-ex_i-e}{3} + \frac{x_i+1}{3}\Big(-I_{x,1}^{\lambda} g(x) - I_{x,1}^{\lambda-1} g(x)\Big) + I_{x,x_i}^{\lambda} g(x)$, $i = 0, 1, \ldots, m$.

For the case of $\lambda = 2$, the error functions $ER_m(x) = |\varphi_m(x) - u^*(x)|$ are depicted in Figure 2 for m = 2–5. The maximum errors of the approximate solutions are 0.069103, 0.007877, 0.000620, and 0.000038, respectively. For the case of $\lambda = 1.5$, the solution approximations $\varphi_m(x)$, m = 2–5, are calculated as

$$\begin{aligned}
\varphi_2(x) &= 0.578503 + 3.00467x - 2.45143x^2, \\
\varphi_3(x) &= 0.659109 + 1.56065x + 1.43569x^2 - 2.61289x^3, \\
\varphi_4(x) &= 0.651626 + 1.81823x + 0.108085x^2 - 0.448696x^3 - 1.09621x^4, \\
\varphi_5(x) &= 0.653112 + 1.75369x + 0.599869x^2 - 1.78975x^3 + 0.411041x^4 - 0.596018x^5.
\end{aligned}$$

The condition numbers of the coefficient matrices W in the derivations of the four solution approximations are 2.85, 3.29, 3.67 and 4.02, respectively. These values show that the coefficient matrices W are well conditioned. We note that the condition number is based on the l_2-matrix norm. The four solution approximations are plotted in Figure 3, where a fast convergence is shown.

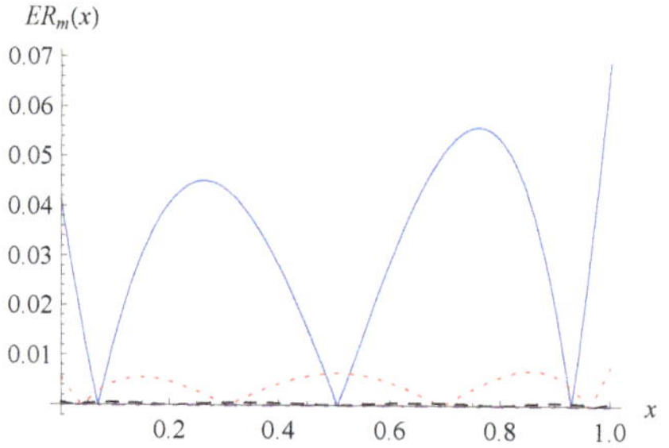

Figure 2. For $\lambda = 2$, the error functions $ER_m(x)$ for $m = 2$ (solid line), $m = 3$ (dot line), $m = 4$ (dash line) and $m = 5$ (dot-dash line).

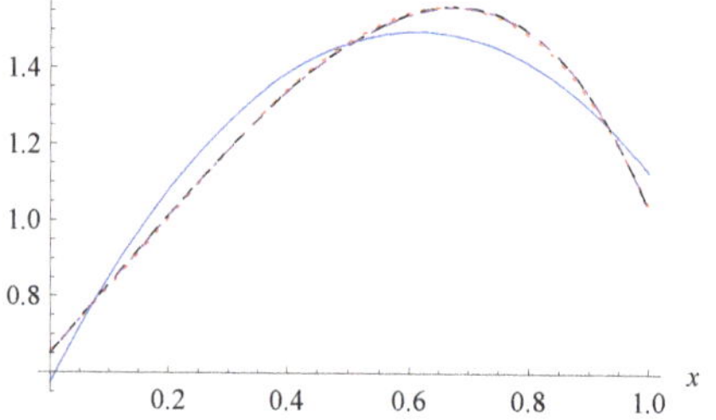

Figure 3. For $\lambda = 1.5$, the solution approximations $\varphi_m(x)$ for $m = 2$ (solid line), $m = 3$ (dot line), $m = 4$ (dash line) and $m = 5$ (dot-dash line).

Example 3. *Consider the BVP for the linear FDE*

$$D_x^{\lambda}u(x) - \frac{x}{1+x}u'(x) - \frac{1}{1+x}u(x) = 0,\ 0 < x < 1,\ 1 < \lambda \le 2, \tag{50}$$
$$u(0) - 2u'(0) = -1,\ u(1) + 2u'(1) = 3e. \tag{51}$$

If $\lambda = 2$, the BVP has the exact solution $u^*(x) = e^x$.

The coefficients and parameters are $c_1(x) = -\frac{x}{1+x}$, $c_0(x) = -\frac{1}{1+x}$, $g(x) = 0$, $p_0 = p_1 = 1, q_0 = q_1 = 2, b_0 = -1, b_1 = 3e$. The collocation equation system in Equation (31) becomes

$$\sum_{n=0}^{m} a_n\left(T_n^*(x_i) - \frac{x_i+2}{5}I_{x,1}^{\lambda}\left(\frac{-x}{1+x}T_n^{*\prime}(x) + \frac{-1}{1+x}T_n^*(x)\right)\right.$$
$$\left. - \frac{2(x_i+2)}{5}I_{x,1}^{\lambda-1}\left(\frac{-x}{1+x}T_n^{*\prime}(x) + \frac{-1}{1+x}T_n^*(x)\right) + I_{x,x_i}^{\lambda}\left(\frac{-x}{1+x}T_n^{*\prime}(x) + \frac{-1}{1+x}T_n^*(x)\right)\right) = h(x_i),$$

where $h(x_i) = \frac{1}{5}(6e - 3 + 3ex_i + x_i)$, $i = 0, 1, \ldots, m$.

For the case of $\lambda = 2$, the error functions $ER_m(x) = |\varphi_m(x) - u^*(x)|$ for $m = 2, 3, 4, 5$, are depicted in Figure 4. The maximum errors of the approximate solutions are 0.011605, 0.000742, 0.000037, and 0.000002, respectively. For the case of $\lambda = 1.5$, the solution approximations $\varphi_m(x)$ for $m = 2, 3, 4, 5$ are calculated as

$$\begin{aligned}
\varphi_2(x) &= 0.627196 + 0.801952x + 0.961626x^2,\\
\varphi_3(x) &= 0.614413 + 0.94835x + 0.55162x^2 + 0.269951x^3,\\
\varphi_4(x) &= 0.615168 + 0.908026x + 0.734701x^2 - 0.0100847x^3 + 0.135331x^4,\\
\varphi_5(x) &= 0.615706 + 0.894049x + 0.828159x^2 - 0.242103x^3 + 0.378859x^4 - 0.0913166x^5.
\end{aligned}$$

The condition numbers of the coefficient matrices W in the derivations of the four solution approximations are 4.87, 7.83, 11.90 and 17.05, respectively. So the coefficient matrices W are well conditioned. The four solution approximations are plotted in Figure 5.

In the three examples, fast convergent rates are shown only using the minor term number with $M = 5$ in Equation (38) for the integral computation of the known functions, and the minor term number with $m = 2, 3, 4$ and 5 in Equation (28) for the truncated Chebyshev series of the unknown function.

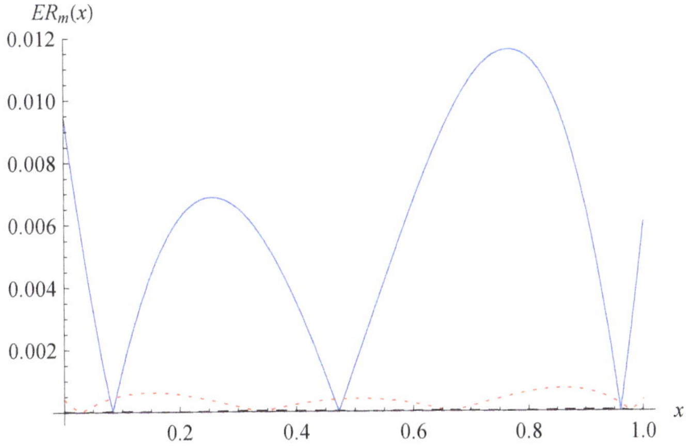

Figure 4. For $\lambda = 2$, the error functions $ER_m(x)$ for $m = 2$ (solid line), $m = 3$ (dot line), $m = 4$ (dash line) and $m = 5$ (dot-dash line).

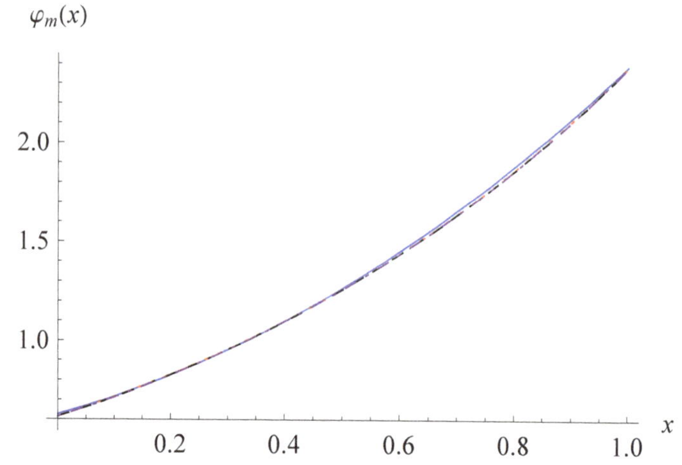

Figure 5. For $\lambda = 1.5$, the solution approximations $\varphi_m(x)$ for $m = 2$ (solid line), $m = 3$ (dot line), $m = 4$ (dash line) and $m = 5$ (dot-dash line).

4. Conclusions

We considered the BVP for the varying coefficient linear Caputo-type fractional ODE subject to the mixed boundary conditions on the interval $0 \le x \le 1$. The BVP was conveniently converted into an equivalent differential–integral equation merging the boundary conditions. Then, the solution was decomposed into a truncated shifted Chebyshev series. The collocation method was used to determine the solution. In order to deal with the involved integrations, the varying coefficients were again decomposed into the truncated shifted Chebyshev series. Thus, the calculations of the integrals are only for polynomials and can be carried out exactly. Three numerical examples were solved by using the proposed method, where fast convergent rates are shown only using the minor term number with $M = 5$ in Equation (38) for the integral computation of the known functions, and the minor term number with $m = 2, 3, 4$ and 5 in Equation (28) for the truncated Chebyshev series of the unknown function.

In the presented method, there is no need to divide the interval commonly used in numerical methods. The collocation points or the zeros of the Chebyshev polynomials have exact explicit expressions. Approximate analytical solutions in the polynomial forms are obtained, which are different from a discrete numerical solution. The obtained approximate analytical solutions in the polynomial forms can be directly checked by substitution. The convergence and effectiveness of solutions can be examined by remainder errors. Convergence order of the approximate solutions could be further consideration in this field.

Author Contributions: Conceptualization, J.-S.D. and M.L.; data curation, L.-X.J. and M.L.; formal analysis, J.-S.D., L.-X.J. and M.L.; funding acquisition, J.-S.D. and M.L.; investigation, J.-S.D. and L.-X.J.; methodology, J.-S.D. and M.L.; software, J.-S.D. and L.-X.J.; supervision, J.-S.D.; validation, M.L.; visualization, L.-X.J.; writing–original draft, J.-S.D. and L.-X.J.; writing–review and editing, J.-S.D. and M.L. All authors have read and agreed to the published version of the manuscript.

Funding: This work was supported by the National Natural Science Foundation of China (Nos. 11772203; 61672238).

Institutional Review Board Statement: Not applicable.

Informed Consent Statement: Not applicable.

Data Availability Statement: Not applicable.

Acknowledgments: Jun-Sheng Duan acknowledges the supports in part by the National Natural Science Foundation of China under the project grant number 11772203. Ming Li acknowledges the supports in part by the National Natural Science Foundation of China under the project grant number 61672238. The authors show their appreciation for the valuable comments from the reviewers on the manuscript.

Conflicts of Interest: The authors declare no conflict of interest.

References

1. Oldham, K.B.; Spanier, J. *The Fractional Calculus*; Academic: New York, NY, USA, 1974.
2. Miller, K.S.; Ross, B. *An Introduction to the Fractional Calculus and Fractional Differential Equations*; Wiley: New York, NY, USA, 1993.
3. Podlubny, I. *Fractional Differential Equations*; Academic: San Diego, CA, USA, 1999.
4. Kilbas, A.A.; Srivastava, H.M.; Trujillo, J.J. *Theory and Applications of Fractional Differential Equations*; Elsevier: Amsterdam, The Netherlands, 2006.
5. Băleanu, D.; Diethelm, K.; Scalas, E.; Trujillo, J.J. *Fractional Calculus Models and Numerical Methods. Series on Complexity, Nonlinearity and Chaos*; World Scientific: Boston, MA, USA, 2012.
6. Mainardi, F. *Fractional Calculus and Waves in Linear Viscoelasticity*; Imperial College: London, UK, 2010.
7. Li, M. *Theory of Fractional Engineering Vibrations*; De Gruyter: Berlin, Germany, 2021.
8. Bagley, R.L.; Torvik, P.J. On the fractional calculus model of viscoelastic behavior. *J. Rheol.* **1986**, *30*, 133–155. [CrossRef]
9. Li, M. Three classes of fractional oscillators. *Symmetry* **2018**, *10*, 40. [CrossRef]
10. Ferras, L.L.; Ford, N.J.; Morgado, M.L.; Rebelo, M.; McKinley, G.H.; Nobrega, J.M. Theoretical and numerical analysis of unsteady fractional viscoelastic flows in simple geometries. *Comput. Fluids* **2018**, *174*, 14–33. [CrossRef]
11. Duan, J.S.; Hu, D.C.; Chen, Y.Q. Simultaneous characterization of relaxation, creep, dissipation, and hysteresis by fractional-order constitutive models. *Fractal Fract.* **2021**, *5*, 36. [CrossRef]
12. Jiang, X.; Xu, M.; Qi, H. The fractional diffusion model with an absorption term and modified Fick's law for non-local transport processes. *Nonlinear Anal. Real World Appl.* **2010**, *11*, 262–269. [CrossRef]
13. Morgado, M.L.; Rebelo, M.; Ferras, L.L.; Ford, N.J. Numerical solution for diffusion equations with distributed order in time using a Chebyshev collocation method. *Appl. Numer. Math.* **2017**, *114*, 108–123. [CrossRef]
14. Atangana, A. *Fractional Operators with Constant and Variable Order with Application to Geo-Hydrology*; Elsevier: London, UK, 2018.
15. Jiao, Z.; Chen, Y.; Podlubny, I. *Distributed-Order Dynamic Systems—Stability, Simulation, Applications and Perspectives*; Springer: London, UK, 2012.
16. Li, Y.; Duan, J.S. The periodic response of a fractional oscillator with a spring-pot and an inerter-pot. *J. Mech.* **2021**, *37*, 108–117. [CrossRef]
17. Duan, J.S.; Hu, D.C. Vibration systems with fractional-order and distributed-order derivatives characterizing viscoinertia. *Fractal Fract.* **2021**, *5*, 67. [CrossRef]
18. Diethelm, K. *The Analysis of Fractional Differential Equations*; Springer: Berlin/Heidelberg, Germany, 2010.
19. Duan, J.S.; Wang, Z.; Liu, Y.L.; Qiu, X. Eigenvalue problems for fractional ordinary differential equations. *Chaos Solitons Fractals* **2013**, *46*, 46–53. [CrossRef]
20. Băleanu, D.; Mustafa, O.G.; Agarwal, R.P. An existence result for a superlinear fractional differential equation. *Appl. Math. Lett.* **2010**, *23*, 1129–1132. [CrossRef]
21. Diethelm, K.; Ford, N.J.; Freed, A.D. Detailed error analysis for a fractional Adams method. *Numer. Algorithms* **2004**, *36*, 31–52. [CrossRef]
22. Liu, F.; Zhuang, P.; Anh, V.; Turner, I.; Burrage, K. Stability and convergence of the difference methods for the space-time fractional advection-diffusion equation. *Appl. Math. Comput.* **2007**, *191*, 12–20. [CrossRef]
23. Wu, G.C. A fractional characteristic method for solving fractional partial differential equations. *Appl. Math. Lett.* **2011**, *24*, 1046–1050. [CrossRef]
24. Atabakzadeh, M.H.; Akrami, M.H.; Erjaee, G.H. Chebyshev operational matrix method for solving multi-order fractional ordinary differential equations. *Appl. Math. Model.* **2013**, *37*, 8903–8911. [CrossRef]
25. Duan, J.S.; Hu, D.C.; Li, M. Comparison of two different analytical forms of response for fractional oscillation equation. *Fractal Fract.* **2021**, *5*, 188. [CrossRef]
26. Jafari, H.; Daftardar-Gejji, V. Positive solutions of nonlinear fractional boundary value problems using Adomian decomposition method. *Appl. Math. Comput.* **2006**, *180*, 700–706. [CrossRef]
27. Rehman, M.U.; Khan, R.A. A numerical method for solving boundary value problems for fractional differential equations. *Appl. Math. Model.* **2012**, *36*, 894–907. [CrossRef]
28. Al-Refai, M.; Hajji, M.A. Monotone iterative sequences for nonlinear boundary value problems of fractional order. *Nonlinear Anal.* **2011**, *74*, 3531–3539. [CrossRef]
29. Doha, E.H.; Bhrawy, A.H.; Ezz-Eldien, S.S. A Chebyshev spectral method based on operational matrix for initial and boundary value problems of fractional order. *Comput. Math. Appl* **2011**, *62*, 2364–2373. [CrossRef]
30. Mason, J.C.; Handscomb, D.C. *Chebyshev Polynomials*; Chapman & Hall/CRC: London, UK, 2003.

fractal and fractional

MDPI

Article

Positive Solutions of a Singular Fractional Boundary Value Problem with r-Laplacian Operators

Alexandru Tudorache [1] and Rodica Luca [2,*]

[1] Department of Computer Science and Engineering, Gh. Asachi Technical University, 700050 Iasi, Romania; alexandru-gabriel.tudorache@academic.tuiasi.ro

[2] Department of Mathematics, Gh. Asachi Technical University, 700506 Iasi, Romania

* Correspondence: rluca@math.tuiasi.ro

Abstract: We investigate the existence and multiplicity of positive solutions for a system of Riemann–Liouville fractional differential equations with r-Laplacian operators and nonnegative singular nonlinearities depending on fractional integrals, supplemented with nonlocal uncoupled boundary conditions which contain Riemann–Stieltjes integrals and various fractional derivatives. In the proof of our main results we apply the Guo–Krasnosel'skii fixed point theorem of cone expansion and compression of norm type.

Keywords: Riemann–Liouville fractional differential equations; nonlocal boundary conditions; singular functions; positive solutions; multiplicity

MSC: 34A08; 34B10; 34B16; 34B18

Citation: Tudorache, A.; Luca, R. Positive Solutions of a Singular Fractional Boundary Value Problem with r-Laplacian Operators. *Fractal Fract.* **2022**, *6*, 18. https://doi.org/10.3390/fractalfract6010018

Academic Editor: Maria Rosaria Lancia

Received: 18 November 2021
Accepted: 29 December 2021
Published: 30 December 2021

1. Introduction

We consider the system of fractional differential equations with r_1-Laplacian and r_2-Laplacian operators

$$\begin{cases} D_{0+}^{\gamma_1}\left(\varphi_{r_1}\left(D_{0+}^{\delta_1}u(\tau)\right)\right) = f(\tau,u(\tau),v(\tau),I_{0+}^{\sigma_1}u(\tau),I_{0+}^{\sigma_2}v(\tau)), \quad \tau\in(0,1), \\ D_{0+}^{\gamma_2}\left(\varphi_{r_2}\left(D_{0+}^{\delta_2}v(\tau)\right)\right) = g(\tau,u(\tau),v(\tau),I_{0+}^{\varsigma_1}u(\tau),I_{0+}^{\varsigma_2}v(\tau)), \quad \tau\in(0,1), \end{cases} \tag{1}$$

subject to the uncoupled nonlocal boundary conditions

$$\begin{cases} u^{(i)}(0)=0, \; i=0,\dots,p-2, \; D_{0+}^{\delta_1}u(0)=0, \\ \varphi_{r_1}(D_{0+}^{\delta_1}u(1)) = \int_0^1 \varphi_{r_1}(D_{0+}^{\delta_1}u(\eta))\,d\mathcal{H}_0(\eta), \; D_{0+}^{\alpha_0}u(1)=\sum_{k=1}^{n}\int_0^1 D_{0+}^{\alpha_k}u(\eta)\,d\mathcal{H}_k(\eta), \\ v^{(i)}(0)=0, \; i=0,\dots,q-2, \; D_{0+}^{\delta_2}v(0)=0, \\ \varphi_{r_2}(D_{0+}^{\delta_2}v(1)) = \int_0^1 \varphi_{r_2}(D_{0+}^{\delta_2}v(\eta))\,d\mathcal{K}_0(\eta), \; D_{0+}^{\beta_0}v(1)=\sum_{k=1}^{m}\int_0^1 D_{0+}^{\beta_k}v(\eta)\,d\mathcal{K}_k(\eta), \end{cases} \tag{2}$$

where $\gamma_1,\gamma_2\in(1,2]$, $\delta_1\in(p-1,p]$, $p\in\mathbb{N}$, $p\geq 3$, $\delta_2\in(q-1,q]$, $q\in\mathbb{N}$, $q\geq 3$, $n,m\in\mathbb{N}$, $\sigma_1,\sigma_2,\varsigma_1,\varsigma_2>0$, $\alpha_k\in\mathbb{R}$, $k=0,\dots,n$, $0\leq\alpha_1<\alpha_2<\cdots<\alpha_n\leq\alpha_0<\delta_1-1$, $\alpha_0\geq 1$, $\beta_k\in\mathbb{R}$, $k=0,\dots,m$, $0\leq\beta_1<\beta_2<\cdots<\beta_m\leq\beta_0<\delta_2-1$, $\beta_0\geq 1$, $\varphi_{r_i}(\eta)=|\eta|^{r_i-2}\eta$, $\varphi_{r_i}^{-1}=\varphi_{\varrho_i}$, $\varrho_i=\frac{r_i}{r_i-1}$, $i=1,2$, $r_i>1$, $i=1,2$, $f,g:(0,1)\times\mathbb{R}_+^4\to\mathbb{R}_+$ are continuous functions, singular at $\tau=0$ and/or $\tau=1$, ($\mathbb{R}_+=[0,\infty)$), I_{0+}^{κ} is the Riemann–Liouville fractional integral of order κ (for $\kappa=\sigma_1,\sigma_2,\varsigma_1,\varsigma_2$), D_{0+}^{κ} is the Riemann-Liouville fractional derivative of order κ (for $\kappa=\gamma_1,\delta_1,\gamma_2,\delta_2,\alpha_0,\dots,\alpha_n,\beta_0,\dots,\beta_m$), and the integrals from the boundary conditions (2) are Riemann–Stieltjes integrals with $\mathcal{H}_i:[0,1]\to\mathbb{R}$, $i=0,\dots,n$ and $\mathcal{K}_i:[0,1]\to\mathbb{R}$, $i=0,\dots,m$ functions of bounded variation.

We give in this paper various conditions for the functions f and g such that problems (1) and (2) have at least one or two positive solutions. From a positive solution of (1) and (2) we understand a pair of functions $(u,v) \in (C([0,1],\mathbb{R}_+))^2$ satisfying the system (1) and the boundary conditions (2), with $u(\tau) > 0$ for all $\tau \in (0,1]$ or $v(\tau) > 0$ for all $\tau \in (0,1]$. In the proof of our main results we use the Guo–Krasnosel'skii fixed point theorem of cone expansion and compression of norm type. We now present some recent results which are connected with our problem. In [1], the authors studied the existence of multiple positive solutions for the system of nonlinear fractional differential equations with a p-Laplacian operator

$$\begin{cases} D_{0+}^{\beta_1}(\varphi_{p_1}(D_{0+}^{\alpha_1}x(\tau))) = f(\tau,x(\tau),y(\tau)), & \tau \in (0,1), \\ D_{0+}^{\beta_2}(\varphi_{p_2}(D_{0+}^{\alpha_2}y(\tau))) = g(\tau,x(\tau),y(\tau)), & \tau \in (0,1), \end{cases}$$

supplemented with the uncoupled boundary conditions

$$\begin{cases} x(0) = 0, \ D_{0+}^{\gamma_1}x(1) = \sum\limits_{i=1}^{m-2} \xi_{1i} D_{0+}^{\gamma_1}x(\eta_{1i}), \\ D_{0+}^{\alpha_1}x(0) = 0, \ \varphi_{p_1}(D_{0+}^{\alpha_1}x(1)) = \sum_{i=1}^{m-2}\zeta_{1i}\varphi_{p_1}(D_{0+}^{\alpha_1}x(\eta_{1i})), \\ y(0) = 0, \ D_{0+}^{\gamma_2}y(1) = \sum\limits_{i=1}^{m-2} \xi_{2i} D_{0+}^{\gamma_2}y(\eta_{2i}), \\ D_{0+}^{\alpha_2}y(0) = 0, \ \varphi_{p_2}(D_{0+}^{\alpha_2}y(1)) = \sum_{i=1}^{m-2}\zeta_{2i}\varphi_{p_2}(D_{0+}^{\alpha_2}y(\eta_{2i})), \end{cases}$$

where $\alpha_i, \beta_i \in (1,2]$, $\gamma_i \in (0,1]$, $\alpha_i + \beta_i \in (3,4]$, $\alpha_i > \gamma_i + 1$, $i = 1,2$, $\xi_{1i}, \eta_{1i}, \zeta_{1i}, \xi_{2i}, \eta_{2i}, \zeta_{2i} \in (0,1)$ for $i = 1,\dots,m-2$, and f and g are nonnegative and nonsingular functions. In the proof of the existence results they use the Leray–Schauder alternative theorem, the Leggett–Williams fixed point theorem and the Avery–Henderson fixed point theorem. In [2], the authors investigated the existence and multiplicity of positive solutions for the system of fractional differential equations with ϱ_1-Laplacian and ϱ_2-Laplacian operators

$$\begin{cases} D_{0+}^{\gamma_1}(\varphi_{\varrho_1}(D_{0+}^{\delta_1}x(\tau))) + f(\tau,x(\tau),y(\tau)) = 0, & \tau \in (0,1), \\ D_{0+}^{\gamma_2}(\varphi_{\varrho_2}(D_{0+}^{\delta_2}y(\tau))) + g(\tau,x(\tau),y(\tau)) = 0, & \tau \in (0,1), \end{cases} \tag{3}$$

subject to the uncoupled nonlocal boundary conditions

$$\begin{cases} x^{(j)}(0) = 0, \ j = 0,\dots,p-2; \ D_{0+}^{\delta_1}x(0) = 0, \ D_{0+}^{\alpha_0}x(1) = \sum\limits_{i=1}^{n}\int_0^1 D_{0+}^{\alpha_i}x(\tau)\,d\mathcal{H}_i(\tau), \\ y^{(j)}(0) = 0, \ j = 0,\dots,q-2; \ D_{0+}^{\delta_2}y(0) = 0, \ D_{0+}^{\beta_0}y(1) = \sum\limits_{i=1}^{m}\int_0^1 D_{0+}^{\beta_i}y(\tau)\,d\mathcal{K}_i(\tau), \end{cases}$$

where $\gamma_1, \gamma_2 \in (0,1]$, $\delta_1 \in (p-1,p]$, $\delta_2 \in (q-1,q]$, $p, q \in \mathbb{N}$, $p, q \geq 3$, $n, m \in \mathbb{N}$, $\alpha_i \in \mathbb{R}$ for all $i = 0,1,\dots,n$, $0 \leq \alpha_1 < \alpha_2 < \cdots < \alpha_n \leq \alpha_0 < \delta_1 - 1$, $\alpha_0 \geq 1$, $\beta_i \in \mathbb{R}$ for all $i = 0,1,\dots,m$, $0 \leq \beta_1 < \beta_2 < \cdots < \beta_m \leq \beta_0 < \delta_2 - 1$, $\beta_0 \geq 1$, $\varrho_1, \varrho_2 > 1$, the functions f and g are nonnegative and continuous, and they may be singular at $\tau = 0$ and/or $\tau = 1$, and $\mathcal{H}_i$, $i = 1,\dots,n$ and $\mathcal{K}_j$, $j = 1,\dots,m$ are functions of bounded variation. In the proof of the main existence results they applied the Guo–Krasnosel'skii fixed point theorem. In [3], the authors studied the existence and nonexistence of positive solutions for the system (3) with two positive parameters λ and μ, supplemented with the coupled nonlocal boundary conditions

$$\begin{cases} x^{(j)}(0) = 0, \ j = 0,\dots,p-2; \ D_{0+}^{\delta_1}x(0) = 0, \ D_{0+}^{\alpha_0}x(1) = \sum\limits_{i=1}^{n}\int_0^1 D_{0+}^{\alpha_i}y(\tau)\,d\mathcal{H}_i(\tau), \\ y^{(j)}(0) = 0, \ j = 0,\dots,q-2; \ D_{0+}^{\delta_2}y(0) = 0, \ D_{0+}^{\beta_0}y(1) = \sum\limits_{i=1}^{m}\int_0^1 D_{0+}^{\beta_i}x(\tau)\,d\mathcal{K}_i(\tau), \end{cases} \tag{4}$$

where $n, m \in \mathbb{N}$, $\alpha_i \in \mathbb{R}$ for all $i = 0, \dots, n$, $0 \le \alpha_1 < \alpha_2 < \cdots < \alpha_n \le \beta_0 < \delta_2 - 1$, $\beta_0 \ge 1$, $\beta_i \in \mathbb{R}$ for all $i = 0, \dots, m$, $0 \le \beta_1 < \beta_2 < \cdots < \beta_m \le \alpha_0 < \delta_1 - 1$, $\alpha_0 \ge 1$, the functions $f, g \in C([0,1] \times \mathbb{R}_+ \times \mathbb{R}_+, \mathbb{R}_+)$, and the functions $\mathcal{H}_i$, $i = 1, \dots, n$ and $\mathcal{K}_j$, $j = 1, \dots, m$ are bounded variation functions. They presented sufficient conditions on the functions f and g, and intervals for the parameters λ and μ such that the problem (3) with these parameters and (4) has positive solutions. In [4], by using the Guo–Krasnosel'skii fixed point theorem, the authors investigated the existence and multiplicity of positive solutions for the nonlinear singular fractional differential equation

$$D_{0+}^{\alpha} w(\tau) + f(\tau, w(\tau), D_{0+}^{\alpha_1} w(\tau), \dots, D_{0+}^{\alpha_{n-2}} w(\tau)) = 0, \ \ \tau \in (0,1),$$

with the nonlocal boundary conditions

$$\begin{cases} w(0) = D_{0+}^{\gamma_1} w(0) = \cdots = D_{0+}^{\gamma_{n-2}} w(0) = 0, \\ D_{0+}^{\beta_1} w(1) = \int_0^{\eta} h(\tau) D_{0+}^{\beta_2} w(\tau)\, dA(\tau) + \int_0^1 a(\tau) D_{0+}^{\beta_3} w(\tau)\, dA(\tau), \end{cases}$$

where $\alpha \in (n-1, n]$, $n \ge 3$, $\alpha_k, \gamma_k \in (k-1, k]$, $k = 1, \dots, n-2$, $\alpha - \gamma_j \in (n-j-1, n-j]$, $j = 1, \dots, n-2$, $\alpha - \alpha_{n-2} - 1 \in (1,2]$, $\gamma_{n-2} \ge \alpha_{n-2}$, $\beta_1 \ge \beta_2$, $\beta_1 \ge \beta_3$, $\alpha \ge \beta_i + 1$, $\beta_i \ge \alpha_{n-2} + 1$, $i = 1,2,3$, $\beta_1 \le n-1$, the function $f : (0,1) \times \mathbb{R}_+^{n-1} \to \mathbb{R}_+$ is continuous, $a, h \in C((0,1), \mathbb{R}_+)$, and A is a function of bounded variation. In [5], the authors studied the existence of a unique positive solution for a system of three Caputo fractional equations with (p,q,r)-Laplacian operators subject to two-point boundary conditions, by using an n-fixed point theorem of ternary operators in partially ordered complete metric spaces. By relying on the properties of the Kuratowski noncompactness measure and the Sadovskii fixed point theorem; in [6], the authors obtained new existence results for the solutions of a Riemann–Liouville fractional differential equation with a p-Laplacian operator in a Banach space, supplemented with multi-point boundary conditions with fractional derivatives. In [7], the authors investigated the existence of solutions for a mixed fractional differential equation with $p(t)$-Laplacian operator and two-point boundary conditions at resonance, by applying the continuation theorem of coincidence degree theory. By using the Leggett–Williams fixed-point theorem, the authors studied in [8] the multiplicity of positive solutions for a Riemann–Liouville fractional differential equation with a p-Laplacian operator, subject to four-point boundary conditions. In [9], the authors established suitable criteria for the existence of positive solutions for a Riemann–Liouville fractional equation with a p-Laplacian operator and infinite-point boundary value conditions, by using the Krasnosel'skii fixed point theorem and Avery–Peterson fixed point theorem. By applying the Guo–Krasnosel'skii fixed point theorem the authors investigated in [10] the existence, multiplicity and the nonexistence of positive solutions for a mixed fractional differential equation with a generalized p-Laplacian operator and a positive parameter, supplemented with two-point boundary conditions. We also mention some recent monographs devoted to the investigation of boundary value problems for fractional differential equations and systems with many examples and applications, namely [11–15].

So in comparison with the above papers, the new characteristics of our problem (1) and (2) consist in a combination between the fractional orders $\gamma_1, \gamma_2 \in (1,2]$ with the arbitrary fractional orders δ_1, δ_2, the existence of the fractional integral terms in equations of (1), and the general uncoupled nonlocal boundary conditions with Riemann–Stieltjes integrals and fractional derivatives. In addition, one of its special feature is the singularity of the nonlinearities from the system (1), that is f, g become unbounded in the vicinity of 0 and/or 1 in the first variable (see Assumption $(I2)$ in Section 3).

The structure of this paper is as follows. In Section 2, some preliminary results including the properties of the Green functions associated to our problem (1) and (2) are presented. In Section 3 we discuss the existence and multiplicity of positive solutions for (1) and (2). Then two examples to illustrate our obtained theorems are given in Section 4, and Section 5 contains the conclusions for this paper.

2. Preliminary Results

We consider the fractional differential equation

$$D_{0+}^{\gamma_1}\left(\varphi_{r_1}\left(D_{0+}^{\delta_1}u(\tau)\right)\right) = x(\tau),\ \ \tau \in (0,1), \tag{5}$$

where $x \in C(0,1) \cap L^1(0,1)$, with the boundary conditions

$$\begin{cases} u^{(i)}(0) = 0,\ \ i = 0,\dots,p-2,\ \ D_{0+}^{\delta_1}u(0) = 0, \\ \varphi_{r_1}(D_{0+}^{\delta_1}u(1)) = \int_0^1 \varphi_{r_1}(D_{0+}^{\delta_1}u(\eta))\, d\mathcal{H}_0(\eta),\ \ D_{0+}^{\alpha_0}u(1) = \sum_{k=1}^{n}\int_0^1 D_{0+}^{\alpha_k}u(\eta)\, d\mathcal{H}_k(\eta). \end{cases} \tag{6}$$

We denote by

$$\mathfrak{a}_1 = 1 - \int_0^1 \eta^{\gamma_1-1}\, d\mathcal{H}_0(\eta),\ \ \mathfrak{a}_2 = \frac{\Gamma(\delta_1)}{\Gamma(\delta_1-\alpha_0)} - \sum_{i=1}^{n}\frac{\Gamma(\delta_1)}{\Gamma(\delta_1-\alpha_i)}\int_0^1 \eta^{\delta_1-\alpha_i-1}\, d\mathcal{H}_i(\eta). \tag{7}$$

Lemma 1. *If $\mathfrak{a}_1 \neq 0$ and $\mathfrak{a}_2 \neq 0$, then the unique solution $u \in C[0,1]$ of problem (5) and (6) is given by*

$$u(\tau) = \int_0^1 \mathcal{G}_2(\tau,\eta)\varphi_{\varrho_1}\left(\int_0^1 \mathcal{G}_1(\eta,\vartheta)x(\vartheta)\, d\vartheta\right)d\eta,\ \ \tau \in [0,1], \tag{8}$$

where

$$\mathcal{G}_1(\tau,\eta) = \mathfrak{g}_1(\tau,\eta) + \frac{\tau^{\gamma_1-1}}{\mathfrak{a}_1}\int_0^1 \mathfrak{g}_1(\vartheta,\eta)\, d\mathcal{H}_0(\vartheta),\ \ (\tau,\eta) \in [0,1]\times[0,1], \tag{9}$$

with

$$\mathfrak{g}_1(\tau,\eta) = \frac{1}{\Gamma(\gamma_1)}\begin{cases} \tau^{\gamma_1-1}(1-\eta)^{\gamma_1-1} - (\tau-\eta)^{\gamma_1-1},\ \ 0 \le \eta \le \tau \le 1, \\ \tau^{\gamma_1-1}(1-\eta)^{\gamma_1-1},\ \ 0 \le \tau \le \eta \le 1, \end{cases} \tag{10}$$

and

$$\mathcal{G}_2(\tau,\eta) = \mathfrak{g}_2(\tau,\eta) + \frac{\tau^{\delta_1-1}}{\mathfrak{a}_2}\sum_{i=1}^{n}\left(\int_0^1 \mathfrak{g}_{2i}(\vartheta,\eta)\, d\mathcal{H}_i(\vartheta)\right),\ \ (\tau,\eta) \in [0,1]\times[0,1], \tag{11}$$

with

$$\begin{aligned} \mathfrak{g}_2(\tau,\eta) &= \frac{1}{\Gamma(\delta_1)}\begin{cases} \tau^{\delta_1-1}(1-\eta)^{\delta_1-\alpha_0-1} - (\tau-\eta)^{\delta_1-1},\ \ 0 \le \eta \le \tau \le 1, \\ \tau^{\delta_1-1}(1-\eta)^{\delta_1-\alpha_0-1},\ \ 0 \le \tau \le \eta \le 1, \end{cases} \\ \mathfrak{g}_{2i}(\tau,\eta) &= \frac{1}{\Gamma(\delta_1-\alpha_i)}\begin{cases} \tau^{\delta_1-\alpha_i-1}(1-\eta)^{\delta_1-\alpha_0-1} - (\tau-\eta)^{\delta_1-\alpha_i-1},\ \ 0 \le \eta \le \tau \le 1, \\ \tau^{\delta_1-\alpha_i-1}(1-\eta)^{\delta_1-\alpha_0-1},\ \ 0 \le \tau \le \eta \le 1, \end{cases} \\ i &= 1,\dots,n. \end{aligned} \tag{12}$$

Proof. We denote by $\varphi_{r_1}(D_{0+}^{\delta_1}u(\tau)) = \phi_1(\tau)$, $\tau \in (0,1)$. Hence problems (5) and (6) are equivalent to the following two boundary value problems

$$(I)\qquad \begin{cases} D_{0+}^{\gamma_1}\phi_1(\tau) = x(\tau),\ \ \tau \in (0,1), \\ \phi_1(0) = 0,\ \ \phi_1(1) = \int_0^1 \phi_1(\eta)\, d\mathcal{H}_0(\eta), \end{cases}$$

and

$$(II)\qquad \begin{cases} D_{0+}^{\delta_1}u(\tau) = \varphi_{\varrho_1}(\phi_1(\tau)),\ \ \tau \in (0,1), \\ u^{(j)}(0) = 0,\ \ j = 0,\dots,p-2,\ \ D_{0+}^{\alpha_0}u(1) = \sum_{k=1}^{n}\int_0^1 D_{0+}^{\alpha_k}u(\eta)\, d\mathcal{H}_k(\eta). \end{cases}$$

By using Lemma 4.1.5 from [14], the unique solution $\phi_1 \in C[0,1]$ of problem (I) is

$$\phi_1(\tau) = -\int_0^1 \mathcal{G}_1(\tau,\vartheta)x(\vartheta)\,d\vartheta, \ \ \tau \in [0,1], \tag{13}$$

where $\mathcal{G}_1$ is given by (9). By using Lemma 2.4.2 from [12], the unique solution $u \in C[0,1]$ of problem (II) is

$$u(\tau) = -\int_0^1 \mathcal{G}_2(\tau,\eta)\varphi_{\varrho_1}(\phi_1(\eta))\,d\eta, \ \ \tau \in [0,1], \tag{14}$$

where $\mathcal{G}_2$ is given by (11). Combining the relations (13) and (14) we obtain the solution u of problem (5) and (6) which is given by relation (8). □

We consider now the fractional differential equation

$$D_{0+}^{\gamma_2}\Big(\varphi_{r_2}\Big(D_{0+}^{\delta_2}v(\tau)\Big)\Big) = y(\tau), \ \ \tau \in (0,1), \tag{15}$$

where $y \in C(0,1) \cap L^1(0,1)$, with the boundary conditions

$$\begin{cases} v^{(i)}(0) = 0, \ \ i = 0,\ldots,q-2, \ \ D_{0+}^{\delta_2}v(0) = 0, \\ \varphi_{r_2}(D_{0+}^{\delta_2}v(1)) = \int_0^1 \varphi_{r_2}(D_{0+}^{\delta_2}v(\eta))\,d\mathcal{K}_0(\eta), \ \ D_{0+}^{\beta_0}v(1) = \sum_{k=1}^{m}\int_0^1 D_{0+}^{\beta_k}v(\eta)\,d\mathcal{K}_k(\eta). \end{cases} \tag{16}$$

We denote by

$$\mathfrak{b}_1 = 1 - \int_0^1 \eta^{\gamma_2-1}\,d\mathcal{K}_0(\eta), \ \ \mathfrak{b}_2 = \frac{\Gamma(\delta_2)}{\Gamma(\delta_2-\beta_0)} - \sum_{i=1}^{m}\frac{\Gamma(\delta_2)}{\Gamma(\delta_2-\beta_i)}\int_0^1 \eta^{\delta_2-\beta_i-1}\,d\mathcal{K}_i(\eta). \tag{17}$$

Similar to Lemma 1 we obtain the next result.

Lemma 2. *If $\mathfrak{b}_1 \neq 0$ and $\mathfrak{b}_2 \neq 0$, then the unique solution $v \in C[0,1]$ of problem (15) and (16) is given by*

$$v(\tau) = \int_0^1 \mathcal{G}_4(\tau,\eta)\varphi_{\varrho_2}\Big(\int_0^1 \mathcal{G}_3(\eta,\vartheta)y(\vartheta)\,d\vartheta\Big)d\eta, \ \ \tau \in [0,1], \tag{18}$$

where

$$\mathcal{G}_3(\tau,\eta) = \mathfrak{g}_3(\tau,\eta) + \frac{\tau^{\gamma_2-1}}{\mathfrak{b}_1}\int_0^1 \mathfrak{g}_3(\vartheta,\eta)\,d\mathcal{K}_0(\vartheta), \ \ (\tau,\eta) \in [0,1]\times[0,1], \tag{19}$$

with

$$\mathfrak{g}_3(\tau,\eta) = \frac{1}{\Gamma(\gamma_2)}\begin{cases} \tau^{\gamma_2-1}(1-\eta)^{\gamma_2-1} - (\tau-\eta)^{\gamma_2-1}, \ \ 0 \le \eta \le \tau \le 1, \\ \tau^{\gamma_2-1}(1-\eta)^{\gamma_2-1}, \ \ 0 \le \tau \le \eta \le 1, \end{cases} \tag{20}$$

and

$$\mathcal{G}_4(\tau,\eta) = \mathfrak{g}_4(\tau,\eta) + \frac{\tau^{\delta_2-1}}{\mathfrak{b}_2}\sum_{i=1}^{m}\Big(\int_0^1 \mathfrak{g}_{4i}(\vartheta,\eta)\,d\mathcal{K}_i(\vartheta)\Big), \ \ (\tau,\eta) \in [0,1]\times[0,1], \tag{21}$$

with

$$\begin{aligned} \mathfrak{g}_4(\tau,\eta) &= \frac{1}{\Gamma(\delta_2)}\begin{cases} \tau^{\delta_2-1}(1-\eta)^{\delta_2-\beta_0-1} - (\tau-\eta)^{\delta_2-1}, \ \ 0 \le \eta \le \tau \le 1, \\ \tau^{\delta_2-1}(1-\eta)^{\delta_2-\beta_0-1}, \ \ 0 \le \tau \le \eta \le 1, \end{cases} \\ \mathfrak{g}_{4i}(\tau,\eta) &= \frac{1}{\Gamma(\delta_2-\beta_i)}\begin{cases} \tau^{\delta_2-\beta_i-1}(1-\eta)^{\delta_2-\beta_0-1} - (\tau-\eta)^{\delta_2-\beta_i-1}, \ \ 0 \le \eta \le \tau \le 1, \\ \tau^{\delta_2-\beta_i-1}(1-\eta)^{\delta_2-\beta_0-1}, \ \ 0 \le \tau \le \eta \le 1, \end{cases} \\ i &= 1,\ldots,m. \end{aligned} \tag{22}$$

Lemma 3. *We assume that* $\mathfrak{a}_1, \mathfrak{a}_2, \mathfrak{b}_1, \mathfrak{b}_2 > 0$*,* $\mathcal{H}_i$*,* $i = 0, \ldots, n$*, and* $\mathcal{K}_j$*,* $j = 0, \ldots, m$ *are non-decreasing functions. Then the functions* $\mathcal{G}_i$*,* $i = 1, \ldots, 4$ *given by (9), (11), (19) and (21) have the properties*

(a) $\mathcal{G}_i : [0,1] \times [0,1] \to [0, \infty)$*,* $i = 1, \ldots, 4$ *are continuous functions;*

(b) $\mathcal{G}_1(\tau, \eta) \le \mathcal{J}_1(\eta)$*,* $\forall (\tau, \eta) \in [0,1] \times [0,1]$*, where*

$$\mathcal{J}_1(\eta) = \mathfrak{h}_1(\eta) + \frac{1}{\mathfrak{a}_1} \int_0^1 \mathfrak{g}_1(\vartheta, \eta)\, d\mathcal{H}_0(\vartheta), \ \forall \eta \in [0,1],$$

with $\mathfrak{h}_1(\eta) = \frac{1}{\Gamma(\gamma_1)}(1-\eta)^{\gamma_1 - 1}$*,* $\eta \in [0,1]$*;*

(c) $\mathcal{G}_2(\tau, \eta) \le \mathcal{J}_2(\eta)$*,* $\forall (\tau, \eta) \in [0,1] \times [0,1]$*, where*

$$\mathcal{J}_2(\eta) = \mathfrak{h}_2(\eta) + \frac{1}{\mathfrak{a}_2} \sum_{i=1}^{n} \int_0^1 \mathfrak{g}_{2i}(\vartheta, \eta)\, d\mathcal{H}_i(\vartheta), \ \forall \eta \in [0,1],$$

with $\mathfrak{h}_2(\eta) = \frac{1}{\Gamma(\delta_1)}(1-\eta)^{\delta_1 - \alpha_0 - 1}(1 - (1-\eta)^{\alpha_0})$*,* $\eta \in [0,1]$*;*

(d) $\mathcal{G}_2(\tau, \eta) \ge \tau^{\delta_1 - 1}\mathcal{J}_2(\eta)$*,* $\forall (\tau, \eta) \in [0,1] \times [0,1]$*;*

(e) $\mathcal{G}_3(\tau, \eta) \le \mathcal{J}_3(\eta)$*,* $\forall (\tau, \eta) \in [0,1] \times [0,1]$*, where*

$$\mathcal{J}_3(\eta) = \mathfrak{h}_3(\eta) + \frac{1}{\mathfrak{b}_1} \int_0^1 \mathfrak{g}_3(\vartheta, \eta)\, d\mathcal{K}_0(\vartheta), \ \forall \eta \in [0,1],$$

with $\mathfrak{h}_3(\eta) = \frac{1}{\Gamma(\gamma_2)}(1-\eta)^{\gamma_2 - 1}$*,* $\eta \in [0,1]$*;*

(f) $\mathcal{G}_4(\tau, \eta) \le \mathcal{J}_4(\eta)$*,* $\forall (\tau, \eta) \in [0,1] \times [0,1]$*, where*

$$\mathcal{J}_4(\eta) = \mathfrak{h}_4(\eta) + \frac{1}{\mathfrak{b}_2} \sum_{i=1}^{m} \int_0^1 \mathfrak{g}_{4i}(\vartheta, \eta)\, d\mathcal{K}_i(\vartheta), \ \forall \eta \in [0,1],$$

with $\mathfrak{h}_4(\eta) = \frac{1}{\Gamma(\delta_2)}(1-\eta)^{\delta_2 - \beta_0 - 1}(1 - (1-\eta)^{\beta_0})$*,* $\eta \in [0,1]$*;*

(g) $\mathcal{G}_4(\tau, \eta) \ge \tau^{\delta_2 - 1}\mathcal{J}_4(\eta)$*,* $\forall (\tau, \eta) \in [0,1] \times [0,1]$*.*

Proof. (a) Based on the continuity of functions $\mathfrak{g}_1, \mathfrak{g}_2, \mathfrak{g}_{2i}$, $i = 1, \ldots, n$, $\mathfrak{g}_3$, $\mathfrak{g}_4$, $\mathfrak{g}_{4i}$, $i = 1, \ldots, m$ (given by (10), (12), (20) and (22)), we obtain that the functions $\mathcal{G}_i$, $i = 1, \ldots, 4$ are continuous.

(b) By the definition of $\mathfrak{g}_1$ we find

$$\begin{aligned} \mathcal{G}_1(\tau, \eta) &\le \frac{1}{\Gamma(\gamma_1)}(1-\eta)^{\gamma_1 - 1} + \frac{1}{\mathfrak{a}_1} \int_0^1 \mathfrak{g}_1(\vartheta, \eta)\, d\mathcal{H}_0(\vartheta) \\ &= \mathfrak{h}_1(\eta) + \frac{1}{\mathfrak{a}_1} \int_0^1 \mathfrak{g}_1(\vartheta, \eta)\, d\mathcal{H}_0(\vartheta) = \mathcal{J}_1(\eta), \ \forall \tau, \eta \in [0,1]. \end{aligned}$$

(c–d) Using our assumptions and the properties of function $\mathfrak{g}_2$ from Lemma 2.1.3 from [12], namely $\mathfrak{g}_2(\tau, \eta) \le \frac{1}{\Gamma(\delta_1)}(1-\eta)^{\delta_1 - \alpha_0 - 1}(1 - (1-\eta)^{\alpha_0}) = \mathfrak{h}_2(\eta)$ and $\mathfrak{g}_2(\tau, \eta) \ge \tau^{\delta_1 - 1}\mathfrak{h}_2(\eta)$ for all τ, $\eta \in [0,1]$, we deduce

$$\begin{aligned} &\mathcal{G}_2(\tau, \eta) \le \mathfrak{h}_2(\eta) + \frac{1}{\mathfrak{a}_2} \sum_{i=1}^{n} \int_0^1 \mathfrak{g}_{2i}(\vartheta, \eta)\, d\mathcal{H}_i(\vartheta) = \mathcal{J}_2(\eta), \\ &\mathcal{G}_2(\tau, \eta) \ge \tau^{\delta_1 - 1}\left(\mathfrak{h}_2(\eta) + \frac{1}{\mathfrak{a}_2} \sum_{i=1}^{n} \mathfrak{g}_{2i}(\vartheta, \eta)\, d\mathcal{H}_i(\vartheta) \right) = \tau^{\delta_1 - 1}\mathcal{J}_2(\eta), \ \forall \tau, \eta \in [0,1]. \end{aligned}$$

(e) By the definition of $\mathfrak{g}_3$ we obtain

$$\begin{aligned}\mathcal{G}_3(\tau,\eta) &\le \frac{1}{\Gamma(\gamma_2)}(1-\eta)^{\gamma_2-1} + \frac{1}{\mathfrak{b}_1}\int_0^1 \mathfrak{g}_3(\vartheta,\eta)\,d\mathcal{K}_0(\vartheta)\\ &= \mathfrak{h}_3(\eta) + \frac{1}{\mathfrak{b}_1}\int_0^1 \mathfrak{g}_3(\vartheta,\eta)\,d\mathcal{K}_0(\vartheta) = \mathcal{J}_3(\eta),\ \ \forall\,\tau,\eta\in[0,1].\end{aligned}$$

(f–g) Using the assumptions of this lemma and the properties of function $\mathfrak{g}_4$ from Lemma 2.1.3 from [12], namely $\mathfrak{g}_4(\tau,\eta) \le \frac{1}{\Gamma(\delta_2)}(1-\eta)^{\delta_2-\beta_0-1}(1-(1-\eta)^{\beta_0}) = \mathfrak{h}_4(\eta)$ and $\mathfrak{g}_4(\tau,\eta) \ge \tau^{\delta_2-1}\mathfrak{h}_4(\eta)$ for all $\tau,\ \eta\in[0,1]$, we find

$$\begin{aligned}&\mathcal{G}_4(\tau,\eta) \le \mathfrak{h}_4(\eta) + \frac{1}{\mathfrak{b}_2}\sum_{i=1}^m \int_0^1 \mathfrak{g}_{4i}(\vartheta,\eta)\,d\mathcal{K}_i(\vartheta) = \mathcal{J}_4(\eta),\\ &\mathcal{G}_4(\tau,\eta) \ge \tau^{\delta_2-1}\left(\mathfrak{h}_4(\eta) + \frac{1}{\mathfrak{b}_2}\sum_{i=1}^m \mathfrak{g}_{4i}(\vartheta,\eta)\,d\mathcal{K}_i(\vartheta)\right) = \tau^{\delta_2-1}\mathcal{J}_4(\eta),\ \ \forall\,\tau,\eta\in[0,1].\end{aligned}$$

□

Lemma 4. *We assume that* $\mathfrak{a}_1,\mathfrak{a}_2,\mathfrak{b}_1,\mathfrak{b}_2 > 0$, $\mathcal{H}_i$, $i=0,\dots,n$, *and* $\mathcal{K}_j$, $j=0,\dots,m$ *are nondecreasing functions,* $x,y\in C(0,1)\cap L^1(0,1)$ *with* $x(\tau)\ge 0$, $y(\tau)\ge 0$ *for all* $\tau\in(0,1)$. *Then the solutions* u *and* v *of problems (5), (6) and (15), (16), respectively, satisfy the inequalities* $u(\tau)\ge 0$, $v(\tau)\ge 0$ *for all* $\tau\in[0,1]$ *and* $u(\tau)\ge \tau^{\delta_1-1}u(s)$ *and* $v(\tau)\ge\tau^{\delta_2-1}v(s)$ *for all* $\tau,s\in[0,1]$.

Proof. Based on the assumptions of this lemma, we obtain that the solutions u and v of problems (5), (6) and (15), (16), respectively, are nonnegative, that is $u(\tau)\ge 0$, $v(\tau)\ge 0$ for all $\tau\in[0,1]$. In addition, by using Lemma 3, we deduce

$$\begin{aligned}u(\tau) &\ge \tau^{\delta_1-1}\int_0^1 \mathcal{J}_2(\eta)\varphi_{\varrho_1}\left(\int_0^1 \mathcal{G}_1(\eta,\vartheta)x(\vartheta)\,d\vartheta\right)d\eta\\ &\ge \tau^{\delta_1-1}\int_0^1 \mathcal{G}_2(s,\eta)\varphi_{\varrho_1}\left(\int_0^1 \mathcal{G}_1(\eta,\vartheta)x(\vartheta)\,d\vartheta\right)d\eta\\ &= \tau^{\delta_1-1}u(s),\\ v(\tau) &\ge \tau^{\delta_2-1}\int_0^1 \mathcal{J}_4(\eta)\varphi_{\varrho_2}\left(\int_0^1 \mathcal{G}_3(\eta,\vartheta)y(\vartheta)\,d\vartheta\right)d\eta\\ &\ge \tau^{\delta_2-1}\int_0^1 \mathcal{G}_4(s,\eta)\varphi_{\varrho_2}\left(\int_0^1 \mathcal{G}_3(\eta,\vartheta)y(\vartheta)\,d\vartheta\right)d\eta\\ &= \tau^{\delta_2-1}v(s),\end{aligned}$$

for all $\tau,\ s\in[0,1]$. □

We present finally in this section the Guo–Krasnosel'skii fixed point theorem, which we will use in the proofs of our main results.

Theorem 1. *([16]). Let* $\mathcal{X}$ *be a real Banach space with the norm* $\|\cdot\|$, *and let* $\mathcal{C}\subset X$ *be a cone in* $\mathcal{X}$. *Assume* Ω_1 *and* Ω_2 *are bounded open subsets of* $\mathcal{X}$ *with* $0\in\Omega_1$, $\overline{\Omega}_1\subset\Omega_2$ *and let* $\mathcal{A}:\mathcal{C}\cap(\overline{\Omega}_2\setminus\Omega_1)\to\mathcal{C}$ *be a completely continuous operator such that, either*

(i) $\|\mathcal{A}u\|\le\|u\|,\ \forall\,u\in\mathcal{C}\cap\partial\Omega_1,$ *and* $\|\mathcal{A}u\|\ge\|u\|,\ \forall\,u\in\mathcal{C}\cap\partial\Omega_2$; *or*

(ii) $\|\mathcal{A}u\|\ge\|u\|,\ \forall\,u\in\mathcal{C}\cap\partial\Omega_1,$ *and* $\|\mathcal{A}u\|\le\|u\|,\ \forall\,u\in\mathcal{C}\cap\partial\Omega_2$.

Then $\mathcal{A}$ *has at least one fixed point in* $\mathcal{C}\cap(\overline{\Omega}_2\setminus\Omega_1)$.

3. Existence of Positive Solutions

According to Lemmas 1 and 2, the pair of functions (u,v) is a solution of problem (1) and (2) if and only if (u,v) is a solution of the system

$$\begin{cases} u(\tau) = \int_0^1 \mathcal{G}_2(\tau,\zeta)\varphi_{\varrho_1}\left(\int_0^1 \mathcal{G}_1(\zeta,\vartheta)f(\vartheta,u(\vartheta),v(\vartheta),I_{0+}^{\sigma_1}u(\vartheta),I_{0+}^{\sigma_2}v(\vartheta))d\vartheta\right)d\zeta, \\ v(\tau) = \int_0^1 \mathcal{G}_4(\tau,\zeta)\varphi_{\varrho_2}\left(\int_0^1 \mathcal{G}_3(\zeta,\vartheta)g(\vartheta,u(\vartheta),v(\vartheta),I_{0+}^{\varsigma_1}u(\vartheta),I_{0+}^{\varsigma_2}v(\vartheta))d\vartheta\right)d\zeta, \end{cases}$$

for all $\tau \in [0,1]$. We introduce the Banach space $\mathcal{X} = C[0,1]$ with supreme norm $\|u\| = \sup_{\tau\in[0,1]}|u(\tau)|$, and the Banach space $\mathcal{Y} = \mathcal{X}\times\mathcal{X}$ with the norm $\|(u,v)\|_{\mathcal{Y}} = \|u\| + \|v\|$. We define the cone

$$\mathcal{P} = \{(u,v) \in \mathcal{Y},\ u(\tau) \geq 0,\ v(\tau) \geq 0,\ \forall\,\tau \in [0,1]\}.$$

We also define the operators $\mathcal{A}_1, \mathcal{A}_2 : \mathcal{Y} \to \mathcal{X}$ and $\mathcal{A} : \mathcal{Y} \to \mathcal{Y}$ by

$$\begin{aligned} \mathcal{A}_1(u,v)(\tau) &= \int_0^1 \mathcal{G}_2(\tau,\zeta)\varphi_{\varrho_1}\left(\int_0^1 \mathcal{G}_1(\zeta,\vartheta)f(\vartheta,u(\vartheta),v(\vartheta),I_{0+}^{\sigma_1}u(\vartheta),I_{0+}^{\sigma_2}v(\vartheta))d\vartheta\right)d\zeta, \\ \mathcal{A}_2(u,v)(\tau) &= \int_0^1 \mathcal{G}_4(\tau,\zeta)\varphi_{\varrho_2}\left(\int_0^1 \mathcal{G}_3(\zeta,\vartheta)g(\vartheta,u(\vartheta),v(\vartheta),I_{0+}^{\varsigma_1}u(\vartheta),I_{0+}^{\varsigma_2}v(\vartheta))d\vartheta\right)d\zeta, \end{aligned}$$

for $\tau \in [0,1]$ and $(u,v) \in \mathcal{Y}$, and $\mathcal{A}(u,v) = (\mathcal{A}_1(u,v), \mathcal{A}_2(u,v))$, $(u,v) \in \mathcal{Y}$. We see that (u,v) is a solution of problem (1) and (2) if and only if (u,v) is a fixed point of operator $\mathcal{A}$.

We introduce now the basic assumptions that we will use in this section.

- $(I1)$ $\gamma_1,\gamma_2 \in (1,2]$, $\delta_1 \in (p-1,p]$, $p \in \mathbb{N}$, $p \geq 3$, $\delta_2 \in (q-1,q]$, $q \in \mathbb{N}$, $q \geq 3$, $n,m \in \mathbb{N}$, $\sigma_1,\sigma_2,\varsigma_1,\varsigma_2 > 0$, $\alpha_j \in \mathbb{R}$, $j = 0,\dots,n$, $0 \leq \alpha_1 < \alpha_2 < \cdots < \alpha_n \leq \alpha_0 < \delta_1 - 1$, $\alpha_0 \geq 1$, $\beta_j \in \mathbb{R}$, $j = 0,\dots,m$, $0 \leq \beta_1 < \beta_2 < \cdots < \beta_m \leq \beta_0 < \delta_2 - 1$, $\beta_0 \geq 1$, $\varphi_{r_i}(\tau) = |\tau|^{r_i-2}\tau$, $\varphi_{r_i}^{-1} = \varphi_{\varrho_i}$, $\varrho_i = \frac{r_i}{r_i-1}$, $i = 1,2$, $r_i > 1$, $i = 1,2$, $\mathcal{H}_i : [0,1] \to \mathbb{R}$, $i = 0,\dots,n$, and $\mathcal{K}_j : [0,1] \to \mathbb{R}$, $j = 0,\dots,m$ are nondecreasing functions, $\mathfrak{a}_1, \mathfrak{a}_2, \mathfrak{b}_1, \mathfrak{b}_2 > 0$ (given by (7) and (17)).
- $(I2)$ The functions $f,g \in C((0,1)\times\mathbb{R}_+^4, \mathbb{R}_+)$ and there exist the functions $\psi_1,\psi_2 \in C((0,1),\mathbb{R}_+)$ and $\chi_1,\chi_2 \in C([0,1]\times\mathbb{R}_+^4,\mathbb{R}_+)$ with $\Lambda_1 = \int_0^1 (1-\tau)^{\gamma_1-1}\psi_1(\tau)\,d\tau \in (0,\infty)$, $\Lambda_2 = \int_0^1 (1-\tau)^{\gamma_2-1}\psi_2(\tau)\,d\tau \in (0,\infty)$, such that

$$\begin{aligned} f(\tau,z_1,z_2,z_3,z_4) &\leq \psi_1(\tau)\chi_1(\tau,z_1,z_2,z_3,z_4), \\ g(\tau,z_1,z_2,z_3,z_4) &\leq \psi_2(\tau)\chi_2(\tau,z_1,z_2,z_3,z_4), \end{aligned}$$

for any $\tau \in (0,1)$, $z_i \in \mathbb{R}_+$, $i = 1,\dots,4$.

Lemma 5. *We assume that assumptions $(I1)$ and $(I2)$ are satisfied. Then operator $\mathcal{A} : \mathcal{P} \to \mathcal{P}$ is completely continuous.*

Proof. We denote by $M_1 = \int_0^1 \mathcal{J}_1(\eta)\psi_1(\eta)\,d\eta$, $M_2 = \int_0^1 \mathcal{J}_3(\eta)\psi_2(\eta)\,d\eta$. By using $(I2)$ and Lemma 3, we deduce that $M_1 > 0$ and $M_2 > 0$. In addition we find

$$M_1 = \int_0^1 \mathcal{J}_1(\eta)\psi_1(\eta)\,d\eta = \int_0^1 \left(\mathfrak{h}_1(\eta) + \frac{1}{\mathfrak{a}_1}\int_0^1 \mathfrak{g}_1(\zeta,\eta)\,d\mathcal{H}_0(\zeta)\right)\psi_1(\eta)\,d\eta$$
$$\leq \frac{1}{\Gamma(\gamma_1)}\int_0^1 (1-\eta)^{\gamma_1-1}\psi_1(\eta)\,d\eta + \frac{1}{\mathfrak{a}_1}\int_0^1\left(\int_0^1 \frac{1}{\Gamma(\gamma_1)}\zeta^{\gamma_1-1}(1-\eta)^{\gamma_1-1}\,d\mathcal{H}_0(\zeta)\right)\psi_1(\eta)d\eta$$
$$= \left[1+\frac{1}{\mathfrak{a}_1}\left(\int_0^1 \zeta^{\gamma_1-1}\,d\mathcal{H}_0(\zeta)\right)\right]\frac{1}{\Gamma(\gamma_1)}\int_0^1 (1-\eta)^{\gamma_1-1}\psi_1(\eta)\,d\eta < \infty,$$
$$M_2 = \int_0^1 \mathcal{J}_3(\eta)\psi_2(\eta)\,d\eta = \int_0^1 \left(\mathfrak{h}_3(\eta) + \frac{1}{\mathfrak{b}_1}\int_0^1 \mathfrak{g}_3(\zeta,\eta)\,d\mathcal{K}_0(\zeta)\right)\psi_2(\eta)\,d\eta$$
$$\leq \frac{1}{\Gamma(\gamma_2)}\int_0^1 (1-\eta)^{\gamma_2-1}\psi_2(\eta)\,d\eta + \frac{1}{\mathfrak{b}_1}\int_0^1\left(\int_0^1 \frac{1}{\Gamma(\gamma_2)}\zeta^{\gamma_2-1}(1-\eta)^{\gamma_2-1}\,d\mathcal{K}_0(\zeta)\right)\psi_2(\eta)d\eta$$
$$= \left[1+\frac{1}{\mathfrak{b}_1}\left(\int_0^1 \zeta^{\gamma_2-1}\,d\mathcal{K}_0(\zeta)\right)\right]\frac{1}{\Gamma(\gamma_2)}\int_0^1 (1-\eta)^{\gamma_2-1}\psi_2(\eta)\,d\eta < \infty.$$

Also, by Lemma 3 we conclude that $\mathcal{A}$ maps $\mathcal{P}$ into $\mathcal{P}$.

We will prove that $\mathcal{A}$ maps bounded sets into relatively compact sets. Let $\mathcal{E} \subset \mathcal{P}$ be an arbitrary bounded set. Then there exists $\Xi_1 > 0$ such that $\|(u,v)\|_{\mathcal{Y}} \leq \Xi_1$ for all $(u,v) \in \mathcal{E}$. By the continuity of χ_1 and χ_2, we deduce that there exists $\Xi_2 > 0$ such that $\Xi_2 = \max\{\sup_{\tau\in[0,1],z_i\in[0,\omega],i=1,\ldots,4}\chi_1(\tau,z_1,z_2,z_3,z_4), \sup_{\tau\in[0,1],z_i\in[0,\omega],i=1,\ldots,4}\chi_2(\tau,z_1,z_2,z_3,z_4)\}$, where $\omega = \Xi_1 \max\left\{1, \frac{1}{\Gamma(\sigma_1+1)}, \frac{1}{\Gamma(\sigma_2+1)}, \frac{1}{\Gamma(\varsigma_1+1)}, \frac{1}{\Gamma(\varsigma_2+1)}\right\}$. Based on the inequality $|I_{0+}^{\xi}w(\eta)| \leq \frac{\|w\|}{\Gamma(\xi+1)}$, for $\xi > 0$ and $w \in C[0,1]$, and by Lemma 3, we find for any $(u,v) \in \mathcal{E}$ and $\eta \in [0,1]$

$$\mathcal{A}_1(u,v)(\eta) \leq \int_0^1 \mathcal{J}_2(\zeta)\varphi_{\varrho_1}\left(\int_0^1 \mathcal{J}_1(\tau)\psi_1(\tau)\chi_1(\tau,u(\tau),v(\tau),I_{0+}^{\sigma_1}u(\tau),I_{0+}^{\sigma_2}v(\tau))d\tau\right)d\zeta$$
$$\leq \Xi_2^{\varrho_1-1}\varphi_{\varrho_1}\left(\int_0^1 \mathcal{J}_1(\tau)\psi_1(\tau)\,d\tau\right)\int_0^1 \mathcal{J}_2(\zeta)\,d\zeta = M_1^{\varrho_1-1}\Xi_2^{\varrho_1-1}M_3,$$
$$\mathcal{A}_2(u,v)(\eta) \leq \int_0^1 \mathcal{J}_4(\zeta)\varphi_{\varrho_2}\left(\int_0^1 \mathcal{J}_3(\tau)\psi_2(\tau)\chi_2(\tau,u(\tau),v(\tau),I_{0+}^{\varsigma_1}u(\tau),I_{0+}^{\varsigma_2}v(\tau))d\tau\right)d\zeta$$
$$\leq \Xi_2^{\varrho_2-1}\varphi_{\varrho_2}\left(\int_0^1 \mathcal{J}_3(\tau)\psi_2(\tau)\,d\tau\right)\int_0^1 \mathcal{J}_4(\zeta)\,d\zeta = M_2^{\varrho_2-1}\Xi_2^{\varrho_2-1}M_4,$$

where $M_3 = \int_0^1 \mathcal{J}_2(\zeta)\,d\zeta$ and $M_4 = \int_0^1 \mathcal{J}_4(\zeta)\,d\zeta$.

Then $\|\mathcal{A}_1(u,v)\| \leq M_1^{\varrho_1-1}\Xi_2^{\varrho_1-1}M_3$, $\|\mathcal{A}_2(u,v)\| \leq M_2^{\varrho_2-1}\Xi_2^{\varrho_2-1}M_4$ for all $(u,v) \in \mathcal{E}$, and $\|\mathcal{A}(u,v)\|_{\mathcal{Y}} \leq M_1^{\varrho_1-1}\Xi_2^{\varrho_1-1}M_3 + M_2^{\varrho_2-1}\Xi_2^{\varrho_2-1}M_4$ for all $(u,v) \in \mathcal{E}$, that is $\mathcal{A}_1(\mathcal{E})$, $\mathcal{A}_2(\mathcal{E})$ and $\mathcal{A}(\mathcal{E})$ are bounded.

We will show that $\mathcal{A}(\mathcal{E})$ is equicontinuous. By using Lemma 1, for $(u,v) \in \mathcal{E}$ and $\eta \in [0,1]$ we obtain

$$\mathcal{A}_1(u,v)(\eta) = \int_0^1 \left(\mathfrak{g}_2(\eta,\zeta) + \frac{\eta^{\delta_1-1}}{\mathfrak{a}_2}\sum_{i=1}^n\left(\int_0^1 \mathfrak{g}_{2i}(\tau,\zeta)\,d\mathcal{H}_i(\tau)\right)\right)\varphi_{\varrho_1}\left(\int_0^1 \mathcal{G}_1(\zeta,\vartheta)\right.$$
$$\left.\times f(\vartheta,u(\vartheta),v(\vartheta),I_{0+}^{\sigma_1}u(\vartheta),I_{0+}^{\sigma_2}v(\vartheta))\,d\vartheta\right)d\zeta$$
$$= \int_0^\eta \frac{1}{\Gamma(\delta_1)}[\eta^{\delta_1-1}(1-\zeta)^{\delta_1-\alpha_0-1} - (\eta-\zeta)^{\delta_1-1}]$$
$$\times\varphi_{\varrho_1}\left(\int_0^1 \mathcal{G}_1(\zeta,\vartheta)f(\vartheta,u(\vartheta),v(\vartheta),I_{0+}^{\sigma_1}u(\vartheta),I_{0+}^{\sigma_2}v(\vartheta))\,d\vartheta\right)d\zeta$$
$$+\int_\eta^1 \frac{1}{\Gamma(\delta_1)}\eta^{\delta_1-1}(1-\zeta)^{\delta_1-\alpha_0-1}\varphi_{\varrho_1}\left(\int_0^1 \mathcal{G}_1(\zeta,\vartheta)f(\vartheta,u(\vartheta),v(\vartheta),\right.$$
$$\left.I_{0+}^{\sigma_1}u(\vartheta),I_{0+}^{\sigma_2}v(\vartheta))\,d\vartheta\right)d\zeta$$
$$+\frac{\eta^{\delta_1-1}}{\mathfrak{a}_2}\int_0^1\sum_{i=1}^n\left(\int_0^1 \mathfrak{g}_{2i}(\tau,\zeta)\,d\mathcal{H}_i(\tau)\right)\varphi_{\varrho_1}\left(\int_0^1 \mathcal{G}_1(\zeta,\vartheta)f(\vartheta,u(\vartheta),v(\vartheta),\right.$$
$$\left.I_{0+}^{\sigma_1}u(\vartheta),I_{0+}^{\sigma_2}v(\vartheta))\,d\vartheta\right)d\zeta.$$

Then for any $\eta \in (0,1)$ we deduce

$$(\mathcal{A}_1(u,v))'(\eta) = \int_0^\eta \frac{1}{\Gamma(\delta_1)}[(\delta_1-1)\eta^{\delta_1-2}(1-\zeta)^{\delta_1-\alpha_0-1} - (\delta_1-1)(\eta-\zeta)^{\delta_1-2}]$$
$$\times\varphi_{\varrho_1}\left(\int_0^1 \mathcal{G}_1(\zeta,\vartheta)f(\vartheta,u(\vartheta),v(\vartheta),I_{0+}^{\sigma_1}u(\vartheta),I_{0+}^{\sigma_2}v(\vartheta))\,d\vartheta\right)d\zeta$$
$$+\int_\eta^1 \frac{1}{\Gamma(\delta_1)}(\delta_1-1)\eta^{\delta_1-2}(1-\zeta)^{\delta_1-\alpha_0-1}\varphi_{\varrho_1}\left(\int_0^1 \mathcal{G}_1(\zeta,\vartheta)f(\vartheta,u(\vartheta),v(\vartheta),\right.$$
$$\left.I_{0+}^{\sigma_1}u(\vartheta),I_{0+}^{\sigma_2}v(\vartheta))\,d\vartheta\right)d\zeta$$
$$+\frac{(\delta_1-1)\eta^{\delta_1-2}}{\mathfrak{a}_2}\int_0^1\sum_{i=1}^n\left(\int_0^1 \mathfrak{g}_{2i}(\tau,\zeta)\,d\mathcal{H}_i(\tau)\right)\varphi_{\varrho_1}\left(\int_0^1 \mathcal{G}_1(\zeta,\vartheta)f(\vartheta,u(\vartheta),v(\vartheta),\right.$$
$$\left.I_{0+}^{\sigma_1}u(\vartheta),I_{0+}^{\sigma_2}v(\vartheta))\,d\vartheta\right)d\zeta.$$

So for any $\eta \in (0,1)$ we find

$$|(\mathcal{A}_1(u,v))'(\eta)| \le \frac{1}{\Gamma(\delta_1-1)}\int_0^\eta [\eta^{\delta_1-2}(1-\zeta)^{\delta_1-\alpha_0-1}+(\eta-\zeta)^{\delta_1-2}]$$
$$\times\varphi_{\varrho_1}\left(\int_0^1 \mathcal{J}_1(\vartheta)\psi_1(\vartheta)\chi_1(\vartheta,u(\vartheta),v(\vartheta),I_{0+}^{\sigma_1}u(\vartheta),I_{0+}^{\sigma_2}v(\vartheta))\,d\vartheta\right)d\zeta$$
$$+\frac{1}{\Gamma(\delta_1-1)}\int_\eta^1 \eta^{\delta_1-2}(1-\zeta)^{\delta_1-\alpha_0-1}\varphi_{\varrho_1}\left(\int_0^1 \mathcal{J}_1(\vartheta)\psi_1(\vartheta)\chi_1(\vartheta,u(\vartheta),v(\vartheta),\right.$$
$$\left.I_{0+}^{\sigma_1}u(\vartheta),I_{0+}^{\sigma_2}v(\vartheta))\,d\vartheta\right)d\zeta$$
$$+\frac{(\delta_1-1)\eta^{\delta_1-2}}{\mathfrak{a}_2}\int_0^1\sum_{i=1}^n\left(\int_0^1 \mathfrak{g}_{2i}(\tau,\zeta)\,d\mathcal{H}_i(\tau)\right)\varphi_{\varrho_1}\left(\int_0^1 \mathcal{J}_1(\vartheta)\chi_1(\vartheta,u(\vartheta),v(\vartheta),\right.$$
$$\left.I_{0+}^{\sigma_1}u(\vartheta),I_{0+}^{\sigma_2}v(\vartheta))\,d\vartheta\right)d\zeta$$
$$\le \Xi_2^{\varrho_1-1}M_1^{\varrho_1-1}\left\{\frac{1}{\Gamma(\delta_1-1)}\int_0^\eta[\eta^{\delta_1-2}(1-\zeta)^{\delta_1-\alpha_0-1}+(\eta-\zeta)^{\delta_1-2}]\,d\zeta\right.$$
$$+\frac{1}{\Gamma(\delta_1-1)}\int_\eta^1\eta^{\delta_1-2}(1-\zeta)^{\delta_1-\alpha_0-1}d\zeta$$
$$\left.+\frac{(\delta_1-1)\eta^{\delta_1-2}}{\mathfrak{a}_2}\int_0^1\sum_{i=1}^n\left(\int_0^1 \mathfrak{g}_{2i}(\tau,\zeta)\,d\mathcal{H}_i(\tau)\right)d\zeta\right\}.$$

Therefore, for $\eta \in (0,1)$ we obtain

$$|(\mathcal{A}_1(u,v))'(\eta)| \le \Xi_2^{\varrho_1-1}M_1^{\varrho_1-1}\left[\frac{1}{\Gamma(\delta_1-1)}\left(\frac{\eta^{\delta_1-2}}{\delta_1-\alpha_0}+\frac{\eta^{\delta_1-1}}{\delta_1-1}\right)\right.$$
$$\left.+\frac{(\delta_1-1)\eta^{\delta_1-2}}{\mathfrak{a}_2}\int_0^1\sum_{i=1}^n\left(\int_0^1\frac{1}{\Gamma(\delta_1-\alpha_i)}(1-\zeta)^{\delta_1-\alpha_0-1}\,d\zeta\right)\tau^{\delta_1-\alpha_i-1}\,d\mathcal{H}_i(\tau)\right]$$
$$=\Xi_2^{\varrho_1-1}M_1^{\varrho_1-1}\left[\frac{1}{\Gamma(\delta_1-1)}\left(\frac{\eta^{\delta_1-2}}{\delta_1-\alpha_0}+\frac{\eta^{\delta_1-1}}{\delta_1-1}\right)+\frac{(\delta_1-1)\eta^{\delta_1-2}}{\mathfrak{a}_2(\delta_1-\alpha_0)}\sum_{i=1}^n\frac{1}{\Gamma(\delta_1-\alpha_i)}\right.$$
$$\left.\times\int_0^1\tau^{\delta_1-\alpha_i-1}\,d\mathcal{H}_i(\tau)\right]. \tag{23}$$

We denote by

$$\Theta_0(\eta) = \frac{1}{\Gamma(\delta_1-1)}\left(\frac{\eta^{\delta_1-2}}{\delta_1-\alpha_0}+\frac{\eta^{\delta_1-1}}{\delta_1-1}\right)$$
$$+\frac{(\delta_1-1)\eta^{\delta_1-2}}{\mathfrak{a}_2(\delta_1-\alpha_0)}\sum_{i=1}^n\frac{1}{\Gamma(\delta_1-\alpha_i)}\int_0^1\tau^{\delta_1-\alpha_i-1}\,d\mathcal{H}_i(\tau),\quad \eta\in(0,1).$$

This function $\Theta_0 \in L^1(0,1)$, because

$$\int_0^1 \Theta_0(\eta)\,d\eta = \frac{1}{\Gamma(\delta_1)}\left(\frac{1}{\delta_1-\alpha_0}+\frac{1}{\delta_1}\right)+\frac{1}{\mathfrak{a}_2(\delta_1-\alpha_0)} \times \sum_{i=1}^{n}\frac{1}{\Gamma(\delta_1-\alpha_i)}\int_0^1 \tau^{\delta_1-\alpha_i-1}\,d\mathcal{H}_i(\tau) < \infty. \quad (24)$$

Then for any $s_1, s_2 \in [0,1]$ with $s_1 < s_2$ and $(u,v) \in \mathcal{E}$, by (23) and (24) we conclude

$$|\mathcal{A}_1(u,v)(s_1) - \mathcal{A}_1(u,v)(s_2)| = \left|\int_{s_1}^{s_2} (\mathcal{A}_1(u,v))'(\tau)\,d\tau\right| \le \Xi_2^{\varrho_1-1} M_1^{\varrho_1-1}\int_{s_1}^{s_2}\Theta_0(\tau)\,d\tau. \quad (25)$$

By (24) and (25), we deduce that $\mathcal{A}_1(\mathcal{E})$ is equicontinuous. By a similar method, we find that $\mathcal{A}_2(\mathcal{E})$ is also equicontinuous, and then $\mathcal{A}(\mathcal{E})$ is equicontinuous too. Using the Arzela–Ascoli theorem, we conclude that $\mathcal{A}_1(\mathcal{E})$ and $\mathcal{A}_2(\mathcal{E})$ are relatively compact sets, and so $\mathcal{A}(\mathcal{E})$ is also relatively compact. In addition, we can show that $\mathcal{A}_1$, $\mathcal{A}_2$ and $\mathcal{A}$ are continuous on $\mathcal{P}$ (see Lemma 1.4.1 from [14]). Hence, $\mathcal{A}$ is a completely continuous operator on $\mathcal{P}$. □

We define now the cone

$$\mathcal{P}_0 = \{(u,v) \in \mathcal{P},\ u(\eta) \ge \eta^{\delta_1-1}\|u\|,\ v(\eta) \ge \eta^{\delta_2-1}\|v\|,\ \eta \in [0,1]\}.$$

Under the assumptions $(I1)$ and $(I2)$, by using Lemma 4, we deduce that $\mathcal{A}(\mathcal{P}) \subset \mathcal{P}_0$, and so $\mathcal{A}|_{\mathcal{P}_0} : \mathcal{P}_0 \to \mathcal{P}_0$ (denoted again by $\mathcal{A}$) is also a completely continuous operator. For $\theta > 0$ we denote by B_θ the open ball centered at zero of radius θ, and by $\overline{B}_\theta$ and ∂B_θ its closure and its boundary, respectively.

We also denote by $M_1 = \int_0^1 \mathcal{J}_1(\tau)\psi_1(\tau)d\tau$, $M_2 = \int_0^1 \mathcal{J}_3(\tau)\psi_2(\tau)d\tau$, $M_3 = \int_0^1 \mathcal{J}_2(\tau)d\tau$, $M_4 = \int_0^1 \mathcal{J}_4(\tau)d\tau$, and for $\theta_1,\theta_2 \in (0,1)$, $\theta_1 < \theta_2$, $M_5 = \int_{\theta_1}^{\theta_2} \mathcal{J}_2(\zeta)\left(\int_{\theta_1}^{\zeta}\mathcal{G}_1(\zeta,\tau)\,d\tau\right)^{\varrho_1-1}d\zeta$, $M_6 = \int_{\theta_1}^{\theta_2} \mathcal{J}_4(\zeta)\left(\int_{\theta_1}^{\zeta}\mathcal{G}_3(\zeta,\tau)\,d\tau\right)^{\varrho_2-1}d\zeta$.

Theorem 2. *We suppose that assumptions $(I1)$, $(I2)$,*

$(I3)$ There exist $c_i \ge 0$, $i = 1,\dots,4$ with $\sum_{i=1}^4 c_i > 0$, $d_i \ge 0$, $i = 1,\dots,4$ with $\sum_{i=1}^4 d_i > 0$, and $\mu_1 \ge 1$, $\mu_2 \ge 1$ such that

$$\chi_{10} = \limsup_{\sum_{i=1}^4 c_i z_i \to 0}\ \max_{\eta\in[0,1]} \frac{\chi_1(\eta,z_1,z_2,z_3,z_4)}{\varphi_{r_1}((c_1z_1+c_2z_2+c_3z_3+c_4z_4)^{\mu_1})} < l_1,$$

and

$$\chi_{20} = \limsup_{\sum_{i=1}^4 d_i z_i \to 0}\ \max_{\eta\in[0,1]} \frac{\chi_2(\eta,z_1,z_2,z_3,z_4)}{\varphi_{r_2}((d_1z_1+d_2z_2+d_3z_3+d_4z_4)^{\mu_2})} < l_2,$$

where $l_1 = (2^{r_1-1}M_1M_3^{r_1-1}\rho_1^{\mu_1(r_1-1)})^{-1}$, $l_2 = (2^{r_2-1}M_2M_4^{r_2-1}\rho_2^{\mu_2(r_2-1)})^{-1}$, with $\rho_1 = 2\max\left\{c_1, c_2, \frac{c_3}{\Gamma(\sigma_1+1)}, \frac{c_4}{\Gamma(\sigma_2+1)}\right\}$, $\rho_2 = 2\max\left\{d_1, d_2, \frac{d_3}{\Gamma(\varsigma_1+1)}, \frac{d_4}{\Gamma(\varsigma_2+1)}\right\}$;

$(I4)$ There exist $p_i \ge 0$, $i = 1,\dots,4$ with $\sum_{i=1}^4 p_i > 0$, $q_i \ge 0$, $i = 1,\dots,4$ with $\sum_{i=1}^4 q_i > 0$, $\theta_1,\theta_2 \in (0,1)$, $\theta_1 < \theta_2$ and $\lambda_1 > 1$, $\lambda_2 > 1$ such that

$$f_\infty = \liminf_{\sum_{i=1}^4 p_i z_i \to \infty}\ \min_{\eta\in[\theta_1,\theta_2]} \frac{f(\eta,z_1,z_2,z_3,z_4)}{\varphi_{r_1}(p_1z_1+p_2z_2+p_3z_3+p_4z_4)} > l_3,$$

or

$$g_\infty = \liminf_{\sum_{i=1}^4 q_i z_i \to \infty}\ \min_{\eta\in[\theta_1,\theta_2]} \frac{g(\eta,z_1,z_2,z_3,z_4)}{\varphi_{r_2}(q_1z_1+q_2z_2+q_3z_3+q_4z_4)} > l_4,$$

where $l_3 = \lambda_1(2\rho_3 M_5 \theta_1^{\delta_1-1})^{1-r_1}$, $l_4 = \lambda_2(2\rho_4 M_6 \theta_1^{\delta_2-1})^{1-r_2}$ *with* $\rho_3 = \min\Big\{p_1\theta_1^{\delta_1-1}, p_2\theta_1^{\delta_2-1}, \frac{p_3\theta_1^{\sigma_1+\delta_1-1}\Gamma(\delta_1)}{\Gamma(\delta_1+\sigma_1)}, \frac{p_4\theta_1^{\sigma_2+\delta_2-1}\Gamma(\delta_2)}{\Gamma(\delta_2+\sigma_2)}\Big\}$, $\rho_4 = \min\Big\{q_1\theta_1^{\delta_1-1}, q_2\theta_1^{\delta_2-1}, \frac{q_3\theta_1^{\varsigma_1+\delta_1-1}\Gamma(\delta_1)}{\Gamma(\delta_1+\varsigma_1)}, \frac{q_4\theta_1^{\varsigma_2+\delta_2-1}\Gamma(\delta_2)}{\Gamma(\delta_2+\varsigma_2)}\Big\}$,

hold. Then there exists a positive solution $(u(\tau), v(\tau))$, $\tau \in [0,1]$ *of problems (1) and (2).*

Proof. By $(I3)$ there exists $R \in (0,1)$ such that

$$\begin{aligned} \chi_1(\eta, z_1, z_2, z_3, z_4) &\le l_1\varphi_{r_1}((c_1z_1 + c_2z_2 + c_3z_3 + c_4z_4)^{\mu_1}), \\ \chi_2(\eta, z_1, z_2, z_3, z_4) &\le l_2\varphi_{r_2}((d_1z_1 + d_2z_2 + d_3z_3 + d_4z_4)^{\mu_2}), \end{aligned} \tag{26}$$

for all $\eta \in [0,1]$, $z_i \ge 0$, $i = 1,\dots,4$ with $\sum_{i=1}^4 c_iz_i \le R$ and $\sum_{i=1}^4 d_iz_i \le R$. We define $R_1 \le \min\{R/\rho_1, R/\rho_2, R\}$. For any $(u,v) \in \overline{B}_{R_1} \cap \mathcal{P}$ and $\zeta \in [0,1]$ we have

$$\begin{aligned} &c_1u(\zeta) + c_2v(\zeta) + c_3I_{0+}^{\sigma_1}u(\zeta) + c_4I_{0+}^{\sigma_2}v(\zeta) \\ &\quad \le 2\max\Big\{c_1, c_2, \frac{c_3}{\Gamma(\sigma_1+1)}, \frac{c_4}{\Gamma(\sigma_2+1)}\Big\}\|(u,v)\|_{\mathcal{Y}} = \rho_1\|(u,v)\|_{\mathcal{Y}} \le \rho_1R_1 \le R, \\ &d_1u(\zeta) + d_2v(\zeta) + d_3I_{0+}^{\varsigma_1}u(\zeta) + d_4I_{0+}^{\varsigma_2}v(\zeta) \\ &\quad \le 2\max\Big\{d_1, d_2, \frac{d_3}{\Gamma(\varsigma_1+1)}, \frac{d_4}{\Gamma(\varsigma_2+1)}\Big\}\|(u,v)\|_{\mathcal{Y}} = \rho_2\|(u,v)\|_{\mathcal{Y}} \le \rho_2R_1 \le R. \end{aligned}$$

Then by (26) and Lemma 3, for any $(u,v) \in \partial B_{R_1} \cap \mathcal{P}_0$ and $\eta \in [0,1]$, we deduce

$$\begin{aligned} (\mathcal{A}_1(u,v))(\eta) &\le \int_0^1 \mathcal{J}_2(\zeta)\varphi_{\varrho_1}\Big(\int_0^1 \mathcal{J}_1(\vartheta)f(\vartheta, u(\vartheta), v(\vartheta), I_{0+}^{\sigma_1}u(\vartheta), I_{0+}^{\sigma_2}v(\vartheta))\,d\vartheta\Big)d\zeta \\ &= M_3\varphi_{\varrho_1}\Big(\int_0^1 \mathcal{J}_1(\vartheta)f(\vartheta, u(\vartheta), v(\vartheta), I_{0+}^{\sigma_1}u(\vartheta), I_{0+}^{\sigma_2}v(\vartheta))\,d\vartheta\Big) \\ &\le M_3\varphi_{\varrho_1}\Big(\int_0^1 \mathcal{J}_1(\vartheta)\psi_1(\vartheta)\chi_1(\vartheta, u(\vartheta), v(\vartheta), I_{0+}^{\sigma_1}u(\vartheta), I_{0+}^{\sigma_2}v(\vartheta))\,d\vartheta\Big) \\ &\le M_3\varphi_{\varrho_1}\Big(\int_0^1 \mathcal{J}_1(\vartheta)\psi_1(\vartheta)l_1\varphi_{r_1}((c_1u(\vartheta) + c_2v(\vartheta) + c_3I_{0+}^{\sigma_1}u(\vartheta) + c_4I_{0+}^{\sigma_2}v(\vartheta))^{\mu_1})d\vartheta\Big) \\ &\le M_3\varphi_{\varrho_1}(\varphi_{r_1}((\rho_1\|(u,v)\|_{\mathcal{Y}})^{\mu_1}))\varphi_{\varrho_1}(l_1)\varphi_{\varrho_1}(M_1) \\ &= M_3M_1^{\varrho_1-1}l_1^{\varrho_1-1}\rho_1^{\mu_1}\|(u,v)\|_{\mathcal{Y}}^{\mu_1} \le M_3M_1^{\varrho_1-1}l_1^{\varrho_1-1}\rho_1^{\mu_1}\|(u,v)\|_{\mathcal{Y}} = \tfrac{1}{2}\|(u,v)\|_{\mathcal{Y}}, \\ (\mathcal{A}_2(u,v))(\eta) &\le \int_0^1 \mathcal{J}_4(\zeta)\varphi_{\varrho_2}\Big(\int_0^1 \mathcal{J}_3(\vartheta)g(\vartheta, u(\vartheta), v(\vartheta), I_{0+}^{\varsigma_1}u(\vartheta), I_{0+}^{\varsigma_2}v(\vartheta))\,d\vartheta\Big)d\zeta \\ &= M_4\varphi_{\varrho_2}\Big(\int_0^1 \mathcal{J}_3(\vartheta)g(\vartheta, u(\vartheta), v(\vartheta), I_{0+}^{\varsigma_1}u(\vartheta), I_{0+}^{\varsigma_2}v(\vartheta))\,d\vartheta\Big) \\ &\le M_4\varphi_{\varrho_2}\Big(\int_0^1 \mathcal{J}_3(\vartheta)\psi_2(\vartheta)\chi_2(\vartheta, u(\vartheta), v(\vartheta), I_{0+}^{\varsigma_1}u(\vartheta), I_{0+}^{\varsigma_2}v(\vartheta))\,d\vartheta\Big) \\ &\le M_4\varphi_{\varrho_2}\Big(\int_0^1 \mathcal{J}_3(\vartheta)\psi_2(\vartheta)l_2\varphi_{r_2}((d_1u(\vartheta) + d_2v(\vartheta) + d_3I_{0+}^{\varsigma_1}u(\vartheta) + d_4I_{0+}^{\varsigma_2}v(\vartheta))^{\mu_2})d\vartheta\Big) \\ &\le M_4\varphi_{\varrho_2}(\varphi_{r_2}((\rho_2\|(u,v)\|_{\mathcal{Y}})^{\mu_2}))\varphi_{\varrho_2}(l_2)\varphi_{\varrho_2}(M_2) \\ &= M_4M_2^{\varrho_2-1}l_2^{\varrho_2-1}\rho_2^{\mu_2}\|(u,v)\|_{\mathcal{Y}}^{\mu_2} \le M_4M_2^{\varrho_2-1}l_2^{\varrho_2-1}\rho_2^{\mu_2}\|(u,v)\|_{\mathcal{Y}} = \tfrac{1}{2}\|(u,v)\|_{\mathcal{Y}}. \end{aligned}$$

Then we conclude that

$$\|\mathcal{A}(u,v)\|_{\mathcal{Y}} = \|\mathcal{A}_1(u,v)\| + \|\mathcal{A}_2(u,v)\| \le \|(u,v)\|_{\mathcal{Y}}, \ \forall\,(u,v) \in \partial B_{R_1} \cap \mathcal{P}_0. \tag{27}$$

Now we suppose in $(I4)$ that $f_\infty > l_3$ (in a similar manner we study the case $g_\infty > l_4$). Then there exists $C_1 > 0$ such that

$$f(\eta, z_1, z_2, z_3, z_4) \ge l_3\varphi_{r_1}(p_1z_1 + p_2z_2 + p_3z_3 + p_4z_4) - C_1, \tag{28}$$

for all $\eta \in [\theta_1, \theta_2]$ and $z_i \geq 0,\ i = 1, \ldots, 4$. By definition of $I_{0+}^{\sigma_1}$, for any $(u, v) \in \mathcal{P}_0$ and $\eta \in [0, 1]$ we have

$$\begin{aligned} I_{0+}^{\sigma_1} u(\eta) &= \frac{1}{\Gamma(\sigma_1)} \int_0^\eta (\eta - \zeta)^{\sigma_1 - 1} u(\zeta)\, d\zeta \geq \frac{1}{\Gamma(\sigma_1)} \int_0^\eta (\eta - \zeta)^{\sigma_1 - 1} \zeta^{\delta_1 - 1} \|u\|\, d\zeta \\ &\overset{\zeta = \eta y}{=} \frac{\|u\|}{\Gamma(\sigma_1)} \int_0^1 (\eta - \eta y)^{\sigma_1 - 1} \eta^{\delta_1 - 1} y^{\delta_1 - 1} \eta\, dy = \frac{\|u\|}{\Gamma(\sigma_1)} \eta^{\sigma_1 + \delta_1 - 1} \int_0^1 y^{\delta_1 - 1} (1 - y)^{\sigma_1 - 1}\, dy \\ &= \frac{\|u\|}{\Gamma(\sigma_1)} \eta^{\sigma_1 + \delta_1 - 1} B(\delta_1, \sigma_1) = \frac{\|u\| \eta^{\sigma_1 + \delta_1 - 1} \Gamma(\delta_1)}{\Gamma(\delta_1 + \sigma_1)}, \end{aligned} \tag{29}$$

and in a similar way

$$I_{0+}^{\sigma_2} v(\eta) \geq \frac{\|v\| \eta^{\sigma_2 + \delta_2 - 1} \Gamma(\delta_2)}{\Gamma(\delta_2 + \sigma_2)},$$

where $B(p, q)$ is the first Euler function. Then by using (28) and (29), for any $(u, v) \in \mathcal{P}_0$ and $\eta \in [\theta_1, \theta_2]$ we obtain

$$\begin{aligned} &(\mathcal{A}_1(u, v))(\eta) \geq \int_{\theta_1}^{\theta_2} \mathcal{G}_2(\eta, \zeta) \varphi_{\varrho_1}\left(\int_{\theta_1}^{\zeta} \mathcal{G}_1(\zeta, \vartheta) f(\vartheta, u(\vartheta), v(\vartheta), I_{0+}^{\sigma_1} u(\vartheta), I_{0+}^{\sigma_2} v(\vartheta))\, d\vartheta \right) d\zeta \\ &\geq \theta_1^{\delta_1 - 1} \int_{\theta_1}^{\theta_2} \mathcal{J}_2(\zeta) \left(\int_{\theta_1}^{\zeta} \mathcal{G}_1(\zeta, \vartheta) \left[l_3 (p_1 u(\vartheta) + p_2 v(\vartheta) + p_3 I_{0+}^{\sigma_1} u(\vartheta) + p_4 I_{0+}^{\sigma_2} v(\vartheta))^{r_1 - 1} \right.\right. \\ &\quad \left.\left. - C_1 \right] d\vartheta \right)^{\varrho_1 - 1} d\zeta \\ &\geq \theta_1^{\delta_1 - 1} \int_{\theta_1}^{\theta_2} \mathcal{J}_2(\zeta) \left(\int_{\theta_1}^{\zeta} \mathcal{G}_1(\zeta, \vartheta) \left[l_3 \left(p_1 \theta_1^{\delta_1 - 1} \|u\| + p_2 \theta_1^{\delta_2 - 1} \|v\| \right.\right.\right. \\ &\quad \left.\left.\left. + p_3 \frac{\theta_1^{\sigma_1 + \delta_1 - 1} \Gamma(\delta_1)}{\Gamma(\delta_1 + \sigma_1)} \|u\| + p_4 \frac{\theta_1^{\sigma_2 + \delta_2 - 1} \Gamma(\delta_2)}{\Gamma(\delta_2 + \sigma_2)} \|v\| \right)^{r_1 - 1} - C_1 \right] d\vartheta \right)^{\varrho_1 - 1} d\zeta \\ &\geq \theta_1^{\delta_1 - 1} \int_{\theta_1}^{\theta_2} \mathcal{J}_2(\zeta) \left(\int_{\theta_1}^{\zeta} \mathcal{G}_1(\zeta, \vartheta) \left[l_3 \left(\min\left\{ p_1 \theta_1^{\delta_1 - 1}, p_2 \theta_1^{\delta_2 - 1}, p_3 \frac{\theta_1^{\sigma_1 + \delta_1 - 1} \Gamma(\delta_1)}{\Gamma(\delta_1 + \sigma_1)}, \right.\right.\right.\right. \\ &\quad \left.\left.\left.\left. \frac{p_4 \theta_1^{\sigma_2 + \delta_2 - 1} \Gamma(\delta_2)}{\Gamma(\delta_2 + \sigma_2)} \right\} 2 \|(u, v)\|_{\mathcal{Y}} \right)^{r_1 - 1} - C_1 \right] d\vartheta \right)^{\varrho_1 - 1} d\zeta \\ &= \theta_1^{\delta_1 - 1} \int_{\theta_1}^{\theta_2} \mathcal{J}_2(\zeta) \left(\int_{\theta_1}^{\zeta} \mathcal{G}_1(\zeta, \vartheta) \left[l_3 (2 \rho_3 \|(u, v)\|_{\mathcal{Y}})^{r_1 - 1} - C_1 \right] d\vartheta \right)^{\varrho_1 - 1} d\zeta \\ &= M_5 \theta_1^{\delta_1 - 1} \left[l_3 (2 \rho_3 \|(u, v)\|_{\mathcal{Y}})^{r_1 - 1} - C_1 \right]^{\varrho_1 - 1} \\ &= \left(M_5^{r_1 - 1} \theta_1^{(\delta_1 - 1)(r_1 - 1)} l_3 2^{r_1 - 1} \rho_3^{r_1 - 1} \|(u, v)\|_{\mathcal{Y}}^{r_1 - 1} - M_5^{r_1 - 1} \theta_1^{(\delta_1 - 1)(r_1 - 1)} C_1 \right)^{\varrho_1 - 1} \\ &= \left(\lambda_1 \|(u, v)\|_{\mathcal{Y}}^{r_1 - 1} - C_2 \right)^{\varrho_1 - 1}, \quad C_2 = M_5^{r_1 - 1} \theta_1^{(\delta_1 - 1)(r_1 - 1)} C_1. \end{aligned}$$

Then we deduce

$$\|\mathcal{A}(u, v)\|_{\mathcal{Y}} \geq \|\mathcal{A}_1(u, v)\| \geq |\mathcal{A}_1(u, v)(\theta_1)| \geq \left(\lambda_1 \|(u, v)\|_{\mathcal{Y}}^{r_1 - 1} - C_2 \right)^{\varrho_1 - 1}, \ \forall (u, v) \in \mathcal{P}_0.$$

We choose $R_2 \geq \max\left\{ 1, C_2^{\varrho_1 - 1} / (\lambda_1 - 1)^{\varrho_1 - 1} \right\}$ and we obtain

$$\|\mathcal{A}(u, v)\|_{\mathcal{Y}} \geq \|(u, v)\|_{\mathcal{Y}}, \ \forall (u, v) \in \partial B_{R_2} \cap \mathcal{P}_0. \tag{30}$$

By Lemma 5, (27), (30) and Theorem 1 (i), we conclude that $\mathcal{A}$ has a fixed point $(u, v) \in (\overline{B}_{R_2} \setminus B_{R_1}) \cap \mathcal{P}_0$, so $R_1 \leq \|(u, v)\|_{\mathcal{Y}} \leq R_2$, and $u(\tau) \geq \tau^{\delta_1 - 1} \|u\|$ and $v(\tau) \geq \tau^{\delta_2 - 1} \|v\|$ for all $\tau \in [0, 1]$. Then $\|u\| > 0$ or $\|v\| > 0$, that is $u(\tau) > 0$ for all $\tau \in (0, 1]$ or $v(\tau) > 0$ for all $\tau \in (0, 1]$. Hence $(u(\tau), v(\tau)),\ \tau \in [0, 1]$ is a positive solution of problem (1) and (2). □

Theorem 3. *We suppose that assumptions* $(I1)$, $(I2)$,

(*I*5) *There exist* $e_i \geq 0,\ i = 1, \dots, 4$ *with* $\sum_{i=1}^4 e_i > 0$, $k_i \geq 0,\ i = 1, \dots, 4$ *with* $\sum_{i=1}^4 k_i > 0$ *such that*

$$\chi_{1\infty} = \limsup_{\sum_{i=1}^4 e_i z_i \to \infty} \max_{\eta \in [0,1]} \frac{\chi_1(\eta, z_1, z_2, z_3, z_4)}{\varphi_{r_1}(e_1 z_1 + e_2 z_2 + e_3 z_3 + e_4 z_4)} < m_1,$$

and

$$\chi_{2\infty} = \limsup_{\sum_{i=1}^4 k_i z_i \to \infty} \max_{\eta \in [0,1]} \frac{\chi_2(\eta, z_1, z_2, z_3, z_4)}{\varphi_{r_2}(k_1 z_1 + k_2 z_2 + k_3 z_3 + k_4 z_4)} < m_2,$$

where $m_1 < \min\{1/(2M_1(\xi_1 M_3)^{r_1-1}), 1/(M_1(2\xi_1 M_3)^{r_1-1})\}$, $m_2 < \min\{1/(2M_2(\xi_2 M_4)^{r_2-1}), 1/(M_2(2\xi_2 M_4)^{r_2-1})\}$ *with* $\xi_1 = 2\max\left\{e_1, e_2, \frac{e_3}{\Gamma(\sigma_1+1)}, \frac{e_4}{\Gamma(\sigma_2+1)}\right\}$, $\xi_2 = 2\max\left\{k_1, k_2, \frac{k_3}{\Gamma(\varsigma_1+1)}, \frac{k_4}{\Gamma(\varsigma_2+1)}\right\}$;

(*I*6) *There exist* $s_i \geq 0,\ i = 1, \dots, 4$ *with* $\sum_{i=1}^4 s_i > 0$, $t_i \geq 0,\ i = 1, \dots, 4$ *with* $\sum_{i=1}^4 t_i > 0$, $\theta_1, \theta_2 \in (0,1)$, $\theta_1 < \theta_2$ *and* $\nu_1 \in (0,1]$, $\nu_2 \in (0,1]$, $\lambda_3 \geq 1$, $\lambda_4 \geq 1$ *such that*

$$f_0 = \liminf_{\sum_{i=1}^4 s_i z_i \to 0} \min_{\eta \in [\theta_1, \theta_2]} \frac{f(\eta, z_1, z_2, z_3, z_4)}{\varphi_{r_1}((s_1 z_1 + s_2 z_2 + s_3 z_3 + s_4 z_4)^{\nu_1})} > m_3,$$

or

$$g_0 = \liminf_{\sum_{i=1}^4 t_i z_i \to 0} \min_{\eta \in [\theta_1, \theta_2]} \frac{g(\eta, z_1, z_2, z_3, z_4)}{\varphi_{r_2}((t_1 z_1 + t_2 z_2 + t_3 z_3 + t_4 z_4)^{\nu_2})} > m_4,$$

where $m_3 = \lambda_3^{r_1-1}(M_5 2^{\nu_1} \xi_3^{\nu_1} \theta_1^{\delta_1-1})^{1-r_1}$, $m_4 = \lambda_4^{r_2-1}(M_6 2^{\nu_2} \xi_4^{\nu_2} \theta_1^{\delta_2-1})^{1-r_2}$, *with* $\xi_3 = \min\left\{s_1\theta_1^{\delta_1-1}, s_2\theta_1^{\delta_2-1}, \frac{s_3\theta_1^{\sigma_1+\delta_1-1}\Gamma(\delta_1)}{\Gamma(\delta_1+\sigma_1)}, \frac{s_4\theta_1^{\sigma_2+\delta_2-1}\Gamma(\delta_2)}{\Gamma(\delta_2+\sigma_2)}\right\}$, $\xi_4 = \min\left\{t_1\theta_1^{\delta_1-1}, t_2\theta_1^{\delta_2-1}, \frac{t_3\theta_1^{\varsigma_1+\delta_1-1}\Gamma(\delta_1)}{\Gamma(\delta_1+\varsigma_1)}, \frac{t_4\theta_1^{\varsigma_2+\delta_2-1}\Gamma(\delta_2)}{\Gamma(\delta_2+\varsigma_2)}\right\}$,

hold. Then there exists a positive solution $(u(\tau), v(\tau))$, $\tau \in [0,1]$ *of problem (1) and (2).*

Proof. From (*I*5) there exist $C_3 > 0$, $C_4 > 0$ such that

$$\begin{aligned} \chi_1(\eta, z_1, z_2, z_3, z_4) &\leq m_1 \varphi_{r_1}(e_1 z_1 + e_2 z_2 + e_3 z_3 + e_4 z_4) + C_3, \\ \chi_2(\eta, z_1, z_2, z_3, z_4) &\leq m_2 \varphi_{r_2}(k_1 z_1 + k_2 z_2 + k_3 z_3 + k_4 z_4) + C_4, \end{aligned} \tag{31}$$

for any $\eta \in [0,1]$ and $z_i \geq 0,\ i = 1, \dots, 4$. By using (*I*2) and (31) for any $(u, v) \in \mathcal{P}_0$ and $\eta \in [0,1]$ we find

$$\begin{aligned} \mathcal{A}_1(u,v)(\eta) &\leq \int_0^1 \mathcal{J}_2(\zeta) \varphi_{\varrho_1}\left(\int_0^1 \mathcal{J}_1(\vartheta) f(\vartheta, u(\vartheta), v(\vartheta), I_{0+}^{\sigma_1} u(\vartheta), I_{0+}^{\sigma_2} v(\vartheta))\, d\vartheta\right) d\zeta \\ &\leq M_3 \varphi_{\varrho_1}\left(\int_0^1 \mathcal{J}_1(\vartheta) \psi_1(\vartheta) \chi_1(\vartheta, u(\vartheta), v(\vartheta), I_{0+}^{\sigma_1} u(\vartheta), I_{0+}^{\sigma_2} v(\vartheta))\, d\vartheta\right) \\ &\leq M_3 \varphi_{\varrho_1}\left(\int_0^1 \mathcal{J}_1(\vartheta) \psi_1(\vartheta) \left[m_1 \varphi_{r_1}(e_1 u(\vartheta) + e_2 v(\vartheta) + e_3 I_{0+}^{\sigma_1} u(\vartheta) + e_4 I_{0+}^{\sigma_2} v(\vartheta)) + C_3\right] d\vartheta\right) \\ &\leq M_3 \varphi_{\varrho_1}\left(\int_0^1 \mathcal{J}_1(\vartheta) \psi_1(\vartheta) \left[m_1\left(e_1\|u\| + e_2\|v\| + \frac{e_3\|u\|}{\Gamma(\sigma_1+1)} + \frac{e_4\|v\|}{\Gamma(\sigma_2+1)}\right)^{r_1-1} + C_3\right] d\vartheta\right) \\ &\leq M_3 \varphi_{\varrho_1}\left[m_1\left(\max\left\{e_1, e_2, \tfrac{e_3}{\Gamma(\sigma_1+1)}, \tfrac{e_4}{\Gamma(\sigma_2+1)}\right\} 2\|(u,v)\|_{\mathcal{Y}}\right)^{r_1-1} + C_3\right] \\ &\quad \times \left(\int_0^1 \mathcal{J}_1(\vartheta) \psi_1(\vartheta)\, d\vartheta\right)^{\varrho_1-1} \\ &= M_1^{\varrho_1-1} M_3 \left(m_1 \xi_1^{r_1-1} \|(u,v)\|_{\mathcal{Y}}^{r_1-1} + C_3\right)^{\varrho_1-1}, \end{aligned}$$

and

$$
\begin{aligned}
\mathcal{A}_2(u,v)(\eta) &\le \int_0^1 \mathcal{J}_4(\zeta)\varphi_{\varrho_2}\left(\int_0^1 \mathcal{J}_3(\vartheta)g(\vartheta,u(\vartheta),v(\vartheta),I_{0+}^{\varsigma_1}u(\vartheta),I_{0+}^{\varsigma_2}v(\vartheta))\,d\vartheta\right)d\zeta \\
&\le M_4\varphi_{\varrho_2}\left(\int_0^1 \mathcal{J}_3(\vartheta)\psi_2(\vartheta)\chi_2(\vartheta,u(\vartheta),v(\vartheta),I_{0+}^{\varsigma_1}u(\vartheta),I_{0+}^{\varsigma_2}v(\vartheta))\,d\vartheta\right) \\
&\le M_4\varphi_{\varrho_2}\left(\int_0^1 \mathcal{J}_3(\vartheta)\psi_2(\vartheta)\left[m_2\varphi_{r_2}(k_1u(\vartheta)+k_2v(\vartheta)+k_3I_{0+}^{\varsigma_1}u(\vartheta)+k_4I_{0+}^{\varsigma_2}v(\vartheta))+C_4\right]d\vartheta\right) \\
&\le M_4\varphi_{\varrho_2}\left(\int_0^1 \mathcal{J}_3(\vartheta)\psi_2(\vartheta)\left[m_2\left(k_1\|u\|+k_2\|v\|+\frac{k_3\|u\|}{\Gamma(\varsigma_1+1)}+\frac{k_4\|v\|}{\Gamma(\varsigma_2+1)}\right)^{r_2-1}+C_4\right]d\vartheta\right) \\
&\le M_4\varphi_{\varrho_2}\left[m_2\left(\max\left\{k_1,k_2,\tfrac{k_3}{\Gamma(\varsigma_1+1)},\tfrac{k_4}{\Gamma(\varsigma_2+1)}\right\}2\|(u,v)\|_{\mathcal{Y}}\right)^{r_2-1}+C_4\right] \\
&\quad\times\left(\int_0^1 \mathcal{J}_3(\vartheta)\psi_2(\vartheta)\,d\vartheta\right)^{\varrho_2-1} \\
&= M_2^{\varrho_2-1}M_4\left(m_2\xi_2^{r_2-1}\|(u,v)\|_{\mathcal{Y}}^{r_2-1}+C_4\right)^{\varrho_2-1}.
\end{aligned}
$$

Then we obtain

$$
\begin{aligned}
\|\mathcal{A}_1(u,v)\| &\le M_1^{\varrho_1-1}M_3\left(m_1\xi_1^{r_1-1}\|(u,v)\|_{\mathcal{Y}}^{r_1-1}+C_3\right)^{\varrho_1-1}, \\
\|\mathcal{A}_2(u,v)\| &\le M_2^{\varrho_2-1}M_4\left(m_2\xi_2^{r_2-1}\|(u,v)\|_{\mathcal{Y}}^{r_2-1}+C_4\right)^{\varrho_2-1},
\end{aligned}
$$

and so

$$
\begin{aligned}
\|\mathcal{A}(u,v)\|_{\mathcal{Y}} &\le M_1^{\varrho_1-1}M_3\left(m_1\xi_1^{r_1-1}\|(u,v)\|_{\mathcal{Y}}^{r_1-1}+C_3\right)^{\varrho_1-1} \\
&\quad+M_2^{\varrho_2-1}M_4\left(m_2\xi_2^{r_2-1}\|(u,v)\|_{\mathcal{Y}}^{r_2-1}+C_4\right)^{\varrho_2-1},
\end{aligned}
$$

for all $(u,v)\in\mathcal{P}_0$. We choose

$$
\begin{aligned}
R_3 \ge \max\Bigg\{&1, \frac{M_1^{\varrho_1-1}M_3 2^{\varrho_1-2}C_3^{\varrho_1-1}+M_2^{\varrho_2-1}M_4 2^{\varrho_2-2}C_4^{\varrho_2-1}}{1-(M_1^{\varrho_1-1}M_3 2^{\varrho_1-2}m_1^{\varrho_1-1}\xi_1+M_2^{\varrho_2-1}M_4 2^{\varrho_2-2}m_2^{\varrho_2-1}\xi_2)}, \\
&\frac{M_1^{\varrho_1-1}M_3C_3^{\varrho_1-1}+M_2^{\varrho_2-1}M_4C_4^{\varrho_2-1}}{1-(M_1^{\varrho_1-1}M_3m_1^{\varrho_1-1}\xi_1+M_2^{\varrho_2-1}M_4m_2^{\varrho_2-1}\xi_2)}, \\
&\frac{M_1^{\varrho_1-1}M_3C_3^{\varrho_1-1}+M_2^{\varrho_2-1}M_4 2^{\varrho_2-2}C_4^{\varrho_2-1}}{1-(M_1^{\varrho_1-1}M_3m_1^{\varrho_1-1}\xi_1+M_2^{\varrho_2-1}M_4 2^{\varrho_2-2}m_2^{\varrho_2-1}\xi_2)}, \\
&\frac{M_1^{\varrho_1-1}M_3 2^{\varrho_1-2}C_3^{\varrho_1-1}+M_2^{\varrho_2-1}M_4C_4^{\varrho_2-1}}{1-(M_1^{\varrho_1-1}M_3 2^{\varrho_1-2}m_1^{\varrho_1-1}\xi_1+M_2^{\varrho_2-1}M_4m_2^{\varrho_2-1}\xi_2)}\Bigg\},
\end{aligned} \tag{32}
$$

and then we conclude

$$
\|\mathcal{A}(u,v)\|_{\mathcal{Y}} \le \|(u,v)\|_{\mathcal{Y}},\ \ \forall\,(u,v)\in\partial B_{R_3}\cap\mathcal{P}_0. \tag{33}
$$

The above number R_3 was chosen based on the inequalities $(x+y)^{\varpi}\le 2^{\varpi-1}(x^{\varpi}+y^{\varpi})$ for $\varpi\ge 1$ and $x,y\ge 0$, and $(x+y)^{\varpi}\le x^{\varpi}+y^{\varpi}$ for $\varpi\in(0,1]$ and $x,y\ge 0$. Here $\varpi=\varrho_1-1$ or ϱ_2-1. We prove the inequality (33) in one case, namely $\varrho_1\in[2,\infty)$ and $\varrho_2\in[2,\infty)$. In this case, by using (32) and the relations $M_1^{\varrho_1-1}M_3 2^{\varrho_1-2}m_1^{\varrho_1-1}\xi_1<1/2$ and

$M_2^{\varrho_2-1}M_4 2^{\varrho_2-2}m_2^{\varrho_2-1}\xi_2 < 1/2$ (from the inequalities for m_1 and m_2 in $(I5)$) we have the inequalities

$$\begin{aligned}
&M_1^{\varrho_1-1}M_3(m_1\xi_1^{r_1-1}R_3^{r_1-1}+C_3)^{\varrho_1-1}+M_2^{\varrho_2-1}M_4(m_2\xi_2^{r_2-1}R_3^{r_2-1}+C_4)^{\varrho_2-1}\\
&\le M_1^{\varrho_1-1}M_3 2^{\varrho_1-2}(m_1^{\varrho_1-1}\xi_1R_3+C_3^{\varrho_1-1})+M_2^{\varrho_2-1}M_4 2^{\varrho_2-2}(m_2^{\varrho_2-1}\xi_2R_3+C_4^{\varrho_2-1})\\
&=(M_1^{\varrho_1-1}M_3 2^{\varrho_1-2}m_1^{\varrho_1-1}\xi_1+M_2^{\varrho_2-1}M_4 2^{\varrho_2-2}m_2^{\varrho_2-1}\xi_2)R_3\\
&\quad+(M_1^{\varrho_1-1}M_3 2^{\varrho_1-2}C_3^{\varrho_1-1}+M_2^{\varrho_2-1}M_4 2^{\varrho_2-2}C_4^{\varrho_2-1})\le R_3.
\end{aligned}$$

In a similar manner we consider the cases $\varrho_1\in(1,2]$ and $\varrho_2\in(1,2]$; $\varrho_1\in[2,\infty)$ and $\varrho_2\in(1,2]$; $\varrho_1\in(1,2]$ and $\varrho_2\in[2,\infty)$.

In $(I6)$, we suppose that $g_0 > m_4$ (in a similar manner we can study the case $f_0 > m_3$). We deduce that there exists $\widetilde{R}_4\in(0,1]$ such that

$$g(\eta,z_1,z_2,z_3,z_4)\ge m_4\varphi_{r_2}((t_1z_1+t_2z_2+t_3z_3+t_4z_4)^{\nu_2}), \tag{34}$$

for all $\eta\in[\theta_1,\theta_2]$, $z_i\ge0$, $i=1,\dots,4$, $\sum_{i=1}^4 t_iz_i\le\widetilde{R}_4$. We take $R_4\le\min\{\widetilde{R}_4/\widetilde{\xi}_4,\widetilde{R}_4\}$, where $\widetilde{\xi}_4=2\max\left\{t_1,t_2,\frac{t_3}{\Gamma(\varsigma_1+1)},\frac{t_4}{\Gamma(\varsigma_2+1)}\right\}$. Then for any $(u,v)\in\overline{B}_{R_4}\cap\mathcal{P}$ and $\eta\in[0,1]$ we have

$$\begin{aligned}
&t_1u(\zeta)+t_2v(\zeta)+t_3I_{0+}^{\varsigma}u(\zeta)+t_4I_{0+}^{\varsigma}v(\zeta)\le t_1\|u\|+t_2\|v\|+\frac{t_3\|u\|}{\Gamma(\varsigma_1+1)}+\frac{t_4\|v\|}{\Gamma(\varsigma_2+1)}\\
&\le\max\left\{t_1,t_2,\frac{t_3}{\Gamma(\varsigma_1+1)},\frac{t_4}{\Gamma(\varsigma_2+1)}\right\}2\|(u,v)\|_{\mathcal{Y}}=\widetilde{\xi}_4\|(u,v)\|_{\mathcal{Y}}\le\widetilde{\xi}_4R_4\le\widetilde{R}_4.
\end{aligned}$$

Therefore by using (34) and (29), we obtain for any $(u,v)\in\partial B_{R_4}\cap\mathcal{P}_0$ and $\eta\in[\theta_1,\theta_2]$

$$\begin{aligned}
&\mathcal{A}_2(u,v)(\eta)\ge\int_{\theta_1}^{\theta_2}\mathcal{G}_4(\eta,\zeta)\varphi_{\varrho_2}\left(\int_{\theta_1}^{\zeta}\mathcal{G}_3(\zeta,\vartheta)g(\vartheta,u(\vartheta),v(\vartheta),I_{0+}^{\varsigma_1}u(\vartheta),I_{0+}^{\varsigma_2}v(\vartheta))d\vartheta\right)d\zeta\\
&\ge\theta_1^{\delta_2-1}\int_{\theta_1}^{\theta_2}\mathcal{J}_4(\zeta)\varphi_{\varrho_2}\left(\int_{\theta_1}^{\zeta}\mathcal{G}_3(\zeta,\vartheta)\left[m_4\varphi_{r_2}((t_1u(\vartheta)+t_2v(\vartheta)+t_3I_{0+}^{\varsigma_1}u(\vartheta)\right.\right.\\
&\quad\left.\left.+t_4I_{0+}^{\varsigma_2}v(\vartheta))^{\nu_2})\right]d\vartheta\right)d\zeta\\
&\ge\theta_1^{\delta_2-1}\int_{\theta_1}^{\theta_2}\mathcal{J}_4(\zeta)\varphi_{\varrho_2}\left(\int_{\theta_1}^{\zeta}\mathcal{G}_3(\zeta,\vartheta)\left[m_4\left(t_1\theta_1^{\delta_1-1}\|u\|+t_2\theta_1^{\delta_2-1}\|v\|\right.\right.\right.\\
&\quad\left.\left.\left.++t_3\frac{\theta_1^{\varsigma_1+\delta_1-1}\Gamma(\delta_1)}{\Gamma(\delta_1+\varsigma_1)}\|u\|+t_4\frac{\theta_1^{\varsigma_2+\delta_2-1}\Gamma(\delta_2)}{\Gamma(\delta_2+\varsigma_2)}\|v\|\right)^{\nu_2(r_2-1)}\right]d\vartheta\right)d\zeta\\
&\ge\theta_1^{\delta_2-1}\int_{\theta_1}^{\theta_2}\mathcal{J}_4(\zeta)\left(\int_{\theta_1}^{\zeta}\mathcal{G}_3(\zeta,\vartheta)m_4(2\xi_4\|(u,v)\|_{\mathcal{Y}})^{\nu_2(r_2-1)}d\vartheta\right)^{\varrho_2-1}d\zeta\\
&=\theta_1^{\delta_2-1}m_4^{\varrho_2-1}(2\xi_4)^{\nu_2(\varrho_2-1)(r_2-1)}\|(u,v)\|_{\mathcal{Y}}^{\nu_2}\left(\int_{\theta_1}^{\theta_2}\mathcal{J}_4(\zeta)\left(\int_{\theta_1}^{\zeta}\mathcal{G}_3(\zeta,\vartheta)\,d\vartheta\right)^{\varrho_2-1}d\zeta\right)\\
&=M_6\theta_1^{\delta_2-1}m_4^{\varrho_2-1}2^{\nu_2}\xi_4^{\nu_2}\|(u,v)\|_{\mathcal{Y}}^{\nu_2}=\lambda_4\|(u,v)\|_{\mathcal{Y}}^{\nu_2}\ge\|(u,v)\|_{\mathcal{Y}}^{\nu_2}\ge\|(u,v)\|_{\mathcal{Y}}.
\end{aligned}$$

Then we deduce $\|\mathcal{A}_2(u,v)\|\ge\|(u,v)\|_{\mathcal{Y}}$ and then

$$\|\mathcal{A}(u,v)\|_{\mathcal{Y}}\ge\|(u,v)\|_{\mathcal{Y}},\ \ \forall(u,v)\in\partial B_{R_4}\cap\mathcal{P}_0. \tag{35}$$

From Lemma 5, (33), (35) and Theorem 1 (ii), we conclude that $\mathcal{A}$ has a fixed point $(u,v)\in(\overline{B}_{R_3}\setminus B_{R_4})\cap\mathcal{P}_0$, so $R_4\le\|(u,v)\|_{\mathcal{Y}}\le R_3$, which is a positive solution of problem (1) and (2). □

Theorem 4. *We suppose that assumptions $(I1)$, $(I2)$, $(I4)$ and $(I6)$ hold. In addition, the functions ψ_i and χ_i, $i=1,2$ satisfy the condition*

(*I7*) $M_3 M_1^{\varrho_1-1} D_0^{\varrho_1-1} < \frac{1}{2}$, $M_4 M_2^{\varrho_2-1} D_0^{\varrho_2-1} < \frac{1}{2}$, *where*

$$D_0 = \max\left\{ \max_{\eta\in[0,1],\, z_i\in[0,\omega_0],\, i=1,\dots,4} \chi_1(\eta, z_1, z_2, z_3, z_4), \max_{\eta\in[0,1],\, z_i\in[0,\omega_0],\, i=1,\dots,4} \chi_2(\eta, z_1, z_2, z_3, z_4) \right\},$$

with $\omega_0 = \max\left\{1, \frac{1}{\Gamma(\sigma_1+1)}, \frac{1}{\Gamma(\sigma_2+1)}, \frac{1}{\Gamma(\varsigma_1+1)}, \frac{1}{\Gamma(\varsigma_2+1)}\right\}$.

Then there exist two positive solutions $(u_1(\tau), v_1(\tau))$, $(u_2(\tau), v_2(\tau))$, $\tau \in [0,1]$ *of problem (1) and (2).*

Proof. Under assumptions $(I1)$, $(I2)$ and $(I4)$, Theorem 2 gives us the existence of $R_2 > 1$ such that

$$\|\mathcal{A}(u,v)\|_{\mathcal{Y}} \geq \|(u,v)\|_{\mathcal{Y}}, \ \forall\,(u,v) \in \partial B_{R_2} \cap \mathcal{P}_0. \tag{36}$$

Under assumptions $(I1)$, $(I2)$ and $(I6)$, Theorem 3 gives us the existence of $R_4 < 1$ such that

$$\|\mathcal{A}(u,v)\|_{\mathcal{Y}} \geq \|(u,v)\|_{\mathcal{Y}}, \ \forall\,(u,v) \in \partial B_{R_4} \cap \mathcal{P}_0. \tag{37}$$

Now we consider the set $B_1 = \{(u,v) \in \mathcal{Y},\ \|(u,v)\|_{\mathcal{Y}} < 1\}$. By $(I7)$, for any $(u,v) \in \partial B_1 \cap \mathcal{P}_0$ and $\eta \in [0,1]$, we obtain

$$\begin{aligned}
&\mathcal{A}_1(u,v)(\eta) \leq \int_0^1 \mathcal{J}_2(\zeta)\varphi_{\varrho_1}\left(\int_0^1 \mathcal{J}_1(\vartheta)\psi_1(\vartheta)\chi_1(\vartheta, u(\vartheta), v(\vartheta), I_{0+}^{\sigma_1}u(\vartheta), I_{0+}^{\sigma_2}v(\vartheta))\,d\vartheta\right)d\zeta \\
&\leq D_0^{\varrho_1-1}\left(\int_0^1 \mathcal{J}_2(\zeta)\,d\zeta\right)\left(\int_0^1 \mathcal{J}_1(\vartheta)\psi_1(\vartheta)\,d\vartheta\right)^{\varrho_1-1} = M_3 D_0^{\varrho_1-1} M_1^{\varrho_1-1} < \tfrac{1}{2}, \\
&\mathcal{A}_2(u,v)(\eta) \leq \int_0^1 \mathcal{J}_4(\zeta)\varphi_{\varrho_2}\left(\int_0^1 \mathcal{J}_3(\vartheta)\psi_2(\vartheta)\chi_2(\vartheta, u(\vartheta), v(\vartheta), I_{0+}^{\varsigma_1}u(\vartheta), I_{0+}^{\varsigma_2}v(\vartheta))\,d\vartheta\right)d\zeta \\
&\leq D_0^{\varrho_2-1}\left(\int_0^1 \mathcal{J}_4(\zeta)\,d\zeta\right)\left(\int_0^1 \mathcal{J}_3(\vartheta)\psi_2(\vartheta)\,d\vartheta\right)^{\varrho_2-1} = M_4 D_0^{\varrho_2-1} M_2^{\varrho_2-1} < \tfrac{1}{2}.
\end{aligned}$$

Then $\|\mathcal{A}_i(u,v)\| < 1/2$ for all $(u,v) \in \partial B_1 \cap \mathcal{P}_0$, $i = 1,2$. Hence

$$\|\mathcal{A}(u,v)\|_{\mathcal{Y}} = \|\mathcal{A}_1(u,v)\| + \|\mathcal{A}_2(u,v)\| < 1 = \|(u,v)\|_{\mathcal{Y}}, \ \forall\,(u,v) \in \partial B_1 \cap \mathcal{P}_0. \tag{38}$$

So from (36), (38) and Theorem 1, we deduce that problem (1) and (2) has one positive solution $(u_1, v_1) \in \mathcal{P}_0$ with $1 < \|(u_1,v_1)\|_{\mathcal{Y}} \leq R_2$. From (37) and (38) and the Guo–Krasnosel'skii fixed point theorem, we conclude that problem (1) and (2) have another positive solution $(u_2, v_2) \in \mathcal{P}_0$ with $R_4 \leq \|(u_2,v_2)\|_{\mathcal{Y}} < 1$. Then problem (1) and (2) have at least two positive solutions $(u_1(\tau), v_1(\tau))$, $(u_2(\tau), v_2(\tau))$, $\tau \in [0,1]$. □

4. Examples

Let $\gamma_1 = 3/2$, $\gamma_2 = 7/6$, $p = 4$, $q = 3$, $\delta_1 = 10/3$, $\delta_2 = 12/5$, $\sigma_1 = 2/5$, $\sigma_2 = 29/7$, $\varsigma_1 = 11/9$, $\varsigma_2 = 21/4$, $n = 2$, $m = 1$, $\alpha_0 = 13/8$, $\alpha_1 = 5/7$, $\alpha_2 = 3/4$, $\beta_0 = 10/9$, $\beta_1 = 7/8$, $r_1 = 17/4$, $r_2 = 25/8$, $\varrho_1 = 17/13$, $\varrho_2 = 25/17$, $\mathcal{H}_0(t) = \{2/7,\ t \in [0,3/4);\ 11/4,\ t \in [3/4,1]\}$, $\mathcal{H}_1(t) = t/2$, $t \in [0,1]$, $\mathcal{H}_2(t) = \{1/2,\ t \in [0,1/2);\ 13/10,\ t \in [1/2,1]\}$, $\mathcal{K}_0(t) = 4t/9$, $t \in [0,1]$, $\mathcal{K}_1(t) = \{1/4,\ t \in [0,1/3);\ 29/20,\ t \in [1/3,1]\}$.

We consider the system of fractional differential equations

$$\begin{cases} D_{0+}^{3/2}\left(\varphi_{17/4}\left(D_{0+}^{10/3}u(\tau)\right)\right) = f(\tau, u(\tau), v(\tau), I_{0+}^{2/5}u(\tau), I_{0+}^{29/7}v(\tau)), & \tau \in (0,1), \\ D_{0+}^{7/6}\left(\varphi_{25/8}\left(D_{0+}^{12/5}v(\tau)\right)\right) = g(\tau, u(\tau), v(\tau), I_{0+}^{11/9}u(\tau), I_{0+}^{21/4}v(\tau)), & \tau \in (0,1), \end{cases} \tag{39}$$

with the boundary conditions

$$\begin{cases} u(0) = u'(0) = u''(0) = 0, \ D_{0+}^{10/3}u(0) = 0, \ D_{0+}^{10/3}u(1) = \frac{1}{2^{4/13}} D_{0+}^{10/3}u(\frac{3}{4}), \\ D_{0+}^{13/8}u(1) = \frac{1}{2}\int_0^1 D_{0+}^{5/7}u(\eta)\,d\eta + \frac{4}{5}D_{0+}^{3/4}u\left(\frac{1}{2}\right), \\ v(0) = v'(0) = 0, \ D_{0+}^{12/5}v(0) = 0, \ \varphi_{25/8}\left(D_{0+}^{12/5}v(1)\right) = \frac{4}{9}\int_0^1 \varphi_{25/8}\left(D_{0+}^{12/5}v(\eta)\right)d\eta, \\ D_{0+}^{10/9}v(1) = \frac{6}{5}D_{0+}^{7/8}v\left(\frac{1}{3}\right). \end{cases} \tag{40}$$

We have here $\mathfrak{a}_1 \approx 0.56698729 > 0$, $\mathfrak{a}_2 \approx 2.16111947 > 0$, $\mathfrak{b}_1 \approx 0.61904762 > 0$, $\mathfrak{b}_2 \approx 0.43774133 > 0$. So, assumption $(I1)$ is satisfied. We also obtain

$$\begin{aligned}
\mathfrak{g}_1(\tau,\eta) &= \frac{1}{\Gamma(3/2)}\begin{cases} \tau^{1/2}(1-\eta)^{1/2} - (\tau-\eta)^{1/2}, \ 0 \le \eta \le \tau \le 1, \\ \tau^{1/2}(1-\eta)^{1/2}, \ 0 \le \tau \le \eta \le 1, \end{cases} \\
\mathfrak{g}_2(\tau,\eta) &= \frac{1}{\Gamma(10/3)}\begin{cases} \tau^{7/3}(1-\eta)^{17/24} - (\tau-\eta)^{7/3}, \ 0 \le \eta \le \tau \le 1, \\ \tau^{7/3}(1-\eta)^{17/24}, \ 0 \le \tau \le \eta \le 1, \end{cases} \\
\mathfrak{g}_{21}(\tau,\eta) &= \frac{1}{\Gamma(55/21)}\begin{cases} \tau^{34/21}(1-\eta)^{17/24} - (\tau-\eta)^{34/21}, \ 0 \le \eta \le \tau \le 1, \\ \tau^{34/21}(1-\eta)^{17/24}, \ 0 \le \tau \le \eta \le 1, \end{cases} \\
\mathfrak{g}_{22}(\tau,\eta) &= \frac{1}{\Gamma(31/12)}\begin{cases} \tau^{19/12}(1-\eta)^{17/24} - (\tau-\eta)^{19/12}, \ 0 \le \eta \le \tau \le 1, \\ \tau^{19/12}(1-\eta)^{17/24}, \ 0 \le \tau \le \eta \le 1, \end{cases} \\
\mathfrak{g}_3(\tau,\eta) &= \frac{1}{\Gamma(7/6)}\begin{cases} \tau^{1/6}(1-\eta)^{1/6} - (\tau-\eta)^{1/6}, \ 0 \le \eta \le \tau \le 1, \\ \tau^{1/6}(1-\eta)^{1/6}, \ 0 \le \tau \le \eta \le 1, \end{cases} \\
\mathfrak{g}_4(\tau,\eta) &= \frac{1}{\Gamma(12/5)}\begin{cases} \tau^{7/5}(1-\eta)^{13/45} - (\tau-\eta)^{7/5}, \ 0 \le \eta \le \tau \le 1, \\ \tau^{7/5}(1-\eta)^{13/45}, \ 0 \le \tau \le \eta \le 1, \end{cases} \\
\mathfrak{g}_{41}(\tau,\eta) &= \frac{1}{\Gamma(61/40)}\begin{cases} \tau^{21/40}(1-\eta)^{13/45} - (\tau-\eta)^{21/40}, \ 0 \le \eta \le \tau \le 1, \\ \tau^{21/40}(1-\eta)^{13/45}, \ 0 \le \tau \le \eta \le 1, \end{cases} \\
\mathcal{G}_1(\tau,\eta) &= \mathfrak{g}_1(\tau,\eta) + \frac{\tau^{1/2}}{2\mathfrak{a}_1}\mathfrak{g}_1\left(\frac{3}{4},\eta\right), \ (\tau,\eta) \in [0,1]\times[0,1], \\
\mathcal{G}_2(\tau,\eta) &= \mathfrak{g}_2(\tau,\eta) + \frac{\tau^{7/3}}{\mathfrak{a}_2}\left(\frac{1}{2}\int_0^1 \mathfrak{g}_{21}(\vartheta,\eta)\,d\vartheta + \frac{4}{5}\mathfrak{g}_{22}\left(\frac{1}{2},\eta\right)\right), \ (\tau,\eta) \in [0,1]\times[0,1], \\
\mathcal{G}_3(\tau,\eta) &= \mathfrak{g}_3(\tau,\eta) + \frac{4\tau^{1/6}}{9\mathfrak{b}_1}\int_0^1 \mathfrak{g}_3(\vartheta,\eta)\,d\vartheta, \ (\tau,\eta) \in [0,1]\times[0,1], \\
\mathcal{G}_4(\tau,\eta) &= \mathfrak{g}_4(\tau,\eta) + \frac{6\tau^{7/5}}{5\mathfrak{b}_2}\mathfrak{g}_{41}\left(\frac{1}{3},\eta\right), \ (\tau,\eta) \in [0,1]\times[0,1], \\
\mathfrak{h}_1(\eta) &= \frac{1}{\Gamma(3/2)}(1-\eta)^{1/2}, \ \mathfrak{h}_2(\eta) = \frac{1}{\Gamma(10/3)}(1-\eta)^{17/24}(1-(1-\eta)^{13/8}), \ \eta \in [0,1], \\
\mathfrak{h}_3(\eta) &= \frac{1}{\Gamma(7/6)}(1-\eta)^{1/6}, \ \mathfrak{h}_4(\eta) = \frac{1}{\Gamma(12/5)}(1-\eta)^{13/45}(1-(1-\eta)^{10/9}), \ \eta \in [0,1].
\end{aligned}$$

Besides we deduce

$$\begin{aligned}
\mathcal{J}_1(\zeta) &= \begin{cases} \mathfrak{h}_1(\zeta) + \frac{1}{2\mathfrak{a}_1\Gamma(3/2)}\left[\left(\frac{3}{4}\right)^{1/2}(1-\zeta)^{1/2} - \left(\frac{3}{4}-\zeta\right)^{1/2}\right], \ 0 \le \zeta \le \frac{3}{4}, \\ \mathfrak{h}_1(\zeta) + \frac{1}{2\mathfrak{a}_1\Gamma(3/2)}\left(\frac{3}{4}\right)^{1/2}(1-\zeta)^{1/2}, \ \frac{3}{4} < \zeta \le 1, \end{cases} \\
\mathcal{J}_2(\zeta) &= \begin{cases} \mathfrak{h}_2(\zeta) + \frac{1}{\mathfrak{a}_2}\left\{\frac{1}{2\Gamma(76/21)}\left[(1-\zeta)^{17/24} - (1-\zeta)^{55/21}\right]\right. \\ \quad \left. + \frac{4}{5\Gamma(31/12)}\left[\left(\frac{1}{2}\right)^{19/12}(1-\zeta)^{17/24} - \left(\frac{1}{2}-\zeta\right)^{19/12}\right]\right\}, \ 0 \le \zeta \le \frac{1}{2}, \\ \mathfrak{h}_2(\zeta) + \frac{1}{\mathfrak{a}_2}\left\{\frac{1}{2\Gamma(76/21)}\left[(1-\zeta)^{17/24} - (1-\zeta)^{55/21}\right]\right. \\ \quad \left. + \frac{4}{5\Gamma(31/12)}\left(\frac{1}{2}\right)^{19/12}(1-\zeta)^{17/24}\right\}, \ \frac{1}{2} < \zeta \le 1, \end{cases} \\
\mathcal{J}_3(\zeta) &= \mathfrak{h}_3(\zeta) + \frac{4}{9\mathfrak{b}_1\Gamma(13/6)}\left[(1-\zeta)^{1/6} - (1-\zeta)^{7/6}\right], \ \zeta \in [0,1], \\
\mathcal{J}_4(\zeta) &= \begin{cases} \mathfrak{h}_4(\zeta) + \frac{6}{5\mathfrak{b}_2\Gamma(61/40)}\left[\left(\frac{1}{3}\right)^{21/40}(1-\zeta)^{13/45} - \left(\frac{1}{3}-\zeta\right)^{21/40}\right], \ 0 \le \zeta \le \frac{1}{3}, \\ \mathfrak{h}_4(\zeta) + \frac{6}{5\mathfrak{b}_2\Gamma(61/40)}\left(\frac{1}{3}\right)^{21/40}(1-\zeta)^{13/45}, \ \frac{1}{3} < \zeta \le 1. \end{cases}
\end{aligned}$$

Example 1. *We consider the functions*

$$f(\eta,z_1,z_2,z_3,z_4)=\frac{(2z_1+z_2+5z_3+7z_4)^{13a/4}}{\eta^{\kappa_1}(1-\eta)^{\kappa_2}},\quad g(\eta,z_1,z_2,z_3,z_4)=\frac{(3z_1+8z_2+2z_3+9z_4)^{17b/8}}{\eta^{\kappa_3}(1-\eta)^{\kappa_4}},\tag{41}$$

for $\eta\in(0,1)$, $z_i\geq 0$, $i=1,\ldots,4$, *where* $a>1$, $b>1$, $\kappa_1\in(0,1)$, $\kappa_2\in(0,3/2)$, $\kappa_3\in(0,1)$, $\kappa_4\in(0,7/6)$. *Here* $\psi_1(\eta)=\frac{1}{\eta^{\kappa_1}(1-\eta)^{\kappa_2}}$, $\psi_2(\eta)=\frac{1}{\eta^{\kappa_3}(1-\eta)^{\kappa_4}}$ *for* $\eta\in(0,1)$, $\chi_1(\eta,z_1,z_2,z_3,z_4)=(2z_1+z_2+5z_3+7z_4)^{13a/4}$ *and* $\chi_2(\eta,z_1,z_2,z_3,z_4)=(3z_1+8z_2+2z_3+9z_4)^{17b/8}$ *for* $\eta\in[0,1]$, $z_i\geq 0$, $i=1,\ldots,4$. *We also find* $\Lambda_1=\int_0^1(1-\tau)^{1/2}\psi_1(\tau)\,d\tau=B(1-\kappa_1,\frac{3}{2}-\kappa_2)\in(0,\infty)$, $\Lambda_2=\int_0^1(1-\tau)^{1/6}\psi_2(\tau)\,d\tau=B(1-\kappa_3,\ \frac{7}{6}-\kappa_4)\in(0,\infty)$. *Then assumption (I2) is also satisfied. Moreover, in (I3), for* $c_1=2$, $c_2=1$, $c_3=5$, $c_4=7$, $\mu_1=1$, $d_1=3$, $d_2=8$, $d_3=2$, $d_4=9$, $\mu_2=1$, *we obtain* $\chi_{10}=0$, $\chi_{20}=0$. *In (I4), for* $[\theta_1,\theta_2]\subset(0,1)$, $p_1=2$, $p_2=1$, $p_3=5$, $p_4=7$, *we have* $f_\infty=\infty$. *By Theorem 2, we deduce that there exists a positive solution* $(u(\tau),v(\tau))$, $\tau\in[0,1]$ *of problems (39) and (40) with the nonlinearities (41).*

Example 2. *We consider the functions*

$$\begin{aligned}f(\eta,z_1,z_2,z_3,z_4)&=\frac{s_0(\eta+2)}{(\eta^2+6)\sqrt[3]{\eta^2}}\left[\left(\tfrac{1}{4}z_1+\tfrac{1}{3}z_2+z_3+\tfrac{1}{2}z_4\right)^{\omega_1}\right.\\&\left.+\left(\tfrac{1}{4}z_1+\tfrac{1}{3}z_2+z_3+\tfrac{1}{2}z_4\right)^{\omega_2}\right],\ \eta\in(0,1],\ z_i\geq 0,\ i=1,\ldots,4,\\g(\eta,z_1,z_2,z_3,z_4)&=\frac{t_0(3+\sin\eta)}{(\eta+2)^4\sqrt[5]{(1-\eta)^3}}\left(e^{z_1}+\ln(z_2+z_3+1)+z_4^{\omega_3}\right),\\&\eta\in[0,1),\ z_i\geq 0,\ i=1,\ldots,4,\end{aligned}\tag{42}$$

where $s_0>0$, $t_0>0$, $\omega_1>\frac{13}{4}$, $\omega_2\in\left(0,\frac{13}{4}\right)$, $\omega_3>0$. *Here, we have* $\psi_1(\eta)=\frac{1}{\sqrt[3]{\eta^2}}$, $\eta\in(0,1]$, $\chi_1(\eta,z_1,z_2,z_3,z_4)=\frac{s_0(\eta+2)}{(\eta^2+6)}\left[\left(\frac{1}{4}z_1+\frac{1}{3}z_2+z_3+\frac{1}{2}z_4\right)^{\omega_1}+\left(\frac{1}{4}z_1+\frac{1}{3}z_2+z_3+\frac{1}{2}z_4\right)^{\omega_2}\right]$, $\eta\in[0,1]$, $z_i\geq 0$, $i=1,\ldots,4$, $\psi_2(\eta)=\frac{1}{\sqrt[5]{(1-\eta)^3}}$, $\eta\in[0,1)$, $\chi_2(\eta,z_1,z_2,z_3,z_4)=\frac{t_0(3+\sin\eta)}{(\eta+2)^4}\left(e^{z_1}+\ln(z_2+z_3+1)+z_4^{\omega_3}\right)$, $\eta\in[0,1]$, $z_i\geq 0$, $i=1,\ldots,4$. *We find* $\Lambda_1=\int_0^1(1-\tau)^{1/2}\frac{1}{\sqrt[3]{\tau^2}}\,d\tau=B\left(\frac{1}{3},\frac{3}{2}\right)\in(0,\infty)$, $\Lambda_2=\int_0^1(1-\tau)^{1/6}\frac{1}{\sqrt[5]{(1-\tau)^3}}\,d\tau=\frac{30}{17}\in(0,\infty)$. *Then assumption (I2) is satisfied. For* $[\theta_1,\theta_2]\subset(0,1)$, $p_1=1/4$, $p_2=1/3$, $p_3=1$, $p_4=1/2$, *we obtain* $f_\infty=\infty$, *and for* $s_1=1/4$, $s_2=1/3$, $s_3=1$, $s_4=1/2$ *and* $\nu_1\in\left(\frac{4\omega_2}{13},1\right]$, *we have* $f_0=\infty$. *So assumptions (I4) and (I6) are satisfied. Then after some computations, we deduce* $M_1=\int_0^1\mathcal{J}_1(\tau)\psi_1(\tau)\,d\tau\approx 3.04682891$, $M_2=\int_0^1\mathcal{J}_3(\tau)\psi_2(\tau)\,d\tau\approx 2.64937892$, $M_3=\int_0^1\mathcal{J}_2(\tau)\,d\tau\approx 0.15582207$, $M_4=\int_0^1\mathcal{J}_4(\tau)\,d\tau\approx 1.25629509$. *In addition, we obtain that* $\omega_0=\frac{1}{\Gamma(7/5)}\approx 1.12706049$, $D_0=\max\left\{\frac{3s_0}{7}\left[\left(\frac{25}{12}\omega_0\right)^{\omega_1}+\left(\frac{25}{12}\omega_0\right)^{\omega_2}\right],t_0m_0[e^{\omega_0}+\ln(2\omega_0+1)+\omega_0^{\omega_3}]\right\}$, *with* $m_0=\max_{\eta\in[0,1]}\frac{3+\sin\eta}{(\eta+2)^4}\approx 3.0123699$. *If*

$$\begin{aligned}s_0&<\min\left\{\frac{7}{3(2M_3)^{13/4}M_1[(25\omega_0/12)^{\omega_1}+(25\omega_0/12)^{\omega_2}]},\frac{7}{3(2M_4)^{17/8}M_2[(25\omega_0/12)^{\omega_1}+(25\omega_0/12)^{\omega_2}]}\right\},\\t_0&<\min\left\{\frac{1}{(2M_3)^{13/4}M_1m_0\left[e^{\omega_0}+\ln(2\omega_0+1)+\omega_0^{\omega_3}\right]},\frac{1}{(2M_4)^{17/8}M_2m_0\left[e^{\omega_0}+\ln(2\omega_0+1)+\omega_0^{\omega_3}\right]}\right\},\end{aligned}$$

then the inequalities $M_3M_1^{4/13}D_0^{4/13}<\frac{1}{2}$, $M_4M_2^{8/17}D_0^{8/17}<\frac{1}{2}$ *are satisfied (that is, assumption (I7) is satisfied). For example, if* $\omega_1=4$, $\omega_2=2$, $\omega_3=3$, *and* $s_0\leq 0.0034$ *and* $t_0\leq 0.0031$, *then the above inequalities are satisfied. By Theorem 4, we conclude that problem (39) and (40) with the nonlinearities (42) has at least two positive solutions* $(u_1(\tau),v_1(\tau))$, $(u_2(\tau),v_2(\tau))$, $\tau\in[0,1]$.

5. Conclusions

In this paper we investigate the system of Riemann–Liouville fractional differential Equations (1) with r_1-Laplacian and r_2-Laplacian operators and fractional integral terms, subject to the uncoupled boundary conditions (2) which contain Riemann–Stieltjes integrals and fractional derivatives of various orders. The nonlinearities f and g from the system are nonnegative functions and they may be singular at $\tau = 0$ and/or $\tau = 1$. First we present the Green functions associated to our problem (1) and (2) and some of their properties. Then we give various conditions for the functions f and g such that (1) and (2) has at least one or two positive solutions. In the proof of our main results we use the Guo–Krasnosel'skii fixed point theorem of cone expansion and compression of norm type. We finally present two examples for illustrating the obtained existence theorems.

Author Contributions: Conceptualization, R.L.; formal analysis, A.T. and R.L.; methodology, A.T. and R.L. All authors have read and agreed to the published version of the manuscript.

Funding: This research received no external funding.

Institutional Review Board Statement: Not applicable.

Informed Consent Statement: Not applicable.

Data Availability Statement: Not applicable.

Acknowledgments: The authors thank the referees for their valuable comments and suggestions.

Conflicts of Interest: The authors declare no conflict of interest.

References

1. Wang, H.; Jiang, J. Existence and multiplicity of positive solutions for a system of nonlinear fractional multi-point boundary value problems with p-Laplacian operator. *J. Appl. Anal. Comput.* **2021**, *11*, 351–366.
2. Alsaedi, A.; Luca, R.; Ahmad, B. Existence of positive solutions for a system of singular fractional boundary value problems with p-Laplacian operators. *Mathematics* **2020**, *8*, 1–18. [CrossRef]
3. Tudorache, A.; Luca, R. Positive solutions for a system of Riemann–Liouville fractional boundary value problems with p-Laplacian operators. *Adv. Differ. Equ.* **2020**, *292*, 1–30. [CrossRef]
4. Liu, L.; Min, D.; Wu, Y. Existence and multiplicity of positive solutions for a new class of singular higher-order fractional differential equations with Riemann–Stieltjes integral boundary value conditions. *Adv. Differ. Equ.* **2020**, *442*, 1–23. [CrossRef]
5. Prasad, K.R.; Leela, I.D.; Khuddush, M. Existence and uniqueness of positive solutions for system of (p,q,r)-Laplacian fractional order boundary value problems. *Adv. Theory Nonlinear Anal. Appl.* **2021**, *5*, 138–157.
6. Tan, J.; Li, M. Solutions of fractional differential equations with p-Laplacian operator in Banach spaces. *Bound. Value Prob.* **2018**, *15*, 1–13. [CrossRef]
7. Tang, X.; Wang, X.; Wang, Z.; Ouyang, P. The existence of solutions for mixed fractional resonant boundary value problem with $p(t)$-Laplacian operator. *J. Appl. Math. Comput.* **2019**, *61*, 559–572. [CrossRef]
8. Tian, Y.; Sun, S.; Bai, Z. Positive Solutions of Fractional Differential Equations with p-Laplacian. *J. Funct. Spaces* **2017**, *2017*, 3187492. [CrossRef]
9. Wang, H.; Liu, S.; Li, H. Positive solutions to p-Laplacian fractional differential equations with infinite-point boundary value conditions. *Adv. Differ. Equ.* **2018**, *425*, 1–15.
10. Wang, Y.; Liu, S.; Han, Z. Eigenvalue problems for fractional differential equationswith mixed derivatives and generalized p-Laplacian. *Nonlinear Anal. Model. Control* **2018**, *23*, 830–850. [CrossRef]
11. Ahmad, B.; Alsaedi, A.; Ntouyas, S.K.; Tariboon, J. *Hadamard-Type Fractional Differential Equations, Inclusions and Inequalities*; Springer: Cham, Switzerland, 2017.
12. Ahmad, B.; Henderson, J.; Luca, R. *Boundary Value Problems for Fractional Differential Equations and Systems, Trends in Abstract and Applied Analysis*; World Scientific: Hackensack, NJ, USA, 2021, Volume 9.
13. Ahmad, B.; Ntouyas, S.K. *Nonlocal Nonlinear Fractional-Order Boundary Value Problems*; World Scientific: Hackensack, NJ, USA, 2021.
14. Henderson, J.; Luca, R. *Boundary Value Problems for Systems of Differential, Difference and Fractional Equations. Positive Solutions*; Elsevier: Amsterdam, The Netherlands, 2016.
15. Zhou, Y.; Wang, J.R.; Zhang, L. *Basic Theory of Fractional Differential Equations*, 2nd. ed.; World Scientific: Singapore, 2016.
16. Guo, D.; Lakshmikantham, V. *Nonlinear Problems in Abstract Cones*; Academic Press: New York, NY, USA, 1988.

fractal and fractional

MDPI

Article

Systems of Riemann–Liouville Fractional Differential Equations with ρ-Laplacian Operators and Nonlocal Coupled Boundary Conditions

Alexandru Tudorache [1] **and Rodica Luca** [2,*]

[1] Department of Computer Science and Engineering, Gh. Asachi Technical University, 700050 Iasi, Romania
[2] Department of Mathematics, Gh. Asachi Technical University, 700506 Iasi, Romania
[*] Correspondence: rluca@math.tuiasi.ro

Abstract: In this paper, we study the existence of positive solutions for a system of fractional differential equations with ρ-Laplacian operators, Riemann–Liouville derivatives of diverse orders and general nonlinearities which depend on several fractional integrals of differing orders, supplemented with nonlocal coupled boundary conditions containing Riemann–Stieltjes integrals and varied fractional derivatives. The nonlinearities from the system are continuous nonnegative functions and they can be singular in the time variable. We write equivalently this problem as a system of integral equations, and then we associate an operator for which we are looking for its fixed points. The main results are based on the Guo–Krasnosel'skii fixed point theorem of cone expansion and compression of norm type.

Keywords: Riemann–Liouville fractional differential equations; nonlocal coupled boundary conditions; singular functions; positive solutions; multiplicity

MSC: 34A08; 34B10; 34B16; 34B18

Citation: Tudorache, A.; Luca, R. Systems of Riemann–Liouville Fractional Differential Equations with ρ-Laplacian Operators and Nonlocal Coupled Boundary Conditions. *Fractal Fract.* **2022**, *6*, 610. https://doi.org/10.3390/fractalfract6100610

Academic Editor: Maria Rosaria Lancia

Received: 25 September 2022
Accepted: 14 October 2022
Published: 19 October 2022

1. Introduction

We consider the system of Riemann–Liouville fractional differential equations with ρ_1-Laplacian and ρ_2-Laplacian operators

$$\begin{cases} D_{0+}^{\delta_1}(\varphi_{\rho_1}(D_{0+}^{\gamma_1}x(t))) = \mathfrak{f}(t,x(t),y(t),I_{0+}^{\mu_1}x(t),I_{0+}^{\mu_2}y(t)), & t\in(0,1), \\ D_{0+}^{\delta_2}(\varphi_{\rho_2}(D_{0+}^{\gamma_2}y(t))) = \mathfrak{g}(t,x(t),y(t),I_{0+}^{\nu_1}x(t),I_{0+}^{\nu_2}y(t)), & t\in(0,1), \end{cases} \tag{1}$$

subject to the nonlocal coupled boundary conditions

$$\begin{cases} x^{(j)}(0)=0,\ j=0,\dots,p-2,\ D_{0+}^{\gamma_1}x(0)=0, \\ \varphi_{\rho_1}(D_{0+}^{\gamma_1}x(1)) = \int_0^1 \varphi_{\rho_1}(D_{0+}^{\gamma_1}x(\tau))\,d\mathfrak{M}_0(\tau),\ D_{0+}^{\alpha_0}x(1) = \sum_{k=1}^{n}\int_0^1 D_{0+}^{\alpha_k}y(\tau)\,d\mathfrak{M}_k(\tau), \\ y^{(j)}(0)=0,\ j=0,\dots,q-2,\ D_{0+}^{\gamma_2}y(0)=0, \\ \varphi_{\rho_2}(D_{0+}^{\gamma_2}y(1)) = \int_0^1 \varphi_{\rho_2}(D_{0+}^{\gamma_2}y(\tau))\,d\mathfrak{N}_0(\tau),\ D_{0+}^{\beta_0}y(1) = \sum_{k=1}^{m}\int_0^1 D_{0+}^{\beta_k}x(\tau)\,d\mathfrak{N}_k(\tau), \end{cases} \tag{2}$$

where $\delta_1,\delta_2\in(1,2]$, $\gamma_1\in(p-1,p]$, $p\in\mathbb{N}$, $p\geq 3$, $\gamma_2\in(q-1,q]$, $q\in\mathbb{N}$, $q\geq 3$, $n,m\in\mathbb{N}$, $\mu_1,\mu_2,\nu_1,\nu_2>0$, $\alpha_k\in\mathbb{R}$, $k=0,\dots,n$, $0\leq\alpha_1<\alpha_2<\cdots<\alpha_n\leq\beta_0<\gamma_2-1$, $\beta_0\geq 1$, $\beta_k\in\mathbb{R}$, $k=0,\dots,m$, $0\leq\beta_1<\beta_2<\cdots<\beta_m\leq\alpha_0<\gamma_1-1$, $\alpha_0\geq 1$, $\varphi_{\rho_i}(s)=|s|^{\rho_i-2}s$, $\varphi_{\rho_i}^{-1}=\varphi_{\varrho_i}$, $\varrho_i=\frac{\rho_i}{\rho_i-1}$, $i=1,2$, $\rho_i>1$, $i=1,2$, $\mathfrak{f},\mathfrak{g}:(0,1)\times\mathbb{R}_+^4\to\mathbb{R}_+$ are continuous functions, singular at $t=0$ and/or $t=1$, ($\mathbb{R}_+=[0,\infty)$), I_{0+}^{θ} is the Riemann–Liouville fractional integral of order θ (for $\theta=\mu_1,\mu_2,\nu_1,\nu_2$), D_{0+}^{θ} is the Riemann–Liouville fractional derivative of order θ (for $\theta=\delta_1,\gamma_1,\delta_2,\gamma_2,\alpha_0,\dots,\alpha_n,\beta_0,\dots,\beta_m$), and the integrals from the boundary conditions (2) are Riemann–Stieltjes integrals with $\mathfrak{M}_i : [0,1] \to \mathbb{R},\ i = 0,\ldots,n$ and $\mathfrak{N}_j : [0,1] \to \mathbb{R},\ j = 0,\ldots,m$ functions of bounded variation. The present work was motivated by the applications of ρ-Laplacian operators in various fields such as nonlinear elasticity, glaciology, nonlinear electrorheological fluids, fluid flows through porous media, etc. see for details the paper [1] and its references.

In this paper, we present varied conditions for the functions $\mathfrak{f}$ and $\mathfrak{g}$ such that problem (1), (2) has a positive solution, and then it has two positive solutions. A positive solution of (1), (2) is a pair of functions $(x,y) \in (C([0,1],\mathbb{R}_+))^2$ satisfying the system (1) and the boundary conditions (2), with $x(s) > 0$ for all $s \in (0,1]$ or $y(s) > 0$ for all $s \in (0,1]$. We apply the Guo–Krasnosel'skii fixed point theorem of cone expansion and compression of norm type (see [2]) in the proof of our main results. Connected to our problem, we mention the following papers. In [3], the authors studied the existence of multiple positive solutions of the system of nonlinear fractional differential equations with p_1-Laplacian and p_2-Laplacian operators

$$\begin{cases} D_{0+}^{\beta_1}(\varphi_{p_1}(D_{0+}^{\alpha_1}x(s))) = \mathfrak{f}(s,x(s),y(s)), & s \in (0,1), \\ D_{0+}^{\beta_2}(\varphi_{p_2}(D_{0+}^{\alpha_2}y(s))) = \mathfrak{g}(s,x(s),y(s)), & s \in (0,1), \end{cases}$$

supplemented with the nonlocal uncoupled boundary conditions

$$\begin{cases} x(0) = 0, \ D_{0+}^{\gamma_1}x(1) = \sum\limits_{k=1}^{m-2} \xi_{1k} D_{0+}^{\gamma_1}x(\eta_{1k}), \\ D_{0+}^{\alpha_1}x(0) = 0, \ \varphi_{p_1}(D_{0+}^{\alpha_1}x(1)) = \sum_{k=1}^{m-2} \zeta_{1k}\varphi_{p_1}(D_{0+}^{\alpha_1}x(\eta_{1k})), \\ y(0) = 0, \ D_{0+}^{\gamma_2}y(1) = \sum\limits_{k=1}^{m-2} \xi_{2k} D_{0+}^{\gamma_2}y(\eta_{2k}), \\ D_{0+}^{\alpha_2}y(0) = 0, \ \varphi_{p_2}(D_{0+}^{\alpha_2}y(1)) = \sum_{k=1}^{m-2} \zeta_{2k}\varphi_{p_2}(D_{0+}^{\alpha_2}y(\eta_{2k})), \end{cases}$$

where $\alpha_i, \beta_i \in (1,2]$, $\gamma_i \in (0,1]$, $\alpha_i + \beta_i \in (3,4]$, $\alpha_i > \gamma_i + 1$, $i = 1,2$, $\xi_{1k}, \eta_{1k}, \zeta_{1k}, \xi_{2k}, \eta_{2k}, \zeta_{2k} \in (0,1)$ for $k = 1,\ldots,m-2$, $p_1, p_2 > 1$, and $\mathfrak{f}$ and $\mathfrak{g}$ are nonnegative and nonsingular functions. They applied the Leray-Schauder alternative theorem, the Leggett-Williams fixed point theorem and the Avery-Henderson fixed point theorem in the proof of the existence results. In [4], the authors studied the existence and nonexistence of positive solutions for the system of Riemann–Liouville fractional differential equations with ϱ_1-Laplacian and ϱ_2-Laplacian operators

$$\begin{cases} D_{0+}^{\gamma_1}(\varphi_{\varrho_1}(D_{0+}^{\delta_1}x(s))) + \lambda\mathfrak{f}(s,x(s),y(s)) = 0, & s \in (0,1), \\ D_{0+}^{\gamma_2}(\varphi_{\varrho_2}(D_{0+}^{\delta_2}y(s))) + \mu\mathfrak{g}(s,x(s),y(s)) = 0, & s \in (0,1), \end{cases} \tag{3}$$

subject to the coupled nonlocal boundary conditions

$$\begin{cases} x^{(j)}(0) = 0, \ j = 0,\ldots,p-2; \ D_{0+}^{\delta_1}x(0) = 0, \ D_{0+}^{\alpha_0}x(1) = \sum\limits_{k=1}^{n} \int_0^1 D_{0+}^{\alpha_k}y(\zeta)\, d\mathfrak{M}_k(\zeta), \\ y^{(j)}(0) = 0, \ j = 0,\ldots,q-2; \ D_{0+}^{\delta_2}y(0) = 0, \ D_{0+}^{\beta_0}y(1) = \sum\limits_{k=1}^{m} \int_0^1 D_{0+}^{\beta_k}x(\zeta)\, d\mathfrak{N}_k(\zeta), \end{cases} \tag{4}$$

where λ and μ are positive parameters, $\gamma_1, \gamma_2 \in (0,1]$, $\delta_1 \in (p-1,p]$, $\delta_2 \in (q-1,q]$, $p, q \in \mathbb{N}$, $p, q \geq 3$, $n, m \in \mathbb{N}$, $\alpha_k \in \mathbb{R}$ for all $k = 0,\ldots,n$, $0 \leq \alpha_1 < \alpha_2 < \cdots < \alpha_n \leq \beta_0 < \delta_2 - 1$, $\beta_0 \geq 1$, $\beta_k \in \mathbb{R}$ for all $k = 0,\ldots,m$, $0 \leq \beta_1 < \beta_2 < \cdots < \beta_m \leq \alpha_0 < \delta_1 - 1$, $\alpha_0 \geq 1$, $\varrho_1, \varrho_2 > 1$, the functions $\mathfrak{f}, \mathfrak{g} \in C([0,1] \times \mathbb{R}_+ \times \mathbb{R}_+, \mathbb{R}_+)$, and the functions $\mathfrak{M}_j$, $j = 1,\ldots,n$ and $\mathfrak{N}_k$, $k = 1,\ldots,m$ are bounded variation functions. They presented sufficient conditions on the functions $\mathfrak{f}$ and $\mathfrak{g}$, and intervals for the parameters λ and μ such that problem (3), (4) has positive solutions. In [5], the authors investigated the existence and multiplicity of positive solutions for the system (3) with $\lambda = \mu = 1$, supplemented with the uncoupled nonlocal boundary conditions

$$\begin{cases} x^{(j)}(0) = 0,\ j = 0, \dots, p-2;\ D_{0+}^{\delta_1} x(0) = 0,\ D_{0+}^{\alpha_0} x(1) = \sum_{k=1}^{n} \int_0^1 D_{0+}^{\alpha_k} x(\zeta)\, d\mathfrak{M}_k(\zeta), \\ y^{(j)}(0) = 0,\ j = 0, \dots, q-2;\ D_{0+}^{\delta_2} y(0) = 0,\ D_{0+}^{\beta_0} y(1) = \sum_{k=1}^{m} \int_0^1 D_{0+}^{\beta_k} y(\zeta)\, d\mathfrak{N}_k(\zeta), \end{cases}$$

where $n, m \in \mathbb{N}$, $\alpha_k \in \mathbb{R}$ for all $k = 0, 1, \dots, n$, $0 \le \alpha_1 < \alpha_2 < \dots < \alpha_n \le \alpha_0 < \delta_1 - 1$, $\alpha_0 \ge 1$, $\beta_k \in \mathbb{R}$ for all $k = 0, 1, \dots, m$, $0 \le \beta_1 < \beta_2 < \dots < \beta_m \le \beta_0 < \delta_2 - 1$, $\beta_0 \ge 1$, the functions $\mathfrak{f}$ and $\mathfrak{g}$ from system (3) are nonnegative and continuous, and they may be singular at $s = 0$ and/or $s = 1$, and $\mathfrak{M}_j$, $j = 1, \dots, n$ and $\mathfrak{N}_k$, $k = 1, \dots, m$ are functions of bounded variation. They applied the Guo–Krasnosel'skii fixed point theorem in the proof of the main existence results. In [6] the authors studied the existence and multiplicity of positive solutions for the system (1) subject to general uncoupled boundary conditions in the point $t = 1$. We mention that our problem (1), (2) is different than the problems from papers [4,6]. Indeed the orders of the first fractional derivatives in the system (3) (from [4]) are positive numbers less than or equal to 1, and in our system (1) the first fractional derivatives are numbers greater than 1 and less than or equal to 2. This difference conducts to the consideration of different boundary conditions (more precisely, for our problem, we have a bigger number of such boundary conditions)—see (2) and (4). Another differences are the presence of the parameters in system (3)—here, we do not have any parameters, and also the nonlinearities $\mathfrak{f}$ and $\mathfrak{g}$ from (3) which are nonsingular functions, as opposed to our problem in which the functions $\mathfrak{f}$ and $\mathfrak{g}$ are singular; so here is a more difficult case to study. On the other hand, the essential difference between the present problem (1), (2) and the problem studied in [6], is given by the boundary conditions. In [6] the last boundary conditions for the unknown functions are uncoupled in the point 1, and here in (2), the last boundary conditions for the unknown functions x and y are coupled in the point 1; that is, the fractional derivative of order α_0 of function x in the point 1 is dependent of varied fractional derivatives of function y, and the fractional derivative of order β_0 of function y in 1 is dependent of various fractional derivatives of function x. Hence the novelty of our problem (1), (2) is represented by a combination between the existence of ρ-Laplacian operators in system (1), the dependence of the nonlinearities in (1) on diverse fractional integrals, and the nature of the last boundary conditions in the point 1 which are coupled here. We also mention the recent papers [7–12] in which the authors study fractional differential equations and systems with ρ-Laplacian operators, and some recent monographs devoted to the investigation of boundary value problems for fractional differential equations and systems, namely [13–17].

The paper is organized in the following way. In Section 2, some auxiliary results which include the properties of the Green functions associated to our problem (1), (2) are given. In Section 3 we present the system of integral equations corresponding to our problem, and the main existence and multiplicity theorems for positive solutions of (1), (2), and Section 4 contains their proofs. Finally, two examples which illustrate our obtained results are presented in Section 5, and the conclusions are given in Section 6.

2. Auxiliary Results

In this section, we consider the system of fractional differential equations

$$\begin{cases} D_{0+}^{\delta_1}(\varphi_{\rho_1}(D_{0+}^{\gamma_1} x(t))) = u(t),\ t \in (0,1), \\ D_{0+}^{\delta_2}(\varphi_{\rho_2}(D_{0+}^{\gamma_2} y(t))) = v(t),\ t \in (0,1), \end{cases} \tag{5}$$

with the coupled boundary conditions (2), where $u, v \in C(0,1) \cap L^1(0,1)$.

We denote $\varphi_{\rho_1}(D_{0+}^{\gamma_1}x(t)) = h(t)$, $\varphi_{\rho_2}(D_{0+}^{\gamma_2}y(t)) = k(t)$. Then problem (2), (5) is equivalent to the following three problems

$$\begin{cases} D_{0+}^{\delta_1}h(t) = u(t), \ t \in (0,1), \\ h(0) = 0, \ h(1) = \int_0^1 h(\tau)\, d\mathfrak{M}_0(\tau), \end{cases} \tag{6}$$

$$\begin{cases} D_{0+}^{\delta_2}k(t) = v(t), \ t \in (0,1), \\ k(0) = 0, \ k(1) = \int_0^1 k(\tau)\, d\mathfrak{N}_0(\tau), \end{cases} \tag{7}$$

and

$$\begin{cases} D_{0+}^{\gamma_1}x(t) = \varphi_{\varrho_1}(h(t)), \ t \in (0,1), \\ D_{0+}^{\gamma_2}y(t) = \varphi_{\varrho_2}(k(t)), \ t \in (0,1), \end{cases} \tag{8}$$

with the boundary conditions

$$\begin{cases} x^{(j)}(0) = 0, \ j = 0,\dots,p-2, \ D_{0+}^{\alpha_0}x(1) = \sum_{k=1}^{n}\int_0^1 D_{0+}^{\alpha_k}y(\tau)\, d\mathfrak{M}_k(\tau), \\ y^{(j)}(0) = 0, \ j = 0,\dots,q-2, \ D_{0+}^{\beta_0}y(1) = \sum_{k=1}^{m}\int_0^1 D_{0+}^{\beta_k}x(\tau)\, d\mathfrak{N}_k(\tau). \end{cases} \tag{9}$$

By Lemma 4.1.5 from [16], the unique solution $h \in C[0,1]$ of problem (6) is

$$h(t) = -\int_0^1 \mathfrak{G}_1(t,\tau)u(\tau)\, d\tau, \ t \in [0,1], \tag{10}$$

where

$$\mathfrak{G}_1(t,\tau) = \mathfrak{g}_1(t,\tau) + \frac{t^{\delta_1-1}}{\mathfrak{a}_1}\int_0^1 \mathfrak{g}_1(\zeta,\tau)\, d\mathfrak{M}_0(\zeta),$$
$$\mathfrak{g}_1(t,\tau) = \frac{1}{\Gamma(\delta_1)}\begin{cases} t^{\delta_1-1}(1-\tau)^{\delta_1-1} - (t-\tau)^{\delta_1-1}, \ 0 \le \tau \le t \le 1, \\ t^{\delta_1-1}(1-\tau)^{\delta_1-1}, \ 0 \le t \le \tau \le 1, \end{cases}$$

for $(t,\tau) \in [0,1] \times [0,1]$, with $\mathfrak{a}_1 = 1 - \int_0^1 \zeta^{\delta_1-1}\, d\mathfrak{M}_0(\zeta) \neq 0$.

By the same lemma (Lemma 4.1.5 from [16]), the unique solution $k \in C[0,1]$ of problem (7) is

$$k(t) = -\int_0^1 \mathfrak{G}_2(t,\tau)v(\tau)\, d\tau, \ t \in [0,1], \tag{11}$$

where

$$\mathfrak{G}_2(t,\tau) = \mathfrak{g}_2(t,\tau) + \frac{t^{\delta_2-1}}{\mathfrak{a}_2}\int_0^1 \mathfrak{g}_2(\zeta,\tau)\, d\mathfrak{N}_0(\zeta),$$
$$\mathfrak{g}_2(t,\tau) = \frac{1}{\Gamma(\delta_2)}\begin{cases} t^{\delta_2-1}(1-\tau)^{\delta_2-1} - (t-\tau)^{\delta_2-1}, \ 0 \le \tau \le t \le 1, \\ t^{\delta_2-1}(1-\tau)^{\delta_2-1}, \ 0 \le t \le \tau \le 1, \end{cases}$$

for $(t,\tau) \in [0,1] \times [0,1]$, with $\mathfrak{a}_2 = 1 - \int_0^1 \zeta^{\delta_2-1}\, d\mathfrak{N}_0(\zeta) \neq 0$.

By Lemma 2.2 from [4], the unique solution $(x,y) \in (C[0,1])^2$ of problem (8), (9) is

$$\begin{cases} x(t) = -\int_0^1 \mathfrak{G}_3(t,\tau)\varphi_{\varrho_1}(h(\tau))\, d\tau - \int_0^1 \mathfrak{G}_4(t,\tau)\varphi_{\varrho_2}(k(\tau))\, d\tau, \ t \in [0,1], \\ y(t) = -\int_0^1 \mathfrak{G}_5(t,\tau)\varphi_{\varrho_1}(h(\tau))\, d\tau - \int_0^1 \mathfrak{G}_6(t,\tau)\varphi_{\varrho_2}(k(\tau))\, d\tau, \ t \in [0,1], \end{cases} \tag{12}$$

where

$$\mathfrak{G}_3(t,\tau) = \mathfrak{g}_3(t,\tau) + \frac{t^{\gamma_1-1}\mathfrak{b}_1}{\mathfrak{b}}\left(\sum_{i=1}^{m}\int_0^1 \mathfrak{g}_{3i}(\vartheta,\tau)\,d\mathfrak{N}_i(\vartheta)\right),$$
$$\mathfrak{G}_4(t,\tau) = \frac{t^{\gamma_1-1}\Gamma(\gamma_2)}{\mathfrak{b}\Gamma(\gamma_2-\beta_0)}\sum_{i=1}^{n}\int_0^1 \mathfrak{g}_{4i}(\vartheta,\tau)\,d\mathfrak{M}_i(\vartheta),$$
$$\mathfrak{G}_5(t,\tau) = \frac{t^{\gamma_2-1}\Gamma(\gamma_1)}{\mathfrak{b}\Gamma(\gamma_1-\alpha_0)}\sum_{i=1}^{m}\int_0^1 \mathfrak{g}_{3i}(\vartheta,\tau)\,d\mathfrak{N}_i(\vartheta),$$
$$\mathfrak{G}_6(t,\tau) = \mathfrak{g}_4(t,\tau) + \frac{t^{\gamma_2-1}\mathfrak{b}_2}{\mathfrak{b}}\left(\sum_{i=1}^{n}\int_0^1 \mathfrak{g}_{4i}(\vartheta,\tau)\,d\mathfrak{M}_i(\vartheta)\right),$$

$$\mathfrak{g}_3(t,\tau) = \frac{1}{\Gamma(\gamma_1)}\begin{cases} t^{\gamma_1-1}(1-\tau)^{\gamma_1-\alpha_0-1} - (t-\tau)^{\gamma_1-1}, & 0\le\tau\le t\le 1,\\ t^{\gamma_1-1}(1-\tau)^{\gamma_1-\alpha_0-1}, & 0\le t\le\tau\le 1,\end{cases}$$
$$\mathfrak{g}_{3i}(\vartheta,\tau) = \frac{1}{\Gamma(\gamma_1-\beta_i)}\begin{cases} \vartheta^{\gamma_1-\beta_i-1}(1-\tau)^{\gamma_1-\alpha_0-1} - (\vartheta-\tau)^{\gamma_1-\beta_i-1}, & 0\le\tau\le\vartheta\le 1,\\ \vartheta^{\gamma_1-\beta_i-1}(1-\tau)^{\gamma_1-\alpha_0-1}, & 0\le\vartheta\le\tau\le 1,\end{cases}$$
$$\mathfrak{g}_4(t,\tau) = \frac{1}{\Gamma(\gamma_2)}\begin{cases} t^{\gamma_2-1}(1-\tau)^{\gamma_2-\beta_0-1} - (t-\tau)^{\gamma_2-1}, & 0\le\tau\le t\le 1,\\ t^{\gamma_2-1}(1-\tau)^{\gamma_2-\beta_0-1}, & 0\le t\le\tau\le 1,\end{cases}$$
$$\mathfrak{g}_{4j}(\vartheta,\tau) = \frac{1}{\Gamma(\gamma_2-\alpha_j)}\begin{cases} \vartheta^{\gamma_2-\alpha_j-1}(1-\tau)^{\gamma_2-\beta_0-1} - (\vartheta-\tau)^{\gamma_2-\alpha_j-1}, & 0\le\tau\le\vartheta\le 1,\\ \vartheta^{\gamma_2-\alpha_j-1}(1-\tau)^{\gamma_2-\beta_0-1}, & 0\le\vartheta\le\tau\le 1,\end{cases}$$

for all $t,\tau,\vartheta \in [0,1]$, $i=1,\dots,m$, $j=1,\dots,n$, and $\mathfrak{b}_1 = \sum_{i=1}^{n}\frac{\Gamma(\gamma_2)}{\Gamma(\gamma_2-\alpha_i)}\int_0^1 \zeta^{\gamma_2-\alpha_i-1}\,d\mathfrak{M}_i(\zeta)$, $\mathfrak{b}_2 = \sum_{i=1}^{m}\frac{\Gamma(\gamma_1)}{\Gamma(\gamma_1-\beta_i)}\int_0^1 \zeta^{\gamma_1-\beta_i-1}\,d\mathfrak{N}_i(\zeta)$, and $\mathfrak{b} = \frac{\Gamma(\gamma_1)\Gamma(\gamma_2)}{\Gamma(\gamma_1-\alpha_0)\Gamma(\gamma_2-\beta_0)} - \mathfrak{b}_1\mathfrak{b}_2 \neq 0$.

Combining the above Formulas (10)–(12) for $h(t)$, $k(t)$, $x(t)$, $y(t)$, $t\in[0,1]$, we obtain the following result.

Lemma 1. *If $\mathfrak{a}_1 \neq 0$, $\mathfrak{a}_2 \neq 0$ and $\mathfrak{b} \neq 0$, then the unique solution $(x,y) \in (C[0,1])^2$ of problem (5), (2) is given by*

$$x(t) = \int_0^1 \mathfrak{G}_3(t,\tau)\varphi_{\varrho_1}\left(\int_0^1 \mathfrak{G}_1(\tau,\zeta)u(\zeta)\,d\zeta\right)d\tau + \int_0^1 \mathfrak{G}_4(t,\tau)\varphi_{\varrho_2}\left(\int_0^1 \mathfrak{G}_2(\tau,\zeta)v(\zeta)\,d\zeta\right)d\tau, \quad \forall t\in[0,1],$$
$$y(t) = \int_0^1 \mathfrak{G}_5(t,\tau)\varphi_{\varrho_1}\left(\int_0^1 \mathfrak{G}_1(\tau,\zeta)u(\zeta)\,d\zeta\right)d\tau + \int_0^1 \mathfrak{G}_6(t,\tau)\varphi_{\varrho_2}\left(\int_0^1 \mathfrak{G}_2(\tau,\zeta)v(\zeta)\,d\zeta\right)d\tau, \quad \forall t\in[0,1].$$

Now by using the properties of functions $\mathfrak{g}_1$, $\mathfrak{g}_2$, $\mathfrak{g}_3$, $\mathfrak{g}_{3i}$, $i = 1,\dots,m$, $\mathfrak{g}_4$, $\mathfrak{g}_{4j}$, $j=1,\dots,n$ (see [14,16]), we deduce the following properties of the functions $\mathfrak{G}_i$, $i = 1,\dots,6$.

Lemma 2. *We suppose that $\mathfrak{a}_1 > 0$, $\mathfrak{a}_2 > 0$ and $\mathfrak{b} > 0$, $\mathfrak{M}_i$, $i=1,\dots,n$ and $\mathfrak{N}_j$, $j=0,\dots,m$ are nondecreasing functions. Then the functions $\mathfrak{G}_i$, $i=1,\dots,6$ have the properties:*

(a) $\mathfrak{G}_i : [0,1]\times[0,1] \to [0,\infty)$, $i=1,\dots,6$ *are continuous functions.*

(b) $\mathfrak{G}_1(t,\tau) \le \mathfrak{J}_1(\tau)$, *for all* $(t,\tau)\in[0,1]\times[0,1]$, *where*

$$\mathfrak{J}_1(\tau) = \mathfrak{h}_1(\tau) + \frac{1}{\mathfrak{a}_1}\int_0^1 \mathfrak{g}_1(\zeta,\tau)\,d\mathfrak{M}_0(\zeta), \quad \forall\tau\in[0,1],$$

with $\mathfrak{h}_1(\tau) = \frac{1}{\Gamma(\delta_1)}(1-\tau)^{\delta_1-1}$, $\tau\in[0,1]$.

(c) $\mathfrak{G}_2(t,\tau) \le \mathfrak{J}_2(\tau)$, *for all* $(t,\tau)\in[0,1]\times[0,1]$, *where*

$$\mathfrak{J}_2(\tau) = \mathfrak{h}_2(\tau) + \frac{1}{\mathfrak{a}_2}\int_0^1 \mathfrak{g}_2(\zeta,\tau)\,d\mathfrak{N}_0(\zeta), \quad \forall\tau\in[0,1],$$

with $\mathfrak{h}_2(\tau) = \frac{1}{\Gamma(\delta_2)}(1-\tau)^{\delta_2-1}$, $\tau \in [0,1]$.

(d) $\mathfrak{G}_3(t,\tau) \le \mathfrak{J}_3(\tau)$, *for all* $(t,\tau) \in [0,1] \times [0,1]$, *where*

$$\mathfrak{J}_3(\tau) = \mathfrak{h}_3(\tau) + \frac{\mathfrak{b}_1}{\mathfrak{b}}\left(\sum_{i=1}^{m}\int_0^1 \mathfrak{g}_{3i}(\vartheta,\tau)\,d\mathfrak{N}_i(\vartheta)\right), \quad \forall \tau \in [0,1],$$

with $\mathfrak{h}_3(\tau) = \frac{1}{\Gamma(\gamma_1)}(1-\tau)^{\gamma_1-\alpha_0-1}(1-(1-\tau)^{\alpha_0})$, $\tau \in [0,1]$.

(e) $\mathfrak{G}_3(t,\tau) \ge t^{\gamma_1-1}\mathfrak{J}_3(\tau)$, *for all* $(t,\tau) \in [0,1] \times [0,1]$.

(f) $\mathfrak{G}_4(t,\tau) \le \mathfrak{J}_4(\tau)$, *for all* $(t,\tau) \in [0,1] \times [0,1]$, *where*

$$\mathfrak{J}_4(\tau) = \frac{\Gamma(\gamma_2)}{\mathfrak{b}\Gamma(\gamma_2-\beta_0)}\sum_{i=1}^{n}\int_0^1 \mathfrak{g}_{4i}(\vartheta,\tau)\,d\mathfrak{M}_i(\vartheta), \quad \forall \tau \in [0,1].$$

(g) $\mathfrak{G}_4(t,\tau) = t^{\gamma_1-1}\mathfrak{J}_4(\tau)$, *for all* $(t,\tau) \in [0,1] \times [0,1]$.

(h) $\mathfrak{G}_5(t,\tau) \le \mathfrak{J}_5(\tau)$, *for all* $(t,\tau) \in [0,1] \times [0,1]$, *where*

$$\mathfrak{J}_5(\tau) = \frac{\Gamma(\gamma_1)}{\mathfrak{b}\Gamma(\gamma_1-\alpha_0)}\sum_{i=1}^{m}\int_0^1 \mathfrak{g}_{3i}(\vartheta,\tau)\,d\mathfrak{N}_i(\vartheta), \quad \forall \tau \in [0,1].$$

(i) $\mathfrak{G}_5(t,\tau) = t^{\gamma_2-1}\mathfrak{J}_5(\tau)$, *for all* $(t,\tau) \in [0,1] \times [0,1]$.

(j) $\mathfrak{G}_6(t,\tau) \le \mathfrak{J}_6(\tau)$, *for all* $(t,\tau) \in [0,1] \times [0,1]$, *where*

$$\mathfrak{J}_6(\tau) = \mathfrak{h}_4(\tau) + \frac{\mathfrak{b}_2}{\mathfrak{b}}\left(\sum_{i=1}^{n}\int_0^1 \mathfrak{g}_{4i}(\vartheta,\tau)\,d\mathfrak{M}_i(\vartheta)\right), \quad \forall \tau \in [0,1],$$

with $\mathfrak{h}_4(\tau) = \frac{1}{\Gamma(\gamma_2)}(1-\tau)^{\gamma_2-\beta_0-1}(1-(1-\tau)^{\beta_0})$, $\tau \in [0,1]$.

(k) $\mathfrak{G}_6(t,\tau) \ge t^{\gamma_2-1}\mathfrak{J}_6(\tau)$, *for all* $(t,\tau) \in [0,1] \times [0,1]$.

Under the assumptions of Lemma 2, we find that $\mathfrak{J}_i(\tau) \ge 0$ for all $\tau \in [0,1]$ and $i = 1,\ldots,6$, and $\mathfrak{J}_1, \mathfrak{J}_2, \mathfrak{J}_3, \mathfrak{J}_6 \not\equiv 0$. In addition, $\mathfrak{J}_4 \equiv 0$ if all the functions $\mathfrak{M}_i$, $i = 1,\ldots,n$ are constant, and $\mathfrak{J}_5 \equiv 0$ if all the functions $\mathfrak{N}_j$, $j = 1,\ldots,m$ are constant.

We also deduce easily the next lemma.

Lemma 3. *We suppose that* $\mathfrak{a}_1 > 0$, $\mathfrak{a}_2 > 0$ *and* $\mathfrak{b} > 0$, $\mathfrak{M}_i$, $i = 1,\ldots,n$ *and* $\mathfrak{N}_j$, $j = 0,\ldots,m$ *are nondecreasing functions,* $u, v \in C(0,1) \cap L^1(0,1)$ *with* $u(s) \ge 0$, $v(s) \ge 0$ *for all* $s \in (0,1)$. *Then the solution* (x,y) *of problem (5), (2) satisfies the inequalities* $x(s) \ge 0$, $y(s) \ge 0$ *for all* $s \in [0,1]$, *and* $x(s) \ge s^{\gamma_1-1}x(\tau)$ *and* $y(s) \ge s^{\gamma_2-1}y(\tau)$ *for all* $s,\tau \in [0,1]$.

3. Main Theorems

By using Lemma 1, the pair of functions (x,y) is a solution of problem (1), (2) if and only if (x,y) is a solution of the system

$$\begin{aligned}
x(t) &= \int_0^1 \mathfrak{G}_3(t,\tau)\varphi_{\varrho_1}\left(\int_0^1 \mathfrak{G}_1(\tau,\zeta)\mathfrak{f}(\zeta,x(\zeta),y(\zeta),I_{0+}^{\mu_1}x(\zeta),I_{0+}^{\mu_2}y(\zeta))\,d\zeta\right)d\tau \\
&+ \int_0^1 \mathfrak{G}_4(t,\tau)\varphi_{\varrho_2}\left(\int_0^1 \mathfrak{G}_2(\tau,\zeta)\mathfrak{g}(\zeta,x(\zeta),y(\zeta),I_{0+}^{\nu_1}x(\zeta),I_{0+}^{\nu_2}y(\zeta))\,d\zeta\right)d\tau, \\
y(t) &= \int_0^1 \mathfrak{G}_5(t,\tau)\varphi_{\varrho_1}\left(\int_0^1 \mathfrak{G}_1(\tau,\zeta)\mathfrak{f}(\zeta,x(\zeta),y(\zeta),I_{0+}^{\mu_1}x(\zeta),I_{0+}^{\mu_2}y(\zeta))\,d\zeta\right)d\tau \\
&+ \int_0^1 \mathfrak{G}_6(t,\tau)\varphi_{\varrho_2}\left(\int_0^1 \mathfrak{G}_2(\tau,\zeta)\mathfrak{g}(\zeta,x(\zeta),y(\zeta),I_{0+}^{\nu_1}x(\zeta),I_{0+}^{\nu_2}y(\zeta))\,d\zeta\right)d\tau,
\end{aligned}$$

for all $t \in [0,1]$. We introduce the Banach space $\mathfrak{U} = C[0,1]$ with supremum norm $\|x\| = \sup_{s\in[0,1]} |x(s)|$, and the Banach space $\mathfrak{V} = \mathfrak{U} \times \mathfrak{U}$ with the norm $\|(x,y)\|_{\mathfrak{V}} = \|x\| + \|y\|$. We define the cone

$$\mathfrak{Q} = \{(x,y) \in \mathfrak{V},\ x(s) \geq 0,\ y(s) \geq 0,\ \forall s \in [0,1]\}.$$

We also define the operators $\mathfrak{E}_1,\ \mathfrak{E}_2 : \mathfrak{V} \to \mathfrak{U}$ and $\mathfrak{E} : \mathfrak{V} \to \mathfrak{V}$ by

$$\begin{aligned}
\mathfrak{E}_1(x,y)(t) &= \int_0^1 \mathfrak{G}_3(t,\tau)\varphi_{\varrho_1}\left(\int_0^1 \mathfrak{G}_1(\tau,\zeta)\mathfrak{f}(\zeta,x(\zeta),y(\zeta),I_{0+}^{\mu_1}x(\zeta),I_{0+}^{\mu_2}y(\zeta))\,d\zeta\right)d\tau \\
&+ \int_0^1 \mathfrak{G}_4(t,\tau)\varphi_{\varrho_2}\left(\int_0^1 \mathfrak{G}_2(\tau,\zeta)\mathfrak{g}(\zeta,x(\zeta),y(\zeta),I_{0+}^{\nu_1}x(\zeta),I_{0+}^{\nu_2}y(\zeta))\,d\zeta\right)d\tau, \\
\mathfrak{E}_2(x,y)(t) &= \int_0^1 \mathfrak{G}_5(t,\tau)\varphi_{\varrho_1}\left(\int_0^1 \mathfrak{G}_1(\tau,\zeta)\mathfrak{f}(\zeta,x(\zeta),y(\zeta),I_{0+}^{\mu_1}x(\zeta),I_{0+}^{\mu_2}y(\zeta))\,d\zeta\right)d\tau \\
&+ \int_0^1 \mathfrak{G}_6(t,\tau)\varphi_{\varrho_2}\left(\int_0^1 \mathfrak{G}_2(\tau,\zeta)\mathfrak{g}(\zeta,x(\zeta),y(\zeta),I_{0+}^{\nu_1}x(\zeta),I_{0+}^{\nu_2}y(\zeta))\,d\zeta\right)d\tau,
\end{aligned}$$

for all $t \in [0,1]$ and $(x,y) \in \mathfrak{V}$, and $\mathfrak{E}(x,y) = (\mathfrak{E}_1(x,y), \mathfrak{E}_2(x,y)),\ (x,y) \in \mathfrak{V}$. We remark that (x,y) is a solution of problem (1), (2) if and only if (x,y) is a fixed point of operator $\mathfrak{E}$.

We define the constants: $\Xi_i = \int_0^1 \mathfrak{J}_i(\tau)\xi_i(\tau)\,d\tau,\ i = 1,2,\ \Xi_j = \int_0^1 \mathfrak{J}_j(\tau)\,d\tau,\ j = 3,\ldots,6$, and for $\sigma_1, \sigma_2 \in (0,1),\ \sigma_1 < \sigma_2,\ \Xi_7 = \int_{\sigma_1}^{\sigma_2} \mathfrak{J}_3(\tau)\left(\int_{\sigma_1}^{\tau} \mathfrak{G}_1(\tau,\zeta)\,d\zeta\right)^{\varrho_1 - 1} d\tau,\ \Xi_8 = \int_{\sigma_1}^{\sigma_2} \mathfrak{J}_6(\tau)\left(\int_{\sigma_1}^{\tau} \mathfrak{G}_2(\tau,\zeta)\,d\zeta\right)^{\varrho_2 - 1} d\tau$.

We now present the assumptions that we will use in our theorems.

$(H1)$ $\delta_1, \delta_2 \in (1,2]$, $\gamma_1 \in (p-1,p]$, $p \in \mathbb{N}$, $p \geq 3$, $\gamma_2 \in (q-1,q]$, $q \in \mathbb{N}$, $q \geq 3$, $n,m \in \mathbb{N}$, $\mu_1, \mu_2, \nu_1, \nu_2 > 0$, $\alpha_k \in \mathbb{R}$, $k = 0,\ldots,n$, $0 \leq \alpha_1 < \alpha_2 < \cdots < \alpha_n \leq \beta_0 < \gamma_2 - 1$, $\beta_0 \geq 1$, $\beta_k \in \mathbb{R}$, $k = 0,\ldots,m$, $0 \leq \beta_1 < \beta_2 < \cdots < \beta_m \leq \alpha_0 < \gamma_1 - 1$, $\alpha_0 \geq 1$, $\mathfrak{M}_i : [0,1] \to \mathbb{R}$, $i = 0,\ldots,n$, and $\mathfrak{N}_j : [0,1] \to \mathbb{R}$, $j = 0,\ldots,m$ are nondecreasing functions, $\varphi_{\rho_i}(\tau) = |\tau|^{\rho_i - 2}\tau$, $\varphi_{\rho_i}^{-1} = \varphi_{\varrho_i}$, $\varrho_i = \frac{\rho_i}{\rho_i - 1}$, $i = 1,2$, $\rho_i > 1$, $i = 1,2$, $\mathfrak{a}_1 > 0$, $\mathfrak{a}_2 > 0$, $\mathfrak{b} > 0$ (given in Section 2).

$(H2)$ The functions $\mathfrak{f},\ \mathfrak{g} \in C((0,1) \times \mathbb{R}_+^4, \mathbb{R}_+)$ and there exist the functions $\xi_1, \xi_2 \in C((0,1), \mathbb{R}_+)$ and $\psi_1, \psi_2 \in C([0,1] \times \mathbb{R}_+^4, \mathbb{R}_+)$ with $M_1 = \int_0^1 (1-t)^{\delta_1 - 1}\xi_1(t)\,dt \in (0,\infty)$, $M_2 = \int_0^1 (1-t)^{\delta_2 - 1}\xi_2(t)\,dt \in (0,\infty)$, such that

$$\begin{aligned}
\mathfrak{f}(t,w_1,w_2,w_3,w_4) &\leq \xi_1(t)\psi_1(t,w_1,w_2,w_3,w_4), \\
\mathfrak{g}(t,w_1,w_2,w_3,w_4) &\leq \xi_2(t)\psi_2(t,w_1,w_2,w_3,w_4),
\end{aligned}$$

for any $t \in (0,1)$, $w_i \in \mathbb{R}_+$, $i = 1,\ldots,4$.

$(H3)$ There exist $l_i \geq 0$, $i = 1,\ldots,4$ with $\sum_{i=1}^4 l_i > 0$, $m_i \geq 0$, $i = 1,\ldots,4$ with $\sum_{i=1}^4 m_i > 0$, and $\theta_1 \geq 1$, $\theta_2 \geq 1$ such that

$$\psi_{10} = \limsup_{\sum_{i=1}^4 l_i w_i \to 0} \max_{t\in[0,1]} \frac{\psi_1(t,w_1,w_2,w_3,w_4)}{\varphi_{\rho_1}((l_1 w_1 + l_2 w_2 + l_3 w_3 + l_4 w_4)^{\theta_1})} < c_1,$$
$$\text{and } \psi_{20} = \limsup_{\sum_{i=1}^4 m_i w_i \to 0} \max_{t\in[0,1]} \frac{\psi_2(t,w_1,w_2,w_3,w_4)}{\varphi_{\rho_2}((m_1 w_1 + m_2 w_2 + m_3 w_3 + m_4 w_4)^{\theta_2})} < c_2,$$

where

$c_1 = \left\{\min\left\{\left(4^{\rho_1 - 1}\Xi_1\Xi_3^{\rho_1 - 1}d_1^{\theta_1(\rho_1 - 1)}\right)^{-1}, \left(4^{\rho_1 - 1}\Xi_1\Xi_5^{\rho_1 - 1}d_1^{\theta_1(\rho_1 - 1)}\right)^{-1}\right\}, \text{ if } \Xi_5 \neq 0;\ \left(4^{\rho_1 - 1}\Xi_1\Xi_3^{\rho_1 - 1}d_1^{\theta_1(\rho_1 - 1)}\right)^{-1}, \text{ if } \Xi_5 = 0\right\}$,
$c_2 = \left\{\min\left\{\left(4^{\rho_2 - 1}\Xi_2\Xi_4^{\rho_2 - 1}d_2^{\theta_2(\rho_2 - 1)}\right)^{-1}, \left(4^{\rho_2 - 1}\Xi_2\Xi_6^{\rho_2 - 1}d_2^{\theta_2(\rho_2 - 1)}\right)^{-1}\right\}, \text{ if } \Xi_4 \neq 0;\ \left(4^{\rho_2 - 1}\Xi_2\Xi_6^{\rho_2 - 1}d_2^{\theta_2(\rho_2 - 1)}\right)^{-1}, \text{ if } \Xi_4 = 0\right\}$, with $d_1 = 2\max\left\{l_1, l_2, \frac{l_3}{\Gamma(\mu_1+1)}, \frac{l_4}{\Gamma(\mu_2+1)}\right\}$, $d_2 = 2\max\left\{m_1, m_2, \frac{m_3}{\Gamma(\nu_1+1)}, \frac{m_4}{\Gamma(\nu_2+1)}\right\}$.

$(H4)$ There exist $s_i \geq 0,\ i = 1, \dots, 4$ with $\sum_{i=1}^{4} s_i > 0$, $t_i \geq 0,\ i = 1, \dots, 4$ with $\sum_{i=1}^{4} t_i > 0$, $\sigma_1, \sigma_2 \in (0,1)$, $\sigma_1 < \sigma_2$ and $\eta_1 > 1$, $\eta_2 > 1$ such that

$$\mathfrak{f}_\infty = \liminf_{\sum_{i=1}^4 s_i w_i \to \infty} \min_{t \in [\sigma_1, \sigma_2]} \frac{\mathfrak{f}(t, w_1, w_2, w_3, w_4)}{\varphi_{\rho_1}(s_1 w_1 + s_2 w_2 + s_3 w_3 + s_4 w_4)} > c_3,$$
$$\text{or } \mathfrak{g}_\infty = \liminf_{\sum_{i=1}^4 t_i w_i \to \infty} \min_{t \in [\sigma_1, \sigma_2]} \frac{\mathfrak{g}(t, w_1, w_2, w_3, w_4)}{\varphi_{\rho_2}(t_1 w_1 + t_2 w_2 + t_3 w_3 + t_4 w_4)} > c_4,$$

where $c_3 = \eta_1 \left(2 d_3 \Xi_7 \sigma_1^{\gamma_1 - 1}\right)^{1-\rho_1}$, $c_4 = \eta_2 \left(2 d_4 \Xi_8 \sigma_1^{\gamma_2 - 1}\right)^{1-\rho_2}$ with $d_3 = \min\left\{ s_1 \sigma_1^{\gamma_1 - 1},\ s_2 \sigma_1^{\gamma_2 - 1}, s_3 \frac{\sigma_1^{\mu_1 + \gamma_1 - 1} \Gamma(\gamma_1)}{\Gamma(\gamma_1 + \mu_1)}, s_4 \frac{\sigma_1^{\mu_2 + \gamma_2 - 1} \Gamma(\gamma_2)}{\Gamma(\gamma_2 + \mu_2)} \right\}$, $d_4 = \min\left\{ t_1 \sigma_1^{\gamma_1 - 1}, t_2 \sigma_1^{\gamma_2 - 1}, t_3 \frac{\sigma_1^{\nu_1 + \gamma_1 - 1} \Gamma(\gamma_1)}{\Gamma(\gamma_1 + \nu_1)},\ t_4 \frac{\sigma_1^{\nu_2 + \gamma_2 - 1} \Gamma(\gamma_2)}{\Gamma(\gamma_2 + \nu_2)} \right\}$.

$(H5)$ There exist $u_i \geq 0,\ i = 1, \dots, 4$ with $\sum_{i=1}^{4} u_i > 0$, $v_i \geq 0,\ i = 1, \dots, 4$ with $\sum_{i=1}^{4} v_i > 0$ such that

$$\psi_{1\infty} = \limsup_{\sum_{i=1}^4 u_i w_i \to \infty} \max_{t \in [0,1]} \frac{\psi_1(t, w_1, w_2, w_3, w_4)}{\varphi_{\rho_1}(u_1 w_1 + u_2 w_2 + u_3 w_3 + u_4 w_4)} < e_1,$$
$$\text{and } \psi_{2\infty} = \limsup_{\sum_{i=1}^4 v_i w_i \to \infty} \max_{t \in [0,1]} \frac{\psi_2(t, w_1, w_2, w_3, w_4)}{\varphi_{\rho_2}(v_1 w_1 + v_2 w_2 + v_3 w_3 + v_4 w_4)} < e_2,$$

where $e_1 < \left[2 \Xi_1^{\varrho_1 - 1} (\Xi_3 + \Xi_5) \Lambda_1 k_1\right]^{1-\rho_1}$, $e_2 < \left[2 \Xi_2^{\varrho_2 - 1} (\Xi_4 + \Xi_6) \Lambda_2 k_2\right]^{1-\rho_2}$, with $\Lambda_1 = \max\{2^{\varrho_1 - 2}, 1\}$, $\Lambda_2 = \max\{2^{\varrho_2 - 2}, 1\}$, $k_1 = 2 \max\left\{ u_1, u_2, \frac{u_3}{\Gamma(\mu_1 + 1)}, \frac{u_4}{\Gamma(\mu_2 + 1)} \right\}$, $k_2 = 2 \max\left\{ v_1, v_2, \frac{v_3}{\Gamma(\nu_1 + 1)}, \frac{v_4}{\Gamma(\nu_2 + 1)} \right\}$.

$(H6)$ There exist $p_i \geq 0,\ i = 1, \dots, 4$ with $\sum_{i=1}^{4} p_i > 0$, $q_i \geq 0,\ i = 1, \dots, 4$ with $\sum_{i=1}^{4} q_i > 0$, $\sigma_1, \sigma_2 \in (0,1)$, $\sigma_1 < \sigma_2$ and $\varsigma_1 \in (0,1]$, $\varsigma_2 \in (0,1]$, $\eta_3 \geq 1$, $\eta_4 \geq 1$ such that

$$\mathfrak{f}_0 = \liminf_{\sum_{i=1}^4 p_i w_i \to 0} \min_{t \in [\sigma_1, \sigma_2]} \frac{\mathfrak{f}(t, w_1, w_2, w_3, w_4)}{\varphi_{\rho_1}((p_1 w_1 + p_2 w_2 + p_3 w_3 + p_4 w_4)^{\varsigma_1})} > e_3,$$
$$\text{or } \mathfrak{g}_0 = \liminf_{\sum_{i=1}^4 q_i w_i \to 0} \min_{t \in [\sigma_1, \sigma_2]} \frac{\mathfrak{g}(t, w_1, w_2, w_3, w_4)}{\varphi_{\rho_2}((q_1 w_1 + q_2 w_2 + q_3 w_3 + q_4 w_4)^{\varsigma_2})} > e_4,$$

where $e_3 = \left(\sigma_1^{\gamma_1 - 1} 2^{\varsigma_1} k_3^{\varsigma_1} \Xi_7\right)^{1-\rho_1}$, $e_4 = \left(\sigma_1^{\gamma_2 - 1} 2^{\varsigma_2} k_4^{\varsigma_2} \Xi_8\right)^{1-\rho_2}$, with $k_3 = \min\left\{ p_1 \sigma_1^{\gamma_1 - 1}, p_2 \sigma_1^{\gamma_2 - 1}, p_3 \frac{\sigma_1^{\mu_1 + \gamma_1 - 1} \Gamma(\gamma_1)}{\Gamma(\gamma_1 + \mu_1)}, p_4 \frac{\sigma_1^{\mu_2 + \gamma_2 - 1} \Gamma(\gamma_2)}{\Gamma(\gamma_2 + \mu_2)} \right\}$, $k_4 = \min\left\{ q_1 \sigma_1^{\gamma_1 - 1}, q_2 \sigma_1^{\gamma_2 - 1}, q_3 \frac{\sigma_1^{\nu_1 + \gamma_1 - 1} \Gamma(\gamma_1)}{\Gamma(\gamma_1 + \nu_1)}, q_4 \frac{\sigma_1^{\nu_2 + \gamma_2 - 1} \Gamma(\gamma_2)}{\Gamma(\gamma_2 + \nu_2)} \right\}$.

$(H7)$ $A_0^{\varrho_1 - 1} \Xi_3 \Xi_1^{\varrho_1 - 1} < \frac{1}{4}$, $A_0^{\varrho_2 - 1} \Xi_4 \Xi_2^{\varrho_2 - 1} < \frac{1}{4}$, $A_0^{\varrho_1 - 1} \Xi_5 \Xi_1^{\varrho_1 - 1} < \frac{1}{4}$, $A_0^{\varrho_2 - 1} \Xi_6 \Xi_2^{\varrho_2 - 1} < \frac{1}{4}$, where $A_0 = \max\left\{ \max_{t \in [0,1],\, w_i \in [0, \varpi],\, i = 1, \dots, 4} \psi_1(t, w_1, w_2, w_3, w_4), \max_{t \in [0,1],\, w_i \in [0, \varpi],\, i = 1, \dots, 4} \psi_2(t, w_1, w_2, w_3, w_4) \right\}$, with $\varpi = \max\left\{ 1, \frac{1}{\Gamma(\mu_1 + 1)}, \frac{1}{\Gamma(\mu_2 + 1)}, \frac{1}{\Gamma(\nu_1 + 1)}, \frac{1}{\Gamma(\nu_2 + 1)} \right\}$.

Lemma 4. *We suppose that* $(H1)$ *and* $(H2)$ *hold. Then* $\mathfrak{E} : \mathfrak{Q} \to \mathfrak{Q}$ *is a completely continuous operator.*

We introduce now the cone

$$\mathfrak{Q}_0 = \{(x, y) \in \mathfrak{Q},\ x(\tau) \geq \tau^{\gamma_1 - 1} \|x\|,\ y(\tau) \geq \tau^{\gamma_2 - 1} \|y\|,\ \forall \tau \in [0,1]\}.$$

If $(H1)$ and $(H2)$ are satisfied, then by Lemma 3 we obtain $\mathfrak{E}(\mathfrak{Q}) \subset \mathfrak{Q}_0$ and then the operator $\mathfrak{E}|_{\mathfrak{Q}_0} : \mathfrak{Q}_0 \to \mathfrak{Q}_0$ (which we will denote again by $\mathfrak{E}$) is completely continuous. For

$\kappa > 0$ we denote by B_κ the open ball centered at zero of radius κ, and by $\overline{B}_\kappa$ and ∂B_κ its closure and its boundary, respectively.

Our main existence results are the following theorems.

Theorem 1. *We suppose that assumptions $(H1)$–$(H4)$ hold. Then there exists a positive solution $(x(t), y(t))$, $t \in [0,1]$ of problem (1), (2).*

Theorem 2. *We suppose that assumptions $(H1)$, $(H2)$, $(H5)$, $(H6)$ hold. Then there exists a positive solution $(x(t), y(t))$, $t \in [0,1]$ of problem (1), (2).*

Theorem 3. *We suppose that assumptions $(H1)$, $(H2)$, $(H4)$, $(H6)$ and $(H7)$ hold. Then there exist two positive solutions $(x_1(t), y_1(t))$, $(x_2(t), y_2(t))$, $t \in [0,1]$ of problem (1), (2).*

4. Proofs of the Results

Proof of Lemma 4. By $(H2)$, we have $\Xi_1 = \int_0^1 \mathfrak{J}_1(\tau)\xi_1(\tau)\,d\tau > 0$ and $\Xi_2 = \int_0^1 \mathfrak{J}_2(\tau)\xi_2(\tau)$ $d\tau > 0$. In addition, by using Lemma 2.2 we find

$$\Xi_1 \le \frac{M_1}{\Gamma(\delta_1)}\left[1 + \frac{1}{\mathfrak{a}_1}\left(\int_0^1 \zeta^{\delta_1 - 1}\,d\mathfrak{M}_0(\zeta)\right)\right] < \infty,$$
$$\Xi_2 \le \frac{M_2}{\Gamma(\delta_2)}\left[1 + \frac{1}{\mathfrak{a}_2}\left(\int_0^1 \zeta^{\delta_2 - 1}\,d\mathfrak{N}_0(\zeta)\right)\right] < \infty.$$

Using now Lemma 3, we deduce that the operator $\mathfrak{E}$ maps $\mathfrak{Q}$ into $\mathfrak{Q}$.

Next, we will show that $\mathfrak{E}$ transforms the bounded sets into relatively compact sets. Let $\mathcal{S} \subset \mathfrak{Q}$ be a bounded set. So there exists $L_1 > 0$ such that $\|(x,y)\|_{\mathfrak{Y}} \le L_1$ for all $(x,y) \in \mathcal{S}$. Because ψ_1 and ψ_2 are continuous functions, we find that there exists $L_2 > 0$ such that $L_2 = \max\Big\{\sup_{\tau \in [0,1],\, w_i \in [0,\Lambda],\, i=1,\dots,4} \psi_1(\tau, w_1, w_2, w_3, w_4), \sup_{\tau \in [0,1],\, w_i \in [0,\Lambda],\, i=1,\dots,4}$ $\psi_2(\tau, w_1, w_2, w_3, w_4)\Big\}$, where $\Lambda = L_1 \max\Big\{1, \frac{1}{\Gamma(\mu_1+1)}, \frac{1}{\Gamma(\mu_2+1)}, \frac{1}{\Gamma(\nu_1+1)}, \frac{1}{\Gamma(\nu_2+1)}\Big\}$. Because $|I_{0+}^{\omega} z(t)| \le \frac{\|z\|}{\Gamma(\omega+1)}$ for $\omega > 0$ and $z \in C[0,1]$, by Lemma 2 we obtain that for any $(x,y) \in \mathcal{S}$ and $t \in [0,1]$

$$\begin{aligned}
\mathfrak{E}_1(x,y)(t) &\le \int_0^1 \mathfrak{J}_3(\tau)\varphi_{\varrho_1}\left(\int_0^1 \mathfrak{J}_1(\zeta)\xi_1(\zeta)\psi_1(\zeta, x(\zeta), y(\zeta), I_{0+}^{\mu_1}x(\zeta), I_{0+}^{\mu_2}y(\zeta))\,d\zeta\right)d\tau \\
&\quad + \int_0^1 \mathfrak{J}_4(\tau)\varphi_{\varrho_2}\left(\int_0^1 \mathfrak{J}_2(\zeta)\xi_2(\zeta)\psi_2(\zeta, x(\zeta), y(\zeta), I_{0+}^{\nu_1}x(\zeta), I_{0+}^{\nu_2}y(\zeta))\,d\zeta\right)d\tau \\
&\le L_2^{\varrho_1 - 1}\varphi_{\varrho_1}\left(\int_0^1 \mathfrak{J}_1(\zeta)\xi_1(\zeta)\,d\zeta\right)\int_0^1 \mathfrak{J}_3(\tau)\,d\tau \\
&\quad + L_2^{\varrho_2 - 1}\varphi_{\varrho_2}\left(\int_0^1 \mathfrak{J}_2(\zeta)\xi_2(\zeta)\,d\zeta\right)\int_0^1 \mathfrak{J}_4(\tau)\,d\tau \\
&= L_2^{\varrho_1 - 1}\Xi_1^{\varrho_1 - 1}\Xi_3 + L_2^{\varrho_2 - 1}\Xi_2^{\varrho_2 - 1}\Xi_4.
\end{aligned}$$

In a similar way we have

$$\mathfrak{E}_2(x,y)(t) \le L_2^{\varrho_1 - 1}\Xi_1^{\varrho_1 - 1}\Xi_5 + L_2^{\varrho_2 - 1}\Xi_2^{\varrho_2 - 1}\Xi_6.$$

Therefore

$$\|\mathfrak{E}_1(x,y)\| \le L_2^{\varrho_1 - 1}\Xi_1^{\varrho_1 - 1}\Xi_3 + L_2^{\varrho_2 - 1}\Xi_2^{\varrho_2 - 1}\Xi_4,$$
$$\|\mathfrak{E}_2(x,y)\| \le L_2^{\varrho_1 - 1}\Xi_1^{\varrho_1 - 1}\Xi_5 + L_2^{\varrho_2 - 1}\Xi_2^{\varrho_2 - 1}\Xi_6,$$

for all $(x,y) \in \mathcal{S}$, and then $\mathfrak{E}_1(\mathcal{S})$, $\mathfrak{E}_2(\mathcal{S})$ and $\mathfrak{E}(\mathcal{S})$ are bounded.

In what follows, we prove that $\mathfrak{E}(\mathcal{S})$ is equicontinuous. By Lemma 1, for $(x,y) \in \mathcal{S}$ and $t \in [0,1]$ we find

$$\begin{aligned}
\mathfrak{E}_1(x,y)(t) &= \int_0^1 \left[\mathfrak{g}_3(t,\tau) + \frac{t^{\gamma_1-1}\mathfrak{b}_1}{\mathfrak{b}} \left(\sum_{i=1}^{m} \int_0^1 \mathfrak{g}_{3i}(\vartheta,\tau)\, d\mathfrak{N}_i(\vartheta) \right) \right] \\
&\times \varphi_{\varrho_1}\left(\int_0^1 \mathfrak{G}_1(\tau,\zeta)\mathfrak{f}\left(\zeta, x(\zeta), y(\zeta), I_{0+}^{\mu_1}x(\zeta), I_{0+}^{\mu_2}y(\zeta)\right) d\zeta \right) d\tau \\
&+ \int_0^1 \frac{t^{\gamma_1-1}\Gamma(\gamma_2)}{\mathfrak{b}\Gamma(\gamma_2-\beta_0)} \left(\sum_{i=1}^{n} \int_0^1 \mathfrak{g}_{4i}(\vartheta,\tau)\, d\mathfrak{M}_i(\vartheta) \right) \\
&\times \varphi_{\varrho_2}\left(\int_0^1 \mathfrak{G}_2(\tau,\zeta)\mathfrak{g}(\zeta, x(\zeta), y(\zeta), I_{0+}^{\nu_1}x(\zeta), I_{0+}^{\nu_2}y(\zeta)) d\zeta \right) d\tau \\
&= \int_0^t \frac{1}{\Gamma(\gamma_1)} \left[t^{\gamma_1-1}(1-\tau)^{\gamma_1-\alpha_0-1} - (t-\tau)^{\gamma_1-1} \right] \\
&\times \varphi_{\varrho_1}\left(\int_0^1 \mathfrak{G}_1(\tau,\zeta)\mathfrak{f}\left(\zeta, x(\zeta), y(\zeta), I_{0+}^{\mu_1}x(\zeta), I_{0+}^{\mu_2}y(\zeta)\right) d\zeta \right) d\tau \\
&+ \int_t^1 \frac{1}{\Gamma(\gamma_1)} t^{\gamma_1-1}(1-\tau)^{\gamma_1-\alpha_0-1} \\
&\times \varphi_{\varrho_1}\left(\int_0^1 \mathfrak{G}_1(\tau,\zeta)\mathfrak{f}(\zeta, x(\zeta), y(\zeta), I_{0+}^{\mu_1}x(\zeta), I_{0+}^{\mu_2}y(\zeta))\, d\zeta \right) d\tau \\
&+ \frac{t^{\gamma_1-1}\mathfrak{b}_1}{\mathfrak{b}} \int_0^1 \left(\sum_{i=1}^{m} \int_0^1 \mathfrak{g}_{3i}(\vartheta,\tau)\, d\mathfrak{N}_i(\vartheta) \right) \\
&\times \varphi_{\varrho_1}\left(\int_0^1 \mathfrak{G}_1(\tau,\zeta)\mathfrak{f}(\zeta, x(\zeta), y(\zeta), I_{0+}^{\mu_1}x(\zeta), I_{0+}^{\mu_2}y(\zeta))\, d\zeta \right) d\tau \\
&+ \frac{t^{\gamma_1-1}\Gamma(\gamma_2)}{\mathfrak{b}\Gamma(\gamma_2-\beta_0)} \int_0^1 \left(\sum_{i=1}^{n} \int_0^1 \mathfrak{g}_{4i}(\vartheta,\tau)\, d\mathfrak{M}_i(\vartheta) \right) \\
&\times \varphi_{\varrho_2}\left(\int_0^1 \mathfrak{G}_2(\tau,\vartheta)\mathfrak{g}(\zeta, x(\zeta), y(\zeta), I_{0+}^{\nu_1}x(\zeta), I_{0+}^{\nu_2}y(\zeta))\, d\zeta \right) d\tau.
\end{aligned}$$

Then for any $t \in (0,1)$, we obtain

$$\begin{aligned}
(\mathfrak{E}_1(x,y))'(t) &= \int_0^t \frac{1}{\Gamma(\gamma_1)} \left[(\gamma_1-1)t^{\gamma_1-2}(1-\tau)^{\gamma_1-\alpha_0-1} - (\gamma_1-1)(t-\tau)^{\gamma_1-2} \right] \\
&\times \varphi_{\varrho_1}\left(\int_0^1 \mathfrak{G}_1(\tau,\zeta)\mathfrak{f}(\zeta, x(\zeta), y(\zeta), I_{0+}^{\mu_1}x(\zeta), I_{0+}^{\mu_2}y(\zeta)) d\zeta \right) d\tau \\
&+ \int_t^1 \frac{1}{\Gamma(\gamma_1)} (\gamma_1-1)t^{\gamma_1-2}(1-\tau)^{\gamma_1-\alpha_0-1} \\
&\times \varphi_{\varrho_1}\left(\int_0^1 \mathfrak{G}_1(\tau,\zeta)\mathfrak{f}(\zeta, x(\zeta), y(\zeta), I_{0+}^{\mu_1}x(\zeta), I_{0+}^{\mu_2}y(\zeta))\, d\zeta \right) d\tau \\
&+ \frac{(\gamma_1-1)t^{\gamma_1-2}\mathfrak{b}_1}{\mathfrak{b}} \int_0^1 \left(\sum_{i=1}^{m} \int_0^1 \mathfrak{g}_{3i}(\vartheta,\tau)\, d\mathfrak{N}_i(\vartheta) \right) \\
&\times \varphi_{\varrho_1}\left(\int_0^1 \mathfrak{G}_1(\tau,\zeta)\mathfrak{f}(\zeta, x(\zeta), y(\zeta), I_{0+}^{\mu_1}x(\zeta), I_{0+}^{\mu_2}y(\zeta))\, d\zeta \right) d\tau \\
&+ \frac{(\gamma_1-1)t^{\gamma_1-2}\Gamma(\gamma_2)}{\mathfrak{b}\Gamma(\gamma_2-\beta_0)} \int_0^1 \left(\sum_{i=1}^{n} \int_0^1 \mathfrak{g}_{4i}(\vartheta,\tau)\, d\mathfrak{M}_i(\vartheta) \right) \\
&\times \varphi_{\varrho_2}\left(\int_0^1 \mathfrak{G}_2(\tau,\zeta)\mathfrak{g}(\zeta, x(\zeta), y(\zeta), I_{0+}^{\nu_1}x(\zeta), I_{0+}^{\nu_2}y(\zeta))\, d\zeta \right) d\tau.
\end{aligned}$$

So for any $t \in (0,1)$ we deduce

$$
\begin{aligned}
|(\mathfrak{E}_1(x,y))'(t)| &\le \frac{1}{\Gamma(\gamma_1-1)} \int_0^t \left[t^{\gamma_1-2}(1-\tau)^{\gamma_1-\alpha_0-1} + (t-\tau)^{\gamma_1-2} \right] \\
&\times \varphi_{\varrho_1}\left(\int_0^1 \mathfrak{J}_1(\zeta)\xi_1(\zeta)\psi_1\left(\zeta, x(\zeta), y(\zeta), I_{0+}^{\mu_1}x(\zeta), I_{0+}^{\mu_2}y(\zeta)\right) d\zeta \right) d\tau \\
&+ \frac{1}{\gamma_1-1} \int_t^1 t^{\gamma_1-2}(1-\tau)^{\gamma_1-\alpha_0-1} \\
&\times \varphi_{\varrho_1}\left(\int_0^1 \mathfrak{J}_1(\zeta)\xi_1(\zeta)\psi_1\left(\zeta, x(\zeta), y(\zeta), I_{0+}^{\mu_1}x(\zeta), I_{0+}^{\mu_2}y(\zeta)\right) d\zeta \right) d\tau \\
&+ \frac{(\gamma_1-1)t^{\gamma_1-2}\mathfrak{b}_1}{\mathfrak{b}} \int_0^1 \left(\sum_{i=1}^m \int_0^1 \mathfrak{g}_{3i}(\vartheta,\tau)\, d\mathfrak{N}_i(\vartheta) \right) \\
&\times \varphi_{\varrho_1}\left(\int_0^1 \mathfrak{J}_1(\zeta)\xi_1(\zeta)\psi_1\left(\zeta, x(\zeta), y(\zeta), I_{0+}^{\mu_1}x(\zeta), I_{0+}^{\mu_2}y(\zeta)\right) d\zeta \right) d\tau \\
&+ \frac{(\gamma_1-1)t^{\gamma_1-2}\Gamma(\gamma_2)}{\mathfrak{b}\Gamma(\gamma_2-\beta_0)} \int_0^1 \left(\sum_{i=1}^n \int_0^1 \mathfrak{g}_{4i}(\vartheta,\tau)\, d\mathfrak{M}_i(\vartheta) \right) \\
&\times \varphi_{\varrho_2}\left(\int_0^1 \mathfrak{J}_2(\zeta)\xi_2(\zeta)\psi_2(\zeta, x(\zeta), y(\zeta), I_{0+}^{\nu_1}x(\zeta), I_{0+}^{\nu_2}y(\zeta))\, d\zeta \right) d\tau \\
&\le L_2^{\varrho_1-1}\Xi_1^{\varrho_1-1} \left\{ \frac{1}{\Gamma(\gamma_1-1)} \int_0^t \left[t^{\gamma_1-2}(1-\tau)^{\gamma_1-\alpha_0-1} + (t-\tau)^{\gamma_1-2} \right] d\tau \right. \\
&+ \frac{1}{\Gamma(\gamma_1-1)} \int_t^1 t^{\gamma_1-2}(1-\tau)^{\gamma_1-\alpha_0-1} d\tau \\
&\left. + \frac{(\gamma_1-1)t^{\gamma_1-2}\mathfrak{b}_1}{\mathfrak{b}} \int_0^1 \left(\sum_{i=1}^m \int_0^1 \mathfrak{g}_{3i}(\vartheta,\tau)\, d\mathfrak{N}_i(\vartheta) \right) d\tau \right\} \\
&+ L_2^{\varrho_2-1}\Xi_2^{\varrho_2-1} \frac{(\gamma_1-1)t^{\gamma_1-2}\Gamma(\gamma_2)}{\mathfrak{b}\Gamma(\gamma_2-\beta_0)} \int_0^1 \left(\sum_{i=1}^n \int_0^1 \mathfrak{g}_{4i}(\vartheta,\tau)\, d\mathfrak{M}_i(\vartheta) \right) d\tau.
\end{aligned}
$$

Hence for any $t \in (0,1)$ we find

$$
\begin{aligned}
|(\mathfrak{E}_1(x,y))'(t)| &\le L_2^{\varrho_1-1}\Xi_1^{\varrho_1-1} \left\{ \frac{1}{\Gamma(\gamma_1-1)} \left(\frac{t^{\gamma_1-2}}{\gamma_1-\alpha_0} + \frac{t^{\gamma_1-1}}{\gamma_1-1} \right) \right. \\
&\left. + \frac{(\gamma_1-1)t^{\gamma_1-2}\mathfrak{b}_1}{\mathfrak{b}} \int_0^1 \left(\sum_{i=1}^m \left(\int_0^1 \frac{1}{\Gamma(\gamma_1-\beta_i)} \vartheta^{\gamma_1-\beta_i-1}(1-\tau)^{\gamma_1-\alpha_0-1}\, d\mathfrak{N}_i(\vartheta) \right) \right) d\tau \right\} \\
&+ L_2^{\varrho_2-1}\Xi_2^{\varrho_2-1} \frac{(\gamma_1-1)t^{\gamma_1-2}\Gamma(\gamma_2)}{\mathfrak{b}\Gamma(\gamma_2-\beta_0)} \\
&\times \int_0^1 \left(\sum_{i=1}^n \left(\int_0^1 \frac{1}{\Gamma(\gamma_2-\alpha_i)} \vartheta^{\gamma_2-\alpha_i-1}(1-\tau)^{\gamma_2-\beta_0-1}\, d\mathfrak{M}_i(\vartheta) \right) \right) d\tau \\
&= L_2^{\varrho_1-1}\Xi_1^{\varrho_1-1} \left[\frac{1}{\Gamma(\gamma_1-1)} \left(\frac{t^{\gamma_1-2}}{\gamma_1-\alpha_0} + \frac{t^{\gamma_1-1}}{\gamma_1-1} \right) + \frac{(\gamma_1-1)t^{\gamma_1-2}\mathfrak{b}_1\mathfrak{b}_2}{\mathfrak{b}(\gamma_1-\alpha_0)\Gamma(\gamma_1)} \right] \\
&+ L_2^{\varrho_2-1}\Xi_2^{\varrho_2-1} \frac{(\gamma_1-1)t^{\gamma_1-2}\mathfrak{b}_1}{\mathfrak{b}\Gamma(\gamma_2-\beta_0+1)} \\
&= L_2^{\varrho_1-1}\Xi_1^{\varrho_1-1} \left[\frac{1}{\Gamma(\gamma_1-1)} \left(\frac{t^{\gamma_1-2}}{\gamma_1-\alpha_0} + \frac{t^{\gamma_1-1}}{\gamma_1-1} \right) + \frac{t^{\gamma_1-2}\mathfrak{b}_1\mathfrak{b}_2}{\mathfrak{b}(\gamma_1-\alpha_0)\Gamma(\gamma_1-1)} \right] \\
&+ L_2^{\varrho_2-1}\Xi_2^{\varrho_2-1} \frac{(\gamma_1-1)t^{\gamma_1-2}\mathfrak{b}_1}{\mathfrak{b}\Gamma(\gamma_2-\beta_0+1)} \\
&= L_2^{\varrho_1-1}\Xi_1^{\varrho_1-1} \left[\frac{(\mathfrak{b}+\mathfrak{b}_1\mathfrak{b}_2)t^{\gamma_1-2}}{\mathfrak{b}(\gamma_1-\alpha_0)\Gamma(\gamma_1-1)} + \frac{t^{\gamma_1-1}}{\Gamma(\gamma_1)} \right] + L_2^{\varrho_2-1}\Xi_2^{\varrho_2-1} \frac{(\gamma_1-1)t^{\gamma_1-2}\mathfrak{b}_1}{\mathfrak{b}\Gamma(\gamma_2-\beta_0+1)}.
\end{aligned}
$$

We denote by

$$
\Theta_1(t) = \frac{(\mathfrak{b}+\mathfrak{b}_1\mathfrak{b}_2)t^{\gamma_1-2}}{\mathfrak{b}(\gamma_1-\alpha_0)\Gamma(\gamma_1-1)} + \frac{t^{\gamma_1-1}}{\Gamma(\gamma_1)}, \quad \Theta_2(t) = \frac{(\gamma_1-1)t^{\gamma_1-2}\mathfrak{b}_1}{\mathfrak{b}\Gamma(\gamma_2-\beta_0+1)}, \quad t \in (0,1).
$$

Then for any $t_1, t_2 \in [0,1]$ with $t_1 < t_2$ and $(x,y) \in \mathcal{S}$, we deduce

$$\begin{aligned} |\mathfrak{E}_1(x,y)(t_1) - \mathfrak{E}_1(x,y)(t_2)| &= \left| \int_{t_1}^{t_2} (\mathfrak{E}_1(x,y))'(\tau)\, d\tau \right| \\ &\le L_2^{\varrho_1-1} \Xi_1^{\varrho_1-1} \int_{t_1}^{t_2} \Theta_1(\tau)\, d\tau + L_2^{\varrho_2-1} \Xi_2^{\varrho_2-1} \int_{t_1}^{t_2} \Theta_2(\tau)\, d\tau. \end{aligned} \tag{13}$$

Because $\Theta_1, \Theta_2 \in L^1(0,1)$, by (13), we conclude that $\mathfrak{E}_1(\mathcal{S})$ is equicontinuous. By using a similar technique, we deduce that $\mathfrak{E}_2(\mathcal{S})$ is also equicontinuous, and so $\mathfrak{E}(\mathcal{S})$ is equicontinuous. We apply now the Arzela-Ascoli theorem and we obtain that $\mathfrak{E}_1(\mathcal{S})$ and $\mathfrak{E}_2(\mathcal{S})$ are relatively compact sets, and then $\mathfrak{E}(\mathcal{S})$ is relatively compact, too. In addition, we can prove that $\mathfrak{E}_1$, $\mathfrak{E}_2$ and $\mathfrak{E}$ are continuous operators on $\mathfrak{Q}$ (see Lemma 1.4.1 from [16]). Therefore, the operator $\mathfrak{E}$ is completely continuous on $\mathfrak{Q}$. □

Proof of Theorem 1. From $(H3)$ we deduce that there exists $r \in (0,1)$ such that

$$\begin{aligned} \psi_1(t, w_1, w_2, w_3, w_4) &\le c_1 \varphi_{\rho_1}((l_1 w_1 + l_2 w_2 + l_3 w_3 + l_4 w_4)^{\theta_1}), \\ \psi_2(t, w_1, w_2, w_3, w_4) &\le c_2 \varphi_{\rho_2}((m_1 w_1 + m_2 w_2 + m_3 w_3 + m_4 w_4)^{\theta_2}), \end{aligned} \tag{14}$$

for all $t \in [0,1]$, $w_i \ge 0$, $i = 1, \ldots, 4$ with $\sum_{i=1}^4 l_i w_i \le r$ and $\sum_{i=1}^4 m_i w_i \le r$. We consider firstly the case $\Xi_4 \ne 0$ and $\Xi_5 \ne 0$. We define $r_1 \le \min\{r/d_1, r/d_2, r\}$. For any $(x,y) \in \overline{B}_{r_1} \cap \mathfrak{Q}$ and $\tau \in [0,1]$ we find

$$\begin{aligned} & l_1 x(\tau) + l_2 y(\tau) + l_3 I_{0+}^{\mu_1} x(\tau) + l_4 I_{0+}^{\mu_2} y(\tau) \\ & \quad \le 2\max\left\{ l_1, l_2, \tfrac{l_3}{\Gamma(\mu_1+1)}, \tfrac{l_4}{\Gamma(\mu_2+1)} \right\} \|(x,y)\|_{\mathfrak{V}} = d_1 \|(x,y)\|_{\mathfrak{V}} \le d_1 r_1 \le r, \\ & m_1 x(\tau) + m_2 y(\tau) + m_3 I_{0+}^{\nu_1} x(\tau) + m_4 I_{0+}^{\nu_2} y(\tau) \\ & \quad \le 2\max\left\{ m_1, m_2, \tfrac{m_3}{\Gamma(\nu_1+1)}, \tfrac{m_4}{\Gamma(\nu_2+1)} \right\} \|(x,y)\|_{\mathfrak{V}} = d_2 \|(x,y)\|_{\mathfrak{V}} \le d_2 r_1 \le r. \end{aligned}$$

Therefore by (14) and Lemma 2, for any $(x,y) \in \partial B_{r_1} \cap \mathfrak{Q}_0$ and $t \in [0,1]$ we deduce

$$\begin{aligned} \mathfrak{E}_1(x,y)(t) &\le \int_0^1 \mathfrak{J}_3(\tau) \varphi_{\varrho_1}\left(\int_0^1 \mathfrak{J}_1(\zeta) \mathfrak{f}(\zeta, x(\zeta), y(\zeta), I_{0+}^{\mu_1} x(\zeta), I_{0+}^{\mu_2} y(\zeta))\, d\zeta \right) d\tau \\ &\quad + \int_0^1 \mathfrak{J}_4(\tau) \varphi_{\varrho_2}\left(\int_0^1 \mathfrak{J}_2(\zeta) \mathfrak{g}(\zeta, x(\zeta), y(\zeta), I_{0+}^{\nu_1} x(\zeta), I_{0+}^{\nu_2} y(\zeta))\, d\zeta \right) d\tau \\ &= \Xi_3 \varphi_{\varrho_1}\left(\int_0^1 \mathfrak{J}_1(\zeta) \mathfrak{f}\left(\zeta, x(\zeta), y(\zeta), I_{0+}^{\mu_1} x(\zeta), I_{0+}^{\mu_2} y(\zeta)\right) d\zeta \right) \\ &\quad + \Xi_4 \varphi_{\varrho_2}\left(\int_0^1 \mathfrak{J}_2(\zeta) \mathfrak{g}(\zeta, x(\zeta), y(\zeta), I_{0+}^{\nu_1} x(\zeta), I_{0+}^{\nu_2} y(\zeta)) d\zeta \right) \\ &\le \Xi_3 \varphi_{\varrho_1}\left(\int_0^1 \mathfrak{J}_1(\zeta) \xi_1(\zeta) \psi_1\left(\zeta, x(\zeta), y(\zeta), I_{0+}^{\mu_1} x(\zeta), I_{0+}^{\mu_2} y(\zeta)\right) d\zeta \right) \\ &\quad + \Xi_4 \varphi_{\varrho_2}\left(\int_0^1 \mathfrak{J}_2(\zeta) \xi_2(\zeta) \psi_2(\zeta, x(\zeta), y(\zeta), I_{0+}^{\nu_1} x(\zeta), I_{0+}^{\nu_2} y(\zeta)) d\zeta \right) \\ &\le \Xi_3 \varphi_{\varrho_1}\left(\int_0^1 \mathfrak{J}_1(\zeta) \xi_1(\zeta) c_1 \varphi_{\rho_1}\left(\left(l_1 x(\zeta) + l_2 y(\zeta) + l_3 I_{0+}^{\mu_1} x(\zeta) + l_4 I_{0+}^{\mu_2} y(\zeta) \right)^{\theta_1} \right) d\zeta \right) \\ &\quad + \Xi_4 \varphi_{\varrho_2}\left(\int_0^1 \mathfrak{J}_2(\zeta) \xi_2(\zeta) c_2 \varphi_{\rho_2}\left(\left(m_1 x(\zeta) + m_2 y(\zeta) + m_3 I_{0+}^{\nu_1} x(\zeta) + m_4 I_{0+}^{\nu_2} y(\zeta) \right)^{\theta_2} \right) d\zeta \right) \\ &\le \Xi_3 \varphi_{\varrho_1}\left(\varphi_{\rho_1}\left((d_1 \|(x,y)\|_{\mathfrak{V}})^{\theta_1} \right) \right) \varphi_{\varrho_1}(c_1) \varphi_{\varrho_1}(\Xi_1) \\ &\quad + \Xi_4 \varphi_{\varrho_2}\left(\varphi_{\rho_2}\left((d_2 \|(x,y)\|_{\mathfrak{V}})^{\theta_2} \right) \right) \varphi_{\varrho_2}(c_2) \varphi_{\varrho_2}(\Xi_2) \\ &= \Xi_3 \Xi_1^{\varrho_1-1} c_1^{\varrho_1-1} d_1^{\theta_1} \|(x,y)\|_{\mathfrak{V}}^{\theta_1} + \Xi_4 \Xi_2^{\varrho_2-1} c_2^{\varrho_2-1} d_2^{\theta_2} \|(x,y)\|_{\mathfrak{V}}^{\theta_2} \\ &\le \Xi_3 \Xi_1^{\varrho_1-1} c_1^{\varrho_1-1} d_1^{\theta_1} \|(x,y)\|_{\mathfrak{V}} + \Xi_4 \Xi_2^{\varrho_2-1} c_2^{\varrho_2-1} d_2^{\theta_2} \|(x,y)\|_{\mathfrak{V}} \\ &\le \tfrac{1}{4} \|(x,y)\|_{\mathfrak{V}} + \tfrac{1}{4} \|(x,y)\|_{\mathfrak{V}} = \tfrac{1}{2} \|(x,y)\|_{\mathfrak{V}}. \end{aligned}$$

In a similar manner we obtain

$$\begin{aligned}\mathfrak{E}_2(x,y)(t) &\le \Xi_5 \Xi_1^{\varrho_1-1} c_1^{\varrho_1-1} d_1^{\theta_1} \|(x,y)\|_{\mathfrak{V}} + \Xi_6 \Xi_2^{\varrho_2-1} c_2^{\varrho_2-1} d_2^{\theta_2} \|(x,y)\|_{\mathfrak{V}} \\ &\le \tfrac{1}{4}\|(x,y)\|_{\mathfrak{V}} + \tfrac{1}{4}\|(x,y)\|_{\mathfrak{V}} = \tfrac{1}{2}\|(x,y)\|_{\mathfrak{V}}.\end{aligned}$$

Then we conclude

$$\|\mathfrak{E}(x,y)\|_{\mathfrak{V}} = \|\mathfrak{E}_1(x,y)\| + \|\mathfrak{E}_2(x,y)\| \le \|(x,y)\|_{\mathfrak{V}}, \ \forall (x,y) \in \partial B_{r_1} \cap \mathfrak{Q}_0. \tag{15}$$

If $\Xi_4 = 0$ or $\Xi_5 = 0$ we also find in a similar manner inequality (15).

In what follows, in $(H4)$ we assume that $\mathfrak{g}_\infty > c_4$ (in a similar manner we study the case $\mathfrak{f}_\infty > c_3$). Then there exists a positive constant $C_1 > 0$ such that

$$\mathfrak{g}(t, w_1, w_2, w_3, w_4) \ge c_4 \varphi_{\rho_2}(t_1 w_1 + t_2 w_2 + t_3 w_3 + t_4 w_4) - C_1, \tag{16}$$

for all $t \in [\sigma_1, \sigma_2]$ and $w_i \ge 0$, $i = 1, \ldots, 4$. From the definition of $I_{0+}^{\nu_1}$, for any $(x,y) \in \mathfrak{Q}_0$ and $\tau \in [0,1]$, we find

$$\begin{aligned} I_{0+}^{\nu_1} x(\tau) &= \frac{1}{\Gamma(\nu_1)} \int_0^\tau (\tau-\zeta)^{\nu_1-1} x(\zeta)\, d\zeta \ge \frac{1}{\Gamma(\nu_1)} \int_0^\tau (\tau-\zeta)^{\nu_1-1} \zeta^{\gamma_1-1} \|x\|\, d\zeta \\ &\overset{\zeta=\tau z}{=} \frac{\|x\|}{\Gamma(\nu_1)} \int_0^1 (\tau-\tau z)^{\nu_1-1} \tau^{\gamma_1-1} z^{\gamma_1-1} \tau\, dz = \frac{\|x\|}{\Gamma(\nu_1)} \tau^{\nu_1+\gamma_1-1} \int_0^1 z^{\gamma_1-1}(1-z)^{\nu_1-1}\, dz \\ &= \frac{\|x\|}{\Gamma(\nu_1)} \tau^{\nu_1+\gamma_1-1} B(\gamma_1,\nu_1) = \frac{\|x\| \tau^{\nu_1+\gamma_1-1}\Gamma(\gamma_1)}{\Gamma(\gamma_1+\nu_1)}, \end{aligned} \tag{17}$$

and similarly

$$I_{0+}^{\nu_2} y(\tau) \ge \frac{\|y\| \tau^{\nu_2+\gamma_2-1}\Gamma(\gamma_2)}{\Gamma(\gamma_2+\nu_2)},$$

where $B(z_1,z_2)$ is the first Euler function defined by $B(z_1,z_2) = \int_0^1 t^{z_1-1}(1-t)^{z_2-1}\, dt$, $z_1, z_2 > 0$. Then by using (16) and (17), for any $(x,y) \in \mathfrak{Q}_0$ and $t \in [\sigma_1,\sigma_2]$ we obtain

$$\begin{aligned} \mathfrak{E}_2(x,y)(t) &\ge \int_{\sigma_1}^{\sigma_2} \mathfrak{G}_6(t,\tau) \varphi_{\varrho_2}\left(\int_{\sigma_1}^{\tau} \mathfrak{G}_2(\tau,\zeta) \mathfrak{g}(\zeta, x(\zeta), y(\zeta), I_{0+}^{\nu_1}x(\zeta), I_{0+}^{\nu_2}y(\zeta))\, d\zeta \right) d\tau \\ &\ge \sigma_1^{\gamma_2-1} \int_{\sigma_1}^{\sigma_2} \mathfrak{J}_6(\tau) \left(\int_{\sigma_1}^{\tau} \mathfrak{G}_2(\tau,\zeta) \Big[c_4 \big(t_1 x(\zeta) + t_2 y(\zeta) + t_3 I_{0+}^{\nu_1}x(\zeta) + t_4 I_{0+}^{\nu_2} y(\zeta)\big)^{\rho_2-1} \right. \\ &\quad \left. - C_1 \Big] d\zeta \right)^{\varrho_2-1} d\tau \\ &\ge \sigma_1^{\gamma_2-1} \int_{\sigma_1}^{\sigma_2} \mathfrak{J}_6(\tau) \left(\int_{\sigma_1}^{\tau} \mathfrak{G}_2(\tau,\zeta) \left[c_4 \left(t_1 \sigma_1^{\gamma_1-1}\|x\| + t_2 \sigma_1^{\gamma_2-1}\|y\| \right.\right.\right. \\ &\quad \left.\left.\left. + t_3 \frac{\sigma_1^{\nu_1+\gamma_1-1}\Gamma(\gamma_1)}{\Gamma(\gamma_1+\nu_1)}\|x\| + t_4 \frac{\sigma_1^{\nu_2+\gamma_2-1}\Gamma(\gamma_2)}{\Gamma(\gamma_2+\nu_2)}\|y\| \right)^{\rho_2-1} - C_1 \right] d\zeta \right)^{\varrho_2-1} d\tau \\ &\ge \sigma_1^{\gamma_2-1} \int_{\sigma_1}^{\sigma_2} \mathfrak{J}_6(\tau) \left(\int_{\sigma_1}^{\tau} \mathfrak{G}_2(\tau,\zeta) \left[c_4 \left(\min\left\{ t_1 \sigma_1^{\gamma_1-1}, t_2 \sigma_1^{\gamma_2-1}, t_3 \frac{\sigma_1^{\nu_1+\gamma_1-1}\Gamma(\gamma_1)}{\Gamma(\gamma_1+\nu_1)}, \right.\right.\right.\right. \\ &\quad \left.\left.\left.\left. t_4 \frac{\sigma_1^{\nu_2+\gamma_2-1}\Gamma(\gamma_2)}{\Gamma(\gamma_2+\nu_2)} \right\} 2\|(x,y)\|_{\mathfrak{V}} \right)^{\rho_2-1} - C_1 \right] d\zeta \right)^{\varrho_2-1} d\tau \\ &= \sigma_1^{\gamma_2-1} \int_{\sigma_1}^{\sigma_2} \mathfrak{J}_6(\tau) \left(\int_{\sigma_1}^{\tau} \mathfrak{G}_2(\tau,\zeta) \left[c_4 (2 d_4 \|(x,y)\|_{\mathfrak{V}})^{\rho_2-1} - C_1 \right] d\zeta \right)^{\varrho_2-1} d\tau \\ &= \Xi_8 \sigma_1^{\gamma_2-1} \left[c_4 (2 d_4 \|(x,y)\|_{\mathfrak{V}})^{\rho_2-1} - C_1 \right]^{\varrho_2-1} \\ &= \left(\Xi_8^{\rho_2-1} \sigma_1^{(\gamma_2-1)(\rho_2-1)} c_4 2^{\rho_2-1} d_4^{\rho_2-1} \|(x,y)\|_{\mathfrak{V}}^{\rho_2-1} - \Xi_8^{\rho_2-1} \sigma_1^{(\gamma_2-1)(\rho_2-1)} C_1 \right)^{\varrho_2-1} \\ &= \left(\eta_2 \|(x,y)\|_{\mathfrak{V}}^{\rho_2-1} - C_2 \right)^{\varrho_2-1}, \quad C_2 = \Xi_8^{\rho_2-1} \sigma_1^{(\gamma_1-1)(\rho_2-1)} C_1. \end{aligned}$$

So we find

$$\|\mathfrak{E}(x,y)\|_{\mathfrak{Y}} \geq \|\mathfrak{E}_2(x,y)\| \geq \mathfrak{E}_2(x,y)(\sigma_1) \geq \left(\eta_2\|(x,y)\|_{\mathfrak{Y}}^{\rho_2-1} - C_2\right)^{\varrho_2-1}, \ \forall (x,y) \in \mathfrak{Q}_0.$$

We choose $r_2 \geq \max\left\{1, C_2^{\varrho_2-1}/(\eta_2-1)^{\varrho_2-1}\right\}$ and we deduce

$$\|\mathfrak{E}(x,y)\|_{\mathfrak{Y}} \geq \|(x,y)\|_{\mathfrak{Y}}, \ \forall (x,y) \in \partial B_{r_2} \cap \mathfrak{Q}_0. \tag{18}$$

Now based on Lemma 4, the relations (15), (18) and the Guo–Krasnosel'skii fixed point theorem we conclude that the operator $\mathfrak{E}$ has a fixed point $(x,y) \in (\overline{B}_{r_2} \setminus B_{r_1}) \cap \mathfrak{Q}_0$ with $r_1 \leq \|(x,y)\|_{\mathfrak{Y}} \leq r_2$ and $x(s) \geq s^{\gamma_1-1}\|x\|$, $y(s) \geq s^{\gamma_2-1}\|y\|$ for all $s \in [0,1]$. So $\|x\| > 0$ or $\|y\| > 0$, that is $x(s) > 0$ for all $s \in (0,1]$ or $y(s) > 0$ for all $s \in (0,1]$. Therefore, $(x(t), y(t))$, $t \in [0,1]$ is a positive solution of problem (1), (2). □

Proof of Theorem 2. From assumption $(H5)$ we deduce that there exist $C_3 > 0$, $C_4 > 0$ such that

$$\begin{aligned} \psi_1(t,w_1,w_2,w_3,w_4) &\leq e_1\varphi_{\rho_1}(u_1w_1+u_2w_2+u_3w_3+u_4w_4)+C_3, \\ \psi_2(t,w_1,w_2,w_3,w_4) &\leq e_2\varphi_{\rho_2}(u_1w_1+u_2w_2+u_3w_3+u_4w_4)+C_4, \end{aligned} \tag{19}$$

for any $t \in [0,1]$ and $w_i \geq 0,\ i = 1,\ldots,4$. By using $(H2)$ and (19), for any $(x,y) \in \mathfrak{Q}_0$ and $t \in [0,1]$ we obtain

$$\begin{aligned}
\mathfrak{E}_1(x,y)(t) &\leq \int_0^1 \mathfrak{J}_3(\tau)\varphi_{\varrho_1}\left(\int_0^1 \mathfrak{J}_1(\zeta)\mathfrak{f}(\zeta,x(\zeta),y(\zeta),I_{0+}^{\mu_1}x(\zeta),I_{0+}^{\mu_2}y(\zeta))\,d\zeta\right)d\tau \\
&\quad + \int_0^1 \mathfrak{J}_4(\tau)\varphi_{\varrho_2}\left(\int_0^1 \mathfrak{J}_2(\zeta)\mathfrak{g}(\zeta,x(\zeta),y(\zeta),I_{0+}^{\nu_1}x(\zeta),I_{0+}^{\nu_2}y(\zeta))\,d\zeta\right)d\tau \\
&\leq \Xi_3\varphi_{\varrho_1}\left(\int_0^1 \mathfrak{J}_1(\zeta)\xi_1(\zeta)\psi_1(\zeta,x(\zeta),y(\zeta),I_{0+}^{\mu_1}x(\zeta),I_{0+}^{\mu_2}y(\zeta))\,d\zeta\right) \\
&\quad +\Xi_4\varphi_{\varrho_2}\left(\int_0^1 \mathfrak{J}_2(\zeta)\xi_2(\zeta)\psi_2(\zeta,x(\zeta),y(\zeta),I_{0+}^{\nu_1}x(\zeta),I_{0+}^{\nu_2}y(\zeta))\,d\zeta\right) \\
&\leq \Xi_3\varphi_{\varrho_1}\left(\int_0^1 \mathfrak{J}_1(\zeta)\xi_1(\zeta)\left[e_1\varphi_{\rho_1}\left(u_1x(\zeta)+u_2y(\zeta)+u_3I_{0+}^{\mu_1}x(\zeta)+u_4I_{0+}^{\mu_2}y(\zeta)\right)+C_3\right]d\zeta\right) \\
&\quad +\Xi_4\varphi_{\varrho_2}\left(\int_0^1 \mathfrak{J}_2(\zeta)\xi_2(\zeta)\left[e_2\varphi_{\rho_2}(v_1x(\zeta)+v_2y(\zeta)+v_3I_{0+}^{\nu_1}x(\zeta)+v_4I_{0+}^{\nu_2}y(\zeta))+C_4\right]d\zeta\right) \\
&\leq \Xi_3\varphi_{\varrho_1}\left(\int_0^1 \mathfrak{J}_1(\zeta)\xi_1(\zeta)\left[e_1\left(u_1\|x\|+u_2\|y\|+\frac{u_3\|x\|}{\Gamma(\mu_1+1)}+\frac{u_4\|y\|}{\Gamma(\mu_2+1)}\right)^{\rho_1-1}+C_3\right]d\zeta\right) \\
&\quad +\Xi_4\varphi_{\varrho_2}\left(\int_0^1 \mathfrak{J}_2(\zeta)\xi_2(\zeta)\left[e_2\left(v_1\|x\|+v_2\|y\|+\frac{v_3\|x\|}{\Gamma(\nu_1+1)}+\frac{v_4\|y\|}{\Gamma(\nu_2+1)}\right)^{\rho_2-1}+C_4\right]d\zeta\right) \\
&\leq \Xi_3\varphi_{\varrho_1}\left[e_1\left(\max\left\{u_1,u_2,\tfrac{u_3}{\Gamma(\mu_1+1)},\tfrac{u_4}{\Gamma(\mu_2+1)}\right\}2\|(x,y)\|_{\mathfrak{Y}}\right)^{\rho_1-1}+C_3\right] \\
&\quad \times\left(\int_0^1 \mathfrak{J}_1(\zeta)\xi_1(\zeta)\,d\zeta\right)^{\varrho_1-1} \\
&\quad +\Xi_4\varphi_{\varrho_2}\left[e_2\left(\max\left\{v_1,v_2,\tfrac{v_3}{\Gamma(\nu_1+1)},\tfrac{v_4}{\Gamma(\nu_2+1)}\right\}2\|(x,y)\|_{\mathfrak{Y}}\right)^{\rho_2-1}+C_4\right] \\
&\quad \times\left(\int_0^1 \mathfrak{J}_2(\zeta)\xi_2(\zeta)\,d\zeta\right)^{\varrho_2-1} \\
&= \Xi_1^{\varrho_1-1}\Xi_3\left(e_1k_1^{\rho_1-1}\|(x,y)\|_{\mathfrak{Y}}^{\rho_1-1}+C_3\right)^{\varrho_1-1} + \Xi_2^{\varrho_2-1}\Xi_4\left(e_2k_2^{\rho_2-1}\|(x,y)\|_{\mathfrak{Y}}^{\rho_2-1}+C_4\right)^{\varrho_2-1}.
\end{aligned}$$

In a similar way we find

$$\begin{aligned} \mathfrak{E}_2(x,y)(t) \leq\ & \Xi_1^{\varrho_1-1}\Xi_5\left(e_1k_1^{\rho_1-1}\|(x,y)\|_{\mathfrak{Y}}^{\rho_1-1}+C_3\right)^{\varrho_1-1} \\ &+\Xi_2^{\varrho_2-1}\Xi_6\left(e_2k_2^{\rho_2-1}\|(x,y)\|_{\mathfrak{Y}}^{\rho_2-1}+C_4\right)^{\varrho_2-1}. \end{aligned}$$

Hence we conclude

$$\|\mathfrak{E}_1(x,y)\| \le \Xi_1^{\varrho_1-1}\Xi_3\Big(e_1k_1^{\rho_1-1}\|(x,y)\|_{\mathfrak{V}}^{\rho_1-1}+C_3\Big)^{\varrho_1-1} + \Xi_2^{\varrho_2-1}\Xi_4\Big(e_2k_2^{\rho_2-1}\|(x,y)\|_{\mathfrak{V}}^{\rho_2-1}+C_4\Big)^{\varrho_2-1},$$
$$\|\mathfrak{E}_2(x,y)\| \le \Xi_1^{\varrho_1-1}\Xi_5\Big(e_1k_1^{\rho_1-1}\|(x,y)\|_{\mathfrak{V}}^{\rho_1-1}+C_3\Big)^{\varrho_1-1} + \Xi_2^{\varrho_2-1}\Xi_6\Big(e_2k_2^{\rho_2-1}\|(x,y)\|_{\mathfrak{V}}^{\rho_2-1}+C_4\Big)^{\varrho_2-1},$$

and then

$$\|\mathfrak{E}(x,y)\|_{\mathfrak{V}} \le \Xi_1^{\varrho_1-1}(\Xi_3+\Xi_5)\Big(e_1k_1^{\rho_1-1}\|(x,y)\|_{\mathfrak{V}}^{\rho_1-1}+C_3\Big)^{\varrho_1-1} + \Xi_2^{\varrho_2-1}(\Xi_4+\Xi_6)\Big(e_2k_2^{\rho_2-1}\|(x,y)\|_{\mathfrak{V}}^{\rho_2-1}+C_4\Big)^{\varrho_2-1}, \tag{20}$$

for all $(x,y)\in\mathfrak{Q}_0$. We choose

$$r_3 \ge \max\left\{1, \frac{\Xi_1^{\varrho_1-1}(\Xi_3+\Xi_5)\Lambda_1C_3^{\varrho_1-1}+\Xi_2^{\varrho_2-1}(\Xi_4+\Xi_6)\Lambda_2C_4^{\varrho_2-1}}{1-\Big[\Xi_1^{\varrho_1-1}(\Xi_3+\Xi_5)\Lambda_1e_1^{\varrho_1-1}k_1+\Xi_2^{\varrho_2-1}(\Xi_4+\Xi_6)\Lambda_2e_2^{\varrho_2-1}k_2\Big]}\right\}.$$

Then by (20) and the inequalities $(a+b)^{\varrho_i-1}\le\Lambda_i(a^{\varrho_i-1}+b^{\varrho_i-1})$, for $a,b\ge 0$, $i=1,2$ we deduce

$$\|\mathfrak{E}(x,y)\|_{\mathfrak{V}} \le \|(x,y)\|_{\mathfrak{V}}, \ \forall\,(x,y)\in\partial B_{r_3}\cap\mathfrak{Q}_0. \tag{21}$$

Now, in $(H6)$ we assume that $\mathfrak{f}_0 > e_3$ (the case $\mathfrak{g}_0 > e_4$ is treated in a similar way). So there exists $\widetilde{r}_4\in(0,1]$ such that

$$\mathfrak{f}(t,w_1,w_2,w_3,w_4) \ge e_4\varphi_{\rho_1}((p_1w_1+p_2w_2+p_3w_3+p_4w_4)^{\varsigma_1}), \tag{22}$$

for all $t\in[\sigma_1,\sigma_2]$, $w_i\ge 0$, $i=1,\dots,4$, $\sum_{i=1}^4 p_iw_i\le\widetilde{r}_4$. We define $r_4\le\min\{\widetilde{r}_4/\widetilde{k}_3,\widetilde{r}_4\}$, where $\widetilde{k}_3=2\max\Big\{p_1,p_2,\frac{p_3}{\Gamma(\mu_1+1)},\frac{p_4}{\Gamma(\mu_2+1)}\Big\}$. Hence for any $(x,y)\in\overline{B}_{r_4}\cap\mathfrak{Q}$ and $t\in[0,1]$ we find

$$p_1x(\tau)+p_2y(\tau)+p_3I_{0+}^{\mu_1}x(\tau)+p_4I_{0+}^{\mu_2}y(\tau) \le 2\max\Big\{p_1,p_2,\tfrac{p_3}{\Gamma(\mu_1+1)},\tfrac{p_4}{\Gamma(\mu_2+1)}\Big\}\|(x,y)\|_{\mathfrak{V}}=\widetilde{k}_3r_4\le\widetilde{r}_4.$$

Therefore, by using (22) and the inequalities $I_{0+}^{\mu_1}x(\tau)\ge\|x\|\frac{\tau^{\mu_1+\gamma_1-1}\Gamma(\gamma_1)}{\Gamma(\gamma_1+\mu_1)}$ and $I_{0+}^{\mu_2}y(\tau)\ge\|y\|\frac{\tau^{\mu_2+\gamma_2-1}\Gamma(\gamma_2)}{\Gamma(\gamma_2+\mu_2)}$, for all $\tau\in[0,1]$ and $(x,y)\in\mathfrak{Q}_0$, we obtain for any $(x,y)\in\overline{B}_{r_4}\cap\mathfrak{Q}_0$ and $t\in[\sigma_1,\sigma_2]$

$$\begin{aligned}
\mathfrak{E}_1(x,y)(t) &\ge \int_{\sigma_1}^{\sigma_2}\mathfrak{G}_3(t,\tau)\varphi_{\varrho_1}\left(\int_{\sigma_1}^{\tau}\mathfrak{G}_1(\tau,\zeta)\mathfrak{f}(\zeta,x(\zeta),y(\zeta),I_{0+}^{\mu_1}x(\zeta),I_{0+}^{\mu_2}y(\zeta))\,d\zeta\right)d\tau\\
&\ge \sigma_1^{\gamma_1-1}\int_{\sigma_1}^{\sigma_2}\mathfrak{J}_3(\tau)\left(\int_{\sigma_1}^{\tau}\mathfrak{G}_1(\tau,\zeta)e_3\Big(p_1x(\zeta)+p_2y(\zeta)+p_3I_{0+}^{\mu_1}x(\zeta)\right.\\
&\quad\left.+p_4I_{0+}^{\mu_2}y(\zeta)\Big)^{\varsigma_1(\rho_1-1)}d\zeta\right)^{\varrho_1-1}d\tau\\
&\ge \sigma_1^{\gamma_1-1}\int_{\sigma_1}^{\sigma_2}\mathfrak{J}_3(\tau)\left(\int_{\sigma_1}^{\tau}\mathfrak{G}_1(\tau,\zeta)e_3\Big(p_1\sigma_1^{\gamma_1-1}\|x\|+p_2\sigma_1^{\gamma_2-1}\|y\|\right.\\
&\quad\left.+\,p_3\frac{\sigma_1^{\mu_1+\gamma_1-1}\Gamma(\gamma_1)}{\Gamma(\gamma_1+\mu_1)}\|x\|+p_4\frac{\sigma_1^{\mu_2+\gamma_2-1}\Gamma(\gamma_2)}{\Gamma(\gamma_2+\mu_2)}\|y\|\Big)^{\varsigma_1(\rho_1-1)}d\zeta\right)^{\varrho_1-1}d\tau
\end{aligned}$$

$$
\begin{aligned}
&\geq \sigma_1^{\gamma_1-1}\int_{\sigma_1}^{\sigma_2}\mathfrak{J}_3(\tau)\left(\int_{\sigma_1}^{\tau}\mathfrak{G}_1(\tau,\zeta)e_3\left(\min\left\{p_1\sigma_1^{\gamma_1-1},p_2\sigma_1^{\gamma_2-1},p_3\frac{\sigma_1^{\mu_1+\gamma_1-1}\Gamma(\gamma_1)}{\Gamma(\gamma_1+\mu_1)},\right.\right.\right.\\
&\quad\left.\left.\left.p_4\frac{\sigma_1^{\mu_2+\gamma_2-1}\Gamma(\gamma_2)}{\Gamma(\gamma_2+\mu_2)}\right\}2\|(x,y)\|_{\mathfrak{V}}\right)^{\varsigma_1(\rho_1-1)}d\zeta\right)^{\varrho_1-1}d\tau\\
&=\sigma_1^{\gamma_1-1}\int_{\sigma_1}^{\sigma_2}\mathfrak{J}_3(\tau)\left(\int_{\sigma_1}^{\tau}\mathfrak{G}_1(\tau,\zeta)e_3(2k_3\|(x,y)\|_{\mathfrak{V}})^{\varsigma_1(\rho_1-1)}d\zeta\right)^{\varrho_1-1}d\tau\\
&=\sigma_1^{\gamma_1-1}e_3^{\varrho_1-1}2^{\varsigma_1}k_3^{\varsigma_1}\|(x,y)\|_{\mathfrak{V}}^{\varsigma_1}\int_{\sigma_1}^{\sigma_2}\mathfrak{J}_3(\tau)\left(\int_{\sigma_1}^{\tau}\mathfrak{G}_1(\tau,\zeta)\,d\zeta\right)^{\varrho_1-1}d\tau\\
&=\sigma_1^{\gamma_1-1}e_3^{\varrho_1-1}2^{\varsigma_1}k_3^{\varsigma_1}\Xi_7\|(x,y)\|_{\mathfrak{V}}^{\varsigma_1}\\
&\geq \sigma_1^{\gamma_1-1}e_3^{\varrho_1-1}2^{\varsigma_1}k_3^{\varsigma_1}\Xi_7\|(x,y)\|_{\mathfrak{V}}=\|(x,y)\|_{\mathfrak{V}}.
\end{aligned}
$$

Then we deduce

$$
\|\mathfrak{E}(x,y)\|_{\mathfrak{V}}\geq\|\mathfrak{E}_1(x,y)\|\geq\mathfrak{E}_1(x,y)(\sigma_1)\geq\|(x,y)\|_{\mathfrak{V}},\ \forall\,(x,y)\in\partial B_{r_4}\cap\mathfrak{Q}_0. \tag{23}
$$

By Lemma 4, (21), (23) and the Guo–Krasnosel'skii fixed point theorem, we conclude that $\mathfrak{E}$ has a fixed point $(x,y)\in(\overline{B}_{r_3}\setminus B_{r_4})\cap\mathfrak{Q}_0$, so $r_4\leq\|(x,y)\|_{\mathfrak{V}}\leq r_3$, and $x(s)\geq s^{\gamma_1-1}\|x\|$, $y(s)\geq s^{\gamma_2-1}\|y\|$ for all $s\in[0,1]$, which is a positive solution of problem (1), (2). □

Proof of Theorem 3. Because assumptions $(H1)$, $(H2)$ and $(H4)$ hold, then by Theorem 1 we deduce that there exists $r_2>1$ such that

$$
\|\mathfrak{E}(x,y)\|_{\mathfrak{V}}\geq\|(x,y)\|_{\mathfrak{V}},\ \forall\,(x,y)\in\partial B_{r_2}\cap\mathfrak{Q}_0. \tag{24}
$$

Next because assumptions $(H1)$, $(H2)$ and $(H6)$ hold, then by Theorem 2 we conclude that there exists $r_4<1$ such that

$$
\|\mathfrak{E}(x,y)\|_{\mathfrak{V}}\geq\|(x,y)\|_{\mathfrak{V}},\ \forall\,(x,y)\in\partial B_{r_4}\cap\mathfrak{Q}_0. \tag{25}
$$

Now, consider the set $B_1=\{(x,y)\in\mathfrak{V},\ \|(x,y)\|_{\mathfrak{V}}<1\}$. By assumption $(H7)$ for any $(x,y)\in\partial B_1\cap\mathfrak{Q}_0$ and $t\in[0,1]$ we find

$$
\begin{aligned}
\mathfrak{E}_1(x,y)(t)&\leq\int_0^1\mathfrak{J}_3(\tau)\varphi_{\varrho_1}\left(\int_0^1\mathfrak{J}_1(\zeta)\xi_1(\zeta)\psi_1\left(\zeta,x(\zeta),y(\zeta),I_{0+}^{\mu_1}x(\zeta),I_{0+}^{\mu_2}y(\zeta)\right)d\zeta\right)d\tau\\
&\quad+\int_0^1\mathfrak{J}_4(\tau)\varphi_{\varrho_2}\left(\int_0^1\mathfrak{J}_2(\zeta)\xi_2(\zeta)\psi_2(\zeta,x(\zeta),y(\zeta),I_{0+}^{\nu_1}x(\zeta),I_{0+}^{\nu_2}y(\zeta))d\zeta\right)d\tau\\
&\leq A_0^{\varrho_1-1}\int_0^1\mathfrak{J}_3(\tau)\varphi_{\varrho_1}\left(\int_0^1\mathfrak{J}_1(\zeta)\xi_1(\zeta)\,d\zeta\right)d\tau+A_0^{\varrho_2-1}\int_0^1\mathfrak{J}_4(\tau)\varphi_{\varrho_2}\left(\int_0^1\mathfrak{J}_2(\zeta)\xi_2(\zeta)\,d\zeta\right)d\tau\\
&=A_0^{\varrho_1-1}\left(\int_0^1\mathfrak{J}_3(\tau)\,d\tau\right)\left(\int_0^1\mathfrak{J}_1(\zeta)\xi_1(\zeta)\,d\zeta\right)^{\varrho_1-1}\\
&\quad+A_0^{\varrho_2-1}\left(\int_0^1\mathfrak{J}_4(\tau)\,d\tau\right)\left(\int_0^1\mathfrak{J}_2(\zeta)\xi_2(\zeta)\,d\zeta\right)^{\varrho_2-1}\\
&=A_0^{\varrho_1-1}\Xi_3\Xi_1^{\varrho_1-1}+A_0^{\varrho_2-1}\Xi_4\Xi_2^{\varrho_2-1}<\tfrac{1}{4}+\tfrac{1}{4}=\tfrac{1}{2},\\
\mathfrak{E}_2(x,y)(t)&\leq\int_0^1\mathfrak{J}_5(\tau)\varphi_{\varrho_1}\left(\int_0^1\mathfrak{J}_1(\zeta)\xi_1(\zeta)\psi_1\left(\zeta,x(\zeta),y(\zeta),I_{0+}^{\mu_1}x(\zeta),I_{0+}^{\mu_2}y(\zeta)\right)d\zeta\right)d\tau\\
&\quad+\int_0^1\mathfrak{J}_6(\tau)\varphi_{\varrho_2}\left(\int_0^1\mathfrak{J}_2(\zeta)\xi_2(\zeta)\psi_2(\zeta,x(\zeta),y(\zeta),I_{0+}^{\nu_1}x(\zeta),I_{0+}^{\nu_2}y(\zeta))d\zeta\right)d\tau\\
&\leq A_0^{\varrho_1-1}\int_0^1\mathfrak{J}_5(\tau)\varphi_{\varrho_1}\left(\int_0^1\mathfrak{J}_1(\zeta)\xi_1(\zeta)\,d\zeta\right)d\tau+A_0^{\varrho_2-1}\int_0^1\mathfrak{J}_6(\tau)\varphi_{\varrho_2}\left(\int_0^1\mathfrak{J}_2(\zeta)\xi_2(\zeta)\,d\zeta\right)d\tau\\
&=A_0^{\varrho_1-1}\left(\int_0^1\mathfrak{J}_5(\tau)\,d\tau\right)\left(\int_0^1\mathfrak{J}_1(\zeta)\xi_1(\zeta)\,d\zeta\right)^{\varrho_1-1}\\
&\quad+A_0^{\varrho_2-1}\left(\int_0^1\mathfrak{J}_6(\tau)\,d\tau\right)\left(\int_0^1\mathfrak{J}_2(\zeta)\xi_2(\zeta)\,d\zeta\right)^{\varrho_2-1}\\
&=A_0^{\varrho_1-1}\Xi_5\Xi_1^{\varrho_1-1}+A_0^{\varrho_2-1}\Xi_6\Xi_2^{\varrho_2-1}<\tfrac{1}{4}+\tfrac{1}{4}=\tfrac{1}{2}.
\end{aligned}
$$

Therefore we deduce $\|\mathfrak{E}_1(x,y)\| < \frac{1}{2}$, $\|\mathfrak{E}_2(x,y)\| < \frac{1}{2}$ for all $(x,y) \in \partial B_1 \cap \mathfrak{Q}_0$. So we obtain

$$\|\mathfrak{E}(x,y)\|_{\mathfrak{B}} = \|\mathfrak{E}_1(x,y)\| + \|\mathfrak{E}_2(x,y)\| < 1 = \|(x,y)\|_{\mathfrak{B}}, \ \forall (x,y) \in \partial B_1 \cap \mathfrak{Q}_0. \tag{26}$$

Then, by (24) and (26) we conclude that there exists a positive solution $(x_1, y_1) \in \mathfrak{Q}_0$ with $1 < \|(x_1,y_1)\|_{\mathfrak{B}} \le r_2$ for problem (1), (2). By (25) and (26) we deduce that there exists another positive solution $(x_2,y_2) \in \mathfrak{Q}_0$ with $r_4 \le \|(x_2,y_2)\|_{\mathfrak{B}} < 1$ for problem (1), (2). Hence problem (1), (2) has at least two positive solutions $(x_1(t), y_1(t))$, $(x_2(t), y_2(t))$, $t \in [0,1]$. □

5. Examples

Let $\delta_1 = \frac{7}{4}$, $\delta_2 = \frac{5}{3}$, $p = 3$, $q = 4$, $\gamma_1 = \frac{5}{2}$, $\gamma_2 = \frac{17}{5}$, $n = 1$, $m = 2$, $\mu_1 = \frac{23}{6}$, $\mu_2 = \frac{19}{7}$, $\nu_1 = \frac{47}{9}$, $\nu_2 = \frac{22}{3}$, $\alpha_0 = \frac{4}{3}$, $\alpha_1 = \frac{2}{3}$, $\beta_0 = \frac{9}{4}$, $\beta_1 = \frac{3}{4}$, $\beta_2 = \frac{5}{6}$, $\rho_1 = \frac{27}{8}$, $\rho_2 = \frac{38}{9}$, $\varrho_1 = \frac{27}{19}$, $\varrho_2 = \frac{38}{29}$, $\mathfrak{M}_0(\tau) = \frac{5\tau}{7}$, $\tau \in [0,1]$, $\mathfrak{N}_0(\tau) = \left\{\frac{1}{2},\ \tau \in \left[0,\frac{1}{3}\right);\ \frac{11}{10},\ \tau \in \left[\frac{1}{3},1\right]\right\}$, $\mathfrak{M}_1(\tau) = \left\{\frac{3}{4},\ \tau \in \left[0,\frac{1}{2}\right);\ \frac{93}{28},\ \tau \in \left[\frac{1}{2},1\right]\right\}$, $\mathfrak{N}_1(\tau) = \left\{\frac{1}{3},\ \tau \in \left[0,\frac{4}{5}\right);\ \frac{29}{24},\ \tau \in \left[\frac{4}{5},1\right]\right\}$, $\mathfrak{N}_2(\tau) = \frac{3\tau}{2}$, $\tau \in [0,1]$.

We consider the system of fractional differential equations

$$\begin{cases} D_{0+}^{7/4}\left(\varphi_{27/8}\left(D_{0+}^{5/2}x(t)\right)\right) = \mathfrak{f}\left(t, x(t), y(t), I_{0+}^{23/6}x(t), I_{0+}^{19/7}y(t)\right), & t \in (0,1), \\ D_{0+}^{5/3}\left(\varphi_{38/9}\left(D_{0+}^{17/5}y(t)\right)\right) = \mathfrak{g}\left(t, x(t), y(t), I_{0+}^{47/9}x(t), I_{0+}^{22/3}y(t)\right), & t \in (0,1), \end{cases} \tag{27}$$

with the boundary conditions

$$\begin{cases} x(0) = x'(0) = 0,\ D_{0+}^{5/2}x(0) = 0,\ \varphi_{27/8}\left(D_{0+}^{5/2}x(1)\right) = \frac{5}{7}\int_0^1 \varphi_{27/8}\left(D_{0+}^{5/2}x(\tau)\right)d\tau, \\ D_{0+}^{4/3}x(1) = \frac{18}{7}D_{0+}^{2/3}y\left(\frac{1}{2}\right), \\ y(0) = y'(0) = y''(0) = 0,\ D_{0+}^{17/5}y(0) = 0,\ D_{0+}^{17/5}y(1) = \left(\frac{3}{5}\right)^{9/29} D_{0+}^{17/5}y\left(\frac{1}{3}\right), \\ D_{0+}^{9/4}y(1) = \frac{7}{8}D_{0+}^{3/4}x\left(\frac{4}{5}\right) + \frac{3}{2}\int_0^1 D_{0+}^{5/6}x(\tau)\,d\tau. \end{cases} \tag{28}$$

We obtain here $\mathfrak{a}_1 \approx 0.59183673 > 0$, $\mathfrak{a}_2 \approx 0.71155008 > 0$, $\mathfrak{b}_1 \approx 1.45311179$, $\mathfrak{b}_2 \approx 2.39587178$, $\mathfrak{b} \approx 1.09690108 > 0$. Then assumption $(H1)$ is satisfied. We also find

$$\mathfrak{g}_1(t,\tau) = \frac{1}{\Gamma(7/4)}\begin{cases} t^{3/4}(1-\tau)^{3/4} - (t-\tau)^{3/4}, & 0 \le \tau \le t \le 1, \\ t^{3/4}(1-\tau)^{3/4}, & 0 \le t \le \tau \le 1, \end{cases}$$
$$\mathfrak{g}_2(t,\tau) = \frac{1}{\Gamma(5/3)}\begin{cases} t^{2/3}(1-\tau)^{2/3} - (t-\tau)^{2/3}, & 0 \le \tau \le t \le 1, \\ t^{2/3}(1-\tau)^{2/3}, & 0 \le t \le \tau \le 1, \end{cases}$$
$$\mathfrak{g}_3(t,\tau) = \frac{1}{\Gamma(5/2)}\begin{cases} t^{3/2}(1-\tau)^{1/6} - (t-\tau)^{3/2}, & 0 \le \tau \le t \le 1, \\ t^{3/2}(1-\tau)^{1/6}, & 0 \le t \le \tau \le 1, \end{cases}$$
$$\mathfrak{g}_{31}(\vartheta,\tau) = \frac{1}{\Gamma(7/4)}\begin{cases} \vartheta^{3/4}(1-\tau)^{1/6} - (\vartheta-\tau)^{3/4}, & 0 \le \tau \le \vartheta \le 1, \\ \vartheta^{3/4}(1-\tau)^{1/6}, & 0 \le \vartheta \le \tau \le 1, \end{cases}$$
$$\mathfrak{g}_{32}(t,\tau) = \frac{1}{\Gamma(5/3)}\begin{cases} \vartheta^{2/3}(1-\tau)^{1/6} - (\vartheta-\tau)^{2/3}, & 0 \le \tau \le \vartheta \le 1, \\ \vartheta^{2/3}(1-\tau)^{1/6}, & 0 \le \vartheta \le \tau \le 1, \end{cases}$$
$$\mathfrak{g}_4(t,\tau) = \frac{1}{\Gamma(17/5)}\begin{cases} t^{12/5}(1-\tau)^{3/20} - (t-\tau)^{12/5}, & 0 \le \tau \le t \le 1, \\ t^{12/5}(1-\tau)^{3/20}, & 0 \le t \le \tau \le 1, \end{cases}$$
$$\mathfrak{g}_{41}(\vartheta,\tau) = \frac{1}{\Gamma(41/15)}\begin{cases} \vartheta^{26/15}(1-\tau)^{3/20} - (\vartheta-\tau)^{26/15}, & 0 \le \tau \le \vartheta \le 1, \\ \vartheta^{26/15}(1-\tau)^{3/20}, & 0 \le \vartheta \le \tau \le 1, \end{cases}$$
$$\mathfrak{G}_1(t,\tau) = \mathfrak{g}_1(t,\tau) + \frac{5t^{3/4}}{7\mathfrak{a}_1}\int_0^1 \mathfrak{g}_1(\zeta,\tau)\,d\zeta,$$
$$\mathfrak{G}_2(t,\tau) = \mathfrak{g}_2(t,\tau) + \frac{3t^{2/3}}{5\mathfrak{a}_2}\mathfrak{g}_2\left(\frac{1}{3},\tau\right),$$

$$
\begin{aligned}
&\mathfrak{G}_3(t,\tau) = \mathfrak{g}_3(t,\tau) + \frac{t^{3/2}\mathfrak{b}_1}{\mathfrak{b}}\left[\frac{7}{8}\mathfrak{g}_{31}\left(\frac{4}{5},\tau\right) + \frac{3}{2}\int_0^1 \mathfrak{g}_{32}(\vartheta,\tau)\,d\vartheta\right],\\
&\mathfrak{G}_4(t,\tau) = \frac{18t^{3/2}\Gamma(17/5)}{7\mathfrak{b}\Gamma(23/20)}\mathfrak{g}_{41}\left(\frac{1}{2},\tau\right),\\
&\mathfrak{G}_5(t,\tau) = \frac{t^{12/5}\Gamma(5/2)}{\mathfrak{b}\Gamma(7/6)}\left[\frac{7}{8}\mathfrak{g}_{31}\left(\frac{4}{5},\tau\right) + \frac{3}{2}\int_0^1 \mathfrak{g}_{32}(\vartheta,\tau)\,d\vartheta\right],\\
&\mathfrak{G}_6(t,\tau) = \mathfrak{g}_4(t,\tau) + \frac{18t^{12/5}\mathfrak{b}_2}{7\mathfrak{b}}\mathfrak{g}_{41}\left(\frac{1}{2},\tau\right),\\
&\mathfrak{h}_1(\tau) = \tfrac{1}{\Gamma(7/4)}(1-\tau)^{3/4},\ \ \mathfrak{h}_2(\tau) = \tfrac{1}{\Gamma(5/3)}(1-\tau)^{2/3},\\
&\mathfrak{h}_3(\tau) = \tfrac{1}{\Gamma(5/2)}(1-\tau)^{1/6}(1-(1-\tau)^{4/3}),\\
&\mathfrak{h}_4(\tau) = \tfrac{1}{\Gamma(17/5)}(1-\tau)^{3/20}(1-(1-\tau)^{9/4}),
\end{aligned}
$$

for all $t,\tau,\vartheta \in [0,1]$. In addition we deduce

$$
\begin{aligned}
&\mathfrak{J}_1(\tau) = \mathfrak{h}_1(\tau) + \tfrac{5}{7\mathfrak{a}_1\Gamma(11/4)}\left[(1-\tau)^{3/4} - (1-\tau)^{7/4}\right],\ \ \tau\in[0,1],\\
&\mathfrak{J}_2(\tau) = \begin{cases} \mathfrak{h}_2(\tau) + \tfrac{3}{5\mathfrak{a}_2\Gamma(5/3)}\left[\left(\tfrac{1}{3}\right)^{2/3}(1-\tau)^{2/3} - \left(\tfrac{1}{3}-\tau\right)^{2/3}\right], & 0\le\tau\le\tfrac{1}{3},\\ \mathfrak{h}_2(\tau) + \tfrac{3}{5\mathfrak{a}_2\Gamma(5/3)}\left(\tfrac{1}{3}\right)^{2/3}(1-\tau)^{2/3}, & \tfrac{1}{3}<\tau\le 1,\end{cases}\\
&\mathfrak{J}_3(\tau) = \begin{cases} \mathfrak{h}_3(\tau) + \tfrac{\mathfrak{b}_1}{\mathfrak{b}}\Big\{\tfrac{7}{8\Gamma(7/4)}\left[\left(\tfrac{4}{5}\right)^{3/4}(1-\tau)^{1/6} - \left(\tfrac{4}{5}-\tau\right)^{3/4}\right] \\ \quad + \tfrac{3}{2\Gamma(8/3)}\left[(1-\tau)^{1/6} - (1-\tau)^{5/3}\right]\Big\}, & 0\le\tau\le\tfrac{4}{5},\\ \mathfrak{h}_3(\tau) + \tfrac{\mathfrak{b}_1}{\mathfrak{b}}\Big\{\tfrac{7}{8\Gamma(7/4)}\left(\tfrac{4}{5}\right)^{3/4}(1-\tau)^{1/6} \\ \quad + \tfrac{3}{2\Gamma(8/3)}\left[(1-\tau)^{1/6} - (1-\tau)^{5/3}\right]\Big\}, & \tfrac{4}{5}<\tau\le 1,\end{cases}\\
&\mathfrak{J}_4(\tau) = \begin{cases} \tfrac{18\Gamma(17/5)}{7\mathfrak{b}\Gamma(23/20)\Gamma(41/15)}\left[\left(\tfrac{1}{2}\right)^{26/15}(1-\tau)^{3/20} - \left(\tfrac{1}{2}-\tau\right)^{26/15}\right], & 0\le\tau\le\tfrac{1}{2},\\ \tfrac{18\Gamma(17/5)}{7\mathfrak{b}\Gamma(23/20)\Gamma(41/15)}\left(\tfrac{1}{2}\right)^{26/15}(1-\tau)^{3/20}, & \tfrac{1}{2}<\tau\le 1,\end{cases}\\
&\mathfrak{J}_5(\tau) = \begin{cases} \tfrac{\Gamma(5/2)}{\mathfrak{b}\Gamma(7/6)}\Big\{\tfrac{7}{8\Gamma(7/4)}\left[\left(\tfrac{4}{5}\right)^{3/4}(1-\tau)^{1/6} - \left(\tfrac{4}{5}-\tau\right)^{3/4}\right] \\ \quad + \tfrac{3}{2\Gamma(8/3)}\left[(1-\tau)^{1/6} - (1-\tau)^{5/3}\right]\Big\}, & 0\le\tau\le\tfrac{4}{5},\\ \tfrac{\Gamma(5/2)}{\mathfrak{b}\Gamma(7/6)}\Big\{\tfrac{7}{8\Gamma(7/4)}\left(\tfrac{4}{5}\right)^{3/4}(1-\tau)^{1/6} \\ \quad + \tfrac{3}{2\Gamma(8/3)}\left[(1-\tau)^{1/6} - (1-\tau)^{5/3}\right]\Big\}, & \tfrac{4}{5}<\tau\le 1,\end{cases}\\
&\mathfrak{J}_6(\tau) = \begin{cases} \mathfrak{h}_4(\tau) + \tfrac{18\mathfrak{b}_2}{7\mathfrak{b}\Gamma(41/15)}\left[\left(\tfrac{1}{2}\right)^{26/15}(1-\tau)^{3/20} - \left(\tfrac{1}{2}-\tau\right)^{26/15}\right], & 0\le\tau\le\tfrac{1}{2},\\ \mathfrak{h}_4(\tau) + \tfrac{18\mathfrak{b}_2}{7\mathfrak{b}\Gamma(41/15)}\left(\tfrac{1}{2}\right)^{26/15}(1-\tau)^{3/20}, & \tfrac{1}{2}<\tau\le 1.\end{cases}
\end{aligned}
$$

Example 1. *We introduce the functions*

$$
\begin{aligned}
\mathfrak{f}(t,w_1,w_2,w_3,w_4) &= \frac{(3w_1+2w_2+w_3+5w_4)^{19a/8}}{t^{z_1}(1-t)^{z_2}},\\
\mathfrak{g}(t,w_1,w_2,w_3,w_4) &= \frac{(w_1+7w_2+4w_3+2w_4)^{29b/9}}{t^{z_3}(1-t)^{z_4}},
\end{aligned}
\tag{29}
$$

for $t\in(0,1)$, $w_i\ge 0$, $i=1,\dots,4$, *where* $a>1$, $b>1$, $z_1\in(0,1)$, $z_2\in(0,\frac{7}{4})$, $z_3\in(0,1)$, $z_4\in(0,\frac{5}{3})$. *Here* $\xi_1(t)=\frac{1}{t^{z_1}(1-t)^{z_2}}$, $\xi_2(t)=\frac{1}{t^{z_3}(1-t)^{z_4}}$ *for* $t\in(0,1)$, $\psi_1(t,w_1,w_2,w_3,w_4) = (3w_1+2w_2+w_3+5w_4)^{19a/8}$ *and* $\psi_2(t,w_1,w_2,w_3,w_4) = (w_1+7w_2+4w_3+2w_4)^{29b/9}$ *for* $t\in[0,1]$, $w_i\ge 0$, $i=1,\dots,4$. *We also obtain* $M_1 = B(1-z_1,7/4-z_2)\in(0,\infty)$, $M_2 = B(1-z_3,5/3-z_4)\in(0,\infty)$. *Then assumption* $(H2)$ *is satisfied. In addition, in* $(H3)$, *for* $l_1=3$, $l_2=2$, $l_3=1$, $l_4=5$, $\theta_1=1$, $m_1=1$, $m_2=7$, $m_3=4$, $m_4=2$, $\theta_2=1$, *we find* $\psi_{10}=0$ *and* $\psi_{20}=0$. *In* $(H4)$, *for* $[\sigma_1,\sigma_2]\subset(0,1)$, $s_1=3$, $s_2=2$, $s_3=1$, $s_4=5$, *we obtain*

$\mathfrak{f}_\infty = \infty$. *Then by Theorem 1 we deduce that problem (27), (28) with the nonlinearities (29) has at least one solution* $(x_1(t), y_1(t))$, $t \in [0,1]$.

Example 2. *We define the functions*

$$\begin{aligned}
&\mathfrak{f}(t, w_1, w_2, w_3, w_4) = \frac{p_0(t+3)}{(t^2+8)\sqrt[4]{t^3}} \left[\left(\frac{1}{2}w_1 + w_2 + \frac{1}{4}w_3 + \frac{1}{5}w_4 \right)^{v_1} \right. \\
&\quad \left. + \left(\tfrac{1}{2}w_1 + w_2 + \tfrac{1}{4}w_3 + \tfrac{1}{5}w_4 \right)^{v_2} \right], \ t \in (0,1], \ w_i \geq 0, \ i = 1, \dots, 4, \\
&\mathfrak{g}(t, w_1, w_2, w_3, w_4) = \frac{q_0(2+\sin t)}{(t+6)^4 \sqrt[7]{(1-t)^5}} \left(w_1^{v_3} + e^{w_2} + \ln(w_3 + w_4 + 1) \right), \\
&\quad t \in [0,1), \ w_i \geq 0, \ i = 1, \dots, 4,
\end{aligned} \tag{30}$$

where $p_0 > 0$, $q_0 > 0$, $v_1 > 19/8$, $v_2 \in (0, 19/8)$, $v_3 > 0$. *Here we have* $\xi_1(t) = \frac{1}{\sqrt[4]{t^3}}$, $t \in (0,1]$, $\psi_1(t, w_1, w_2, w_3, w_4) = \frac{p_0(t+3)}{(t^2+8)} \left[\left(\frac{1}{2}w_1 + w_2 + \frac{1}{4}w_3 + \frac{1}{5}w_4 \right)^{v_1} + \left(\frac{1}{2}w_1 + w_2 + \frac{1}{4}w_3 + \frac{1}{5}w_4 \right)^{v_2} \right]$, $t \in [0,1]$, $w_i \geq 0$, $i = 1, \dots, 4$, $\xi_2(t) = \frac{1}{\sqrt[7]{(1-t)^5}}$, $t \in [0,1)$, $\psi_2(t, w_1, w_2, w_3, w_4) = \frac{q_0(2+\sin t)}{(t+6)^4} (w_1^{v_3} + e^{w_2} + \ln(w_3 + w_4 + 1))$, $t \in [0,1]$, $w_i \geq 0$, $i = 1, \dots, 4$. *We obtain* $M_1 = B(1/4, 7/4) \in (0, \infty)$, $M_2 = \frac{21}{20} \in (0, \infty)$. *Then assumption (H2) is satisfied. For* $[\sigma_1, \sigma_2] \subset (0,1)$, $s_1 = \frac{1}{2}$, $s_2 = 1$, $s_3 = \frac{1}{4}$, $s_4 = \frac{1}{5}$, *we find* $\mathfrak{f}_\infty = \infty$ *(in (H4)), and for* $p_1 = \frac{1}{2}$, $p_2 = 1$, $p_3 = \frac{1}{4}$, $p_4 = \frac{1}{5}$, $\varsigma_1 \in \left(\frac{8v_2}{19}, 1 \right]$, *we have* $\mathfrak{f}_0 = \infty$ *(in (H6)). So assumptions (H4) and (H6) are satisfied. Then after some computations we deduce* $\Xi_1 \approx 3.93816256$, $\Xi_2 \approx 1.53523525$, $\Xi_3 \approx 1.40740842$, $\Xi_4 \approx 0.97489748$, $\Xi_5 \approx 1.04873754$, $\Xi_6 \approx 0.92404828$, $\varpi = 1$, *and* $A_0 = \max\left\{ \frac{4p_0}{9} \left(\left(\frac{39}{20}\right)^{v_1} + \left(\frac{39}{20}\right)^{v_2} \right), q_0 m_0 (1 + e + \ln 3) \right\}$, *where* $m_0 = \max_{t \in [0,1]} \frac{2+\sin t}{(t+6)^4} \approx 2.00035047$. *If*

$$\begin{aligned}
p_0 &< \frac{9}{\left(\frac{39}{20}\right)^{v_1} + \left(\frac{39}{20}\right)^{v_2}} \min\left\{ \frac{1}{4^{27/8} \Xi_3^{19/8} \Xi_1}, \frac{1}{4^{38/9} \Xi_4^{29/9} \Xi_2}, \frac{1}{4^{27/8} \Xi_5^{19/8} \Xi_1}, \frac{1}{4^{38/9} \Xi_6^{29/9} \Xi_2} \right\}, \\
q_0 &< \frac{1}{m_0(1 + e + \ln 3)} \min\left\{ \frac{1}{4^{19/8} \Xi_3^{19/8} \Xi_1}, \frac{1}{4^{29/9} \Xi_4^{29/9} \Xi_2}, \frac{1}{4^{19/8} \Xi_5^{19/8} \Xi_1}, \frac{1}{4^{29/9} \Xi_6^{29/9} \Xi_2} \right\},
\end{aligned}$$

then the inequalities $A_0^{8/19} \Xi_3 \Xi_1^{8/19} < \frac{1}{4}$, $A_0^{9/29} \Xi_4 \Xi_2^{9/29} < \frac{1}{4}$, $A_0^{8/19} \Xi_5 \Xi_1^{8/19} < \frac{1}{4}$, $A_0^{9/29} \Xi_6 \Xi_2^{9/29} < \frac{1}{4}$ *are satisfied, (that is, assumption (H7) is satisfied). For example, if* $v_1 = 2$, $v_2 = 3$ *and* $p_0 \leq 0.0008$, $q_0 \leq 0.0004$, *then the above inequalities are verified. By Theorem 3, we conclude that problem (27), (28) with the nonlinearities (30) has at least two positive solutions* $(x_1(t), y_1(t))$, $(x_2(t), y_2(t))$, $t \in [0,1]$.

6. Conclusions

In this paper we investigated the system of coupled fractional differential equations (1) with ϱ-Laplacian operators and Riemann–Liouville fractional derivatives of varied orders, supplemented with general nonlocal boundary conditions (2) containing Riemann–Stieltjes integrals and fractional derivatives of differing orders. The nonlinearities from the system are dependent on various fractional integrals and they are nonnegative and singular in the points $t = 0$ and $t = 1$. The last boundary conditions for the unknown functions x and y are coupled in the point 1, in contrast to the boundary conditions from paper [6] in which they are uncoupled in the point 1. We presented diverse assumptions on the functions $\mathfrak{f}$ and $\mathfrak{g}$ so that problem (1), (2) has one positive solution (in Theorems 1 and 2), and two positive solutions (in Theorem 3). We also gave the corresponding Green functions and their properties used in the proof of the main results. We transformed our problem into a system of integral equations and we associated an operator $\mathfrak{C}$ for which we looked for the fixed points by applying the Guo–Krasnosel'skii fixed point theorem of cone expansion and compression of norm type. We presented finally two examples for illustrating our main theorems. For some future research directions we have in mind the study of some systems of fractional differential equations with other nonlocal coupled or uncoupled boundary conditions.

Author Contributions: Conceptualization, R.L.; Formal analysis, A.T. and R.L.; Methodology, A.T. and R.L. All authors have read and agreed to the published version of the manuscript.

Funding: This research received no external funding.

Institutional Review Board Statement: Not applicable.

Informed Consent Statement: Not applicable.

Data Availability Statement: Not applicable.

Conflicts of Interest: The authors declare no conflict of interest.

References

1. Wang, G.; Ren, X.; Zhang, L.; Ahmad, B. Explicit iteration and unique positive solution for a Caputo-Hadamard fractional turbulent flow model. *IEEE Access* **2019**, *7*, 109833–109839. [CrossRef]
2. Guo, D.; Lakshmikantham, V. *Nonlinear Problems in Abstract Cones*; Academic Press: New York, NY, USA, 1988.
3. Wang, H.; Jiang, J. Existence and multiplicity of positive solutions for a system of nonlinear fractional multi-point boundary value problems with p-Laplacian operator. *J. Appl. Anal. Comput.* **2021**, *11*, 351–366.
4. Tudorache, A.; Luca, R. Positive solutions for a system of Riemann–Liouville fractional boundary value problems with p-Laplacian operators. *Adv. Differ. Equ.* **2020**, *292*, 1–30. 10.1186/s13662-020-02750-6. [CrossRef]
5. Alsaedi, A.; Luca, R.; Ahmad, B. Existence of positive solutions for a system of singular fractional boundary value problems with p-Laplacian operators. *Mathematics* **2020**, *8*, 1890. [CrossRef]
6. Tudorache, A.; Luca, R. Positive solutions of a singular fractional boundary value problem with r-Laplacian operators. *Fractal Fract.* **2022**, *6*, 18. [CrossRef]
7. Prasad, K.R.; Leela, I.D.; Khuddush, M. Existence and uniqueness of positive solutions for system of (p,q,r)-Laplacian fractional order boundary value problems. *Adv. Theory Nonlinear Anal. Appl.* **2021**, *5*, 138–157.
8. Tan, J.; Li, M. Solutions of fractional differential equations with p-Laplacian operator in Banach spaces. *Bound. Value Prob.* **2018**, *15*, 1–13. [CrossRef]
9. Tang, X.; Wang, X.; Wang, Z.; Ouyang, P. The existence of solutions for mixed fractional resonant boundary value problem with $p(t)$-Laplacian operator. *J. Appl. Math. Comput.* **2019**, *61*, 559–572. [CrossRef]
10. Tian, Y.; Sun, S.; Bai, Z. Positive Solutions of Fractional Differential Equations with p-Laplacian. *J. Funct. Spaces* **2017**, *2017*, 3187492. [CrossRef]
11. Wang, H.; Liu, S.; Li, H. Positive solutions to p-Laplacian fractional differential equations with infinite-point boundary value conditions. *Adv. Differ. Equ.* **2018**, *425*, 1–15. [CrossRef]
12. Wang, Y.; Liu, S.; Han, Z. Eigenvalue problems for fractional differential equationswith mixed derivatives and generalized p-Laplacian. *Nonlinear Anal. Model. Control* **2018**, *23*, 830–850. [CrossRef]
13. Ahmad, B.; Alsaedi, A.; Ntouyas, S.K.; Tariboon, J. *Hadamard-Type Fractional Differential Equations, Inclusions and Inequalities*; Springer: Cham, Switzerland, 2017.
14. Ahmad, B.; Henderson, J.; Luca, R. *Boundary Value Problems for Fractional Differential Equations and Systems*; Trends in Abstract and Applied Analysis; World Scientific: Hackensack, NJ, USA, 2021; Volume 9.
15. Ahmad, B.; Ntouyas, S.K. *Nonlocal Nonlinear Fractional-Order Boundary Value Problems*; World Scientific: Hackensack, NJ, USA, 2021.
16. Henderson, J.; Luca, R. *Boundary Value Problems for Systems of Differential, Difference and Fractional Equations. Positive Solutions*; Elsevier: Amsterdam, The Netherlands, 2016.
17. Zhou, Y.; Wang, J.R.; Zhang, L. *Basic Theory of Fractional Differential Equations*, 2nd ed.; World Scientific: Singapore, 2016.

fractal and fractional

Article

On a System of Riemann–Liouville Fractional Boundary Value Problems with ϱ-Laplacian Operators and Positive Parameters

Johnny Henderson [1], **Rodica Luca** [2,*] and **Alexandru Tudorache** [3]

1 Department of Mathematics, Baylor University, Waco, TX 76798-7328, USA; johnny_henderson@baylor.edu
2 Department of Mathematics, Gheorghe Asachi Technical University, 700506 Iasi, Romania
3 Department of Computer Science and Engineering, Gheorghe Asachi Technical University, 700050 Iasi, Romania; alexandru.tudorache93@gmail.com
* Correspondence: rluca@math.tuiasi.ro

Abstract: In this paper, we study the existence and nonexistence of positive solutions of a system of Riemann–Liouville fractional differential equations with ϱ-Laplacian operators, supplemented with coupled nonlocal boundary conditions containing Riemann–Stieltjes integrals, fractional derivatives of various orders, and positive parameters. We apply the Schauder fixed point theorem in the proof of the existence result.

Keywords: Riemann–Liouville fractional differential equations; nonlocal coupled boundary conditions; positive solutions; existence; nonexistence; positive parameters

MSC: 34A08; 34B10; 34B18

Citation: Henderson, J.; Luca, R.; Tudorache, A. On a System of Riemann–Liouville Fractional Boundary Value Problems with ϱ-Laplacian Operators and Positive Parameters. *Fractal Fract.* **2022**, *6*, 299. https://doi.org/10.3390/fractalfract6060299

Academic Editor: Maria Rosaria Lancia

Received: 22 April 2022
Accepted: 27 May 2022
Published: 29 May 2022

1. Introduction

We consider the system of fractional differential equations with ϱ_1-Laplacian and ϱ_2-Laplacian operators

$$\begin{cases} D_{0+}^{\gamma_1}(\varphi_{\varrho_1}(D_{0+}^{\delta_1}\mathrm{u}(t))) + \mathfrak{a}(t)\mathfrak{f}(\mathrm{v}(t)) = 0, \ \ t \in (0,1), \\ D_{0+}^{\gamma_2}(\varphi_{\varrho_2}(D_{0+}^{\delta_2}\mathrm{v}(t))) + \mathfrak{b}(t)\mathfrak{g}(\mathrm{u}(t)) = 0, \ \ t \in (0,1), \end{cases} \tag{1}$$

subject to the coupled nonlocal boundary conditions

$$\begin{cases} \mathrm{u}^{(j)}(0) = 0, \ j = 0, \dots, p-2; \ D_{0+}^{\delta_1}\mathrm{u}(0) = 0, \ D_{0+}^{\alpha_0}\mathrm{u}(1) = \sum_{j=1}^{n} \int_0^1 D_{0+}^{\alpha_j}\mathrm{v}(\tau)\, d\mathfrak{H}_j(\tau) + \mathfrak{c}_0, \\ \mathrm{v}^{(j)}(0) = 0, \ j = 0, \dots, q-2; \ D_{0+}^{\delta_2}\mathrm{v}(0) = 0, \ D_{0+}^{\beta_0}\mathrm{v}(1) = \sum_{j=1}^{m} \int_0^1 D_{0+}^{\beta_j}\mathrm{u}(\tau)\, d\mathfrak{K}_j(\tau) + \mathfrak{d}_0, \end{cases} \tag{2}$$

where $\gamma_1, \gamma_2 \in (0,1]$, $\delta_1 \in (p-1,p]$, $\delta_2 \in (q-1,q]$, $p, q \in \mathbb{N}$, $p, q \geq 3$, $n, m \in \mathbb{N}$, $\alpha_j \in \mathbb{R}$ for all $j = 0,1,\dots,n$, $0 \leq \alpha_1 < \alpha_2 < \cdots < \alpha_n \leq \beta_0 < \delta_2 - 1$, $\beta_0 \geq 1$, $\beta_j \in \mathbb{R}$ for all $j = 0,1,\dots,m$, $0 \leq \beta_1 < \beta_2 < \cdots < \beta_m \leq \alpha_0 < \delta_1 - 1$, $\alpha_0 \geq 1$, the functions $\mathfrak{f}, \mathfrak{g} : \mathbb{R}_+ \to \mathbb{R}_+$ and $\mathfrak{a}, \mathfrak{b} : [0,1] \to \mathbb{R}_+$ are continuous, ($\mathbb{R}_+ = [0,\infty)$), $\mathfrak{c}_0$ and $\mathfrak{d}_0$ are positive parameters, $\varrho_1, \varrho_2 > 1$, $\varphi_{\varrho_i}(\zeta) = |\zeta|^{\varrho_i - 2}\zeta$, $\varphi_{\varrho_i}^{-1} = \varphi_{\rho_i}$, $\rho_i = \frac{\varrho_i}{\varrho_i - 1}$, and $i = 1,2$. The integrals from the conditions (2) are Riemann–Stieltjes integrals with $\mathfrak{H}_j$, $j = 1,\dots,n$ and $\mathfrak{K}_i$, $i = 1,\dots,m$ functions of bounded variation, and D_{0+}^{k} denotes the Riemann–Liouville derivative of order k (for $k = \gamma_1, \delta_1, \gamma_2, \delta_2, \alpha_j$; for $j = 0,1,\dots,n$, β_i; and for $i = 0,1,\dots,m$).

We present in this paper sufficient conditions for the functions $\mathfrak{f}$ and $\mathfrak{g}$, and intervals for the parameters $\mathfrak{c}_0$ and $\mathfrak{d}_0$ such that problem (1) and (2) has at least one positive solution, or it has no positive solutions. We apply the Schauder fixed point theorem in the proof of the main existence result. A positive solution of (1) and (2) is a pair of functions $(\mathrm{u},\mathrm{v}) \in (C([0,1];\mathbb{R}_+))^2$ that satisfy the system (1) and the boundary conditions (2), with

$u(t) > 0$ and $v(t) > 0$ for all $t \in (0,1]$. Now, we present some recent results related to our problem. By using the Guo–Krasnosel'skii fixed point theorem, in [1], the authors investigated the system of fractional differential equations

$$\begin{cases} D_{0+}^{\gamma_1}(\varphi_{\varrho_1}(D_{0+}^{\delta_1}u(t))) + \lambda f(t,u(t),v(t)) = 0, \ t \in (0,1), \\ D_{0+}^{\gamma_2}(\varphi_{\varrho_2}(D_{0+}^{\delta_2}v(t))) + \mu g(t,u(t),v(t)) = 0, \ t \in (0,1), \end{cases} \tag{3}$$

supplemented with the boundary conditions (2) with $\mathfrak{c}_0 = \mathfrak{d}_0 = 0$, where λ and μ are positive parameters, and $f, g \in C([0,1] \times \mathbb{R}_+ \times \mathbb{R}_+, \mathbb{R}_+)$. They presented various intervals for λ and μ such that problem (2) and (3) with $\mathfrak{c}_0 = \mathfrak{d}_0 = 0$ has at least one positive solution ($u(t) > 0$ for all $t \in (0,1]$, or $v(t) > 0$ for all $t \in (0,1]$). They also studied the nonexistence of positive solutions. In [2], the author investigated the existence and nonexistence of positive solutions for the system (3) with the uncoupled boundary conditions

$$\begin{cases} u^{(j)}(0) = 0, \ j = 0,\ldots,p-2; \ D_{0+}^{\delta_1}u(0) = 0, \ D_{0+}^{\alpha_0}u(1) = \sum_{j=1}^{n}\int_0^1 D_{0+}^{\alpha_j}u(\tau)\, d\mathfrak{H}_j(\tau), \\ v^{(j)}(0) = 0, \ j = 0,\ldots,q-2; \ D_{0+}^{\delta_2}v(0) = 0, \ D_{0+}^{\beta_0}v(1) = \sum_{j=1}^{m}\int_0^1 D_{0+}^{\beta_j}v(\tau)\, d\mathfrak{K}_j(\tau), \end{cases}$$

where $\alpha_j \in \mathbb{R}$ for all $j = 0,1,\ldots,n$, $0 \le \alpha_1 < \alpha_2 < \cdots < \alpha_n \le \alpha_0 < \delta_1 - 1$, $\alpha_0 \ge 1$, $\beta_j \in \mathbb{R}$ for all $j = 0,1,\ldots,m$, $0 \le \beta_1 < \beta_2 < \cdots < \beta_m \le \beta_0 < \delta_2 - 1$, $\beta_0 \ge 1$, $\mathfrak{H}_i$, $i = 1,\ldots,n$, and $\mathfrak{K}_j$, $j = 1,\cdots,m$ are functions of bounded variation. In [3], the authors studied the positive solutions for the system of nonlinear fractional differential equations

$$\begin{cases} D_{0+}^{\alpha}u(t) + \mathfrak{a}(t)\mathfrak{f}(v(t)) = 0, \ t \in (0,1), \\ D_{0+}^{\beta}v(t) + \mathfrak{b}(t)\mathfrak{g}(u(t)) = 0, \ t \in (0,1), \end{cases}$$

subject to the coupled integral boundary conditions

$$\begin{cases} u(0) = u'(0) = \cdots = u^{(n-2)}(0) = 0, \ u(1) = \int_0^1 v(\tau)d\mathfrak{H}(\tau) + \mathfrak{c}_0, \\ v(0) = v'(0) = \cdots = v^{(m-2)}(0) = 0, \ v(1) = \int_0^1 u(\tau)d\mathfrak{K}(\tau) + \mathfrak{d}_0, \end{cases}$$

where $n-1 < \alpha \le n$, $m-1 < \beta \le m$, $n, m \in \mathbb{N}$, $n, m \ge 3$, $\mathfrak{a}, \mathfrak{b}, \mathfrak{f}, \mathfrak{g}$ are nonnegative continuous functions, $\mathfrak{c}_0$ and $\mathfrak{d}_0$ are positive parameters, and $\mathfrak{H}$ and $\mathfrak{K}$ are bounded variation functions. In [4], the authors investigated the existence and nonexistence of positive solutions for the system (1) with the nonlocal uncoupled boundary conditions with positive parameters

$$\begin{cases} u^{(j)}(0) = 0, \ j = 0,\ldots,p-2; \ D_{0+}^{\delta_1}u(0) = 0, \ D_{0+}^{\alpha_0}u(1) = \sum_{j=1}^{n}\int_0^1 D_{0+}^{\alpha_j}u(\tau)\, d\mathfrak{H}_j(\tau) + \mathfrak{c}_0, \\ v^{(j)}(0) = 0, \ j = 0,\ldots,q-2; \ D_{0+}^{\delta_2}v(0) = 0, \ D_{0+}^{\beta_0}v(1) = \sum_{j=1}^{m}\int_0^1 D_{0+}^{\beta_j}v(\tau)\, d\mathfrak{K}_j(\tau) + \mathfrak{d}_0. \end{cases}$$

We note that our problem (1) and (2) is different than the problem studied in [4], because of the boundary conditions, which are coupled in (2) and uncoupled in [4]. Based on this difference, here, we will use, for problem (1) and (2), other Green functions, different systems of integral equations, and different operators than those in [4]. We would also like to mention the papers [5–10], and the monographs [11–13], which contain other recent results for fractional differential equations and systems of fractional differential equations with or without Laplacian operators, and for various applications. The novelties of our problem (1) and (2) with respect to the above papers consist in the consideration of positive parameters $\mathfrak{c}_0$ and $\mathfrak{d}_0$ in the coupled nonlocal boundary conditions (2) containing fractional derivatives of various orders and Riemann–Stieltjes integrals, combined with the system of fractional differential Equation (1), which has ϱ-Laplacian operators.

The paper is structured as follows. In Section 2, we present some auxiliary results, which include the Green functions associated with our problem (1) and (2) and their properties. In Section 3, we give the main theorems for the existence and nonexistence of positive solutions for (1) and (2), and Section 4 contains an example illustrating our results. Finally, in Section 5, we present the conclusions of this work.

2. Auxiliary Results

In this section, we present some results from [1], which will be used in our main theorems in the next section.

We consider the system of fractional differential equations

$$\begin{cases} D_{0+}^{\gamma_1}(\varphi_{\varrho_1}(D_{0+}^{\delta_1}\mathrm{u}(t))) + \widetilde{\mathrm{h}}(t) = 0, \ \ t \in (0,1), \\ D_{0+}^{\gamma_2}(\varphi_{\varrho_2}(D_{0+}^{\delta_2}\mathrm{v}(t))) + \widetilde{\mathrm{k}}(t) = 0, \ \ t \in (0,1), \end{cases} \tag{4}$$

with the coupled boundary conditions

$$\begin{cases} \mathrm{u}^{(j)}(0) = 0, \ j = 0, \dots, p-2; \ D_{0+}^{\delta_1}\mathrm{u}(0) = 0, \ D_{0+}^{\alpha_0}\mathrm{u}(1) = \sum_{j=1}^{n}\int_0^1 D_{0+}^{\alpha_j}\mathrm{v}(\tau)\,d\mathfrak{H}_j(\tau), \\ \mathrm{v}^{(j)}(0) = 0, \ j = 0, \dots, q-2; \ D_{0+}^{\delta_2}\mathrm{v}(0) = 0, \ D_{0+}^{\beta_0}\mathrm{v}(1) = \sum_{j=1}^{m}\int_0^1 D_{0+}^{\beta_j}\mathrm{u}(\tau)\,d\mathfrak{K}_j(\tau), \end{cases} \tag{5}$$

where $\widetilde{\mathrm{h}}, \widetilde{\mathrm{k}} \in C[0,1]$. We denote this by

$$\Delta_1 = \sum_{i=1}^{n} \frac{\Gamma(\delta_2)}{\Gamma(\delta_2 - \alpha_i)} \int_0^1 \tau^{\delta_2 - \alpha_i - 1}\, d\mathfrak{H}_i(\tau), \ \ \Delta_2 = \sum_{i=1}^{m} \frac{\Gamma(\delta_1)}{\Gamma(\delta_1 - \beta_i)} \int_0^1 \tau^{\delta_1 - \beta_i - 1}\, d\mathfrak{K}_i(\tau),$$
$$\Delta = \frac{\Gamma(\delta_1)\Gamma(\delta_2)}{\Gamma(\delta_1 - \alpha_0)\Gamma(\delta_2 - \beta_0)} - \Delta_1\Delta_2.$$

Lemma 1 ([1]). *If $\Delta \neq 0$, then the unique solution $(\mathrm{u}, \mathrm{v}) \in (C[0,1])^2$ of problem (4) and (5) is given by*

$$\begin{cases} \mathrm{u}(t) = \int_0^1 \mathfrak{G}_1(t,\zeta)\varphi_{\rho_1}(I_{0+}^{\gamma_1}\widetilde{\mathrm{h}}(\zeta))\,d\zeta + \int_0^1 \mathfrak{G}_2(t,\zeta)\varphi_{\rho_2}(I_{0+}^{\gamma_2}\widetilde{\mathrm{k}}(\zeta))\,d\zeta, \ \ \forall t \in [0,1], \\ \mathrm{v}(t) = \int_0^1 \mathfrak{G}_3(t,\zeta)\varphi_{\rho_1}(I_{0+}^{\gamma_1}\widetilde{\mathrm{h}}(\zeta))\,d\zeta + \int_0^1 \mathfrak{G}_4(t,\zeta)\varphi_{\rho_2}(I_{0+}^{\gamma_2}\widetilde{\mathrm{k}}(\zeta))\,d\zeta, \ \ \forall t \in [0,1], \end{cases} \tag{6}$$

where

$$\begin{aligned} \mathfrak{G}_1(t,\zeta) &= \mathfrak{g}_1(t,\zeta) + \frac{t^{\delta_1-1}\Delta_1}{\Delta}\left(\sum_{j=1}^{m}\int_0^1 \mathfrak{g}_{1j}(\tau,\zeta)\,d\mathfrak{K}_j(\tau)\right), \\ \mathfrak{G}_2(t,\zeta) &= \frac{t^{\delta_1-1}\Gamma(\delta_2)}{\Delta\Gamma(\delta_2-\beta_0)}\sum_{j=1}^{n}\int_0^1 \mathfrak{g}_{2j}(\tau,\zeta)\,d\mathfrak{H}_j(\tau), \\ \mathfrak{G}_3(t,\zeta) &= \frac{t^{\delta_2-1}\Gamma(\delta_1)}{\Delta\Gamma(\delta_1-\alpha_0)}\sum_{j=1}^{m}\int_0^1 \mathfrak{g}_{1j}(\tau,\zeta)\,d\mathfrak{K}_j(\tau), \\ \mathfrak{G}_4(t,\zeta) &= \mathfrak{g}_2(t,\zeta) + \frac{t^{\delta_2-1}\Delta_2}{\Delta}\left(\sum_{j=1}^{n}\int_0^1 \mathfrak{g}_{2j}(\tau,\zeta)\,d\mathfrak{H}_j(\tau)\right), \end{aligned} \tag{7}$$

for all $(t,\zeta) \in [0,1] \times [0,1]$ and

$$\mathfrak{g}_1(t,\zeta) = \frac{1}{\Gamma(\delta_1)}\begin{cases} t^{\delta_1-1}(1-\zeta)^{\delta_1-\alpha_0-1} - (t-\zeta)^{\delta_1-1}, \ 0 \le \zeta \le t \le 1, \\ t^{\delta_1-1}(1-\zeta)^{\delta_1-\alpha_0-1}, \ 0 \le t \le \zeta \le 1, \end{cases}$$
$$\mathfrak{g}_{1j}(\tau,\zeta) = \frac{1}{\Gamma(\delta_1-\beta_j)}\begin{cases} \tau^{\delta_1-\beta_j-1}(1-\zeta)^{\delta_1-\alpha_0-1} - (\tau-\zeta)^{\delta_1-\beta_j-1}, \ 0 \le \zeta \le \tau \le 1, \\ \tau^{\delta_1-\beta_j-1}(1-\zeta)^{\delta_1-\alpha_0-1}, \ 0 \le \tau \le \zeta \le 1, \end{cases}$$

$$\mathfrak{g}_2(t,\zeta) = \frac{1}{\Gamma(\delta_2)} \begin{cases} t^{\delta_2-1}(1-\zeta)^{\delta_2-\beta_0-1} - (t-\zeta)^{\delta_2-1}, & 0 \le \zeta \le t \le 1, \\ t^{\delta_2-1}(1-\zeta)^{\delta_2-\beta_0-1}, & 0 \le t \le \zeta \le 1, \end{cases}$$
$$\mathfrak{g}_{2k}(\tau,\zeta) = \frac{1}{\Gamma(\delta_2-\alpha_k)} \begin{cases} \tau^{\delta_2-\alpha_k-1}(1-\zeta)^{\delta_2-\beta_0-1} - (\tau-\zeta)^{\delta_2-\alpha_k-1}, & 0 \le \zeta \le \tau \le 1, \\ \tau^{\delta_2-\alpha_k-1}(1-\zeta)^{\delta_2-\beta_0-1}, & 0 \le \tau \le \zeta \le 1, \end{cases}$$

for all $j = 1, \dots, m$ *and* $k = 1, \dots, n$.

Lemma 2 ([1]). *We suppose that* $\Delta > 0$, $\mathfrak{H}_j$, $j = 1, \dots, n$, $\mathfrak{K}_j$, $j = 1, \dots, m$ *are nondecreasing functions. Therefore, the functions* $\mathfrak{G}_i$, $i = 1, \dots, 4$ *(given by (7)) have the following properties:*

(1) $\mathfrak{G}_i : [0,1] \times [0,1] \to \mathbb{R}_+$, $i = 1, \dots, 4$ *are continuous functions;*
(2) $\mathfrak{G}_1(t,\zeta) \le \mathfrak{J}_1(\zeta)$ *for all* $(t,\zeta) \in [0,1] \times [0,1]$, *where*
$$\mathfrak{J}_1(\zeta) = \mathfrak{h}_1(\zeta) + \frac{\Delta_1}{\Delta}\left(\sum_{j=1}^{m} \int_0^1 g_{1j}(\tau,\zeta)\, d\mathfrak{K}_j(\tau)\right), \ \forall \zeta \in [0,1],$$
and $\mathfrak{h}_1(\zeta) = \frac{1}{\Gamma(\delta_1)}(1-\zeta)^{\delta_1-\alpha_0-1}(1-(1-\zeta)^{\alpha_0})$, *for all* $\zeta \in [0,1]$.
(3) $\mathfrak{G}_1(t,\zeta) \ge t^{\delta_1-1}\mathfrak{J}_1(\zeta)$ *for all* $(t,\zeta) \in [0,1] \times [0,1]$;
(4) $\mathfrak{G}_2(t,\zeta) \le \mathfrak{J}_2(\zeta)$, *for all* $(t,\zeta) \in [0,1] \times [0,1]$, *where*
$$\mathfrak{J}_2(\zeta) = \frac{\Gamma(\delta_2)}{\Delta\Gamma(\delta_2-\beta_0)} \sum_{j=1}^{n} \int_0^1 g_{2j}(\tau,\zeta)\, d\mathfrak{H}_j(\tau), \ \forall \zeta \in [0,1];$$
(5) $\mathfrak{G}_2(t,\zeta) = t^{\delta_1-1}\mathfrak{J}_2(\zeta)$ *for all* $(t,\zeta) \in [0,1] \times [0,1]$;
(6) $\mathfrak{G}_3(t,\zeta) \le \mathfrak{J}_3(\zeta)$ *for all* $(t,\zeta) \in [0,1] \times [0,1]$, *where*
$$\mathfrak{J}_3(\zeta) = \frac{\Gamma(\delta_1)}{\Delta\Gamma(\delta_1-\alpha_0)} \sum_{j=1}^{m} \int_0^1 g_{1j}(\tau,\zeta)\, d\mathfrak{K}_j(\tau), \ \forall \zeta \in [0,1];$$
(7) $\mathcal{G}_3(t,\zeta) = t^{\delta_2-1}\mathfrak{J}_3(\zeta)$ *for all* $(t,\zeta) \in [0,1] \times [0,1]$;
(8) $\mathfrak{G}_4(t,\zeta) \le \mathfrak{J}_4(\zeta)$ *for all* $(t,\zeta) \in [0,1] \times [0,1]$, *where*
$$\mathfrak{J}_4(\zeta) = \mathfrak{h}_2(\zeta) + \frac{\Delta_2}{\Delta}\left(\sum_{j=1}^{n} \int_0^1 g_{2j}(\tau,\zeta)\, dH_j(\tau)\right), \ \forall \zeta \in [0,1],$$
and $\mathfrak{h}_2(\zeta) = \frac{1}{\Gamma(\delta_2)}(1-\zeta)^{\delta_2-\beta_0-1}(1-(1-\zeta)^{\beta_0})$, *for all* $\zeta \in [0,1]$.
(9) $\mathfrak{G}_4(t,\zeta) \ge t^{\delta_2-1}\mathfrak{J}_4(\zeta)$, *for all* $(t,\zeta) \in [0,1] \times [0,1]$.

Lemma 3. *We suppose that* $\Delta > 0$, $\mathfrak{H}_i$, $i = 1, \dots, n$, $\mathfrak{K}_j$, $j = 1, \dots, m$ *are nondecreasing functions, and* $\widetilde{\mathrm{h}}, \widetilde{\mathrm{k}} \in C([0,1];\mathbb{R}_+)$. *Therefore, the solution* $(\mathrm{u}(t), \mathrm{v}(t))$, $t \in [0,1]$ *of problem (4) and (5) (given by (6)) satisfies the inequalities* $\mathrm{u}(t) \ge 0$, $\mathrm{v}(t) \ge 0$, $\mathrm{u}(t) \ge t^{\delta_1-1}\mathrm{u}(\nu)$, $\mathrm{v}(t) \ge t^{\delta_2-1}\mathrm{v}(\nu)$ *for all* $t, \nu \in [0,1]$.

Proof. Under the assumptions of this lemma, by using relations (6) and Lemma 2, we find that $\mathrm{u}(t) \ge 0$ and $\mathrm{v}(t) \ge 0$ for all $t \in [0,1]$. In addition, for all t, $\nu \in [0,1]$, we obtain the following inequalities:

$$\begin{aligned}
\mathrm{u}(t) &\ge t^{\delta_1-1}\left(\int_0^1 \mathfrak{J}_1(\zeta)\varphi_{\rho_1}(I_{0+}^{\gamma_1}\widetilde{\mathrm{h}}(\zeta))\, d\zeta + \int_0^1 \mathfrak{J}_2(\zeta)\varphi_{\rho_2}(I_{0+}^{\gamma_2}\widetilde{\mathrm{k}}(\zeta))\, d\zeta\right) \\
&\ge t^{\delta_1-1}\left(\int_0^1 \mathfrak{G}_1(\nu,\zeta)\varphi_{\rho_1}(I_{0+}^{\gamma_1}\widetilde{\mathrm{h}}(\zeta))\, d\zeta + \int_0^1 \mathfrak{G}_2(\nu,\zeta)\varphi_{\rho_2}(I_{0+}^{\gamma_2}\widetilde{\mathrm{k}}(\zeta))\, d\zeta\right) \\
&= t^{\delta_1-1}\mathrm{u}(\nu), \\
\mathrm{v}(t) &\ge t^{\delta_2-1}\left(\int_0^1 \mathfrak{J}_3(\zeta)\varphi_{\rho_1}(I_{0+}^{\gamma_1}\widetilde{\mathrm{h}}(\zeta))\, d\zeta + \int_0^1 \mathcal{J}_4(\zeta)\varphi_{\rho_2}(I_{0+}^{\gamma_2}\widetilde{\mathrm{k}}(\zeta))\, d\zeta\right) \\
&\ge t^{\delta_2-1}\left(\int_0^1 \mathfrak{G}_3(\nu,\zeta)\varphi_{\rho_1}(I_{0+}^{\gamma_1}\widetilde{\mathrm{h}}(\zeta))\, d\zeta + \int_0^1 \mathfrak{G}_4(\nu,\zeta)\varphi_{\rho_2}(I_{0+}^{\gamma_2}\widetilde{\mathrm{k}}(\zeta))\, d\zeta\right) \\
&= t^{\delta_2-1}\mathrm{v}(\nu).
\end{aligned}$$

□

3. Main Results

In this section, we study the existence and nonexistence of positive solutions for problem (1) and (2) under some conditions on $\mathfrak{a}, \mathfrak{b}, \mathfrak{f}$, and $\mathfrak{g}$, when the positive parameters $\mathfrak{c}_0$ and $\mathfrak{d}_0$ belong to some intervals.

We now give the assumptions that we will use in the next part.

$(K1)$ $\gamma_1, \gamma_2 \in (0,1]$, $\delta_1 \in (p-1, p]$, $\delta_2 \in (q-1, q]$, $p, q \in \mathbb{N}$, $p, q \geq 3$, $n, m \in \mathbb{N}$, $\alpha_j \in \mathbb{R}$ for all $j = 0, 1, \ldots, n$, $0 \leq \alpha_1 < \alpha_2 < \cdots < \alpha_n \leq \beta_0 < \delta_2 - 1$, $\beta_0 \geq 1$, $\beta_j \in \mathbb{R}$ for all $j = 0, 1, \ldots, m$, $0 \leq \beta_1 < \beta_2 < \cdots < \beta_m \leq \alpha_0 < \delta_1 - 1$, $\alpha_0 \geq 1$, $\mathfrak{c}_0 > 0$ and $\mathfrak{d}_0 > 0$, $\mathfrak{H}_i$, $i = 1, \ldots, n$ and $\mathfrak{K}_j$, $j = 1, \ldots, m$ are nondecreasing functions, and $\Delta > 0$.

$(K2)$ The functions $\mathfrak{a}, \mathfrak{b} : [0,1] \to \mathbb{R}_+$ are continuous, and there exist $\tau_1, \tau_2 \in (0,1)$ such that $\mathfrak{a}(\tau_1) > 0$, $\mathfrak{b}(\tau_2) > 0$.

$(K3)$ The functions $\mathfrak{f}, \mathfrak{g} : \mathbb{R}_+ \to \mathbb{R}_+$ are continuous, and there exists $\mathfrak{e}_0 > 0$ such that $\mathfrak{f}(z) < \frac{\mathfrak{e}_0^{\varrho_1 - 1}}{L}$, $\mathfrak{g}(z) < \frac{\mathfrak{e}_0^{\varrho_2 - 1}}{L}$ for all $z \in [0, \mathfrak{e}_0]$, where

$$L = \max\left\{ \frac{2^{\varrho_1 - 1}\Xi_1}{\Gamma(\gamma_1 + 1)} \left(\int_0^1 \mathfrak{J}_i(\zeta)\zeta^{\gamma_1(\rho_1 - 1)}\, d\zeta \right)^{\varrho_1 - 1}, \; i \in \{1,3\}; \right.$$
$$\left. \frac{2^{\varrho_2 - 1}\Xi_2}{\Gamma(\gamma_2 + 1)} \left(\int_0^1 \mathfrak{J}_j(\zeta)\zeta^{\gamma_2(\rho_2 - 1)}\, d\zeta \right)^{\varrho_2 - 1}, \; j \in \{2,4\} \right\},$$

with $\Xi_1 = \sup_{\tau \in [0,1]} \mathfrak{a}(\tau)$, $\Xi_2 = \sup_{\tau \in [0,1]} \mathfrak{b}(\tau)$.

$(K4)$ The functions $\mathfrak{f}, \mathfrak{g} : \mathbb{R}_+ \to \mathbb{R}_+$ are continuous and satisfy the conditions $\lim_{w \to \infty} \frac{\mathfrak{f}(w)}{w^{\varrho_1 - 1}} = \infty$ and $\lim_{w \to \infty} \frac{\mathfrak{g}(w)}{w^{\varrho_2 - 1}} = \infty$.

By assumptions $(K1)$ and $(K2)$ and Lemma 2, we obtain that the constant L from assumption $(K3)$ is positive.

Now, we consider the following system of fractional differential equations:

$$\begin{cases} D_{0+}^{\gamma_1}(\varphi_{\varrho_1}(D_{0+}^{\delta_1} x(t))) = 0, & t \in (0,1), \\ D_{0+}^{\gamma_2}(\varphi_{\varrho_2}(D_{0+}^{\delta_2} y(t))) = 0, & t \in (0,1), \end{cases} \tag{8}$$

subject to the coupled boundary conditions

$$\begin{cases} x^{(j)}(0) = 0, \; j = 0, \ldots, p-2; \; D_{0+}^{\delta_1} x(0) = 0, \; D_{0+}^{\alpha_0} x(1) = \sum_{j=1}^{n} \int_0^1 D_{0+}^{\alpha_j} y(\tau)\, d\mathfrak{H}_j(\tau) + \mathfrak{c}_0, \\ y^{(j)}(0) = 0, \; j = 0, \ldots, q-2; \; D_{0+}^{\delta_2} y(0) = 0, \; D_{0+}^{\beta_0} y(1) = \sum_{j=1}^{m} \int_0^1 D_{0+}^{\beta_j} x(\tau)\, d\mathfrak{K}_j(\tau) + \mathfrak{d}_0. \end{cases} \tag{9}$$

Lemma 4. *Under assumption $(K1)$, the unique solution $(x,y) \in (C[0,1])^2$ of problem (8) and (9) is*

$$x(t) = \frac{t^{\delta_1 - 1}}{\Delta}\left(\mathfrak{c}_0 \frac{\Gamma(\delta_2)}{\Gamma(\delta_2 - \beta_0)} + \mathfrak{d}_0 \Delta_1 \right), \; y(t) = \frac{t^{\delta_2 - 1}}{\Delta}\left(\mathfrak{c}_0 \Delta_2 + \mathfrak{d}_0 \frac{\Gamma(\delta_1)}{\Gamma(\delta_1 - \alpha_0)} \right), \; t \in [0,1], \tag{10}$$

which satisfies the conditions $x(t) > 0$ and $y(t) > 0$ for all $t \in (0,1]$.

Proof. We note that $\varphi_{\varrho_1}(D_{0+}^{\delta_1} x(t)) = \phi(t)$, $\varphi_{\varrho_2}(D_{0+}^{\delta_2} y(t)) = \psi(t)$. Therefore, the problem (8) and (9) is equivalent to the following three problems:

$$(I) \begin{cases} D_{0+}^{\gamma_1} \phi(t) = 0, \\ \phi(0) = 0, \end{cases} \qquad (II) \begin{cases} D_{0+}^{\gamma_2} \psi(t) = 0, \\ \psi(0) = 0, \end{cases}$$

and

$$(III)\begin{cases} \begin{cases} D_{0+}^{\delta_1}x(t) = \varphi_{\rho_1}(\phi(t)), \ t \in (0,1), \\ D_{0+}^{\delta_2}y(t) = \varphi_{\rho_2}(\psi(t)), \ t \in (0,1), \end{cases} & (III)_1 \\ \text{with} \\ \begin{cases} x^{(j)}(0) = 0, \ j = 0, \dots, p-2, \ D_{0+}^{\alpha_0}x(1) = \sum_{j=1}^{n} \int_0^1 D_{0+}^{\alpha_j}y(\tau)\,d\mathfrak{H}_j(\tau) + \mathfrak{c}_0, \\ y^{(j)}(0) = 0, \ j = 0, \dots, q-2, \ D_{0+}^{\beta_0}y(1) = \sum_{j=1}^{m} \int_0^1 D_{0+}^{\beta_j}x(\tau)\,d\mathfrak{K}_j(\tau) + \mathfrak{d}_0. \end{cases} & (III)_2 \end{cases}$$

Problem (I) has the solution $\phi(t) = 0$ for all $t \in [0,1]$, and problem (II) has the solution $\psi(t) = 0$ for all $t \in [0,1]$. Therefore, problem (III) can be written as

$$\begin{cases} D_{0+}^{\delta_1}x(t) = 0, \ t \in (0,1), \\ D_{0+}^{\delta_2}y(t) = 0, \ t \in (0,1), \end{cases} \quad (11)$$

supplemented with the boundary conditions $(III)_2$. The solutions of system (11) are

$$\begin{array}{l} x(t) = a_1 t^{\delta_1 - 1} + a_2 t^{\delta_1 - 2} + \cdots + a_p t^{\delta_1 - p}, \ t \in [0,1], \\ y(t) = b_1 t^{\delta_2 - 1} + b_2 t^{\delta_2 - 2} + \cdots + b_q t^{\delta_2 - q}, \ t \in [0,1], \end{array} \quad (12)$$

with $a_1, \dots, a_p, b_1, \dots, b_q \in \mathbb{R}$. By using the boundary conditions $x^{(j)}(0) = 0, \ j = 0, \dots, p-2$, $y^{(j)}(0) = 0, \ j = 0, \dots, q-2$ (from $(III)_2$), we obtain $a_2 = \cdots = a_p = 0$ and $b_2 = \cdots = b_q = 0$. Then, the functions in Equation (12) become $x(t) = a_1 t^{\delta_1 - 1}, \ t \in [0,1]$, $y(t) = b_1 t^{\delta_2 - 1}, \ t \in [0,1]$. For these functions, we find

$$\begin{array}{l} D_{0+}^{\alpha_0}x(t) = a_1 \dfrac{\Gamma(\delta_1)}{\Gamma(\delta_1 - \alpha_0)} t^{\delta_1 - \alpha_0 - 1}, \ D_{0+}^{\beta_0}y(t) = b_1 \dfrac{\Gamma(\delta_2)}{\Gamma(\delta_2 - \beta_0)} t^{\delta_2 - \beta_0 - 1}, \\ D_{0+}^{\alpha_j}y(t) = b_1 \dfrac{\Gamma(\delta_2)}{\Gamma(\delta_2 - \alpha_j)} t^{\delta_2 - \alpha_j - 1}, \ D_{0+}^{\beta_j}x(t) = a_1 \dfrac{\Gamma(\delta_1)}{\Gamma(\delta_1 - \beta_j)} t^{\delta_1 - \beta_j - 1}. \end{array}$$

Therefore, by now using the above fractional derivatives and the conditions $D_{0+}^{\alpha_0}x(1) = \sum_{j=1}^{n} \int_0^1 D_{0+}^{\alpha_j}y(\tau)\,d\mathfrak{H}_j(\tau) + \mathfrak{c}_0$ and $D_{0+}^{\beta_0}y(1) = \sum_{j=1}^{m} \int_0^1 D_{0+}^{\beta_j}x(\tau)\,d\mathfrak{K}_j(\tau) + \mathfrak{d}_0$ (from $(III)_2$), we deduce the following system for a_1 and b_1:

$$\begin{cases} a_1 \dfrac{\Gamma(\delta_1)}{\Gamma(\delta_1 - \alpha_0)} = \sum_{j=1}^{n} \int_0^1 b_1 \dfrac{\Gamma(\delta_2)}{\Gamma(\delta_2 - \alpha_j)} \tau^{\delta_2 - \alpha_j - 1}\,d\mathfrak{H}_j(\tau) + \mathfrak{c}_0, \\ b_1 \dfrac{\Gamma(\delta_2)}{\Gamma(\delta_2 - \beta_0)} = \sum_{j=1}^{m} \int_0^1 a_1 \dfrac{\Gamma(\delta_1)}{\Gamma(\delta_1 - \beta_j)} \tau^{\delta_1 - \beta_j - 1}\,d\mathfrak{K}_j(\tau) + \mathfrak{d}_0, \end{cases}$$

or equivalently

$$\begin{cases} a_1 \dfrac{\Gamma(\delta_1)}{\Gamma(\delta_1 - \alpha_0)} = b_1 \Delta_1 + \mathfrak{c}_0, \\ b_1 \dfrac{\Gamma(\delta_2)}{\Gamma(\delta_2 - \beta_0)} = a_1 \Delta_2 + \mathfrak{d}_0. \end{cases}$$

The determinant of the above system in the unknown a_1 and b_1 is

$$\begin{vmatrix} \dfrac{\Gamma(\delta_1)}{\Gamma(\delta_1 - \alpha_0)} & -\Delta_1 \\ -\Delta_2 & \dfrac{\Gamma(\delta_2)}{\Gamma(\delta_2 - \beta_0)} \end{vmatrix} = \frac{\Gamma(\delta_1)\Gamma(\delta_2)}{\Gamma(\delta_1 - \alpha_0)\Gamma(\delta_2 - \beta_0)} - \Delta_1 \Delta_2 = \Delta.$$

Then, we obtain

$$a_1 = \frac{1}{\Delta}\left(\mathfrak{c}_0 \frac{\Gamma(\delta_2)}{\Gamma(\delta_2-\beta_0)} + \mathfrak{d}_0\Delta_1\right), \; b_1 = \frac{1}{\Delta}\left(\mathfrak{d}_0 \frac{\Gamma(\delta_1)}{\Gamma(\delta_1-\alpha_0)} + \mathfrak{c}_0\Delta_2\right).$$

Therefore, we deduce the solution $(x(t), y(t))$ of problem (8) and (9) presented in (10). By assumption $(K1)$, we find that $x(t) > 0$ and $y(t) > 0$ for all $t \in (0,1]$. □

We use the functions $x(t)$ and $y(t)$, $t \in [0,1]$ (given by (10)), and we make a change of unknown functions for our boundary value problem (1) and (2) such that the new boundary conditions have no positive parameters. For a solution (u, v) of problem (1) and (2), we define the functions $h(t)$ and $k(t)$, $t \in [0,1]$ by

$$\begin{aligned} h(t) &= \mathrm{u}(t) - x(t) = \mathrm{u}(t) - \frac{t^{\delta_1-1}}{\Delta}\left(\mathfrak{c}_0 \frac{\Gamma(\delta_2)}{\Gamma(\delta_2-\beta_0)} + \mathfrak{d}_0\Delta_1\right), \; t \in [0,1], \\ k(t) &= \mathrm{v}(t) - y(t) = \mathrm{v}(t) - \frac{t^{\delta_2-1}}{\Delta}\left(\mathfrak{c}_0\Delta_2 + \mathfrak{d}_0 \frac{\Gamma(\delta_1)}{\Gamma(\delta_1-\alpha_0)}\right), \; t \in [0,1]. \end{aligned}$$

Then, problem (1) and (2) can be equivalently written as the system of fractional differential equations

$$\begin{cases} D_{0+}^{\gamma_1}(\varphi_{\varrho_1}(D_{0+}^{\delta_1}h(t))) + \mathfrak{a}(t)\mathfrak{f}(k(t)+y(t)) = 0, \; t \in (0,1), \\ D_{0+}^{\gamma_2}(\varphi_{\varrho_2}(D_{0+}^{\delta_2}k(t))) + \mathfrak{b}(t)\mathfrak{g}(h(t)+x(t)) = 0, \; t \in (0,1), \end{cases} \tag{13}$$

with the boundary conditions without parameters

$$\begin{cases} h^{(j)}(0) = 0, \; j = 0,\ldots,p-2; \; D_{0+}^{\delta_1}h(0) = 0, \; D_{0+}^{\alpha_0}h(1) = \sum_{j=1}^{n}\int_0^1 D_{0+}^{\alpha_j}k(\tau)\,d\mathfrak{H}_j(\tau), \\ k^{(j)}(0) = 0, \; j = 0,\ldots,q-2; \; D_{0+}^{\delta_2}k(0) = 0, \; D_{0+}^{\beta_0}k(1) = \sum_{j=1}^{m}\int_0^1 D_{0+}^{\beta_j}h(\tau)\,d\mathfrak{K}_j(\tau). \end{cases} \tag{14}$$

Using the Green functions $\mathfrak{G}_i$, $i = 1,\ldots,4$ and Lemma 1, a pair of functions (h,k) is a solution of problem (13) and (14) if and only if (h,k) is a solution of the system of integral equations

$$\begin{aligned} h(t) &= \int_0^1 \mathfrak{G}_1(t,\zeta)\varphi_{\rho_1}(I_{0+}^{\gamma_1}(\mathfrak{a}(\zeta)\mathfrak{f}(k(\zeta)+y(\zeta))))\,d\zeta \\ &\quad + \int_0^1 \mathfrak{G}_2(t,\zeta)\varphi_{\rho_2}(I_{0+}^{\gamma_2}(\mathfrak{b}(\zeta)\mathfrak{g}(h(\zeta)+x(\zeta))))\,d\zeta, \; t \in [0,1], \\ k(t) &= \int_0^1 \mathfrak{G}_3(t,\zeta)\varphi_{\rho_1}(I_{0+}^{\gamma_1}(\mathfrak{a}(\zeta)\mathfrak{f}(k(\zeta)+y(\zeta))))\,d\zeta \\ &\quad + \int_0^1 \mathfrak{G}_4(t,\zeta)\varphi_{\rho_2}(I_{0+}^{\gamma_2}(\mathfrak{b}(\zeta)\mathfrak{g}(h(\zeta)+x(\zeta))))\,d\zeta, \; t \in [0,1]. \end{aligned} \tag{15}$$

We consider the Banach space $\mathcal{X} = C[0,1]$ with the supremum norm $\|z\| = \sup_{\tau\in[0,1]}|z(\tau)|$ for $z \in \mathcal{X}$, and the Banach space $\mathcal{Y} = \mathcal{X} \times \mathcal{X}$ with the norm $\|(h,k)\|_{\mathcal{Y}} = \max\{\|h\|, \|k\|\}$ for $(h,k) \in \mathcal{Y}$. We define the set $\mathcal{V} = \{(h,k) \in \mathcal{Y}, \; 0 \le h(t) \le \mathfrak{e}_0, \; 0 \le k(t) \le \mathfrak{e}_0, \; \forall t \in [0,1]\}$. We also define the operator $\mathcal{S}: \mathcal{V} \to \mathcal{Y}$, $\mathcal{S} = (\mathcal{S}_1, \mathcal{S}_2)$,

$$\begin{aligned} \mathcal{S}_1(h,k)(t) &= \int_0^1 \mathfrak{G}_1(t,\zeta)\varphi_{\rho_1}(I_{0+}^{\gamma_1}(\mathfrak{a}(\zeta)\mathfrak{f}(k(\zeta)+y(\zeta))))\,d\zeta \\ &\quad + \int_0^1 \mathfrak{G}_2(t,\zeta)\varphi_{\rho_2}(I_{0+}^{\gamma_2}(\mathfrak{b}(\zeta)\mathfrak{g}(h(\zeta)+x(\zeta))))\,d\zeta, \; t \in [0,1], \\ \mathcal{S}_2(h,k)(t) &= \int_0^1 \mathfrak{G}_3(t,\zeta)\varphi_{\rho_1}(I_{0+}^{\gamma_1}(\mathfrak{a}(\zeta)\mathfrak{f}(k(\zeta)+y(\zeta))))\,d\zeta \\ &\quad + \int_0^1 \mathfrak{G}_4(t,\zeta)\varphi_{\rho_2}(I_{0+}^{\gamma_2}(\mathfrak{b}(\zeta)\mathfrak{g}(h(\zeta)+x(\zeta))))\,d\zeta, \; t \in [0,1], \end{aligned}$$

for $(h,k) \in \mathcal{V}$. We easily see that (h,k) is a solution of system (15) if and only if (h,k) is a fixed point of operator $\mathcal{S}$. Therefore, our next task is the detection of the fixed points of operator $\mathcal{S}$. The first result is the following existence theorem for problem (1) and (2):

Theorem 1. *We assume that assumptions $(K1)-(K3)$ are satisfied. Therefore, there exist $\mathfrak{c}_1 > 0$ and $\mathfrak{d}_1 > 0$ such that for any $\mathfrak{c}_0 \in (0, \mathfrak{c}_1]$ and $\mathfrak{d}_0 \in (0, \mathfrak{d}_1]$, the problem (1) and (2) has at least one positive solution.*

Proof. By assumption $(K3)$ we deduce that there exist $\mathfrak{s}_0 > 0$ and $\mathfrak{t}_0 > 0$ such that $\mathfrak{f}(w) \le \frac{\mathfrak{e}_0^{\varrho_1-1}}{L}$ for all $w \in [0, \mathfrak{e}_0 + \mathfrak{s}_0]$, and $\mathfrak{g}(w) \le \frac{\mathfrak{e}_0^{\varrho_2-1}}{L}$ for all $w \in [0, \mathfrak{e}_0 + \mathfrak{t}_0]$. We define now $\mathfrak{c}_1$ and $\mathfrak{d}_1$ as follows:

- If $\Delta_1 \neq 0$ and $\Delta_2 \neq 0$, then

$$\mathfrak{c}_1 = \min\left\{\frac{\mathfrak{s}_0\Delta}{2\Delta_2}, \frac{\mathfrak{t}_0\Delta\Gamma(\delta_2-\beta_0)}{2\Gamma(\delta_2)}\right\}, \ \mathfrak{d}_1 = \min\left\{\frac{\mathfrak{s}_0\Delta\Gamma(\delta_1-\alpha_0)}{2\Gamma(\delta_1)}, \frac{\mathfrak{t}_0\Delta}{2\Delta_1}\right\}.$$

- If $\Delta_1 = 0$ and $\Delta_2 \neq 0$, then

$$\mathfrak{c}_1 = \min\left\{\frac{\mathfrak{s}_0\Delta}{2\Delta_2}, \frac{\mathfrak{t}_0\Delta\Gamma(\delta_2-\beta_0)}{\Gamma(\delta_2)}\right\}, \ \mathfrak{d}_1 = \frac{\mathfrak{s}_0\Delta\Gamma(\delta_1-\alpha_0)}{2\Gamma(\delta_1)}.$$

- If $\Delta_1 \neq 0$ and $\Delta_2 = 0$, then

$$\mathfrak{c}_1 = \frac{\mathfrak{t}_0\Delta\Gamma(\delta_2-\beta_0)}{2\Gamma(\delta_2)}, \ \mathfrak{d}_1 = \min\left\{\frac{\mathfrak{s}_0\Delta\Gamma(\delta_1-\alpha_0)}{\Gamma(\delta_1)}, \frac{\mathfrak{t}_0\Delta}{2\Delta_1}\right\}.$$

- If $\Delta_1 = 0$ and $\Delta_2 = 0$, then

$$\mathfrak{c}_1 = \frac{\mathfrak{t}_0\Delta\Gamma(\delta_2-\beta_0)}{\Gamma(\delta_2)}, \ \mathfrak{d}_1 = \frac{\mathfrak{s}_0\Delta\Gamma(\delta_1-\alpha_0)}{\Gamma(\delta_1)}.$$

Let $\mathfrak{c}_0 \in (0, \mathfrak{c}_1]$ and $\mathfrak{d}_0 \in (0, \mathfrak{d}_1]$. Then, for $(h,k) \in \mathcal{V}$ and $\zeta \in [0,1]$, we have

$$\begin{aligned} k(\zeta)+y(\zeta) &\le \mathfrak{e}_0 + \tfrac{1}{\Delta}\left(\mathfrak{c}_0\Delta_2 + \mathfrak{d}_0\tfrac{\Gamma(\delta_1)}{\Gamma(\delta_1-\alpha_0)}\right) \le \mathfrak{e}_0 + \tfrac{1}{\Delta}\left(\mathfrak{c}_1\Delta_2 + \mathfrak{d}_1\tfrac{\Gamma(\delta_1)}{\Gamma(\delta_1-\alpha_0)}\right) \le \mathfrak{e}_0 + \mathfrak{s}_0, \\ h(\zeta)+x(\zeta) &\le \mathfrak{e}_0 + \tfrac{1}{\Delta}\left(\mathfrak{c}_0\tfrac{\Gamma(\delta_2)}{\Gamma(\delta_2-\beta_0)} + \mathfrak{d}_0\Delta_1\right) \le \mathfrak{e}_0 + \tfrac{1}{\Delta}\left(\mathfrak{c}_1\tfrac{\Gamma(\delta_2)}{\Gamma(\delta_2-\beta_0)} + \mathfrak{d}_1\Delta_1\right) \le \mathfrak{e}_0 + \mathfrak{t}_0, \end{aligned}$$

and so

$$\mathfrak{f}(k(\zeta)+y(\zeta)) \le \frac{\mathfrak{e}_0^{\varrho_1-1}}{L}, \ \mathfrak{g}(h(\zeta)+x(\zeta)) \le \frac{\mathfrak{e}_0^{\varrho_2-1}}{L}. \tag{16}$$

By using Lemma 3, we deduce that $\mathcal{S}_i(h,k)(t) \ge 0$, $i = 1,2$ for all $t \in [0,1]$ and $(h,k) \in \mathcal{V}$. By inequalities (16), for all $(h,k) \in \mathcal{V}$, we obtain

$$\begin{aligned} I_{0+}^{\gamma_1}(\mathfrak{a}(\zeta)\mathfrak{f}(k(\zeta)+y(\zeta))) &= \frac{1}{\Gamma(\gamma_1)}\int_0^\zeta (\zeta-\tau)^{\gamma_1-1}\mathfrak{a}(\tau)\mathfrak{f}(k(\tau)+y(\tau))\,d\tau \\ &\le \frac{\mathfrak{e}_0^{\varrho_1-1}}{L\Gamma(\gamma_1)}\int_0^\zeta (\zeta-\tau)^{\gamma_1-1}\mathfrak{a}(\tau)\,d\tau \le \frac{\Xi_1\mathfrak{e}_0^{\varrho_1-1}}{L\Gamma(\gamma_1)}\int_0^\zeta (\zeta-\tau)^{\gamma_1-1}\,d\tau \\ &= \frac{\Xi_1\mathfrak{e}_0^{\varrho_1-1}\zeta^{\gamma_1}}{L\Gamma(\gamma_1+1)}, \ \forall \zeta \in [0,1], \end{aligned}$$

and

$$\begin{aligned} I_{0+}^{\gamma_2}(\mathfrak{b}(\zeta)\mathfrak{g}(h(\zeta)+x(\zeta))) &= \frac{1}{\Gamma(\gamma_2)}\int_0^\zeta (\zeta-\tau)^{\gamma_2-1}\mathfrak{b}(\tau)\mathfrak{g}(h(\tau)+x(\tau))\,d\tau \\ &\le \frac{\mathfrak{e}_0^{\varrho_2-1}}{L\Gamma(\gamma_2)}\int_0^\zeta (\zeta-\tau)^{\gamma_2-1}\mathfrak{b}(\tau)\,d\tau \le \frac{\Xi_2\mathfrak{e}_0^{\varrho_2-1}}{L\Gamma(\gamma_2)}\int_0^\zeta (\zeta-\tau)^{\gamma_2-1}\,d\tau \\ &= \frac{\Xi_2\mathfrak{e}_0^{\varrho_2-1}\zeta^{\gamma_2}}{L\Gamma(\gamma_2+1)}, \ \forall \zeta \in [0,1]. \end{aligned}$$

Then, by Lemma 2 and the definition of L from $(K3)$, we find

$$\mathcal{S}_1(h,k)(t) \le \int_0^1 \mathfrak{J}_1(\zeta)\varphi_{\rho_1}\left(\frac{\Xi_1 \mathfrak{e}_0^{\varrho_1-1}\zeta^{\gamma_1}}{L\Gamma(\gamma_1+1)}\right)d\zeta + \int_0^1 \mathfrak{J}_2(\zeta)\varphi_{\rho_2}\left(\frac{\Xi_2 \mathfrak{e}_0^{\varrho_2-1}\zeta^{\gamma_2}}{L\Gamma(\gamma_2+1)}\right)d\zeta$$
$$= \left(\frac{\Xi_1 \mathfrak{e}_0^{\varrho_1-1}}{L\Gamma(\gamma_1+1)}\right)^{\rho_1-1}\int_0^1 \mathfrak{J}_1(\zeta)\zeta^{\gamma_1(\rho_1-1)}\,d\zeta$$
$$+\left(\frac{\Xi_2 \mathfrak{e}_0^{\varrho_2-1}}{L\Gamma(\gamma_2+1)}\right)^{\rho_2-1}\int_0^1 \mathfrak{J}_2(\zeta)\zeta^{\gamma_2(\rho_2-1)}\,d\zeta \le \frac{\mathfrak{e}_0}{2}+\frac{\mathfrak{e}_0}{2} = \mathfrak{e}_0, \quad \forall t\in[0,1],$$

and

$$\mathcal{S}_2(h,k)(t) \le \int_0^1 \mathfrak{J}_3(\zeta)\varphi_{\rho_1}\left(\frac{\Xi_1 \mathfrak{e}_0^{\varrho_1-1}\zeta^{\gamma_1}}{L\Gamma(\gamma_1+1)}\right)d\zeta + \int_0^1 \mathfrak{J}_4(\zeta)\varphi_{\rho_2}\left(\frac{\Xi_2 \mathfrak{e}_0^{\varrho_2-1}\zeta^{\gamma_2}}{L\Gamma(\gamma_2+1)}\right)d\zeta$$
$$= \left(\frac{\Xi_1 \mathfrak{e}_0^{\varrho_1-1}}{L\Gamma(\gamma_1+1)}\right)^{\rho_1-1}\int_0^1 \mathfrak{J}_3(\zeta)\zeta^{\gamma_1(\rho_1-1)}\,d\zeta$$
$$+\left(\frac{\Xi_2 \mathfrak{e}_0^{\varrho_2-1}}{L\Gamma(\gamma_2+1)}\right)^{\rho_2-1}\int_0^1 \mathfrak{J}_4(\zeta)\zeta^{\gamma_2(\rho_2-1)}\,d\zeta \le \frac{\mathfrak{e}_0}{2}+\frac{\mathfrak{e}_0}{2} = \mathfrak{e}_0, \quad \forall t\in[0,1].$$

Therefore, we find that $\mathcal{S}(\mathcal{V}) \subset \mathcal{V}$. By using a standard method, we conclude that $\mathcal{S}$ is a completely continuous operator. Therefore, by the Schauder fixed point theorem, we deduce that $\mathcal{S}$ has a fixed point $(h,k) \in \mathcal{V}$, which is a non-negative solution for problem (15), or equivalently, for problem (13) and (14). Hence, (u,v), where $\mathrm{u}(t) = h(t) + x(t)$ and $\mathrm{v}(t) = k(t) + y(t)$ for all $t \in [0,1]$, is a positive solution of problem (1) and (2). This solution (u,v) satisfies the conditions $\frac{t^{\delta_1-1}}{\Delta}(\mathfrak{c}_0\frac{\Gamma(\delta_2)}{\Gamma(\delta_2-\beta_0)} + \mathfrak{d}_0\Delta_1) \le \mathrm{u}(t) \le \frac{t^{\delta_1-1}}{\Delta}(\mathfrak{c}_0\frac{\Gamma(\delta_2)}{\Gamma(\delta_2-\beta_0)} + \mathfrak{d}_0\Delta_1) + \mathfrak{e}_0$ and $\frac{t^{\delta_2-1}}{\Delta}(\mathfrak{c}_0\Delta_2 + \mathfrak{d}_0\frac{\Gamma(\delta_1)}{\Gamma(\delta_1-\alpha_0)}) \le \mathrm{v}(t) \le \frac{t^{\delta_2-1}}{\Delta}(\mathfrak{c}_0\Delta_2 + \mathfrak{d}_0\frac{\Gamma(\delta_1)}{\Gamma(\delta_1-\alpha_0)}) + \mathfrak{e}_0$ for all $t \in [0,1]$. □

The second result is the following nonexistence theorem for the boundary value problem (1) and (2).

Theorem 2. *We assume that assumptions $(K1)$, $(K2)$, and $(K4)$ are satisfied. Then, there exist $\mathfrak{c}_2 > 0$ and $\mathfrak{d}_2 > 0$ such that for any $\mathfrak{c}_0 \ge \mathfrak{c}_2$ and $\mathfrak{d}_0 \ge \mathfrak{d}_2$, the problem (1) and (2) has no positive solution.*

Proof. By assumption $(K2)$, there exist $[\eta_1,\eta_2] \subset (0,1)$, $\eta_1 < \eta_2$ such that $\tau_1,\tau_2 \in (\eta_1,\eta_2)$, and then

$$\Lambda_1 = \int_{\eta_1}^{\eta_2} \mathfrak{J}_1(\zeta)\left(\int_{\eta_1}^{\zeta}\mathfrak{a}(\tau)(\zeta-\tau)^{\gamma_1-1}\,d\tau\right)^{\rho_1-1} d\zeta > 0,$$
$$\Lambda_4 = \int_{\eta_1}^{\eta_2} \mathfrak{J}_4(\zeta)\left(\int_{\eta_1}^{\zeta}\mathfrak{b}(\tau)(\zeta-\tau)^{\gamma_2-1}\,d\tau\right)^{\rho_2-1} d\zeta > 0.$$

We define the number

$$R_0 = \max\left\{\frac{2^{\varrho_1-1}\Gamma(\gamma_1)}{\eta_1^{(\delta_1+\delta_2-2)(\varrho_1-1)}\Lambda_1^{\varrho_1-1}}, \frac{2^{\varrho_2-1}\Gamma(\gamma_2)}{\eta_1^{(\delta_1+\delta_2-2)(\varrho_2-1)}\Lambda_4^{\varrho_2-1}}\right\}.$$

By using $(K4)$, for R_0 defined above, we obtain that there exists $L_0 > 0$ such that $\mathfrak{f}(w) \ge R_0 w^{\varrho_1-1}$ and $\mathfrak{g}(w) \ge R_0 w^{\varrho_2-1}$ for all $w \ge L_0$. We define now $\mathfrak{c}_2$ and $\mathfrak{d}_2$ as follows:

- If $\Delta_1 \ne 0$ and $\Delta_2 \ne 0$, then

$$\mathfrak{c}_2 = \max\left\{\frac{L_0\Delta\Gamma(\delta_2-\beta_0)}{2\eta_1^{\delta_1-1}\Gamma(\delta_2)}, \frac{L_0\Delta}{2\eta_1^{\delta_2-1}\Delta_2}\right\}, \quad \mathfrak{d}_2 = \max\left\{\frac{L_0\Delta}{2\eta_1^{\delta_1-1}\Delta_1}, \frac{L_0\Delta\Gamma(\delta_1-\alpha_0)}{2\eta_1^{\delta_2-1}\Gamma(\delta_1)}\right\}.$$

- If $\Delta_1 = 0$ and $\Delta_2 \neq 0$, then

$$\mathfrak{c}_2 = \max\left\{\frac{L_0\Delta\Gamma(\delta_2-\beta_0)}{\eta_1^{\delta_1-1}\Gamma(\delta_2)}, \frac{L_0\Delta}{2\eta_1^{\delta_2-1}\Delta_2}\right\}, \quad \mathfrak{d}_2 = \frac{L_0\Delta\Gamma(\delta_1-\alpha_0)}{2\eta_1^{\delta_2-1}\Gamma(\delta_1)}.$$

- If $\Delta_1 \neq 0$ and $\Delta_2 = 0$, then

$$\mathfrak{c}_2 = \frac{L_0\Delta\Gamma(\delta_2-\beta_0)}{2\eta_1^{\delta_1-1}\Gamma(\delta_2)}, \quad \mathfrak{d}_2 = \max\left\{\frac{L_0\Delta}{2\eta_1^{\delta_1-1}\Delta_1}, \frac{L_0\Delta\Gamma(\delta_1-\alpha_0)}{\eta_1^{\delta_2-1}\Gamma(\delta_1)}\right\}.$$

- If $\Delta_1 = 0$ and $\Delta_2 = 0$, then

$$\mathfrak{c}_2 = \frac{L_0\Delta\Gamma(\delta_2-\beta_0)}{\eta_1^{\delta_1-1}\Gamma(\delta_2)}, \quad \mathfrak{d}_2 = \frac{L_0\Delta\Gamma(\delta_1-\alpha_0)}{\eta_1^{\delta_2-1}\Gamma(\delta_1)}.$$

Let $\mathfrak{c}_0 \geq \mathfrak{c}_2$ and $\mathfrak{d}_0 \geq \mathfrak{d}_2$. We assume that (u,v) is a positive solution of (1) and (2). Then, the pair (h,k), where $h(t) = \mathrm{u}(t) - x(t)$, $k(t) = \mathrm{v}(t) - y(t)$, $t \in [0,1]$, with x and y given by (10), is a solution of problem (13) and (14), or equivalently, of system (15). By using Lemma 3, we find that $h(t) \geq t^{\delta_1-1}\|h\|$, $k(t) \geq t^{\delta_2-1}\|k\|$ for all $t \in [0,1]$. Then, $\inf_{s\in[\eta_1,\eta_2]} h(s) \geq \eta_1^{\delta_1-1}\|h\|$, $\inf_{s\in[\eta_1,\eta_2]} k(s) \geq \eta_1^{\delta_2-1}\|k\|$. By the definition of the functions x and y, we obtain

$$\inf_{s\in[\eta_1,\eta_2]} x(s) = \frac{\eta_1^{\delta_1-1}}{\Delta}\left(\mathfrak{c}_0\frac{\Gamma(\delta_2)}{\Gamma(\delta_2-\beta_0)} + \mathfrak{d}_0\Delta_1\right) = \eta_1^{\delta_1-1}\|x\|,$$
$$\inf_{s\in[\eta_1,\eta_2]} y(s) = \frac{\eta_1^{\delta_2-1}}{\Delta}\left(\mathfrak{c}_0\Delta_2 + \mathfrak{d}_0\frac{\Gamma(\delta_1)}{\Gamma(\delta_1-\alpha_0)}\right) = \eta_1^{\delta_2-1}\|y\|.$$

Hence, we deduce

$$\begin{aligned}&\inf_{s\in[\eta_1,\eta_2]}(h(s)+x(s)) \geq \inf_{s\in[\eta_1,\eta_2]} h(s) + \inf_{s\in[\eta_1,\eta_2]} x(s) \geq \eta_1^{\delta_1-1}\|h\| + \eta_1^{\delta_1-1}\|x\| \\ &= \eta_1^{\delta_1-1}(\|h\|+\|x\|) \geq \eta_1^{\delta_1-1}\|h+x\|, \\ &\inf_{s\in[\eta_1,\eta_2]}(k(s)+y(s)) \geq \inf_{s\in[\eta_1,\eta_2]} k(s) + \inf_{s\in[\eta_1,\eta_2]} y(s) \geq \eta_1^{\delta_2-1}\|k\| + \eta_1^{\delta_2-1}\|y\| \\ &= \eta_1^{\delta_2-1}(\|k\|+\|y\|) \geq \eta_1^{\delta_2-1}\|k+y\|.\end{aligned}$$

In addition we have

$$\begin{aligned}&\inf_{s\in[\eta_1,\eta_2]}(h(s)+x(s)) \geq \eta_1^{\delta_1-1}\|x\| = \eta_1^{\delta_1-1}\frac{1}{\Delta}\left(\mathfrak{c}_0\frac{\Gamma(\delta_2)}{\Gamma(\delta_2-\beta_0)} + \mathfrak{d}_0\Delta_1\right) \\ &\geq \eta_1^{\delta_1-1}\frac{1}{\Delta}\left(\mathfrak{c}_2\frac{\Gamma(\delta_2)}{\Gamma(\delta_2-\beta_0)} + \mathfrak{d}_2\Delta_1\right) \geq L_0,\end{aligned}$$

$$\begin{aligned}&\inf_{s\in[\eta_1,\eta_2]}(k(s)+y(s)) \geq \eta_1^{\delta_2-1}\|y\| = \eta_1^{\delta_2-1}\frac{1}{\Delta}\left(\mathfrak{c}_0\Delta_2 + \mathfrak{d}_0\frac{\Gamma(\delta_1)}{\Gamma(\delta_1-\alpha_0)}\right) \\ &\geq \eta_1^{\delta_2-1}\frac{1}{\Delta}\left(\mathfrak{c}_2\Delta_2 + \mathfrak{d}_2\frac{\Gamma(\delta_1)}{\Gamma(\delta_1-\alpha_0)}\right) \geq L_0.\end{aligned}$$

By using Lemma 3 and the above inequalities we find

$$\begin{aligned}
&I_{0+}^{\gamma_1}(\mathfrak{a}(\zeta)\mathfrak{f}(k(\zeta)+y(\zeta))) \\
&\geq \frac{1}{\Gamma(\gamma_1)}\int_{\eta_1}^{\zeta}(\zeta-\tau)^{\gamma_1-1}\mathfrak{a}(\tau)\mathfrak{f}(k(\tau)+y(\tau))\,d\tau \\
&\geq \frac{R_0}{\Gamma(\gamma_1)}\int_{\eta_1}^{\zeta}(\zeta-\tau)^{\gamma_1-1}\mathfrak{a}(\tau)(k(\tau)+y(\tau))^{\varrho_1-1}\,d\tau \\
&\geq \frac{R_0}{\Gamma(\gamma_1)}\int_{\eta_1}^{\zeta}(\zeta-\tau)^{\gamma_1-1}\mathfrak{a}(\tau)\left(\inf_{\tau\in[\eta_1,\eta_2]}(k(\tau)+y(\tau))\right)^{\varrho_1-1}\,d\tau \\
&\geq \frac{R_0L_0^{\varrho_1-1}}{\Gamma(\gamma_1)}\int_{\eta_1}^{\zeta}(\zeta-\tau)^{\gamma_1-1}\mathfrak{a}(\tau)\,d\tau,\ \ \forall\zeta\in[\eta_1,\eta_2],
\end{aligned}$$

and then

$$\begin{aligned}
h(\eta_1) &\geq \int_0^1 \eta_1^{\delta_1-1}\mathfrak{J}_1(\zeta)\varphi_{\rho_1}(I_{0+}^{\gamma_1}(\mathfrak{a}(\zeta)\mathfrak{f}(k(\zeta)+y(\zeta))))\,d\zeta \\
&\geq \int_{\eta_1}^{\eta_2}\eta_1^{\delta_1-1}\mathfrak{J}_1(\zeta)\left(\frac{R_0L_0^{\varrho_1-1}}{\Gamma(\gamma_1)}\int_{\eta_1}^{\zeta}(\zeta-\tau)^{\gamma_1-1}\mathfrak{a}(\tau)\,d\tau\right)^{\rho_1-1}d\zeta \\
&= \frac{R_0^{\rho_1-1}L_0\eta_1^{\delta_1-1}\Lambda_1}{(\Gamma(\gamma_1))^{\rho_1-1}} > 0.
\end{aligned}$$

We deduce that $\|h\| \geq h(\eta_1) > 0$. In a similar manner, we obtain

$$\begin{aligned}
&I_{0+}^{\gamma_2}(\mathfrak{b}(\zeta)\mathfrak{g}(h(\zeta)+x(\zeta))) \\
&\geq \frac{R_0}{\Gamma(\gamma_2)}\int_{\eta_1}^{\zeta}(\zeta-\tau)^{\gamma_2-1}\mathfrak{b}(\tau)\left(\inf_{\tau\in[\eta_1,\eta_2]}(h(\tau)+x(\tau))\right)^{\varrho_2-1}\,d\tau \\
&\geq \frac{R_0L_0^{\varrho_2-1}}{\Gamma(\gamma_2)}\int_{\eta_1}^{\zeta}(\zeta-\tau)^{\gamma_2-1}\mathfrak{b}(\tau)\,d\tau,\ \ \forall\zeta\in[\eta_1,\eta_2],
\end{aligned}$$

and so

$$\begin{aligned}
k(\eta_1) &\geq \int_0^1 \eta_1^{\delta_2-1}\mathfrak{J}_4(\zeta)\varphi_{\rho_2}(I_{0+}^{\gamma_2}(\mathfrak{b}(\zeta)\mathfrak{g}(h(\zeta)+x(\zeta))))\,d\zeta \\
&\geq \int_{\eta_1}^{\eta_2}\eta_1^{\delta_2-1}\mathfrak{J}_4(\zeta)\left(\frac{R_0L_0^{\varrho_2-1}}{\Gamma(\gamma_2)}\int_{\eta_1}^{\zeta}(\zeta-\tau)^{\gamma_2-1}\mathfrak{b}(\tau)\,d\tau\right)^{\rho_2-1}d\zeta \\
&= \frac{R_0^{\rho_2-1}L_0\eta_1^{\delta_2-1}\Lambda_4}{(\Gamma(\gamma_2))^{\rho_2-1}} > 0.
\end{aligned}$$

We deduce that $\|k\| \geq k(\eta_1) > 0$.

In addition, from the above inequalities we have

$$\begin{aligned}
&I_{0+}^{\gamma_1}(\mathfrak{a}(\zeta)\mathfrak{f}(k(\zeta)+y(\zeta))) \\
&\geq \frac{R_0}{\Gamma(\gamma_1)}\int_{\eta_1}^{\zeta}(\zeta-\tau)^{\gamma_1-1}\mathfrak{a}(\tau)\left(\inf_{\tau\in[\eta_1,\eta_2]}(k(\tau)+y(\tau))\right)^{\varrho_1-1}\,d\tau \\
&\geq \frac{R_0\eta_1^{(\delta_2-1)(\varrho_1-1)}}{\Gamma(\gamma_1)}\|k+y\|^{\varrho_1-1}\int_{\eta_1}^{\zeta}(\zeta-\tau)^{\gamma_1-1}\mathfrak{a}(\tau)\,d\tau,\ \ \forall\zeta\in[\eta_1,\eta_2],
\end{aligned}$$

and so

$$\begin{aligned}
h(\eta_1) &\geq \int_{\eta_1}^{\eta_2}\eta_1^{\delta_1-1}\mathfrak{J}_1(\zeta)\left(\frac{R_0\eta_1^{(\delta_2-1)(\varrho_1-1)}}{\Gamma(\gamma_1)}\right)^{\rho_1-1}\|k+y\|\left(\int_{\eta_1}^{\zeta}(\zeta-\tau)^{\gamma_1-1}\mathfrak{a}(\tau)\,d\tau\right)^{\rho_1-1}d\zeta \\
&= \frac{\eta_1^{\delta_1+\delta_2-2}R_0^{\rho_1-1}}{(\Gamma(\gamma_1))^{\rho_1-1}}\Lambda_1\|k+y\| \geq 2\|k+y\| \geq 2\|k\|.
\end{aligned}$$

Hence,

$$\|k\| \le \frac{1}{2}h(\eta_1) \le \frac{1}{2}\|h\|. \tag{17}$$

In a similar manner, we deduce

$$\begin{aligned} &I_{0+}^{\gamma_2}(\mathfrak{b}(\zeta)\mathfrak{g}(h(\zeta)+x(\zeta))) \\ &\ge \frac{R_0}{\Gamma(\gamma_2)}\int_{\eta_1}^{\zeta}(\zeta-\tau)^{\gamma_2-1}\mathfrak{b}(\tau)\left(\inf_{\tau\in[\eta_1,\eta_2]}(h(\tau)+x(\tau))\right)^{\varrho_2-1}d\tau \\ &\ge \frac{R_0\eta_1^{(\delta_1-1)(\varrho_2-1)}}{\Gamma(\gamma_2)}\|h+x\|^{\varrho_2-1}\int_{\eta_1}^{\zeta}(\zeta-\tau)^{\gamma_2-1}\mathfrak{b}(\tau)\,d\tau,\ \ \forall\zeta\in[\eta_1,\eta_2], \end{aligned}$$

and then

$$\begin{aligned} k(\eta_1) &\ge \int_{\eta_1}^{\eta_2}\eta_1^{\delta_2-1}\mathfrak{J}_4(\zeta)\left(\frac{R_0\eta_1^{(\delta_1-1)(\varrho_2-1)}}{\Gamma(\gamma_2)}\right)^{\rho_2-1}\|h+x\|\left(\int_{\eta_1}^{\zeta}(\zeta-\tau)^{\gamma_2-1}\mathfrak{b}(\tau)\,d\tau\right)^{\rho_2-1}d\zeta \\ &= \frac{\eta_1^{\delta_1+\delta_2-2}R_0^{\rho_2-1}}{(\Gamma(\gamma_2))^{\rho_2-1}}\Lambda_4\|h+x\| \ge 2\|h+x\| \ge 2\|h\|. \end{aligned}$$

Therefore,

$$\|h\| \le \frac{1}{2}k(\eta_1) \le \frac{1}{2}\|k\|. \tag{18}$$

Hence, by (17) and (18), we conclude that $\|h\| \le \frac{1}{2}\|k\| \le \frac{1}{4}\|h\|$, which is a contradiction (we saw before that $\|h\| > 0$). Therefore, problem (1) and (2) has no positive solution. □

4. An Example

We consider $\gamma_1 = \frac{3}{4}$, $\gamma_2 = \frac{2}{5}$, $\delta_1 = \frac{14}{3}$, $(p = 5)$, $\delta_2 = \frac{11}{2}$, $(q = 6)$, $n = 2$, $m = 1$, $\alpha_0 = \frac{17}{8}$, $\beta_0 = \frac{19}{6}$, $\alpha_1 = \frac{3}{2}$, $\alpha_2 = \frac{16}{7}$, $\beta_1 = \frac{3}{7}$, $\varrho_1 = \frac{73}{12}$, $\varrho_2 = \frac{59}{8}$, $\rho_1 = \frac{73}{61}$, $\rho_2 = \frac{59}{51}$, $\mathfrak{a}(t) = 1$, $\mathfrak{b}(t) = 1$ for all $t \in [0,1]$, $\mathfrak{H}_1(t) = \frac{91}{6}t$ for all $t \in [0,1]$, $\mathfrak{H}_2(t) = \left\{\frac{1}{3},\ t \in \left[0,\frac{2}{3}\right);\ \frac{17}{15},\ t \in \left[\frac{2}{3},1\right]\right\}$, $\mathfrak{K}_1(t) = \left\{\frac{1}{2},\ t \in \left[0,\frac{8}{11}\right);\ \frac{33}{26},\ t \in \left[\frac{8}{11},1\right]\right\}$. We introduce the functions $\mathfrak{f}, \mathfrak{g}; [0,\infty) \to [0,\infty)$, $\mathfrak{f}(z) = \omega_1 z^{\sigma_1}$, $\mathfrak{g}(z) = \omega_2 z^{\sigma_2}$ for all $z \in [0,\infty)$ with $\omega_1, \omega_2 > 0$, $\sigma_1, \sigma_2 > 0$, $\sigma_1 > \frac{61}{12}$, $\sigma_2 > \frac{51}{8}$. We have $\lim_{z\to\infty}\frac{\mathfrak{f}(z)}{z^{\varrho_1-1}} = \infty$ and $\lim_{z\to\infty}\frac{\mathfrak{g}(z)}{z^{\varrho_2-1}} = \infty$.

We consider the system of Riemann–Liouville fractional differential equations

$$\begin{cases} D_{0+}^{3/4}\left(\varphi_{73/12}\left(D_{0+}^{14/3}\mathrm{u}(t)\right)\right) + \omega_1(\mathrm{v}(t))^{\sigma_1} = 0,\ \ t \in (0,1), \\ D_{0+}^{2/5}\left(\varphi_{59/8}\left(D_{0+}^{11/2}\mathrm{v}(t)\right)\right) + \omega_2(\mathrm{u}(t))^{\sigma_2} = 0,\ \ t \in (0,1), \end{cases} \tag{19}$$

subject to the coupled boundary conditions

$$\begin{cases} \mathrm{u}^{(i)}(0) = 0,\ i = 0,\ldots,3,\ \ D_{0+}^{14/3}\mathrm{u}(0) = 0, \\ D_{0+}^{17/8}\mathrm{u}(1) = \frac{91}{6}\int_0^1 D_{0+}^{3/2}\mathrm{v}(t)\,dt + \frac{4}{5}D_{0+}^{16/7}\mathrm{v}\left(\frac{2}{3}\right) + \mathfrak{c}_0, \\ \mathrm{v}^{(i)}(0) = 0,\ i = 0,\ldots,4,\ \ D_{0+}^{11/2}\mathrm{v}(0) = 0,\ \ D_{0+}^{19/6}\mathrm{v}(1) = \frac{10}{13}D_{0+}^{3/7}\mathrm{u}\left(\frac{8}{11}\right) + \mathfrak{d}_0. \end{cases} \tag{20}$$

We obtain here $\Delta_1 \approx 40.01662964$, $\Delta_2 \approx 0.49478575$, and $\Delta \approx 452.46647281 > 0$. Therefore, assumptions $(K1)$, $(K2)$, and $(K4)$ are satisfied. In addition, we deduce

$$
\begin{aligned}
\mathfrak{g}_1(t,\zeta) &= \frac{1}{\Gamma(14/3)}\begin{cases} t^{11/3}(1-\zeta)^{37/24}-(t-\zeta)^{11/3}, & 0\le\zeta\le t\le 1,\\ t^{11/3}(1-\zeta)^{37/24}, & 0\le t\le\zeta\le 1,\end{cases}\\
\mathfrak{g}_{11}(\tau,\zeta) &= \frac{1}{\Gamma(89/21)}\begin{cases} \tau^{68/21}(1-\zeta)^{37/24}-(\tau-\zeta)^{68/21}, & 0\le\zeta\le\tau\le 1,\\ \tau^{68/21}(1-\zeta)^{37/24}, & 0\le\tau\le\zeta\le 1,\end{cases}\\
\mathfrak{g}_2(t,\zeta) &= \frac{1}{\Gamma(11/2)}\begin{cases} t^{9/2}(1-\zeta)^{4/3}-(t-\zeta)^{9/2}, & 0\le\zeta\le t\le 1,\\ t^{9/2}(1-\zeta)^{4/3}, & 0\le t\le\zeta\le 1,\end{cases}\\
\mathfrak{g}_{21}(\tau,\zeta) &= \frac{1}{6}\begin{cases} \tau^{3}(1-\zeta)^{4/3}-(\tau-\zeta)^{3}, & 0\le\zeta\le\tau\le 1,\\ \tau^{3}(1-\zeta)^{4/3}, & 0\le\tau\le\zeta\le 1,\end{cases}\\
\mathfrak{g}_{22}(\tau,\zeta) &= \frac{1}{\Gamma(45/14)}\begin{cases} \tau^{31/14}(1-\zeta)^{4/3}-(\tau-\zeta)^{31/14}, & 0\le\zeta\le\tau\le 1,\\ \tau^{31/14}(1-\zeta)^{4/3}, & 0\le\tau\le\zeta\le 1,\end{cases}\\
\mathfrak{G}_1(t,\zeta) &= \mathfrak{g}_1(t,\zeta)+\frac{10\Delta_1 t^{11/3}}{13\Delta}\mathfrak{g}_{11}\left(\frac{8}{11},\zeta\right),\\
\mathfrak{G}_2(t,\zeta) &= \frac{t^{11/3}\Gamma(11/2)}{\Delta\Gamma(7/3)}\left(\frac{91}{6}\int_0^1 \mathfrak{g}_{21}(\tau,\zeta)\,d\tau+\frac{4}{5}\mathfrak{g}_{22}\left(\frac{2}{3},\zeta\right)\right),\\
\mathfrak{G}_3(t,\zeta) &= \frac{10t^{9/2}\Gamma(14/3)}{13\Delta\Gamma(61/24)}\mathfrak{g}_{11}\left(\frac{8}{11},\zeta\right),\\
\mathfrak{G}_4(t,\zeta) &= \mathfrak{g}_2(t,\zeta)+\frac{t^{9/2}\Delta_2}{\Delta}\left(\frac{91}{6}\int_0^1 \mathfrak{g}_{21}(\tau,\zeta)\,d\tau+\frac{4}{5}\mathfrak{g}_{22}\left(\frac{2}{3},\zeta\right)\right),\\
\mathfrak{h}_1(\zeta) &= \frac{1}{\Gamma(14/3)}(1-\zeta)^{37/24}\left(1-(1-\zeta)^{17/8}\right),\\
\mathfrak{h}_2(\zeta) &= \frac{1}{\Gamma(11/2)}(1-\zeta)^{4/3}\left(1-(1-\zeta)^{19/6}\right),
\end{aligned}
$$

for all $t,\tau,\zeta\in[0,1]$. In addition, we find

$$
\mathfrak{J}_1(\zeta) = \begin{cases} \mathfrak{h}_1(\zeta)+\frac{10\Delta_1}{13\Delta\Gamma(89/21)}\left[\left(\frac{8}{11}\right)^{68/21}(1-\zeta)^{37/24}-\left(\frac{8}{11}-\zeta\right)^{68/21}\right], & 0\le\zeta<\frac{8}{11},\\ \mathfrak{h}_1(\zeta)+\frac{10\Delta_1}{13\Delta\Gamma(89/21)}\left(\frac{8}{11}\right)^{68/21}(1-\zeta)^{37/24}, & \frac{8}{11}\le\zeta\le 1,\end{cases}
$$

$$
\mathfrak{J}_2(\zeta) = \begin{cases} \frac{\Gamma(11/2)}{\Delta\Gamma(7/3)}\Big\{\frac{91}{144}(1-\zeta)^{4/3}-\frac{91}{144}(1-\zeta)^4+\frac{4}{5\Gamma(45/14)}\\ \quad\times\left[\left(\frac{2}{3}\right)^{31/14}(1-\zeta)^{4/3}-\left(\frac{2}{3}-\zeta\right)^{31/14}\right]\Big\}, & 0\le\zeta<\frac{2}{3},\\ \frac{\Gamma(11/2)}{\Delta\Gamma(7/3)}\Big[\frac{91}{144}(1-\zeta)^{4/3}-\frac{91}{144}(1-\zeta)^4+\frac{4}{5\Gamma(45/14)}\\ \quad\times\left(\frac{2}{3}\right)^{31/14}(1-\zeta)^{4/3}\Big], & \frac{2}{3}\le\zeta\le 1,\end{cases}
$$

$$
\mathfrak{J}_3(\zeta) = \begin{cases} \frac{10\Gamma(14/3)}{13\Delta\Gamma(61/24)\Gamma(89/21)}\left[\left(\frac{8}{11}\right)^{68/21}(1-\zeta)^{37/24}-\left(\frac{8}{11}-\zeta\right)^{68/21}\right], & 0\le\zeta<\frac{8}{11},\\ \frac{10\Gamma(14/3)}{13\Delta\Gamma(61/24)\Gamma(89/21)}\left(\frac{8}{11}\right)^{68/21}(1-\zeta)^{37/24}, & \frac{8}{11}\le\zeta\le 1,\end{cases}
$$

$$
\mathfrak{J}_4(\zeta) = \begin{cases} \mathfrak{h}_2(\zeta)+\frac{\Delta_2}{\Delta}\Big\{\frac{91}{144}(1-\zeta)^{4/3}-\frac{91}{144}(1-\zeta)^4+\frac{4}{5\Gamma(45/14)}\\ \quad\times\left[\left(\frac{2}{3}\right)^{31/14}(1-\zeta)^{4/3}-\left(\frac{2}{3}-\zeta\right)^{31/14}\right]\Big\}, & 0\le\zeta<\frac{2}{3},\\ \mathfrak{h}_2(\zeta)+\frac{\Delta_2}{\Delta}\Big[\frac{91}{144}(1-\zeta)^{4/3}-\frac{91}{144}(1-\zeta)^4+\frac{4}{5\Gamma(45/14)}\\ \quad\times\left(\frac{2}{3}\right)^{31/14}(1-\zeta)^{4/3}\Big], & \frac{2}{3}\le\zeta\le 1.\end{cases}
$$

We also obtain $\Xi_1 = 1$ and $\Xi_2 = 1$. After some computations, we find

$$
\begin{aligned}
P_1 &:= \frac{2^{61/12}}{\Gamma(7/4)}\left(\int_0^1 \mathfrak{J}_1(\zeta)\zeta^{9/61}\,d\zeta\right)^{61/12} \approx 4.11609161\times 10^{-9},\\
P_2 &:= \frac{2^{51/8}}{\Gamma(7/5)}\left(\int_0^1 \mathfrak{J}_2(\zeta)\zeta^{16/255}\,d\zeta\right)^{51/8} \approx 3.11233481\times 10^{-10},
\end{aligned}
$$

$$P_3 := \frac{2^{61/12}}{\Gamma(7/4)} \left(\int_0^1 \mathfrak{J}_3(\zeta)\zeta^{9/61}\, d\zeta \right)^{61/12} \approx 1.39796164 \times 10^{-18},$$
$$P_4 := \frac{2^{51/8}}{\Gamma(7/5)} \left(\int_0^1 \mathfrak{J}_4(\zeta)\zeta^{16/255}\, d\zeta \right)^{51/8} \approx 1.16007238 \times 10^{-13},$$

and so $L = \max\{P_i,\ i = 1, \ldots, 4\} = P_1$. We choose $\mathfrak{e}_0 = 10$, $\sigma_1 = \frac{31}{6}$, $\sigma_2 = \frac{13}{2}$, and if we select $\omega_1 < \frac{1}{L}10^{-1/12}$ and $\omega_2 < \frac{1}{L}10^{-1/8}$, then we deduce that $\mathfrak{f}(z) < \frac{10^{61/12}}{L}$ and $\mathfrak{g}(z) < \frac{10^{51/8}}{L}$ for all $z \in [0, 10]$. For example, if $\omega_1 \le 2.0053 \times 10^8$ and $\omega_2 \le 1.8218 \times 10^8$, then the above conditions for $\mathfrak{f}$ and $\mathfrak{g}$ are satisfied. Therefore, assumption $(K3)$ is also satisfied. By Theorem 1, we conclude that there exist positive constants $\mathfrak{c}_1$ and $\mathfrak{d}_1$ such that for any $\mathfrak{c}_0 \in (0, \mathfrak{c}_1]$ and $\mathfrak{d}_0 \in (0, \mathfrak{d}_1]$, problem (19) and (20) has at least one positive solution $(\mathfrak{u}(t), \mathfrak{v}(t))$, $t \in [0, 1]$. By Theorem 2, we deduce that there exist positive constants $\mathfrak{c}_2$ and $\mathfrak{d}_2$ such that for any $\mathfrak{c}_0 \ge \mathfrak{c}_2$ and $\mathfrak{d}_0 \ge \mathfrak{d}_2$, problem (19) and (20) has no positive solution.

5. Conclusions

In this paper, we studied the system of coupled Riemann–Liouville fractional differential Equation (1) with ϱ_1-Laplacian and ϱ_2-Laplacian operators, subject to the nonlocal coupled boundary conditions (2), which contain fractional derivatives of various orders, Riemann–Stieltjes integrals, and two positive parameters $\mathfrak{c}_0$ and $\mathfrak{d}_0$. Under some assumptions for the nonlinearities $\mathfrak{f}$ and $\mathfrak{g}$ of system (1), we established intervals for the parameters $\mathfrak{c}_0$ and $\mathfrak{d}_0$ such that our problem (1) and (2) has at least one positive solution. First, we made a change of unknown functions such that the new boundary conditions have no positive parameters. By using the corresponding Green functions, the new boundary value problem was then written equivalently as a system of integral equations (namely the system (15)). We associated to this integral system an operator $(\mathcal{S})$, and we proved the existence of at least one fixed point for it by applying the Schauder fixed point theorem. Intervals for parameters $\mathfrak{c}_0$ and $\mathfrak{d}_0$ were also given such that problem (1) and (2) has no positive solution. Finally, we presented an example to illustrate our main results.

Author Contributions: Conceptualization, R.L.; formal analysis, J.H., R.L. and A.T.; methodology, J.H., R.L. and A.T. All authors have read and agreed to the published version of the manuscript.

Funding: This research received no external funding.

Institutional Review Board Statement: Not applicable.

Informed Consent Statement: Not applicable.

Data Availability Statement: Not applicable.

Conflicts of Interest: The authors declare no conflict of interest.

References

1. Tudorache, A.; Luca, R. Positive solutions for a system of Riemann–Liouville fractional boundary value problems with p-Laplacian operators. *Adv. Differ. Equ.* **2020**, *2022*, 292. [CrossRef]
2. Luca, R. On a system of fractional differential equations with p-Laplacian operators and integral boundary conditions. *Revue Roum. Math. Pures Appl.* **2021**, *66*, 749–766.
3. Henderson, J.; Luca, R.; Tudorache, A. Positive solutions for systems of coupled fractional boundary value problems. *Open J. Appl. Sci.* **2015**, *5*, 600–608. [CrossRef]
4. Tudorache, A.; Luca, R. Positive solutions for a system of fractional boundary value problems with r-Laplacian operators, uncoupled nonlocal conditions and positive parameters. *Axioms* **2022**, *11*, 164. [CrossRef]
5. Tan, J.; Li, M. Solutions of fractional differential equations with p-Laplacian operator in Banach spaces. *Bound. Value Prob.* **2018**, *2018*, 15. [CrossRef]
6. Tang, X.; Wang, X.; Wang, Z.; Ouyang, P. The existence of solutions for mixed fractional resonant boundary value problem with $p(t)$-Laplacian operator. *J. Appl. Math. Comput.* **2019**, *61*, 559–572. [CrossRef]
7. Tian, Y.; Sun, S.; Bai, Z. Positive Solutions of Fractional Differential Equations with p-Laplacian. *J. Funct. Spaces* **2017**, *2017*, 3187492. [CrossRef]

8. Wang, G.; Ren, X.; Zhang, L.; Ahmad, B. Explicit iteration and unique positive solution for a Caputo-Hadamard fractional turbulent flow model. *IEEE Access* **2019**, *7*, 109833–109839. [CrossRef]
9. Wang, H.; Jiang, J. Existence and multiplicity of positive solutions for a system of nonlinear fractional multi-point boundary value problems with *p*-Laplacian operator. *J. Appl. Anal. Comput.* **2021**, *11*, 351–366.
10. Wang, Y.; Liu, S.; Han, Z. Eigenvalue problems for fractional differential equationswith mixed derivatives and generalized *p*-Laplacian. *Nonlinear Anal. Model. Control* **2018**, *23*, 830–850. [CrossRef]
11. Ahmad, B.; Alsaedi, A.; Ntouyas, S.K.; Tariboon, J. *Hadamard-Type Fractional Differential Equations, Inclusions and Inequalities*; Springer: Cham, Switzerland, 2017.
12. Ahmad, B.; Ntouyas, S.K. *Nonlocal Nonlinear Fractional-Order Boundary Value Problems*; World Scientific: Hackensack, NJ, USA, 2021.
13. Zhou, Y.; Wang, J.R.; Zhang, L. *Basic Theory of Fractional Differential Equations*, 2nd ed.; World Scientific: Singapore, 2016.

fractal and fractional

MDPI

Article

Study on Infinitely Many Solutions for a Class of Fredholm Fractional Integro-Differential System

Dongping Li [1], Yankai Li [2,*] and Fangqi Chen [3,4]

1 Department of Mathematics, Xi'an Technological University, Xi'an 710021, China
2 School of Automation and Information Engineering, Xi'an University of Technology, Xi'an 710048, China
3 Department of Mathematics, Nanjing University of Aeronautics and Astronautics, Nanjing 211106, China
4 College of Mathematics and Systems Science, Shandong University of Science and Technology, Qingdao 266590, China
* Correspondence: liyankai@xaut.edu.cn

Abstract: This paper deals with a class of nonlinear fractional Sturm–Liouville boundary value problems. Each sub equation in the system is a fractional partial equation including the second kinds of Fredholm integral equation and the p-Laplacian operator, simultaneously. Infinitely many solutions are derived due to perfect involvements of fractional calculus theory and variational methods with some simpler and more easily verified assumptions.

Keywords: fractional integro-differential equation; Sturm–Liouville boundary condition; variational method

MSC: 26A33; 34B15; 35A15

Citation: Li, D.; Li, Y.; Chen, F. Study on Infinitely Many Solutions for a Class of Fredholm Fractional Integro-Differential System. *Fractal Fract.* **2022**, *6*, 467. https://doi.org/10.3390/fractalfract6090467

Academic Editor: Rodica Luca

Received: 8 July 2022
Accepted: 22 August 2022
Published: 26 August 2022

1. Introduction

Nano/microactuators, as an indispensable portion of nano/microelectromechanical systems, are always subject to different inherent nonlinear forces. Many studies show that an integro-differential equation is generated in the modeling process of the nano/microactuator governing equation owing to axial forces ([1–3]). In [4,5], the following nanoactuator beam equation augmented to boundary conditions and containing an integro-differential expression, was discussed

$$\begin{cases} \frac{d^4 f}{dt^4} - (\mu \int_0^1 (\frac{df}{dt})^2 dt + L)\frac{d^2 f}{dt^2} + \frac{\theta}{f^\eta} + \frac{\kappa}{(r+f)^2} + \frac{s}{f} = 0, \ t \in [0,1], \\ f(0) = f(1) = 0, \ \ f'(0) = f'(1) = 0, \end{cases} \tag{1}$$

where f and t denote the deflection and length of the beam, respectively. μ, L, κ and r denote some inherent nonlinear forces. Actually, in practical engineering applications, actuators are constructed by the billions for chipsets, therefore, developing more effective and accurate strategies for the study of nano/microactuator structures is of great significance.

Furthermore, it is often not appropriate to establish models with delayed behaviors by ordinary differential equations or partial differential equations, while integral equations are ideal tools. Moreover, fractional calculus operators are convolution operators (For details, please refer to the definitions of fractional integral and differential operators in [6], in which the definitions involving convolution integrals.), because they are nonlocal and have full-memory function, and those characteristics can be well used to describe various phenomena and complex processes involving delay and global correlations. For this reason, fractional calculus has been extensively applied in interdisciplinary fields such as fluid and viscoelastic mechanics, control theory, signal and image processing, electricity, physical, etc., (see [7–9]). Therefore, matching fractional calculus operators and integro-differential equations is ideal to complete the mathematical modeling of practical problems. Taking into account the effect of a full-memory system, the integer derivatives in Equation (1) can be substituted for fractional ones. Inspired by this fact in Equation (1), Shivanian [10] introduced the following overdetermined Fredholm fractional integro-differential equations

$$\begin{cases} {}_tD_T^{\alpha_j}(a_j(t){}_0D_t^{\alpha_j}u_j(t)) = \lambda F_{u_j}(t,u_1(t),\dots,u_m(t)) + \int_0^T k_j(t,s)u_j(s)ds, \ t\in(0,T),\ j=1,2,\dots,m, \\ u_j(t) = \int_0^T k_j(t,s)u_j(s)ds, \ t\in(0,T),\ j=1,2,\dots,m, \\ u_j(0)=u_j(T)=0, \ j=1,2,\dots,m, \end{cases} \tag{2}$$

where $\alpha_j \in (0,1]$, $a_j(t) \in L^\infty[0,T]$, $j=1,2,\dots,m$. The existence of at least three weak solutions was obtained through the three critical points theorem.

Committed to fully considering more general systems, this paper studies a class of nonlinear Fredholm fractional integro-differential equations with p-Laplacian operator and Sturm–Liouville boundary conditions as below

$$\begin{cases} {}_tD_T^{\gamma_j}(k_j(t)\Phi_p({}_0^CD_t^{\gamma_j}z_j(t))) + l_j(t)\Phi_p(z_j(t)) \\ = \lambda f_{z_j}(t,z_1(t),\dots,z_m(t)) + \int_0^T g_j(t,s)\Phi_p(z_j(s))ds, \ t\in[0,T],\ j=1,2,\dots,m, \\ z_j(t) = \int_0^T g_j(t,s)\Phi_p(z_j(s))ds, \ t\in[0,T],\ j=1,2,\dots,m, \\ c_jk_j(0)\Phi_p(z_j(0)) - c_j'{}_tD_T^{\gamma_j-1}(k_j(0)\Phi_p({}_0^CD_t^{\gamma_j}z_j(0))) = 0, \ j=1,2,\dots,m, \\ d_jk_j(T)\Phi_p(z_j(T)) + d_j'{}_tD_T^{\gamma_j-1}(k_j(T)\Phi_p({}_0^CD_t^{\gamma_j}z_j(T))) = 0, \ j=1,2,\dots,m, \end{cases} \tag{3}$$

where c_j, c_j', d_j and d_j' are positive constants, $\lambda \in (0,+\infty)$ is a parameter, $k_j, l_j \in L^\infty[0,T]$ with $\widehat{k_j} = ess\inf_{[0,T]} k_j(t) > 0$ and $\widehat{l_j} = ess\inf_{[0,T]} l_j(t) \geq 0$, $j=1,2,\dots,m$. For $1<p<\infty$, $\Phi_p(s) = |s|^{p-2}s (s \neq 0)$, $\Phi_p(0)=0$, $f: [0,T]\times\mathbb{R}^m \to \mathbb{R}$ satisfies $f(\cdot,z_1(t),\dots,z_m(t)) \in C[0,T]$ and $f(t,\cdot,\dots,\cdot) \in C^1[\mathbb{R}^m]$, $g_j(\cdot,\cdot) \in C([0,T],[0,T])$. ${}_0^CD_t^{\gamma_j}$ and ${}_tD_T^{\gamma_j}$ denote the left Caputo fractional derivative and right Riemann–Liouville fractional derivative of order γ_j, respectively, which are defined by Kilbas et al. in [6]

$${}_tD_T^{\gamma_j}u(t) = (-1)^n\frac{d^n}{dt^n}{}_tD_T^{\gamma_j-n}u(t) = \frac{(-1)^n}{\Gamma(n-\gamma_j)}\frac{d^n}{dt^n}\int_t^T(\zeta-t)^{n-\gamma_j-1}u(\zeta)d\zeta, \tag{4}$$

$${}_0^CD_t^{\gamma_j}u(t) = {}_0D_t^{\gamma_j-n}u^{(n)}(t) = \frac{1}{\Gamma(n-\gamma_j)}\int_0^t(t-\zeta)^{n-\gamma_j-1}u^{(n)}(\zeta)d\zeta, \tag{5}$$

for $\forall u(t) \in AC([0,T],\mathbb{R})$, $n-1 \leq \gamma_j < n$, $n \in \mathrm{N}$.

We emphasize that this paper extends previous results in several directions, which are listed as follows: (i) In recent years, a large number of existence results for fractional differential equations have been acquired by variational methods and critical point theory ([11–14]). However, not many research works are available in related references to handle fractional integro-differential equations, let alone involving the p-Laplacian operator and Sturm–Liouville boundary conditions. (ii) It is not hard to see that Equation (3) can turn into the Dirichlet boundary value problem Equation (2) under $p=2, c_j'=d_j'=0, l_j(t)\equiv 0, j=1,2,\dots,m$, which means that Equation (2) is a special case of Equation (3). Furthermore, since the p-Laplacian operator is considered with $1<p<\infty$ in the paper, the linear differential operator ${}_tD_T^{\gamma}{}_0^CD_t^{\gamma}$ is extended to the nonlinear differential operator ${}_tD_T^{\gamma}\Phi_p({}_0^CD_t^{\gamma})$. In short, the form of Equation (3) is more generalized, as well as the boundary value conditions. (iii) Infinitely many solutions are obtained in this paper with some simpler and more easily verified assumptions. Hence, our work improves and replenishes some existing results form the literature.

2. Preliminaries

Assume H is a Banach space and $\mathcal{F} \in C^1(H,\mathbb{R})$. Functional $\mathcal{F}$ satisfies the Palais–Smale condition if each sequence $\{z_k\}_{k=1}^\infty \subset H$ such that $\{\mathcal{F}(z_k)\}$ is bounded and $\lim_{k\to\infty}\mathcal{F}'(z_k)=0$ possesses strongly convergent subsequence in H.

Theorem 1 ([15]). *Let H be an infinite-dimensional Banach space, $\mathcal{F} \in C^1(H, \mathbb{R})$ is an even functional and satisfies the Palais–Smale condition. Assume that:*

(*i*) $\mathcal{F}(0) = 0$. *There exist $\tau > 0$ and $\eta > 0$ such that $\overline{\Upsilon}_\tau \subset \{z \in H \mid \mathcal{F}(z) \geq 0\}$ and $\mathcal{F}(z) \geq \eta$ for all $z \in \partial\Upsilon_\tau$, where $\Upsilon_\tau = \{z \in H \mid \|z\| < \tau\}$;*

(*ii*) *For any finite dimensional subspace $H_0 \subset H$, the set $H_0 \bigcap \{z \in H \mid \mathcal{F}(z) \geq 0\}$ is bounded.*

Then, $\mathcal{F}$ has infinitely many critical points.

Definition 1. *Let $1 < p < \infty$, $\frac{1}{p} < \gamma_j \leq 1$, $j = 1, 2, \ldots, m$. Define the fractional derivative space $H = \Pi_{j=1}^{j=m} H^{\gamma_j,p}$ with the weighted norm*

$$\|Z\|_H = \sum_{j=1}^{j=m} \|z_j\|_{(\gamma_j,p)},\ z_j \in H^{\gamma_j,p},\ Z = (z_1, \ldots, z_m) \in H, \tag{6}$$

where

$$H^{\gamma_j,p} = \{z_j \in AC([0,T], \mathbb{R}) : {}_0^C D_t^{\gamma_j} z_j(t) \in L^p([0,T], \mathbb{R})\}$$

as the closure of $C^\infty([0,T], \mathbb{R})$ endowed with the norm

$$\|z_j\|_{(\gamma_j,p)} := \left(\int_0^T \mid z_j(t) \mid^p dt + \int_0^T \mid {}_0^C D_t^{\gamma_j} z_j(t) \mid^p dt \right)^{\frac{1}{p}}, \forall z_j \in H^{\gamma_j,p}. \tag{7}$$

$H^{\gamma_j,p}$ is a reflexive and separable Banach space [16]. Therefore, H also is a reflexive and separable Banach space.

Lemma 1 ([13]). *For any $z_j(t) \in H^{\gamma_j,p}$, $1 < p, q < \infty$ with $\frac{1}{p} + \frac{1}{q} = 1$, there exists a constant $W_{(\gamma_j,p)} = \max\left\{ \frac{T^{\gamma_j - \frac{1}{p}}}{\Gamma(\gamma_j)((\gamma_j-1)q+1)^{\frac{1}{q}}}, 1 \right\} + \left[\frac{2^{p-1}}{T} \max\left\{ 1, \left(\frac{T^{\gamma_j}}{\Gamma(\gamma_j+1)} \right)^p \right\} \right]^{\frac{1}{p}}$ such that $\|z_j\|_\infty \leq W_{(\gamma_j,p)} \|z_j\|_{(\gamma_j,p)}$, $j = 1, 2, \ldots, m$.*

Taking into account Lemma 1, one has

$$\|z_j\|_\infty \leq \frac{W_{(\gamma_j,p)}}{(\min\{\widehat{k}_j, \widehat{l}_j\})^{\frac{1}{p}}} \left(\int_0^T l_j(t) \mid z_j(t) \mid^p dt + \int_0^T k_j(t) \mid {}_0^C D_t^{\gamma_j} z_j(t) \mid^p dt \right)^{\frac{1}{p}},\ \forall\, z_j(t) \in H^{\gamma_j,p}, \tag{8}$$

$j = 1, 2, \ldots, m$. In order to describe it more easily for the further analysis, denote

$$W_j = \frac{W_{(\gamma_j,p)}}{(\min\{\widehat{k}_j, \widehat{l}_j\})^{\frac{1}{p}}},\ \widehat{W} = \max_{1 \leq j \leq m} \{W_j\}. \tag{9}$$

Obviously, the norm defined by (7) is equivalent to

$$\|z_j\|_{(\gamma_j,p)} = \left(\int_0^T l_j(t) \mid z_j(t) \mid^p dt + \int_0^T k_j(t) \mid {}_0^C D_t^{\gamma_j} z_j(t) \mid^p dt \right)^{\frac{1}{p}},\ j = 1, 2, \ldots, m. \tag{10}$$

We work with the norm (10) hereinafter.

Lemma 2 ([17]). *Let $1 < p < \infty$, $\gamma_j \in (\frac{1}{p}, 1]$, $j = 1, 2, \ldots, m$. Suppose that any sequence $\{z_{k,j}\}$ converges to z_j in $H^{\gamma_j,p}$ weakly. Then, $z_{k,j} \to z_j$ in $C([0,T])$ as $k \to \infty$.*

Lemma 3 ([18]). *Let H_j be any finite-dimensional subspace of $H^{\gamma_j,p}$, $j = 1, 2, \ldots, m$. There exists a constant $\zeta_0 > 0$ such that $meas\{t \in [0,T] : \mid z_j(t) \mid \geq \zeta_0 \|z_j\|_{(\gamma_j,p)}\} \geq \zeta_0$, $\forall z_j(t) \in H_j \setminus \{0\}$.*

Lemma 4 ([6])**.** *Let $\gamma > 0$, $p \geq 1$, $q \geq 1$ and $\frac{1}{p} + \frac{1}{q} \leq 1 + \gamma$ ($p \neq 1, q \neq 1$ in the case when $\frac{1}{p} + \frac{1}{q} = 1 + \gamma$). If $z_1 \in L^p([a,b])$ and $z_2 \in L^q([a,b])$, then, $\int_a^b ({}_aD_t^{-\gamma} z_1(t)) z_2(t)dt = \int_a^b z_1(t)({}_tD_b^{-\gamma} z_2(t))dt$.*

Lemma 5. *It is said $Z = (z_1, \ldots, z_m) \in H$ is a weak solution of Equations (3), if the following equation holds*

$$\sum_{j=1}^{m} \left\{ \int_0^T k_j(t)\Phi_p({}_0^C D_t^{\gamma_j} z_j(t)){}_0^C D_t^{\gamma_j} y_j(t) + l_j(t)\Phi_p(z_j(t))y_j(t)dt + \frac{c_j}{c_j'} k_j(0)\Phi_p(z_j(0))y_j(0) + \frac{d_j}{d_j'} k_j(T)\Phi_p(z_j(T))y_j(T) \right\}$$
$$= \sum_{j=1}^{m} \left\{ \int_0^T \int_0^T g_j(t,s)\Phi_p(z_j(s))y_j(t)dsdt + \lambda \int_0^T f_{z_j}(t, z_1(t), \ldots, z_m(t))y_j(t)dt \right\}, \forall Y = (y_1, \ldots, y_m) \in H. \quad (11)$$

Proof. Consider (4) and (5), the boundary conditions in Equation (3) and Lemma 4 yield:

$$\begin{aligned}
&\int_0^T {}_tD_T^{\gamma_j}(k_j(t)\Phi_p({}_0^C D_t^{\gamma_j} z_j(t)))y_j(t)dt \\
&= -\int_0^T y_j(t)d[{}_tD_T^{\gamma_j-1}(k_j(t)\Phi_p({}_0^C D_t^{\gamma_j} z_j(t)))] \\
&= {}_tD_T^{\gamma_j-1}\Big(k_j(0)\Phi_p({}_0^C D_t^{\gamma_j} z_j(0))\Big)y_j(0) - {}_tD_T^{\gamma_j-1}\Big(k_j(T)\Phi_p({}_0^C D_t^{\gamma_j} z_j(T))\Big)y_j(T) + \int_0^T {}_tD_T^{\gamma_j-1}(k_j(t)\Phi_p({}_0^C D_t^{\gamma_j} z_j(t)))y_j'(t)dt \qquad (12) \\
&= \frac{c_j}{c_j'} k_j(0)\Phi_p(z_j(0))y_j(0) + \frac{d_j}{d_j'} k_j(T)\Phi_p(z_j(T))y_j(T) + \int_0^T k_j(t)\Phi_p({}_0^C D_t^{\gamma_j} z_j(t)){}_0^C D_t^{\gamma_j} y_j(t)dt.
\end{aligned}$$

Substituting $y_j(t)$ into Equation (3) and integrating on both sides from 0 to T, then summing from $j = 1$ to $j = m$ and combining with (12), we can obtain Equation (11). The proof is completed.
□

Remark 1. *For any $z_j \in H^{\gamma_j, p} \subset C([0,T])$, $j = 1, 2, \ldots, m$, from Equation (3) we have*

$${}_tD_T^{\gamma_j}(k_j(t)\Phi_p({}_0^C D_t^{\gamma_j} z_j(t))) + l_j(t)\Phi_p(z_j(t)) = \lambda f_{z_j}(t, z_1(t), \ldots, z_m(t)) + \int_0^T g_j(t,s)\Phi_p(z_j(s))ds, t \in [0,T],$$

because $f(t, \cdot, \ldots, \cdot) \in C^1[R^m]$, $z_j(t) = \int_0^T g_j(t,s)\Phi_p(z_j(s))ds \in H^{\gamma_j, p}$ and

$${}_tD_T^{\gamma_j}(k_j(t)\Phi_p({}_0^C D_t^{\gamma_j} z_j(t))) = \left({}_tD_T^{\gamma_j-1}(k_j(t)\Phi_p({}_0^C D_t^{\gamma_j} z_j(t)))\right)',$$

one gets

$${}_tD_T^{\gamma_j-1}(k_j(t)\Phi_p({}_0^C D_t^{\gamma_j} z_j(t))) \in AC([0,T]).$$

Hence, the terms ${}_tD_T^{\gamma_j-1}(k_j(0)\Phi_p({}_0^C D_t^{\gamma_j} z_j(0)))$ and ${}_tD_T^{\gamma_j-1}(k_j(T)\Phi_p({}_0^C D_t^{\gamma_j} z_j(T)))$ exist in this paper.

Consider the functional $\mathcal{F} : H \to \mathbb{R}$ with

$$\mathcal{F}(Z) := \frac{1}{p}\sum_{j=1}^{j=m}\int_0^T k_j(t) \mid {}_0^C D_t^{\gamma_j} z_j(t) \mid^p + l_j(t) \mid z_j(t) \mid^p dt + \sum_{j=1}^{j=m}\left[\frac{c_j}{pc_j'}k_j(0) \mid z_j(0) \mid^p + \frac{d_j}{pd_j'}k_j(T) \mid z_j(T) \mid^p\right]$$
$$-\sum_{j=1}^{j=m}\int_0^T G_j(z_j(t))dt - \lambda\int_0^T f(t, z_1(t), \dots, z_m(t))dt$$
$$= \frac{1}{p}\sum_{j=1}^{j=m}\|z_j\|^p_{(\gamma_j, p)} + \sum_{j=1}^{j=m}\left[\frac{c_j}{pc_j'}k_j(0) \mid z_j(0) \mid^p + \frac{d_j}{pd_j'}k_j(T) \mid z_j(T) \mid^p\right]$$
$$-\sum_{j=1}^{j=m}\int_0^T G_j(z_j(t))dt - \lambda\int_0^T f(t, z_1(t), \dots, z_m(t))dt, \tag{13}$$

where $G_j(z_j(t)) = \frac{1}{2}\int_0^T g_j(t,s)\Phi_p(z_j(s))z_j(t)ds$, $t \in (0,T)$, $j = 1, 2, \dots, m$. Owing to $z_j(t) = \int_0^T g_j(t,s)\Phi_p(z_j(s))ds$, $j = 1, 2, \dots, m$, the Gâteaux derivative of G_j is

$$G_j'(z_j)(y_j) = \lim_{h\to 0}\frac{G_j(z_j + hy_j) - G_j(z_j)}{h} \tag{14}$$
$$= \lim_{h\to 0}\frac{\frac{1}{2}\int_0^T g_j(t,s)\Phi_p(z_j(s) + hy_j(s))(z_j(t) + hy_j(t)) - g_j(t,s)\Phi_p(z_j(s))z_j(t)ds}{h}$$
$$= \lim_{h\to 0}\frac{\frac{1}{2}h^2 y_j^2(t) + hz_j(t)y_j(t)}{h} = z_j(t)y_j(t) = \int_0^T g_j(t,s)\Phi_p(z_j(s))y_j(t)ds, j = 1, 2, \dots, m.$$

Then, combining the continuity of f and (14), we can see that $\mathcal{F} \in C^1(H, \mathbb{R})$ and

$$\mathcal{F}'(Z)(Y) = \sum_{j=1}^{j=m}\Bigg\{\int_0^T k_j(t)\Phi_p({}_0^C D_t^{\gamma_j} z_j(t)){}_0^C D_t^{\gamma_j} y_j(t) + l_j(t)\Phi_p(z_j(t))y_j(t)dt + \frac{c_j}{c_j'}k_j(0)\Phi_p(z_j(0))y_j(0) \tag{15}$$
$$+ \frac{d_j}{d_j'}k_j(T)\Phi_p(z_j(T))y_j(T) - \int_0^T\int_0^T g_j(t,s)\Phi_p(z_j(s))y_j(t)dsdt - \lambda\int_0^T f_{z_j}(t, Z(t))y_j(t)dt\Bigg\}, \forall Z, Y \in H.$$

Notice that, the critical point of $\mathcal{F}$ is the weak solution of Equation (3).

3. Main Results

First, some hypotheses related to nonlinearity f are given, which play important roles in the remaining discussion.

(H_0) $\lim\limits_{\forall j: |z_j| \to \infty}\frac{f(t, Z(t))}{\sum_{j=1}^{j=m}|z_j|^p} = \infty$ uniformly for $t \in [0,T]$, $Z(t) = (z_1(t), \dots, z_m(t)) \in \mathbb{R}^m$;

(H_1) $0 \le f(t, Z(t)) = o(\sum_{j=1}^{j=m} \mid z_j \mid^p)$ as $\sum_{j=1}^{j=m} \mid z_j \mid \to 0$ uniformly for $t \in [0,T]$;

(H_2) For any $Z(t) = (z_1(t), \dots, z_m(t)) \in \mathbb{R}^m$, $f(t, Z(t)) = \sum_{j=1}^{j=m}\frac{\eta_j}{p} \mid z_j \mid^p - J(t, Z(t))$ with $J(t, 0) \equiv 0$, and

$$\min_{1\le j\le m}\{\eta_j\} > \frac{1}{\lambda\zeta_0^{p+1}}\left(\frac{3}{2} + p\sum_{j=1}^{j=m}\left[\frac{c_j}{pc_j'}k_j(0) + \frac{d_j}{pd_j'}k_j(T)\right]W_j^p\right),$$
$$\sum_{j=1}^{j=m}\left(\frac{\eta_j}{p} + \frac{\beta_j}{2\lambda}\right) \mid z_j \mid^{\omega_j} \le J(t, Z(t)) \le \sum_{j=1}^{j=m}\delta_j \mid z_j \mid^{\omega_j},$$

where $\omega_j \in (0,p)$, $\delta_j > 0$, $\zeta_0 > 0$ is a constant and $\widehat{\beta}$ is introduced thereinafter, $j = 1, 2, \dots, m$.

Lemma 6. *$\mathcal{F}$ satisfies the Palais–Smale condition under (H_0).*

Proof. Suppose that sequence $\{\mathcal{F}(Z_k)\}_{k\in\mathrm{N}}$ is bounded and $\lim\limits_{k\to\infty}\mathcal{F}'(Z_k) = 0$, $Z_k(t) = (z_{k,1}(t), \dots, z_{k,m}(t))$. We claim that $\{Z_k\}_{k\in\mathrm{N}}$ is bounded in H. Indeed, assume

$\forall j : \|z_{k,j}\|_{(\gamma_j,p)} \to \infty (k \to \infty)$. From (H_0), for any $L > 0$, there exists $k_0 \in \mathrm{N}$ such that

$$\frac{f(t, Z_k(t))}{\sum_{j=1}^{j=m} \|z_{k,j}\|^p_{(\gamma_j,p)}} \geq L,\ \forall\, k > k_0,\ t \in [0, T]. \tag{16}$$

For any fixed $k_* \in \mathrm{N}$ with $k_* > k_0$, from the integral mean value theorem, there exists $\xi(k_*) \in (0, 1]$ such that

$$\int_0^T f(t, Z_{k_*}(t))dt = Tf(\xi(k_*)T, Z_{k_*}(\xi(k_*)T)). \tag{17}$$

Combining (16) and (17) yields

$$\frac{\int_0^T f(t, Z_{k_*}(t))dt}{\sum_{j=1}^{j=m} \|z_{k_*,j}\|^p_{(\gamma_j,p)}} = \frac{Tf(\xi(k_*)T, Z_{k_*}(\xi(k_*)T))}{\sum_{j=1}^{j=m} \|z_{k_*,j}\|^p_{(\gamma_j,p)}} \geq \frac{TL\sum_{j=1}^{j=m} \|z_{k_*,j}\|^p_{(\gamma_j,p)}}{\sum_{j=1}^{j=m} \|z_{k_*,j}\|^p_{(\gamma_j,p)}} = TL.$$

Hence, we can get

$$\frac{\int_0^T f(t, Z_k(t))dt}{\sum_{j=1}^{j=m} \|z_{k,j}\|^p_{(\gamma_j,p)}} \geq TL,\ \forall\, k > k_0,\ t \in [0, T]. \tag{18}$$

In view of (8), (9), (13) and (18) we have

$$\begin{aligned}
\frac{\mathcal{F}(Z_k(t))}{\sum_{j=1}^{j=m} \|z_{k,j}\|^p_{(\gamma_j,p)}} =& \frac{1}{p} + \frac{\sum_{j=1}^{j=m} \left[\frac{c_j}{pc'_j} k_j(0) \mid z_{k,j}(0) \mid^p + \frac{d_j}{pd'_j} k_j(T) \mid z_{k,j}(T) \mid^p\right]}{\sum_{j=1}^{j=m} \|z_{k,j}\|^p_{(\gamma_j,p)}} \\
&- \frac{\sum_{j=1}^{j=m} \int_0^T G_j(z_{k,j}(t))dt + \lambda \int_0^T f(t, Z_k(t))dt}{\sum_{j=1}^{j=m} \|z_{k,j}\|^p_{(\gamma_j,p)}} \\
\leq& \frac{1}{p} + \frac{\sum_{j=1}^{j=m} [\frac{c_j}{pc'_j} k_j(0) + \frac{d_j}{pd'_j} k_j(T)] W_j^p \|z_{k,j}\|^p_{(\gamma_j,p)}}{\sum_{j=1}^{j=m} \|z_{k,j}\|^p_{(\gamma_j,p)}} - \lambda TL \\
\leq& \frac{1}{p} + \sum_{j=1}^{j=m} [\frac{c_j}{pc'_j} k_j(0) + \frac{d_j}{pd'_j} k_j(T)] W_j^p - \lambda TL.
\end{aligned} \tag{19}$$

Choose L large enough such that $\frac{1}{p} + \sum_{j=1}^{j=m} [\frac{c_j}{pc'_j} k_j(0) + \frac{d_j}{pd'_j} k_j(T)] W_j^p - \lambda TL < -1$, then combining (19) yields that $\mathcal{F}(Z_k(t)) \leq -\sum_{j=1}^{j=m} \|z_{k,j}\|^p_{(\gamma_j,p)}$, which means that $\mathcal{F}(Z_k(t)) \to -\infty$ as $\|z_{k,j}\|_{(\gamma_j,p)} \to \infty, \forall j = 1, 2, \ldots, m$. It contradicts that $\{\mathcal{F}(Z_k)\}$ is bounded. Hence, $\{Z_k\}$ is bounded in H. Because of the reflexivity of H, we get that $Z_k \rightharpoonup Z^*$ in H (up to subsequences). From Lemma 2, we have $Z_k \to Z^*$ uniformly in $C([0, T]^m)$ and $L^p([0, T]^m)$. Then,

$$\begin{cases}
(\mathcal{F}'(Z_k) - \mathcal{F}'(Z^*))(Z_k - Z^*) \to 0,\ k \to \infty, \\
\int_0^T (f_{z_j}(t, Z_k(t)) - f_{z_j}(t, Z^*(t)))(z_{k,j}(t) - z_j^*(t))dt \to 0,\ k \to \infty,, j = 1, 2, \ldots, m, \\
\int_0^T \mid z_{k,j}(t) - z_j^*(t) \mid^2 dt \to 0, z_{k,j}(0) - z_j^*(0) \to 0, z_{k,j}(T)) - z_j^*(T) \to 0,\ k \to \infty, j = 1, 2, \ldots, m.
\end{cases} \tag{20}$$

From (15), we obtain that

$$
\begin{aligned}
&(\mathcal{F}'(Z_k)-\mathcal{F}'(Z^*))(Z_k-Z^*)=\mathcal{F}'(Z_k)(Z_k-Z^*)-\mathcal{F}'(Z^*)(Z_k-Z^*)\\
&=\sum_{j=1}^{j=m}\Big\{\int_0^T k_j(t)\Big(\Phi_p({}_0^CD_t^{\gamma_j}z_{k,j}(t))-\Phi_p({}_0^CD_t^{\gamma_j}z_j^*(t))\Big){}_0^CD_t^{\gamma_j}(z_{k,j}(t)-z_j^*(t))+l_j(t)\Big(\Phi_p(z_{k,j}(t))-\Phi_p(z_j^*(t))\Big)(z_{k,j}(t)-z_j^*(t))dt \quad (21)\\
&-\int_0^T\int_0^T g_j(t,s)\Big(\Phi_p(z_{k,j}(s))-\Phi_p(z_j^*(s))\Big)(z_{k,j}(t)-z_j^*(t))dsdt+\frac{c_j}{c_j'}k_j(0)\Big(\Phi_p(z_{k,j}(0))-\Phi_p(z_j^*(0))\Big)(z_{k,j}(0)-z_j^*(0))\\
&+\frac{d_j}{d_j'}k_j(T)\Big(\Phi_p(z_{k,j}(T))-\Phi_p(z_j^*(T))\Big)(z_{k,j}(T)-z_j^*(T))-\lambda\int_0^T(f_{z_j}(t,Z_k(t))-f_{z_j}(t,Z^*(t)))(z_{k,j}(t)-z_j^*(t))dt\Big\};
\end{aligned}
$$

moreover,

$$
\int_0^T\int_0^T g_j(t,s)\Big(\Phi_p(z_{k,j}(s))-\Phi_p(z_j^*(s))\Big)(z_{k,j}(t)-z_j^*(t))dsdt=\int_0^T\mid z_{k,j}(t)-z_j^*(t)\mid^2 dt. \quad (22)
$$

Denote

$$
\begin{aligned}
\Psi_{k,j}(\gamma_j,p)&=\int_0^T k_j(t)\Big(\Phi_p({}_0^CD_t^{\gamma_j}z_{k,j}(t))-\Phi_p({}_0^CD_t^{\gamma_j}z_j^*(t))\Big){}_0^CD_t^{\gamma_j}(z_{k,j}(t)-z_j^*(t))dt,\\
\Psi_{k,j}(p)&=\int_0^T l_j(t)\Big(\Phi_p(z_{k,j}(t))-\Phi_p(z_j^*(t))\Big)(z_{k,j}(t)-z_j^*(t))dt,
\end{aligned}
$$

combining (20), (21) and (22), we obtain $\sum_{j=1}^{j=m}\{\Psi_{k,j}(\gamma_j,p)+\Psi_{k,j}(p)\}\to 0$ as $k\to\infty$. As in the discussion of $\Theta(\alpha,p),\Theta(p)$ in [19], we can get

$$
\Psi_{k,j}(\gamma_j,p)+\Psi_{k,j}(p)\geq\begin{cases} e_j\|z_{k,j}-z_j^*\|^p_{\gamma_j,p}, & p\geq 2,\\ e_j'\|z_{k,j}-z_j^*\|^2_{(\gamma_j,p)}(\|z_{k,j}\|^p_{L^p}+\|z_j^*\|^p_{L^p})^{\frac{p-2}{p}}, & 1<p<2,\end{cases}
$$

where e_j,e_j' are constants, $j=1,2,\ldots,m$. Based on the above discussion, we can obtain $\|z_{k,j}-z_j^*\|_{(\gamma_j,p)}\to 0$, $j=1,2,\ldots,m$, for all $1<p<\infty$. Hence, the Palais–Smale condition holds. □

Theorem 2. *Assume that (H_0) and (H_1) hold and $f(t,Z)=f(t,-Z)$. Then, Equation (3) has infinitely many solutions with $\frac{1}{Tp\widehat{W}^p}-\widehat{\beta}>0$ and $0<\lambda<\infty$.*

Proof. Due to $f(t,Z)=f(t,-Z)$, it is easy to verify that $\mathcal{F}$ is even. Obviously, $\mathcal{F}(0)=0$. Taking into account (H_1) that, for any $\varepsilon>0$, there exists $r(\varepsilon)$ such that

$$
f(t,Z(t))\leq\varepsilon\sum_{j=1}^{j=m}\mid z_j\mid^p,\ \forall t\in[0,T],\ \sum_{j=1}^{j=m}\mid z_j\mid\leq r(\varepsilon). \quad (23)
$$

Further, $g_j(\cdot,\cdot)\in C([0,T],[0,T])$ means that the kernel g_j is bounded by, say β_j, i.e., $\mid g_j(t,s)\mid\leq\beta_j$, and

$$
G_j(z_j(t))=\frac{1}{2}\int_0^T g_j(t,s)\Phi_p(z_j(s))z_j(t)ds\leq\frac{\beta_j}{2}z_j(t)\parallel z_j\parallel_\infty^{p-1}\leq\frac{\beta_j}{2}\parallel z_j\parallel_\infty^p, j=1,2,\ldots,m. \quad (24)
$$

Let $\tau=\frac{r}{\widehat{W}}$. For any $Z\in\overline{\Upsilon}_\tau$, one has $\|Z\|_H=\sum_{j=1}^{j=m}\|z_j\|_{(\gamma_j,p)}\leq\frac{r}{\widehat{W}}$. Then,

$$
\frac{r}{\widehat{W}}\geq\sum_{j=1}^{j=m}\|z_j\|_{(\gamma_j,p)}\geq\sum_{j=1}^{j=m}\frac{1}{W_j}\|z_j\|_\infty\geq\frac{1}{\widehat{W}}\sum_{j=1}^{j=m}\|z_j\|_\infty, \quad (25)
$$

which means that $\sum_{j=1}^{j=m} \|z_j\|_\infty \le r(\varepsilon)$. At this point, from (13), (23) and (24) we can see

$$\begin{aligned} \mathcal{F}(Z) \ge & \frac{1}{p}\sum_{j=1}^{j=m} \|z_j\|^p_{(\gamma_j,p)} - \sum_{j=1}^{j=m}\int_0^T \frac{\beta_j}{2} \| z_j \|^p_\infty dt - \lambda \int_0^T \varepsilon \sum_{j=1}^{j=m} | z_j |^p dt \\ \ge & \frac{1}{p}\sum_{j=1}^{j=m} \|z_j\|^p_{(\gamma_j,p)} - \sum_{j=1}^{j=m}(\frac{T\beta_j}{2} + \lambda\varepsilon T)W_j^p \|z_j\|^p_{(\gamma_j,p)} \\ \ge & [\frac{1}{p} - (\frac{T\widehat{\beta}}{2} + \lambda\varepsilon T)\widehat{W}^p]\frac{1}{m^p}\left(\sum_{j=1}^{j=m}\|z_j\|_{(\gamma_j,p)}\right)^p \\ = & [\frac{1}{p} - (\frac{T\widehat{\beta}}{2} + \lambda\varepsilon T)\widehat{W}^p]\frac{1}{m^p}\|Z\|^p_H, \ \forall Z \in \overline{Y}_\tau, \end{aligned} \tag{26}$$

where $\widehat{\beta} = \max_{1\le j\le m}\{\beta_j\}$. Choose $\varepsilon = \frac{1}{2\lambda}(\frac{1}{Tp\widehat{W}^p} - \widehat{\beta})$, from (26), we get

$$\mathcal{F}(Z) \ge \frac{1}{2pm^p}\|Z\|^p_H \ge 0. \tag{27}$$

Hence, $\overline{Y}_\tau \subset \{Z \in H \mid \mathcal{F}(Z) \ge 0\}$ and $\mathcal{F}(Z) \ge \frac{1}{2pm^p}\|Z\|^p_H, \forall Z \in \partial Y_\tau$. Therefore, the condition (i) in Theorem 1 holds.

For any finite-dimensional space $H_0 \subset H$, we claim that $\widetilde{H} = H_0 \bigcap \{Z \in H \mid \mathcal{F}(Z) \ge 0\}$ is bounded. Assume that there exists at least a sequence $\{Z_k\} \subset \widetilde{H}$ such that $\|Z_k\|_H \to \infty$ as $k \to \infty$. From $\mathcal{F}(Z_k) \ge 0$ and (19), we obtain

$$0 \le \frac{\mathcal{F}(Z_k(t))}{\sum_{j=1}^{j=m}\|z_{k,j}\|^p_{(\gamma_j,p)}} \le \frac{1}{p} + \sum_{j=1}^{j=m}[\frac{c_j}{pc'_j}k_j(0) + \frac{d_j}{pd'_j}k_j(T)]W_j^p - \lambda TL.$$

Since L is arbitrary, we draw a contradiction. Therefore, $\widetilde{H} = H_0 \bigcap \{Z \in H \mid \mathcal{F}(Z) \ge 0\}$ is bounded. Based on Theorem 1, functional $\mathcal{F}$ has infinitely many critical points, which means that Equation (3) has infinitely many solutions in H. □

Theorem 3. *Assume that* (H_2) *holds and* $J(t, Z) = J(t, -Z)$*. Then, Equation (3) has infinitely many solutions with* $\sum_{j=1}^{j=m} \frac{1}{p} - \left(\frac{\beta_j T}{2} + \frac{\lambda T\eta_j}{p}\right)W_j^p > 0$.

Proof. Suppose that the sequence $\{\mathcal{F}(Z_k)\}_{k\in N}$ is bounded and $\lim_{k\to\infty}\mathcal{F}'(Z_k) = 0$, $Z_k(t) = (z_{k,1}(t), \dots, z_{k,m}(t))$. In what follows, we prove that $\mathcal{F}$ satisfies the Palais–Smale condition. Indeed, assume $\forall j : \|z_{k,j}\|_{(\gamma_j,p)} \to \infty (k \to \infty)$, from (13), (24), (H_2) and (8), we have

$$\begin{aligned} \frac{1}{p}\sum_{j=1}^{j=m}\|z_{k,j}\|^p_{(\gamma_j,p)} \le & \mathcal{F}(Z_k) + \sum_{j=1}^{j=m}\int_0^T G_j(z_j(t))dt + \lambda\int_0^T f(t, z_1(t), \dots, z_m(t))dt \\ \le & \mathcal{F}(Z_k) + \sum_{j=1}^{j=m}\int_0^T \frac{\beta_j}{2} | z_{k,j} |^p dt + \lambda\sum_{j=1}^{j=m}\int_0^T \frac{\eta_j}{p} | z_{k,j} |^p - (\frac{\eta_j}{p} + \frac{\beta_j}{2\lambda}) | z_{k,j} |^{\omega_j} dt \\ \le & \mathcal{F}(Z_k) + \sum_{j=1}^{j=m}\left(\frac{\beta_j T}{2} + \frac{\lambda T\eta_j}{p}\right)W_j^p\|z_{k,j}\|^p_{(\gamma_j,p)} + \lambda T\sum_{j=1}^{j=m}(\frac{\eta_j}{p} + \frac{\beta_j}{2\lambda})W_j^{\omega_j}\|z_{k,j}\|^{\omega_j}_{(\gamma_j,p)}, \end{aligned} \tag{28}$$

namely

$$\sum_{j=1}^{j=m}\left[\frac{1}{p} - \left(\frac{\beta_j T}{2} + \frac{\lambda T\eta_j}{p}\right)W_j^p\right]\|z_{k,j}\|^p_{(\gamma_j,p)} - \lambda T\sum_{j=1}^{j=m}(\frac{\eta_j}{p} + \frac{\beta_j}{2\lambda})W_j^{\omega_j}\|z_{k,j}\|^{\omega_j}_{(\gamma_j,p)} \le \mathcal{F}(Z_k). \tag{29}$$

Recall that $\sum_{j=1}^{j=m}\frac{1}{p}-\left(\frac{\beta_j T}{2}+\frac{\lambda T\eta_j}{p}\right)W_j^p>0$, $\omega_j\in(0,p)$ and $\{\mathcal{F}(Z_k)\}$ is bounded, we get a contradiction. Hence, $\{Z_k\}$ is bounded on H. The rest of the proof for the Palais–Smale condition is similar to that of Lemma 6, so we do not repeat it.

Let $\tau'\in(0,\frac{1}{W})$. For any $Z\in\overline{Y}_{\tau'}$, one has $\|Z\|_H=\sum_{j=1}^{j=m}\|z_j\|_{(\gamma_j,p)}\le\tau'<\frac{1}{W}$. A similar analysis with (25) yields $\sum_{j=1}^{j=m}\|z_j\|_\infty<1$. From (28), we get

$$\begin{aligned}
\mathcal{F}(Z)&\geq\frac{1}{p}\sum_{j=1}^{j=m}\|z_j\|^p_{(\gamma_j,p)}-\sum_{j=1}^{j=m}\int_0^T\frac{\beta_j}{2}\mid z_j\mid^p dt-\lambda\sum_{j=1}^{j=m}\int_0^T\frac{\eta_j}{p}\mid z_j\mid^p-(\frac{\eta_j}{p}+\frac{\beta_j}{2\lambda})\mid z_j\mid^{\omega_j}dt\\
&=\frac{1}{p}\sum_{j=1}^{j=m}\|z_j\|^p_{(\gamma_j,p)}-\sum_{j=1}^{j=m}\left[\int_0^T\frac{\beta_j}{2}\mid z_j\mid^p dt+\lambda\int_0^T\frac{\eta_j}{p}\mid z_j\mid^p-(\frac{\eta_j}{p}+\frac{\beta_j}{2\lambda})\mid z_j\mid^{\omega_j}dt\right]\\
&=\frac{1}{p}\sum_{j=1}^{j=m}\|z_j\|^p_{(\gamma_j,p)}-\sum_{j=1}^{j=m}\left[\int_0^T(\frac{\beta_j}{2}+\frac{\lambda\eta_j}{p})\mid z_j\mid^p-(\frac{\lambda\eta_j}{p}+\frac{\beta_j}{2})\mid z_j\mid^{\omega_j}dt\right]\\
&=\frac{1}{p}\sum_{j=1}^{j=m}\|z_j\|^p_{(\gamma_j,p)}+\sum_{j=1}^{j=m}\int_0^T(\frac{\lambda\eta_j}{p}+\frac{\beta_j}{2})\mid z_j\mid^{\omega_j}-(\frac{\lambda\eta_j}{p}+\frac{\beta_j}{2})\mid z_j\mid^p dt\\
&\geq\frac{1}{p}\sum_{j=1}^{j=m}\|z_j\|^p_{(\gamma_j,p)}+\sum_{j=1}^{j=m}\int_0^T(\frac{\lambda\eta_j}{p}+\frac{\beta_j}{2})\mid z_j\mid^p-(\frac{\lambda\eta_j}{p}+\frac{\beta_j}{2})\mid z_j\mid^p dt\\
&=\frac{1}{p}\sum_{j=1}^{j=m}\|z_j\|^p_{(\gamma_j,p)}\geq\frac{1}{pm^p}(\sum_{j=1}^{j=m}\|z_j\|_{(\gamma_j,p)})^p=\frac{1}{pm^p}\|Z\|^p_H\geq 0,\ \forall\, Z\in\overline{Y}_{\tau'}.
\end{aligned}$$

Clearly, $\overline{Y}_{\tau'}\subset\{Z\in H\mid\mathcal{F}(Z)\geq 0\}$ and $\mathcal{F}(Z)\geq\frac{1}{pm^p}\|Z\|^p_{H'}\forall Z\in\partial Y_{\tau'}$.

For any finite-dimensional space $H_0'\subset H$, we claim that $\widehat{H}=H_0'\bigcap\{Z\in H\mid\mathcal{F}(Z)\geq 0\}$ is bounded. Assume that there exists at least a sequence $\{Z_k\}\subset\widehat{H}$ such that $\|Z_k\|_H\to\infty$ as $k\to\infty$. Then, according to (19), (H_2) and Lemma 3 we obtain

$$\begin{aligned}
0\leq\frac{\mathcal{F}(Z_k(t))}{\sum_{j=1}^{j=m}\|z_{k,j}\|^p_{(\gamma_j,p)}}&\leq\frac{1}{p}+\sum_{j=1}^{j=m}[\frac{c_j}{pc_j'}k_j(0)+\frac{d_j}{pd_j'}k_j(T)]W_j^p-\frac{\lambda\int_0^T\sum_{j=1}^{j=m}\frac{\eta_j}{p}\mid z_{k,j}\mid^p-J(t,Z_k(t))dt}{\sum_{j=1}^{j=m}\|z_{k,j}\|^p_{(\gamma_j,p)}}\\
&\leq\frac{1}{p}+\sum_{j=1}^{j=m}[\frac{c_j}{pc_j'}k_j(0)+\frac{d_j}{pd_j'}k_j(T)]W_j^p-\frac{\sum_{j=1}^{j=m}\frac{\lambda\eta_j}{p}\int_{\Omega_{z_{k,j}}}\zeta_0^p\|z_{k,j}\|^p_{(\gamma_j,p)}dt}{\sum_{j=1}^{j=m}\|z_{k,j}\|^p_{(\gamma_j,p)}}+\frac{\lambda\int_0^T\sum_{j=1}^{j=m}\delta_j\mid z_{k,j}\mid^{\omega_j}dt}{\sum_{j=1}^{j=m}\|z_{k,j}\|^p_{(\gamma_j,p)}}\\
&\leq\frac{1}{p}+\sum_{j=1}^{j=m}[\frac{c_j}{pc_j'}k_j(0)+\frac{d_j}{pd_j'}k_j(T)]W_j^p-\frac{\lambda\zeta_0^{p+1}}{p}\min_{1\leq j\leq m}\{\eta_j\}+\frac{\lambda T\sum_{j=1}^{j=m}\delta_j W_j^{\omega_j}\|z_{k,j}\|^{\omega_j}_{(\gamma_j,p)}}{\sum_{j=1}^{j=m}\|z_{k,j}\|^p_{(\gamma_j,p)}},
\end{aligned}\tag{30}$$

where $\Omega_{z_{k,j}}=\{t\in[0,T]:\mid z_{k,j}(t)\mid\geq\zeta_0\|z_{k,j}\|_{(\gamma_j,p)}\}$ and $meas\{\Omega_{z_{k,j}}\}\geq\zeta_0$. Since $\min_{1\le j\le m}\{\eta_j\}>\frac{1}{\lambda\zeta_0^{p+1}}(\frac{3}{2}+p\sum_{j=1}^{j=m}[\frac{c_j}{pc_j'}k_j(0)+\frac{d_j}{pd_j'}k_j(T)]W_j^p)$, then

$$\frac{1}{p}+\sum_{j=1}^{j=m}[\frac{c_j}{pc_j'}k_j(0)+\frac{d_j}{pd_j'}k_j(T)]W_j^p-\frac{\lambda\zeta_0^{p+1}}{p}\min_{1\leq j\leq m}\{\eta_j\}<-\frac{1}{2p},\tag{31}$$

based on $\omega_j\in(0,p)$ and $\|Z_k\|_H\to\infty$ as $k\to\infty$, we get

$$\frac{\lambda T\sum_{j=1}^{j=m}\delta_j W_j^{\omega_j}\|z_{k,j}\|^{\omega_j}_{(\gamma_j,p)}}{\sum_{j=1}^{j=m}\|z_{k,j}\|^p_{(\gamma_j,p)}}\to 0,k\to\infty.\tag{32}$$

Combining (31) and (32), we obtain that $0 \leq \frac{\mathcal{F}(Z_k(t))}{\sum_{j=1}^{j=m} \|z_{k,j}\|^p_{(\gamma_j,p)}} < -\frac{1}{2p}$ as $k \to \infty$, which draws a contradiction. Hence, $\widehat{H}$ is bounded. Based on Theorem 1, functional $\mathcal{F}$ has infinitely many critical points, which means that Equation (3) has infinitely many solutions in H. $\square$

Example 1. *Focus on the following Fredholm fractional partial integro-differential equations with* $m = 3$ *and* $p = 4$:

$$\begin{cases} {}_tD_1^{0.5}((t+1)\Phi_4({}_0^CD_t^{0.5}z_1(t))) + (\frac{1}{2}+t)\Phi_4(z_1(t)) = D_{z_1}f(t,z_1(t),z_2(t),z_3(t)) + \int_0^1 10^{-5}t\sin(s)\Phi_4(z_1(s))ds, t \in [0,1], \\ z_1(t) = \int_0^1 10^{-5}t\sin(s)\Phi_4(z_1(s))ds, \ t \in [0,1], \\ {}_tD_1^{0.6}((t^2+1)\Phi_4({}_0^CD_t^{0.6}z_2(t))) + (\frac{1}{3}+t^2)\Phi_4(z_2(t)) = D_{z_2}f(t,z_1(t),z_2(t),z_3(t)) + \int_0^1 10^{-5}t^2\sin(s)\Phi_4(z_2(s))ds, t \in [0,1], \\ z_2(t) = \int_0^1 10^{-5}t^2\sin(s)\Phi_4(z_2(s))ds, \ t \in [0,1], \\ {}_tD_1^{0.75}((t^3+1)\Phi_4({}_0^CD_t^{0.75}z_3(t))) + (\frac{1}{4}+t^3)\Phi_4(z_3(t)) = D_{z_3}f(t,z_1(t),z_2(t),z_3(t)) + \int_0^1 10^{-5}t^3\sin(s)\Phi_4(z_3(s))ds, t \in [0,1], \\ z_3(t) = \int_0^1 10^{-5}t^3\sin(s)\Phi_4(z_3(s))ds, \ t \in [0,1], \\ \Phi_4(z_1(0)) - {}_tD_1^{-0.5}(\Phi_4({}_0^CD_t^{0.5}z_1(0))) = 0, \ \Phi_4(z_1(1)) + {}_tD_1^{-0.5}(\Phi_4({}_0^CD_t^{0.5}z_1(1))) = 0, \\ \Phi_4(z_2(0)) - {}_tD_1^{-0.4}(\Phi_4({}_0^CD_t^{0.6}z_2(0))) = 0, \ \Phi_4(z_2(1)) + {}_tD_1^{-0.4}(\Phi_4({}_0^CD_t^{0.6}z_2(1))) = 0, \\ \Phi_4(z_3(0)) - {}_tD_1^{-0.25}(\Phi_4({}_0^CD_t^{0.75}z_3(0))) = 0, \ \Phi_4(z_3(1)) + {}_tD_1^{-0.25}(\Phi_4({}_0^CD_t^{0.75}z_3(1))) = 0, \end{cases} \tag{33}$$

where $c_j = c_{j'} = 1, d_j = d_{j'} = \frac{1}{2}, j = 1,2,3,$

$$f(t,z_1,z_2,z_3) = (1+t)\begin{cases} (z_1^4+z_2^4+z_3^4)^2, \ z_1^4+z_2^4+z_3^4 \leq 1, \\ 2(z_1^4+z_2^4+z_3^4)^2 - (z_1^4+z_2^4+z_3^4)^{\frac{1}{2}}, \ z_1^4+z_2^4+z_3^4 > 1. \end{cases}$$

It is easy to verify that f is continuous with respect to t and continuously differentiable with respect to z_1, z_2 and z_3 (see Figures 1 and 2) and satisfies (H_0) and (H_1). Obviously, $k_1(0) = k_2(0) = k_3(0) = 1, k_1(1) = k_2(1) = k_3(1) = 2, \beta = 10^{-5}$. By direct calculation we have $\widehat{k}_1 = \widehat{k}_2 = \widehat{k}_3 = 1, \widehat{l}_1 = \frac{1}{2}, \widehat{l}_2 = \frac{1}{3}, \widehat{l}_3 = \frac{1}{4}$, and

$$W_{(0.5,4)} = \max\left\{\frac{1}{\Gamma(0.5)[(-\frac{1}{2})\frac{4}{3}+1]^{\frac{3}{4}}}, 1\right\} + \left[8\max\left\{1, \left(\frac{1}{\Gamma(1.5)}\right)^4\right\}\right]^{\frac{1}{4}} = 3.184,$$

$$W_{(0.6,4)} = \max\left\{\frac{1}{\Gamma(0.6)[(-\frac{2}{5})\frac{4}{3}+1]^{\frac{3}{4}}}, 1\right\} + \left[8\max\left\{1, \left(\frac{1}{\Gamma(1.6)}\right)^4\right\}\right]^{\frac{1}{4}} = 3.072,$$

$$W_{(0.75,4)} = \max\left\{\frac{1}{\Gamma(0.75)[(-\frac{1}{4})\frac{4}{3}+1]^{\frac{3}{4}}}, 1\right\} + \left[8\max\left\{1, \left(\frac{1}{\Gamma(1.75)}\right)^4\right\}\right]^{\frac{1}{4}} = 2.936,$$

then

$$\frac{W^4_{(0.5,4)}}{\min\{\widehat{k}_1, \widehat{l}_1\}} = 206, \frac{W^4_{(0.6,4)}}{\min\{\widehat{k}_2, \widehat{l}_2\}} = 267, \frac{W^4_{(0.75,4)}}{\min\{\widehat{k}_3, \widehat{l}_3\}} = 297,$$

namely, $\widehat{W} = 297$, $\frac{1}{p\widehat{W}} = 8.4 \times 10^{-5}$, then $\frac{1}{p\widehat{W}} - \beta > 0$. Hence, from Theorem 2 we can see that Equation (33) has infinitely many solutions.

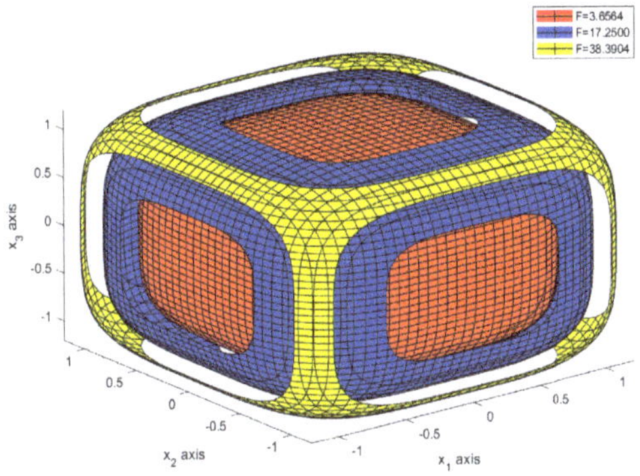

Figure 1. the contour-plot of Equation (33) for $t = 0$.

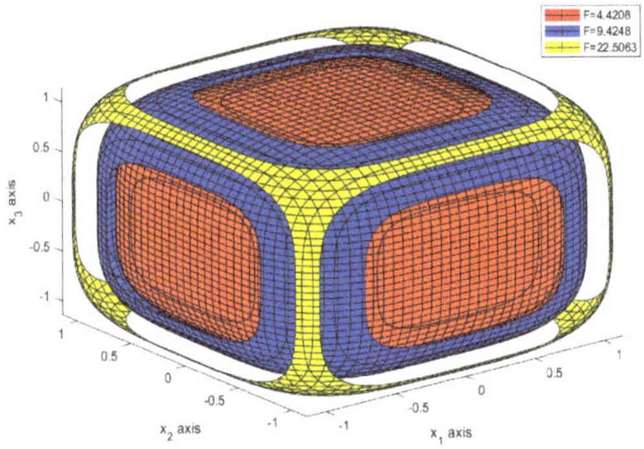

Figure 2. the contour-plot of Equation (33) for $t = 1$.

Author Contributions: Conceptualization, Y.L.; Investigation, D.L.; Writing—original draft, D.L.; Writing—review and editing, Y.L. and F.C. All authors have read and agreed to the published version of the manuscript.

Funding: This research was funded by National Natural Science Foundation of China grant numbers 12101481, 62103327, 11872201; Young Talent Fund of Association for Science and Technology in Shaanxi, China grant number 20220529; Young Talent Fund of Association for Science and Technology in Xi'an, China grant number 095920221344.

Institutional Review Board Statement: Not applicable.

Informed Consent Statement: Not applicable.

Data Availability Statement: Not applicable.

Acknowledgments: The authors would like to thank the editor and reviewers greatly for their precious comments and suggestions.

Conflicts of Interest: The authors declare no conflict of interest.

References

1. Abbasnejad, B.; Rezazadeh, G.; Shabani, R. Stability analysis of a capacitive FGM micro-beam using modified couple stress theory. *Acta Mech. Solida Sin.* **2013**, *26*, 427–440. [CrossRef]
2. Noghrehabadi, A.; Ghalambaz, M.; Vosough, A. A hybrid power series—Cuckoo search optimization algorithm to electrostatic deflection of micro fixed-fixed actuators. *Int. J. Multidiscip. Sci. Eng.* **2011**, *2*, 22–26.

3. Noghrehabadi, A.; Ghalambaz, M.; Beni, Y.T.; Abadyan, M.; Abadi, M.N. A new solution on the buckling and stable length of multi wall carbon nanotube probes near graphite sheets. *Procedia Eng.* **2011**, *10*, 3725–3733. [CrossRef]
4. Ghalambaz, M.; Ghalambaz, M.; Edalatifar, M. A new analytic solution for buckling of doubly clamped nano-actuators with integro differential governing equation using Duan—Rach adomian decomposition method. *Appl. Math. Model.* **2016**, *40*, 7293–7302. [CrossRef]
5. Shivanian, E.; Ansari, M. Buckling of doubly clamped nano-actuators in general form through optimized Chebyshev polynomials with interior point algorithm. *Acta Phys. Pol. A* **2019**, *135*, 444–450. [CrossRef]
6. Kilbas, A.; Srivastava, H.; Trujillo, J. *Theory and Applications of Fractional Differential Equations;* North-Holland Mathematics Studies; Elsevier Science B.V.: Amsterdam, The Netherlands, 2006; pp. 2453–2461.
7. Mirceski, V.; Tomovski, Z. Modeling of a voltammetric experiment in a limiting diffusion space. *J. Solid State Electrochem.* **2011**, *15*, 197–204. [CrossRef]
8. Khiabani E.D., Ghaffarzadeh H., Shiri B.; Katebi, J. Spline collocation methods for seismic analysis of multiple degree of freedom systems with visco-elastic dampers using fractional models. *J. Vib. Control.* **2020**, *26*, 1445–1462. [CrossRef]
9. Ameen, I.; Novati, P. The solution of fractional order epidemic model by implicit Adams methods. *Appl. Math. Model.* **2017**, *43*, 78–84. [CrossRef]
10. Shivanian, E. To study existence of at least three weak solutions to a system of over-determined Fredholm fractional integro-differential equations. *Commun. Nonlinear Sci. Numer. Simulat.* **2021**, *101*, 105892. [CrossRef]
11. Li, D.; Chen, F.; Wu, Y.; An,Y. Multiple solutions for a class of p-Laplacian type fractional boundary value problems with instantaneous and non-instantaneous impulses. *Appl. Math. Lett.* **2020**, *106*, 106352. [CrossRef]
12. Li, D.; Chen, F.; Wu, Y.; An, Y. Variational formulation for nonlinear impulsive fractional differential equations with (p, q)-Laplacian operator. *Math. Meth. Appl. Sci.* **2022**, *45*, 515–531. [CrossRef]
13. Nyamoradi, N.; Tersian, S. Existence of solutions for nonlinear fractional order p-Laplacian differential equations via critical point theory. *Fract. Calc. Appl. Anal.* **2019**, *22*, 945–967. [CrossRef]
14. Zhang, W.; Liu, W. Variational approach to fractional dirichlet problem with instantaneous and non-instantaneous impulses. *Appl. Math. Lett.* **2020**, *99*, 105993. [CrossRef]
15. Guo, D. *Nonlinear Functional Analysis;* Science and Technology Press of Shan Dong: Jinan, China, 2004
16. Tian, Y.; Nieto, J.J. The applications of critical-point theory to discontinuous fractional-order differential equations. *Proc. Edinb. Math. Soc.* **2017**, *60*, 1021–1051. [CrossRef]
17. Jiao, F.; Zhou, Y. Existence results for fractional boundary value problem via critical point theory. *Int. J. Bifurcation Chaos.* **2017**, *22*, 1250086. [CrossRef]
18. Wang, Y.; Liu, Y.; Cui, Y. Infinitely many solutions for impulsive fractional boundary value problem with p-Laplacian. *Bound. Value Probl.* **2018**, *94*, 1–16. [CrossRef]
19. Li, D.; Chen, F.; An Y. The existence of solutions for an impulsive fractional coupled system of (p, q)-Laplacian type without the Ambrosetti-Rabinowitz condition. *Math. Meth. Appl. Sci.* **2019**, *42*, 1449–1464. [CrossRef]

fractal and fractional

Article

Existence and Approximate Controllability of Mild Solutions for Fractional Evolution Systems of Sobolev-Type

Yue Liang

Center for Quantitative Biology, College of Science, Gansu Agricultural University, Lanzhou 730070, China; liangy@gsau.edu.cn; Tel.: +86-139-1915-6640

Abstract: This paper investigates the existence and approximate controllability of Riemann–Liouville fractional evolution systems of Sobolev-type in abstract spaces. At first, a group of sufficient conditions is established for the existence of mild solutions without the compactness of operator semigroup. Then the approximate controllability is studied under the assumption that the corresponding linear system is approximate controllability. The proof is based on the fixed point theory and the method of operator semigroup. An example is given as an application of the obtained results.

Keywords: fractional evolution systems; approximate controllability; Sobolev operator; compactness; Schauder fixed point theorem

MSC: 26A33; 93B05

Citation: Liang, Y. Existence and Approximate Controllability of Mild Solutions for Fractional Evolution Systems of Sobolev-Type. *Fractal Fract.* **2022**, *6*, 56. https://doi.org/10.3390/fractalfract6020056

Academic Editor: Rodica Luca

Received: 5 January 2022
Accepted: 18 January 2022
Published: 22 January 2022

1. Introduction

Let X be a Hilbert space, whose norm is denoted by $\|\cdot\|$. We consider the fractional evolution equation of sobolev type with the Riemann–Liouville derivative of the form

$$\begin{cases} {}^{L}D_t^{\alpha}(Ex(t)) = Ax(t) + f(t,x(t)) + Bu(t), \quad t \in J' := (0,b], \\ I_t^{1-\alpha}(Ex(t))|_{t=0} + g(x) = x_0, \end{cases} \tag{1}$$

where ${}^{L}D_t^{\alpha}$ is the Riemann–Liouville fractional derivative operator of order $\alpha \in (0,1)$, $I_t^{1-\alpha}$ is the fractional integral operator of order $1-\alpha$, $A : D(A) \subset X \to X$ and $E : D(E) \subset X \to X$ are linear operators, B is a linear bounded operator from U to X; here U is another Hilbert space, the control function $u \in L^p(J,U)$ for $p\alpha > 1$, $x_0 \in X$, f is the nonlinear function and g represents the nonlocal function which satisfies specific conditions.

Fractional differential equations, including of the Caputo type and Riemann–Liouville type, have been proved to be crucial tools in portraying the hereditary and memory property of various materials and processes. In 2011, Du et al. [1] pointed out that Riemann–Liouville fractional derivatives are more suitable to describe certain characteristics of viscoelastic materials than Caputo ones. Therefore, it is significant to study Riemann–Liouville fractional differential systems. In 2013, Zhou et al. [2], applying the Laplace transform technique and probability density functions, presented a suitable concept of mild solutions of Riemann–Liouville fractional evolution equations, and proved the existence of mild solutions for the fractional Cauchy problems under the cases that the C_0-semigroup is compact or noncompact. For the existence of mild solutions of fractional evolution equations, we refer to [3–8] and the references therein. In these papers, the compactness of operator semigroup or the measure of non-compactness conditions on nonlinearity are required. Sometimes, in order to obtain the uniqueness of mild solutions, the Lipschitz condition is also assumed.

In recent years, the controllability of fractional evolution equations has gained considerable attention. Generally speaking, the controllability of fractional evolution equations in abstract spaces includes two cases: the exact controllability and the approximate controllability. When we study the exact controllability of fractional evolution systems in abstract spaces, we assume that the control operator has a bounded inverse operator in a quotient space. However, if the state space is infinite dimensional and the operator semigroup is compact, the inverse of the control operator may not exist, see [9]. Hence, the assumptions for the exact controllability are too strong. Contrasting with the exact controllability, approximate controllability is more suitable to describe the natural phenomena. There are many research works focusing on the approximate controllability of fractional evolution systems, see [10–12] and the references therein. In [10], Chang et al. investigated the approximate controllability of fractional differential systems of Sobolev type in Banach spaces under the assumption that the resolvent operators, generated by the linear part, are compact. Sakthivel et al. [11] studied the approximate controllability of nonlinear fractional stochastic evolution systems when the linear part generates a compact semigroup. Recently, In [12], Yang demonstrated the existence and approximate controllability of mild solutions for $\alpha \in (1,2)$-order fractional evolution equations of Sobolev type when the pair (A, E) generates a compact resolvent family.

Inspired by the above mentioned papers, the aim of this work is to investigate the existence and approximate controllability of Riemann–Liouville fractional evolution system (1) in Hilbert space X. By using the Schauder fixed point theorem and the operator semigroup theory, we first prove the existence of mild solutions of the considered system without the compactness of operator semigroup and the measure of non-compactness conditions on nonlinearity. Then the approximate controllability is studied under the assumption that the corresponding linear system is approximate controllability. It is emphasized that the compactness of the operator semigroup and the Lipschitz continuity of nonlinearity are deleted in our work. The redundant assumptions on the linear operator E, such as the conditions $[C_1]$ and $[C_4]$ of [13], are removed in this paper.

2. Preliminaries

Let $J = [0, b]$ and $C(J, X)$ be the continuous function space. Denote by

$$C_{1-\alpha}(J, X) := \{x : \cdot^{1-\alpha}x(\cdot) \in C(J, X)\}.$$

Then $C_{1-\alpha}(J, X)$ is a Banach space endowed with the norm $\|x\|_{C_{1-\alpha}} = \sup\limits_{t\in J} t^{1-\alpha}\|x(t)\|$.

At first, for any $h \in L^p(J, X)$ with $p\alpha > 1$, we consider the following linear fractional initial value problem

$$\begin{cases} {}^{L}D_t^{\alpha}(Ex(t)) = Ax(t) + h(t), \quad t \in J', \\ I_t^{1-\alpha}(Ex(t))|_{t=0} + g(x) = x_0. \end{cases} \tag{2}$$

Throughout this paper, we suppose the following assumptions on A and E.

$(A1)$ The linear operator A is densely defined and closed.

$(A2)$ $D(E) \subset D(A)$ and E is bijective.

$(A3)$ The linear operator $E^{-1} : X \to D(E) \subset X$ is compact.

By $(A1)$–$(A3)$, the linear operator $AE^{-1} : X \to X$ is bounded due to the closed graph theorem. Hence, AE^{-1} generates a C_0-semigroup $T(t)(t \geq 0)$, which is expressed by $T(t) = e^{AE^{-1}t}$ for $t \geq 0$. We suppose that $M := \sup\limits_{t\geq 0} \|T(t)\| < +\infty$.

Remark 1. *Contrasting with [13], we delete the redundant conditions $[C_1]$ and $[C_4]$ of [13] in our paper. Hence, the results obtained in this work extends the results of [13].*

Applying the Riemann–Liouville fractional integral operator on both sides of (2), we obtain

$$\begin{aligned} Ex(t) &= \frac{t^{\alpha-1}}{\Gamma(\alpha)} I_t^{1-\alpha}(Ex(t))|_{t=0} + I_t^{\alpha} Ax(t) + I_t^{\alpha} h(t) \\ &= \frac{t^{\alpha-1}}{\Gamma(\alpha)}[x_0 - g(x)] + \frac{1}{\Gamma(\alpha)} \int_0^t (t-s)^{\alpha-1} \big[Ax(s) + h(s)\big] ds. \end{aligned}$$

Let $\lambda > 0$. Taking the Laplace transform

$$\widehat{x}(\lambda) = \int_0^\infty e^{-\lambda t} x(t) dt$$

and

$$\widehat{h}(\lambda) = \int_0^\infty e^{-\lambda t} h(t) dt$$

on both sides of the above equality, we can obtain

$$\begin{aligned} E\widehat{x}(t) &= \frac{1}{\lambda^\alpha}[x_0 - g(x)] + \frac{1}{\lambda^\alpha} AE^{-1} E\widehat{x}(\lambda) + \frac{1}{\lambda^\alpha}\widehat{h}(\lambda) \\ &= (\lambda^\alpha I - AE^{-1})^{-1}[x_0 - g(x)] + (\lambda^\alpha I - AE^{-1})^{-1}\widehat{h}(\lambda) \\ &= \int_0^\infty e^{-\lambda^\alpha s} T(s)[x_0 - g(x)] ds + \int_0^\infty e^{-\lambda^\alpha s} T(s)\widehat{h}(\lambda) ds, \end{aligned}$$

where $(\lambda^\alpha I - AE^{-1})^{-1} = \int_0^\infty e^{-\lambda^\alpha s} T(s) ds$. Consider the one-side stable probability density function

$$\xi_\alpha(\theta) = \frac{1}{\pi} \sum_{n=1}^{\infty} (-1)^{n-1} \theta^{-\alpha n - 1} \frac{\Gamma(n\alpha + 1)}{n!} \sin(n\pi\alpha),\ \theta \in (0, +\infty),$$

whose Laplace transform is given by

$$\int_0^\infty e^{-\lambda\theta} \xi_\alpha(\theta) d\theta = e^{-\lambda^\alpha}, \quad \alpha \in (0,1).$$

A similar argument as in [2] shows that

$$\begin{aligned} E\widehat{x}(\lambda) &= \int_0^\infty e^{-\lambda t} \int_0^\infty \alpha\theta\xi_\alpha(\theta) T(t^\alpha\theta) t^{\alpha-1}[x_0 - g(x)] d\theta dt \\ &\quad + \int_0^\infty e^{-\lambda t} \int_0^t \int_0^\infty \alpha\theta\xi_\alpha(\theta) T((t-s)^\alpha\theta)(t-s)^{\alpha-1} h(s) d\theta ds dt, \end{aligned}$$

where $\xi_\alpha(\theta) = \frac{1}{\alpha}\theta^{-1-\frac{1}{\alpha}}\varpi_\alpha(\theta^{-\frac{1}{\alpha}})$. This fact implies that

$$\begin{aligned} Ex(t) &= \int_0^\infty \alpha\theta\xi_\alpha(\theta) T(t^\alpha\theta) t^{\alpha-1}[x_0 - g(x)] d\theta \\ &\quad + \int_0^t \int_0^\infty \alpha\theta\xi_\alpha(\theta) T((t-s)^\alpha\theta)(t-s)^{\alpha-1} h(s) d\theta ds. \end{aligned}$$

Thus, we obtain

$$x(t) = t^{\alpha-1} T_E(t)[x_0 - g(x)] + \int_0^t (t-s)^{\alpha-1} T_E(t-s) h(s) ds,$$

where

$$T_E(t) = E^{-1} \int_0^\infty \alpha\theta\xi_\alpha(\theta) T(t^\alpha\theta) d\theta.$$

Remark 2. *When $E = I$, $I : X \to X$ is the identity operator, we have*

$$T_I(t) = \int_0^\infty \alpha\theta\xi_\alpha(\theta) T(t^\alpha\theta) d\theta,\ t \geq 0.$$

Therefore, $T_E(t) = E^{-1}T_I(t)$ *for all* $t \geq 0$.

From the above arguments, we introduce the definition of mild solution of the system (1) as follows.

Definition 1. *For each* $u \in L^p(J, U)$, $p\alpha > 1$, *a function* $x \in C_{1-\alpha}(J, X)$ *is called a mild solution of the system (1) if* $I_t^{1-\alpha}(Ex(t))|_{t=0} + g(x) = x_0$ *and*

$$x(t) = t^{\alpha-1}T_E(t)[x_0 - g(x)] + \int_0^t (t-s)^{\alpha-1}T_E(t-s)[f(s, x(s)) + Bu(s)]ds, \ t \in J'. \quad (3)$$

For the operator family $\{T_E(t)\}_{t\geq 0}$, we have the following lemma.

Lemma 1. *Let the assumptions* $(A1)$*–*$(A3)$ *hold. Then* $\{T_E(t)\}_{t\geq 0}$ *has the following properties:*
(i) *For fixed* $t \geq 0$, $T_E(t)$ *is a linear and bounded operator, i.e., for any* $x \in X$,

$$\|T_E(t)x\| \leq \frac{M\|E^{-1}\|}{\Gamma(\alpha)}\|x\|.$$

(ii) $\{T_E(t)\}_{t\geq 0}$ *is continuous in the uniform operator topology for* $t \geq 0$.
(iii) $\{T_E(t)\}_{t\geq 0}$ *is compact.*

Proof. From Proposition 3.1 of [2] and Remark 2, it is easy to verify that (i) holds. By virtue of the definition of the operator $T(t)(t \geq 0)$ and the Lebesgue dominated convergence theorem, we can deduce (ii). Next, we prove (iii). For any $r > 0$, $x \in X$ with $\|x\| \leq r$, we have

$$\begin{aligned} \|T_I(t)x\| &\leq \alpha M \int_0^\infty \theta\xi_\alpha(\theta)d\theta\|x\| \\ &\leq \frac{\alpha M}{\Gamma(\alpha+1)}\|x\| \\ &\leq \frac{Mr}{\Gamma(\alpha)}. \end{aligned}$$

This fact means that $T_I(t)$ maps bounded subset of X into the bounded set. Then $E^{-1}T_I(t)$ maps the bounded subset of X into relatively compact set due to the compactness of E^{-1}. Thus, $\{T_E(t)\}_{t\geq 0}$ is compact. □

Definition 2. *Let* $K_f(b) = \{x(b) : x$ *be a mild solution of the system* (1) *for some* $u \in L^p(J, U)\}$. *If* $\overline{K_f(b)} = X$, *the system* (1) *is said to be approximate controllability on* J.

We consider the linear fractional control system corresponding to (1) in the form

$$\begin{cases} {}^L D_t^\alpha(Ex(t)) = Ax(t) + Bu(t), & t \in J', \\ I_t^{1-\alpha}(Ex(t)) = x_0. \end{cases} \quad (4)$$

Define two operators Π_0^b and $R(\epsilon, \Pi_0^b)$ by

$$\Pi_0^b = \int_0^b (b-s)^{\alpha-1}T_E(b-s)BB^*T_E^*(b-s)ds,$$

$$R(\epsilon, \Pi_0^b) = (\epsilon I + \Pi_0^b)^{-1}, \quad \epsilon > 0,$$

where B^* and $T_E^*(t)$ denote the adjoint operators of B and $T_E(t)$, respectively. Then, Π_0^b is a linear operator. From [14], we obtain the following result.

Lemma 2. *The following conditions are equivalent:*
(i) The linear fractional control system (4) is approximately controllable on J.
(ii) The operator Π_0^b is positive, that is, $\langle x^*, \Pi_0^b x^* \rangle > 0$ for all nonzero $x^* \in X^*$.
(iii) For any $x \in X$, $\|\epsilon R(\epsilon, \Pi_0^b)x\| \to 0$ as $\epsilon \to 0^+$.

3. Existence and Approximate Controllability

In order to study the approximate controllability of the fractional control system (1), we first investigate the existence of solutions for the following integral system

$$\begin{cases} x(t) = t^{\alpha-1}T_E(t)[x_0 - g(x)] + \int_0^t (t-s)^{\alpha-1}T_E(t-s)[f(s,x(s)) + Bu(s;x)]ds, \quad t \in J', \\ u(t;x) = B^*T_E^*(b-t)R(\epsilon, \Pi_0^b)\mathcal{P}(x), \\ \mathcal{P}(x) = x_b - b^{\alpha-1}T_E(b)(x_0 - g(x)) - \int_0^b (b-s)^{\alpha-1}T_E(b-s)f(s,x(s))ds, \end{cases} \tag{5}$$

where x_b is an arbitrary element in X which is different from x_0. By Definition 1, the mild solution of the system (1) is equivalent to the solution of the integral system (5) for $u(\cdot;x) \in L^p(J,X)$.

For this purpose, we make the following assumptions.

$(A4)$ $f : J \times X \to X$ satisfies the following conditions.

(i) For each $x \in X$, $f(\cdot,x) : J \to X$ is strongly measurable, and for every $t \in J$, $f(\cdot,x) : X \to X$ is continuous.

(ii) For any $r > 0$, there is a function $\phi \in L^p(J,\mathbb{R}^+)$, $p\alpha > 1$ such that

$$\|f(t,x)\| \le \phi(t)$$

for any $t \in J$ and $x \in X$ with $\|x\| \le r$.

$(A5)$ $g : C_{1-\alpha}(J,X) \to X$ is continuous and maps bounded subset of $C_{1-\alpha}(J,X)$ into the bounded set.

$(A6)$ $B : U \to X$ is a bounded linear operator, i.e., $\exists\, M_B > 0$ such that $\|B\| \le M_B$.

$(A7)$ $\|R(\epsilon, \Pi_0^b)\| \le \frac{1}{\epsilon}$ for all $\epsilon > 0$.

For any $r > 0$, let $B_r = \left\{x \in C_{1-\alpha}(J,X) : \|x\|_{C_{1-\alpha}} \le r\right\}$. Then B_r is a nonempty bounded, closed and convex subset of $C_{1-\alpha}(J,X)$. By the assumption $(A5)$ we know that there exists a constant $M_1 > 0$ such that $\|g(x)\| \le M_1$ for any $x \in B_r$. From the assumption $(A6)$ we deduce that $Bu \in L^p(J,X)$ for any $u \in L^p(J,X)$ with $p\alpha > 1$.

Lemma 3. *For any $\mathcal{F} \in L^p(J,X)$, the operator $\aleph : L^p(J,X) \to C(J,X)$, defined by*

$$(\aleph\mathcal{F})(\cdot) = \cdot^{1-\alpha}\int_0^{\cdot} (\cdot - s)^{\alpha-1}T_E(\cdot - s)\mathcal{F}(s)ds,$$

is compact.

Proof. Denote by

$$(\aleph_0\mathcal{F})(t) = t^{1-\alpha}\int_0^t (t-s)^{\alpha-1}T_I(t-s)\mathcal{F}(s)ds.$$

It follows from Lemma 1 that

$$\|(\aleph_0\mathcal{F})(t)\| \quad \le \quad \frac{M}{\Gamma(\alpha)}\left(\frac{bp-b}{p\alpha-1}\right)^{1-\frac{1}{p}}\|\mathcal{F}\|_{L^p}.$$

So, owing to the compactness of E^{-1}, we conclude that the set

$$\{(\aleph\mathcal{F})(t) = E^{-1}(\aleph_0\mathcal{F})(t) : \mathcal{F} \in L^p(J,X), t \in J\}$$

is relatively compact in X.

Next, we will prove that the set $\{\aleph\mathcal{F} : \mathcal{F} \in L^p(J,X)\}$ is equi-continuous in $C(J,X)$. For $t_1, t_2 \in J$ with $0 \leq t_1 < t_2 < b$, we have

$$\begin{aligned}
\|(\aleph\mathcal{F})(t_2) - (\aleph\mathcal{F})(t_1)\| &\leq \|(t_2^{1-\alpha} - t_1^{1-\alpha}) \int_0^{t_2} (t_2-s)^{\alpha-1} T_E(t_2-s)\mathcal{F}(s)ds\| \\
&+ t_1^{1-\alpha}\| \int_0^{t_1} [(t_2-s)^{\alpha-1} - (t_1-s)^{\alpha-1}] T_E(t_2-s)\mathcal{F}(s)ds\| \\
&+ t_1^{1-\alpha}\| \int_0^{t_1} (t_1-s)^{\alpha-1} [T_E(t_2-s) - T_E(t_1-s)]\mathcal{F}(s)ds\| \\
&+ t_1^{1-\alpha}\| \int_{t_1}^{t_2} (t_2-s)^{\alpha-1} T_E(t_2-s)\mathcal{F}(s)ds\| \\
&= \sum_{i=1}^{4} I_i.
\end{aligned}$$

Obviously, if $t_2 - t_1 \to 0$, we have

$$\begin{aligned}
I_1 &= \|(t_2^{1-\alpha} - t_1^{1-\alpha}) \int_0^{t_2} (t_2-s)^{\alpha-1} T_E(t_2-s)\mathcal{F}(s)ds\| \\
&\leq \frac{M\|E^{-1}\|}{\Gamma(\alpha)} (\frac{p-1}{p\alpha-1})^{1-\frac{1}{p}} \|\mathcal{F}\|_{L^p} (t_2-t_1)^{1-\alpha} \\
&\to 0,
\end{aligned}$$

$$\begin{aligned}
I_2 &= t_1^{1-\alpha}\| \int_0^{t_1} [(t_2-s)^{\alpha-1} - (t_1-s)^{\alpha-1}] T_E(t_2-s)\mathcal{F}(s)ds\| \\
&\leq \frac{M\|E^{-1}\|b^{1-\alpha}}{\Gamma(\alpha)} \int_0^{t_1} [(t_2-s)^{\alpha-1} - (t_1-s)^{\alpha-1}]\mathcal{F}(s)ds \\
&\to 0
\end{aligned}$$

and

$$\begin{aligned}
I_4 &= t_1^{1-\alpha}\| \int_{t_1}^{t_2} (t_2-s)^{\alpha-1} T_E(t_2-s)\mathcal{F}(s)ds\| \\
&\leq \frac{M\|E^{-1}\|b^{1-\alpha}}{\Gamma(\alpha)} (\frac{p-1}{p\alpha-1})^{1-\frac{1}{p}} \|\mathcal{F}\|_{L^p} (t_2-t_1)^{\frac{p\alpha-1}{p}} \\
&\to 0.
\end{aligned}$$

Since $T_E(t)$ is continuous in the uniform operator topology for $t \geq 0$, we obtain that

$$\begin{aligned}
I_3 &= t_1^{1-\alpha}\| \int_0^{t_1} (t_1-s)^{\alpha-1} [T_E(t_2-s) - T_E(t_1-s)]\mathcal{F}(s)ds\| \\
&\leq \sup_{s\in[0,t_1]} \|T_E(t_2-s) - T_E(t_1-s)\| (\frac{bp-b}{p\alpha-1})^{1-\frac{1}{p}} \|\mathcal{F}\|_{L^p} \\
&\to 0
\end{aligned}$$

as $t_2 - t_1 \to 0$. Consequently, we have

$$\|(\aleph\mathcal{F})(t_2) - (\aleph\mathcal{F})(t_1)\| \to 0 \;\; (t_2 - t_1 \to 0).$$

This fact yields that the set $\{\aleph\mathcal{F} : \mathcal{F} \in L^p(J,X)\}$ is equi-continuous in $C(J,X)$. According to the Ascoli–Arzela theorem, the set $\{\aleph\mathcal{F} : \mathcal{F} \in L^p(J,X)\}$ is relatively compact in $C(J,X)$. □

Theorem 1. *Let the assumptions* $(A1)$–$(A7)$ *hold. Then, the system* (1) *has at least one mild solution on* J.

Proof. For any $\epsilon > 0$, let $r > 0$ be large enough such that

$$r \geq N^*\|x_b\| + \frac{M\|E^{-1}\|}{\Gamma(\alpha)}(N^*b^{\alpha-1}+1)(\|x_0\|+M_1) + \frac{M\|E^{-1}\|}{\Gamma(\alpha)}(\frac{bp-b}{p\alpha-1})^{1-\frac{1}{p}}(\|\phi\|_{L^p}(N^*+1), \tag{6}$$

where $N^* = \frac{b}{\epsilon}(\frac{MM_B\|E^{-1}\|}{\Gamma(\alpha)})^2(\frac{p-1}{p\alpha-1})^{1-\frac{1}{p}}$. Define an operator $\Phi : B_r \to C_{1-\alpha}(J, X)$ by

$$(\Phi x)(t) = t^{\alpha-1}T_E(t)[x_0 - g(x)] + \int_0^t (t-s)^{\alpha-1}T_E(t-s)[f(s,x(s)) + Bu(s;x)]ds,$$

where

$$u(s;x) = B^*T_E^*(b-s)R(\epsilon, \Pi_0^b)\mathcal{P}(x),$$

$$\mathcal{P}(x) = x_b - b^{\alpha-1}T_E(b)(x_0 - g(x)) - \int_0^b (b-s)^{\alpha-1}T_E(b-s)f(s,x(s))ds.$$

Step 1. We will prove $\Phi : B_r \to B_r$.
For any $\epsilon > 0$, by assumptions $(A4)$–$(A7)$ and Lemma 1, we have

$$\|u(t;x)\| \leq \frac{MM_B\|E^{-1}\|}{\epsilon\Gamma(\alpha)}\|\mathcal{P}(x)\|, \quad x \in B_r, \ t \in J'$$

and

$$\|\mathcal{P}(x)\| \leq \|x_b\| + \frac{M\|E^{-1}\|b^{\alpha-1}}{\Gamma(\alpha)}(M_1 + \|x_0\|) + \frac{M\|E^{-1}\|}{\Gamma(\alpha)}(\frac{bp-b}{p\alpha-1})^{1-\frac{1}{p}}\|\phi\|_{L^p}, \quad x \in B_r.$$

Together this fact with (6), for any $\epsilon > 0$, we have

$$\begin{aligned}
t^{1-\alpha}\|(\Phi x)(t)\| &\leq \|T_E(t)[x_0 - g(x)]\| + t^{1-\alpha}\|\int_0^t (t-s)^{\alpha-1}T_E(t-s)[f(s,x(s)) + Bu(s)]ds\| \\
&\leq \frac{M\|E^{-1}\|}{\Gamma(\alpha)}(\|x_0\| + M_1) + b^{1-\alpha}\frac{M\|E^{-1}\|}{\Gamma(\alpha)}\int_0^t (t-s)^{\alpha-1}(\phi(s) + M_B\|u(s)\|)ds \\
&\leq \frac{M\|E^{-1}\|}{\Gamma(\alpha)}(\|x_0\| + M_1) + \frac{M\|E^{-1}\|}{\Gamma(\alpha)}(\frac{bp-b}{p\alpha-1})^{1-\frac{1}{p}}(\|\phi\|_{L^p} + M_B\|u\|_{L^p}) \\
&\leq N^*\|x_b\| + \frac{M\|E^{-1}\|}{\Gamma(\alpha)}(N^*b^{\alpha-1}+1)(\|x_0\| + M_1) \\
&\quad + \frac{M\|E^{-1}\|}{\Gamma(\alpha)}(\frac{bp-b}{p\alpha-1})^{1-\frac{1}{p}}\|\phi\|_{L^p}(N^*+1) \\
&\leq r.
\end{aligned}$$

Thus, $\|\Phi x\|_{C_{1-\alpha}} = \sup_{t \in J} t^{1-\alpha}\|(\Phi x)(t)\| \leq r$, which implies $\Phi : B_r \to B_r$.

Step 2. $\Phi : B_r \to B_r$ is continuous.
Let $\{x_n\} \subset B_r$ with $x_n \to \overline{x}$ as $n \to \infty$. From the continuity of f and g, we have

$$f(t, x_n(t)) \to f(t, \overline{x}(t)), \quad t \in J$$

and

$$g(x_n) \to g(\overline{x})$$

as $n \to \infty$. Since

$$\|(t-s)^{\alpha-1}[f(s,x_n(s)) - f(s,\overline{x}(s))]\| \leq 2(t-s)^{\alpha-1}\phi(s) \in L^1(J, \mathbb{R}^+),$$

it follows from the Lebesgue dominated convergence theorem that

$$\begin{aligned} & t^{1-\alpha}\|(\Phi x_n)(t) - (\Phi\overline{x})(t)\| \\ \leq \ & \|T_E(t)(g(x_n) - g(\overline{x}))\| + b^{1-\alpha}\frac{M\|E^{-1}\|}{\Gamma(\alpha)}\int_0^t (t-s)^{\alpha-1}\|f(s,x_n(s)) - f(s,\overline{x}(s))\|ds \\ \to \ & 0 \quad (n\to\infty). \end{aligned}$$

Hence,

$$\|\Phi x_n - \Phi\overline{x}\|_{C_{1-\alpha}} \to 0$$

as $n \to \infty$ and $\Phi : B_r \to B_r$ is continuous.

Step 3. The set $\{\Phi x : x \in B_r\}$ is relatively compact in $C_{1-\alpha}(J, X)$.

In order to prove the relative compactness of $\{\Phi x : x \in B_r\}$ in $C_{1-\alpha}(J, X)$, we prove that the set $\{\cdot^{1-\alpha}\Phi x(\cdot) : x \in B_r\}$ is relatively compact in $C(J, X)$.

Denote by

$$(\Phi_1 x)(t) = T_E(t)(x_0 - g(x)), \quad t \in J$$

and

$$(\Phi_2 x)(t) = t^{1-\alpha}\int_0^t (t-s)^{\alpha-1}T_E(t-s)[f(s,x(s)) + Bu(s)]ds, \quad t \in J.$$

Then for any $t \in J$, we have

$$t^{1-\alpha}\Phi x(t) = (\Phi_1 x)(t) + (\Phi_2 x)(t).$$

It is sufficient to prove that $\{\Phi_1 x : x \in B_r\}$ and $\{\Phi_2 x : x \in B_r\}$ are relatively compact in $C(J, X)$.

For any $x \in B_r$ and $t \in J$, by virtue of

$$\|T_I(t)(x_0 - g(x))\| \leq \frac{M}{\Gamma(\alpha)}(\|x_0\| + M_1),$$

we obtain that $\{(\Phi_1 x)(t) : x \in B_r, t \in J\}$ is relatively compact in X owing to the compactness of E^{-1}. It is obvious that the set $\{\Phi_1 x : x \in B_r\}$ is equi-continuous in $C(J, X)$ because $T_E(t)$ is continuous in the uniform operator topology for $t \geq 0$. Hence, it follows from the Ascoli–Arzela theorem that the set $\{\Phi_1 x : x \in B_r\}$ is relatively compact in $C(J, X)$.

By assumptions $(A4)$ and $(A6)$, we know that

$$f(t, x(t)) + Bu(t) \in L^p(J, X).$$

By Lemma 3, the set $\{\Phi_2 x : x \in B_r\}$ is relatively compact in $C(J, X)$. Consequently, the set $\{\Phi x : x \in B_r\}$ is relatively compact in $C_{1-\alpha}(J, X)$.

Hence, Φ is completely continuous in $C_{1-\alpha}(J, X)$. By the Schauder fixed point theorem, Φ has at least one fixed point in B_r, which is the mild solution of the system (1). □

Remark 3. *In [15], Lian et al. proved the existence of mild solutions of fractional evolution equations under the assumption that the nonlocal function g is continuous, uniformly bounded and satisfies some other conditions. In [2], Zhou et al. investigated the existence of mild solutions of fractional evolution equations when the nonlocal function g is Lipschitz continuous or completely continuous. In our Theorem 1, we only assume that the nonlocal function g is continuous and maps bounded subset into bounded set, without the Lipschitz continuity and the complete continuity and any other extra conditions we obtain the existence of mild solutions of the fractional evolution Equation (1). Hence, Theorem 1 greatly extends the main results in [2,15].*

If the assumptions $(A4)$ and $(A5)$ are replaced by the following conditions:

$(A4)'$ $f : J \times X \to X$ satisfies the following conditions.

(i) For each $x \in X$, $f(\cdot, x) : J \to X$ is strongly measurable, and for every $t \in J$, $f(\cdot, x) : X \to X$ is continuous.

(ii) There exists a function $\psi \in L^p(J, \mathbb{R}^+)$, $p\alpha > 1$ and a constant $\rho > 0$ such that

$$\|f(t,x)\| \le \psi(t) + \rho t^{1-\alpha}\|x\|, \quad t \in J, \ x \in X.$$

$(A5)'$ $g : C_{1-\alpha}(J, X) \to X$ is continuous and there exists a constant $M_2 > 0$ such that $\|g(x)\| \le M_2$ for any $x \in C_{1-\alpha}(J, X)$.
then by Theorem 1 we can obtain the following existence theorem.

Theorem 2. *Let the assumptions $(A1)$–$(A3)$, $(A4)'$, $(A5)'$, $(A6)$ and $(A7)$ hold. Then the system (1) has at least one mild solution in $C_{1-\alpha}(J, X)$.*

Proof. It is clear that $(A5)' \Rightarrow (A5)$ and $(A4)' \Rightarrow (A4)$ with $\phi(\cdot) = \psi(\cdot) + r\rho\cdot^{1-\alpha} \in L^p(J, X)$ for any $r > 0$ and $x \in B_r$. Therefore, by Theorem 1 we can prove that the system (1) has a mild solution $x \in C_{1-\alpha}(J, X)$. □

Now, we state and prove the approximate controllability of the fractional control system (1).

Theorem 3. *Let the conditions $(A1)$–$(A3)$, $(A4)''$, $(A5)'$ and $(A6)$ be satisfied, where*

$(A4)''$ $f : J \times X \to X$ satisfies the following conditions.

(i) For each $x \in X$, $f(\cdot, x) : J \to X$ is strongly measurable, and for every $t \in J$, $f(\cdot, x) : X \to X$ is continuous.

(ii) There exist a function $\varphi \in L^p(J, \mathbb{R}^+)$ with $p\alpha > 1$ such that

$$\|f(t,x)\| \le \varphi(t), \quad \forall t \in J, \ x \in X.$$

In addition, the linear fractional control system (4) is approximately controllable on J. Then the fractional control system (1) is approximately controllable on J.

Proof. It is clear that $(A4)'' \Rightarrow (A4)$ and $(A5)' \Rightarrow (A5)$. By Lemma 2 we know that the condition $(H7)$ holds. It follows from Theorem 1 that the system (1) has a mild solution $x_\epsilon \in C_{1-\alpha}(J, X)$ for every $\epsilon > 0$, which is expressed by

$$\begin{aligned} x_\epsilon(t) &= t^{\alpha-1}T_E(t)[x_0 - g(x)] + \int_0^t (t-s)^{\alpha-1}T_E(t-s)f(s, x_\epsilon(s))ds \\ &+ \int_0^t (t-s)^{\alpha-1}T_E(t-s)BB^*T_E^*(b-s)R(\epsilon, \Pi_0^b)\big[x_b - b^{\alpha-1}T_E(b)(x_0 - g(x)) \\ &- \int_0^b (b-\theta)^{\alpha-1}T_E(b-\theta)f(\theta, x_\epsilon(\theta))d\theta\big]ds. \end{aligned}$$

In view of $I - \Pi_0^b(\epsilon I + \Pi_0^b)^{-1} = \epsilon R(\epsilon, \Pi_0^b)$, we have

$$x_\epsilon(b) = x_b - \epsilon R(\epsilon, \Pi_0^b)p(x_\epsilon),$$

where

$$p(x_\epsilon) = x_b - b^{\alpha-1}T_E(b)(x_0 - g(x_\epsilon)) - \int_0^b (b-s)^{\alpha-1}T_E(b-s)f(s, x_\epsilon(s))ds.$$

By the assumption $(A5)'$, we have

$$\|b^{\alpha-1}(x_0 - g(x_\epsilon))\| \le b^{\alpha-1}(\|x_0\| + M_2).$$

Then the set $\{b^{\alpha-1}T_E(b)(x_0 - g(x_\epsilon))\}$ is relatively compact since $T_E(b)$ is a compact operator. There exists a subsequence of $\{b^{\alpha-1}T_E(b)(x_0 - g(x_\epsilon))\}$, still denoted by itself, and a function g^* such that

$$b^{\alpha-1}T_E(b)(x_0 - g(x_\epsilon)) \to g^* \quad (\epsilon \to 0^+).$$

By means of $(A4)''$ we have

$$\|f(\cdot, x_\epsilon(\cdot))\|_{L^p} = (\int_0^b \|f(s, x_\epsilon(s))\|^p ds)^{\frac{1}{p}} \leq \|\varphi\|_{L^p}.$$

Hence, the set $\{f(\cdot, x_\epsilon(\cdot))\}$ is bounded in $L^p(J, X)$. So there is a subsequence, still denoted by $\{f(\cdot, x_\epsilon(\cdot))\}$, converges weakly to some $f^*(\cdot) \in L^p(J, X)$, that is,

$$f(s, x_\epsilon(s)) \xrightarrow{w} f^*(s), \quad a.e.\ s \in J$$

as $\epsilon \to 0$. By Lemma 3 and the Lebesgue dominated convergence theorem, we can obtain

$$\int_0^b (b-s)^{\alpha-1}T_E(b-s)f(s, x_\epsilon(s))ds \to \int_0^b (b-s)^{\alpha-1}T_E(b-s)f^*(s)ds$$

as $\epsilon \to 0$. Denote by

$$h = x_b - g^* - \int_0^b (b-s)^{\alpha-1}T_E(b-s)f^*(s)ds.$$

Then by the definition of $p(x_\epsilon)$, we obtain that

$$p(x_\epsilon) \to h \ (\epsilon \to 0).$$

Consequently, we have

$$\begin{aligned} \|x_\epsilon(b) - x_b\| &= \|\epsilon R(\epsilon, \Pi_0^b)p(x_\epsilon)\| \\ &= \|\epsilon R(\epsilon, \Pi_0^b)(p(x_\epsilon) - h)\| + |\epsilon R(\epsilon, \Pi_0^b)h\| \\ &\to 0 \quad (\epsilon \to 0). \end{aligned}$$

By Definition 2, the fractional control system (1) is approximately controllable on J. □

4. An Example

Consider the Sobolev-type partial differential equation with Riemann-Liouville fractional derivatives

$$\begin{cases} {}^L D_t^{\frac{3}{4}}[(I - \frac{\partial^2}{\partial y^2})x(t,y)] = \frac{\partial^2}{\partial y^2}x(t,y) + \frac{e^{-3t}\sqrt{\sin x(t,y)}}{3+|x(t,y)|} + u(t), \quad (t,y) \in (0,1] \times [0,\pi], \\ x(t,0) = x(t,\pi) = 0, \quad t \in [0,1], \\ I_{0^+}^{1-\alpha}[(I - \frac{\partial^2}{\partial y^2})x(t,y)]|_{t=0} + \sum\limits_{i=1}^{m} c_i \sqrt[3]{\sin(t^{1-\alpha}x(t,y)) + 7} = x_0(y), \end{cases} \tag{7}$$

where $c_i > 0, i = 1, 2, \cdots, m$ are given positive constants.

Let $X = U := L^2[0,\pi]$. Denote $D(A) = D(E) := \{x \in X : x, x'$ are absolutely continuous, $x'' \in X$ and $x(t,0) = x(t,\pi) = 0\}$. We define two operators $A : D(A) \subset X \to X$ and $E : D(E) \subset X \to X$ by

$$Ax = \frac{\partial^2}{\partial y^2}x, \quad x \in D(A); \quad Ex = (I - \frac{\partial^2}{\partial y^2})x, \quad x \in D(E).$$

Let $e_n(y) = \sqrt{\frac{2}{\pi}} \sin ny, n \in \mathbb{N}$ be the orthonormal set of eigenvectors of A. By [4,16], we have

$$Ax = -\Sigma_{n=1}^{\infty} n^2 \langle x, e_n \rangle e_n, \quad x \in D(A)$$

and

$$Ex = \Sigma_{n=1}^{\infty} (1+n^2) \langle x, e_n \rangle e_n, \quad x \in D(E).$$

This implies, for any $x \in H$, that

$$E^{-1}x = \Sigma_{n=1}^{\infty} \frac{1}{1+n^2} \langle x, e_n \rangle e_n,$$

$$AE^{-1}x = \Sigma_{n=1}^{\infty} \frac{-n^2}{1+n^2} \langle x, e_n \rangle e_n$$

and

$$T(t)x = \Sigma_{n=1}^{\infty} e^{\frac{-n^2}{1+n^2}t} \langle x, e_n \rangle e_n,$$

where $T(t)x = e^{AE^{-1}t}x, t \geq 0$. Then E^{-1} is a linear operator which is compact and $\|E^{-1}\| \leq 1$. Hence,

$$T_E(t) = \frac{3}{4} \int_0^{\infty} E^{-1} \theta \xi_{\frac{3}{4}}(\theta) T(t^{\frac{3}{4}} \theta) d\theta$$

with

$$\|T_E(t)x\| \leq \frac{1}{\Gamma(\frac{3}{4})} \|x\|,$$

where

$$\xi_{\frac{3}{4}}(\theta) = \frac{1}{\pi} \sum_{n=1}^{\infty} (-1)^{n-1} \theta^{-\frac{3}{4}n-1} \frac{\Gamma(\frac{3}{4}n+1)}{n!} \sin(\frac{3}{4}n\pi), \ \theta \in (0, +\infty).$$

Let $x(t)(y) = x(t, y)$. Denote

$$f(t, x(t))(y) = \frac{e^{-3t}\sqrt{\sin x(t,y)}}{3 + |x(t,y)|}$$

and

$$g(x)(y) = \sum_{i=1}^{m} c_i \sqrt[3]{\sin(t^{1-\alpha} x(t,y)) + 7}.$$

Then the problem (7) can be rewritten as the abstract control system (1). Moreover, the assumptions $(A1)$–$(A6)$ are fulfilled with $\|f(t,x)\|_X = \frac{1}{3}$ and $\|g(x)\|_X \leq 2 \sum_{i=1}^{m} c_i$. If the linear system corresponding to (7) is approximately controllable on $[0,1]$, then by Theorem 3, the fractional partial differential equation of (7) is approximately controllable on $[0,1]$.

5. Conclusions

In this paper, with the aid of the compactness of the operator E^{-1}, we prove the existence of mild solutions of the fractional evolution system (1) without the compactness of operator semigroup. The Lipschitz continuity and the compactness of the nonlocal function g are not needed in our main results. Under the assumption that the associate linear control system (4) is approximately controllable, the approximate controllability of the fractional evolution system (1) is also studied.

Funding: The research is supported by the National Natural Science Function of China (No. 11701457).

Institutional Review Board Statement: Not applicable.

Informed Consent Statement: Not applicable.

Data Availability Statement: Not applicable.

Conflicts of Interest: The author declares no conflict of interest.

References

1. Du, M.L.; Wang, Z.H. Initialized fractional differential equations with Riemann-Liouville fractional-order derivative. *Eur. Phys. J. Spec. Top.* **2011**, *193*, 49–60. [CrossRef]
2. Zhou, Y.; Zhang, L.; Shen, X.H. Existence of mild solutions for fractional evolution equations. *J. Int. Equ. Appl.* **2013**, *25*, 557–585. [CrossRef]
3. Benchaabane, A.; Sakthivel, R. Sobolev-type fractional stochastic differential equations with non-Lipschitz coefficients. *J. Comput. Appl. Math.* **2017**, *312*, 65–73. [CrossRef]
4. Fečkan, M.; Wang, J.R.; Zhou, Y. Controllability of fractional functional evolution equations of Sobolev type via characteristic solution operators. *J. Optim. Theory Appl.* **2013**, *156*, 79–95.
5. Liang, J.; Yang, H. Controllability of fractional integro-differential evolution equations with nonlocal conditions. *Appl. Math. Comput.* **2015**, *254*, 20–29. [CrossRef]
6. Shu, X.B.; Wang, Q.Q. The existence and uniqueness of mild solutions for fractional differential equations with nonlocal conditions of order $1 < \alpha < 2$. *Comput. Math. Appl.* **2012**, *64*, 2100–2110.
7. Yang, H. Existence results of mild solutions for the fractional stochastic evolution equations of Sobolev type. *Symmetry* **2020**, *12*, 1031. [CrossRef]
8. Yang, H.; Zhao, Y.J. Controllability of fractional evolution systems of Sobolev type via resolvent operators. *Bound. Value Prob.* **2020**, *2020*, 119. [CrossRef]
9. Hernández, E.; O'Regan, D. Controllability of Volterra-Fredholm type systmes in Banach spaces. *J. Frankl. Inst.* **2009**, *346*, 95–101. [CrossRef]
10. Chang, Y.K.; Pereira, A.; Ponce, R. Approximate controllability for fractional differential equations of Sobolev type via properties on resolvent operators. *Fract. Calc. Appl. Anal.* **2017**, *20*, 963–987. [CrossRef]
11. Sakthivel, R.; Suganya, S.; Anthoni, S.M. Approximate controllability of fractional stochastic evolution equations. *Comput. Math. Appl.* **2012**, *63*, 660–668. [CrossRef]
12. Yang, H. Approximate controllability of Sobolev type fractional evolutin equations of order $\alpha \in (1,2)$ via resolvent operator. *J. Appl. Anal. Comput.* **2021**, *11*, 2981–3000.
13. Balachandran, K.; Dauer, J.P. Controllability of functional differential systems of Sobolev type in Banach spaces. *Kybernetika* **1998**, *34*, 349–357.
14. Mahmudov, N.I. Approximate controllability of semilinear deterministic and stochastic evolution equation in abstract spaces. *SIAM J. Control Optim.* **2003**, *42*, 1604–1622. [CrossRef]
15. Lian, T.T.; Fan, Z.B.; Li, G. Approximate controllability of semilinear fractional differential systems of order $1 < q < 2$ via resolvent operators. *Filomat* **2017**, *18*, 5769–5781.
16. Lightbourne, J.H.; Rankin, S.M. A partial functional differential equation of Sobolev type. *J. Math. Anal. Appl.* **1983**, *93*, 328–337. [CrossRef]

fractal and fractional

Article

New Discussion on Approximate Controllability for Semilinear Fractional Evolution Systems with Finite Delay Effects in Banach Spaces via Differentiable Resolvent Operators

Daliang Zhao * and Yongyang Liu

School of Mathematics and Statistics, Shandong Normal University, Jinan 250014, China; 2020020448@stu.sdnu.edu.cn
* Correspondence: dlzhao928@sdnu.edu.cn

Abstract: This manuscript mainly discusses the approximate controllability for certain fractional delay evolution equations in Banach spaces. We introduce a suitable complete space to deal with the disturbance due to the time delay. Compared with many related papers on this issue, the major tool we use is a set of differentiable properties based on resolvent operators, rather than the theory of C_0-semigroup and the properties of some associated characteristic solution operators. By implementing an iterative method, some new controllability results of the considered system are derived. In addition, the system with non-local conditions and a parameter is also discussed as an extension of the original system. An instance is proposed to support the theoretical results.

Keywords: approximate controllability; resolvent operator; delay; nonlocal conditions; parameter

Citation: Zhao, D.; Liu, Y. New Discussion on Approximate Controllability for Semilinear Fractional Evolution Systems with Finite Delay Effects in Banach Spaces via Differentiable Resolvent Operators. *Fractal Fract.* **2022**, *6*, 424. https://doi.org/10.3390/fractalfract6080424

Academic Editor: Rodica Luca

Received: 7 July 2022
Accepted: 28 July 2022
Published: 30 July 2022

1. Introduction

This manuscript mainly investigates the sufficient conditions of the approximate controllability of some fractional control systems as below:

$$\begin{cases} {}^C D^{\beta} x(t) = Ax(t) + f(t, x_t) + Bu(t), & t \in I := [0, a], \\ x(t) = \phi(t), & t \in [-b, 0], \end{cases} \tag{1}$$

and

$$\begin{cases} {}^C D^{\beta} x(t) = Ax(t) + f(t, x_t) + Bu(t), & t \in I := [0, a], \\ x(t) + \lambda g_t(x) = \phi(t), & t \in [-b, 0], \end{cases} \tag{2}$$

where ${}^C D^{\beta}$ means the Caputo derivative with order $\frac{1}{2} < \beta \leq 1$. X and U are Banach spaces. Linear operator $A : \mathcal{D} \subset X \to X$ is unbounded with dense domain $\mathcal{D}$. The delay term x_t is explained in Equation (5). The control u takes values in $L^2(I; U)$. For any $t \in [-b, 0]$, the non-local term $g_t : C([-b, a]; X) \to X$ satisfies some given conditions. λ is a parameter. Let $\phi \in L^1([-b, 0]; X)$. $B : L^2(I; U) \to L^2(I; \mathcal{D})$ is a bounded linear operator. f is a non-linearity that will be specified later.

Fractional differential systems and evolution systems have been studied extensively owing to its widespread backgrounds of some scientific and engineering realms, such as signal processing, finance, anomalous diffusion phenomena, heat conduction, etc. We refer readers to [1–4] for further detailed information. On the other side, controllability has gained a lot of importance and interest, and it plays a significant role in the description of various dynamical problems [5–8]. It is known to all that the fractional evolution system is closely related to time. In this regard, it has something in common with the controllability problem. Therefore, the controllability of some kinds of fractional evolution systems has become an important research hotspot. For example, exact controllability and approximate controllability are two mainstream research directions and they have important differences from the viewpoint of mathematics. Exact controllability can steer the control system to any given final time point. The control operator is usually assumed to be reversible. Then, the controllability problem is transformed into a fixed point problem [9–13]. Furthermore, an induced inverse of the control operator is not necessarily true in infinite-dimensional space. In consideration of these strong assumptions, more and more scholars begin to study the approximate controllability in various abstract spaces, which means that it can steer the control system to an any small neighborhood of final time point [14–20]. In addition, controllability of fractional evolution systems also has important applications in the research areas of logical control networks or Boolean networks.

For instance, S. Ji [16] and F. Ge et al. [17] studied the approximate controllability of fractional semi-linear non-local evolution systems and fractional differential systems with impulsive conditions via approximating method under the assumption that A generated a C_0-semigroup, respectively. Moreover, the approximate controllability of some other fractional systems, such as stochastic equations, neutral equations, etc., have also been deeply investigated (one can see [18–20] for more details). However, approximate controllability of the linear systems correspondence to the considered systems is necessary in this method. Therefore, some other approaches, such as the iterative method, are used to solve the approximate controllability problems for some evolution systems. For example, H. Zhou [21] obtained a sufficient condition of the approximate controllability for certain first-order evolution equations by utilizing iterative approach and the theory of strongly continuous semigroup. Authors in [22] dealt with the approximate controllability of some evolution systems with fractional order without delay by using iterative method. The properties of C_0-semigroup are also included. By applying the same method, [23] also derived some appropriate controllability conclusions for some fractional differential equations with no delay effects.

It is noted that the results of approximate controllability discussed above are based on the C_0-semigroup together with some associated characteristic solution operators [24]. However, in many cases, infinitesimal generator A may not be able to generate a C_0-semigroup, but it can generate a resolvent operator instead [25]. On the other side, a resolvent operator can degenerate into a C_0-semigroup when the integral kernel is equal to 1, that is, a resolvent operator covers a C_0-semigroup as a special case. Of course, this can also be explained by the subordinate principle [26].

In comparision with results in [27] considering the influence of delay, we shall study the approximate controllability for some fractional control systems on the supposition that A is an infinitesimal generator of a differentiable resolvent operator rather than a C_0-semigroup; we shall consider a control problem with variable delay, not fixed delay by contrast; the function $\phi(t)$ is supposed to be integrable rather than continuous. Under these generalized conditions, the difficulty mainly lies in how to overcome the obstacles caused by the variable delay and how to make use of the differentiability of resolvent operators. We solve this problem by means of a new special complete space we introduced and the theory of differentiable resolvent operator developed in [25].

Motivated by the aforementioned discussions, we shall establish a set of new approximate controllability results for systems (1) and (2) by using iterative method. As far as we know, the approximate controllability for the fractional evolution equations with finite variable delay and with non-local conditions and a parameter under the hypothesis that A generate a differentiable resolvent operator is still an untreated topic in the existing literature. Therefore, it is necessary to make further investigations to fill the gap in this regard.

Summarily, different from the above discussed papers, some highlights of the manuscript are presented as follows. (i) The approximate controllability of considered systems is studied on the supposition that the resolvent operator is differentiable, rather than utilizing the theory of C_0-semigroup together with the properties of associated characteristic solution operators; (ii) The delay-induced-difficulty is overcome by introducing a special complete integrable space since we generalize the delay term from continuity to integrability compared with some other papers; (iii) The system (2) discussed in this manuscript is provided with some more generalized nonlocal conditions compared with many related papers [5,9,11,16,17] ($\lambda = 1,\ t = 0$).

This manuscript is arranged as below. In the next part, we include some necessary preparations for the main controllability results. InSection 3, some existence results of the mild solution of the considered systems are obtained. In Section 4, we investigate the approximate controllability for the fractional delay control systems, and the case with non-local conditions and a parameter is discussed in Section 5. An instance is proposed in Section 6 to illustrate our abstract conclusions.

2. Preparations

Let X be a Banach space with norm $\|x\|$, $x \in X$. The linear operator $A : \mathcal{D} \subset X \to X$ is closed and unbounded, in which $\mathcal{D}$ means the domain of A equipped with graph norm $\|x\|_{\mathcal{D}} = \|x\| + \|Ax\|$. $C(I;X)$ stands for the space with all the continuous functions mapping I into X equipped with the sup-norm $\|x\|_C$, $L^2(I;X)$ stands for the space of all Bochner integrable functions mapping I into X equipped with the norm $\|x\|_{L^2(I;X)} = \left(\int_0^a \|x(t)\|^2 dt\right)^{1/2}$, and $C^\beta(I;X)$ denotes the space of all the β-Hölder continuous functions mapping I into X provided with the norm $\|x\|_{C^\beta(I;X)} = \|x\|_{C(I;X)} + [|x|]_{C^\beta(I;X)}$, where

$$[|x|]_{C^\beta(I;X)} = \sup_{t,s \in I, t \neq s} \frac{\|x(t) - x(s)\|}{(t-s)^\beta}.$$

In the next discussion, the following equation

$$x(t) = \frac{1}{\Gamma(\beta)} \int_0^t \frac{Ax(s)}{(t-s)^{1-\beta}} ds,\ t \geq 0, \tag{3}$$

is assumed to possess an resolvent operator $\{\mathfrak{R}(t)\}_{t \geq 0}$ on X.

Definition 1 ([28]). *The fractional integral of order $\beta > 0$ with the lower limit zero is written as*

$$I_{0^+}^\beta x(t) = \frac{1}{\Gamma(\beta)} \int_0^t (t-s)^{\beta-1} x(s) ds,\ t > 0,$$

where Γ denotes the Gamma function.

Definition 2 ([28]). *The fractional derivative of the function $x \in C((0,+\infty);\mathbb{R})$ in the Caputo sense can be defined by*

$${}^C D_{0^+}^\beta x(t) = \frac{1}{\Gamma(n-\beta)} \int_0^t \frac{x^{(n)}(s)}{(t-s)^{\beta-n+1}} ds,\ t > 0,$$

where $n = [\beta] + 1$, $[\beta]$ represents the integer part of the positive constant β.

Definition 3 ([25]). *Suppose a set of operators $\{\mathfrak{R}(t)\}_{t \geq 0}$ to be bounded and linear on space X. If it fulfills hypotheses as below:*
(i) $\mathfrak{R}(t)$ is strongly continuous on $\mathbb{R}_+$ and $\mathfrak{R}(0) = \mathcal{I}$;
(ii) $\mathfrak{R}(t)\mathcal{D} \subset \mathcal{D}$; for each $x \in \mathcal{D}$, $t \geq 0$, it satisfies $A\mathfrak{R}(t)x = \mathfrak{R}(t)Ax$;
(iii) The following equality can be established

$$\mathfrak{R}(t)x = x + \frac{1}{\Gamma(\beta)} \int_0^t \frac{Ax(s)}{(t-s)^{1-\beta}} ds,$$

then we define it as a resolvent operator of Equation (3).

Definition 4 ([25]). *A resolvent operator $\mathfrak{R}(t)$ of Equation (3) is known as differentiable, if it satisfies $\mathfrak{R}(\cdot)x \in W^{1,1}_{loc}(\mathbb{R}_+;X)$, $\forall x \in \mathcal{D}$. In addition, for $\forall x \in \mathcal{D}$, there exists a function $\omega \in L^1_{loc}(\mathbb{R}_+)$ satisfying*

$$\|\dot{\mathfrak{R}}(t)x\| \leq \omega(t)\|x\|_{\mathcal{D}} \text{ a.e. on } \mathbb{R}_+.$$

Consider the following equality

$$x(t) = w(t) + \frac{1}{\Gamma(\beta)}\int_0^t \frac{Ax(s)}{(t-s)^{1-\beta}}ds, \ t \in I, \tag{4}$$

where $w \in L^1(I;X)$.

Definition 5 ([25]). *A function $x \in C(I;X)$ is said to be a mild solution of equality Equation (4) if it satisfies $\int_0^t \frac{x(s)}{(t-s)^{1-\beta}}ds \in \mathcal{D}$ and*

$$x(t) = w(t) + \frac{1}{\Gamma(\beta)}A\int_0^t \frac{x(s)}{(t-s)^{1-\beta}}ds, \ \forall t \in I.$$

The following result provides another equivalent form of mild solution for Equation (4).

Lemma 1 ([25]). *If the resolvent operator $\mathfrak{R}(t)$ of Equation (4) is differentiable, then for $w \in C(I;\mathcal{D})$, the following function*

$$x(t) = \int_0^t \dot{\mathfrak{R}}(t-s)w(s)ds + w(t), \ t \in I,$$

is called a mild solution of Equation (4).

To end this section, the set $L^1([-b,0];X)$ is proposed which stands for a space of all the integrable functions mapping $[-b,0]$ into X equipped with norm $\|\cdot\|_{L^1[-b,0]} = \int_{-b}^0 \|\cdot(t)\|dt$. Obviously, it is complete. Considering Equation (1), for any $x \in C(I;X)$, $t \in I$, let

$$x_t(\theta) = \begin{cases} x(t+\theta), & t+\theta \geq 0, \\ \phi(t+\theta), & t+\theta \leq 0, \end{cases} \tag{5}$$

for any $\theta \in [-b,0]$, where $\phi(t)$ denotes the function mentioned in Equation (1). Obviously, we can check that $x_t \in L^1([-b,0];X)$.

On the basis of Equation (5), we give the following result.

Lemma 2. *Assume that $x_n \to x_0$ $(n \to +\infty)$ for $x_n, x_0 \in C(I;X)$. Then, for any $t \in I$, one can derive that $(x_n)_t \to (x_0)_t$ $(n \to +\infty)$ for $(x_n)_t, (x_0)_t \in L^1([-b,0];X)$.*

Proof. In view of (5), we can easily derive

$$\|(x_n)_t - (x_0)_t\|_{L^1[-b,0]} = \begin{cases} \int_0^t \|x_n(s) - x_0(s)\|ds, & t \leq b, \\ \int_{t-b}^t \|x_n(s) - x_0(s)\|ds, & t \geq b, \end{cases}$$

which indicates that

$$\|(x_n)_t - (x_0)_t\|_{L^1[-b,0]} \leq b\|x_n - x_0\|_C, \tag{6}$$

for any $t \in I$. □

3. Existence Results

This part establishes the existence results of mild solution of Equation (1). Now, assume resolvent operator $\{\mathfrak{R}(t)\}_{t\geq 0}$ to be differentiable. Let ω_A be the function mentioned in Definition 4.

From Definition 1 and Definition 5, we can obtain

Definition 6. *For any $u \in L^2(I;U)$, a function $x \in C(I;X)$ is called a mild solution of Equation (1) on I, provided that*

$$x(t) = \phi(0) + \frac{1}{\Gamma(\beta)} A \int_0^t \frac{x(s)}{(t-s)^{1-\beta}} ds + \frac{1}{\Gamma(\beta)} \int_0^t \frac{f(s,x_s)}{(t-s)^{1-\beta}} ds + \frac{1}{\Gamma(\beta)} \int_0^t \frac{Bu(s)}{(t-s)^{1-\beta}} ds,$$

where $\int_0^t \frac{x(s)}{(t-s)^{1-\beta}} ds \in \mathcal{D}$, $\forall t \in I$, and x_s is defined by Equation (5).

In the next content, we will need the following assumptions.

Hypothesis 1 (H1). *f is a continuous function from $I \times L^1([-b,0];X)$ into $\mathcal{D}$ and $\phi(0) \in \mathcal{D}$. There is a real number $\beta_1 \in (0,\beta)$ and a function $m \in L^{\frac{1}{\beta_1}}(I;\mathbb{R}_+)$ satisfying $\|f(t,x)\|_{\mathcal{D}} \leq m(t)$ for any $t \in I$ and $x \in L^1([-b,0];X)$.*

Hypothesis 2 (H2). *For any $x, y \in L^1([-b,0];X)$, there exists a constant $L > 0$ satisfying*

$$\|f(t,x) - f(t,y)\|_{\mathcal{D}} \leq L\|x-y\|_{L^1[-b,0]}.$$

For simplicity, we denote

$$\mathfrak{F}_x(t) = \frac{1}{\Gamma(\beta)} \int_0^t \frac{f(s,x_s)}{(t-s)^{1-\beta}} ds, \quad \mathfrak{B}_u(t) = \frac{1}{\Gamma(\beta)} \int_0^t \frac{Bu(s)}{(t-s)^{1-\beta}} ds, \quad \vartheta = \frac{\beta-1}{1-\beta_1}.$$

From Lemma 1 and Definition 6, we can derive the mild solution of Equation (1) on I of another expression as follows.

Definition 7. *For any $u \in L^2(I;U)$, a function $x \in C(I;X)$ is called a mild solution of Equation (1) on I, provided that*

$$x(t) = \phi(0) + \mathfrak{F}_x(t) + \mathfrak{B}_u(t) + \int_0^t \dot{\mathfrak{R}}(t-s)(\phi(0) + \mathfrak{F}_x(s) + \mathfrak{B}_u(s)) ds.$$

Remark 1. *It follows from Definition 1 that the classical solution of system Equation (1) is a convolution equation. Hence, it is natural to apply Laplace transform on it to express an appropriate formula for the mild solution representation of the considered system. For this purpose, we suppose that resolvent operator $\mathfrak{R}(t)$ is exponentially bounded. By utilizing the theory of the Laplace transform and inverse Laplace transform, the mild solution of Equation (1) could be defined by*

$$x(t) = \begin{cases} \mathfrak{R}(t)\phi(0) + \int_0^t \mathcal{K}_{\odot}(t-s) f(s,x_s) ds + \int_0^t \mathcal{K}_{\odot}(t-s) Bu(s) ds, & t \in I = [0,a], \\ \phi(t), \quad t \in [-b,0], \end{cases}$$

where $\mathcal{K}_{\odot}(t) = \frac{d}{dt}(I_{0+}^{\beta}\mathfrak{R}(t))$ and x_s is defined by Equation (5).

Lemma 3. *(i) If hypothesis (H1) holds, then for arbitrarily given $x \in C(I;X)$, we have $\mathfrak{F}_x \in C^{\beta-\beta_1}(I;\mathcal{D})$, and*

$$[|\mathfrak{F}_x|]_{C^{\beta-\beta_1}(I;\mathcal{D})} \leq \frac{2\|m\|_{L^{\frac{1}{\beta_1}}}}{\Gamma(\beta)(1+\vartheta)^{1-\beta_1}}.$$

(ii) For any $u \in L^2(I;U)$, we have $\mathfrak{B}_u \in C^{\beta-\frac{1}{2}}(I;\mathcal{D})$, and

$$[|\mathfrak{B}_u|]_{C^{\beta-\frac{1}{2}}(I;\mathcal{D})} \leq \frac{2\|Bu\|_{L^2(I;\mathcal{D})}}{\Gamma(\beta)(2\beta-1)^{\frac{1}{2}}}.$$

Proof. (i) For arbitrarily given $x \in C(I;X)$, $\forall t \in [0,a)$, $\forall h > 0$ satisfying $t+h \in [0,a]$, by using Hölder inequality, one can derive

$$\begin{aligned}
& \|\mathfrak{F}_x(t+h) - \mathfrak{F}_x(t)\|_{\mathcal{D}} \\
\leq\ & \frac{1}{\Gamma(\beta)}\int_0^t [(t-s)^{\beta-1} - (t+h-s)^{\beta-1}]\|f(s,x_s)\|_{\mathcal{D}}ds \\
& + \frac{1}{\Gamma(\beta)}\int_t^{t+h}(t+h-s)^{\beta-1}\|f(s,x_s)\|_{\mathcal{D}}ds \\
\leq\ & \frac{1}{\Gamma(\beta)}\left(\int_0^t \left[(t-s)^{\beta-1} - (t+h-s)^{\beta-1}\right]^{\frac{1}{1-\beta_1}}ds\right)^{1-\beta_1}\|m\|_{L^{\frac{1}{\beta_1}}} \\
& + \frac{1}{\Gamma(\beta)}\left(\int_t^{t+h}\left[(t+h-s)^{\beta-1}\right]^{\frac{1}{1-\beta_1}}ds\right)^{1-\beta_1}\|m\|_{L^{\frac{1}{\beta_1}}} \\
\leq\ & \frac{1}{\Gamma(\beta)}\left(\int_0^t \left[(t-s)^{\vartheta} - (t+h-s)^{\vartheta}\right]ds\right)^{1-\beta_1}\|m\|_{L^{\frac{1}{\beta_1}}} \\
& + \frac{1}{\Gamma(\beta)}\left(\int_t^{t+h}(t+h-s)^{\vartheta}ds\right)^{1-\beta_1}\|m\|_{L^{\frac{1}{\beta_1}}} \\
\leq\ & \frac{\|m\|_{L^{\frac{1}{\beta_1}}}}{\Gamma(\beta)(1+\vartheta)^{1-\beta_1}}(t^{1+\vartheta} - (t+h)^{1+\vartheta} + h^{1+\vartheta})^{1-\beta_1} + \frac{\|m\|_{L^{\frac{1}{\beta_1}}}}{\Gamma(\beta)(1+\vartheta)^{1-\beta_1}}h^{(1+\vartheta)(1-\beta_1)} \\
\leq\ & \frac{2\|m\|_{L^{\frac{1}{\beta_1}}}}{\Gamma(\beta)(1+\vartheta)^{1-\beta_1}}h^{(1+\vartheta)(1-\beta_1)} \\
=\ & \frac{2\|m\|_{L^{\frac{1}{\beta_1}}}}{\Gamma(\beta)(1+\vartheta)^{1-\beta_1}}h^{\beta-\beta_1},
\end{aligned}$$

which indicates that $[|\mathfrak{F}_x|]_{C^{\beta-\beta_1}(I;\mathcal{D})} \leq \frac{2\|m\|_{L^{\frac{1}{\beta_1}}}}{\Gamma(\beta)(1+\vartheta)^{1-\beta_1}}$ and $\mathfrak{F}_x \in C^{\beta-\beta_1}(I;\mathcal{D})$.

(ii) In the light of the proof for (i), it can be obtained similarly. □

Lemma 4. *(i) If Hypotheses (H1) and (H2) hold, then for $\forall x, y \in C(I;X)$,*

$$\|\mathfrak{F}_x(t) - \mathfrak{F}_y(t)\|_{\mathcal{D}} \leq \frac{La^{\beta}b}{\Gamma(\beta+1)}\|x-y\|_C,\ \forall t \in I,$$

and

$$\|\mathfrak{F}_x(t)\|_{\mathcal{D}} \leq \frac{a^{\beta-\beta_1}\|m\|_{L^{\frac{1}{\beta_1}}}}{\Gamma(\beta)(1+\vartheta)^{1-\beta_1}},\ \forall t \in I.$$

(ii) For any $u, v \in L^2(I;U)$,

$$\|\mathfrak{B}_u(t) - \mathfrak{B}_v(t)\|_{\mathcal{D}} \leq \frac{1}{\Gamma(\beta)}\sqrt{\frac{a^{2\beta-1}}{2\beta-1}}\|Bu - Bv\|_{L^2(I;\mathcal{D})},\ \forall t \in I,$$

and

$$\|\mathfrak{B}_u(t)\|_{\mathcal{D}} \leq \frac{1}{\Gamma(\beta)}\sqrt{\frac{a^{2\beta-1}}{2\beta-1}}\|Bu\|_{L^2(I;\mathcal{D})},\ \forall t \in I.$$

Proof. (i) In view of Lemma 2, we can obtain

$$\begin{aligned}\|\mathfrak{F}_x(t)-\mathfrak{F}_y(t)\|_{\mathcal{D}} &\leq \frac{1}{\Gamma(\beta)}\int_0^t (t-s)^{\beta-1}\|f(s,x_s)-f(s,y_s)\|_{\mathcal{D}}ds \\ &\leq \frac{L}{\Gamma(\beta)}\int_0^t (t-s)^{\beta-1}\|x_s-y_s\|_{L[-b,0]}ds \\ &\leq \frac{Lb}{\Gamma(\beta)}\int_0^t (t-s)^{\beta-1}\|x-y\|_C ds \\ &= \frac{La^\beta b}{\Gamma(\beta+1)}\|x-y\|_C, \ \forall t\in I.\end{aligned}$$

In addition,

$$\begin{aligned}\|\mathfrak{F}_x(t)\|_{\mathcal{D}} &\leq \frac{1}{\Gamma(\beta)}\int_0^t (t-s)^{\beta-1}\|f(s,x_s)\|_{\mathcal{D}}ds \\ &\leq \frac{1}{\Gamma(\beta)}\left(\int_0^t [(t-s)^{\beta-1}]^{\frac{1}{1-\beta_1}}ds\right)^{1-\beta_1}\|m\|_{L^{\frac{1}{\beta_1}}} \\ &\leq \frac{t^{(1+\vartheta)(1-\beta_1)}}{\Gamma(\beta)(1+\vartheta)^{1-\beta_1}}\|m\|_{L^{\frac{1}{\beta_1}}} \\ &\leq \frac{a^{\beta-\beta_1}\|m\|_{L^{\frac{1}{\beta_1}}}}{\Gamma(\beta)(1+\vartheta)^{1-\beta_1}}, \ \forall t\in I.\end{aligned}$$

(ii) Obviously, we can obtain that

$$\begin{aligned}\|\mathfrak{B}_u(t)-\mathfrak{B}_v(t)\|_{\mathcal{D}} &\leq \frac{1}{\Gamma(\beta)}\int_0^t (t-s)^{\beta-1}\|Bu(s)-Bv(s)\|_{\mathcal{D}}ds \\ &\leq \frac{1}{\Gamma(\beta)}\left(\int_0^t [(t-s)^{\beta-1}]^2 ds\right)^{\frac{1}{2}}\|\mathfrak{B}_u-\mathfrak{B}_v\|_{L^2(I;\mathcal{D})} \\ &= \frac{1}{\Gamma(\beta)}\sqrt{\frac{a^{2\beta-1}}{2\beta-1}}\|\mathfrak{B}_u-\mathfrak{B}_v\|_{L^2(I;\mathcal{D})}, \ \forall t\in I.\end{aligned}$$

Similarly, we can obtain

$$\|\mathfrak{B}_u(t)\|_{\mathcal{D}} \leq \frac{1}{\Gamma(\beta)}\sqrt{\frac{a^{2\beta-1}}{2\beta-1}}\|Bu\|_{L^2(I;\mathcal{D})}, \ \forall t\in I.$$

□

Theorem 1. *If the Hypotheses (H1) and (H2) hold, then for any given control $u \in L^2(I;U)$, fractional evolution system Equation (1) has an unique mild solution on I, provided that*

$$\frac{La^\beta b(1+\|\omega_A\|_{L^1(I)})}{\Gamma(\beta+1)} < 1. \quad (7)$$

Proof. In view of Definition 7, for any $t \in I$, define an operator $\Psi : C(I;X) \to C(I;X)$ as below

$$(\Psi x)(t) = \phi(0) + \mathfrak{F}_x(t) + \mathfrak{B}_u(t) + \int_0^t \dot{\mathfrak{R}}(t-s)(\phi(0)+\mathfrak{F}_x(s)+\mathfrak{B}_u(s))ds. \quad (8)$$

Evidently, we only need to consider the fixed point of Ψ.

Step 1. Ψ maps $C(I;X)$ into $C(I;X)$.

For every $x \in C(I;X),\ 0 < t < t+h \leq a$, we have

$$\begin{aligned}(\Psi x)(t+h) - (\Psi x)(t) &= \mathfrak{F}_x(t+h) - \mathfrak{F}_x(t) + \mathfrak{B}_u(t+h) - \mathfrak{B}_u(t) \\ &+ \int_0^{t+h} \dot{\mathfrak{R}}(t+h-s)\phi(0)ds - \int_0^t \dot{\mathfrak{R}}(t-s)\phi(0)ds \\ &+ \int_0^{t+h} \dot{\mathfrak{R}}(t+h-s)\mathfrak{F}_x(s)ds - \int_0^t \dot{\mathfrak{R}}(t-s)\mathfrak{F}_x(s)ds \\ &+ \int_0^{t+h} \dot{\mathfrak{R}}(t+h-s)\mathfrak{B}_u(s)ds - \int_0^t \dot{\mathfrak{R}}(t-s)\mathfrak{B}_u(s)ds \\ &= \sum_{i=1}^{5} \Upsilon_i,\end{aligned}$$

where

$\Upsilon_1 = \mathfrak{F}_x(t+h) - \mathfrak{F}_x(t)$,
$\Upsilon_2 = \mathfrak{B}_u(t+h) - \mathfrak{B}_u(t)$,
$\Upsilon_3 = \int_0^{t+h} \dot{\mathfrak{R}}(t+h-s)\phi(0)ds - \int_0^t \dot{\mathfrak{R}}(t-s)\phi(0)ds$,
$\Upsilon_4 = \int_0^{t+h} \dot{\mathfrak{R}}(t+h-s)\mathfrak{F}_x(s)ds - \int_0^t \dot{\mathfrak{R}}(t-s)\mathfrak{F}_x(s)ds$,
$\Upsilon_5 = \int_0^{t+h} \dot{\mathfrak{R}}(t+h-s)\mathfrak{B}_u(s)ds - \int_0^t \dot{\mathfrak{R}}(t-s)\mathfrak{B}_u(s)ds$.

By Lemma 3, we can obtain

$$\|\Upsilon_1\| \leq \frac{2\|m\|_{L^{\frac{1}{\beta_1}}}}{\Gamma(\beta)(1+\vartheta)^{1-\beta_1}} h^{\beta-\beta_1} \to 0,\ as\ h \to 0,$$

and

$$\|\Upsilon_2\| \leq \frac{2\|Bu\|_{L^2(I;\mathcal{D})}}{\Gamma(\beta)(2\beta-1)^{\frac{1}{2}}} h^{\beta-\frac{1}{2}} \to 0,\ as\ h \to 0.$$

Notice that

$$\begin{aligned}\Upsilon_3 &= \int_0^h \dot{\mathfrak{R}}(t+h-s)\phi(0)ds + \int_h^{t+h} \dot{\mathfrak{R}}(t+h-s)\phi(0)ds - \int_0^t \dot{\mathfrak{R}}(t-s)\phi(0)ds \\ &= \int_0^h \dot{\mathfrak{R}}(t+h-s)\phi(0)ds.\end{aligned}$$

Then, we have

$$\|\Upsilon_3\| \leq \|\phi(0)\|_{\mathcal{D}} \int_0^h \omega_A(t+h-s)ds \to 0,\ as\ h \to 0.$$

In addition, since

$$\begin{aligned}\Upsilon_4 &= \int_0^h \dot{\mathfrak{R}}(t+h-s)\mathfrak{F}_x(s)ds + \int_h^{t+h} \dot{\mathfrak{R}}(t+h-s)\mathfrak{F}_x(s)ds - \int_0^t \dot{\mathfrak{R}}(t-s)\mathfrak{F}_x(s)ds \\ &= \int_0^h \dot{\mathfrak{R}}(t+h-s)\mathfrak{F}_x(s)ds + \int_0^t \dot{\mathfrak{R}}(s)\mathfrak{F}_x(t+h-s)ds - \int_0^t \dot{\mathfrak{R}}(s)\mathfrak{F}_x(t-s)ds,\end{aligned}$$

we thus can derive from Definition 4, Lemma 3 and Lemma 4 that

$$\begin{aligned}
\|Y_4\| &\leq \int_0^h \|\dot{\mathfrak{R}}(t+h-s)\mathfrak{F}_x(s)\|ds + \int_0^t \|\dot{\mathfrak{R}}(s)(\mathfrak{F}_x(t-s+h) - \mathfrak{F}_x(t-s))\|ds \\
&\leq \int_0^h \omega_A(t+h-s)\|\mathfrak{F}_x(s)\|_{\mathcal{D}}ds + \int_0^t \omega_A(s)[|\mathfrak{F}_x|]_{C^{\beta-\beta_1}(I;\mathcal{D})}h^{\beta-\beta_1}ds \\
&\leq \frac{a^{\beta-\beta_1}\|m\|_{L^{\frac{1}{\beta_1}}}}{\Gamma(\beta)(1+\vartheta)^{1-\beta_1}}\int_0^h \omega_A(t+h-s)ds + \frac{2\|m\|_{L^{\frac{1}{\beta_1}}}h^{\beta-\beta_1}}{\Gamma(\beta)(1+\vartheta)^{1-\beta_1}}\int_0^t \omega_A(s)ds \\
&\leq \frac{\|m\|_{L^{\frac{1}{\beta_1}}}}{\Gamma(\beta)(1+\vartheta)^{1-\beta_1}}\left(a^{\beta-\beta_1}\int_0^h \omega_A(t+h-s)ds + 2h^{\beta-\beta_1}\|\omega_A\|_{L^1(I)}\right) \\
&\quad \to 0,\ as\ h \to 0.
\end{aligned}$$

It is not difficult to have

$$\begin{aligned}
Y_5 &= \int_0^h \dot{\mathfrak{R}}(t+h-s)\mathfrak{B}_u(s)ds + \int_h^{t+h} \dot{\mathfrak{R}}(t+h-s)\mathfrak{B}_u(s)ds - \int_0^t \dot{\mathfrak{R}}(t-s)\mathfrak{B}_u(s)ds \\
&= \int_0^h \dot{\mathfrak{R}}(t+h-s)\mathfrak{B}_u(s)ds + \int_0^t \dot{\mathfrak{R}}(s)\mathfrak{B}_u(t+h-s)ds - \int_0^t \dot{\mathfrak{R}}(s)\mathfrak{B}_u(t-s)ds,
\end{aligned}$$

which together with Lemma 3 and Lemma 4 implies

$$\begin{aligned}
\|Y_5\| &\leq \int_0^h \|\dot{\mathfrak{R}}(t+h-s)\mathfrak{B}_u(s)\|ds + \int_0^t \|\dot{\mathfrak{R}}(s)(\mathfrak{B}_u(t-s+h) - \mathfrak{B}_u(t-s))\|ds \\
&\leq \int_0^h \omega_A(t+h-s)\|\mathfrak{B}_u(s)\|_{\mathcal{D}}ds + \int_0^t \omega_A(s)[|\mathfrak{B}_u|]_{C^{\beta-\frac{1}{2}}(I;\mathcal{D})}h^{\beta-\frac{1}{2}}ds \\
&\leq \frac{1}{\Gamma(\beta)}\sqrt{\frac{a^{2\beta-1}}{2\beta-1}}\|Bu\|_{L^2(I;\mathcal{D})}\int_0^h \omega_A(t+h-s)ds \\
&\quad + \frac{2\|Bu\|_{L^2(I;\mathcal{D})}h^{\beta-\frac{1}{2}}}{\Gamma(\beta)(2\beta-1)^{\frac{1}{2}}}\int_0^t \omega_A(s)ds \\
&\leq \frac{\|Bu\|_{L^2(I;\mathcal{D})}}{\Gamma(\beta)(2\beta-1)^{\frac{1}{2}}}\left(a^{\beta-\frac{1}{2}}\int_0^h \omega_A(t+h-s)ds + 2h^{\beta-\frac{1}{2}}\|\omega_A\|_{L^1(I)}\right) \\
&\quad \to 0,\ as\ h \to 0.
\end{aligned}$$

Hence, $\|(\Psi x)(t+h) - (\Psi x)(t)\| \to 0,\ h \to 0$, which indicates that $\Psi x \in C(I;X)$, $\forall x \in C(I;X)$.

Step 2. Ψ is contractive on $C(I;X)$.

In fact, Lemma 2 indicates that

$$\begin{aligned}
\|(\Psi x)(t) - (\Psi y)(t)\| &\leq \|\mathfrak{F}_x(t) - \mathfrak{F}_y(t)\|_{\mathcal{D}} + \int_0^t \omega_A(t-s)\|\mathfrak{F}_x(s) - \mathfrak{F}_y(s)\|_{\mathcal{D}}ds \\
&\leq \frac{1}{\Gamma(\beta)}\int_0^t (t-s)^{\beta-1}\|f(s,x_s) - f(s,y_s)\|_{\mathcal{D}}ds \\
&\quad + \frac{1}{\Gamma(\beta)}\int_0^t \omega_A(t-s)\left(\int_0^s (s-\tau)^{\beta-1}\|f(\tau,x_\tau) - f(\tau,y_\tau)\|_{\mathcal{D}}d\tau\right)ds \\
&\leq \frac{L}{\Gamma(\beta)}\int_0^t (t-s)^{\beta-1}\|x_s - y_s\|_{L^1[-b,0]}ds \\
&\quad + \frac{L}{\Gamma(\beta)}\int_0^t \omega_A(t-s)\left(\int_0^s (s-\tau)^{\beta-1}\|x_\tau - y_\tau\|_{L^1[-b,0]}d\tau\right)ds \\
&\leq \frac{La^\beta b}{\Gamma(\beta+1)}\|x-y\|_C + \frac{La^\beta b\|\omega_A\|_{L^1(I)}}{\Gamma(\beta+1)}\|x-y\|_C \\
&= \frac{La^\beta b(1+\|\omega_A\|_{L^1(I)})}{\Gamma(\beta+1)}\|x-y\|_C,\ \forall t \in I,
\end{aligned}$$

which shows that

$$\|\Psi x - \Psi y\|_C \leq \frac{La^\beta b(1 + \|\omega_A\|_{L^1(I)})}{\Gamma(\beta+1)}\|x - y\|_C.$$

Hence, Ψ is contractive on $C(I;X)$ due to the Hypothesis (1). By utilizing the Banach's fixed point theorem, we find that Ψ has a unique fixed point on $C(I;X)$. □

4. Main Results

This part gives the results of approximate controllability of Equation (1). Let us show the next definitions which is critical to our work.

Definition 8. *The set $K(a,f) = \{x(a;u) : u \in L^2(I;U)\}$ is said to be the reachable set of Equation (1) at final point a, where $x(t;u)$ is the state value of Equation (1) at time point t corresponding to control $u \in L^2(I;U)$. If $\overline{K(a,f)} = X$, we call that Equation (1) is approximately controllable on I, where $\overline{K(a,f)}$ stands for the closure of $K(a,f)$.*

Denote Nemytskii operator $\mathcal{F} : C(I;X) \to L^2(I;\mathcal{D})$ corresponding to the non-linearity f by

$$\mathcal{F}x(t) = f(t, x_t), \ \ t \in I,$$

and define the continuous operator $\mathcal{P} : L^2(I;\mathcal{D}) \to X$ by

$$\mathcal{P}y = \frac{1}{\Gamma(\beta)}\int_0^a \frac{y(t)}{(a-t)^{1-\beta}}dt + \frac{1}{\Gamma(\beta)}\int_0^a \dot{\mathfrak{R}}(a-t)\left(\int_0^t \frac{y(s)}{(t-s)^{1-\beta}}ds\right)dt, \ \ y \in L^2(I;\mathcal{D}). \tag{9}$$

It is not difficult to see that the approximate controllability of Equation (1) on I is equivalent to that the set $K(a,f)$ is dense on X. That is to say, we can obtain an equivalent definition as below.

Definition 9. *System (1) is said to be approximately controllable on I, provided that for any $\varepsilon > 0$ and any final value $\xi \in X$, there exists a control term $u_\varepsilon \in L^2(I;U)$ satisfying*

$$\|\xi - \mathfrak{R}(a)\phi(0) - \mathcal{P}(\mathcal{F}x_\varepsilon) - \mathcal{P}(Bu_\varepsilon)\| < \varepsilon,$$

where $x_\varepsilon(t) = x(t;u_\varepsilon)$ is a mild solution of Equation (1) corresponding to $u_\varepsilon \in L^2(I;U)$.

In addition, following hypotheses to obtain our approximate controllability results are presented.

Hypothesis 3 (H3). *For arbitrarily given $\varepsilon > 0$ and $\psi \in L^2(I;\mathcal{D})$, there is a function $u \in L^2(I;U)$ satisfying*

$$\|\mathcal{P}\psi - \mathcal{P}(Bu)\| < \varepsilon,$$

and

$$\|Bu\|_{L^2(I;\mathcal{D})} < \mu\|\psi\|_{L^2(I;\mathcal{D})},$$

where $\mu > 0$ is a real number independent of ψ.

Hypothesis 4 (H4). *Under Equation (7), the following inequality holds*

$$\mu La^{\frac{1}{2}}b\left(1 - \frac{La^\beta b(1 + \|\omega_A\|_{L^1(I)})}{\Gamma(\beta+1)}\right)^{-1}\frac{1 + \|\omega_A\|_{L^1(I)}}{\Gamma(\beta)}\sqrt{\frac{a^{2\beta-1}}{2\beta-1}} < 1.$$

Next, to demonstrate our main result, we still need a lemma as below.

Lemma 5. *If the Hypotheses (H1) and (H2) hold, then for any mild solutions of Equation (1), the following result holds*

$$\|x_1 - x_2\|_C \le \left(1 - \frac{La^\beta b(1 + \|\omega_A\|_{L^1(I)})}{\Gamma(\beta+1)}\right)^{-1} \frac{1 + \|\omega_A\|_{L^1(I)}}{\Gamma(\beta)} \sqrt{\frac{a^{2\beta-1}}{2\beta-1}} \|Bu_1 - Bu_2\|_{L^2(I;\mathcal{D})},$$

for any $u_1, u_2 \in L^2(I;U)$.

Proof. The mild solution $x_i(t) = x(t;u_i)$ $(i = 1,2)$ of system (1) corresponding to u_i $(i = 1,2)$ satisfy

$$x_i(t) = \phi(0) + \mathfrak{F}_{x_i}(t) + \mathfrak{B}_{u_i}(t) + \int_0^t \dot{\mathfrak{R}}(t-s)(\phi(0) + \mathfrak{F}_{x_i}(s) + \mathfrak{B}_{u_i}(s))ds, \ \forall t \in I.$$

From Lemma 4, one can obtain

$$\begin{aligned}
& \|x_1(t) - x_2(t)\| \\
\le\ & \|\mathfrak{F}_{x_1}(t) - \mathfrak{F}_{x_2}(t)\| + \|\mathfrak{B}_{u_1}(t) - \mathfrak{B}_{u_2}(t)\| \\
& + \int_0^t \|\dot{\mathfrak{R}}(t-s)(\mathfrak{F}_{x_1}(s) - \mathfrak{F}_{x_2}(s))\|ds + \int_0^t \|\dot{\mathfrak{R}}(t-s)(\mathfrak{B}_{u_1}(t) - \mathfrak{B}_{u_2}(t))\|ds \\
\le\ & \|\mathfrak{F}_{x_1}(t) - \mathfrak{F}_{x_2}(t)\|_{\mathcal{D}} + \|\mathfrak{B}_{u_1}(t) - \mathfrak{B}_{u_2}(t)\|_{\mathcal{D}} \\
& + \int_0^t \omega_A(t-s)\|\mathfrak{F}_{x_1}(s) - \mathfrak{F}_{x_2}(s)\|_{\mathcal{D}}ds + \int_0^t \omega_A(t-s)\|\mathfrak{B}_{u_1}(s) - \mathfrak{B}_{u_2}(s)\|_{\mathcal{D}}ds \\
\le\ & \frac{La^\beta b(1 + \|\omega_A\|_{L^1(I)})}{\Gamma(\beta+1)}\|x_1 - x_2\|_C + \frac{1 + \|\omega_A\|_{L^1(I)}}{\Gamma(\beta)} \sqrt{\frac{a^{2\beta-1}}{2\beta-1}} \|Bu_1 - Bu_2\|_{L^2(I;\mathcal{D})}, \forall t \in I,
\end{aligned}$$

which implies that

$$\|x_1 - x_2\|_C \le \left(1 - \frac{La^\beta b(1 + \|\omega_A\|_{L^1(I)})}{\Gamma(\beta+1)}\right)^{-1} \frac{1 + \|\omega_A\|_{L^1(I)}}{\Gamma(\beta)} \sqrt{\frac{a^{2\beta-1}}{2\beta-1}} \|Bu_1 - Bu_2\|_{L^2(I;\mathcal{D})}.$$

□

Theorem 2. *If the Hypotheses (H1)–(H4) hold, then system (1) is approximately controllable on I.*

Proof. It is only needed to prove that $\mathcal{D} \subset \overline{K(a,f)}$ due to the fact that $\mathcal{D}$ is dense, i.e., for $\forall \varepsilon > 0$ and $\xi \in \mathcal{D}$, there is a control term $u_\varepsilon \in L^2(I;U)$ satisfying

$$\|\xi - \mathfrak{R}(a)\phi(0) - \mathcal{P}(\mathcal{F}x_\varepsilon) - \mathcal{P}(Bu_\varepsilon)\| < \varepsilon. \tag{10}$$

It follows from the Definition 3 that $\mathfrak{R}(a)\phi(0) \in \mathcal{D}$ for $\phi(0) \in \mathcal{D}$, which indicates that $\xi - \mathfrak{R}(a)\phi(0) \in \mathcal{D}$. Then, it can be see that there exists some $\psi \in L^2(I;\mathcal{D})$, such that $\mathcal{P}\psi = \xi - \mathfrak{R}(a)\phi(0)$. Next, we are to show that there is a control $u_\varepsilon \in L^2(I;U)$ satisfying (4.2). Actually, for $\forall \varepsilon > 0$ and $u_1 \in L^2(I;U)$, in view of (H3), we can find a function $u_2 \in L^2(I;U)$, such that

$$\|\xi - \mathfrak{R}(a)\phi(0) - \mathcal{P}(\mathcal{F}x_1) - \mathcal{P}(Bu_2)\| < \frac{\varepsilon}{2^2},$$

where $x_1(t) = x(t;u_1)$, $t \in I$. Further, for $u_2 \in L^2(I;U)$, we can find a function $v_2 \in L^2(I;U)$ by (H3) again, such that

$$\|\mathcal{P}(\mathcal{F}x_2 - \mathcal{F}x_1) - \mathcal{P}(Bv_2)\| < \frac{\varepsilon}{2^3},$$

where $x_2(t) = x(t; u_2),\ t \in I$. Then, from Lemma 5, we derive

$$\begin{aligned} & \|Bv_2\|_{L^2(I;\mathcal{D})} \\ \leq\ & \mu\|\mathcal{F}x_2 - \mathcal{F}x_1\|_{L^2(I;\mathcal{D})} \\ \leq\ & \mu L a^{\frac{1}{2}} b \|x_2 - x_1\|_C \\ \leq\ & \mu L a^{\frac{1}{2}} b \left(1 - \frac{La^{\beta} b(1 + \|\omega_A\|_{L^1(I)})}{\Gamma(\beta+1)}\right)^{-1} \frac{1 + \|\omega_A\|_{L^1(I)}}{\Gamma(\beta)} \sqrt{\frac{a^{2\beta-1}}{2\beta-1}} \|Bu_1 - Bu_2\|_{L^2(I;\mathcal{D})}. \end{aligned}$$

Next, define $u_3 = u_2 - v_2 \in L^2(I; U)$, and, thus, it has

$$\begin{aligned} & \|\xi - \mathfrak{R}(a)\phi(0) - \mathcal{P}(\mathcal{F}x_2) - \mathcal{P}(Bu_3)\| \\ \leq\ & \|\xi - \mathfrak{R}(a)\phi(0) - \mathcal{P}(\mathcal{F}x_1) - \mathcal{P}(Bu_2)\| + \|\mathcal{P}(Bv_2) - \mathcal{P}(\mathcal{F}x_2 - \mathcal{F}x_1)\| \\ \leq\ & \left(\frac{1}{2^2} + \frac{1}{2^3}\right)\varepsilon. \end{aligned}$$

Utilizing induction, it is not hard to find a sequence $\{u_n : n \geq 1\} \subset L^2(I; U)$ satisfying

$$\|\xi - \mathfrak{R}(a)\phi(0) - \mathcal{P}(\mathcal{F}x_n) - \mathcal{P}(Bu_{n+1})\| < \left(\frac{1}{2^2} + \frac{1}{2^3} + \cdots + \frac{1}{2^{n+1}}\right)\varepsilon, \tag{11}$$

where $x_n(t) = x(t; u_n),\ t \in I$, and

$$\begin{aligned} & \|Bu_{n+1} - Bu_n\|_{L^2(I;\mathcal{D})} \\ \leq\ & \mu L a^{\frac{1}{2}} b \left(1 - \frac{La^{\beta} b(1 + \|\omega_A\|_{L^1(I)})}{\Gamma(\beta+1)}\right)^{-1} \frac{1 + \|\omega_A\|_{L^1(I)}}{\Gamma(\beta)} \sqrt{\frac{a^{2\beta-1}}{2\beta-1}} \|Bu_n - Bu_{n-1}\|_{L^2(I;\mathcal{D})}. \end{aligned}$$

From Hypothesis (H4), we know that $\{Bu_n : n \geq 1\}$ is a Cauchy sequence on $L^2(I; \mathcal{D})$, and, thus, there exists a function $u^* \in L^2(I; \mathcal{D})$ satisfying

$$\lim_{n \to \infty} Bu_n = u^* \ \ in \ L^2(I; \mathcal{D}).$$

Hence, for every $\varepsilon > 0$, we can obtain a number $N > 0$ satisfying

$$\|\mathcal{P}(Bu_{N+1}) - \mathcal{P}(Bu_N)\| < \frac{\varepsilon}{2}. \tag{12}$$

Then, from Equations (11) and (12), it is easy to deduce

$$\begin{aligned} & \|\xi - \mathfrak{R}(a)\phi(0) - \mathcal{P}(\mathcal{F}x_N) - \mathcal{P}(Bu_N)\| \\ \leq\ & \|\xi - \mathfrak{R}(a)\phi(0) - \mathcal{P}(\mathcal{F}x_N) - \mathcal{P}(Bu_{N+1})\| + \|\mathcal{P}(Bu_{N+1}) - \mathcal{P}(Bu_N)\| \\ \leq\ & \left(\frac{1}{2^2} + \frac{1}{2^3} + \cdots + \frac{1}{2^{N+1}}\right)\varepsilon + \frac{\varepsilon}{2} < \varepsilon, \end{aligned}$$

where $x_N(t) = x(t; u_N),\ t \in I$. Consequently, the fractional evolution system (1) is approximately controllable on I. □

5. Non-Local Conditions

The practical usefulness and significance of non-local conditions in the field of technology and mechanical engineering have been demonstrated [5,9,11]. It has been proved that the non-local initial condition can provide more accurate descriptions than the classical initial conditions. Therefore, we concern the following system involving non-local conditions and a parameter as below:

$$\begin{cases} {}^C D^{\beta} x(t) = Ax(t) + f(t, x_t) + Bu(t), & t \in I := [0, a], \\ x(t) + \lambda g_t(x) = \phi(t), & t \in [-b, 0]. \end{cases}$$

Firstly, we present the following hypothesis about the non-local conditions.

Hypothesis 5 (H5). *$g_t : C([-b,a];X) \to \mathcal{D}$, for any $t \in [-b,0]$;*
(i) For $\forall x, y \in C(I;X)$, there has a number $l > 0$ satisfying

$$\|g_t(x) - g_t(y)\|_{\mathcal{D}} \leq l\|x - y\|_C;$$

(ii) The non-local term $g_t(x)$ is continuous in $t \in [-b,0]$ for all $x \in C([-b,a];X)$, and there has a constant $C > 0$ satisfying $\|g_t(x)\|_{\mathcal{D}} \leq C$.

Next, for $\forall x \in C(I;X)$ and $t \in I$, let

$$x_t(\theta) = \begin{cases} x(t+\theta), & t+\theta \geq 0, \\ \phi(t+\theta) - \lambda g_{t+\theta}(x), & t+\theta \leq 0, \end{cases} \tag{13}$$

for $\forall\theta \in [-b,0]$. Obviously, we can check that $x_t \in L^1([-b,0];X)$. On the basis of Equation (13) and (H5), we have the following result similar to Lemma 2.

Lemma 6. *Assume that $x_n \to x_0$ $(n \to +\infty)$ for $x_n, x_0 \in C(I;X)$. Then, for any $t \in I$, one can derive that $(x_n)_t \to (x_0)_t$ $(n \to +\infty)$ for $(x_n)_t, (x_0)_t \in L^1([-b,0];X)$, and satisfies*

$$\|(x_n)_t - (x_0)_t\|_{L^1[-b,0]} \leq (|\lambda| l + 1)b\|x_n - x_0\|_C,\ t \in I.$$

Proof. In accordance with Equation (13) and condition (H5), we can draw the inequalities as below:

$$\begin{aligned} \|(x_n)_t - (x_0)_t\|_{L^1[-b,0]} &= \int_{-b}^{0} \|(x_n)_t(\theta) - (x_0)_t(\theta)\| d\theta \\ &= \int_{t-b}^{0} |\lambda| \|g_s(x_n) - g_s(x_0)\| ds + \int_0^t \|x_n(s) - x_0(s)\| ds \\ &\leq |\lambda| l b\|x_n - x_0\|_C + b\|x_n - x_0\|_C \\ &= (|\lambda| l + 1)b\|x_n - x_0\|_C,\ t \leq b, \end{aligned}$$

and

$$\begin{aligned} \|(x_n)_t - (x_0)_t\|_{L^1[-b,0]} &= \int_{-b}^{0} \|(x_n)_t(\theta) - (x_0)_t(\theta)\| d\theta \\ &= \int_{t-b}^{t} \|x_n(s) - x_0(s)\| ds \\ &\leq b\|x_n - x_0\|_C,\ t \geq b, \end{aligned}$$

which imply that

$$\|(x_n)_t - (x_0)_t\|_{L^1[-b,0]} \leq (|\lambda| l + 1)b\|x_n - x_0\|_C,$$

for any $t \in I$. □

Definition 10. *(i) For any $u \in L^2(I;U)$, a function $x \in C(I;X)$ is called a mild solution of Equation (2) on I, provided that*

$$x(t) = \phi(0) - \lambda g_0(x) + \mathfrak{F}_x(t) + \mathfrak{B}_u(t) + \int_0^t \dot{\mathfrak{R}}(t-s)(\phi(0) - \lambda g_0(x) + \mathfrak{F}_x(s) + \mathfrak{B}_u(s))ds,\ t \in I.$$

(ii) System (2) is said to be approximately controllable on I, provided that for any $\varepsilon > 0$ and any final value $\xi \in X$, there exists a control term $u_\varepsilon \in L^2(I;U)$ satisfying

$$\|\xi - \mathfrak{R}(a)(\phi(0) - \lambda g_0(x_\varepsilon)) - \mathcal{P}(\mathcal{F}x_\varepsilon) - \mathcal{P}(Bu_\varepsilon)\| < \varepsilon,$$

where $x_\varepsilon(t) = x(t;u_\varepsilon)$ is a mild solution of Equation (2) corresponding to $u_\varepsilon \in L^2(I;U)$.

Theorem 3. *In accordance with the proof steps of Theorem 1, one finds that if the Hypotheses (H1)–(H2) hold, then for any given control $u \in L^2(I;U)$, system (2) has an unique mild solution on I, provided that*

$$(1 + \|\omega_A\|_{L^1(I)})\left(|\lambda|l + \frac{La^\beta(|\lambda|l+1)b}{\Gamma(\beta+1)}\right) < 1. \tag{14}$$

Under the condition Equation (14), we further suppose the following hypothesis:

Hypothesis 6 (H6). *The following inequality holds*

$$\mu La^{\frac{1}{2}}(|\lambda|l+1)b\left(1-(1+\|\omega_A\|_{L^1(I)})\left(|\lambda|l+\frac{La^\beta(|\lambda|l+1)b}{\Gamma(\beta+1)}\right)\right)^{-1}\frac{1+\|\omega_A\|_{L^1(I)}}{\Gamma(\beta)}\sqrt{\frac{a^{2\beta-1}}{2\beta-1}} < 1.$$

In addition, to obtain the non-local results, we still need a lemma as below.

Lemma 7. *If the hypotheses (H1)–(H2) hold, then for any mild solutions of system (2), the following result holds*

$$\|x_1 - x_2\|_C \le \left(1-(1+\|\omega_A\|_{L^1(I)})\left(|\lambda|l+\frac{La^\beta(|\lambda|l+1)b}{\Gamma(\beta+1)}\right)\right)^{-1}\frac{1+\|\omega_A\|_{L^1(I)}}{\Gamma(\beta)}\sqrt{\frac{a^{2\beta-1}}{2\beta-1}}\|Bu_1 - Bu_2\|_{L^2(I;\mathcal{D})},$$

for any $u_1, u_2 \in L^2(I;U)$.

By means of iterative method utilized in Theorem 2 similarly, we now can obtain the main controllability result of the non-local case:

Theorem 4. *If the Hypotheses (H1)–(H3) and (H5) hold, then system (2) is approximately controllable on I.*

Remark 2. *Usually, the non-local condition can be given as follows*

$$\lambda g_t(x) = \lambda \sum_{i=1}^{q} l_i x(t + \iota_i),\ t \in [-b, 0],$$

where l_i $(i = 1, \cdots, q)$ are some real numbers; $0 < \iota_1 < \iota_2 < \cdots < \iota_q \le a$. When $\lambda = 1$ and at time $t = 0$, it is evident that

$$g_0(x) = g(x) = \sum_{i=1}^{q} l_i x(\iota_i),$$

which is exactly the case in [5,9,11,16,17].

6. Applications

Evolutionary fractional behavior has widespread backgrounds of some practical fields of science and engineering. For example, in an electrical circuit, the voltage produced by some non-linear device can be expressed by the non-linear term f in the evolution systems; some related resistances can be represented by A; and linear operator B can denote some inductances. On the other hand, non-local conditions are more extensive in practical applications because they usually includes many other conditions, such as conditions of initial value, multipoint average, and periodic, etc. In this part, we consider the following fractional non-local delayed evolution systems

$$\begin{cases} \frac{\partial^{\frac{3}{4}}}{\partial t^{\frac{3}{4}}}x(t,\xi) = \frac{\partial^2}{\partial \xi^2}x(t,\xi) + \frac{\omega(t)e^{-t}}{1+e^{2t}}\int_{t-b}^{t} \varrho(t-s)\sin(x(s,\xi))ds + Bu(t,\xi), \ (t,\xi) \in [0,a]\times(0,\pi), \\ x(t,0) = x(t,\pi) = 0, \ t \in [0,a], \\ x(t,\xi) + \lambda\sum_{j=1}^{m} k_j \sin(x(\varsigma_j + t,\xi)) = \phi(t,\xi), \ (t,\xi) \in [-b,0]\times[0,\pi], \ \varsigma_j \in [0,a], \end{cases} \tag{15}$$

where $\omega \in C([0,a];\mathbb{R})$, $\varrho \in L^1_{loc}(\mathbb{R}_+)$, and $\phi \in C^{2,1}([-b,0]\times[0,\pi];\mathbb{R})$. $\phi(t,0) = \phi(t,\pi) = 0, \forall t \in [-b,0]$.

Let $X = U = L^2([0,\pi])$, $Ax = x''$ for $x \in \mathcal{D}$, where

$$\mathcal{D} = \{x \in X : x, x' \mathit{are\ absolutely\ continuous}, x'' \in X, x(0) = x(\pi) = 0\}.$$

Evidently, A is an infinitesimal generator of a semigroup $\{T(t)\}_{t\geq 0}$ satisfying

$$T(t)x = \sum_{n=1}^{\infty} e^{-n^2 t}\langle x,\delta_n\rangle\delta_n, \ x \in X.$$

In view of subordinate principle (Chapter 3, [26]), we know that A is also an infinitesimal generator of a continuous differentiable bounded linear operators family $\{\mathfrak{R}(t)\}_{t\geq 0}$ satisfying $\mathfrak{R}(0) = \mathcal{I}$, and

$$\mathfrak{R}(t) = \int_0^{\infty} \eta_{t,\beta}(s)T(s)ds, \ t > 0,$$

where $\eta_{t,\beta}(s) = t^{-\beta}\Phi_\beta(st^{-\beta})$, and

$$\Phi_\beta(y) = \sum_{n=0}^{\infty} \frac{(-y)^n}{n!\Gamma(-\beta n + 1 - \beta)} = \frac{1}{2\pi i}\int_{\mathcal{H}} \zeta^{\beta-1} exp(\zeta - y\zeta^\beta)d\zeta, \ 0 < \beta < 1,$$

where $\mathcal{H}$ is a contour which encircles the origin once counterclockwise.

For each $u \in L^2([0,a];U)$, one has

$$u(t) = \sum_{n=0}^{\infty} u_n(t)\delta_n, \ u_n(t) = \langle u(t),\delta_n\rangle.$$

Then, an operator B can be defined by

$$Bu = \sum_{n=1}^{\infty} \overline{u}_n\delta_n,$$

where

$$\overline{u}_n(t) = \begin{cases} 0, & 0 \leq t < a - \frac{a}{n^2}, \\ u_n(t), & a - \frac{a}{n^2} \leq t \leq a, \end{cases}$$

for every $n = 1, 2, \cdots$. This ensures that B is a bounded linear operator. In addition, the operator $\mathcal{P}$ in Equation (9) is exactly the case of the operator in [29] when $B = \mathcal{I}$ and $t = a$. Furthermore, denote by

$$\begin{aligned} &\beta = \frac{3}{4} \in (\frac{1}{2}, 1], \\ &{}^C D^{\frac{3}{4}} x(t)(\xi) = \frac{\partial^{\frac{3}{4}}}{\partial t^{\frac{3}{4}}} x(t,\xi), \\ &x(t)(\xi) = x(t,\xi), \\ &Bu(t)(\xi) = Bu(t,\xi), \\ &\phi(t)(\xi) = \phi(t,\xi), \end{aligned}$$

$$g_t(x)(\xi) = \sum_{j=1}^{m} k_j \sin(x(\varsigma_j + t, \xi)),$$

$$f(t, x_t)(\xi) = \frac{\varpi(t)e^{-t}}{1+e^{2t}} \int_{t-b}^{t} \varrho(t-s)\sin(x(s,\xi))ds.$$

Hence, Equation (15) can be regarded as

$$\begin{cases} {}^{C}D^{\beta}x(t) = Ax(t) + f(t, x_t) + Bu(t), & t \in [0, a], \\ x(t) + \lambda g_t(x) = \phi(t), & t \in [-b, 0], \end{cases}$$

In addition, it can be checked that f, B, g_t, ϕ satisfy all assumptions in Theorem 4. Therefore, system (15) is approximately controllable on $[0, a]$. In addition, it is well known to all that the prospect of digital signal processing (DSP) is widespread and developmental, and digital filters play a significant role in it. Therefore, in this part, we also present the filter pattern of the system we studied which is given in Figure 1.

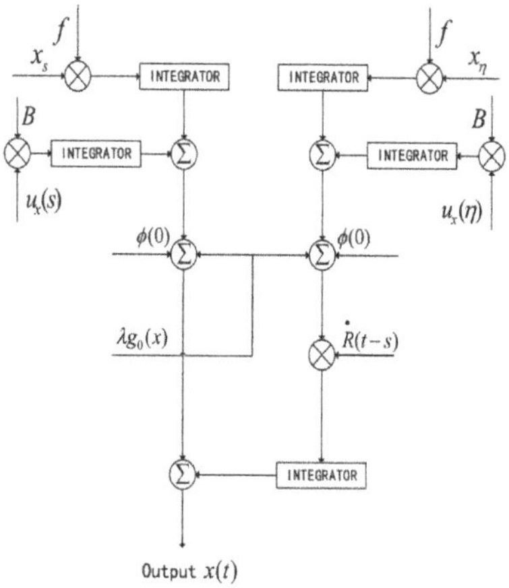

Figure 1. Filter system.

For any time t, the resultant values of samples x_t and $f(t)$ are produced and transferred to the integrators I_1 and I_2, where the signals are integrated over time 0 to t. The signals of resultant values of B and $u_x(t)$ are integrated in integrators I_3 and I_4. Integrators I_1 and I_3 are entered into summer network-1; Integrators I_2 and I_4 are entered into summer network-2. Inputs $\phi(t)$ and $\lambda g_t(x)$ at time $t = 0$ are added up in the summer network-3 and summer network-4. The integral for the product of $\mathfrak{R}(t-s)$ and the signals in summer network-4 over time 0 to t is performed in integrators I_5. At last, move the above outputs and integrators I_5 to summer network-5, and, thus, the final outputs $x(t)$ is derived, which is bounded and approximately controllable.

7. Conclusions

In this manuscript, some approximate controllability results of fractional delay systems with non-local conditions and a parameter are derived by using an iterative method. We substitute for the theory of C_0-semigroup and its associated characteristic solution operators by utilizing differentiability properties about resolvent operator. A special complete space is used to assist in solving the disturbance due to delay effects. Then, the current results seem to be more general and generalize some recent analogous outcomes, e.g., [21–23,27].

By means of iterative method, some further new study can be devoted to the approximate controllability of fractional impulsive systems as below:

$$\begin{cases} {}^C D^{\beta} x(t) = Ax(t) + f(t, x_t, Q_x(t)) + Bu(t), \ \ a.e.\, t \in I = [0, a], \\ \Delta x(t_i) = x(t_i^+) - x(t_i^-) = I_i(x(t_i^-)), \ \ i = 1, 2, \cdots, m, \\ x(t) + \lambda g_t(x) = \phi(t), \ \ t \in [-b, 0], \end{cases}$$

where $Q_x(t) = \int_0^t q(t, s, x_s) ds$, $q : \Lambda \times L([-b, 0]; X) \to X$ and $\Lambda = \{(t, s) \in I \times I : s \leq t\}$. The impulsive items I_i $(i = 1, 2, \cdots, m)$ are given functions that satisfy some appropriate hypotheses. $\phi \in L^1([-b, 0]; X)$. The main tools we are about to use here can be the theory of differentiable resolvent operators or analytic resolvent operators [25,30,31]. Furthermore, evolutionary fractional behavior is more accurately captured by variable-order fractional calculus. To this end, extending the present results to the more generalized variable-order fractional system will be an interesting problem.

Author Contributions: Investigation, D.Z.; writing-original draft, D.Z.; writing-review and editing, Y.L.; software, Y.L.; conception of the work, D.Z.; Validation, D.Z.; Revising, D.Z. and Y.L. All authors have read and agreed to the published version of the manuscript.

Funding: This research was funded by the National Natural Science Foundation of China under grant number 62073204.

Data Availability Statement: Not applicable.

Conflicts of Interest: The authors declare no conflict of interest.

References

1. Mao, J.; Zhao, D. Multiple positive solutions for nonlinear fractional differential equations with integral boundary value conditions and a parameter. *J. Funct. Spaces* **2019** *2019*, 2787569. [CrossRef]
2. Hu, B.; Song, Q.; Zhao, Z. Robust state estimation for fractional-order complex-valued delayed neural networks with interval parameter uncertainties: LMI approach. *Appl. Math. Comput.* **2020**, *373*, 125033. [CrossRef]
3. Cai, C.; Hu, J.; Wang, Y. Asymptotics of Karhunen-Loève eigenvalues for sub-fractional Brownian motion and its application. *Fractal Fract.* **2021**, *5*, 226. [CrossRef]
4. Zhao, D.; Liu, Y. Controllability of nonlinear fractional evolution systems in Banach spaces: A survey. *Electron. Res. Arch.* **2021**, *29*, 3551–3580. [CrossRef]
5. Liang, J.; Yang, H. Controllability of fractional integro-differential evolition equations with nonlocal conditions. *Appl. Math. Comput.* **2015**, *254*, 20–29. [CrossRef]
6. Liu, Y.; O'Regan, D. Controllability of impulsive functional differential systems with nonlocal conditions. *Electron. J. Differ. Equ.* **2013**, *2013*, 194.
7. Vijayakumar, V.; Selvakumar, A.; Murugesu, R. Controllability for a class of fractional neutral integro-differential equations with unbounded delay. *Appl. Math. Comput.* **2014**, *232*, 303–312. [CrossRef]
8. Sathiyaraj, T.; Fečkan, M.; Wang, J. Null controllability results for stochastic delay systems with delayed perturbation of matrices. *Chaos Solitons Fractals* **2020**, *138*, 11. [CrossRef]
9. Debbouche, A.; Baleanu, D. Controllability of fractional evolution nonlocal impulsive quasilinear delay integro-differential systems. *Comput. Math. Appl.* **2011**, *62*, 1442–1450. [CrossRef]
10. Nirmala, R.J.; Balachandran, K.; Rodríguez-Germa, L.; Trujillo, J.J. Controllability of nonlinear fractional delay dynamical systems. *Rep. Math. Phys.* **2016**, *77*, 87–104. [CrossRef]
11. Ji, S.; Li, G.; Wang, M. Controllability of impulsive differential systems with nonlocal conditions. *Appl. Math. Comput.* **2011**, *217*, 6981–6989. [CrossRef]
12. Wang, J.; Zhou, Y. Complete controllability of fractional evolution systems. *Commun. Nonlinear Sci. Numer. Simulat.* **2012**, *17*, 4346–4355. [CrossRef]
13. Zhao, D. New results on controllability for a class of fractional integrodifferential dynamical systems with delay in Banach spaces. *Fractal Fract.* **2021**, *5*, 89. [CrossRef]
14. Dineshkumar, C.; Udhayakumar, R.; Vijayakumar, V.; Shukla, A.; Nisar, K.S. A note on approximate controllability for nonlocal fractional evolution stochastic integrodifferential inclusions of order $r \in (1, 2)$ with delay. *Chaos Solitons Fractals* **2021**, *153*, 111565. [CrossRef]
15. Ge, Z.; Ge, X.; Zhang, J. Approximate controllability and approximate observability of singular distributed parameter systems. *IEEE Trans. Autom. Control* **2020**, *5*, 2294–2299. [CrossRef]

16. Ji, S. Approximate controllability of semilinear nonlocal fractional differential systems via an approximating method. *Appl. Math. Comput.* **2014**, *236*, 43–53. [CrossRef]
17. Ge, F.; Zhou, H.; Kou, C. Approximate controllability of semilinear evolution equations of fractional order with nonlocal and impulsive conditions via an approximating technique. *Appl. Math. Comput.* **2016**, *275*, 107–120. [CrossRef]
18. Dineshkumar, C.; Udhayakumar, R.; Vijayakumar, V.; Nisar, K.S. A discussion on the approximate controllability of Hilfer fractional neutral stochastic integro-differential systems. *Chaos Solitons Fractals* **2021**, *142*, 110472. [CrossRef]
19. Sakthivel, R.; Suganya, S.; Anthoni, S.M. Approximate controllability of fractional stochastic evolution equations. *Comput. Math. Appl.* **2012**, *63*, 660–668. [CrossRef]
20. Kavitha, K.; Vijayakumar, V.; Udhayakumar, R. Results on controllability of Hilfer fractional neutral differential equations with infinite delay via measures of noncompactness.*Chaos Solitons Fractals* **2020**, *139*, 110035. [CrossRef]
21. Zhou, H. Approximate controllability for a class of semilinear abstract equations. *SIAM J. Control Optim.* **1983**, *21*, 551–565. [CrossRef]
22. Liu, Z.; Li, X. Approximate controllability of fractional evolution systems with Riemann-Liouville fractional derivative. *SIAM J. Control Optim.* **2015**, *53*, 1920–1933. [CrossRef]
23. Ibrahim, B.H.E.; Fan, Z.; Li, G. Approximate controllability for functional equations with Riemann-Liouville derivative by iterative and approximate method. *J. Funct. Spaces* **2017**, *2017*, 2508165. [CrossRef]
24. El-Borai, M.M. Some probability densities and fundamental solutions of fractional evolution equations. *Chaos Solitons Fractals* **2002**, *14*, 433–440. [CrossRef]
25. Prüss, J. Evolutionary Integral Equations and Applications. In *Monographs in Mathematics*, Birkhäuser Verlag: Basel, Switherlands, 1993; Volume 87.
26. Bazhlekova, E. *Fractional Evolution Equations in Banach Spaces*; University Press Facilities, University of Technology: Eindhoven, The Netherlands, 2001.
27. Li, X.; Liu, Z.; Tisdell, C.C. Approximate controllability of fractional control systems with time delay using the sequence method. *Electron. J. Differ. Equ.* **2017**, *2017*, 272.
28. Podlubny, I. *Fractional Differential Equations, Mathematics in Science and Engineering*; Academic Press: New York, NY, USA, 1999.
29. Zhao, D.; Liu, Y.; Li, X. Controllability for a class of semilinear fractional evolution systems via resolvent operators. *Commun. Pure Appl. Anal.* **2019**, *18*, 455–478. [CrossRef]
30. Zhao, D. A study on controllability of a class of impulsive fractional nonlinear evolution equations with delay in Banach spaces. *Fractal Fract.* **2021**, *5*, 279. [CrossRef]
31. Zhao, D.; Liu, Y.; Li, H. Fast-time complete controllability of nonlinear fractional delay integrodifferential evolution equations with nonlocal conditions and a parameter. *Math. Methords Appl. Sci.* **2022**, *45*, 5649–5669. [CrossRef]

fractal and fractional

MDPI

Article

Topological Structure of the Solution Sets for Impulsive Fractional Neutral Differential Inclusions with Delay and Generated by a Non-Compact Demi Group

Zainab Alsheekhhussain [1,*], Ahmed Gamal Ibrahim [2] and Akbar Ali [1]

1 Department of Mathematics, Faculty of Science, University of Ha'il, Hail 55476, Saudi Arabia; ak.ali@uoh.edu.sa
2 Department of Mathematics, College of Sciences, King Faisal University, P.O. Box 400, Al-Ahsa 31982, Saudi Arabia; agamal@kfu.edu.sa
* Correspondence: za.hussain@uoh.edu.sa

Abstract: In this paper, we give an affirmative answer to a question about the sufficient conditions which ensure that the set of mild solutions for a fractional impulsive neutral differential inclusion with state-dependent delay, generated by a non-compact semi-group, are not empty compact and an R_δ-set. This means that the solution set may not be a singleton, but it has the same homology group as a one-point space from the point of view of algebraic topology. In fact, we demonstrate that the solution set is an intersection of a decreasing sequence of non-empty compact and contractible sets. Up to now, proving that the solution set for fractional impulsive neutral semilinear differential inclusions in the presence of impulses and delay and generated by a non-compact semigroup is an R_δ-set has not been considered in the literature. Since fractional differential equations have many applications in various fields such as physics and engineering, the aim of our work is important. Two illustrative examples are given to clarify the wide applicability of our results.

Keywords: impulsive fractional differential inclusions; neutral differential inclusions; mild solutions; contractible sets; R_δ-set

Citation: Alsheekhhussain, Z.; Ibrahim, A.G.; Ali, A. Topological Structure of the Solution Sets for Impulsive Fractional Neutral Differential Inclusions with Delay and Generated by a Non-Compact Demi Group. *Fractal Fract.* **2022**, *6*, 188. https://doi.org/10.3390/fractalfract6040188

Academic Editor: Rodica Luca

Received: 12 March 2022
Accepted: 24 March 2022
Published: 28 March 2022

1. Introduction

Impulsive differential equations and inclusions describe phenomena in which states are changing rapidly at certain moments. In [1–8], the authors examined whether a mild solution for different types of impulsive differential inclusions exist.

The study of neutral differential equations appears in many applied mathematical sciences, such as viscoelasticity and equations that describe the distribution of heat. The structure of neutral equations involve derivatives related to delay beside the function. Neutral differential equations and inclusions were studied in [9–12]. These papers examined the mild solutions and controllability of the system.

Because the set of mild solutions for a differential inclusion having the same initial point may not be a singleton, many authors are interested in investigating the structure of this set in a topological point of view. An important aspect of such structure is the R_δ-property, which means that the homology group of the set of mild solutions is the same as a one-point space. We list some studies in which the authors demonstrated the solution sets satisfying R_δ-property: Gabor [13] considered impulsive semilinear differential inclusions with finite delay on the half-line of order one generated by a non-compact semi-group; Djebali et al. [14] worked on impulsive differential inclusions on unbounded domains; Zhou et al. [15] studied the neutral evolution inclusions of order one generated by a non-compact semi-group; Zhou et al. [16] considered fractional stochastic evolution inclusions generated by a compact semi-group; Zhao et al. [17] studied a stochastic differential equation of Sobolev-type which is semilinear with Poisson jumps of order

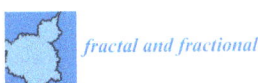

$\alpha \in (1,2)$; Beddani [18] examined a differential inclusion involving Riemann–Liouville fractional derivatives; Wang et al. [19] worked on semilinear fractional differential inclusions with non-instantaneous impulses; Ouahab et al. [20] considered fractional inclusions that are non-local and have impulses at different times; Zaine [21] studied weighted fractional differential equations. Recently, Zhang et al. [22] proved that the set of C^0-solutions for impulsive evolution inclusions of order one is an R_δ-set and generated by m–dissipative operator. Wang et al. [23] proved that the solution for evolution equations that have nonlinear delay and multivalued perturbation on a non-compact interval is an R_δ-set.

In [6,24–26], the authors studied different kinds of fractional differential inclusions, and, in all cases, they showed that the set of solutions is a compact set. For more work related to this, the reader can consult the book in [27] about the topological properties for evolution inclusions.

However, up to now, proving that the solution set for fractional impulsive neutral semilinear differential inclusions involving delay and generated by a non-compact semigroup is an R_δ-set has not been considered in the literature. Thus, this topic is new and interesting and, hence, the question whether there exists a solution set carrying an R_δ-structure remains unsolved for fractional differential inclusions when there are impulses, delay (finite or infinite) and the operator families generated by the linear part lack compactness. Therefore, our main goal is to give an affirmative answer to this question. In fact, we study a neutral fractional impulsive differential inclusion with delay which is generated by a non-compact semigroup, and we show that the set of solutions is non-empty and equal to an intersection of a decreasing sequence of sets each of which is non-empty compact and has a homotopy equivalent to a point.

Let $\alpha \in (0,1)$, $r > 0$, $J = [0,b]$, $T = \{Y(\eta) : \eta \geq 0\}$ a semigroup on E, which is Banach space, and A the infinitesimal generator of T. Let $F : J \times \Theta \to 2^E - \{\phi\}$ be a multifunction, $h : J \times \Theta \to E$, $0 = \eta_0 < \eta_1 < \cdots < \eta_m < \eta_{m+1} = b$, and $\psi \in \Theta$ be given. For every $\eta \in J$, let $\varkappa(\eta) : \mathcal{H} \to \Theta$, $(\varkappa(\eta)x)(\theta) = x(\eta+\theta); \theta \in [-r,0]$; where Θ and $\mathcal{H}$ are defined later.

The present paper shows the solution set of a fractional neutral impulsive semilinear differential inclusion with delay having details as follows:

$$\begin{cases} {}^cD^{\alpha}_{0,\eta}[x(\eta) - h(\eta,\varkappa(\eta)x)] \in Ax(\eta) + F(\eta,\varkappa(\eta)x), \ a.e.\ \eta \in [0,b] - \{\eta_1,\ldots,\eta_m\}, \\ I_i x(\eta_i^-) = x(\eta_i^-) - x(\eta_i^+), i = 1,\ldots,m, \\ x(\eta) = \psi(\eta), \eta \in [-r,0], \end{cases} \tag{1}$$

is not empty, compact and an R_δ-set, where $I_i : E \longrightarrow E, i = 1,\ldots,m$, and $x(\eta_i^+)$, $x(\eta_i^-)$ are the limits of the function x evaluated at η_i from the right and the left. Furthermore, ${}^cD^{\alpha}_{0,\eta}$ denotes the Caputo derivative that has order $\alpha \in (0,1)$ and lower limit at zero [28].

In the following points, we clarify the originality, importance and the main contributions of this article:

1. Up to now, proving that the solution set is an R_δ-set for fractional impulsive neutral semilinear differential inclusions involving delay and generated by a non- compact semigroup has not been considered in the literature.
2. Demonstrating that the set of solutions is an R_δ-set for fractional neutral differential inclusions involving impulses and delay has not been considered yet.
3. We do not assume that the semi-group which generates the linear part is compact.
4. Proving that the set of solutions is an R_δ-set for neutral differential inclusions (without impulses) with a finite delay, $\alpha = 1$, and generated by a non-compact semigroup, has been investigated in [15], while stochastic neutral differential inclusions (without impulsive effects) with finite delay of order $\alpha \in (0,1)$ and generated by a compact semigroup has been examined in [16].
5. Gabor [13] considered Problem 1 on the half-line when $\alpha = 1$ and $h \equiv 0$.
6. Problem 1 is investigated in [19] when $h \equiv 0$ and in the absence of delay.

7. Our technique can be used to derive suitable conditions, which implies that the solution set is an R_δ-set for the problems studied in [13–23] when they contain impulses and delay.

In order to clarify the difficulties encountered to achieve our aim, we point to the normed space $\mathcal{PC}([-r,b],E]$, which consists of piecewise continuous bounded functions defined on $[-r,b]$ with a finite number of discontinuity points and is left continuous at the discontinuity points, and is not necessarily complete. Moreover, unlike the Banach spaces $C([-r,b],E)$ and $PC(J,E)$, the Hausdorff measure of noncompactness on $\mathcal{PC}([-r,b],E]$ is not specific. Thus, when the problem involves delay and impulses, we cannot consider $\mathcal{PC}([-r,b],E]$ as the space of solutions. To overcome these difficulties, a complete metric space H is introduced as the space of mild solutions (see the next section). In addition, the function $\eta \to \varkappa(\eta)\overline{x}; \overline{x} \in H$ is not necessarily measurable (see Remark 1, and so, a norm different from the uniform convergence norm is introduced (see Equation (2) below).

For recent contributions on neutral differential inclusions of fractional order, Burqan et al. [29] give a numerical approach in solving fractional neutral pantograph equations via the ARA integral transform. Ma et al. [30] studied the controllability for a neutral differential inclusion with Hilfer derivative, and Etmad et al. [31] investigated a neutral fractional differential inclusion of Katugampola-type involving both retarded and advanced arguments.

For more recent papers we cite [32–34].

The sections of the paper are organized as follows: We include some background materials in Section 2 as we need them in the main sections. Section 3 is assigned for proving that the solution set of Problem (1) is non-empty and compact. In Section 4, we show that this set is an R_δ-set in the complete metric space H. In Section 5, e give an example as an application of the obtained results. Sections 6 and 7 are the discussion and conclusion sections.

2. Preliminaries and Notation

In all the text we denote for the set of mild solutions for Problem 1 by $\Sigma_\psi^F[-r,b]$ and by $L^1(J,E)$ to the quotient space consisting of $E-$valued Bohner integrable functions defined on J having the norm $\|f\|_{L^1(J,E)} = \int_0^b \|f(\theta)\|d\theta$. Let $P_{ck}(E) = \{B \subseteq E : B$ be non-empty, convex and compact$\}$.

Definition 1. *(Ref. [35]) Let $h : J \to E$, $\{\Upsilon(\eta) : \eta \geq 0\}$ a C_0-semigroup and A be the infinitesimal generator of it. A continuous function $x : J \to E$ is called a mild solution for the problem:*

$$\begin{cases} {}^cD^{\alpha}z(\eta) = Az(\eta) + h(\eta), \eta \in J, \\ z(0) = z_0 \in E, \end{cases}$$

if

$$z(\eta) = \mathfrak{K}_1(\eta)z_0 + \int_0^{\eta} (\eta-\tau)^{\alpha-1}\mathfrak{K}_2(\eta-\tau)h(\tau)d\tau, \eta \in J,$$

where $\mathfrak{K}_1(\eta) = \int_0^\infty \xi_\alpha(\theta)\Upsilon(\eta^{\alpha}\theta)d\theta, \mathfrak{K}_2(\eta) = \alpha\int_0^\infty \theta\xi_\alpha(\theta)\Upsilon(\eta^\alpha\theta)d\theta,$

$\xi_\alpha(\theta) = \frac{1}{\alpha}\theta^{-1-\frac{1}{\alpha}}w_\alpha(\theta^{-\frac{1}{\alpha}}) \geq 0, w_\alpha(\theta) = \frac{1}{\pi}\sum_{n=1}^\infty(-1)^{n-1}\theta^{-\alpha n-1}\frac{\Gamma(n\alpha+1)}{n!}\sin(n\pi\alpha), \theta \in (0,\infty)$ *and* $\int_0^\infty \xi_\alpha(\theta)d\theta = 1.$

Lemma 1. *(Ref. [35] (lemma 3.1)) The properties stated below are held:*

(i) For every fixed $\eta \geq 0$, $\mathfrak{K}_1(\eta), \mathfrak{K}_2(\eta)$ are linear and bounded.
(ii) Assuming $||\eta(\eta)|| \leq M, \eta \geq 0$, we have that for any $x \in E, ||\mathfrak{K}_1(\eta)x|| \leq M||x||$ and $||\mathfrak{K}_2(\eta)x|| \leq \frac{M}{\Gamma(\alpha)}||x||$.
(iii) If $\eta, \tau \geq 0$; then for any $x \in E$,

$$\lim_{\eta\to\tau} ||\mathfrak{K}_1(\eta)x - \mathfrak{K}_1(\tau)x|| = 0, \textit{ and } \lim_{\eta\to\tau} ||\mathfrak{K}_2(\eta)x - \mathfrak{K}_2(\tau)x|| = 0.$$

Consider the spaces:

1. The normed space

$$\Theta \quad : \quad = \{x : [-r, 0] \to E, \text{ where } x \text{ is discontinuous at finite number of points } \tau \neq 0, \text{ and all the limits } x(\tau^+) \text{ and } x(\tau^-) \text{ are less than } \infty\}$$

endowed with the norm:

$$||x||_\Theta := \int_{-r}^{0} ||x(\tau)||d\tau. \tag{2}$$

2. The Banach space

$$PC(J, E) \quad : \quad = \{u : J \to E : u_{|J_i} \in C(J_i, E), i = 0, 1, 2, \ldots, m, \text{ and } u(\eta_i^+), u(\eta_i) = u(\eta_i^-) \text{ are finite for every } i = 1, 2, \ldots .m\},$$

where $J_0 = [0, \eta_1], J_i = (\eta_i, \eta_{i+1}], i = 1, 2, \ldots, m,$ and $||v||_{PC(J;E)} = \tau up_{\eta \in J}||v(\eta)||$.

3. The complete metric space

$$H = \{x : [-r, b] \to E : \text{ where } x \text{ is continuous at } \eta = 0, \; x_{|_{[-r,0]}} = \psi, x_{|_{J_i}} \in PC\,(J, E)\},$$

where the metric function is given by:

$$d_H(x, y) = \tau up_{\eta \in J}||x(\eta) - y(\eta)||.$$

4. The Banach space

$$\mathcal{H} := \{x : [-r, b] \to E \text{ where } x(\eta) = 0, \forall \eta \in [-r, 0], x_{|_{J_i}} \in PC\,(J, E)\}$$

together with the norm $||x||_{\mathcal{H}} = \tau up_{\eta \in J}||x(\eta)|| + ||x_{|_{[-r,0]}}||_\Theta = \tau up_{\eta \in J}||x(\eta)||$.

The Hausdorff measure of noncompactness on a Banach space $PC(J, E)$ is given by

$$\chi_{PC}(B) := \max_{i=0,1,2,\ldots,m} \chi_i(B_{|\overline{J_i}}),$$

where B is a bounded subset of $PC(J, E)$ and χ_i is the Hausdorff measure of noncompactness on the Banach space $C(\overline{J_i}, E)$ and

$$B_{|\overline{J_i}} := \{x^* : \overline{J_i} \to E : x^*(\eta) = x(\eta), \eta \in J_i \text{ and } x^*(\eta_i) = x(\eta_i^+), x \in B\}.$$

The Hausdorff measure of noncompactness on $\mathcal{H}$ is defined by:

$$\chi_{\mathcal{H}}(B) = \max_{i=0,1,2,\ldots,m} \chi_i(B_{|\overline{J_i}}),$$

where B is a bounded subset of $\mathcal{H}$.

Remark 1. *Since the function $\eta \to \varkappa(\eta)x; \overline{x} \in H$ is not necessarily measurable, we do not consider the uniform convergence norm to be the norm defined on the space Θ (see Example 3.1, [36]). Therefore, the multivalued superposition operator*

$$x \to S^1_{F(.,\varkappa(.)x)} = \{f \in L^1(J, E) : f(\eta) \in F(\eta, \varkappa(\eta)x), a.e., \eta \in J\}$$

would not be well defined. Therefore, we consider a norm defined by Equation (2).

Definition 2. *A function $\overline{x} \in H$ is said to be a mild solution for* (1) *if*

$$\overline{x}(\eta) = \begin{cases} \psi(\eta), \eta \in [-r, 0], \\ \mathfrak{K}_1(\eta)[\psi(0) - h(0, \psi)] + h(\eta, \varkappa(\eta)\overline{x}) \\ + \int_0^\eta (\eta - \tau)^{\alpha-1} A\mathfrak{K}_2(\eta - \tau) h(\tau, \varkappa(\tau)\overline{x}) d\tau \\ + \int_0^\eta (\eta - \tau)^{\alpha-1} \mathfrak{K}_2(\eta - \tau) f(\tau) d\tau \\ + \sum_{0<\eta_i<\eta} \mathfrak{K}_1(\eta - \eta_i) I_i(\overline{x}(\eta_i^-)), \eta \in J = [0, b], \end{cases} \tag{3}$$

where $f \in S^1_{F(.,\varkappa(.)x)}$.

We assume the following conditions:

(HA) A is the infinitesimal generator of T, 0 is an element of the resolvent of $A, \rho(A)$ and $\sup_{\eta \geq 0} ||\Upsilon(\eta)|| \leq M$, where $M \geq 1$.

(HF) $F : J \times \Theta \to P_{ck}(E)$ where:

(HF_1) For any $z \in \Theta$, the multifunction $\eta \longrightarrow F(\eta, z)$ has a measurable selection, and for $\eta \in J, a.e.$, the multifunction $z \longrightarrow F(\eta, z)$ is upper semicontinuous.

(HF_2) There exists a $\varphi \in L^P(I, \mathbb{R}^+)(P > \frac{1}{\alpha})$ satisfying

$$||F(\eta, z)|| \leq \varphi(\eta)\ (1 + \|z\|_\Theta), \forall z \in \Theta \text{ and for } a.e.\ \eta \in J.$$

(HF_3) There is a $\beta \in L^P([0, b], E), p > \frac{1}{\alpha}$ such that, for any $D \subset \Theta$ that is bounded, we have

$$\chi_E(F(\eta, D)) \leq \beta(\eta) \sup_{\theta \in [-r, 0]} \chi_E\{z(\theta) : z \in D\}, a.e. \text{ for } \eta \in J. \tag{4}$$

(HI) For any $i = 1, \ldots, m$, the function $I_i : E \to E$ is continuous, and there are $\sigma_i > 0$ and $\varsigma_i > 0$ satisfying $||I_i(x)|| \leq \sigma_i ||x||$, and for any bounded subset $D \subseteq E$,

$$\chi_E(I_i(D)) \leq \varsigma_i \chi_E(I_i(D)).$$

Lemma 2. *(Ref. [37]) Under condition (HA), for any $\gamma \in (0, 1)$, the fractional power A^γ can be defined, and it is linear and closed on its domain $D(A^\gamma)$. In addition, the following properties are satisfied:*

(i) *$D(A^\gamma)$ is a Banach space with the norm*

$$||x||_\gamma = ||A^\gamma x||.$$

(ii) *For any $\eta > 0$, $x \in E$, we have $\Upsilon(\eta)x \in D(A^\gamma)$ and, assuming $x \in D(A^\gamma)$, we get $A^\gamma \Upsilon(\eta)x = \Upsilon(\eta) A^\gamma x$.*

(iii) *For every $\eta > 0$, $A^\gamma \Upsilon(\eta)$ is bounded on E, and there is a constant $C_\gamma > 0$ such that*

$$||A^\gamma \Upsilon(\eta)|| \leq \frac{C_\gamma}{\eta^\gamma}. \tag{5}$$

(iv) *$A^{-\gamma}$ is a bounded linear operator on E.*

(v) *For every $x \in E$,*

$$A\mathfrak{K}_2(\eta)x = A^{1-\gamma}\mathfrak{K}_2(\eta) A^\gamma x, \eta \in J, \tag{6}$$

and

$$||A^\gamma \mathfrak{K}_2(\eta)|| \leq \frac{\alpha C_\gamma \Gamma(2-\gamma)}{\eta^{\alpha\gamma}\Gamma(1 + \alpha(1-\gamma))}, \eta \in (0, b]. \tag{7}$$

We need the next lemmas in order to prove our main results.

Lemma 3. *Assume $W \subseteq E$ to be bounded, closed and convex, $\Phi_1 : W \to E$ is a single-valued function, $\Phi_2 : W \to P_{ck}(E)$ is a multifunction, and for any $x \in W$, $\Phi_1(x) + y \in W$, $\forall y \in \Phi_2(x)$. Suppose that*

(a) *Φ_1 is a contraction with the contraction constant $k < \frac{1}{2}$;*

(b) *Φ_2 is a closed and completely continuous multifunction.*

Then, the fixed point set of $\Phi_1 + \Phi_2$ is not empty. Moreover, the set of fixed points for $\Phi_1 + \Phi_2$ is compact if it is bounded.

Proof. Φ_1 is continuous on W since it is a contraction and, hence, it follows by the closeness of Φ_2, that the multifunction $R = \Phi_1 + \Phi_2$ is closed. We show that R is χ_E-condensing, where χ_E is the Hausdorff measure of noncompactness on E. Let Z be a bounded set of W. Since Φ_1 is a contraction with the contraction constant k, we get $\mu_E(\Phi_1(Z)) \leq k\mu_E(Z) \leq 2k\chi_E(Z) < \chi_E(Z)$, where μ_E is the Kuratowski measure of noncompactness on E. Because Φ_2 is compact, $\chi_E(\Phi_2(Z)) = 0$. Therefore,

$$\begin{aligned}\chi_E(R(Z)) &= \chi_E(\Phi_1(Z)) + \chi_E(\Phi_2(Z) \\ &= \chi_E(\Phi_1(Z)) \leq \mu_E(\Phi_1(Z)) \\ &< \chi_E(Z).\end{aligned}$$

This means that R is χ_E-condensing. By Proposition 3.5.1 in [38], the fixed point set of $\Phi_1 + \Phi_2$ is not empty. The second part follows from Proposition 3.5.1 in [38]. □

3. The Compactness of $\Sigma_\psi^F[-r, b]$

In this section, we show that the set of mild solutions for Problem 1 is nonempty and compact.

For any $x \in \mathcal{H}$ with $x(0) = \psi(0)$, let $\overline{x} \in H$ be defined by

$$\overline{x}(\eta) := \begin{cases} \psi(\eta), \eta \in [-r, 0], \\ x(\eta), \eta \in (0, b]. \end{cases} \tag{8}$$

Lemma 4. *For any $\overline{x} \in H$, the function $\eta \to \varkappa(\eta)\overline{x}$ is continuous from J to Θ.*

Proof. Assume $\eta, \tau \in J, \eta \leq \tau$. Then,

$$||\varkappa(\eta)\overline{x} - \varkappa(\tau)\overline{x}||_\Theta = \int_{-r}^{0} ||\overline{x}(\eta+\theta) - \overline{x}(\tau+\theta)||d\theta.$$

Because $\overline{x}$ is continuous on $[-r, b]$ except for a finite number of points, it follows that $\lim_{\eta\to\tau} ||\overline{x}(\eta+\theta) - \overline{x}(\tau+\theta)|| = 0$, a.e. Since $\overline{x} \in H$, $lim_{\eta\to\tau} \int_{-r}^{0} ||\overline{x}(\eta+\theta) - \overline{x}(\tau+\theta)||d\theta = 0$, and the proof is completed. □

Theorem 1. *Assume that (HA) and (HF) are held and that $\{\Upsilon(\eta) : \eta \geq 0\}$ is equicontinuous. Assume also that the following conditions are satisfied.*

(Hh) The function $h : J \times \Theta \to E$ is continuous and there exists a $\gamma \in (0, 1)$ satisfying $h(\eta, u) \in D(A^\gamma), \forall(\eta, u) \in J \times \Theta$ and

(i) For any $\eta \in J$, $A^\gamma h(\eta, .)$ is strongly measurable.
(ii) There are $d_1 > 0$ and $d_2 > 0$ with

$$d_1||A^{-\gamma}|| + \frac{d_1 b^{\alpha\gamma} C_{1-\gamma}\Gamma(1+\gamma)}{\gamma\Gamma(1+\alpha\gamma)} < \frac{1}{2r}, \tag{9}$$

$$||A^\gamma h(\eta, u)|| \leq d_2(1 + ||u||_\Theta), \forall(\eta, u) \in J \times \Theta, \tag{10}$$

and

$$||A^\gamma h(\eta, u_1) - A^\gamma h(\eta, u_2)|| \leq d_1||u_1 - u_2||_\Theta, \forall\eta \in J. \tag{11}$$

Then, $\Sigma_\psi^F[-r, b]$ is not empty and a compact subset of H provided that

$$||A^{-\gamma}||d_2 r + d_2\frac{C_{1-\gamma}\Gamma(1+\gamma)b^{\alpha\gamma}}{\Gamma(1+\alpha\gamma)\gamma}r + \frac{M}{\Gamma(\alpha)}\Delta||\varphi||_{L^p_{(J,,\mathbb{R}^+)}} r + \sigma M < 1, \tag{12}$$

and

$$\frac{4\Delta M}{\Gamma(\alpha)}||\beta||_{L^P(J,\mathbb{R}^+)}+2M\sum_{i=1}^{i=m}\varsigma_i<\frac{1}{2}, \quad (13)$$

where $\sigma=\sum_{i=1}^{i=m}\sigma_i$ and $\Delta=(\frac{P-1}{\alpha P-1})^{\frac{P-1}{P}}b^{\alpha-\frac{1}{P}}$.

Proof. A multioperator $\Phi:\mathcal{H}\to P(\mathcal{H})$ is defined as the following: let $x\in\mathcal{H}$, hence, as a consequence of (HF_1), the multifunction $\eta\longrightarrow F(\eta,\varkappa(\eta)\overline{x})$ admits a measurable selection which, by (HF_2), belongs to $S^1_{F(.,\varkappa(.)\overline{x})}$, and, therefore, $y\in\Phi(x)$ can be defined by

$$y(\eta)=\begin{cases}0,\eta\in[-r,0],\\ \mathfrak{K}_1(\eta)[\psi(0)-h(0,\psi)]+h(\eta,\varkappa(\eta)\overline{x})\\ +\int_0^\eta(\eta-\tau)^{\alpha-1}A\mathfrak{K}_2(\eta-\tau)h(\tau,\varkappa(\tau)\overline{x})d\tau\\ +\int_0^\eta(\eta-\tau)^{\alpha-1}\mathfrak{K}_2(\eta-\tau)f(\tau)d\tau\\ +\sum_{0<\eta_i<\eta}\mathfrak{K}_1(\eta-\eta_i)I_i(\overline{x}(\eta_i^-)),\eta\in J,\end{cases} \quad (14)$$

where $f\in S^1_{F(.,\varkappa(.)\overline{x})}$ and $\overline{x}$ is defined by (8).

We show that a point x is a fixed point for Φ if and only if $\overline{x}\in\Sigma^F_\psi[-r,b]$. Assume x is a fixed point to Φ. Hence,

$$x(\eta)=\begin{cases}0,\eta\in[-r,0],\\ \mathfrak{K}_1(\eta)[\psi(0)-h(0,\psi)]+h(\eta,\varkappa(\eta)\overline{x})\\ +\int_0^\eta(\eta-\tau)^{\alpha-1}A\mathfrak{K}_2(\eta-\tau)h(\tau,\varkappa(\tau)\overline{x})d\tau\\ +\int_0^\eta(\eta-\tau)^{\alpha-1}\mathfrak{K}_2(\eta-\tau)f(\tau)d\tau\\ +\sum_{0<\eta_i<\eta}\mathfrak{K}_1(\eta-\eta_i)I_i(\overline{x}(\eta_i^-)),\eta\in J.\end{cases}$$

Therefore,

$$\overline{x}(\eta)=\begin{cases}\psi(\eta),\eta\in[-r,0],\\ \mathfrak{K}_1(\eta)[\psi(0)-h(0,\psi)]+h(\eta,\varkappa(\eta)\overline{x})\\ +\int_0^\eta(\eta-\tau)^{\alpha-1}A\mathfrak{K}_2(\eta-\tau)h(\tau,\varkappa(\tau)\overline{x})d\tau\\ +\int_0^\eta(\eta-\tau)^{\alpha-1}\mathfrak{K}_2(\eta-\tau)f(\tau)d\tau\\ +\sum_{0<\eta_i<\eta}\mathfrak{K}_1(\eta-\eta_i)I_i(\overline{x}(\eta_i^-)),\eta\in J,\end{cases}$$

which means that $\overline{x}$ satisfies (3), and, thus, it is a mild solution for problem (1). In a similar way, it can be seen that if $\overline{x}$ satisfies (3), then x is a fixed point for Φ. Let $\Phi_1:\mathcal{H}\to\mathcal{H}$ and $\Phi_2:\Phi_2\to P(\mathcal{H})$ be such that

$$\Phi_1(x)(\eta)=\begin{cases}0,\eta\in[-r,0],\\ \mathfrak{K}_1(\eta)[\psi(0)-h(0,\psi)]+h(\eta,\varkappa(\eta)\overline{x})\\ +\int_0^\eta(\eta-\tau)^{\alpha-1}A\mathfrak{K}_2(\eta-\tau)h(\tau,\varkappa(\tau)\overline{x})d\tau,\eta\in J,\end{cases} \quad (15)$$

and a function $y\in\Phi_2(x)$ if and only if

$$y(\eta)=\begin{cases}0,\eta\in[-r,0],\\ +\int_0^\eta(\eta-\tau)^{\alpha-1}\mathfrak{K}_2(\eta-\tau)f(\tau)d\tau\\ +\sum_{0<\eta_i<\eta}\mathfrak{K}_1(\eta-\eta_i)I_i(\overline{x}(\eta_i^-)),\eta\in J,\end{cases} \quad (16)$$

where $f\in S^1_{F(.,\varkappa(.)\overline{x})}$. Notice that $\Phi=\Phi_1+\Phi_2$. Let $\xi=\sup_{\theta\in[-r,0]}||\psi(\theta)||$,

$$\begin{aligned}\omega &= M\,[\xi+||A^{-\gamma}||d_2(1+r\xi)]\\ &\quad+(1+r\xi)[||A^{-\gamma}||d_2+d_2\frac{C_{1-\gamma}\Gamma(1+\gamma)b^{\alpha\gamma}}{\Gamma(1+\alpha\gamma)\gamma}+\frac{M}{\Gamma(\alpha)}\Delta||\varphi||_{L^P_{(J,,\mathbb{R}^+)}}]\end{aligned}$$

and v be a positive real number satisfying

$$v > \frac{\omega}{1-[||A^{-\gamma}||d_2 r + d_2\frac{C_{1-\gamma}\Gamma(1+\gamma)b^{\alpha\gamma}}{\Gamma(1+\alpha\gamma)\gamma}r + \frac{M}{\Gamma(\alpha)}\Delta||\varphi||_{L^P_{(J,,\mathbb{R}^+)}}r + \sigma M]}. \quad (17)$$

Put $B_v = \{u \in \mathcal{H} : ||u||_{\mathcal{H}} \leq v\}$. Due to (12), v is well defined. The rest of the proof is divided in the following steps:

Step 1. This step shows that $\Phi(B_v) \subseteq B_v$. Let $x \in B_v$ and $y \in \Phi(x)$. There exists $f \in S^1_{F(.,\varkappa(.)x)}$ where

$$y(\eta) = \begin{cases} 0, \eta \in [-r,0], \\ \mathfrak{K}_1(\eta)[\psi(0) - h(0,\psi)] + h(\eta,\varkappa(\eta)\overline{x}) \\ + \int_0^\eta (\eta-\tau)^{\alpha-1} A\mathfrak{K}_2(\eta-\tau)h(\tau,\varkappa(\tau)\overline{x})d\tau \\ + \int_0^\eta (\eta-\tau)^{\alpha-1}\mathfrak{K}_2(\eta-\tau)f(\tau)d\tau \\ + \sum_{0<\eta_i<\eta}\mathfrak{K}_1(\eta-\eta_i)I_i(\overline{x}(\eta_i^-)), \eta \in J. \end{cases}$$

Let $\eta \in J$. For every $x \in \mathcal{H}$, we get

$$||\varkappa(\eta)\overline{x}||_\Theta = \int_{-r}^0 ||\overline{x}(\eta+\theta)||d\theta \leq r(\xi+v),$$

which implies that (HF_2), $||f(\tau)|| \leq \varphi(\tau)(1+||\varkappa(\eta)\overline{x}||_\Theta) \leq r(\xi+v); a.e. \tau \in J$. So, by (ii) of Lemma 1, and the Holder inequality, it follows that

$$\begin{aligned} & ||\int_0^\eta (\eta-\tau)^{\alpha-1}\mathfrak{K}_2(\eta-\tau)f(\tau)d\tau|| \\ \leq & \frac{M}{\Gamma(\alpha)}(1+r(\xi+v))\int_0^\eta(\eta-\tau)^{\alpha-1}\varphi(\tau)d\tau \\ \leq & \frac{M}{\Gamma(\alpha)}\Delta||\varphi||_{L^P_{(J,,\mathbb{R}^+)}}(1+r(\xi+v)). \end{aligned}$$

Then, from (6), (7), (10) and (HI), one has, for $\eta \in J$,

$$\begin{aligned} ||y(\eta)|| \leq & M[\xi + ||A^{-\gamma}A^\gamma h(0,\psi)||] + ||A^{-\gamma}A^\gamma h(\eta,\varkappa(\eta)\overline{x})|| \\ & + \int_0^\eta (\eta-\tau)^{\alpha-1}||A^{1-\gamma}\mathfrak{K}_2(\eta-\tau)A^\gamma h(\tau,\varkappa(\tau)\overline{x})||d\tau \\ & + \frac{M}{\Gamma(\alpha)}\Delta||\varphi||_{L^P_{(J,,\mathbb{R}^+)}}(1+r(\xi+v)) + Mv\sigma \\ \leq & M[\xi + ||A^{-\gamma}||d_2(1+r\xi)] + ||A^{-\gamma}||d_2(1+||\varkappa(\eta)\overline{x}||_\Theta) \\ & + d_2(1+r(\xi+v))\frac{\alpha C_{1-\gamma}\Gamma(2-(1-\gamma))}{\Gamma(1+\alpha(1-(1-\gamma))}\int_0^\eta \frac{(\eta-\tau)^{\alpha-1}}{(\eta-\tau)^{\alpha(1-\gamma)}}d\tau \\ & + \frac{M}{\Gamma(\alpha)}(1+r(\xi+v))\Delta||\varphi||_{L^P_{(J,,\mathbb{R}^+)}} + Mv\sigma \\ \leq & M[\xi + ||A^{-\gamma}||d_2(1+r\xi)] + ||A^{-\gamma}||d_2(1+r(\xi+v)) \\ & + d_2(1+r(\xi+v))\frac{C_{1-\gamma}\Gamma(1+\gamma)b^{\alpha\gamma}}{\Gamma(1+\alpha\gamma)\gamma} \\ & + \frac{M}{\Gamma(\alpha)}(1+r(\xi+v))\Delta||\varphi||_{L^P_{(J,,\mathbb{R}^+)}} + Mv\sigma. \end{aligned}$$

This equation with (12) leads to

$$\begin{aligned} ||y||_{\mathcal{H}} &\leq M\,[\xi + ||A^{-\gamma}||d_2(1+r\xi)] \\ &+(1+r\xi)[||A^{-\gamma}||d_2 + d_2\frac{C_{1-\gamma}\Gamma(1+\gamma)b^{\alpha\gamma}}{\Gamma(1+\alpha\gamma)\gamma} + \frac{M}{\Gamma(\alpha)}\Delta||\varphi||_{L^P_{(J,,\mathbb{R}^+)}}] \\ &+v[||A^{-\gamma}||d_2 r + d_2\frac{C_{1-\gamma}\Gamma(1+\gamma)b^{\alpha\gamma}}{\Gamma(1+\alpha\gamma)\gamma}r + \frac{M}{\Gamma(\alpha)}\Delta||\varphi||_{L^P_{(J,,\mathbb{R}^+)}}r + \sigma M] \\ &< v. \end{aligned}$$

Then, $\Phi(B_v) \subseteq B_v$.

Step 2. Φ_1 is a contraction with a contraction constant $k < \frac{1}{2}$.

Let $u, v \in B_v$ and $\eta \in J$. Then, $||\varkappa(\eta)\overline{u} - \varkappa(\eta)\overline{v}||_{\Theta} = \int_{-r}^{0} ||\overline{u}(\eta+\theta) - \overline{v}(\eta+\theta)||d\theta \leq r||u-v||_{\mathcal{H}}$. From (6), (7) and (11), for every $u, v \in B_v$ and any $\eta \in J$, we have that

$$\begin{aligned} & ||\Phi_1(u)(\eta) - \Phi_1(v)(\eta)|| \\ \leq\ & ||h(\eta,\varkappa(\eta)\overline{u}) - h(\eta,\varkappa(\eta)\overline{v})|| \\ & +||\int_0^{\eta}(\eta-\tau)^{\alpha-1}A\mathfrak{K}_2(\eta-\tau)[h(\tau,\varkappa(\tau)\overline{u}) - h(\tau,\varkappa(\tau)\overline{v})]d\tau \\ \leq\ & ||A^{-\gamma}A^{\gamma}[h(\eta,\varkappa(\eta)\overline{u}) - h(\eta,\varkappa(\eta)\overline{v})]|| \\ & +||\int_0^{\eta}(\eta-\tau)^{\alpha-1}A^{1-\gamma}\mathfrak{K}_2(\eta-\tau)A^{\gamma}[h(\tau,\varkappa(\tau)\overline{u}) - h(\tau,\varkappa(\tau)\overline{v})]d\tau \\ \leq\ & ||A^{-\gamma}||\ ||A^{\gamma}h(\eta,\varkappa(\eta)\overline{u}) - A^{\gamma}h(\eta,\varkappa(\eta)v)|| \\ & +\frac{\alpha C_{1-\gamma}\Gamma(1+\gamma)}{\Gamma(1+\alpha\gamma)}\int_0^{\eta}(\eta-\tau)^{\alpha\gamma-1}||A^{\gamma}h(\tau,\varkappa(\tau)\overline{u}) - A^{\gamma}h(\tau,\varkappa(\tau)\overline{v})||d\tau \\ \leq\ & d_1||A^{-\gamma}||\ ||\varkappa(\eta)\overline{u} - \varkappa(\eta)\overline{v}||_{\Theta} \\ & +\frac{d_1\alpha C_{1-\gamma}\Gamma(2-\gamma)}{\Gamma(1+\alpha\gamma)}\sup_{\tau\in[0,\eta]}||\varkappa(\tau)\overline{u} - \varkappa(\tau)\overline{v}||_{\Theta}\frac{b^{\alpha\gamma}}{\alpha\gamma} \\ \leq\ & ||u-v||_{\mathcal{H}}[d_1||A^{-\gamma}|| + \frac{d_1 b^{\alpha\gamma}C_{1-\gamma}\Gamma(1+\gamma)}{\gamma\Gamma(1+\alpha\gamma)}]r, \end{aligned}$$

which yields with (9) that Φ_1 is a contraction with a contraction constant $k < \frac{1}{2}$.

Step 3. Φ_2 has a closed graph and $\Phi_2(x); x \in B_v$ is compact.

Assume $(x_n)_{n\geq 1}$ and $(y_n)_{n\geq 1}$ are sequences in B_v where $x_n \to x, y_n \to y$ and $y_n \in \Phi_2(x_n); n \geq 1$. Then,

$$y_n(\eta) = \begin{cases} 0, \eta \in [-r,0], \\ +\int_0^{\eta}(\eta-\tau)^{\alpha-1}\mathfrak{K}_2(\eta-\tau)f_n(\tau)d\tau \\ +\sum_{0<\eta_k<\eta}\mathfrak{K}_1(\eta-\eta_k)I_i(x_n(\eta_k^-)), \eta \in J, \end{cases} \tag{18}$$

where $f_n \in \tau^1_{F(.,\varkappa(.)\overline{x}_n)}$. Using (HF_2), it yields that

$$||f_n(\eta)|| \leq \varphi(\eta)(1 + r(v+\xi)), \text{a.e.}\eta \in J.$$

So, $(f_n)_{n\geq 1}$ is bounded in $L^P(J,E)$ and, hence, there exists a subsequence of $\{f_n\}_{n=1}^{\infty}$. We denote them by $(f_n)_{n\geq 1}$, where $f_n \longrightarrow f \in L^P(J,E)$. From Mazur's Lemma, there exists a sequence of convex combination, $\{z_n\}_{n=1}^{\infty}$ of $\{f_n\}_{n=1}^{\infty}$ that converges almost everywhere to f. Note that by (HF_2), again, for any $\eta \in J, \tau \in (0,\eta]$ and any $n \geq 1$,

$$||(\eta-\tau)^{\alpha-1}f_n(\tau)|| \leq |\eta-\tau)|^{\alpha-1}\ \varphi(\tau)(1+r(v+\xi)) \in L^P((0,\eta],\mathbb{R}^+).$$

Set

$$\widetilde{y}_n(\eta) = \begin{cases} 0, \eta \in [-r,0], \\ + \int_0^\eta (\eta-\tau)^{\alpha-1}\mathfrak{K}_2(\eta-\tau)z_n(\tau)d\tau \\ + \sum_{0<\eta_i<\eta} \mathfrak{K}_1(\eta-\eta_i)I_i(x_n(\eta_i^-)), \eta \in J. \end{cases} \tag{19}$$

Note that by (18), $\widetilde{y}_n(\eta) \to y(\eta)$, $\eta \in J$. Moreover, since $\varkappa(\eta)\overline{x}_n \to \varkappa(\eta)\overline{x}; \eta \in J$, $F(\eta,.); a.e.\ \eta \in J$ is upper semicontinuous, it yields $f(\eta) \in F(\eta, \varkappa(\eta)x), a.e.$ Therefore, from the continuity of $\mathfrak{K}_2(\eta-\tau); \tau \in [0,\eta]$, I_i $(i = 1,2,\dots)$, and by taking the limit of (19) as $n \to \infty$, one gets $y \in \Phi_2(x)$.

To prove that the values of Φ_2 are compact, assume $x \in \mathcal{H}$ and $y_n \in \Phi_2(x), n \geq 1$. Using similar arguments to the above, we get that $\{y_n : n \geq 1\}$ has a convergent subsequence $(\widetilde{y})_{n\geq1}$. So, $\Phi_2(x)$ is relatively compact. Since the graph of Φ_2 is closed its values are closed and, hence, $\Phi_2(x)$ is relatively compact in $\mathcal{H}$.

Step 4. We claim that the subsets $Z_{|\overline{J_i}}$ $(i = 0,1,\dots,m)$ are equicontinuous, where

$$Z_{|\overline{J_i}} = \{y^* \in C(\overline{J_i}, E) : y^*(\eta) = y(\eta), \eta \in (\eta_i, \eta_{i+1}], y^*(\eta_i) = y(\eta_i^+), y \in \Phi_2(x), x \in B_v\}.$$

Assume $y^* \in Z_{|\overline{J_i}}$. Then, there exists $x \in B_v$ and $f \in S^1_{F(.,\varkappa(.)\overline{x})}$, where, for $\eta \in J_i$,

$$\begin{aligned} y^*(\eta) &= \int_0^\eta (\eta-\tau)^{\alpha-1}\mathfrak{K}_2(\eta-\tau)f(\tau)d\tau \\ &\quad + \sum_{0<\eta_k<\eta} \mathfrak{K}_1(\eta-\eta_k)I_k(\overline{x}(\eta_k^-)), \end{aligned}$$

and $y^*(\eta_i) = y(\eta_i^+)$.

Case 1. Let η_1, η_2 $(\eta_1 < \eta_2)$ be two points in $(\eta_i, \eta_{i+1}]$. Then,

$$\begin{aligned} & ||y^*(\eta_2) - y^*(\eta_1)|| \\ \leq\ & ||\int_0^{\eta_2} (\eta_2-\tau)^{\alpha-1}\mathfrak{K}_2(\eta_2-\tau)f(\tau)d\tau \\ & - \int_0^{\eta_1} (\eta_1-\tau)^{\alpha-1}\mathfrak{K}_2(\eta_1-\tau)f(\tau)|| \\ & +|| \sum_{0<\eta_k<\eta_2} \mathfrak{K}_1(\eta_2-\eta_k)I_k(\overline{x}(\eta_k^-)) - \sum_{0<\eta_i<\eta_1} \mathfrak{K}_1(\eta_1-\eta_k)I_k(\overline{x}(\eta_k^-))|| \\ \leq\ & ||\int_{\eta_1}^{\eta_2} (\eta_2-\tau)^{\alpha-1}\mathfrak{K}_2(\eta_2-\tau)f(\tau)d\tau|| \\ & + \int_0^{\eta_1} |(\eta_2-\tau)^{\alpha-1} - (\eta_1-\tau)^{\alpha-1}|\ ||\mathfrak{K}_2(\eta_2-\tau)f(\tau)||d\tau \\ & +|| \int_0^{\eta_1} (\eta_1-\tau)^{\alpha-1}||\mathfrak{K}_2(\eta_2-\tau)f(\tau) - \mathfrak{K}_2(\eta_1-\tau)f(\tau)||\, d\tau\,. \\ & + \sum_{0<\eta_k<\eta_2} ||\mathfrak{K}_1(\eta_2-\eta_k) - \mathfrak{K}_1(\eta_1-\eta_k)||\ ||I_i(\overline{x}(\eta_i^-))|| \\ =\ & \sum_{i=1}^{i=4} I_i. \end{aligned}$$

The hypothesis (HF_2) implies $||f(\eta)|| \leq \varphi(\eta)\ (1 + r(v+\xi)), a.e. \eta \in J$, and, hence, by Lemma 1, we get

$$\begin{aligned} \lim_{\eta_2\to\eta_1} I_1 &= \lim_{\eta_2\to\eta_1} ||\int_{\eta_1}^{\eta_2} (\eta_2-\tau)^{\alpha-1}\mathfrak{K}_2(\eta_2-\tau)f(\tau)d\tau|| \\ &\leq \frac{M(1+r(v+\xi))}{\Gamma(\alpha)} \lim_{\eta_2\to\eta_1} \int_{\eta_1}^{\eta_2} (\eta_2-\tau)^{\alpha-1}\varphi(\tau)d\tau \\ &= \frac{M(1+r(v+\xi))}{\Gamma(\alpha)} ||\varphi||_{L^P([J,\mathbb{R}^+)} \lim_{\eta_2\to\eta_1} (\int_{\eta_1}^{\eta_2} (\eta_2-\tau)^{\frac{P(\alpha-1)}{P-1}} d\tau)^{\frac{P-1}{P}} = 0. \end{aligned}$$

For I_2, we have

$$\begin{aligned}\lim_{\eta_2\to\eta_1} I_2 &\leq \lim_{\eta_2\to\eta_1}\int_0^{\eta_1}|(\eta_2-\tau)^{\alpha-1}-(\eta_1-\tau)^{\alpha-1}|\,||\mathfrak{K}_2(\eta_2-\tau)f(\tau)||d\tau\\ &= \frac{M(1+r(v+\xi))}{\Gamma(\alpha)}\lim_{\eta_2\to\eta_1}\int_0^{\eta_1}|(\eta_2-\tau)^{\alpha-1}-(\eta_1-\tau)^{\alpha-1}|\varphi(\tau)d\tau.\end{aligned}$$

Note that $\overline{\omega}=\frac{\alpha-1}{1-\frac{1}{P}}\in(-1,0)$, then, for $\tau<\eta_1$, we have $(\eta_1-\tau)^{\overline{\omega}}\geq(\eta_2-\tau)^{\overline{\omega}}$. As an application of Lemma 3 in [8] and considering $\frac{P-1}{P}\in(0,1)$, we get

$$|\left[(\eta_1-\tau)^{\overline{\omega}}\right]^{1-\frac{1}{P}}-\left[(\eta_2-\tau)^{\overline{\omega}}\right]^{\frac{P-1}{P}}|\leq\left[(\eta_1-\tau)^{\overline{\omega}}-(\eta-\tau)^{\overline{\omega}}\right]^{\frac{P-1}{P}}.$$

Then,

$$|(\eta_1-\tau)^{\alpha-1}-(\eta_2-\tau)^{\alpha-1}|\leq\left[(\eta_1-\tau)^{\overline{\omega}}-(\eta_2-\tau)^{\overline{\omega}}\right]^{\frac{P-1}{P}}.$$

This leads to

$$|(\eta-\tau)^{\alpha-1}-(\eta+\lambda-\tau)^{\alpha-1}|^{\frac{P-1}{P}}\leq\left[(\eta-\tau)^{\overline{\omega}}-(\eta+\lambda-\tau)^{\overline{\omega}}\right].$$

Therefore,

$$\begin{aligned}&\lim_{\eta_2\to\eta_1} I_2\\ \leq\;&\frac{M(1+r(v+\xi))}{\Gamma(\alpha)}\lim_{\eta_2\to\eta_1}\int_0^{\eta_1}|(\eta_2-\tau)^{\alpha-1}-(\eta_1-\tau)^{\alpha-1}|\varphi(\tau)d\tau\\ \leq\;&\frac{M(1+r(v+\xi)))}{\Gamma(\alpha)}\lim_{\eta_2\to\eta_1}\left[\int_0^{\eta_1}|(\eta_2-\tau)^{\alpha-1}-(\eta_1-\tau)^{\alpha-1}|^{\frac{P}{P-1}}d\tau\right]^{\frac{P-1}{P}}\|\varphi\|_{L^P_{(J,\mathbb{R}^+)}}\\ \leq\;&\frac{M(1+r(v+\xi)))}{\Gamma(\alpha)}\lim_{\eta_2\to\eta_1}\left[\int_0^{\eta_1}[(\eta_2-\tau)^{\overline{\omega}}-(\eta_1-\tau)^{\overline{\omega}}]d\tau\right]^{\frac{P-1}{P}}\|\varphi\|_{L^P_{(J,\mathbb{R}^+)}}\\ \leq\;&\frac{M(1+r(v+\xi))}{\Gamma(\alpha)}\lim_{\eta_2\to\eta_1}\left[\frac{1}{\omega+1}[\eta_2^{\overline{\omega}+1}-(\eta_2-\eta_1)^{\overline{\omega}+1}-\eta_1^{\overline{\omega}+1}\right]^{\frac{P-1}{P}}\|\varphi\|_{L^P_{(J,\mathbb{R}^+)}}\\ =\;&0.\end{aligned}$$

For I_3,

$$\lim_{\eta_2\to\eta_1} I_3\leq\lim_{\eta_2\to\eta_1}||\int_0^{\eta_1}(\eta_1-\tau)^{\alpha-1}||\mathfrak{K}_2(\eta_2-\tau)f(\tau)-\mathfrak{K}_2(\eta_1-\tau)f(\tau)||\,d\tau.$$

Observe that for every $\tau\in[0,\eta]$,

$$\begin{aligned}&(\eta_1-\tau)^{\alpha-1}||K_\alpha(\eta_2-\tau)f(\tau)-K_\alpha(\eta_1-\tau)f(\tau)||\\ \leq\;&\frac{2M(\nu+1)}{\Gamma(\alpha)}(\eta_1-\tau)^{\alpha-1}\varphi(\tau)\in L^P(J,\mathbb{R}^+).\end{aligned}$$

Moreover, since $\{\eta(\eta):\eta>0\}$ is equicontinuous, and, using the Lebesgue-dominated convergence theorem, one gets

$$
\begin{aligned}
\lim_{\eta_2\to\eta_1} I_3 &\leq \frac{M(1+r(v+\xi))}{\Gamma(\alpha)} \lim_{\eta_2\to\eta_1} \int_0^{\eta_1} (\eta_1-\tau)^{\alpha-1}||\mathfrak{K}_2(\eta_2-\tau)-\mathfrak{K}_2(\eta_1-\tau)||\varphi(\tau)d\tau \\
&= \frac{M(1+r(v+\xi))}{\Gamma(\alpha)} \int_0^{\eta_1}\int_0^{\infty} \theta(\eta_1-\tau)^{\alpha-1}\zeta_\alpha(\theta)\times \\
&\quad [\lim_{\eta_2\to\eta_1} ||(\Upsilon((\eta_2-\tau)^\alpha\theta)-\Upsilon(\eta_1-\tau)^\alpha\theta))||]\, d\theta\varphi(\tau)d\tau \\
&= 0.
\end{aligned}
$$

For I_4,

$$
\lim_{\eta_2\to\eta_1} I_4 \leq \sigma v \lim_{\eta_2\to\eta_1} \sum_{0<\eta_k<\eta_2} ||\mathfrak{K}_1(\eta_2-\eta_k)-\mathfrak{K}_1(\eta_1-\eta_k)|| = 0.
$$

Case 2. $\eta=\eta_i$, $i=1,\ldots,m$. Assume $\delta>0$, $\eta_i+\delta\in(\eta_i,\eta_{i+1}]$ and $\lambda>0$ where $\eta_i<\lambda<\eta_i+\delta\leq\eta_{i+1}$. Hence, as above, it can be shown that

$$
||y^*(\eta_i+\delta)-y^*(\eta_i)|| = \lim_{\lambda\to\eta_i^+} ||y(\eta_i+\delta)-y(\lambda)|| = 0.
$$

Then, $Z_{|\overline{J_i}}$ $(i=0,1,\ldots,m)$ are equicontinuous.

Step 5. Set $B_1=\overline{conv}\Phi(B_v)$ and $B_n=\overline{conv}\Phi(B_{n-1})$, $n\geq 2$. Then, the sequence (B_n), $n\geq 1$ is a decreasing sequence of not empty, closed and bounded subsets of $\mathcal{H}$. So, the set $B=\bigcap_{n\geq 1} B_n$ is bounded, closed, convex and $\Phi(B)\subset B$. Next, we show that B is compact. According to the generalized Cantor's intersection property, we only need to prove that

$$
\lim_{n\to\infty}\chi_{\mathcal{H}}(B_n)=0, \tag{20}
$$

where $\chi_{\mathcal{H}}$ is the Hausdorff measure of noncompactness on $\mathcal{H}$. Assume $n\in\mathbb{N}$ and $n\geq 1$ are fixed. From the fact that Φ_1 is a contraction with a contraction constant $k<\frac{1}{2}$, it follows that

$$
\begin{aligned}
&\chi_{\mathcal{H}}\Phi(B_{n-1}) \\
\leq\ &\chi_{\mathcal{H}}\Phi_1(B_{n-1})+\chi_{\mathcal{H}}\Phi_2(B_{n-1}) \\
\leq\ &\frac{1}{2}\chi_{\mathcal{H}}(B_{n-1})+\chi_{\mathcal{H}}\Phi_2(B_{n-1}).
\end{aligned} \tag{21}
$$

Let $\varepsilon>0$. Using Lemma 5 in [39], there is a $(y_k)_{k\geq 1}$ in $\Phi_2(B_{n-1})$ with

$$
\chi_{\mathcal{H}}\Phi_2(B_{n-1})\leq 2\chi_{\mathcal{H}}\{y_k:k\geq 1\}+\varepsilon.
$$

From the fact that the subsets $Z_{|\overline{J_i}}$ $(i=0,1,\ldots,m)$ are equicontinuous, one obtains

$$
\begin{aligned}
&\chi_{\mathcal{H}}\Phi_2(B_{n-1}) \\
\leq\ &2\chi_{\mathcal{H}}\{y_k:k\geq 1\}+\varepsilon \\
\leq\ &2\sup_{\eta\in[0,b]}\chi_E\{y_k(\eta):k\geq 1\}+\varepsilon.
\end{aligned} \tag{22}
$$

Now, let $x_k\in B_{n-1}$ and $y_k\in\Phi_2(x_k)$, $k\geq 1$. Then, for every $k\geq 1$, there is a $f_k\in\tau^1_{F(.,\varkappa(\eta)\overline{x}_k)}$ such that, for any $\eta\in J$,

$$
y_k(\eta)=\begin{cases} 0, \eta\in[-r,0], \\ \int_0^\eta(\eta-\tau)^{\alpha-1}\mathfrak{K}_2(\eta-\tau)f_k(\tau)d\tau \\ +\sum_{0<\eta_i<\eta}\mathfrak{K}_1(\eta-\eta_i)I_i(\overline{x}_k(\eta_i^-)), \eta\in J. \end{cases}
$$

Note that the assumption (HI) implies that for $\eta \in J$,

$$\begin{aligned}\chi_E\{\sum_{0<\eta_i<\eta} \mathfrak{K}_1(\eta-\eta_i)I_i(\overline{x}_k(\eta_i^-)) \quad &: \quad k\geq 1\}\\ &\leq M\sum_{i=1}^{i=m} \varsigma_i\, \chi_E\{\overline{x}_k(\eta_i^-)) : k\geq 1\}\\ &\leq M\sum_{i=1}^{i=m} \varsigma_i\, \chi_E\{x_k(\eta_i^-)) : k\geq 1\}\\ &\leq M\,\chi_{\mathcal{H}}(B_{n-1})\sum_{i=1}^{i=m} \varsigma_i\,. \end{aligned} \tag{23}$$

Moreover, from (4) , we have that for $a.e.\tau \in J$,

$$\begin{aligned}\chi_E\{f_k(\tau) \quad &: \quad k\geq 1\}\leq \chi\{F(\tau,\varkappa(\tau)\overline{x}_k) : k\geq 1\}\\ &\leq \beta(\tau)\sup_{\theta\in[-r,0]}\chi\{\overline{x}_k(\tau+\theta) : k\geq 1\}\\ &\leq \beta(\tau)\sup_{\delta\in[-r,\tau]}\chi\{\overline{x}_k(\delta) : k\geq 1\}\\ &\leq \beta(\tau)\sup_{\delta\in[0,\tau]}\chi\{x_k(\delta) : k\geq 1\}\\ &\leq \beta(\tau)\chi_{\mathcal{H}}(B_{n-1})=\gamma(\eta).\end{aligned} \tag{24}$$

Again, by $(HF_2)^*$, for every $k \geq 1$, and for almost $\eta \in J$, $||f_k(\eta)|| \leq \varphi(\eta)\ (1+r(v+\xi))$ and, hence, $\{f_k : k \geq 1\}$ is integrably bounded. As a consequence of Lemma 4 in [40], there is a compact set $K_\epsilon \subseteq E$, a measurable set $J_\epsilon \subset J$ having a measure less than ϵ and $\{z_k^\epsilon\} \subset L^P(J,E)$ such that for every $\tau \in J$, $\{z_k^\epsilon(\tau) : k \geq 1\} \subseteq K_\epsilon$ and

$$||f_k(\tau)-z_k^\epsilon(\tau)||\ < 2\gamma(\tau)+\epsilon \text{ for all } k\geq 1 \text{ and all } \tau\in J-J_\epsilon. \tag{25}$$

Then, by (24) and (25) and Minkowski's inequality, it follows that for $k \geq 1$,

$$\begin{aligned}&||\int_{J-J_\epsilon}(\eta-\tau)^{\alpha-1}\mathfrak{K}_2(\eta-\tau)(f_k(\tau)-z_k^\epsilon(\tau))d\tau||\\ \leq\ &\frac{M}{\Gamma(\alpha)}||f_k-z_k^\epsilon||_{L^P(J_0-J_\epsilon,\mathbb{R}^+)}(\int_{J-\ J_\epsilon}(\eta-\tau)^{\frac{(\alpha-1)P}{P-1}}d\tau)^{\frac{P-1}{P}}\\ \leq\ &\frac{\Delta M}{\Gamma(\alpha)}||f_k-z_k^\epsilon||_{L^P(J_0-J_\epsilon,\mathbb{R}^+)}\\ \leq\ &\frac{\Delta M}{\Gamma(\alpha)}(2||\gamma||_{L^P(J-\ J_\epsilon,\ \mathbb{R}^+)}+\epsilon b^{\frac{1}{P}})\\ =\ &\frac{\Delta M}{\Gamma(\alpha)}\ (2||\beta||_{L^P(J,\ \mathbb{R}^+)}\,\chi_{\mathcal{H}}(B_{n-1})+\epsilon b^{\frac{1}{P}}),\end{aligned} \tag{26}$$

and

$$\begin{aligned}&||\int_{J_\epsilon}(\eta-\tau)^{\alpha-1}\mathfrak{K}_2(\eta-\tau)f_k(\tau)d\tau||\\ \leq\ &\frac{M}{\Gamma(\alpha)}(1+r(v+\xi))\int_{J_\epsilon}(\eta-\tau)^{\alpha-1}\varphi(\tau)d\tau\\ \leq\ &\frac{M}{\Gamma(\alpha)}(1+r(v+\xi))||\varphi||_{L^P(J_\epsilon,\ \mathbb{R}^+)}(\int_{J_\epsilon}(\eta-\tau)^{\frac{(\alpha-1)P}{P-1}}d\tau)^{\frac{P-1}{P}}.\end{aligned} \tag{27}$$

Moreover, from the fact that $\{z_k^\epsilon(\tau) : k \geq 1\}; \tau \in J$ is contained in a compact subset, we get

$$\chi\{\int_{J-J_\epsilon}(\eta-\tau)^{\alpha-1}\mathfrak{K}_2(\eta-\tau)z_k^\epsilon(\tau)d\tau : k\geq 1\} = 0.$$

Combining this relation with (26) and (27), it follows that

$$\begin{aligned}\chi\{\int_0^\eta(\eta-\tau)^{\alpha-1}\mathfrak{K}_2(\eta-\tau)f_k(\tau)d\tau \quad &: \quad k\geq 1\} \\ &\leq \frac{\Delta M}{\Gamma(\alpha)}(2||\beta||_{L^P(J,\,\mathbb{R}^+)}\,\chi_{\mathcal{H}}(B_{n-1})+\epsilon b^{\frac{1}{P}}) \\ &+\frac{(1+r(v+\xi)M}{\Gamma(\alpha)}||\varphi||_{L^P(J_\epsilon,\,\mathbb{R}^+)}\Delta_\epsilon, \qquad (28)\end{aligned}$$

where $\Delta_\epsilon = (\int_{J_\epsilon}(\eta-\tau)^{\frac{(\alpha-1)P}{P-1}}d\tau)^{\frac{P-1}{P}}$. Using the fact that ε is chosen arbitrary, relation (28) becomes

$$\begin{aligned}\chi\{\int_0^\eta(\eta-\tau)^{\alpha-1}\mathfrak{K}_2(\eta-\tau)f_k(\tau)d\tau \quad &: \quad k\geq 1\} \\ &\leq \frac{2\Delta M}{\Gamma(\alpha)}\,||\beta||_{L^P(J,\,\mathbb{R}^+)}\,\chi_{\mathcal{H}}(B_{n-1}).\end{aligned}$$

Using the above inequality and (21)–(23), in addition to the fact that ε is arbitrary, it follows that

$$\chi_{\mathcal{H}}(B_n)\leq(\frac{4\Delta M}{\Gamma(\alpha)}\,||\beta||_{L^P(J,\,\mathbb{R}^+)}\,+2M\sum_{i=1}^{i=m}\varsigma_i+\frac{1}{2})\chi_{\mathcal{H}}(B_{n-1}).$$

This leads to

$$\chi_{\mathcal{H}}(B_n)\leq(\frac{4\Delta M}{\Gamma(\alpha)}\,||\beta||_{L^P(J,\,\mathbb{R}^+)}+M\sum_{i=1}^{i=m}\varsigma_i+\frac{1}{2})^{n-1}\chi_{\mathcal{H}}(B_1),\ \forall n\geq 1.$$

The above inequality holds for any natural number n, and by (13) together with taking the limit as $n\to\infty$, we get (20). Then, B is not empty and a compact subset of $\mathcal{H}$. So, $\Phi : B\to P_{ck}(B)$ is completely continuous. By applying Lemma 3, we conclude that the fixed points set of Φ is not an empty subset of $\mathcal{H}$. Furthermore, by arguing as in Step 1, we can prove that the set of fixed points of Φ is bounded and, hence, by Lemma 3, it is compact in $\mathcal{H}$. Therefore, the set $\Sigma_\psi^F[-r,b]$ is not empty and a compact subset of H. □

4. The Structure Topological of $\Sigma_\psi^F[-r,b]$

In the section we prove that $\Sigma_\psi^F[-r,b]$ is an R_δ-set

Definition 3 ([41]). *A topological space X, which is homotopy equivalent to a point, is called contractible. In other words, there is a continuous map $h : [0,1]\times X\to X$, $h(0,.x) = x$ and $h(1,x) = x_0\in X$.*

Lemma 5 ([41]). *Let $A\subseteq X$, where A is not empty and X is a complete metric space. Then, A is said to be R_δ-set if and only if it is an intersection of a decreasing sequence $\{A_n\}$ of contractible sets and $\chi_X(A_n)\to 0$, as $n\to\infty$.*

Now, consider the multi-valued function $\widetilde{F} : J\times\Theta\to P_{ck}(E)$ that is given by:

$$\widetilde{F}(\eta,u) := \begin{cases} F(\eta,u), ||u|| < v, \\ F(\eta,\frac{vu}{||u||}), ||u||\geq v,\end{cases}$$

where v is defined by (17). Since $\widetilde{F} = F$ on D_v, the set of solutions consisting of mild solutions for Problem (1) is equal to the set of solutions consisting of mild solutions for the problem:

$$\begin{cases} {}^cD^{\alpha}_{0,\eta}[x(\eta) - h(\eta, \varkappa(\eta)x)] \in Ax(\eta) + \widetilde{F}(\eta, \varkappa(\eta)x), \ a.e.\ \eta \in [0,b] - \{\eta_1, \dots, \eta_m\}, \\ I_i(x(\eta_i^-)) = x(\eta_i^-) - x(\eta_i^+), i = 1, \dots, m, \\ x(\eta) = \psi(\eta), \eta \in [-r, 0]. \end{cases}$$

Obviously, $\widetilde{F}$ verifies (HF_1) and, for $\eta \in J, a.e.,$

$$||\widetilde{F}(\eta, u)|| \leq \begin{cases} \varphi(\eta)(1 + ||u||) \leq \varphi(\eta)(1 + r(\xi + v)) = \zeta(\eta), ||u|| < v, \\ \varphi(\eta)(1 + ||\frac{vu}{||u||}||) = \varphi(\eta)(1 + r(\xi + v)) = \zeta(\eta), ||u|| \geq v. \end{cases}$$

Then, we can assume that F verifies the next condition:
$(HF_2)^*$ There exists a function $\xi \in L^P(I, \mathbb{R}^+)(P > \frac{1}{\alpha})$, where for every $z \in \Theta$,

$$||F(\eta, z)|| \leq \zeta(\eta), \ a.e.\ \eta \in J.$$

We recall the next Lemma. For its proof, we refer the reader to the second step in the proof of Theorem 3.5 in [13].

Lemma 6. *Assume that (HF_1) and $(HF_2)^*$ are satisfied. Then, there exists a sequence of multi-functions $\{F_i\}_{i=1}^{\infty}$ with $F_i : J \times \Theta \to P_{ck}(E)$ such that:*

(i) *Every $F_i\,(\eta, .)$ is continuous for almost $\eta \in J$.*
(ii) *$F(\eta, x) \subseteq \dots. \subseteq F_{i+1}(\eta, x) \subseteq F_i(\eta, \varkappa(\eta)x) \subseteq \dots \subseteq \overline{co}F(\eta, \{y \in \Theta : ||y - x|| \leq 3^{1-i}\}), i \geq 1,$ for each $\eta \in J$ and $x \in \Theta$.*
(iii) *$F(\eta, z) = \cap_{i\,\geq 1} F_i(\eta, z)$.*
(iv) *For all $i \geq 1$, there is a selection $g_i : J \times \Theta \to E$ of F_i such that $g_i(., x)$ is measurable for each $x \in \Theta$ and for $g_i(\eta, .)$ is locally Lipschitz.*

Remark 2. *(Ref. [19]) The property (iv) in Lemma 6 implies that, for almost $\eta \in J$, $g_i(\eta, .), i \geq 1$ is continuous.*

Assume $\Sigma_{\psi}^{F_i}[-r, b]$ is the mild solutions set of the following fractional neutral impulsive semilinear differential inclusions with delay:

$$\begin{cases} {}^cD^{\alpha}_{0,\eta}[x(\eta) - h(\eta, \varkappa(\eta)x)] \in Ax(\eta) + F_i(\eta, \varkappa(\eta)x), \ a.e.\ \eta \in [0,b] - \{\eta_1, \dots, \eta_m\}, \\ I_i(x(\eta_i^-)) = x(\eta_i^-) - x(\eta_i^+), i = 1, \dots, m, \\ x(\eta) = \psi(\eta), \eta \in [-r, 0]. \end{cases} \tag{29}$$

Theorem 2. *Assume that the conditions in Theorem 1 after substituting $(HF2)$ by $(HF2)^*$ are held. Then, there exists $N_0 \in \mathbb{N}$ such that, for $i \geq N_0$, the set $\Sigma_{\psi}^{F_i}[-r, b]$ is compact and not empty in H.*

Proof. Let i be a fixed natural number. We define a multioperator $\Phi_i : \mathcal{H} \to P(\mathcal{H})$ as the following : $y \in \Phi_i(x)$ if and only if

$$y(\eta) = \begin{cases} 0, \eta \in [-r, 0], \\ \mathfrak{K}_1(\eta)[\psi(0) - h(0, \psi)] + h(\eta, \varkappa(\eta)\overline{x}) \\ + \int_0^{\eta} (\eta - \tau)^{\alpha - 1} A\mathfrak{K}_2(\eta - \tau) h(\tau, \varkappa(\tau)\overline{x}) d\tau \\ + \int_0^{\eta} (\eta - \tau)^{\alpha - 1} \mathfrak{K}_2(\eta - \tau) f(\tau) d\tau \\ + \sum_{0 < \eta_i < \eta} \mathfrak{K}_1(\eta - \eta_i) I_i(\overline{x}(\eta_i^-)), \eta \in J, \end{cases}$$

where $f \in \tau^1_{F_i(.,\varkappa(.)\overline{x})}$. Due to Lemma 5, F_i verifies (F_1), $(F_2)^*$. As a result of Theorem 1, Φ_i is closed , $\Phi_i(B_v) \subseteq B_v$ and $\Phi_i(B_v)$ is equicontinuous. Set $B_{1,i} = \overline{conv}\Phi_i(B_v)$ and $B_{n,i} = \overline{conv}\Phi_i(B_{n-1,i})$, $n \geq 2$. As in Theorem 1, the sequence $(B_{n,i})$, $n \geq 1$ is a decreasing sequence of non-empty, closed and bounded subsets of $\mathcal{H}$. We show that

$$\lim_{n\to\infty} \chi_{C([-r,b],E)}(B_{n,i}) = 0. \tag{30}$$

Let $\varepsilon > 0$. Choose a natural number N_0 with $3^{1-N_0} < \frac{\varepsilon}{2||\beta||_{L^P(J,\,\mathbb{R}^+)}}$ and let $i > N_0$ be a fixed natural number. Using a similar argument as the one used in the proof of Theorem 1, one gets

$$\begin{aligned} &\chi_{\mathcal{H}}(B_{n,i}) \\ \leq\ & 2\sup_{\eta\in J} \chi_E\{y_k(\eta) : k \geq 1\} + \frac{\varepsilon}{2}, \end{aligned}$$

where

$$y_k(\eta) = \begin{cases} 0, \eta \in [-r, 0] \\ \int_0^\eta (\eta-\tau)^{\alpha-1}\mathfrak{K}_2(\eta-\tau) f_k(\tau)d\tau \\ +\sum_{0<\eta_i<\eta} \mathfrak{K}_1(\eta-\eta_i) I_i(\overline{x}(\eta_i^-)), \eta \in J, \end{cases}$$

and $f_k \in \tau^1_{F_i(.,\varkappa(\eta)x_k)}$. Next, due to Remark 4.2 in [7], it follows that for any bounded subset $D \subset \Theta$,

$$\chi_E(F_i(\eta, D)) \leq \beta(\eta)[\sup_{\theta\in[-r,\eta]} \chi_E\{z(\theta) : z \in D\} + 3^{1-i}]. \tag{31}$$

Then, it yields from (ii) in Lemma 5 and (31), for $a.e. \tau \in J$,

$$\begin{aligned} \chi_E(\{f_k(\tau) \ \ :\ \ & k \geq 1\} \\ \leq\ & \chi_E\{F_i(\tau, \varkappa(\tau)x_k) : k \geq 1\} \\ \leq\ & \beta(\tau)[\sup_{\theta\in[-r,0]} \chi_E\{x_k(\tau+\theta) : k \geq 1\} + 3^{1-N_0}] \\ \leq\ & \beta(\tau)[\sup_{\delta\in[-r,\tau]} \chi_E\{x_k(\delta) : k \geq 1\} + 3^{1-N_0}] \\ \leq\ & \beta(\tau)[\sup_{\theta\in[0,,\tau]} \chi_E\{x_k(\delta) : k \geq 1\} + 3^{1-N_0}] \\ \leq\ & \beta(\tau)\chi_{\mathcal{H}}(B_{n-1,i}) + \beta(\tau)3^{1-N_0} = \overline{\gamma}(\tau). \end{aligned} \tag{32}$$

As in (28) but by using (32) instead of (24), we get

$$\begin{aligned} \chi\{\int_0^\eta (\eta-\tau)^{\alpha-1}\mathfrak{K}_2(\eta-\tau)f_k(\tau)d\tau \ \ :\ \ & k \geq 1\} \\ \leq\ & \frac{\Delta M}{\Gamma(\alpha)}(2||\beta||_{L^P(J,\,\mathbb{R}^+)}\,\chi_{\mathcal{H}}(B_{n-1}) + \epsilon b^{\frac{1}{P}}) + \frac{\epsilon}{2} \\ & + \frac{M}{\Gamma(\alpha)}(1 + rv + r\xi) \times \\ & ||\varphi||_{L^P(J_\epsilon,\,\mathbb{R}^+)}(\int_{J_\epsilon} (\eta-\tau)^{\frac{P}{P-1}}d\tau)^{\frac{P-1}{P}}. \end{aligned}$$

Similarly, as in the proof of Theorem 1, we confirm the validity of (30). Therefore, by the generalized Cantor's intersection property, the set B_i is not empty and compact in $\mathcal{H}$. As in Theorem 1, the fixed points set of the multivalued function $\Phi_i : B_i \to P_{ck}(B_i)$ is not empty and a compact subset in $\mathcal{H}$. Consequently, the set $\sum_{\psi}^{F_n}[-r, b]$ is not empty and a compact subset of H. □

Theorem 3. *Under the conditions of Theorem 2,* $\sum_{\psi}^{F}[-r, b] = \cap_{n=N_0}^{\infty} \sum_{\psi}^{F_n}[-r, b]$.

Proof. In view of (iii) in Lemma 8, it can be seen that $\sum_{\psi}^{F}[-r,b] \subseteq \cap_{n=N_0}^{\infty} \sum_{\psi}^{F_n}[-r,b]$. Let $\overline{x} \in \cap_{n=N_0}^{\infty} \sum_{\psi}^{F_n}[-r,b]$. Then, there is $\mathfrak{f}_n \in \tau^1_{F_n(.,\varkappa(.)\overline{x})}, n \geq N_0$ such that

$$\overline{x}(\eta) = \begin{cases} \psi(\eta), \eta \in [-r,0], \\ \mathfrak{K}_1(\eta)[\psi(0) - h(0,\psi)] + h(\eta,\varkappa(\eta)\overline{x}) \\ + \int_0^\eta (\eta-\tau)^{\alpha-1} A\mathfrak{K}_2(\eta-\tau)h(\tau,\varkappa(\tau)\overline{x})d\tau \\ + \int_0^\eta (\eta-\tau)^{\alpha-1}\mathfrak{K}_2(\eta-\tau)\mathfrak{f}_n(\tau)d\tau \\ + \sum_{0<\eta_i<\eta} \mathfrak{K}_1(\eta-\eta_i)I_i(\overline{x}(\eta_i^-)), \eta \in J. \end{cases} \tag{33}$$

It follows from $(HF2)^*$ that

$$||\mathfrak{f}_n(\eta)|| \leq \zeta(\eta), \text{for } a.e. \eta \in J.$$

This means that the sequence $(\mathfrak{f}_n)_{n\geq 1}$ is weakly relatively compact in $L^P(J,E)$, so we can assume $\mathfrak{f}_n \rightharpoonup f$ weakly, where $f \in L^P(J,\mathbb{R}^+)$. As in the proof of Theorem 1, there is a sequence of convex combinations $(z_n)_{n\geq 1}$ of $(\mathfrak{f}_n)_{n\geq 1}$ that converges almost everywhere to f. Note that

$$\overline{x}(\eta) = \begin{cases} \psi(\eta), \eta \in [-r,0], \\ \mathfrak{K}_1(\eta)[\psi(0) - h(0,\psi)] + h(\eta,\varkappa(\eta)\overline{x}) \\ + \int_0^\eta (\eta-\tau)^{\alpha-1} A\mathfrak{K}_2(\eta-\tau)h(\tau,\varkappa(\tau)\overline{x})d\tau \\ + \int_0^\eta (\eta-\tau)^{\alpha-1}\mathfrak{K}_2(\eta-\tau)z_n(\tau)d\tau \\ + \sum_{0<\eta_i<\eta} \mathfrak{K}_1(\eta-\eta_i)I_i(\overline{x}(\eta_i^-)), \eta \in J, \end{cases} \tag{34}$$

and $z_n(\eta) \in F_n\,(\eta,\varkappa(\eta)\overline{x}), n \geq 1$. It yields, from (ii) of Lemma 8, that for almost $\eta \in J$,

$$z_n(\eta) \in \overline{co}F(\eta, \{y \in \Theta : ||y - \varkappa(\eta)\overline{x}|| \leq 3^{1-n}\}), n \geq 1,$$

which implies that $f(\eta) \in F(\eta,\varkappa(\eta)\overline{x})$, for *a.e.* $\eta \in J$. Moreover, using the fact that $\mathfrak{K}_2(\eta)(\eta > 0)$ is continuous, and taking the limit as $n \to \infty$ in (34), one gets

$$\overline{x}(\eta) = \begin{cases} \psi(\eta), \eta \in [-r,0], \\ \mathfrak{K}_1(\eta)[\psi(0) - h(0,\psi)] + h(\eta,\varkappa(\eta)\overline{x}) \\ + \int_0^\eta (\eta-\tau)^{\alpha-1} A\mathfrak{K}_2(\eta-\tau)h(\tau,\varkappa(\tau)\overline{x})d\tau \\ + \int_0^\eta (\eta-\tau)^{\alpha-1}\mathfrak{K}_2(\eta-\tau)f(\tau)d\tau \\ + \sum_{0<\eta_i<\eta} \mathfrak{K}_1(\eta-\eta_i)I_i(\overline{x}(\eta_i^-)), \eta \in J. \end{cases}$$

This means that $\overline{x} \in \sum_{\psi}^{F}[-r,b]$. □

To prove our main results, we need the next lemma.

Lemma 7 ([19], Lemma 4.5). *Assume that (X,d) and (Y,ρ) are two metric spaces. Then, if $f:(M,d) \to (Y,\rho)$ is locally Lipschitz, then it is Lipschitz on all subsets of X that are compact.*

Theorem 4. *Under the assumptions of Theorem 2, the set $\sum_{\psi}^{F}[-r,b]$ is an R_δ-set in H provided that $rd_1||A^{-\gamma}|| < 1$.*

Proof. Using Lemma 4 and Theorems 1–3, we only need to prove that $\sum_{\psi}^{F_n}[-r,b]$, where $n \geq N_0$ is contractible. Assume that $n \in \mathbb{N}$ and $n \geq N_0$. Consider the following fractional neutral impulsive semilinear:

$$\begin{cases} {}^cD_{0,\eta}^{\alpha}[x(\eta) - h(\eta,\varkappa(\eta)x)] = Ax(\eta) + g_n(\eta,\varkappa(\eta)x), \ a.e. \ \eta \in [0,b] - \{\eta_1,\ldots,\eta_m\}, \\ I_i(x(\eta_i^-)) = x(\eta_i^-) - x(\eta_i^+), i = 1,\ldots,m, \\ x(\eta) = \psi(\eta), \eta \in [-r,0]. \end{cases} \tag{35}$$

Using Lemma 6 and Remark 3, $g_n(.,u)$ is measurable, and for $\eta \in J, a.e., g_n(\eta,.)$ is continuous. Since the multi-valued F satisfies $(F_2)^*$and (F_3), then, following the arguments employed in the proof of Theorem 2, the fractional differential Equation (35) has a mild solution $\overline{y} \in \sum_{\psi}^{F_n}[-r,b]$ satisfying the following integral equation:

$$\overline{y}(\eta) = \begin{cases} \psi(\eta), \eta \in [-r,0], \\ \mathfrak{K}_1(\eta)[\psi(0) - h(0,\psi)] + h(\eta, \varkappa(\eta)\overline{y}) \\ + \int_0^\eta (\eta-\tau)^{\alpha-1} A\mathfrak{K}_2(\eta-\tau)h(\tau,\varkappa(\tau)\overline{y})d\tau \\ + \int_0^\eta (\eta-\tau)^{\alpha-1}\mathfrak{K}_2(\eta-\tau)g_n(\eta,\varkappa(\eta)\overline{y})d\tau \\ + \sum_{0<\eta_i<\eta} \mathfrak{K}_1(\eta-\eta_i)I_i(\overline{y}(\eta_i^-)), \eta \in J. \end{cases} \tag{36}$$

Next, we show that the solution is unique. Assume that $\overline{x} \in \sum_{\psi}^{F_n}[-r,b]$ is another mild solution for (35). Then,

$$\overline{x}(\eta) = \begin{cases} \psi(\eta), \eta \in [-r,0], \\ \mathfrak{K}_1(\eta)[\psi(0) - h(0,\psi)] + h(\eta, \varkappa(\eta)\overline{x}) \\ + \int_0^\eta (\eta-\tau)^{\alpha-1} A\mathfrak{K}_2(\eta-\tau)h(\tau,\varkappa(\tau)\overline{x})d\tau \\ + \int_0^\eta (\eta-\tau)^{\alpha-1}\mathfrak{K}_2(\eta-\tau)g_n(\eta,\varkappa(\eta)\overline{x})d\tau \\ + \sum_{0<\eta_i<\eta} \mathfrak{K}_1(\eta-\eta_i)I_i(\overline{x}(\eta_i^-)), \eta \in J. \end{cases} \tag{37}$$

Let $\eta \in [0,\eta_1]$ be fixed. Due to (6), (7), (11) (36) and (37), it yields

$$\begin{aligned}
& ||\overline{y}(\eta) - \overline{x}(\eta)|| \\
\leq\ & ||h(\eta,\varkappa(\eta)\overline{y}) - h(\eta,\varkappa(\eta)\overline{x})|| \\
& +|| \int_0^\eta (\eta-\tau)^{\alpha-1} A\mathfrak{K}_2(\eta-\tau)(h(\tau,\varkappa(\tau)\overline{y}) - h(\tau,\varkappa(\tau)\overline{x}))d\tau|| \\
& +|| \int_0^\eta (\eta-\tau)^{\alpha-1} \mathfrak{K}_2(\eta-\tau)(g_n(\tau,\varkappa(\tau)\overline{y}) - g_n(\tau,\varkappa(\tau)\overline{x}))d\tau|| \\
\leq\ & ||A^{-\gamma}|| ||A^\gamma h(\eta,\varkappa(\eta)\overline{y}) - A^\gamma h(\eta,\varkappa(\eta)\overline{x})|| \\
& + \int_0^\eta (\eta-\tau)^{\alpha-1}||A^{1-\gamma}\mathfrak{K}_2(\eta-\tau)||\ ||A^\gamma h(\tau,\varkappa(\tau)\overline{y}) - A^\gamma h(\tau,\varkappa(\tau)\overline{x}))||d\tau \\
& + \frac{M}{\Gamma(\alpha)} \int_0^\eta (\eta-\tau)^{\alpha-1}||g_n(\tau,\varkappa(\tau)\overline{y}) - g_n(\tau,\varkappa(\tau)\overline{x}))||d\tau. \\
\leq\ & d_1||A^{-\gamma}||\ ||\varkappa(\eta)\overline{y} - \varkappa(\eta)\overline{x}||_\Theta \\
& +d_1||A^{-\gamma}|| \frac{\alpha C_{1-\gamma}\Gamma(1+\gamma)}{\Gamma(1+\alpha\gamma))} \int_0^\eta (\eta-\tau)^{\alpha\gamma-1}||\varkappa(\tau)\overline{y} - \varkappa(\tau)\overline{x}||_\Theta d\tau \\
& + \frac{M}{\Gamma(\alpha)} \int_0^\eta (\eta-\tau)^{\alpha-1}||g_n(\tau,\varkappa(\tau)\overline{y}) - g_n(\tau,\varkappa(\tau)\overline{x}))||d\tau.
\end{aligned} \tag{38}$$

Now, from Lemma 5, the function $\tau \rightarrow \varkappa(\tau)\overline{x}$ is continuous from $[0,\eta_1]$ to Θ and, hence, the subset $Z_{\overline{x}} = \{\varkappa(\tau)\overline{x} : \tau \in [0,\eta_1]\}$ is compact in Θ. Similarly, the set $Z_{\overline{y}} = \{\varkappa(\tau)\overline{y} : \tau \in [0,\eta_1]\}$ is compact in Θ and, therefore, the set $Z_{\overline{x},\overline{y}} = Z_{\overline{x}} \cup Z_{\overline{y}}$ is compact in Θ, and consequently, $[0,\eta_1] \times Z_{\overline{x},\overline{y}}$ is compact in $[0,\eta_1] \times \Theta$. Thus, by (iv) in Lemma 6 and Lemma 7, there exists $c_{\eta_1} > 0$, for which the estimate

$$||g_n(\tau,\varkappa(\tau)\overline{y}) - g_n(\tau,\varkappa(\tau)\overline{x})|| \leq c_{\eta_1}||\varkappa(\tau)\overline{y} - \varkappa(\tau)\overline{x}||_\Theta,$$

holds for $\tau \in J$. Therefore, from (38), it yields

$$\begin{aligned}
& ||\overline{x}(\eta) - \overline{y}(\eta)|| \\
\leq \; & d_1||A^{-\gamma}|| \, ||\varkappa(\eta)\overline{y} - \varkappa(\eta)\overline{x}||_\Theta \\
& + d_1||A^{-\gamma}||\frac{\alpha C_{1-\gamma}\Gamma(1+\gamma)}{\Gamma(1+\alpha\gamma))}\int_0^\eta (\eta-\tau)^{\alpha\gamma-1}||\varkappa(\tau)\overline{y} - \varkappa(\tau)\overline{x}||_\Theta d\tau \\
& + \frac{Mc_{\eta_1}}{\Gamma(\alpha)}\int_0^\eta (\eta-\tau)^{\alpha-1}||\varkappa(\tau)\overline{y} - \varkappa(\tau)\overline{x}||_\Theta d\tau.
\end{aligned}$$

Note that when $\tau \in [0,\eta]$, we have

$$\begin{aligned}
||\varkappa(\tau)\overline{y} - \varkappa(\tau)\overline{x}||_\Theta &= \int_{-r}^0 ||\overline{y}(\tau+\theta) - \overline{x}(\tau+\theta)||d\theta \\
&\leq r \sup_{\delta\in[0,\tau]} ||\overline{y}(\delta) - \overline{x}(\delta)||.
\end{aligned}$$

It yields

$$\begin{aligned}
& ||\overline{x}(\eta) - \overline{y}(\eta)|| \\
\leq \; & d_1||A^{-\gamma}|| \, ||\varkappa(\eta)\overline{y} - \varkappa(\eta)\overline{x}||_\Theta \\
& + rd_1||A^{-\gamma}||\frac{\alpha C_{1-\gamma}\Gamma(1+\gamma)}{\Gamma(1+\alpha\gamma))}\int_0^\eta (\eta-\tau)^{\alpha\gamma-1}\sup_{\delta\in[a,\tau]}||\overline{y}(\delta) - \overline{x}(\delta)||d\tau \\
& + \frac{rMc_{\eta_1}}{\Gamma(\alpha)}\int_0^\eta (\eta-\tau)^{\alpha-1}\sup_{\delta\in[0,\tau]}||\overline{y}(\delta) - \overline{x}(\delta)||d\tau.
\end{aligned}$$

Since $\overline{x}$ and $\overline{y}$ are continuous on $[0,\eta]$, there is $\rho \in [0,\eta]$ with $||\overline{x}(\rho) - \overline{y}(\rho)|| = \sup_{\delta\in[0,\eta]}||\overline{x}(\delta) - \overline{y}(\delta)||$. Then,

$$\begin{aligned}
& \sup_{\delta\in[0,\eta]}||\overline{x}(\delta) - \overline{y}(\delta)|| = ||\overline{x}(\rho) - \overline{y}(\rho)|| \\
\leq \; & d_1||A^{-\gamma}|| \, ||\varkappa(\rho)\overline{y} - \varkappa(\rho)\overline{x}||_\Theta \\
& + rd_1||A^{-\gamma}||\frac{\alpha C_{1-\gamma}\Gamma(1+\gamma)}{\Gamma(1+\alpha\gamma))}\int_0^\rho (\rho-\tau)^{\alpha\gamma-1}\sup_{\delta\in[0,\tau]}||\overline{y}(\delta) - \overline{x}(\delta)||d\tau \\
& + \frac{rMc_{\eta_1}}{\Gamma(\alpha)}\int_0^\rho (\rho-\tau)^{\alpha-1}\sup_{\delta\in[0,\tau]}||\overline{y}(\delta) - \overline{x}(\delta)||d\tau \\
\leq \; & rd_1||A^{-\gamma}|| \sup_{\delta\in[0,\eta]}||\overline{x}(\delta) - \overline{y}(\delta)|| \\
& + rd_1||A^{-\gamma}||\frac{\alpha C_{1-\gamma}\Gamma(1+\gamma)}{\Gamma(1+\alpha\gamma))}\int_a^\rho (\rho-\tau)^{\alpha\gamma-1}\sup_{\delta\in[a,\tau]}||\overline{y}(\delta) - \overline{x}(\delta)||d\tau \\
& + \frac{rMc_{\eta_1}}{\Gamma(\alpha)}\int_a^\rho (\rho-\tau)^{\alpha-1}\sup_{\delta\in[a,\tau]}||\overline{y}(\delta) - \overline{x}(\delta)||d\tau.
\end{aligned}$$

Since $rd_1||A^{-\gamma}|| < 1$, the last relations lead to

$$\begin{aligned}
& \sup_{\delta\in[0,\eta]}||\overline{x}(\delta) - \overline{y}(\delta)|| \\
\leq \; & \frac{1}{1-rd_1||A^{-\gamma}||}[\int_0^\rho (\rho-\tau)^{\alpha\gamma-1}d_1||A^{-\gamma}||\frac{r\alpha C_{1-\gamma}\Gamma(1+\gamma)}{\Gamma(1+\alpha\gamma))} \\
& + \int_0^\rho (\rho-\tau)^{\alpha-1}\frac{rMc_V}{\Gamma(\alpha)}]\sup_{\delta\in[0,\tau]}||\overline{y}(\delta) - \overline{x}(\delta)||d\tau.
\end{aligned}$$

Using the generalized Gronwall inequality [42], one has $\sup_{\delta\in[0,\eta]} ||\overline{x}(\delta) - \overline{y}(\delta)|| = 0$. Since $\eta \in [0, \eta_1]$ is arbitrary, we conclude that $\overline{x} = \overline{y}$ on $[0, \eta_1]$.

Next, let $\eta \in [\eta_1, \eta_2]$ be fixed. Note that $x(\eta_1^-) = y(\eta_1^-)$. Then,

$$\begin{aligned}
& ||\overline{y}(\eta) - \overline{x}(\eta)|| \\
\leq\ & ||h(\eta, \varkappa(\eta)\overline{y}) - h(\eta, \varkappa(\eta)\overline{x})||_{\Theta} \\
& +|| \int_{\eta_1}^{\eta} (\eta - \tau)^{\alpha-1} A\mathfrak{K}_2(\eta - \tau)(h(\tau, \varkappa(\tau)\overline{y}) - h(\tau, \varkappa(\tau)\overline{x}))d\tau|| \\
& +|| \int_{\eta_1}^{\eta} (\eta - \tau)^{\alpha-1} \mathfrak{K}_2(\eta - \tau)(g_n(\tau, \varkappa(\tau)\overline{y}) - g_n(\tau, \varkappa(\tau)\overline{x}))d\tau|| \\
\leq\ & d_1||A^{-\gamma}||\ ||\varkappa(\eta)\overline{y} - \varkappa(\eta)\overline{x}||_{\Theta} \\
& +d_1||A^{-\gamma}|| \frac{\alpha C_{1-\gamma}\Gamma(1+\gamma)}{\Gamma(1+\alpha\gamma))} \int_a^{\eta} (\eta - \tau)^{\alpha\gamma-1} ||\varkappa(\tau)\overline{y} - \varkappa(\tau)\overline{x}||_{\Theta} d\tau \\
& + \frac{M}{\Gamma(\alpha)} \int_{\eta_1}^{\eta} (\eta - \tau)^{\alpha-1} ||g_n(\tau, \varkappa(\tau)\overline{y}) - g_n(\tau, \varkappa(\tau)\overline{x}))||d\tau.
\end{aligned}$$

By repeating the arguments employed above, we get $\overline{x} = \overline{y}$ on $[\eta_1, \eta_2]$. Continuing with the same processes, we arrive to $\overline{x} = \overline{y}$ on J.

Next, we prove that $\sum_{\psi}^{F_n}[-r, b]$ is homotopically equivalent to $\overline{y}$. To this end, we define a continuous function $Z_n : [0,1] \times \sum_{\psi}^{F_n}[-r, b] \to \sum_{\psi}^{F_n}[-r, b]$, where $Z_n(0, \widetilde{x}) = \widetilde{x}$ and $(1, \widetilde{x}) = y$. Assume $(\lambda, \widetilde{x}) \in [0,1] \times \sum_{\psi}^{F_n}[-r, b]$ is fixed. Then, there exists a $f \in \tau^1_{F_n(.,\varkappa(.)\widetilde{x})}$ such that

$$\widetilde{x}(\eta) = \begin{cases} \psi(\eta), \eta \in [-r, 0], \\ \mathfrak{K}_1(\eta)[\psi(0) - h(0, \psi)] + h(\eta, \varkappa(\eta)\widetilde{x}) \\ + \int_0^{\eta} (\eta - \tau)^{\alpha-1} A\mathfrak{K}_2(\eta - \tau)h(\tau, \varkappa(\tau)\widetilde{x})d\tau \\ + \int_0^{\eta} (\eta - \tau)^{\alpha-1} \mathfrak{K}_2(\eta - \tau)f(\tau)d\tau \\ + \sum_{0<\eta_i<\eta} \mathfrak{K}_1(\eta - \eta_i)I_i(\widetilde{x}(\eta_i^-)), \eta \in J. \end{cases} \tag{39}$$

Consider the partition $\{0, \frac{1}{m+1}, \frac{2}{m+1}, \ldots, \frac{m+1}{m+1}\}$ for $J = [0,1]$. We consider the following cases:

(i) $\lambda \in [0, \frac{1}{m+1}]$. Put $a_\lambda^1 = \eta_{m+1} - \lambda\ (m+1)(\eta_{m+1} - \eta_m)$. The following fractional neutral differential inclusion is a result of the above discussion:

$$\begin{cases} {}^cD^{\alpha}_{a_\lambda^1,\eta}[x(\eta) - h(\eta, \varkappa(\eta)x)] = Ax(\eta) + g_n(\eta, \varkappa(\eta)x),\ a.e.\ \eta \in [a_{\lambda,1}, b], \\ x(\eta) = \widetilde{x}(\eta), \eta \in [-r, a_\lambda^1], \end{cases}$$

has a unique mild solution $x_\lambda^1 \in \sum_{\psi}^{F_n}[-r, b]$ satisfying the next integral equation:

$$x_\lambda^1(\eta) = \begin{cases} \widetilde{x}(\eta),\ \eta \in [-r, a_\lambda^1], \\ \mathfrak{K}_1(\eta - a_\lambda^1)[\widetilde{x}(a_\lambda^1) - h(a_\lambda^1, \varkappa(a_\lambda^1)\widetilde{x}(a_\lambda^1)] \\ +h(\eta, \varkappa(\eta)x_\lambda^1(\eta)) \\ + \int_{a_\lambda^1}^{\eta} (\eta - \tau)^{\alpha-1} A\mathfrak{K}_2(\eta - \tau)h(\tau, \varkappa(\tau)x_\lambda^1(\eta))d\tau \\ + \int_{a_\lambda^1}^{\eta} (\eta - \tau)^{\alpha-1} \mathfrak{K}_2(\eta - \tau)g_n(\eta, \varkappa(\eta)x_\lambda^1)d\tau, \eta \in [a_{\lambda,1}, b]. \end{cases} \tag{40}$$

Note that $x_0^1(\eta) = \widetilde{x}(\eta);\ \eta \in [-r, b]$.

(ii) $\lambda \in (\frac{1}{m+1}, \frac{2}{m+1}]$.Put $a_\lambda^2 = \eta_m - (m+1)(\lambda - \frac{1}{m+1})(\eta_m - \eta_{m-1})$. Again, the following fractional neutral differential inclusion:

$$\begin{cases} {}^cD^{\alpha}_{a_\lambda^2,\eta}[x(\eta) - h(\eta, \varkappa(\eta)x)] = Ax(\eta) + g_n(\eta, \varkappa(\eta)x),\ a.e.\ \eta \in [a_\lambda^2, b] - \{\eta_m\}, \\ I_m(x(\eta_m^-)) = x(\eta_m^-) - x(\eta_m^+), \\ x(\eta) = \widetilde{x}(\eta), \eta \in [-r, a_\lambda^2], \end{cases}$$

has a unique mild solution $x_\lambda^2 \in \sum_\psi^{F_n}[-r,b]$ and

$$x_\lambda^2(\eta) = \begin{cases} \widetilde{x}(\eta),\ \eta \in [-r, a_\lambda^2], \\ \mathfrak{K}_1(\eta - a_\lambda^2)[\widetilde{x}(a_\lambda^2) - h(a_{\lambda,1}, \varkappa(a_\lambda^2)\widetilde{x}(a_\lambda^2)] \\ +h(\eta, \varkappa(\eta)x_\lambda^2(\eta)) \\ +\int_{a_\lambda^2}^{\eta}(\eta-\tau)^{\alpha-1}A\mathfrak{K}_2(\eta-\tau)h(\tau, \varkappa(\tau)x_\lambda^2(\eta))d\tau \\ +\int_{a_\lambda^2}^{\eta}(\eta-\tau)^{\alpha-1}\mathfrak{K}_2(\eta-\tau)g_n(\eta, \varkappa(\eta)x_\lambda^2)d\tau \\ +\sum_{a_\lambda^2<\eta_i<\eta}\mathfrak{K}_1(\eta-\eta_i)I_i(x_\lambda^2(\eta_i^-)), \eta \in [a_\lambda^2, b]. \end{cases}$$

We continue up to $m+1-$step. That is $\lambda \in (\frac{m}{m+1}, 1]$ and put $a_\lambda^{m+1} = \eta_1 - (m+1)(\lambda - \frac{m}{m+1})\eta_1$. Let $x_\lambda^{m+1} \in \sum_\psi^{F_n}[-r,b\ ]$ be the unique mild solution for the impulsive fractional neutral differential inclusion:

$$\begin{cases} {}^cD^{\alpha}_{a_\lambda^{m+1},\eta}[x(\eta) - h(\eta, \varkappa(\eta)x)] = Ax(\eta) + g_n(\eta, \varkappa(\eta)x),\ a.e.\ \eta \in [a_\lambda^{m+1}, b] - \{\eta_1, \eta_2, \ldots \eta_m\}, \\ I_i(x(\eta_i^-)) = x(\eta_i^-) - x(\eta_i^+), i = 1, 2, \ldots, m \\ x(\eta) = \widetilde{x}(\eta), \eta \in [-r, a_\lambda^{m+1}]. \end{cases}$$

Then,

$$x_\lambda^{m+1}(\eta) = \begin{cases} \widetilde{x}(\eta),\ \eta \in [-r, a_\lambda^{m+1}], \\ \mathfrak{K}_1(\eta)[\widetilde{x}(a_\lambda^{m+1}) - h(a_{\lambda,1}, \varkappa(a_\lambda^{m+1})\widetilde{x}(a_\lambda^{m+1})] \\ +h(\eta, \varkappa(\eta)x_\lambda^{m+1}) \\ +\int_{a_\lambda^{m+1}}^{\eta}(\eta-\tau)^{\alpha-1}A\mathfrak{K}_2(\eta-\tau)h(\tau, \varkappa(\tau)x_\lambda^{m+1}(\eta))d\tau \\ +\int_{a_\lambda^{m+1}}^{\eta}(\eta-\tau)^{\alpha-1}\mathfrak{K}_2(\eta-\tau)g_n(\eta, \varkappa(\eta)x_\lambda^{m+1})d\tau \\ +\sum_{a_\lambda^{m+1}<\eta_i<\eta}\mathfrak{K}_1(\eta-\eta_i)I_i(x_\lambda^{m+1}(\eta_i^-)), \eta \in [a_\lambda^{m+1}, b]. \end{cases} \tag{41}$$

Note that $a_1^{m+1} = 0$ and $x_1^{m+1} = y$. Now, we define Z_n at $(\lambda, \widetilde{x})$ as

$$Z_n(\lambda, \widetilde{x}) = \begin{cases} x_\lambda^1, \quad \text{if } \lambda \in [0, \frac{1}{m+1}], \\ x_\lambda^2, \text{if } \lambda \in (\frac{1}{m+1}, \frac{2}{m+1}], \\ . \\ . \\ . \\ x_\lambda^{m+1}, \quad \text{if } \lambda \in (\frac{m}{m+1}, 1]. \end{cases} \tag{42}$$

Therefore, $Z_n(0, \widetilde{x}) = x_\lambda^1 = \widetilde{x}$ and $Z_n(1, \widetilde{x}) = x_1^{m+1} = y$.

It remains to clarify the continuity of Z_n. Let $(\lambda, u\ ), (\varrho, v) \in [0,1] \times \sum_\psi^{F_n}[-r,b]$. Let $\lambda = \varrho = 0$. Then, by (42), $\lim_{u\to v} Z_n(\lambda, u) = \lim_{u\to v} u = v = Z_n(\varrho, v)$. Let $\lambda, \varrho \in (0, \frac{1}{m+1}]$. So, $Z_n(\lambda, u) = \overline{u}_\lambda^1$ and $Z_n(\lambda, v) = \overline{v}_\mu^1$, where

$$\overline{u}_\lambda^1(\eta) = \begin{cases} \widetilde{x}(\eta),\ \eta \in [-r, a_\lambda^1], \\ \mathfrak{K}_1(\eta - a_\lambda^1)[\widetilde{x}(a_\lambda^1) - h(a_\lambda^1, \varkappa(a_\lambda^1)\widetilde{x}(a_\lambda^1)] \\ +h(\eta, \varkappa(\eta)\overline{u}_\lambda^1(\eta)) \\ +\int_{a_\lambda^1}^{\eta}(\eta-\tau)^{\alpha-1}A\mathfrak{K}_2(\eta-\tau)h(\tau, \varkappa(\tau)\overline{u}_\lambda^1(\eta))d\tau \\ +\int_{a_\lambda^1}^{\eta}(\eta-\tau)^{\alpha-1}\mathfrak{K}_2(\eta-\tau)g_n(\eta, \varkappa(\eta)\overline{u}_\lambda^1)d\tau, \eta \in [a_{\lambda,1}, b], \end{cases} \tag{43}$$

and

$$\overline{v}_{\mu}^{1}(\eta)=\begin{cases}\widetilde{x}(\eta),\ \eta\in[-r,a_{\mu}^{1}],\\ \mathfrak{K}_1(\eta-a_{\lambda}^{1})[\widetilde{x}(a_{\lambda}^{1})-h(a_{\mu}^{1},\varkappa(a_{\mu}^{1})\widetilde{x}(a_{\mu}^{1})]\\ +h(\eta,\varkappa(\eta)\overline{v}_{\mu}^{1}(\eta))\\ +\int_{a_{\mu}^{1}}^{\eta}(\eta-\tau)^{\alpha-1}A\mathfrak{K}_2(\eta-\tau)h(\tau,\varkappa(\tau)\overline{v}_{\mu}^{1}(\eta))d\tau\\ +\int_{a_{\mu}^{1}}^{\eta}(\eta-\tau)^{\alpha-1}\mathfrak{K}_2(\eta-\tau)g_n(\eta,\varkappa(\eta)\overline{v}_{\mu}^{1})d\tau,\eta\in[a_{\mu}^{1},b],\end{cases} \tag{44}$$

$a_{\lambda}^{1}=b-\mu(m+1)(b-\tau_m)$ and $a_{\mu}^{1}=b-\mu(m+1)(b-\tau_m)$. Obviously, $\lim_{\lambda\to\mu}a_{\lambda}^{1}=a_{\mu}^{1}$ and, hence, by (43) and (44), and by arguing as above, we get

$$\lim_{\substack{\lambda\to\mu\\ u\to v}}Z_n(\lambda,u)=Z_n(\mu,v),$$

which implies the continuity of $Z_n(.,.)$, when $\lambda\in[0,\frac{1}{m+1}]$. Similarly, we can show the continuity of Z_n and consequently, $\sum_{\psi}^{F_n}[-r,b]$ is contractible. This completes the proof. □

5. Example

Example 1. *Assume that* $E=L^2([0,\pi],\mathbb{R})$, $J=[0,1]$, $r=\frac{1}{2}$, $m=1$, $\eta_0=0$ *and* $\eta_1=\frac{1}{2}$, $\eta_2=1$. *For any* $x:J\to E=L^2([0,\pi],\mathbb{R})$, *we denote by* $x(\eta,\omega);\eta\in J,\omega\in[0,\pi]$ *the value of* $x(\eta)$ *at* ω. *Let* $A:D(A)\subseteq L^2[0,\pi]\to L^2[0,\pi]$, $Ax(\eta,\omega):=-\frac{\partial^2}{\partial\omega^2}x(\eta,\omega)$ *and domain* A *be defined as*

$$\begin{aligned}D(A)&=\{x\in L^2[0,\pi]:x,x'\ \textit{are absolutely continuous},\ x''\in L^2[0,1],\\ x(\eta,0)&=x(\eta,\pi)=0\}.\end{aligned}$$

Using [37], there is a compact analytic semi-group $\{Y(\eta):\eta\geq 0\}$ generated by A and

$$Ax=\sum_{n=1}^{\infty}n^2<x,\ x_n>x_n,x\in D(A), \tag{45}$$

where $x_n(y)=\sqrt{2}\ \sin ny, n=1,2,\ldots$ is the orthonormal set of eigenvalues of A. In addition, for all $x\in L^2[0,1]$, one gets

$$Y(\eta)(x)=\sum_{n=1}^{\infty}e^{-n^2\eta}<x,\ x_n>x_n.$$

So, $M=\sup\{||Y(\eta)||:\eta\geq 0\}=1$. Furthermore, for each $x\in L^2([0,\pi],\mathbb{R})$,

$$A^{\frac{-1}{2}}x=\sum_{n=1}^{\infty}\frac{1}{n}<x,\ x_n>x_n.$$

$$A^{\frac{1}{2}}x=\sum_{n=1}^{\infty}n<x,\ x_n>x_n,$$

and $||A^{\frac{-1}{2}}||=1$. The domain of $A^{\frac{1}{2}}$ is defined as

$$D(A^{\frac{1}{2}})=\{x\in L^2([0,\pi],\mathbb{R}):\sum_{n=1}^{\infty}n<x,\ x_n>x_n\in L^2([0,\pi],\mathbb{R})\}.$$

Let $h:J\times\Theta\to E$ be such that

$$h(\eta,u):=A^{\frac{-1}{2}}(\int_{-r}^{0}\lambda u(\theta)d\theta), \tag{46}$$

where $\lambda > 0$. We have

$$\begin{aligned} ||A^{\frac{1}{2}}h(\eta,u_1) - A^{\frac{1}{2}}h(\eta,u_2)||_E &\leq \lambda || \int_{-r}^{0} (u_1(\theta) - u_2(\theta))d\theta|| \\ &\leq \lambda \int_{-r}^{0} ||u_1(\theta) - u_2(\theta)||d\theta \\ &\leq \lambda||u_1 - u_2||_\Theta, \end{aligned}$$

and

$$||A^\gamma h(\eta,u)|| \leq \lambda || \int_{-r}^{0} (u(\theta)d\theta|| \leq \lambda||u||_\Theta.$$

Then, (10) and (11) are satisfied with $d_1 = d_2 = \lambda$.

Let Λ be a convex compact subset in E, $\sup\{||z|| : z \in Z\} = \varrho$ and $\kappa > 0$. Define $F : J \times \Theta \to 2^{L^2[0,\pi]}$ by

$$F(\eta,u) := \frac{e^{-\kappa\eta}||u||}{\varrho}\Lambda. \tag{47}$$

We have

$$||F(\eta,u)|| = \sup\{||\frac{e^{\kappa\eta}||u||}{\varrho}z : z \in \Lambda\} \leq e^{\kappa\eta}; \eta \in J.$$

Moreover, for any bounded subset $D \subset \Theta$, we have $F(\eta,D) \subseteq \varsigma\frac{e^{\kappa\eta}}{\varrho}\Lambda$, where $\varsigma = \sup\{||u|| : u \in D\}$ and, hence, $\chi_E(F(\eta,D)) = 0$. Then, F satisfies $(HF1), (HF2)^*$and $(HF3)$ with $\xi(\eta) = e^{-\kappa\eta}, \beta(\eta) = 0; \eta \in J$.

Next, let

$$I : E \to E, I_i(x) := \sigma\ proj_\Lambda x, \tag{48}$$

where σ is a positive number. Obviously, I verifies (HI) with $\varsigma_i = 0\,; i = 1,2,\ldots$.

Therefore, by applying Theorems 1 and 4, the set of solutions for the following fractional neutral impulsive semilinear differential inclusions with delay:

$$\begin{cases} {}^cD^\alpha_{0,\eta}[x(\eta) - h(\eta,\varkappa(\eta)x)] \\ \in -\frac{\partial^2}{\partial\omega^2}x(\eta,\omega) + F(\eta,\varkappa(\eta)x),\ a.e.\ \eta \in [0,1] - \{\frac{1}{2},1\}, \\ I_i x(\eta_i^-,\omega) = x(\eta_i^-,\omega) - x(\eta_i^+,\omega), i = 1,2, \omega \in [0,\pi], \\ x(\eta,\omega) = \psi(\eta,\omega), \eta \in [-r,0], \eta \in [0,1] - \{\frac{1}{2},1\}, \end{cases} \tag{49}$$

is a not empty, compact and an R_δ-set provided that

$$\lambda(1 + \frac{C_{1-\gamma}\Gamma(\frac{3}{2})}{\Gamma(1+\frac{\alpha}{2})}) < 1, \tag{50}$$

and

$$\frac{\lambda}{2} + 2\lambda\frac{C_{1-\gamma}\Gamma(\frac{3}{2})}{\Gamma(1+\frac{\alpha}{2})} + \frac{1}{2\Gamma((\alpha)}(\frac{P-1}{\alpha P - 1})^{\frac{P-1}{P}}||\xi||_{L^P_{(J,,\mathbb{R}^+)}} + \sigma < 1, \tag{51}$$

where $F, h\ I$ are given by (45)–(47). By choosing λ and σ small enough and κ large enough, we arrive to (50) and (51).

Example 2. *Let $J, E, A, r, \eta_0, \eta_1, \eta_2\ \Lambda$, and ϱ be as in Example (1) and $\theta \in [-r,0]$ be a fixed element.*

Let $h : J \times \Theta \to E$ be such that

$$h((\eta,\varkappa(\eta)x)(\omega) := \lambda \int_0^\pi U(\omega,y)x(\theta+\eta)(\omega)dy; \omega \in [0,\pi]; \eta \in [0,1], \tag{52}$$

where $\lambda > 0$, $U : [0, \pi] \times [0, \pi] \to \mathbb{R}$ is measurable, $\int_0^{\pi} \int_0^{\pi} U(\omega, y) dy d\omega < \infty$, $\frac{\partial U(\omega,\eta)}{\partial \omega}$ is measurable, $U(0, y) = U(\pi, y) = 0, \forall y \in [0, \pi]$ and $(\int_0^{\pi} \int_0^{\pi} (\frac{\partial U(\omega,\eta)}{\partial \omega})^2 dy d\omega)^{\frac{1}{2}} < \infty$.

Next, let $F : J \times \Theta \to 2^{L^2[0,\pi]}$, $F((\eta, \varkappa(\eta)x)(\omega) = \frac{\gamma G(\eta, x(\theta+\eta)(\omega))|}{\varrho}\Lambda$, where $\gamma > 0$, $G : J \times \mathbb{R} \to \mathbb{R}$ is a continuous function. Then, by choosing λ and σ small enough, one can show that h and F satisfy all assumptions of Theorems 2 (see [15,43]) and, hence, the set of mild solutions for the partial differential inclusions of impulsive neutral type with delay:

$$\begin{cases} {}^{c}D^{\alpha}_{0,\eta}[x(\eta,\omega) - \int_0^{\pi} U(\omega,y)x(\theta+\eta)(\omega)dy,] \\ \in -\frac{\partial^2}{\partial \omega^2}x(\eta,\omega) + \frac{G(\eta,x(\theta+\eta)(\omega))|}{\varrho}\Lambda, \ a.e.\ \eta \in [0,1] - \{\frac{1}{2}, 1\}, \\ I_i x(\eta_i^-, \omega) = x(\eta_i^-, \omega) - x(\eta_i^+, \omega), i = 1, 2, \omega \in [0, \pi], \\ x(\eta, \omega) = \psi(\eta, \omega), \eta \in [-r, 0], \eta \in [0,1] - \{\frac{1}{2}, 1\}, \end{cases} \tag{53}$$

is an R_δ-set.

6. Discussion

The neutral differential equations and inclusions appear in many applied mathematical sciences such as viscoelasticity, and the equations describe the distribution of heat. Since the set of mild solutions for a differential inclusion having the same initial point may not be a singleton, many authors are interested to investigate the structure of this set in a topological point of view. An important aspect of such structure is the R_δ- property, which means that the homology group of the set of mild solutions is the same as a one-point space. In the literature, there are many results on this subject but no result about the topological properties of the set of mild solutions for a fractional neutral differential inclusion generated by a non-compact semigroup in the presence of impulses and delay. As cited in the introduction, when the problem involves delay and impulses, we cannot consider the space $\mathcal{PC}([-r, b], E]$ as the space of solutions. To overcome these difficulties, a complete metric space H is introduced as the space of mild solutions. In addition, the function $\eta \to \varkappa(\eta)\overline{x}; \overline{x} \in H$ is not necessarily measurable, therefore, a norm different from the uniform convergence norm is introduced on Θ (see Equation (2)).

7. Conclusions

During the past two decades, fractional differential equations and fractional differential inclusions have gained considerable importance due to their applications in various fields, such as physics, mechanics and engineering. For some of these applications, one can see [28] and the references therein. In this paper, we have given an affirmative answer for a basic question, which is whether there exists a solution set carrying an R_δ-structure when there are impulsive effects and delay on the system, the operator families generated by the linear part lack compactness and the order is fractional. More specifically,

1. By utilizing the properties of both multivalued functions, fraction powers of operators, measures of non-compactness and analytic semi-groups, we showed that the mild solutions set for a fractional impulsive neutral semilinear differential inclusions with delay and generated by a non-compact semi-group is not empty, compact and an R_δ-set. This means that, from an algebraic topological perspective, it is equivalent to a point.
2. Our work generalizes the obtained results in [19], where Problem 1 is investigated without delay and $h \equiv 0$.
3. Our work generalizes the obtained results in [15] to the case when there are impulsive effects on the system.
4. Our technique can be used to prove that the solutions set is an R_δ-set for problems considered in [13–23,30] when it is generated by a non-compact semi-group, the order is fractional and there are impulsive effects and delay.
5. As a future work, we suggest to extend the work conducted in [24–26] to find the sufficient conditions that guarantee that the solution set is an R_δ-set.

Author Contributions: Funding acquisition, Z.A. and A.G.I.; investigation, Z.A. and A.G.I.; methodology, Z.A., A.G.I. and A.A.; writing—original draft, Z.A. and A.G.I.; writing—review and editing, Z.A., A.G.I. and A.A. All authors have read and agreed to the published version of the manuscript.

Funding: This research received no external funding.

Data Availability Statement: Not applicable.

Acknowledgments: This research has been funded by the Scientific Research Deanship at University of Ha'il—Saudi Arabia through project number RG-21 101.

Conflicts of Interest: The authors declare no conflict of interest.

References

1. Aissani, K.; Benchohra, M. Impulsive fractional differential inclusions with state-dependent delay. *Math. Moravica* **2019**, *23*, 97–113. [CrossRef]
2. Chen, Y.; Wang, J.R. Continuous dependence of solutions of integer and fractional order non-instantaneous impulsive equations with random impulsive and junction points. *Mathematics* **2019**, *7*, 331. [CrossRef]
3. Ibrahim, A.G. Differential Equations and inclusions of fractional order with impulse effect in Banach spaces. *Bull. Malays. Math. Sci. Soc.* **2020**, *43*, 69–109. [CrossRef]
4. Liu, S.; Wang, J.R.; Shen,D.; O'Regan, D. Iterative learning control for differential inclusions of parabolic type with non-instantaneous impulses. *Appl. Math. Comput.* **2019**, *350*, 48–59. [CrossRef]
5. Wang, J.R.; Li, M.; O'Regan, D. Robustness for linear evolution equation with non-instantaneous impulsive effects. *Bull. Sci. Math.* **2020**, *150*, 102827. [CrossRef]
6. Wang, J.R.; Ibrahim, A.G.; O'Regan, D. Nonempties and compactness of the solution set for fractional evolution inclusions with of non-instantaneous impulses. *Electron. J. Differ. Equ.* **2019**, *37*, 1–17.
7. Wang, J.R.; Ibrahim, A.G.; O'Regan, D. Global attracting solutions to Hilfer fractional differential inclusions of Sobolev type with non-instantaneous impulses and nonlocal conditions. *Nonlinear Anal. Model. Control* **2019**, *24*, 775–803.
8. Wang, J.R.; Ibrahim, A.G.; O'Regan, D. Controllability of Hilfer Fractional Noninstantaneous Impulsive Semilinear Differential Inclusions with Nonlocal Conditions. *Nonlinear Anal. Model. Control* **2019**, *24*, 958–984. [CrossRef]
9. Zhou, Y.; Vijayakumar, V.; Ravichandran, C.; Murugesu, R. Controllability results for fractional order neutral functional differential inclusions with infinite delay. *Fixed Point Theory* **2017**, *18*, 773–798. [CrossRef]
10. Yang, M.; Wang, Q. Approximate controllability of Caputo fractional neutral stochastic differential inclusions with state dependent delay. *IMA J. Math. Control Inf.* **2018**, *35*, 1061–1085. [CrossRef]
11. Yan, Z.; Jia, X. Approximate controllability of fractional impulsive partial neutral integro-differential inclusions with infinite delay in Hilbert spaces. *Adv. Differ. Equ.* **2015**, 1–31. [CrossRef]
12. Chalishajar, D.; Anguraj, A.; Malar, K.; Karthikeyan, K. Study of controllability of impulsive neutral evolution integro-differential equations with state-dependent delay in Banach Spaces. *Mathematics* **2016**, *4*, 1–16. [CrossRef]
13. Gabor, G.; Grudzka, A. Structure of the solution set to impulsive functional differential inclusions on the half-line. *Nonlinear Differ. Equ. Appl.* **2012**, *19*, 609–627. [CrossRef]
14. Djebali, S.; Gorniewicz, L.; Ouahab, A. Topological structure of solution sets for impulsive differential inclusions in Fré chet spaces. *Nonlinear Anal.* **2011**, *74*, 2141–2169. [CrossRef]
15. Zhou, Y.; Peng, L. Topological properties of solution sets for partial functional evolution inclusions. *C. R. Math.* **2017**, *1*, 45–64. [CrossRef]
16. Zhou, Y.; Peng, L.; Ahmed, B.; Alsaedi, A. Topological properties of solution sets of fractional stochastic evolution inclusions. *Adv. Differ. Equ.* **2017**, *90*, 1–20. [CrossRef]
17. Zhao, Z.H.; Chang, Y.-k. Topological properties of solution sets for Sobolev type fractional stochastic differential inclusions with Poisson jumps. *Appl. Anal.* **2020**, *99*, 1373–1401. [CrossRef]
18. Beddani, M.; Hedia, B. Solution sets for fractional differential inclusions. *J. Fract. Calc. Appl.* **2019**, *10*, 273–289.
19. Wang, J.R.; Ibrahim, A.G.; O'Regan, D. Topological structure of the solution set for fractional non-instantaneous impulsive evolution inclusions. *J. Fixed Point Theory Appl.* **2018**, *20*, 20–59. [CrossRef]
20. Ouahab, A.; Seghiri, S. Nonlocal fractional differential inclusions with impulses at variable times. *Surv. Math. Its Appl.* **2019**, *14*, 307–325.
21. Ziane, M. On the Solution Set for Weighted Fractional Differential Equations in Banach Spaces. *Differ Equ. Dyn. Syst.* **2020**, *28*, 419–430. [CrossRef]
22. Zhang, L.; Zhou, Y.; Ahmad, B. Topological properties of C_0-solution set for impulsive evolution inclusions. *Bound. Value Probl.* **2018**, *2018*, 182. [CrossRef]
23. Wang, R.N.; Ma, Z.X.; Miranville, A. Topological Structure of the Solution Sets for a Nonlinear Delay. *Int. Math. Res. Not.* **2021**, *2022*, 4801–4889. [CrossRef]
24. Castaing, C.; Godet-Thobie, C.; Phung, P.D.; Truong, L.X. On fractional differential inclusions with Nonlocal boundary conditions. *Fract. Calc. Appl. Anal.* **2019**, *22*, 444–478. [CrossRef]

25. Xiang, O.; Zhu, P. Some New Results for the Sobolev-Type Fractional Order Delay Systems with Noncompact Semigroup. *J. Funct. Spaces* **2020**, *2020*. [CrossRef]
26. Zhu, P.; Xiang, Q. Topological structure of solution sets for fractional evolution inclusions of Sobolev type. *Bound. Value Probl.* **2018**, *2018*, 1–3. [CrossRef]
27. Zhou, Y.; Wang, R-N.; Peng, L. *Topological Structure of the Solution Set for Evolution Inclusions, Developments in Mathematics*; Springer: Singapore, 2017.
28. Kilbas, A.A.; Srivastava, H.M.; Trujillo, J.J. *Theory and Applications of Fractional Differential Equations, North Holland Mathematics Studies*; Elsevier Science: Amsterdam, The Netherlands, 2006.
29. Burqan, A.; Saadeh, R.; Qazza, A.A. Novel numerical approach in solving fractional neutral pantograph equations via the ARA integral transform. *Symmetry* **2022**, *14*, 50. [CrossRef]
30. Ma, Y.K.; Kavitha, K.; Albalawi, W.; Shukla, A.; Nisar, K.S.; Vijayakumar, V. An analysis on the approximate controllability of Hilfer fractional neutral differential systems in Hilbert spaces. *Alex. Eng. J.* 2022, *in press*. [CrossRef]
31. Etemad, S.; Souid, M.S.; Telli, B.; Kaabar, M.; Rezapour, S. Investigation of the neutral fractional differential inclusions of Katugampola-type involving both retarded and advanced arguments via Kuratowski MNC technique. *Adv. Differ. Equ.* **2021**, *2021*, 214. [CrossRef]
32. Sindhu, T.N.; Atangana, A. Reliability analysis incorporating exponentiated inverse Weibull distribution and inverse power law. *Qual. Reliab. Eng. Int.* **2021**, *37*, 2399–2422. [CrossRef]
33. Rahman, A.; Sindhu, T.N.; Lone, S.A.; Kamal, M. Statistical inference for Burr Type X distribution using geometric process in accelerated life testing design for time censored data. *Pak. J. Stat. Oper. Res.* **2020**, *16*, 577–586. [CrossRef]
34. Shafiq, A.; Sindhu, T.N.; Al-Mdallal, Q.M. A sensitivity study on carbon nanotubes significance in Darcy–Forchheimer flow towards a rotating disk by response surface methodology. *Sci. Rep.* **2021**, *11*, 1–26. [CrossRef] [PubMed]
35. Wang, J.R.; Zhou, Y. Existence and controllability results for fractional semilinear differential inclusions. *Nonlinear Anal. Real World Appl.* **2011**, *12*, 3642–3653. [CrossRef]
36. Guedda, L. Some remarks in the study of impulsive differential equations and inclusions with delay. *Fixed Point Theory* **2011**, *12*, 349–354.
37. Pazy, A. *Semigroup of Linear Operators and Applications to Partial Differential Equations*; Springer: New York, NY, USA, 1983.
38. Kamenskii, M.; Obukhowskii, V.; Zecca, P. *Condensing Multivalued Maps and Semilinear Differential Inclusions in Banach Spaces*; De Gruyter Series in Nonlinear Analysis and Applications; De Gruyter: Berlin, NY, USA, 2001; Volume 7.
39. Bothe, D. Multivalued perturbation of m-accerative differential inclusions. *Israel J. Math.* **1998**, *108*, 109–138. [CrossRef]
40. Bader, K.M.; Obukhowskii, V. On some class of operator inclusions with lower semicontinuous nonlinearity: Nonlinear Analysis. *J. Jul. Schauder Cent.* **2001**, *17*, 143–156.
41. Hyman, D.H. On decreasing sequence of compact absolute Retract. *Fund. Math.* **1969**, *64*, 91–97. [CrossRef]
42. Ye, H.; Gao, J.; Ding, J.Y. A generalized Gronwall inequality and its application to a fractional differential equation. *J. Math. Anal. Appl.* **2007**, *328*, 1075–1081. [CrossRef]
43. Zhou, Y.; Jiao, F. Existence of mild solutions for fractional neutral evolution equations. *Comput. Math. Appl.* **2010**, *59*, 1063–1077. [CrossRef]

fractal and fractional

MDPI

Article

Existence of Mild Solutions for Hilfer Fractional Neutral Integro-Differential Inclusions via Almost Sectorial Operators

Chandra Bose Sindhu Varun Bose and **Ramalingam Udhayakumar** *

Department of Mathematics, School of Advanced Sciences, Vellore Institute of Technology, Vellore 632 014, Tamil Nadu, India
* Correspondence: udhayaram.v@gmail.com or udhayakumar.r@vit.ac.in

Abstract: This manuscript focuses on the existence of a mild solution Hilfer fractional neutral integro-differential inclusion with almost sectorial operator. By applying the facts related to fractional calculus, semigroup, and Martelli's fixed point theorem, we prove the primary results. In addition, the application is provided to demonstrate how the major results might be applied.

Keywords: Hilfer fractional system; neutral system; multi-valued maps; sectorial operators

MSC: 26A33; 34A08; 34K30; 47D09

Citation: Varun Bose, C.B.S.; Udhayakumar, R. Existence of Mild Solutions for Hilfer Fractional Neutral Integro-Differential Inclusions via Almost Sectorial Operators. *Fractal Fract.* **2022**, *6*, 532. https://doi.org/10.3390/fractalfract6090532

Academic Editor: Rodica Luca

Received: 18 August 2022
Accepted: 16 September 2022
Published: 19 September 2022

1. Introduction

In modern mathematics, the fundamentals surrounding fractional computation and the fractional differential equation have taken center stage. The idea of fractional computation has now been put to the test in a wide variety of social, physical, signal, image processing, biological, control theory, engineering, etc., challenges. However, it has been demonstrated that fractional differential equations may be a valuable tool for describing a variety of situations. For many different types of realistic applications, fractional-order models are superior to integer-order models. The research articles [1–15] are concerned with the theory of fractional differential systems, and readers will find a number of fascinating findings about fractional dynamical systems. Please refer to [16–21] for more information.

Other fractional derivatives introduced by Hilfer [22] include the R-L derivative and Caputo fractional derivative. Many scholars have recently shown tremendous interest in this area, e.g., [23–25]; researchers have established their results with the help of Schauder's fixed point theorem. In [26–28], the authors worked on the existence and controllability of differential inclusions via the fixed point theorem approach. In references [29–31], the authors discussed the existence of a mild solution by using Martelli's fixed point theorem. As a result of these findings, we expand on the literature's earlier findings to a class of Hilfer fractional differential (HFD) systems in which the closed operator is almost sectorial.

In [32], M. Zhou, C. Li, and Y. Zhou studied the existence of mild solutions to Hilfer fractional differential equations with the order $\lambda \in (0,1)$ and type $\nu \in [0,1]$ in the abstract sense, as follows:

$$\begin{aligned} &{}^{H}D_{0^+}^{\lambda,\nu} y(t) = Ay(t) + g(t, y(t)),\ t \in (0,T], \\ &I_{0^+}^{(1-\lambda)(1-\nu)} y(0) = y_0, \end{aligned}$$

here, A denotes the almost sectorial operator of the semigroup and the Schauder fixed point theorem is used.

In [33], Zhang and Zhou demonstrated the existence of fractional Cauchy problems using almost sectorial operators of the type,

$$
\begin{aligned}
{}^{L}D^{q}_{0+}x(t) &= Ax(t) + f(t, x(t))\; t \in [0, a], \\
I^{(1-q)}_{0+}x(0) &= x_0,
\end{aligned}
$$

where ${}^{L}D^{q}_{0+}$ is the $R-L$ derivative of order q, $0 < q < 1$, $I^{(1-q)}_{0+}$ is the $R-L$ integral of order $1-q$, A is an almost sectorial operator on a complex Banach space. We refer the reader to [34–37] for information. These discoveries led us to extend past findings in the literature to Hilfer fractional Volterra–Fredholm integro-differential inclusions.

We will examine the following subject in the article: The almost sectorial operators are contained in the HF neutral integro-differential inclusion,

$$
D^{\kappa,\varepsilon}_{0+}[\mathrm{y}(\mathfrak{z}) - \mathcal{N}(\mathfrak{z}, \mathrm{y}(\mathfrak{z}))] \in \mathtt{A}\mathrm{y}(\mathfrak{z}) + \mathcal{G}\left(\mathfrak{z}, \mathrm{y}(\mathfrak{z}), \int_0^{\mathfrak{z}} e(\mathfrak{z}, s, \mathrm{y}(s))ds\right), \qquad \mathfrak{z} \in \mathcal{J}' = (0, d], \quad (1)
$$

$$
I^{(1-\kappa)(1-\varepsilon)}_{0+}\mathrm{y}(0) = \mathrm{y}_0, \quad (2)
$$

where $D^{\kappa,\varepsilon}_{0+}$ notates the HFD of order κ, $0 < \kappa < 1$, type ε, $0 \le \varepsilon \le 1$; and $\mathtt{A}$ is an almost sectorial operator of the analytic semigroup $\{\mathtt{T}(\mathfrak{z}), \mathfrak{z} \ge 0\}$ on Y. State $\mathrm{y}(\cdot)$ takes the value in a Banach space Y with norm $\|\cdot\|$. Let $\mathcal{J} = [0, d]$, $\mathcal{N} : \mathcal{J} \times Y$ be the appropriate function, $\mathcal{G} : \mathcal{J} \times Y \times Y \to 2^{Y}\backslash\{\emptyset\}$ be a non-empty, bounded, closed convex multi-valued map, $\mathcal{N} : \mathcal{J} \times Y \to Y$ and $e : \mathcal{J} \times \mathcal{J} \times Y \to Y$ are the appropriate functions.

This article is structured as follows: In Section 2, we present the fundamentals of fractional differential systems, semigroup, and closed linear operators. In Section 3, we present the existence of the required solution. In Section 4, we provide an application to demonstrate our main arguments and some inferences are established in the end.

2. Preliminaries

Here, we introduce some basic definitions, theorems, and lemmas that are applied to every part of the paper.

Let $\mathtt{C}$ be the collection of all continuous functions from $\mathcal{J}$ to Y, where $\mathcal{J} = [0, d]$ and $\mathcal{J}' = (0, d]$ with $d > 0$. Take $\mathcal{X} = \{\mathrm{y} \in \mathtt{C} : \lim_{\mathfrak{z}\to 0} \mathfrak{z}^{1-\varepsilon+\kappa\varepsilon-\kappa\xi}\mathrm{y}(\mathfrak{z})$ exists and finite $\}$, which is the Banach space and its norm on $\|\cdot\|_{\mathcal{X}}$, defined as $\|\mathrm{y}\|_{\mathcal{X}} = \sup_{\mathfrak{z}\in\mathcal{I}'}\{\mathfrak{z}^{1-\varepsilon+\kappa\varepsilon-\kappa\xi}\|\mathrm{y}(\mathfrak{z})\|\}$. Let $\mathrm{y}(\mathfrak{z}) = \mathfrak{z}^{-1+\varepsilon-\kappa\varepsilon+\kappa\xi}u(\mathfrak{z})$, $\mathfrak{z} \in (0, d]$ then, $\mathrm{y} \in \mathcal{X}$ *iff* $y \in \mathtt{C}$ *and* $\|\mathrm{y}\|_{\mathcal{X}} = \|\mathrm{y}\|$. Moreover, define $B_P(\mathcal{J}) = \{\mathrm{y} \in \mathtt{C}$ *such that* $\|\mathrm{y}\| \le P\}$.

Definition 1 ([19])**.** *The left side of the R-L fractional integral of order κ with the lower limit d for function $\mathcal{G} : [d, \infty) \to \mathbb{R}$ is presented by*

$$
I^{\kappa}_{d+}\mathcal{G}(\mathfrak{z}) = \frac{1}{\Gamma(\kappa)}\int_d^{\mathfrak{z}} \frac{\mathcal{G}(w)}{(\mathfrak{z} - w)^{1-\kappa}}dw, \; \mathfrak{z} > 0, \; \kappa > 0,
$$

provided the right side is pointwise determined on $[d, +\infty)$, $\Gamma(\cdot)$ is the gamma function.

Definition 2 ([19])**.** *The left-sided R-L fractional derivative of order $\kappa > 0$, $m - 1 \le \kappa < m$, $m \in \mathbb{N}$, for a function $\mathcal{G} : [d, +\infty) \to \mathbb{R}$ is presented by*

$$
{}^{L}D^{\kappa}_{d+}\mathcal{G}(\mathfrak{z}) = \frac{1}{\Gamma(m - \kappa)}\frac{d^m}{d\mathfrak{z}^m}\int_d^{\mathfrak{z}} \frac{\mathcal{G}(w)}{(\mathfrak{z} - w)^{\kappa+1-m}}dw, \; \mathfrak{z} > d,
$$

where $\Gamma(\cdot)$ is the gamma function.

Definition 3 ([19]). *The left-sided Caputo derivative of the type of order $\kappa > 0$, $m - 1 \leq \kappa < m$, $m \in \mathbb{N}$ for a function $\mathcal{G} : [d, +\infty) \to \mathbb{R}$, is defined as*

$$ {}^{C}D^{\kappa}_{d^+}\mathcal{G}(\mathfrak{z}) = \frac{1}{\Gamma(m-\kappa)} \int_d^{\mathfrak{z}} \frac{\mathcal{G}^m(w)}{(\mathfrak{z}-w)^{\kappa+1-m}} dw = I^{m-\kappa}_{d+}\mathcal{G}^m(\mathfrak{z}),\ \mathfrak{z} > d, $$

where $\Gamma(\cdot)$ is the gamma function.

Definition 4 ([22]). *The left-sided HFD of order $0 < \kappa < 1$ and type $\varepsilon \in [0,1]$, of function $\mathcal{G} : [d, +\infty) \to \mathbb{R}$, is defined as*

$$ D^{\kappa,\varepsilon}_{d^+}\mathcal{G}(\mathfrak{z}) = [I^{(1-\kappa)\varepsilon}_{d^+} D(I^{(1-\kappa)(1-\varepsilon)}_{d^+}\mathcal{G})](\mathfrak{z}). $$

Remark 1 ([22]). *1. If $\varepsilon = 0$, $0 < \kappa < 1$, and $d = 0$, then the HFD corresponds to the classical R-L fractional derivative:*

$$ D^{\kappa,0}_{0^+}\mathcal{G}(\mathfrak{z}) = \frac{d}{d\mathfrak{z}} I^{1-\kappa}_{0+}\mathcal{G}(\mathfrak{z}) =^{L} D^{\kappa}_{0^+}\mathcal{G}(\mathfrak{z}). $$

2. *If $\varepsilon = 1$, $0 < \kappa < 1$, and $d = 0$, then the HFD corresponds to the classical Caputo fractional derivative:*

$$ D^{\kappa,1}_{0^+}\mathcal{G}(\mathfrak{z}) = I^{1-\kappa}_{0^+} \frac{d}{d\mathfrak{z}}\mathcal{G}(\mathfrak{z}) =^{C} D^{\kappa}_{0^+}\mathcal{G}(\mathfrak{z}). $$

Definition 5 ([38]). *For $0 < \xi < 1$, $0 < \omega < \frac{\pi}{2}$, $\Theta^{-\xi}_{\omega}$ is the family of closed linear operators, the sector $S_\omega = \{v \in \mathbb{C}\backslash\{0\}$ with $|arg\ v| \leq \omega\}$, and $\mathtt{A} : D(\mathtt{A}) \subset Y \to Y$, which satisfy*

(i) $\sigma(\mathtt{A}) \subseteq S_\omega$;

(ii) *For any $\omega < \delta < \pi\ \exists\ \Lambda_\delta$ is a constant, such that,*

$$ \|(vI - \mathtt{A})^{-1}\| \leq \Lambda_\delta |v|^{-\xi} $$

then $\mathtt{A} \in \Theta^{-\xi}_{\omega}$ is called an almost sectorial operator on Y.

Lemma 1 ([38]). *Let $0 < \xi < 1$ and $0 < \omega < \frac{\pi}{2}$, $\mathtt{A} \in \Theta^{-\xi}_{\omega}(Y)$. Then*

1. $T(\mathfrak{z}_1 + \mathfrak{z}_2) = T(\mathfrak{z}_1) + T(\mathfrak{z}_2)$, *for any* $\mathfrak{z}_1, \mathfrak{z}_2 \in S^0_{\frac{\pi}{2}-\omega}$;
2. $\exists\ \Lambda_0 > 0$ *is the constant, such that* $\|T(\mathfrak{z})\|_{\mathtt{C}} \leq \Lambda_0 \mathfrak{z}^{\xi-1}$, *for any* $\mathfrak{z} > 0$;
3. *The range $R(T(\mathfrak{z}))$ of $T(\mathfrak{z})$, $\mathfrak{z} \in S^0_{\frac{\pi}{2}-\omega}$ is contained in $D(\mathtt{A}^\infty)$. Particularly, $R(T(\mathfrak{z})) \subset D(\mathtt{A}^\theta)$ for all $\theta \in \mathbb{C}$ with $Re(\theta) > 0$,*

$$ \mathtt{A}^\theta T(\mathfrak{z})\mathrm{y} = \frac{1}{2\pi i} \int_{\Gamma_\gamma} z^\theta e^{-\mathfrak{z}z} R(z;\mathtt{A})\mathrm{y}dz,\ \textit{for all } \mathrm{y} \in Y, $$

   and, hence, $\exists$ is a constant $\Lambda' = \Lambda'(\beta,\theta) > 0$, such that

$$ \|\mathtt{A}^\theta T(\mathfrak{z})\|_{B(Y)} \leq \Lambda' \mathfrak{z}^{-\beta-Re(\theta)-1}, \textit{for all } \mathfrak{z} > 0; $$

4. *If $\theta > 1 - \xi$, then $D(\mathtt{A}^\theta) \subset \Sigma_T = \{y \in Y : \lim_{\mathfrak{z}\to 0+} T(\mathfrak{z})y = y\}$;*
5. $R(\kappa', \mathtt{A}) = \int_0^\infty e^{-\kappa'\mathfrak{z}} T(\mathfrak{z}) d\mathfrak{z}$, $\forall\ \kappa' \in C$ *with* $Re(\kappa') > 0$.

Consider the operator families $\{\mathcal{S}_\kappa(\mathfrak{z})\}_{\mathfrak{z}\in S_{\frac{\pi}{2}-\omega}}, \{\mathcal{Q}_\kappa(\mathfrak{z})\}_{\mathfrak{z}\in S_{\frac{\pi}{2}-\omega}}$ *is defined as follows:*

$$\mathcal{S}_\kappa(\mathfrak{z}) = \int_0^\infty W_\kappa(\nu)T(\mathfrak{z}^\kappa \nu)d\nu,$$
$$\mathcal{Q}_\kappa(\mathfrak{z}) = \int_0^\infty \kappa\nu W_\kappa(\nu)T(\mathfrak{z}^\kappa \nu)d\nu,$$

where $W_\kappa(\beta)$ *is the Wright-type function:*

$$W_\kappa(\beta) = \sum_{n\in\mathbb{N}} \frac{(-\beta)^{n-1}}{\Gamma(1-\kappa n)(n-1)!}, \qquad \beta \in \mathbb{C}. \tag{3}$$

Let $-1 < \iota < \infty$, $p > 0$, *the succeeding properties are satisfied.*

(a) $W_\kappa(\theta) \geq 0, \quad \mathfrak{z} > 0;$

(b) $\int_0^\infty \theta^\iota W_\kappa(\theta)d\theta = \frac{\Gamma(1+\iota)}{\Gamma(1+\kappa\iota)};$

(c) $\int_0^\infty \frac{\kappa}{\theta^{(\kappa+1)}} e^{-p\theta} W_\kappa(\frac{1}{\theta^\kappa})d\theta = e^{-p^\kappa}.$

Theorem 1 ([19])**.** $\mathcal{S}_\kappa(\mathfrak{z})$ *and* $\mathcal{Q}_\kappa(\mathfrak{z})$ *are continuous in the uniform operator topology, for* $\mathfrak{z} > 0$, *for every* $c > 0$, *the continuity is uniform on* $[c, \infty)$.

Definition 6 ([16])**.** *A multi-valued map* $\mathcal{G}$ *is called u.s.c. on* Y *if for each* $y_0 \in Y$ *the set* $\mathcal{G}(y_0)$ *is a non-empty, closed subset of* Y, *and if for each open set* $\mathcal{U}$ *of* Y *containing* $\mathcal{G}(y_0)$, *there exists an open neighborhood* $\mathcal{V}$ *of* y_0, *such that* $\mathcal{G}(\mathcal{V}) \subseteq \mathcal{U}$.

Definition 7 ([16])**.** $\mathcal{G}$ *is said to be completely continuous if* $\mathcal{G}(C)$ *is relatively compact for each bounded subset* C *of* Y. *If a multi-valued map* $\mathcal{G}$ *is completely continuous with non-empty compact values, then* $\mathcal{G}$ *is upper semi-continuous if and only if* $\mathcal{G}$ *has a closed graph i.e.,* $y_m \to y_0$, $\mathfrak{z}_m \to \mathfrak{z}_0$, $\mathfrak{z}_m \in \mathcal{G}(y_m)$ *imply* $\mathfrak{z}_0 \in \mathcal{G}(y_0)$.

Definition 8 ([16])**.** *A multi-valued mapping* $\mathcal{G} : Y \to 2^Y$ *is said to be condensing, if for any bounded subset* $D \subset Y$ *with* $\beta(D) \neq 0$, *we have* $\beta(F(D)) < \beta(D)$, *where* $\beta(\cdot)$ *denotes the Kuratowski measure of non-compactness, defined as follows:*

$$\beta(D) = \inf\{d > 0 : \ D \text{ covered by a finite number of balls of radius } d\}.$$

Lemma 2. *System* (1)–(2) *is equivalent to an integral inclusion given by*

$$y(\mathfrak{z}) \in \frac{y_0 - \mathcal{N}(0, y(0))}{\Gamma(\varepsilon(1-\kappa)+\kappa)} \mathfrak{z}^{(1-\kappa)(\varepsilon-1)} + \mathcal{N}(\mathfrak{z}, y(\mathfrak{z})) + \frac{1}{\Gamma(\kappa)} \int_0^{\mathfrak{z}} (\mathfrak{z}-w)^{\kappa-1} \mathrm{A}\mathcal{N}(w, y(w))dw$$
$$+ \frac{1}{\Gamma(\kappa)} \int_0^{\mathfrak{z}} (\mathfrak{z}-w)^{\kappa-1} \left[\mathrm{A}y(w) + \mathcal{G}\left(w, y(w), \int_0^w e(w,s,y(s))ds\right)dw\right].$$

Definition 9. *By a mild solution of the Cauchy problem* (1)–(2), *the function* $y(\mathfrak{z}) \in C(\mathcal{J}', Y)$ *satisfies*

$$y(\mathfrak{z}) = \mathcal{S}_{\kappa,\varepsilon}(\mathfrak{z})[y_0 - \mathcal{N}(0, y(0))] + \mathcal{N}(\mathfrak{z}, y(\mathfrak{z})) + \int_0^{\mathfrak{z}} \mathcal{K}_\kappa(\mathfrak{z}-w)\mathrm{A}\mathcal{N}(w, y(w))dw$$
$$+ \int_0^{\mathfrak{z}} \mathcal{K}_\kappa(\mathfrak{z}-w)\mathcal{G}\left(w, y(w), \int_0^w e(w,s,y(s))ds\right)dw, \quad \mathfrak{z} \in \mathcal{J},$$

where $\mathcal{S}_{\kappa,\varepsilon}(\mathfrak{z}) = I_0^{\varepsilon(1-\kappa)} \mathcal{K}_\kappa(\mathfrak{z})$, $\mathcal{K}_\kappa(\mathfrak{z}) = \mathfrak{z}^{\kappa-1}\mathcal{Q}_\kappa(\mathfrak{z})$.

Lemma 3 ([32]). *For any fixed $\nu > 0$, $\mathcal{Q}_\kappa(\nu)$, $\mathcal{K}_\kappa(\nu)$ and $\mathcal{S}_{\kappa,\varepsilon}(\nu)$ are linear operators, and for any $y \in Y$,*

$$\|\mathcal{Q}_\kappa(\mathfrak{z})\| \leq L'\mathfrak{z}^{-\kappa+\kappa\xi}, \ \|\mathcal{K}_\kappa(\mathfrak{z})\mathrm{y}\| \leq L'\mathfrak{z}^{-1+\kappa\xi}\|\mathrm{y}\|, \ \|\mathcal{S}_{\kappa,\varepsilon}(\mathfrak{z})\mathrm{y}\| \leq L''\mathfrak{z}^{-1+\varepsilon-\kappa\varepsilon+\kappa\xi}\|\mathrm{y}\|,$$

where

$$L' = \Lambda_0\frac{\Gamma(\xi)}{\Gamma(\kappa\xi)}, \ L'' = \Lambda_0\frac{\Gamma(\xi)}{\Gamma(\varepsilon(1-\kappa)+\kappa\xi)}.$$

Lemma 4 ([32]). *Let $\{T(\mathfrak{z})\}_{\mathfrak{z}>0}$ be equicontinuous, then $\{\mathcal{Q}_\kappa(\mathfrak{z})\}_{\mathfrak{z}>0}$, $\{\mathcal{K}_\kappa(\mathfrak{z})\}_{\mathfrak{z}>0}$, and $\{\mathcal{S}_{\kappa,\varepsilon}(\mathfrak{z})\}_{\mathfrak{z}>0}$ are strongly continuous, i.e., for any $\mathrm{y} \in Y$ and $\mathfrak{z}_2 > \mathfrak{z}_1 > 0$,*

$$\|\mathcal{Q}_\kappa(\mathfrak{z}_2)\mathrm{y} - \mathcal{Q}_\kappa(\mathfrak{z}_1)\mathrm{y}\| \to 0, \ \|\mathcal{K}_\kappa(\mathfrak{z}_2)\mathrm{y} - \mathcal{K}_\kappa(\mathfrak{z}_1)\mathrm{y}\| \to 0$$
$$\|\mathcal{S}_{\kappa,\varepsilon}(\mathfrak{z}_2)\mathrm{y} - \mathcal{S}_{\kappa,\varepsilon}(\mathfrak{z}_1)\mathrm{y}\| \to 0, \text{ as } \mathfrak{z}_2 \to \mathfrak{z}_1.$$

Proposition 1 ([39]). *Let $\kappa \in (0,1), \mu \in (0,1]$ and for all $\mathrm{y} \in D(\mathtt{A})$, there exists a $\Lambda_\mu > 0$, such that*

$$\|\mathtt{A}^\mu \mathcal{Q}_\kappa(\mathfrak{z})\mathrm{y}\| \leq \frac{\kappa\Lambda_\mu\Gamma(2-\mu)}{\mathfrak{z}^{\kappa\mu}\Gamma(1+\kappa(1-\mu))}\|\mathrm{y}\|, \ 0 < \mathfrak{z} < d.$$

Lemma 5 ([40]). *Let $\mathcal{J}$ be a compact real interval and $\mathcal{P}_{bd,cv,cl}(Y)$ be the set of all non-empty, bounded, convex, and closed subsets of Y. Let $\mathcal{G}$ be the L^1-Carathéodory multi-valued map, measurable to $\mathfrak{z}$ for each $\mathrm{y} \in Y$, u.s.c. to y for each $\mathfrak{z} \in C(\mathcal{J}, Y)$, the set*

$$S_{\mathcal{G},\mathrm{y}} = \left\{g \in L^1(\mathcal{J}, Y) : g(\mathfrak{z}) \in \mathcal{G}\left(\mathfrak{z}, \mathrm{y}(\mathfrak{z}), \int_0^w e(w,s,\mathrm{y}(s))ds\right), \mathfrak{z} \in \mathcal{J}\right\}, \tag{4}$$

is non-empty. Let Ybe the linear continuous function from $L^1(\mathcal{J}, Y)$ to $\mathtt{C}$, then

$$\mathrm{Y} \circ S_{\mathcal{G}} : \mathtt{C} \to \mathcal{P}_{bd,cv,cl}(\mathtt{C}), \quad \mathrm{y} \to (\mathrm{Y} \circ S_{\mathcal{G}})(\mathrm{y}) = \mathrm{Y}(S_{\mathcal{G},\mathrm{y}}), \tag{5}$$

is a closed graph operator in $\mathtt{C} \times \mathtt{C}$.

Lemma 6 (Martelli's fixed point theorem [17]). *Let Y be a Banach space and $F : Y \to \mathcal{P}_{bd,cv,cl}(Y)$ be an upper semi-continuous and condensing map. If the set*

$$\mathcal{M} = \{\mathrm{y} \in Y : \lambda\mathrm{y} \in F(\mathrm{y}) \text{ for some } \lambda > 1\}$$

is bounded, then F has a fixed point.

3. Existence

We need the succeeding hypotheses:

(H_1) The almost sectorial operator $\mathtt{A}$ produces an analytic semigroup $\mathtt{T}(\mathfrak{z})$, where $\mathfrak{z} \geq 0$ in Y and $\|\mathtt{T}(\mathfrak{z})\| \leq M$, for some $M > 0$.

(H_2) (a) Let $\mathcal{G} : \mathcal{J} \times Y \times Y \to \mathcal{P}_{bd,cv,cl}(Y)$ be measurable to $\mathfrak{z}$ for each fixed $\mathrm{y} \in Y$, upper semi-continuous to y for each $\mathfrak{z} \in \mathcal{J}$, and each $\mathrm{y} \in \mathtt{C}$, take

$$S_{\mathcal{G},\mathrm{y}} = \left\{g \in L^1(\mathcal{J}, Y) : g(\mathfrak{z}) \in \mathcal{G}\left(\mathfrak{z}, \mathrm{y}(\mathfrak{z}), \int_0^w e(w,s,\mathrm{y}(s))ds\right), \mathfrak{z} \in \mathcal{J}\right\},$$

is non-empty.

(b) For $\mathfrak{z} \in \mathcal{J}$, $\mathcal{G}(\mathfrak{z},\cdot,\cdot) : Y \times Y \to Y$, $e(\mathfrak{z},s,\cdot) : Y \to Y$ are continuous functions and for each $\mathrm{y} \in \mathtt{C}$, $\mathcal{G}(\cdot,\mathrm{y},\int e) : \mathcal{J} \to \mathcal{I}$ and $e(\cdot,\cdot,\mathrm{y}) : \mathcal{I} \times \mathcal{J} \to Y$ are strongly measurable.

(c) There exists a function $\phi(\mathfrak{z}) \in C(\mathcal{J}', \mathbb{R}^+)$ satisfying

$$\lim_{\mathfrak{z}\to 0^+} \mathfrak{z}^{1-\varepsilon+\kappa\varepsilon-\kappa\xi} I_{0^+}^{\kappa\xi}\phi(\mathfrak{z}) = 0$$

$$\begin{aligned}\|\mathcal{G}(\mathfrak{z}, \mathfrak{z}_1, \mathfrak{z}_2)\| &= \sup\left\{\|\mathcal{G}\| : \mathcal{G}(\mathfrak{z}) \in \mathcal{G}\left(\mathfrak{z}, y(\mathfrak{z}), \int_0^{\mathfrak{z}} e(\mathfrak{z}, s, y(s))ds\right)\right\} \\ &\leq \phi(\mathfrak{z})\Phi(\|\mathfrak{z}_1\| + \|\mathfrak{z}_2\|).\end{aligned}$$

for a.e. $\mathfrak{z} \in \mathcal{J}$ and $\mathfrak{z}_1, \mathfrak{z}_2 \in Y$, where $\Phi : \mathbb{R}^+ \to (0, \infty)$ is a continuous, additive, and non-decreasing function, satisfying $\Phi(\gamma_1(\mathfrak{z})(y)) \leq \gamma_1(\mathfrak{z})\Phi(y)$, where $\gamma \in C(\mathcal{J}', \mathbb{R}^+)$.

(d) There exists $\psi \in C(\mathcal{J}', \mathbb{R}^+)$, such that

$$\left\| \int_0^{\mathfrak{z}} e(\mathfrak{z}, s, y(s)) \right\| \leq \psi(\mathfrak{z})\|y\| \text{ for each } \mathfrak{z} \in \mathcal{J},\ y \in Y.$$

(H_3) For any $\mathfrak{z} \in \mathcal{J}$, multi-valued map $\mathcal{N} : \mathcal{J} \times Y \to Y$ is a continuous function and there exists $\mu \in (0, 1)$, such that $\mathcal{N} \in D(\mathtt{A}^\mu)$ and all $y \in Y$, $\mathfrak{z} \in \mathcal{J}$, $\mathtt{A}^\mu\mathcal{N}(\mathfrak{z}, \cdot)$ satisfy the following:

$$\|\mathtt{A}^\mu\mathcal{N}(\mathfrak{z}, y(\mathfrak{z}))\| \leq M_g(1 + \mathfrak{z}^{1-\varepsilon+\kappa\varepsilon-\kappa\xi}\|y(\mathfrak{z})\|) \ and\ \|\mathtt{A}^{-\mu}\| \leq M_0,\ (\mathfrak{z}, y) \in \mathcal{J} \times Y.$$

(H_4) $\mathcal{N}$ is completely continuous, and for any bounded set $D \subset \mathbb{C}$, the set $\{\mathfrak{z} \to \mathcal{N}(\mathfrak{z}, y(\mathfrak{z})),\ y \in D\}$ is equicontinuous in Y.

Theorem 2. *Assume that $(H_1) - (H_4)$ hold. Then the HF system* (1)–(2) *has a mild solution on $\mathcal{J}$, provided*

$$L'\int_0^{\mathfrak{z}} (\mathfrak{z} - w)^{\kappa\xi-1}\phi(\mathfrak{z})(1 + \psi(\mathfrak{z}))dw < \int_{M_1^*}^{\infty} \frac{du}{\Phi(u)},$$

where

$$M_1^* = d^{1-\varepsilon+\kappa\varepsilon-\kappa\xi}\left[L''d^{-1+\varepsilon-\kappa\varepsilon+\kappa\xi}(y_0 - M_0M_g) + M_0M_g(1 + P)\right]$$

and $y_0 \in D(\mathtt{A}^\theta)$ with $\theta > 1 - \xi$.

Proof. We define the multi-valued operator $\Psi : \mathcal{X} \to \mathcal{P}(\mathcal{X})$ by

$$\begin{aligned}\Psi(y(\mathfrak{z})) = \Big\{z \in \mathcal{X} : z(\mathfrak{z}) = \mathfrak{z}^{1-\varepsilon+\kappa\varepsilon-\kappa\xi}\Big[&\mathcal{S}_{\kappa,\varepsilon}(\mathfrak{z})[y_0 - \mathcal{N}(0, y(0))] + \mathcal{N}(\mathfrak{z}, y(\mathfrak{z})) \\ &+ \int_0^{\mathfrak{z}} (\mathfrak{z} - w)^{\kappa-1}\mathcal{Q}_\kappa(\mathfrak{z} - w)\mathtt{A}\mathcal{N}(w, y(w))dw \\ &+ \int_0^{\mathfrak{z}} (\mathfrak{z} - w)^{\kappa-1}\mathcal{Q}_\kappa(\mathfrak{z} - w)\mathcal{G}\left(w, y(w), \int_0^w e(w, s, y(s))ds\right)\Big]dw,\ \mathfrak{z} \in (0, d]\Big\}.\end{aligned}$$

To show that the fixed point of Ψ exists.

Step:1 Convexity of $\Psi(y)$ $\forall$ $y \in B_P(\mathcal{J})$.

Let $z_1, z_2 \in \{\Psi y(\mathfrak{z})\}$ and $h_1, h_2 \in S_{\mathcal{G},y}$ such that $\mathfrak{z} \in \mathcal{J}$. We know

$$\begin{aligned}z_i =& \mathfrak{z}^{1-\varepsilon+\kappa\varepsilon-\kappa\xi}\Big[\mathcal{G}_{\kappa,\varepsilon}(\mathfrak{z})[y_0 - \mathcal{N}(0, y(0))] + \mathcal{N}(\mathfrak{z}, y(\mathfrak{z})) \\ &+ \int_0^{\mathfrak{z}} (\mathfrak{z} - w)^{\kappa-1}\mathcal{Q}_\kappa(\mathfrak{z} - w)\mathtt{A}\mathcal{N}(w, y(w))dw + \int_0^{\mathfrak{z}} (\mathfrak{z} - w)^{\kappa-1}\mathcal{Q}_\kappa(\mathfrak{z} - w)h_i(w)dw\Big],\quad i = 1, 2.\end{aligned}$$

Let $0 \leq \lambda \leq 1$; then for each of $\mathfrak{z} \in \mathcal{J}$, we have

$$\begin{aligned}\lambda z_1 + (1-\lambda)z_2(\mathfrak{z}) =& \mathfrak{z}^{1-\varepsilon+\kappa\varepsilon-\kappa\xi}\Big(\mathcal{S}_{\kappa,\varepsilon}(\mathfrak{z})\left[\mathrm{y}_0 - \mathcal{N}(0,\mathrm{y}(0))\right] + \mathcal{N}(\mathfrak{z},\mathrm{y}(\mathfrak{z})) \\ &+ \int_0^{\mathfrak{z}} (\mathfrak{z}-w)^{\kappa-1}\mathcal{Q}_\kappa(\mathfrak{z}-w)\mathtt{A}(w,\mathrm{y}(w))dw\Big) \\ &+ \mathfrak{z}^{1-\varepsilon+\kappa\varepsilon-\kappa\xi}\int_0^{\mathfrak{z}}(\mathfrak{z}-w)^{\kappa-1}\mathcal{Q}_\kappa(\mathfrak{z}-w)\left[\lambda h_1(w) + (1-\lambda)h_2(w)\right]dw.\end{aligned}$$

We know that $\mathcal{N}$ has a convex value, then $S_{\mathcal{G},\mathrm{y}}$ is convex. So, $\lambda h_1 + (1-\lambda)h_2 \in S_{\mathcal{G},\mathrm{y}}$. Therefore,

$$\lambda z_1 + (1-\lambda)z_2 \in \Psi\mathrm{y}(\mathfrak{z}),$$

hence Ψ is convex.
Step 2: Boundness of Ψ on $B_P(\mathcal{J})$. Consider, $\forall\ \mathrm{y} \in B_P(\mathcal{J})$, we have

$$\begin{aligned}\|z(\mathfrak{z})\| \leq& \sup \mathfrak{z}^{1-\varepsilon+\kappa\varepsilon-\kappa\xi}\Big\|\mathcal{S}_{\kappa,\varepsilon}(\mathfrak{z})\left[\mathrm{y}_0 - \mathcal{N}(0,\mathrm{y}(0))\right] + \mathcal{N}(\mathfrak{z},\mathrm{y}(\mathfrak{z})) \\ &+ \int_0^{\mathfrak{z}}(\mathfrak{z}-w)^{\kappa-1}\mathcal{Q}_\kappa(\mathfrak{z}-w)\mathtt{A}\mathcal{N}(w,\mathrm{y}(w))dw \\ &+ \int_0^{\mathfrak{z}}(\mathfrak{z}-w)^{\kappa-1}\mathcal{Q}_\kappa(\mathfrak{z}-w)\mathcal{G}\Big(w,\mathrm{y}(w),\int_0^w e(w,s,\mathrm{y}(s))ds\Big)dw\Big\| \\ \leq& d^{1-\varepsilon+\kappa\varepsilon-\kappa\xi}\Big(\sup\Big\|\mathcal{S}_{\kappa,\varepsilon}(\mathfrak{z})\left[\mathrm{y}_0 - \mathcal{N}(0,\mathrm{y}(0))\right]\Big\| + \|\mathcal{N}(\mathfrak{z},\mathrm{y}(\mathfrak{z}))\| \\ &+ \sup\int_0^{\mathfrak{z}}(\mathfrak{z}-w)^{\kappa-1}\Big\|\mathtt{A}^{1-\mu}\mathcal{Q}_\kappa(\mathfrak{z}-w)\Big\|\Big\|\mathtt{A}^{\mu}\mathcal{N}(w,\mathrm{y}(w))\Big\|dw \\ &+ \sup\int_0^{\mathfrak{z}}(\mathfrak{z}-w)^{\kappa-1}\Big\|\mathcal{Q}_\kappa(\mathfrak{z}-w)\Big\|\Big\|\mathcal{G}\Big(w,\mathrm{y}(w),\int_0^w e(w,s,\mathrm{y}(w))ds\Big)\Big\|dw\Big) \\ \leq& d^{1-\varepsilon+\kappa\varepsilon-\kappa\xi}\Big[L'' d^{-1+\varepsilon-\kappa\varepsilon+\kappa\xi}(\mathrm{y}_0 - M_0M_g) + M_0M_g(1+P)\Big] \\ &+ d^{1-\varepsilon+\kappa\varepsilon-\kappa\xi}\Big[\Big(\Lambda_{1-\mu}\frac{d^{\kappa\mu}\Gamma(1+\mu)}{\mu\Gamma(1+\kappa\mu)}(M_g(1+P))\Big) + L'\phi(\mathfrak{z})\Phi(\mathrm{y})[1+\psi(\mathfrak{z})]\frac{d^{\kappa\xi}}{\kappa\xi}\Big] \\ \leq& \mathcal{M}_1^* + d^{\varepsilon(1-\kappa)-\kappa\xi-1}\Big[\Big(\Lambda_{1-\mu}\frac{d^{\kappa\mu}\Gamma(1+\mu)}{\mu\Gamma(1+\kappa\mu)}(M_g(1+P))\Big) \\ &+ L'\phi(\mathfrak{z})\Phi(\mathrm{y})[1+\psi(\mathfrak{z})]\frac{d^{\kappa\xi}}{\kappa\xi}\Big].\end{aligned}$$

From Lemma 2 and hypotheses (H_3), we have the boundness of the operators. Hence, it is bounded.
Step 3: Next, we show that the $z(\mathfrak{z})$ bounded maps are set to the equicontinuous set of $B_P(\mathcal{J})$.
Consider $0 < \mathfrak{z}_1 < \mathfrak{z}_2 \leq d$ and $\exists\ \mathcal{G} \in S_{\mathcal{G},\mathrm{y}}$, we have

$$
\begin{aligned}
&\left\| z(\mathfrak{z}_2) - z(\mathfrak{z}_1) \right\| \\
&\leq \Bigg\| \mathfrak{z}_2^{1-\varepsilon+\kappa\varepsilon-\kappa\xi} \Bigg[\mathcal{S}_{\kappa,\varepsilon}(\mathfrak{z}_2)[\mathbf{y}_0 - \mathcal{N}(0,\mathbf{y}(0))] + \mathcal{N}(\mathfrak{z}_2, \mathbf{y}(\mathfrak{z}_2)) \\
&\quad + \int_0^{\mathfrak{z}_2} (\mathfrak{z}_2 - w)^{\kappa-1} \mathcal{Q}_\kappa(\mathfrak{z}_2 - w) \mathbf{A}\mathcal{N}(w, \mathbf{y}(w)) dw \\
&\quad + \int_0^{\mathfrak{z}_2} (\mathfrak{z}_2 - w)^{\kappa-1} \mathcal{Q}_\kappa(\mathfrak{z}_2 - w) \mathcal{G}\left(w, \mathbf{y}(w), \int_0^w e(w,s,\mathbf{y}(s)) ds \right) dw \Bigg] \\
&\quad - \mathfrak{z}_1^{1-\varepsilon+\kappa\varepsilon-\kappa\xi} \Bigg[\mathcal{S}_{\kappa,\varepsilon}(\mathfrak{z}_1)[\mathbf{y}_0 - \mathcal{N}(0,\mathbf{y}(0))] + \mathcal{N}(\mathfrak{z}_1, \mathbf{y}(\mathfrak{z}_1)) \\
&\quad + \int_0^{\mathfrak{z}_1} (\mathfrak{z}_1 - w)^{\kappa-1} \mathcal{Q}_\kappa(\mathfrak{z}_1 - w) \mathbf{A}\mathcal{N}(w, \mathbf{y}(w)) dw \\
&\quad + \int_0^{\mathfrak{z}_1} (\mathfrak{z}_1 - w)^{\kappa-1} \mathcal{Q}_\kappa(\mathfrak{z}_1 - w) \mathcal{G}\left(w, \mathbf{y}(w), \int_0^w e(w,s,\mathbf{y}(s)) ds \right) dw \Bigg] \Bigg\| \\
&\leq \left\| [\mathfrak{z}_2^{1-\varepsilon+\kappa\varepsilon-\kappa\xi} \mathcal{S}_{\kappa,\varepsilon}(\mathfrak{z}_2) - \mathfrak{z}_1^{1-\varepsilon+\kappa\varepsilon-\kappa\xi} \mathcal{S}_{\kappa,\varepsilon}(\mathfrak{z}_1)][\mathbf{y}_0 - \mathcal{N}(0,\mathbf{y}(0))] \right\| \\
&\quad + \left\| \mathfrak{z}_2^{1-\varepsilon+\kappa\varepsilon-\kappa\xi} \mathcal{N}(\mathfrak{z}_2, \mathbf{y}(\mathfrak{z}_2)) - \mathfrak{z}_1^{1-\varepsilon+\kappa\varepsilon-\kappa\xi} \mathcal{N}(\mathfrak{z}_1, \mathbf{y}(\mathfrak{z}_1)) \right\| \\
&\quad + \Bigg\| \mathfrak{z}_2^{1-\varepsilon+\kappa\varepsilon-\kappa\xi} \int_0^{\mathfrak{z}_1} (\mathfrak{z}_2 - w)^{\kappa-1} \mathcal{Q}_\kappa(\mathfrak{z}_2 - w) \mathbf{A}\mathcal{N}(w, \mathbf{y}(w)) dw \\
&\quad + \mathfrak{z}_2^{1-\varepsilon+\kappa\varepsilon-\kappa\xi} \int_{\mathfrak{z}_1}^{\mathfrak{z}_2} (\mathfrak{z}_2 - w)^{\kappa-1} \mathcal{Q}_\kappa(\mathfrak{z}_2 - w) \mathbf{A}\mathcal{N}(w, \mathbf{y}(w)) dw \\
&\quad - \mathfrak{z}_1^{1-\varepsilon+\kappa\varepsilon-\kappa\xi} \int_0^{\mathfrak{z}_1} (\mathfrak{z}_1 - w)^{\kappa-1} \mathcal{Q}_\kappa(\mathfrak{z}_1 - w) \mathbf{A}\mathcal{N}(w, \mathbf{y}(w)) dw \Bigg\| \\
&\quad + \Bigg\| \mathfrak{z}_2^{1-\varepsilon+\kappa\varepsilon-\kappa\xi} \int_0^{\mathfrak{z}_1} (\mathfrak{z}_2 - w)^{\kappa-1} \mathcal{Q}_\kappa(\mathfrak{z}_2 - w) \mathcal{G}\left(w, \mathbf{y}(w), \int_0^w e(w,s,\mathbf{y}(s)) ds \right) dw \\
&\quad + \mathfrak{z}_2^{1-\varepsilon+\kappa\varepsilon-\kappa\xi} \int_{\mathfrak{z}_1}^{\mathfrak{z}_2} (\mathfrak{z}_2 - w)^{\kappa-1} \mathcal{Q}_\kappa(\mathfrak{z}_2 - w) \mathcal{G}\left(w, \mathbf{y}(w), \int_0^w e(w,s,\mathbf{y}(s)) ds \right) dw \\
&\quad - \mathfrak{z}_1^{1-\varepsilon+\kappa\varepsilon-\kappa\xi} \int_0^{\mathfrak{z}_1} (\mathfrak{z}_1 - w)^{\kappa-1} \mathcal{Q}_\kappa(\mathfrak{z}_1 - w) \mathcal{G}\left(w, \mathbf{y}(w), \int_0^w e(w,s,\mathbf{y}(s)) ds \right) dw \Bigg\| \\
&\leq \left\| [\mathfrak{z}_2^{1-\varepsilon+\kappa\varepsilon-\kappa\xi} \mathcal{S}_{\kappa,\varepsilon}(\mathfrak{z}_2) - \mathfrak{z}_1^{1-\varepsilon+\kappa\varepsilon-\kappa\xi} \mathcal{S}_{\kappa,\varepsilon}(\mathfrak{z}_1)][\mathbf{y}_0 - \mathcal{N}(0,\mathbf{y}(0))] \right\| \\
&\quad + \left\| \mathfrak{z}_2^{1-\varepsilon+\kappa\varepsilon-\kappa\xi} \mathcal{N}(\mathfrak{z}_2, \mathbf{y}(\mathfrak{z}_2)) - \mathfrak{z}_1^{1-\varepsilon+\kappa\varepsilon-\kappa\xi} \mathcal{N}(\mathfrak{z}_1, \mathbf{y}(\mathfrak{z}_1)) \right\| \\
&\quad + \left\| \mathfrak{z}_2^{1-\varepsilon+\kappa\varepsilon-\kappa\xi} \int_{\mathfrak{z}_1}^{\mathfrak{z}_2} (\mathfrak{z}_2 - w)^{\kappa-1} \mathcal{Q}_\kappa(\mathfrak{z}_2 - w) \mathcal{N}(w, \mathbf{y}(w)) dw \right\| \\
&\quad + \Bigg\| \mathfrak{z}_2^{1-\varepsilon+\kappa\varepsilon-\kappa\xi} \int_0^{\mathfrak{z}_1} (\mathfrak{z}_2 - w)^{\kappa-1} \mathcal{Q}_\kappa(\mathfrak{z}_2 - w) \mathbf{A}\mathcal{N}(w, \mathbf{y}(w)) dw \\
&\quad - \mathfrak{z}_1^{1-\varepsilon+\kappa\varepsilon-\kappa\xi} \int_0^{\mathfrak{z}_1} (\mathfrak{z}_1 - w)^{\kappa-1} \mathcal{Q}_\kappa(\mathfrak{z}_2 - w) \mathbf{A}\mathcal{N}(w, \mathbf{y}(w)) dw \Bigg\| \\
&\quad + \Bigg\| \mathfrak{z}_1^{1-\varepsilon+\kappa\varepsilon-\kappa\xi} \int_0^{\mathfrak{z}_1} (\mathfrak{z}_1 - w)^{\kappa-1} \mathcal{Q}_\kappa(\mathfrak{z}_2 - w) \mathbf{A}\mathcal{N}(w, \mathbf{y}(w)) dw \\
&\quad - \mathfrak{z}_1^{1-\varepsilon+\kappa\varepsilon-\kappa\xi} \int_0^{\mathfrak{z}_1} (\mathfrak{z}_1 - w)^{\kappa-1} \mathcal{Q}_\kappa(\mathfrak{z}_1 - w) \mathbf{A}\mathcal{N}(w, \mathbf{y}(w)) dw \Bigg\| \\
&\quad + \left\| \mathfrak{z}_2^{1-\varepsilon+\kappa\varepsilon-\kappa\xi} \int_{\mathfrak{z}_1}^{\mathfrak{z}_2} (\mathfrak{z}_2 - w)^{\kappa-1} \mathcal{Q}_\kappa(\mathfrak{z}_2 - w) \mathcal{G}\left(w, \mathbf{y}(w), \int_0^w e(w,s,\mathbf{y}(s)) ds \right) dw \right\| \\
&\quad + \Bigg\| \mathfrak{z}_2^{1-\varepsilon+\kappa\varepsilon-\kappa\xi} \int_0^{\mathfrak{z}_1} (\mathfrak{z}_2 - w)^{\kappa-1} \mathcal{Q}_\kappa(\mathfrak{z}_2 - w) \mathcal{G}\left(w, \mathbf{y}(w), \int_0^w e(w,s,\mathbf{y}(s)) ds \right) dw \\
&\quad - \mathfrak{z}_1^{1-\varepsilon+\kappa\varepsilon-\kappa\xi} \int_0^{\mathfrak{z}_1} (\mathfrak{z}_1 - w)^{\kappa-1} \mathcal{Q}_\kappa(\mathfrak{z}_2 - w) \mathcal{G}\left(w, \mathbf{y}(w), \int_0^w e(w,s,\mathbf{y}(s)) ds \right) dw \Bigg\| \\
&\quad + \Bigg\| \mathfrak{z}_1^{1-\varepsilon+\kappa\varepsilon-\kappa\xi} \int_0^{\mathfrak{z}_1} (\mathfrak{z}_1 - w)^{\kappa-1} \mathcal{Q}_\kappa(\mathfrak{z}_2 - w) \mathcal{G}\left(w, \mathbf{y}(w), \int_0^w e(w,s,\mathbf{y}(s)) ds \right) dw \\
&\quad - \mathfrak{z}_1^{1-\varepsilon+\kappa\varepsilon-\kappa\xi} \int_0^{\mathfrak{z}_1} (\mathfrak{z}_1 - w)^{\kappa-1} \mathcal{Q}_\kappa(\mathfrak{z}_1 - w) \mathcal{G}\left(w, \mathbf{y}(w), \int_0^w e(w,s,\mathbf{y}(s)) ds \right) dw \Bigg\| \\
&= \sum_{i=1}^{8} I_i.
\end{aligned}
$$

Since $\mathcal{S}_{\kappa,\varepsilon}(\mathfrak{z})(y_0 - M_0 M_g)$ is strong-continuous, we have

$$I_1 \textit{ tends to } 0 \textit{ as } \mathfrak{z}_2 \to \mathfrak{z}_1.$$

The equicontinuity of $\mathcal{N}$ ensures that

$$I_2 \textit{ tends to } 0, \textit{ as } \mathfrak{z}_2 \to \mathfrak{z}_1.$$

$$\begin{aligned}
I_3 &= \left\| \mathfrak{z}_2^{1-\varepsilon+\kappa\varepsilon-\kappa\xi} \int_{\mathfrak{z}_1}^{\mathfrak{z}_2} (\mathfrak{z}_2 - w)^{\kappa-1} \mathcal{Q}_\kappa(\mathfrak{z}_2 - w) A\mathcal{N}(w, y(w)) dw \right\| \\
&\leq \mathfrak{z}_2^{1-\varepsilon+\kappa\varepsilon-\kappa\xi} \Lambda_{1-\mu} M_g (1+P) \frac{\Gamma(1+\mu)}{\mu\Gamma(1+\kappa\mu)} (\mathfrak{z}_2 - \mathfrak{z}_1)^{\kappa\mu}
\end{aligned}$$

Then, I_3 *tends* 0 *as* $\mathfrak{z}_2 \to \mathfrak{z}_1$.

$$\begin{aligned}
I_4 &= \Bigg\| \mathfrak{z}_2^{1-\varepsilon+\kappa\varepsilon-\kappa\xi} \int_0^{\mathfrak{z}_1} (\mathfrak{z}_2 - w)^{\kappa-1} \mathcal{Q}_\kappa(\mathfrak{z}_2 - w) A\mathcal{N}(w, y(w)) dw \\
&\quad - \mathfrak{z}_1^{1-\varepsilon+\kappa\varepsilon-\kappa\xi} \int_0^{\mathfrak{z}_1} (\mathfrak{z}_1 - w)^{\kappa-1} \mathcal{Q}_\kappa(\mathfrak{z}_2 - w) A\mathcal{N}(w, y(w)) dw \Bigg\| \\
&\leq \kappa \Lambda_{1-\mu} M_g (1+P) \frac{\Gamma(1+\mu)}{\mu\Gamma(1+\kappa\mu)} \\
&\quad \times \left\| \int_0^{\mathfrak{z}_1} \left(\mathfrak{z}_2^{1-\varepsilon+\kappa\varepsilon-\kappa\xi} (\mathfrak{z}_2 - w)^{\kappa-1} - \mathfrak{z}_1^{1-\varepsilon+\kappa\varepsilon-\kappa\xi} (\mathfrak{z}_1 - w)^{\kappa-1} \right) (\mathfrak{z}_2 - w)^{\kappa(\mu-1)} dw \right\|.
\end{aligned}$$

We have, I_4 *tends* 0 *as* $\mathfrak{z}_2 \to \mathfrak{z}_1$. *Also,*

$$\begin{aligned}
I_5 &= \Bigg\| \mathfrak{z}_1^{1-\varepsilon+\kappa\varepsilon-\kappa\xi} \int_0^{\mathfrak{z}_1} \Big((\mathfrak{z}_1 - w)^{\kappa-1} \mathcal{Q}_\kappa(\mathfrak{z}_2 - w) A\mathcal{N}(w, y(w)) \\
&\qquad - (\mathfrak{z}_1 - w)^{\kappa-1} \mathcal{Q}_\kappa(\mathfrak{z}_1 - w) A\mathcal{N}(w, y(w)) \Big) dw \Bigg\| \\
&\leq M_0' M_g (1+P) \mathfrak{z}_1^{1-\varepsilon+\kappa\varepsilon-\kappa\xi} \int_0^{\mathfrak{z}_1} (\mathfrak{z}_1 - w)^{\kappa-1} \| [\mathcal{Q}_\kappa(\mathfrak{z}_2 - w) - \mathcal{Q}_\kappa(\mathfrak{z}_1 - w)] \|.
\end{aligned}$$

By Theorem 1 and strong continuity of $\mathcal{Q}_\kappa(\mathfrak{z})$, I_5 *tends to* 0, *as* $\mathfrak{z}_2 \to \mathfrak{z}_1$.

$$\begin{aligned}
I_6 &= \left\| \mathfrak{z}_2^{1-\varepsilon+\kappa\varepsilon-\kappa\xi} \int_{\mathfrak{z}_1}^{\mathfrak{z}_2} (\mathfrak{z}_2 - w)^{\kappa-1} \mathcal{Q}_\kappa(\mathfrak{z}_2 - w) \mathcal{G}\left(w, y(w), \int_0^w e(w, s, y(s)) ds \right) dw \right\| \\
&\leq L' \left| \mathfrak{z}_2^{1-\varepsilon+\kappa\varepsilon-\kappa\xi} \int_{\mathfrak{z}_1}^{\mathfrak{z}_2} (\mathfrak{z}_2 - w)^{\kappa\xi-1} \phi(w) \Phi(y) [1 + \psi(\mathfrak{z})] dw \right| \\
&\leq L' \int_0^{\mathfrak{z}_1} \left[\mathfrak{z}_1^{1-\varepsilon+\kappa\varepsilon-\kappa\xi} (\mathfrak{z}_1 - w)^{\kappa\xi-1} - \mathfrak{z}_2^{(1+\kappa\xi)(1-\kappa)} (\mathfrak{z}_2 - w)^{\kappa\xi-1} \right] \\
&\quad \times \phi(w) \Phi(y) [1 + \psi(\mathfrak{z})] dw.
\end{aligned}$$

Then I_6 *tends to* 0 as $\mathfrak{z}_2 \to \mathfrak{z}_1$ by using (H_2) and the Lebesgue-dominated convergent theorem.

$$\begin{aligned}
I_7 &= \Bigg\| \mathfrak{z}_2^{1-\varepsilon+\kappa\varepsilon-\kappa\xi} \int_0^{\mathfrak{z}_1} (\mathfrak{z}_2 - w)^{\kappa-1} \mathcal{Q}_\kappa(\mathfrak{z}_2 - w) \mathcal{G}\left(w, y(w), \int_0^w e(w, s, y(s)) ds \right) dw \\
&\quad - \mathfrak{z}_1^{1-\varepsilon+\kappa\varepsilon-\kappa\xi} \int_0^{\mathfrak{z}_1} (\mathfrak{z}_1 - w)^{\kappa-1} \mathcal{Q}_\kappa(\mathfrak{z}_2 - w) \mathcal{G}\left(w, y(w), \int_0^w e(w, s, y(s)) ds \right) dw \Bigg\| \\
&\leq L' \int_0^{\mathfrak{z}_1} (\mathfrak{z}_2 - w)^{-\kappa+\kappa\xi} \left| \mathfrak{z}_2^{1-\varepsilon+\kappa\varepsilon-\kappa\xi} (\mathfrak{z}_2 - w)^{\kappa-1} - \mathfrak{z}_1^{1-\varepsilon+\kappa\varepsilon-\kappa\xi} (\mathfrak{z}_1 - w)^{\kappa-1} \right| \\
&\quad \times \phi(w) \Phi(y) [1 + \psi(\mathfrak{z})] dw,
\end{aligned}$$

and $\int_0^{\mathfrak{z}_1} 2\mathfrak{z}_1^{(1+\kappa\xi)(1-\kappa)}(\mathfrak{z}_1 - w)^{\kappa\xi-1}\phi(w)\Phi(\mathrm{y})[1+\psi(\mathfrak{z})]dw$ exists ($w \in (0, \mathfrak{z}_1]$), then from Lebesgue's dominated convergence theorem, we obtain

$$\int_0^{\mathfrak{z}_1} (\mathfrak{z}_2 - w)^{-\kappa+\kappa\xi} \left| \mathfrak{z}_2^{1-\varepsilon+\kappa\varepsilon-\kappa\xi}(\mathfrak{z}_2 - w)^{\kappa-1} - \mathfrak{z}_1^{1-\varepsilon+\kappa\varepsilon-\kappa\xi}(\mathfrak{z}_1 - w)^{\kappa-1} \right| \phi(w)\Phi(\mathrm{y})\left[1+\psi(\mathfrak{z})\right]dw$$
$$\to 0 \text{ as } \mathfrak{z}_2 \to \mathfrak{z}_1,$$

so we conclude $\lim_{\mathfrak{z}_2 \to \mathfrak{z}_1} I_7 = 0$.

For any $\epsilon > 0$, we have

$$\begin{aligned} I_8 &= \left\| \int_0^{\mathfrak{z}_1} \mathfrak{z}_1^{1-\varepsilon+\kappa\varepsilon-\kappa\xi} \left[\mathcal{Q}_\kappa(\mathfrak{z}_2 - w) - \mathcal{Q}_\kappa(\mathfrak{z}_1 - w)\right](\mathfrak{z}_1 - w)^{\kappa-1}\mathcal{G}\left(w, \mathrm{y}(w), \int_0^w e(w,s,\mathrm{y}(s))ds\right)dw \right\| \\ &\le \mathfrak{z}_1^{1-\varepsilon+\kappa\varepsilon-\kappa\xi+\kappa(1+\xi)} \int_0^{\mathfrak{z}_1} (\mathfrak{z}_1 - w)^{\kappa\xi-1}\phi(w)\Phi(\mathrm{y})\left[1+\psi(\mathfrak{z})\right]dw \\ &\quad \times \sup_{w\in[0,\mathfrak{z}_1-\epsilon]} \left\| \mathcal{Q}_\kappa(\mathfrak{z}_2 - w) - \mathcal{Q}_\kappa(\mathfrak{z}_1 - w) \right\| \\ &\quad + 2L' \int_{\mathfrak{z}_1-\epsilon}^{\mathfrak{z}_1} \mathfrak{z}_1^{1-\varepsilon+\kappa\varepsilon+\kappa\xi}(\mathfrak{z}_1 - w)^{\kappa\xi-1}\phi(w)\Phi(\mathrm{y})\left[1+\psi(\mathfrak{z})\right]dw. \end{aligned}$$

From Theorem (1) and $\lim_{\mathfrak{z}_2\to\mathfrak{z}_1} I_6 = 0$, we have $I_8 \to 0$ independently of $\mathrm{y} \in B_P(\mathcal{J})$ as $\mathfrak{z}_2 \to \mathfrak{z}_1$, $\epsilon \to 0$. Hence, $\|z(\mathfrak{z}_2) - z(\mathfrak{z}_1)\| \to 0$ independently of $\mathrm{y} \in B_P(\mathcal{J})$ as $\mathfrak{z}_2 \to \mathfrak{z}_1$. Therefore, $\{\Psi\mathrm{y}(\mathfrak{z}) : \mathrm{y} \in B_P(\mathcal{J})\}$ is equicontinuous on $\mathcal{J}$.

Step 4: Show the relative compact of $V(\mathfrak{z}) = \{z(\mathfrak{z}) : z \in \Psi(B_P(\mathcal{J}))\}$ for $\mathfrak{z} \in \mathcal{J}$.

Let $0 < \alpha < \mathfrak{z}$, and there is a positive value q, assume an operator $z'(\mathfrak{z})$ on $B_P(\mathcal{J})$ by

$$\begin{aligned} z'_{\alpha,q}(\mathfrak{z}) &= \mathfrak{z}^{1-\varepsilon+\kappa\varepsilon-\kappa\xi}\Big[\mathcal{S}_{\kappa,\varepsilon}(\mathfrak{z})\left[\mathrm{y}_0 - \mathcal{N}(0,\mathrm{y}(0))\right] + \mathcal{N}(\mathfrak{z},\mathrm{y}(\mathfrak{z})) \\ &\quad + \int_0^{\mathfrak{z}-\alpha} (\mathfrak{z}-w)^{\kappa-1}\mathcal{Q}_\kappa(\mathfrak{z}-w)\mathrm{A}\mathcal{N}(w,\mathrm{y}(w))dw \\ &\quad + \int_0^{\mathfrak{z}-\alpha} (\mathfrak{z}-w)^{\kappa-1}\mathcal{Q}_\kappa(\mathfrak{z}-w)\mathcal{G}\left(w,\mathrm{y}(w),\int_0^w e(w,s,\mathrm{y}(s))ds\right)dw\Big] \\ &= \mathfrak{z}^{1-\varepsilon+\kappa\varepsilon-\kappa\xi}\Big[\mathcal{S}_{\kappa,\varepsilon}(\mathfrak{z})\left[\mathrm{y}_0 - \mathcal{N}(0,\mathrm{y}(0))\right] + \mathcal{N}(\mathfrak{z},\mathrm{y}(\mathfrak{z})) \\ &\quad + \int_0^{\mathfrak{z}-\alpha}\int_q^\infty \kappa\theta M_\kappa(\theta)(\mathfrak{z}-w)^{\kappa-1}T((\mathfrak{z}-w)^\kappa\theta)\mathrm{A}\mathcal{N}(w,\mathrm{y}(w))dw \\ &\quad + \int_0^{\mathfrak{z}-\alpha}\int_q^\infty \kappa\theta M_\kappa(\theta)(\mathfrak{z}-w)^{\kappa-1}T((\mathfrak{z}-w)^\kappa\theta)\mathcal{G}\left(w,\mathrm{y}(w),\int_0^w e(w,s,\mathrm{y}(s))ds\right)d\theta dw\Big] \\ &= \mathfrak{z}^{1-\varepsilon+\kappa\varepsilon-\kappa\xi}\Big[\mathcal{S}_{\kappa,\varepsilon}(\mathfrak{z})\left[\mathrm{y}_0 - \mathcal{N}(0,\mathrm{y}(0))\right] + \mathcal{N}(\mathfrak{z},\mathrm{y}(\mathfrak{z}))\Big] \\ &\quad + \kappa\mathfrak{z}^{1-\varepsilon+\kappa\varepsilon-\kappa\xi}T(\alpha^\kappa q)\int_0^{\mathfrak{z}-q}\int_q^\infty \theta M_\kappa(\theta)(\mathfrak{z}-w)^{\kappa-1} \\ &\quad \times T((\mathfrak{z}-w)^\kappa\theta - \alpha^\kappa q)\left[\mathrm{A}\mathcal{N}(w,\mathrm{y}(w)) + \mathcal{G}\left(w,\mathrm{y}(w),\int_0^w e(w,s,\mathrm{y}(s))\right)d\theta dw.\right. \end{aligned}$$

From the compactness of $T(\alpha^{\kappa}q)$, we note that $V_{\alpha,\xi}(\mathfrak{z}) = \{(z'_{\alpha,q}(\mathfrak{z}))\mathrm{y}(\mathfrak{z}) : \mathrm{y} \in B_P(\mathcal{J})\}$ is pre-compact in Y. $\forall$ y $\in B_P(\mathcal{J})$, we have

$$\begin{aligned}
&\left\|z(\mathfrak{z}) - z'_{\alpha,q}(\mathfrak{z})\right\| \\
&\leq \Bigg\|\kappa\mathfrak{z}^{1-\varepsilon+\kappa\varepsilon-\kappa\xi}\int_0^{\mathfrak{z}}\int_0^{q}\theta M_\kappa(\theta)(\mathfrak{z}-w)^{\kappa-1}T((\mathfrak{z}-w)^{\kappa}\theta) \\
&\qquad \left[\mathrm{A}\mathcal{N}(w,\mathrm{y}(w)) + \mathcal{G}\left(w,\mathrm{y}(w),\int_0^w e(w,s,\mathrm{y}(s))ds\right)\right]d\theta dw\Bigg\| \\
&+ \Bigg\|\kappa\mathfrak{z}^{1-\varepsilon+\kappa\varepsilon-\kappa\xi}\int_{\mathfrak{z}-\alpha}^{\mathfrak{z}}\int_q^{\infty}(\mathfrak{z}-w)^{\kappa-1}\theta M_\kappa(\theta)T((\mathfrak{z}-w)^{\kappa}\theta) \\
&\qquad \left[\mathrm{A}\mathcal{N}(w,\mathrm{y}(w)) + \mathcal{G}\left(w,\mathrm{y}(w),\int_0^w e(w,s,\mathrm{y}(s))ds\right)\right]d\theta dw\Bigg\| \\
&\leq \kappa\Lambda_0\mathfrak{z}^{1-\varepsilon+\kappa\varepsilon-\kappa\xi}\Bigg(\int_0^{\mathfrak{z}}\int_0^{q}\theta M_\kappa(\theta)(\mathfrak{z}-w)^{\kappa-1}(\mathfrak{z}-w)^{\kappa\xi-\kappa}\theta^{\xi-1} \\
&\quad \times\left[M'_0M_g(1+P) + \phi(w)\Phi(\mathrm{y})[1+\psi(\mathfrak{z})]\right]d\theta dw \\
&\quad + \int_{\mathfrak{z}-\alpha}^{\mathfrak{z}}\int_q^{\infty}(\mathfrak{z}-w)^{\kappa-1}\theta M_\kappa(\theta)(\mathfrak{z}-w)^{\kappa\xi-\kappa}\theta^{\xi-1}\left[M'_0M_g(1+P) + \phi(w)\Phi(\mathrm{y})[1+\psi(\mathfrak{z})]\right]dw\Bigg) \\
&\leq \kappa\Lambda_0\mathfrak{z}^{1-\varepsilon+\kappa\varepsilon-\kappa\xi}\Bigg(\int_0^{\mathfrak{z}}(\mathfrak{z}-w)^{\kappa\xi-1}\left[M'_0M_g(1+P) + \phi(w)\Phi(\mathrm{y})[1+\psi(\mathfrak{z})]\right]dw\int_0^q\theta^{\xi}M_\kappa(\theta)d\theta \\
&\quad + \int_{\mathfrak{z}-\alpha}^{\mathfrak{z}}(\mathfrak{z}-w)^{\kappa\xi-1}\left[M'_0M_g(1+P) + \phi(w)\Phi(\mathrm{y})[1+\psi(\mathfrak{z})]\right]dw\int_0^{\infty}\theta^{\xi}M_\kappa(\theta)d\theta\Bigg) \\
&\leq \kappa\Lambda_0\mathfrak{z}^{1-\varepsilon+\kappa\varepsilon-\kappa\xi}\Bigg(\int_0^{\mathfrak{z}}(\mathfrak{z}-w)^{\kappa\xi-1}\left[M'_0M_g(1+P) + \phi(w)\Phi(\mathrm{y})[1+\psi(\mathfrak{z})]\right]dw\int_0^q\theta^{\xi}M_\kappa(\theta)d\theta \\
&\quad + \frac{\Gamma(1-\xi)}{\Gamma(1-\kappa\xi)}\int_{\mathfrak{z}-\alpha}^{\mathfrak{z}}(\mathfrak{z}-w)^{\kappa\xi-1}\left[M'_0M_g(1+P) + \phi(w)\Phi(\mathrm{y})[1+\psi(\mathfrak{z})]\right]dw\Bigg) \\
&\to 0 \text{ as } \alpha \textit{ tends to } 0, q \textit{ tends to } 0.
\end{aligned}$$

So, $V_{\alpha,q}(\mathfrak{z}) = \{z_{\alpha,q}(\mathfrak{z}) : \mathfrak{z} \in B_P(\mathcal{J})\}$ are arbitrary closed to $V(\mathfrak{z}) = \{z(\mathfrak{z}) : \mathfrak{z} \in B_P(\mathcal{I})\}$. Therefore, $\{z(\mathfrak{z}) : \mathfrak{z} \in B_P(\mathcal{J})\}$ is relatively compact by the Arzela–Ascoli theorem. Thus, the continuity of $z(\mathfrak{z})$ and relative compactness of $\{z(\mathfrak{z}) : \mathfrak{z} \in B_P(\mathcal{J})\}$ imply that $z(\mathfrak{z})$ is a completely continuous operator.

Step 5: Ψ has a closed graph.

Take $\mathrm{y}_n \to \mathrm{y}_*$ as $n \to \infty$, $z_n(\mathfrak{z}) \in \Psi(\mathrm{y}_n)$ and $z_n \to z_*$ as $n \to \infty$, we have to show that $z_* \in \Psi(\mathrm{y}_*)$. Since $z_n \in \Psi(\mathrm{y}_n)$ then $\exists$ a function $\mathcal{G}_n \in S_{\mathcal{G},\mathrm{y}_n}$, such that

$$\begin{aligned}
z_n(\mathfrak{z}) = \mathfrak{z}^{1-\varepsilon+\kappa\varepsilon-\kappa\xi}&\Bigg[\mathcal{S}_{\kappa,\varepsilon}(\mathfrak{z})[\mathrm{y}_0 - \mathcal{N}(0,\mathrm{y}(0))] + \mathcal{N}(\mathfrak{z},\mathrm{y}_n(\mathfrak{z})) \\
&+ \int_0^{\mathfrak{z}}(\mathfrak{z}-w)^{\kappa-1}\mathcal{Q}_\kappa(\mathfrak{z}-w)\mathrm{A}\mathcal{N}(w,\mathrm{y}_n(w))dw + \int_0^{\mathfrak{z}}(\mathfrak{z}-w)^{\kappa-1}\mathcal{Q}_\kappa(\mathfrak{z}-w)\mathcal{G}_n(w)dw\Bigg].
\end{aligned}$$

We need to show that $\exists\, \mathcal{G}_* \in S_{\mathcal{G},\mathrm{y}_*}$, such that

$$\begin{aligned}
z_*(\mathfrak{z}) = \mathfrak{z}^{1-\varepsilon+\kappa\varepsilon-\kappa\xi}&\Bigg[\mathcal{S}_{\kappa,\varepsilon}(\mathfrak{z})[\mathrm{y}_0 - \mathcal{N}(0,\mathrm{y}(0))] + \mathcal{N}(\mathfrak{z},\mathrm{y}_*(\mathfrak{z})) \\
&+ \int_0^{\mathfrak{z}}(\mathfrak{z}-w)^{\kappa-1}\mathcal{Q}_\kappa(\mathfrak{z}-w)\mathrm{A}\mathcal{N}(w,\mathrm{y}_*(w))dw + \int_0^{\mathfrak{z}}(\mathfrak{z}-w)^{\kappa-1}\mathcal{Q}_\kappa(\mathfrak{z}-w)\mathcal{G}_*(w)dw\Bigg].
\end{aligned}$$

Clearly,

$$\left\| \left[z_n(\mathfrak{z}) - \mathfrak{z}^{1-\varepsilon+\kappa\varepsilon-\kappa\xi} \Big(\mathcal{S}_{\kappa,\varepsilon}(\mathfrak{z})[\mathrm{y}_0 + \mathcal{N}(0,\mathrm{y}(0))] - \mathcal{N}(\mathfrak{z},\mathrm{y}_n(\mathfrak{z})) - \int_0^{\mathfrak{z}} (\mathfrak{z}-w)^{\mathfrak{z}-1} \mathcal{Q}_\kappa(\mathfrak{z}-w) \mathrm{A}\mathcal{N}(w,\mathrm{y}_n(w))dw \Big) \right] - \left[z_*(\mathfrak{z}) - \mathfrak{z}^{1-\varepsilon+\kappa\varepsilon-\kappa\xi} \Big(\mathcal{S}_{\kappa,\varepsilon}(\mathfrak{z})[\mathrm{y}_0 - \mathcal{N}(0,\mathrm{y}(0))] - \mathcal{N}(\mathfrak{z},\mathrm{y}_*(\mathfrak{z})) - \int_0^{\mathfrak{z}} (\mathfrak{z}-w)^{\mathfrak{z}-1} \mathcal{Q}_\kappa(\mathfrak{z}-w) \mathrm{A}\mathcal{N}(w,\mathrm{y}_*(w))dw \Big) \right] \right\| \to 0 \text{ as } n \to \infty.$$

Next, we define the operator $\Upsilon : L'(\mathcal{J},Y) \to \mathcal{X}$,

$$\Upsilon(g)(\mathfrak{z}) = \int_0^{\mathfrak{z}} (\mathfrak{z}-w)^{\kappa-1} \mathcal{Q}_\kappa(\mathfrak{z}-w) \mathcal{G}\Big(w, \mathrm{y}(w), \int_0^w e(w,s,\mathrm{y}(w))ds \Big) dw.$$

We have (by (5)) that $\Upsilon \circ S_{\mathcal{G},\mathrm{y}}$ is a closed graph operator. So, by referring to *ypsilon*, we know

$$\left[z_n(\mathfrak{z}) - \mathfrak{z}^{1-\varepsilon+\kappa\varepsilon-\kappa\xi} \Big(\mathcal{S}_{\kappa,\varepsilon}(\mathfrak{z})[\mathrm{y}_0 + \mathcal{N}(0,\mathrm{y}(0))] - \mathcal{N}(\mathfrak{z},\mathrm{y}_n(\mathfrak{z})) - \int_0^{\mathfrak{z}} (\mathfrak{z}-w)^{\mathfrak{z}-1} \mathcal{Q}_\kappa(\mathfrak{z}-w) \mathrm{A}\mathcal{N}(w,\mathrm{y}_n(w))dw \Big) \right] \in \Upsilon(S_{\mathcal{G},\mathrm{y}_n}),$$

since $\mathcal{G}_n \to \mathcal{G}_*$, we follow from (5) that

$$\left[z_*(\mathfrak{z}) - \mathfrak{z}^{1-\varepsilon+\kappa\varepsilon-\kappa\xi} \Big(\mathcal{S}_{\kappa,\varepsilon}(\mathfrak{z})[\mathrm{y}_0 - \mathcal{N}(0,\mathrm{y}(0))] - \mathcal{N}(\mathfrak{z},\mathrm{y}_*(\mathfrak{z})) - \int_0^{\mathfrak{z}} (\mathfrak{z}-w)^{\mathfrak{z}-1} \mathcal{Q}_\kappa(\mathfrak{z}-w) \mathrm{A}\mathcal{N}(w,\mathrm{y}_*(w))dw \Big) \right] \in \Upsilon(S_{\mathcal{G},u_*}).$$

Therefore, Ψ is a closed graph.
Step:6 Set Λ is bounded.

$$\Lambda = \{\mathrm{y} \in \partial B_P(\mathcal{J}) : \lambda\mathrm{y} = \Psi(\mathrm{y}) \text{ for some } \lambda > 1\}.$$

Let $\mathrm{y} \in \Lambda$. Then $\lambda w \in \Psi(\mathrm{y})$ for some $\lambda > 1$. Thus, there exists $\mathcal{G} \in S_{\mathcal{G},\mathrm{y}}$ in ways that for each $\mathfrak{z} \in [0,d]$ and $\|\mathrm{A}^{1-\mu}\| \leq M_0'$, we have

$$\mathrm{y}(\mathfrak{z}) = \lambda^{-1}\mathfrak{z}^{1-\varepsilon+\kappa\varepsilon-\kappa\xi} \Big[\mathcal{S}_{\kappa,\varepsilon}(\mathfrak{z})[\mathrm{y}_0 - \mathcal{N}(0,\mathrm{y}(0))] + \mathcal{N}(\mathfrak{z},\mathrm{y}(\mathfrak{z})) + \int_0^{\mathfrak{z}} (\mathfrak{z}-w)^{\kappa-1} \mathcal{Q}_\kappa(\mathfrak{z}-w) \mathrm{A}\mathcal{N}(w,\mathrm{y}(w))dw + \int_0^{\mathfrak{z}} (\mathfrak{z}-w)^{\kappa-1} \mathcal{Q}_\kappa(\mathfrak{z}-w) \mathcal{G}\Big(w, \mathrm{y}(w), \int_0^w e(w,s,\mathrm{y}(s))ds \Big) \Big] dw.$$

By assumptions $(H_2) - (H_4)$, we have

$$
\begin{aligned}
\|y(\mathfrak{z})\| = & \Bigg\| \lambda^{-1}\mathfrak{z}^{1-\varepsilon+\kappa\varepsilon-\kappa\xi}\Bigg[\mathcal{S}_{\kappa,\varepsilon}(\mathfrak{z})[y_0-\mathcal{N}(0,y(0))]+\mathcal{N}(\mathfrak{z},y(\mathfrak{z})) \\
& + \int_0^{\mathfrak{z}}(\mathfrak{z}-w)^{\kappa-1}\mathcal{Q}_\kappa(\mathfrak{z}-w)\mathrm{A}\mathcal{N}(w,y(w))dw \\
& + \int_0^{\mathfrak{z}}(\mathfrak{z}-w)^{\kappa-1}\mathcal{Q}_\kappa(\mathfrak{z}-w)\mathcal{G}\left(w,y(w),\int_0^w e(w,s,y(s))ds\right)\Bigg]dw\Bigg\| \\
\leq & \, d^{1-\varepsilon+\kappa\varepsilon-\kappa\xi}\Bigg[\sup\Big\|\mathcal{S}_{\kappa,\varepsilon}(\mathfrak{z})[y_0-\mathcal{N}(0,y(0))]\Big\|+\Big\|\mathcal{N}(\mathfrak{z},y(\mathfrak{z}))\Big\| \\
& + \sup\int_0^{\mathfrak{z}}(\mathfrak{z}-w)^{\kappa-1}\Big\|\mathcal{Q}_\kappa(\mathfrak{z}-w)\Big\|\left(\Big\|A\mathcal{N}(w,y(w))\Big\|+\Big\|\mathcal{G}\left(w,y(w),\int_0^w e(w,s,y(s))ds\right)\Big\|\right)dw\Bigg] \\
\leq & \, d^{1-\varepsilon+\kappa\varepsilon-\kappa\xi}\Big[L''d^{-1+\varepsilon-\kappa\varepsilon+\kappa\xi}(y_0-M_0M_g)+M_0M_g(1+P)\Big] \\
& + d^{1-\varepsilon+\kappa\varepsilon-\kappa\xi}L'\int_0^{\mathfrak{z}}(\mathfrak{z}-w)^{\kappa\xi-1}[M_0'M_g(1+P)+\phi(w)\Phi(\|y(w)\|)(1+\psi(w))]dw \\
\leq & \, M_1^*+L'M_2^*+d^{1-\varepsilon+\kappa\varepsilon-\kappa\xi}L'\int_0^{\mathfrak{z}}(\mathfrak{z}-w)^{\kappa\xi-1}\phi(w)\Phi(\|y(w)\|)(1+\psi(w))dw,
\end{aligned}
$$

$$
\begin{aligned}
& \textit{where } M_1^* = d^{1-\varepsilon+\kappa\varepsilon-\kappa\xi}\Big[L''d^{-1+\varepsilon-\kappa\varepsilon+\kappa\xi}(y_0-M_0M_g)+M_0M_g(1+P)\Big] \\
& \textit{and } M_2^* = d^{1-\varepsilon(1+\kappa\xi)}\frac{M_0'M_g(1+P)}{\kappa\xi}.
\end{aligned}
$$

Consider the RHS of the above inequality as $\gamma(\mathfrak{z})$. Then, we have

$$
\begin{aligned}
& \gamma(0) = M_1^*,\ \|y(\mathfrak{z})\| \leq \gamma(\mathfrak{z}),\ \mathfrak{z} \in [0,d], \\
& \gamma'(\mathfrak{z}) = d^{1-\varepsilon+\kappa\varepsilon-\kappa\xi}L'(w-\mathfrak{z})^{\kappa\xi-1}\phi(\mathfrak{z})\Phi(\|y(\mathfrak{z})\|)(1+\psi(\mathfrak{z})).
\end{aligned}
$$

By the non-decreasing character of Φ, we obtain

$$
\gamma'(\mathfrak{z}) = d^{1-\varepsilon+\kappa\varepsilon-\kappa\xi}L'(w-\mathfrak{z})^{\kappa\xi-1}\phi(\mathfrak{z})\Phi(\gamma(\mathfrak{z}))(1+\psi(\mathfrak{z})).
$$

Then the above inequality implies (for each $\mathfrak{z} \in \mathcal{J}$) that

$$
\int_{\gamma(0)}^{\gamma(\mathfrak{z})}\frac{du}{\Phi(u)} \leq L'\int_0^{\mathfrak{z}}(\mathfrak{z}-w)^{\kappa\xi-1}\phi(\mathfrak{z})(1+\psi(\mathfrak{z}))dw < \int_{M_1^*}^{\infty}\frac{du}{\Phi(u)}.
$$

This inequality implies that there exists a constant $\mathcal{L}$, such that $\gamma(\mathfrak{z}) \leq \mathcal{L}$, $\mathfrak{z} \in \mathcal{J}$, and, hence, $y(\mathfrak{z}) \leq \mathcal{L}$. From this we notice that set Λ is bounded. Therefore, by [17], Martelli's fixed point theorem Ψ has a fixed point, which is the mild solution of the system (1)–(2). □

4. Example

As an idea of how our findings may be used, think about the following Hilfer fractional neutral integro-differential inclusion,

$$
\begin{aligned}
& D_{0^+}^{\frac{4}{7},\varepsilon}[\Delta(\mathfrak{z},v)-\overline{\mathcal{N}}(\mathfrak{z},\Delta(\mathfrak{z},v))] \in \frac{\partial^2}{\partial\mathfrak{z}^2}\Delta(\mathfrak{z},v)+\bar{\mathcal{G}}(\mathfrak{z},\Delta(\mathfrak{z},v),(E\Delta)(\mathfrak{z},v))\mathfrak{z} \in (0,d], v \in [0,\pi], \\
& \Delta(\mathfrak{z},0) = \Delta(\mathfrak{z},\pi) = 0\mathfrak{z} \in [0,d], \qquad (6) \\
& I^{(1-\frac{4}{7})(1-\varepsilon)}y(w,0) = y_0(v), v \in [0,\pi],
\end{aligned}
$$

where $D_{0^+}^{\frac{4}{7},\varepsilon}$ is the HFD of order $\frac{4}{7}$, type ε, $I^{(1-\frac{4}{7})(1-\varepsilon)}$ is the Riemann–Liouville integral of order $\frac{3}{7}(1-\varepsilon)$, $\bar{\mathcal{G}}(\mathfrak{z},\Delta(\mathfrak{z},v),(E\Delta)(\mathfrak{z},v)),(E\Delta)(\mathfrak{z},v),$ *and* $\bar{\mathcal{N}}(\mathfrak{z},\Delta(\mathfrak{z},v))$ are the required functions.

To write the system (6) in the abstract form of (1)–(2), we chose the space $Y = L^2[0,\pi]$. Define an almost sectorial operator $\mathtt{A}$ by $\mathtt{A}\Delta = \Delta_{\mathfrak{z}\mathfrak{z}}$ with the domain

$$D(\mathtt{A}) = \left\{\Delta \in Y : \frac{\partial\Delta}{\partial\mathfrak{z}}, \frac{\partial^2\Delta}{\partial\mathfrak{z}^2} \in Y : \Delta(\mathfrak{z},0) = \Delta(\mathfrak{z},\pi) = 0\right\}.$$

Then $\mathtt{A}$ produces a compact semigroup that is analytic and self-adjoint, $\mathtt{T}(\mathfrak{z})\mathfrak{z} \geq 0$. Additionally, the discrete spectrum of $\mathtt{A}$ contains eigenvalues of $k^2, k \in \mathbb{N}$ and orthogonal eigenvectors $\zeta_k(z) = \sqrt{\frac{2}{\pi}}\sin(kz)$, then

$$\mathtt{A}z = \sum_{k=0}^{\infty} k^2\langle z,\zeta_k\rangle\zeta_k.$$

Moreover, we have each $v \in Y, \mathtt{T}(\mathfrak{z})v = \sum_{k=1}^{\infty}\zeta^{-k^2\mathfrak{z}}\langle v,\zeta_k\rangle\zeta_k$. In particular, $\mathtt{T}(\cdot)$ is uniformly stable semigroup and $\|\mathtt{T}(\mathfrak{z})\| \leq M$, which satisfies (H_1).

$\mathtt{y}(\mathfrak{z})(v) = \Delta(\mathfrak{z},v)$, $\mathfrak{z} \in \mathcal{J} = [0,d]$, $v \in [0,\pi]$. Take $\mathtt{y} \in Y = L^2[0,\pi]$, $v \in [0,\pi]$, we consider the multi-valued mapping $\mathcal{G} : \mathcal{J} \times Y \times Y \to Y$,

$$\begin{aligned}\mathcal{G}(\mathfrak{z},\mathtt{y}(\mathfrak{z}),(E\mathtt{y})(\mathfrak{z})) &= \overline{\mathcal{G}}(\mathfrak{z},\Delta(\mathfrak{z},v),(E\Delta)(\mathfrak{z},v)) \\ &= \frac{e^{-\mathfrak{z}}}{1+e^{-\mathfrak{z}}}\sin\left(w(\mathfrak{z},v) + \int_0^{\mathfrak{z}}\cos(\mathfrak{z}s)\Delta(s,v)ds\right),\end{aligned}$$

where

$$(E\mathtt{y})(\mathfrak{z})(v) = \int_0^{\mathfrak{z}} e(\mathfrak{z},s,\Delta(s,v))ds = \int_0^{\mathfrak{z}}\cos(\mathfrak{z}s)\Delta(s,v)ds.$$

Since, mapping $\overline{\mathcal{G}}$ is measurable, upper semi-continuous, and strongly measurable,

$$\overline{\mathcal{G}}(\mathfrak{z},\Delta(\mathfrak{z},v),(E\Delta)(\mathfrak{z},v)) \leq \mathcal{M}_1^*.$$

So $\overline{\mathcal{G}}$ is satisfied (H_2). Additionally, $\mathcal{N} : \mathcal{J} \times Y \to Y$ must have completely continuous mapping, which is defined as $\mathcal{N}(\mathfrak{z},u(\mathfrak{z})) = \overline{\mathcal{N}}(\mathfrak{z},\Delta(\mathfrak{z},v))$, satisfying the necessary hypotheses. Therefore, the required mapping satisfied all hypotheses. As a result, the nonlocal Cauchy problem (1)–(2) may be used to rephrase the fractional system (6). It is clear that the boundary of $\mathcal{G}(\mathfrak{z},\Delta(\mathfrak{z},u),(E\Delta)(\mathfrak{z},u))$ is uniform. The problem has a mild solution on $\mathcal{J}$, according to Theorem 2 .

5. Conclusions

In this study, Martelli's fixed point theorem was used to examine the possibility of a mild solution for an abstract Hilfer fractional differential system via almost sectorial operators. Adequate criteria were applied to the present findings and were satisfied. The controllability of the Hilfer fractional neutral derivative (via almost sectorial operators) will be investigated in the future using a fixed point technique.

Author Contributions: Conceptualisation, C.B.S.V.B. and R.U.; methodology, C.B.S.V.B.; validation, C.B.S.V.B. and R.U.; formal analysis, C.B.S.V.B.; investigation, R.U.; resources, C.B.S.V.B.; writing original draft preparation, C.B.S.V.B.; writing review and editing, R.U.; visualisation, R.U.; supervision, R.U.; project administration, R.U. All authors have read and agreed to the published version of the manuscript.

Funding: There are no funders to report for this submission.

Institutional Review Board Statement: Not applicable.

Informed Consent Statement: Not applicable.

Data Availability Statement: Data sharing is not applicable to this article as no datasets were generated or analyzed during the current study.

Acknowledgments: The authors are grateful to the reviewers of this article who provided insightful comments and advice that allowed us to revise and improve the content of the paper. The first author would like to thank the management of VIT University for providing a teaching cum research assistant fellowship.

Conflicts of Interest: The authors have no conflict of interest to declare.

Abbreviations

The following abbreviations are used in this manuscript:

HFD	Hilfer fractional derivative
HF	Hilfer fractional

References

1. Agarwal, R.P.; Lakshmikantham, V.; Nieto, J.J. On the concept of solution for fractional differential equations with uncertainty. *Nonlinear Anal.* **2010**, *72*, 2859–2862. [CrossRef]
2. Ahmad, B.; Alsaedi, A.; Ntouyas, S.K.J.; Tariboon, J. *Hadamard-Type Fractional Differential Equations, Inclusions and Inequalities*; Springer International Publishing AG: Cham, Switzerland, 2017.
3. Chang, Y. K.; Chalishajar, D. N. Controllability of mixed Volterra-Fredholm-type integro-differential inclusions in Banach spaces. *J. Franklin Inst.* **2008**, *345*, 499–507. [CrossRef]
4. Diemling, K. *Multivalued Differential Equations*; De Gruyter Series in Nonlinear Analysis and Applications; De Gruyter: Berlin, Germany, 1992.
5. Diethelm, K. *The Analysis of Fractional Differential Equations: An Application-Oriented Exposition Using Differential Operators of Caputo Type*; Lecture Notes in Mathematics; Springer: Berlin, Germany, 2010.
6. Ding, X.L.; Ahmad, B. Analytical solutions to fractional evolution equations with almost sectorial operators. *Adv. Differ. Equ.* **2016**, *2016*, 203. [CrossRef]
7. Du, J.; Jiang, W.; Niazi, A.U.K. Approximate controllability of impulsive Hilfer fractional differential inclusions. *J. Nonlinear Sci. Appl.* **2017**, *10*, 595–611. [CrossRef]
8. Furati, K.M.; Kassim, M.D.; Tatar, N.E. Existence and uniqueness for a problem involving Hilfer fractional derivative. *Comput. Math. Appl.* **2012**, *641*, 616–626. [CrossRef]
9. Ganesh, R.; Sakthivel, R.; Mahmudov, N.I.; Anthoni, S.M. Approximate controllability of fractional integro-differential evolution equations. *J. Appl. Math.* **2013**, *225*, 708–717.
10. Gu, H.; Trujillo, J.J. Existence of integral solution for evolution equation with Hilfer fractional derivative. *Appl. Math. Comput.* **2015**, *257*, 344–354.
11. Pazy, A. *Semigroups of Linear Operators and Applications to Partial Differential Equations*; Applied Mathematical Sciences; Springer: New York, NY, USA, 1983.
12. Podlubny, I. *Fractional Differential Equations*; Academic Press: San Diego, CA, USA, 1999.
13. Khaminsou, B.; Thaiprayoon, C.; Sudsutad, W.; Jose, S.A. Qualitative analysis of a proportional Caputo fractional Pantograph differential equation with mixed nonlocal conditions. *Nonlinear Funct. Anal. Appl.* **2021**, *26*, 197–223.
14. Mallika Arjunan, M.; Abdeljawad, T.; Kavitha. K.; Yousef, A. On a class of Atangana-Boleanu fractional Volterra-Fredholm integro-differential inclusions with non-instantaneous impulses. *Chaos Solitons Fractals* **2021**, *148*, 1–13. [CrossRef]
15. Salmon, N.; SenGupta, I. Fractional Barndorff-Nielsen and Shephard model: Applications in variance and volatility swaps, and hedging. *Ann. Financ.* **2021**, *17*, 529–558. [CrossRef]
16. Yang, M.; Wang, Q. Approximate controllability of Hilfer fractional differential inclusions with nonlocal conditions. *Math. Methods Appl. Sci.* **2017**, *40*, 1126–1138. [CrossRef]
17. Martelli, M. A Rothe's type theorem for non-compact acyclic-valued map. *Boll. Dell'unione Math. Ital.* **1975**, *2*, 70–76.
18. Wan, X.J.; Zhang, Y.P.; Sun, J.T. Controllability of impulsive neutral fractional differential inclusions in Banach Space. *Abstr. Appl. Anal.* **2013**, *2013*, 861568. [CrossRef]
19. Zhou, Y. *Basic Theory of Fractional Differential Equations*; World Scientific: Singapore, 2014.
20. Zhou, Y. *Fractional Evolution Equations and Inclusions: Analysis and Control*; Elsevier: New York, NY, USA, 2015.
21. Zhou, Y,; Vijayakumar. V.; Murugesu, R. Controllability for fractional evolution inclusions without compactness. *Evol. Equ. Control Theory* **2015**, *4*, 507–524. [CrossRef]
22. Hilfer, R. *Application of Fractional Calculus in Physics*; World Scientific: Singapore, 2000.

23. Bedi, P.; Kumar, A.; Abdeljawad, T.; Khan, Z.A.; Khan, A. Existence and approaximate controllability of Hilfer fractional evolution equations with almost sectorial operators. *Adv. Differ. Equ.* **2020**, *2020*, 615. [CrossRef]
24. Jaiswal, A.; Bahuguna, D. Hilfer fractional differantial equations with almost sectorial operators. *Differ. Equ. Dyn. Syst.* **2020**, 1–17. [CrossRef]
25. Karthikeyan, K.A.; Debbouche, A.; Torres, D.F.M. Analysis of Hilfer fractional integro-differential equations with almost sectorial operators. *Fractal Fract.* **2021**, *5*, 22. [CrossRef]
26. Kavitha, K.; Vijayakumar, V.; Udhayakumar, R.; Sakthivel, N.; Nissar, K.S. A note on approaximate controllability of the Hilfer fractional neutral differential inclusions with infinite delay. *Math. Methods Appl. Sci.* **2021**, *44*, 4428–4447. [CrossRef]
27. Sakthivel, R.; Ganesh, R.; Anthoni, S.M. Approximate controllability of fractional nonlinear differential inclusions. *Appl. Math. Comput.* **2013**, *225*, 708–717. [CrossRef]
28. Wang, J.; Zhou, Y. Existence and controllability results for fractional semilinear differential inclusions. *Nonlinear Anal.* **2011**, *12*, 3642–3653. [CrossRef]
29. Benchohra, M.; Henderson, J.; Ntouyas, S.K. Existence results for impulsive multivalued semilinear neutral functional differential inclusions in Banach Spaces. *J. Math. Anal. Appl.* **2001**, *263*, 763–780. [CrossRef]
30. Li, F.; Xiao, T.J.; Xu, H.K. On nonlinear neutral fractional integro-differential inclusions with infinite delay. *J. Appl. Math.* **2012**, *2012*, 916543. [CrossRef]
31. Fu, X.; Cao, Y. Existence for neutral impulsive differential inclusions with nonlocal conditions. *Nonlinear Anal.* **2008**, *68*, 3707–3718. [CrossRef]
32. Zhou, M.; Li, C.; Zhou, Y. Existence of mild solutions for Hilfer fractional evolution equations with almost sectorial operators. *Axioms* **2022**, *11*, 144. doi10.3390/axioms11040144. [CrossRef]
33. Zhang, L.; Zhou, Y. Fractional Cauchy problems with almost sectorial operators. *Appl. Math. Comput.* **2014**, *257*, 145–157. [CrossRef]
34. Li, F. Mild solutions for abstract differential equations with almost sectorial operators and infinite delay. *Adv. Differ. Equ.* **2013**, *2013*, 327. [CrossRef]
35. Sivasankar, S.; Udhayakumar, R. Hilfer fractional neutral stochastic Volterra integro-differential inclusions via almost sectorial operators. *Mathematics* **2022**, *10*, 2074. [CrossRef]
36. Varun Bose, C.S.; Udhayakumar, R. A note on the existence of Hilfer fractional differential inclusions with almost sectorial operators. *Math. Methods Appl. Sci.* **2022**, *45*, 2530–2541. [CrossRef]
37. Wang, R.N.; De-Han Chen.; Xiao, T.J. Abstract fractional Cauchy problems with almost sectorial operators. *J. Differ. Equ.* **2002**, *252*, 202–235 . [CrossRef]
38. Periago, F.; Straub, B. A functional calculus for almost sectorial operators and applications to abstract evolution equations. *J. Evol. Equ.* **2002**, *2*, 41–68. [CrossRef]
39. Yang, M.; Wang, Q. Existence of mild solutions for a class of Hilfer fractional evolution equations with nonlocal conditions. *Fract. Calc. Appl. Anal.* **2017**, *20*, 679–705. [CrossRef]
40. Lasota, A.; Opial, Z. An application of the Kakutani-Ky-Fan theorem in the theory of ordinary differential equations or noncompact acyclic-valued map. *Bull. Acad. Pol. Sci. Ser. Sci. Math. Astron. Phys.* **1965**, *13*, 781–786.

fractal and fractional

MDPI

Article

Nonexistence of Global Solutions to Time-Fractional Damped Wave Inequalities in Bounded Domains with a Singular Potential on the Boundary

Areej Bin Sultan †, Mohamed Jleli † and Bessem Samet *,†

Department of Mathematics, College of Science, King Saud University, P.O. Box 2455, Riyadh 11451, Saudi Arabia; 437203645@student.ksu.edu.sa (A.B.S.); jleli@ksu.edu.sa (M.J.)
* Correspondence: bsamet@ksu.edu.sa
† These authors contributed equally to this work.

Abstract: We first consider the damped wave inequality $\frac{\partial^2 u}{\partial t^2} - \frac{\partial^2 u}{\partial x^2} + \frac{\partial u}{\partial t} \geq x^\sigma |u|^p$, $t > 0$, $x \in (0,L)$, where $L > 0$, $\sigma \in \mathbb{R}$, and $p > 1$, under the Dirichlet boundary conditions $(u(t,0), u(t,L)) = (f(t), g(t))$, $t > 0$. We establish sufficient conditions depending on σ, p, the initial conditions, and the boundary conditions, under which the considered problem admits no global solution. Two cases of boundary conditions are investigated: $g \equiv 0$ and $g(t) = t^\gamma$, $\gamma > -1$. Next, we extend our study to the time-fractional analogue of the above problem, namely, the time-fractional damped wave inequality $\frac{\partial^\alpha u}{\partial t^\alpha} - \frac{\partial^2 u}{\partial x^2} + \frac{\partial^\beta u}{\partial t^\beta} \geq x^\sigma |u|^p$, $t > 0$, $x \in (0,L)$, where $\alpha \in (1,2)$, $\beta \in (0,1)$, and $\frac{\partial^\tau}{\partial t^\tau}$ is the time-Caputo fractional derivative of order τ, $\tau \in \{\alpha, \beta\}$. Our approach is based on the test function method. Namely, a judicious choice of test functions is made, taking in consideration the boundedness of the domain and the boundary conditions. Comparing with previous existing results in the literature, our results hold without assuming that the initial values are large with respect to a certain norm.

Keywords: time-fractional damped wave inequalities; bounded domain; singularity; nonexistence

MSC: 35B44; 35B33; 26A33

Citation: Bin Sultan, A.; Jleli, M.; Samet, B. Nonexistence of Global Solutions to Time-Fractional Damped Wave Inequalities in Bounded Domains with a Singular Potential on the Boundary. *Fractal Fract.* **2021**, *5*, 258. https://doi.org/10.3390/fractalfract5040258

Academic Editor: Rodica Luca

Received: 1 November 2021
Accepted: 29 November 2021
Published: 6 December 2021

1. Introduction

In this paper, we first consider the damped wave inequality

$$\begin{cases} \dfrac{\partial^2 u}{\partial t^2} - \dfrac{\partial^2 u}{\partial x^2} + \dfrac{\partial u}{\partial t} \geq x^\sigma |u|^p, & t > 0,\ x \in (0,L), \\ (u(t,0), u(t,L)) = (f(t), g(t)), & t > 0, \\ \left(u(0,x), \dfrac{\partial u}{\partial t}(0,x)\right) = (u_0(x), u_1(x)), & x \in (0,L), \end{cases} \tag{1}$$

where $L > 0$, $\sigma \in \mathbb{R}$, and $p > 1$. It is supposed that $u_0, u_1 \in L^1([0,L])$, $f \in L^1_{loc}([0,\infty))$, and $g(t) = C_g t^\gamma$, where $C_g \geq 0$ and $\gamma > -1$, are constants. Namely, we establish sufficient conditions depending on the initial values, the boundary conditions, p, and σ, under which (1) admits no global weak solution, in a sense that will be specified later.

Next, we study the time-fractional analogue of (1), namely the time-fractional damped wave inequality

$$
\begin{cases}
\frac{\partial^\alpha u}{\partial t^\alpha} - \frac{\partial^2 u}{\partial x^2} + \frac{\partial^\beta u}{\partial t^\beta} \geq x^\sigma |u|^p, & t > 0,\ x \in (0, L), \\
(u(t,0), u(t,L)) = (f(t), g(t)), & t > 0, \\
\left(u(0,x), \frac{\partial u}{\partial t}(0,x) \right) = (u_0(x), u_1(x)), & x \in (0, L),
\end{cases}
\tag{2}
$$

where $\alpha \in (1,2)$, $\beta \in (0,1)$, and $\frac{\partial^\tau}{\partial t^\tau}$, $\tau \in \{\alpha, \beta\}$, is the time-Caputo fractional derivative of order τ.

The investigation of the question of blow-up of solutions to initial boundary value problems for semilinear wave equations started in the 1970s. For example, Tsutsumi [1] considered the nonlinear damped wave equation

$$
\frac{\partial^2 u}{\partial t^2} - \Delta u + b \frac{\partial u}{\partial t} = F(u),
$$

under homogeneous Dirichlet boundary conditions, where $b \geq 0$ and

$$
F(s)s - 2(2\kappa + 1) \int_0^s F(\tau)\, d\tau \geq d_0 |s|^{\rho+2}, \quad s \in \mathbb{R},
$$

for some $\kappa > 0$ and $\rho > 0$. By means of the energy method, the author established sufficient conditions for the blow-up of solutions. In [2], using a concavity argument, Levine established sufficient conditions for the blow-up of solutions to an abstract Cauchy problem in a Hilbert space, of the form

$$
P \frac{\partial^2 u}{\partial t^2} + Au + Q \frac{\partial u}{\partial t} = F(u),
$$

where P and A are positive symmetric operators and F is a nonlinear operator satisfying certain conditions. Later, the concavity method was used and developed by many authors in order to study more general problems. For further blow-up results for nonlinear wave equations, obtained by means of the energy/concavity method, see e.g., [3–11] and the references therein.

Fractional operators arise in various applications, such as chemistry, biology, continuum mechanics, anomalous diffusion, and materials science, see for instance [12–16]. Consequently, many mathematicians dealt with the study of fractional differential equations in both theoretical and numerical aspects, see e.g., [17–21].

In [22], Kirane and Tatar considered the time-fractional damped wave equation

$$
\begin{cases}
\frac{\partial^2 u}{\partial t^2} - \Delta u + \frac{\partial^{1+\alpha} u}{\partial t^{1+\alpha}} = a|u|^{p-1}u, & t > 0,\ x \in \Omega, \\
u(t,x) = 0, \quad t > 0,\ x \in \partial\Omega, \\
\left(u(0,x), \frac{\partial u}{\partial t}(0,x) \right) = (u_0(x), u_1(x)), & x \in \Omega,
\end{cases}
\tag{3}
$$

where $p > 1$, $\alpha \in (-1,1)$, and Ω is a bounded domain of $\mathbb{R}^N$. Using some arguments based on Fourier transforms and the Hardy–Littlewood inequality, it was shown that the energy grows exponentially for sufficiently large initial data.

By combining an argument due to Georgiev and Todorova [23] with the techniques used in [22], Tatar [24] proved that the solutions to (3) blow up in finite-time for sufficiently large initial data.

In all the above cited references, the blow-up results were obtained for sufficiently large initial data. In this paper, we use a different approach than those used in the above mentioned references. Namely, our approach is based on the test function method introduced by Mitidieri and Pohozaev [25]. Taking into consideration the boundedness of the domain as well as the boundary conditions, adequate test functions are used to obtain sufficient conditions for the nonexistence of global weak solutions to problems (1) and (2). Notice that our results hold without assuming that the initial values are large with respect to a certain norm.

Let us mention also that recently, methods for the numerical diagnostics of the solution's blow-up have been actively developing (see e.g., [26–28]), which make it possible to refine the theoretical estimates.

The rest of the paper is organized as follows: In Section 2, we provide some preliminaries on fractional calculus, and some useful lemmas. We state our main results in Section 3. The proofs are presented in Section 4.

2. Preliminaries on Fractional Calculus

For the reader's convenience, we recall below some notions from fractional calculus, see e.g., [17,20].

Let $T > 0$ be fixed. Given $\rho > 0$ and $v \in L^1([0,T])$, the left-sided and right-sided Riemann–Liouville fractional integrals of order ρ of v, are defined, respectively, by

$$(I_0^\rho v)(t) = \frac{1}{\Gamma(\rho)} \int_0^t (t-s)^{\rho-1} v(s)\,ds \quad \text{and} \quad (I_T^\rho v)(t) = \frac{1}{\Gamma(\rho)} \int_t^T (s-t)^{\rho-1} v(s)\,ds,$$

for almost everywhere $t \in [0,T]$, where Γ denotes the Gamma function. It can be easily seen that, if $v \in C([0,T])$, then

$$\lim_{t \to 0^+} (I_0^\rho v)(t) = \lim_{t \to T^-} (I_T^\rho v)(t) = 0.$$

In this case, we may consider $I_0^\rho v$ and $I_T^\rho v$ as continuous functions in $[0,T]$, by taking

$$(I_0^\rho v)(0) = (I_T^\rho v)(T) = 0.$$

Given a positive integer n, $\tau \in (n-1,n)$, and $v \in C^n([0,T])$, the (left-sided) Caputo fractional derivative of order τ of v, is defined by

$$\frac{d^\tau v}{dt^\tau}(t) = \left(I_0^{n-\tau} \frac{d^n v}{dt^n} \right)(t) = \frac{1}{\Gamma(n-\tau)} \int_0^t (t-s)^{n-\tau-1} \frac{d^n v}{dt^n}(s)\,ds,$$

for all $t \in [0,L]$.

We have the following integration by parts rule.

Lemma 1 (see the Corollary in [17], p. 67). *Let $\rho > 0$, $q, r \geq 1$, and $\frac{1}{q} + \frac{1}{r} \leq 1 + \rho$ ($q \neq 1$, $r \neq 1$, in the case $\frac{1}{q} + \frac{1}{r} = 1 + \rho$). If $(v,w) \in L^q([0,T]) \times L^r([0,T])$, then*

$$\int_0^T (I_0^\rho v)(t) w(t)\,dt = \int_0^T v(t) (I_T^\rho w)(t)\,dt.$$

Lemma 2. *For sufficiently large λ, let*

$$\eta(t) = T^{-\lambda}(T-t)^\lambda, \quad 0 \leq t \leq T. \tag{4}$$

Let $\rho \in (0,1)$. Then

$$(I_T^\rho \eta)(t) = \frac{\Gamma(\lambda+1)}{\Gamma(\rho+\lambda+1)} T^{-\lambda}(T-t)^{\rho+\lambda}, \tag{5}$$

$$(I_T^\rho \eta)'(t) = -\frac{\Gamma(\lambda+1)}{\Gamma(\rho+\lambda)} T^{-\lambda}(T-t)^{\rho+\lambda-1}, \tag{6}$$

$$(I_T^\rho \eta)''(t) = \frac{\Gamma(\lambda+1)}{\Gamma(\rho+\lambda-1)} T^{-\lambda}(T-t)^{\rho+\lambda-2}. \tag{7}$$

Proof. We have

$$\begin{aligned}
(I_T^\rho \eta)(t) &= \frac{1}{\Gamma(\rho)} \int_t^T (s-t)^{\rho-1} \eta(s)\, ds \\
&= \frac{T^{-\lambda}}{\Gamma(\rho)} \int_t^T (s-t)^{\rho-1} (T-s)^\lambda\, ds \\
&= \frac{T^{-\lambda}}{\Gamma(\rho)} \int_t^T (s-t)^{\rho-1} ((T-t)-(s-t))^\lambda\, ds \\
&= \frac{T^{-\lambda}(T-t)^\lambda}{\Gamma(\rho)} \int_t^T (s-t)^{\rho-1} \left(1-\frac{s-t}{T-t}\right)^\lambda ds.
\end{aligned}$$

Using the change of variable $z = \frac{s-t}{T-t}$, we obtain

$$\begin{aligned}
(I_T^\rho \eta)(t) &= \frac{T^{-\lambda}(T-t)^{\lambda+\rho}}{\Gamma(\rho)} \int_0^1 z^{\rho-1}(1-z)^\lambda\, dz \\
&= \frac{T^{-\lambda}(T-t)^{\lambda+\rho}}{\Gamma(\rho)} B(\rho, \lambda+1),
\end{aligned}$$

where B denotes the Beta function. Using the property (see e.g., [20])

$$B(a,b) = \frac{\Gamma(a)\Gamma(b)}{\Gamma(a+b)}, \quad a,b>0,$$

we obtain

$$\begin{aligned}
(I_T^\rho \eta)(t) &= \frac{T^{-\lambda}(T-t)^{\lambda+\rho}}{\Gamma(\rho)} \frac{\Gamma(\rho)\Gamma(\lambda+1)}{\Gamma(\rho+\lambda+1)} \\
&= \frac{\Gamma(\lambda+1)}{\Gamma(\rho+\lambda+1)} T^{-\lambda}(T-t)^{\rho+\lambda},
\end{aligned}$$

which proves (5).

Next, calculating the derivative of $I_T^\rho \eta$, we obtain

$$(I_T^\rho \eta)'(t) = -\frac{(\rho+\lambda)\Gamma(\lambda+1)}{\Gamma(\rho+\lambda+1)} T^{-\lambda}(T-t)^{\rho+\lambda-1}.$$

On the other hand, by the property (see e.g., [20])

$$\Gamma(a+1) = a\Gamma(a), \quad a>0, \tag{8}$$

we obtain

$$\Gamma(\rho+\lambda+1) = (\rho+\lambda)\Gamma(\rho+\lambda).$$

Hence, we deduce that

$$(I_T^\rho \eta)'(t) = -\frac{\Gamma(\lambda+1)}{\Gamma(\rho+\lambda)} T^{-\lambda}(T-t)^{\rho+\lambda-1},$$

which proves (6).

Differentiating $(I_T^\rho \eta)'$ and using (8), we obtain

$$\begin{aligned}
(I_T^\rho \eta)''(t) &= \frac{(\rho+\lambda-1)\Gamma(\lambda+1)}{\Gamma(\rho+\lambda)} T^{-\lambda}(T-t)^{\rho+\lambda-2} \\
&= \frac{(\rho+\lambda-1)\Gamma(\lambda+1)}{(\rho+\lambda-1)\Gamma(\rho+\lambda-1)} T^{-\lambda}(T-t)^{\rho+\lambda-2} \\
&= \frac{\Gamma(\lambda+1)}{\Gamma(\rho+\lambda-1)} T^{-\lambda}(T-t)^{\rho+\lambda-2},
\end{aligned}$$

which proves (7). □

The following inequality will be useful later.

Lemma 3 (Young's Inequality with Epsilon, see [29], p. 36). *Let $\varepsilon > 0$ and $p > 1$. Then, for all $a, b \geq 0$, there holds*

$$ab \leq \varepsilon a^p + C_{\varepsilon,p} b^{\frac{p}{p-1}},$$

where $C_{\varepsilon,p} = (p-1)p^{-1}(\varepsilon p)^{\frac{-1}{p-1}}$.

Remark 1. *For a function $u : (0,\infty) \times (0,L) \to \mathbb{R}$, the notation $\frac{\partial^\alpha u}{\partial t^\alpha}$ used in (2), where $1 < \alpha < 2$, means the following:*

$$\frac{\partial^\alpha u}{\partial t^\alpha}(t,x) = \left(I_0^{2-\alpha} \frac{\partial^2 u}{\partial t^2}(\cdot, x) \right)(t), \quad t > 0,\ 0 < x < L,$$

i.e.,

$$\frac{\partial^\alpha u}{\partial t^\alpha}(t,x) = \frac{1}{\Gamma(2-\alpha)} \int_a^t (t-s)^{1-\alpha} \frac{\partial^2 u}{\partial t^2}(s,x)\, ds.$$

Similarly, the notation $\frac{\partial^\beta u}{\partial t^\beta}$ used in (2), where $0 < \beta < 1$, means the following:

$$\frac{\partial^\beta u}{\partial t^\beta}(t,x) = \left(I_0^{1-\beta} \frac{\partial u}{\partial t}(\cdot, x) \right)(t), \quad t > 0,\ 0 < x < L,$$

i.e.,

$$\frac{\partial^\beta u}{\partial t^\beta}(t,x) = \frac{1}{\Gamma(1-\beta)} \int_a^t (t-s)^{-\beta} \frac{\partial u}{\partial t}(s,x)\, ds.$$

3. Statement of the Main Results

We first consider problem (1). Let

$$Q = [0,\infty) \times [0,L].$$

We introduce the test function space

$$\Phi = \left\{ \varphi \in C^2(Q) : \varphi \geq 0,\ \varphi(\cdot,0) = \varphi(\cdot,L) \equiv 0,\ \varphi(t,\cdot) \equiv 0 \text{ for sufficiently large } t \right\}.$$

Definition 1. *Let $u_0, u_1 \in L^1([0,L])$ and $f, g \in L^1_{loc}([0,\infty))$. We say that u is a global weak solution to (1), if*

(i) $x^\sigma |u|^p \in L^1_{loc}(Q)$, $u \in L^1_{loc}(Q)$;

(ii) *for every* $\varphi \in \Phi$,

$$\begin{aligned}&\int_Q x^\sigma |u|^p \varphi\,dx\,dt + \int_0^\infty \left(f(t)\frac{\partial \varphi}{\partial x}(t,0) - g(t)\frac{\partial \varphi}{\partial x}(t,L)\right) dt \\ &+ \int_0^L \left(u_1(x)\varphi(0,x) - u_0(x)\frac{\partial \varphi}{\partial t}(0,x) + u_0(x)\varphi(0,x)\right) dx \\ &\leq -\int_Q u \frac{\partial^2 \varphi}{\partial x^2}\,dx\,dt + \int_Q u\frac{\partial^2 \varphi}{\partial t^2}\,dx\,dt - \int_Q u\frac{\partial \varphi}{\partial t}\,dx\,dt.\end{aligned} \tag{9}$$

Remark 2. *The weak formulation* (9) *is obtained by multiplying the differential inequality in* (1) *by* φ, *integrating over* Q, *and using the initial conditions in* (1). *So, clearly, any global solution to* (1) *is a global weak solution to* (1) *in the sense of Definition 1.*

We first consider the case $g \equiv 0$.

Theorem 1. *Let* $u_0, u_1 \in L^1([0,L])$, $f \in L^1_{loc}([0,\infty))$, *and* $g \equiv 0$. *Suppose that*

$$\int_0^L (u_0(x) + u_1(x))(L-x)\,dx > 0. \tag{10}$$

If

$$\sigma < -(p+1), \tag{11}$$

then (1) *admits no global weak solution.*

Remark 3. *Comparing with the existing results in the literature, in Theorem 1, it is not required that the initial data are sufficiently large with respect to a certain norm. The same remark holds for the next theorems.*

Example 1. *Consider problem* (1) *with*

$$f(t) = \frac{1}{\sqrt{t}},\ t>0, \quad g\equiv 0, \quad u_0(x) = -(L-x), \quad u_1(x) = 2(L-x), \quad \sigma=-4, \quad p=2.$$

Then, all the assumptions of Theorem 1 are satisfied. Consequently, we deduce that (1) *admits no global weak solution.*

Next, we consider the case when

$$g(t) = C_g t^\gamma, \quad \gamma > -1, \quad t>0, \tag{12}$$

where $C_g > 0$ is a constant.

Theorem 2. *Let* $u_0, u_1 \in L^1([0,L])$, $f \in L^1_{loc}([0,\infty))$, *and* g *be the function defined by* (12). *If one of the following conditions is satisfied:*

(i) $\sigma < -(p+1)$;

(ii) $\sigma \geq -(p+1)$, $\gamma > 0$,

then (1) *admits no global weak solution.*

Example 2. *Consider problem* (1) *with*

$$f(t) = \frac{e^t}{\sqrt{t}},\ t>0, \quad u_0(x) = x, \quad u_1(x) = x^2, \quad g(t) = \sqrt{t},\ t>0, \quad \sigma = -2, \quad p=2.$$

Then, by the statement (ii) of Theorem 2, we deduce that (1) *admits no global weak solution.*

Consider now problem (2). For all $T > 0$, let

$$Q_T = [0, T] \times [0, L].$$

We introduce the test function space

$$\Phi_T = \left\{ \varphi \in C^2(Q_T) : \varphi \geq 0, \, \varphi(\cdot, 0) = \varphi(\cdot, L) \equiv 0, \, \frac{\partial (I_T^{2-\alpha}\varphi)}{\partial t}(T, \cdot) \equiv 0 \right\}.$$

Definition 2. *Let $u_0, u_1 \in L^1([0, L])$ and $f, g \in L^1_{loc}([0, \infty))$. We say that u is a global weak solution to (2), if*

(i) $x^\sigma |u|^p \in L^1_{loc}(Q)$, $u \in L^1_{loc}(Q)$;
(ii) *for all $T > 0$ and $\varphi \in \Phi_T$,*

$$\begin{aligned} &\int_{Q_T} x^\sigma |u|^p \varphi \, dx \, dt + \int_0^T \left(f(t) \frac{\partial \varphi}{\partial x}(t, 0) - g(t) \frac{\partial \varphi}{\partial x}(t, L) \right) dt \\ &+ \int_0^L \left(u_1(x) (I_T^{2-\alpha}\varphi)(0, x) - u_0(x) \frac{\partial (I_T^{2-\alpha}\varphi)}{\partial t}(0, x) + u_0(x) (I_T^{1-\beta}\varphi)(0, x) \right) dx \quad (13) \\ &\leq - \int_{Q_T} u \frac{\partial^2 \varphi}{\partial x^2} \, dx \, dt + \int_{Q_T} u \frac{\partial^2 (I_T^{2-\alpha}\varphi)}{\partial t^2} \, dx \, dt - \int_{Q_T} u \frac{\partial (I_T^{1-\beta}\varphi)}{\partial t} \, dx \, dt. \end{aligned}$$

Remark 4. *The weak formulation (13) is obtained by multiplying the differential inequality in (2) by φ, integrating over Q_T, using the initial conditions in (2), and using the fractional integration by parts rule provided by Lemma 1. So, clearly, any global solution to (2) is a global weak solution to (2) in the sense of Definition 2.*

As for problem (1), we first consider the case $g \equiv 0$.

Theorem 3. *Let $u_0, u_1 \in L^1([0, L])$, $f \in L^1_{loc}([0, \infty))$, and $g \equiv 0$. If*

$$\sigma < -(p + 1),$$

and one of the following conditions is satisfied:

$$\alpha < \beta + 1, \quad \int_0^L u_1(x)(L - x) \, dx > 0; \quad (14)$$

$$\alpha = \beta + 1, \quad \int_0^L (u_0(x) + u_1(x))(L - x) \, dx > 0; \quad (15)$$

$$\alpha > \beta + 1, \quad \int_0^L u_0(x)(L - x) \, dx > 0, \quad (16)$$

then (2) admits no global weak solution.

Example 3. *Consider problem (2) with*

$$f(t) = \frac{1}{\sqrt{t}}, \quad t > 0, \quad u_0 \equiv 0, \quad u_1(x) = 2(L - x), \quad \alpha = \frac{3}{2}, \quad \beta = \frac{3}{4}, \quad \sigma = -4, \quad p = 2.$$

Since (14) is satisfied and $\sigma < -(p + 1)$, by Theorem 3, we deduce that (2) admits no global weak solution.

Next, we consider the inhomogeneous case, where the function g is given by (12).

Theorem 4. *Let $u_0, u_1 \in L^1([0,L])$, $f \in L^1_{loc}([0,\infty))$, and g be the function defined by (12). If*

$$\alpha > \max\{1-\gamma, 1\}, \quad \beta > \max\{-\gamma, 0\}, \tag{17}$$

and one of the following conditions is satisfied:
(i) $\sigma < -(p+1)$;
(ii) $\sigma \geq -(p+1)$, $\gamma > 0$,
then (2) *admits no global weak solution.*

Example 4. *Consider problem* (2) *with*

$$f(t) = \frac{1}{\sqrt{t}}, \ t > 0, \quad u_0(x) = -x, \quad u_1(x) = x^2, \quad g(t) = t^{\frac{2}{3}}, \ t > 0, \quad \alpha = \frac{3}{2}, \quad \beta = \frac{1}{2},$$

and

$$\sigma = -3, \quad p = 3.$$

Then (17) *is satisfied, $\sigma \geq -(p+1)$, and $\gamma > 0$. Then, by Theorem 4, we deduce that* (2) *admits no global weak solution.*

4. Proof of the Main Results

Throughout this section, any positive constant independent on T and R, is denoted by C. Namely, in the proofs, we use several asymptotic estimates as $T \to \infty$ and $R \to \infty$; therefore, the value of any positive constant independent of T and R has no influence in our analysis.

4.1. Proof of Theorem 1

Proof. Suppose that u is a global weak solution to (1). Then, by (9), for every $\varphi \in \Phi$, there holds

$$\begin{aligned} &\int_Q x^\sigma |u|^p \varphi \, dx \, dt + \int_0^\infty \left(f(t) \frac{\partial \varphi}{\partial x}(t,0) - g(t) \frac{\partial \varphi}{\partial x}(t,L) \right) dt \\ &+ \int_0^L \left(u_1(x)\varphi(0,x) - u_0(x) \frac{\partial \varphi}{\partial t}(0,x) + u_0(x)\varphi(0,x) \right) dx \\ &\leq \int_Q |u| \left| \frac{\partial^2 \varphi}{\partial x^2} \right| dx \, dt + \int_Q |u| \left| \frac{\partial^2 \varphi}{\partial t^2} \right| dx \, dt + \int_Q |u| \left| \frac{\partial \varphi}{\partial t} \right| dx \, dt. \end{aligned} \tag{18}$$

On the other hand, using Lemma 3 with $\varepsilon = \frac{1}{3}$ and adequate choices of a and b, we obtain

$$\int_Q |u| \left| \frac{\partial^2 \varphi}{\partial x^2} \right| dx \, dt \leq \frac{1}{3} \int_Q x^\sigma |u|^p \varphi \, dx \, dt + C \int_Q x^{\frac{-\sigma}{p-1}} \varphi^{\frac{-1}{p-1}} \left| \frac{\partial^2 \varphi}{\partial x^2} \right|^{\frac{p}{p-1}} dx \, dt, \tag{19}$$

$$\int_Q |u| \left| \frac{\partial^2 \varphi}{\partial t^2} \right| dx \, dt \leq \frac{1}{3} \int_Q x^\sigma |u|^p \varphi \, dx \, dt + C \int_Q x^{\frac{-\sigma}{p-1}} \varphi^{\frac{-1}{p-1}} \left| \frac{\partial^2 \varphi}{\partial t^2} \right|^{\frac{p}{p-1}} dx \, dt, \tag{20}$$

$$\int_Q |u| \left| \frac{\partial \varphi}{\partial t} \right| dx \, dt \leq \frac{1}{3} \int_Q x^\sigma |u|^p \varphi \, dx \, dt + C \int_Q x^{\frac{-\sigma}{p-1}} \varphi^{\frac{-1}{p-1}} \left| \frac{\partial \varphi}{\partial t} \right|^{\frac{p}{p-1}} dx \, dt. \tag{21}$$

Using (18)–(21), we obtain

$$\begin{aligned}&\int_0^\infty \left(f(t)\frac{\partial \varphi}{\partial x}(t,0)-g(t)\frac{\partial \varphi}{\partial x}(t,L)\right)dt\\&+\int_0^L \left(u_1(x)\varphi(0,x)-u_0(x)\frac{\partial \varphi}{\partial t}(0,x)+u_0(x)\varphi(0,x)\right)dx\\&\leq C\sum_{j=1}^3 I_j(\varphi),\end{aligned} \tag{22}$$

where

$$\begin{aligned}I_1(\varphi) &= \int_Q x^{\frac{-\sigma}{p-1}}\varphi^{\frac{-1}{p-1}}\left|\frac{\partial^2\varphi}{\partial x^2}\right|^{\frac{p}{p-1}},\\ I_2(\varphi) &= \int_Q x^{\frac{-\sigma}{p-1}}\varphi^{\frac{-1}{p-1}}\left|\frac{\partial^2\varphi}{\partial t^2}\right|^{\frac{p}{p-1}},\\ I_3(\varphi) &= \int_Q x^{\frac{-\sigma}{p-1}}\varphi^{\frac{-1}{p-1}}\left|\frac{\partial\varphi}{\partial t}\right|^{\frac{p}{p-1}}.\end{aligned}$$

Consider now two cut-off functions $\xi,\mu\in C^\infty([0,\infty))$ satisfying the following properties:

$$0\leq \xi,\mu\leq 1,\quad \xi(s)=\begin{cases}1 & \text{if } 0\leq s\leq \frac{1}{2}\\ 0 & \text{if } s\geq 1\end{cases},\quad \mu(s)=\begin{cases}0 & \text{if } 0\leq s\leq \frac{1}{2}\\ 1 & \text{if } s\geq 1\end{cases}.$$

For sufficiently large ℓ and R, let

$$\varphi_1(t)=\xi^\ell(R^{-\theta}t),\quad \varphi_2(x)=(L-x)\mu^\ell(Rx),\quad t\geq 0,\, x\in[0,L], \tag{23}$$

where $\theta>0$ is a constant that will be determined later. Consider the function

$$\varphi(t,x)=\varphi_1(t)\varphi_2(x),\quad t\geq 0,\, x\in[0,L]. \tag{24}$$

By the properties of the cut-off functions ξ and μ, it can be easily seen that the function φ defined by (24), belongs to Φ. Thus, the estimate (22) holds for this function.

Now, let us estimate the terms $I_j(\varphi)$, $j=1,2,3$. For $j=1$, by (24), we obtain

$$I_1(\varphi)=\left(\int_0^\infty \varphi_1(t)\,dt\right)\left(\int_0^L x^{\frac{-\sigma}{p-1}}\varphi_2^{\frac{-1}{p-1}}(x)|\varphi_2''(x)|^{\frac{p}{p-1}}\,dx\right):=I_1^{(1)}(\varphi_1)I_1^{(2)}(\varphi_2). \tag{25}$$

On the other hand, by the definitions of the function φ_1 and the cut-off function ξ, there holds

$$\begin{aligned}I_1^{(1)}(\varphi_1) &= \int_0^\infty \xi^\ell\left(R^{-\theta}t\right)dt\\ &= \int_0^{R^\theta} \xi^\ell\left(R^{-\theta}t\right)dt\\ &\leq R^\theta.\end{aligned} \tag{26}$$

By the definitions of the function φ_2 and the cut-off function μ, we obtain

$$\begin{aligned}\varphi_2''(x) &= \ell R^2\mu^{\ell-2}(Rx)\times\\ &\quad [(L-x)((\ell-1)\mu'^2(Rx)+\mu(Rx)\mu''(Rx))-2R^{-1}\mu(Rx)\mu'(Rx)]\chi_{[\frac{1}{2}R^{-1},R^{-1}]}(x),\end{aligned}$$

which yields

$$|\varphi_2''(x)|\leq CR^2\mu^{\ell-2}(Rx)\chi_{[\frac{1}{2}R^{-1},R^{-1}]}(x),$$

where $\chi_{[\frac{1}{2}R^{-1},R^{-1}]}$ is the indicator function of the interval $\left[\frac{1}{2}R^{-1},R^{-1}\right]$. Then, there holds

$$\begin{aligned} I_1^{(2)}(\varphi_2) &\le CR^{\frac{2p}{p-1}}\int_{\frac{1}{2}R^{-1}}^{R^{-1}} x^{\frac{-\sigma}{p-1}}(L-x)^{\frac{-1}{p-1}}\mu^{\ell-\frac{2p}{p-1}}(Rx)\,dx \\ &\le CR^{\frac{2p}{p-1}}\int_{\frac{1}{2}R^{-1}}^{R^{-1}} x^{\frac{-\sigma}{p-1}}\,dx \\ &\le CR^{\frac{\sigma}{p-1}+\frac{2p}{p-1}-1}. \end{aligned} \tag{27}$$

Thus, it follows from (25)–(27) that

$$I_1(\varphi) \le CR^{\theta+\frac{p+1+\sigma}{p-1}}. \tag{28}$$

For $j=2$, $I_j(\varphi)$ can be written as

$$I_2(\varphi) = \left(\int_0^\infty \varphi_1^{\frac{-1}{p-1}}(t)|\varphi_1''(t)|^{\frac{p}{p-1}}\,dt\right)\left(\int_0^L x^{\frac{-\sigma}{p-1}}\varphi_2(x)\,dx\right) := I_2^{(1)}(\varphi_1)I_2^{(2)}(\varphi_2). \tag{29}$$

By the definitions of the function φ_1 and the cut-off function ξ, we obtain

$$\varphi_1''(t) = \ell R^{-2\theta}\xi^{\ell-2}(R^{-\theta}t)\left[(\ell-1)\xi'^2(R^{-\theta}t)+\xi^{\ell-1}(R^{-\theta}t)\xi''(R^{-\theta}t)\right]\chi_{[\frac{1}{2}R^\theta,R^\theta]}(t),$$

which yields

$$|\varphi_1''(t)| \le CR^{-2\theta}\xi^{\ell-2}(R^{-\theta}t)\chi_{[\frac{1}{2}R^\theta,R^\theta]}(t).$$

Thus, there holds

$$\begin{aligned} I_2^{(1)}(\varphi_1) &\le CR^{\frac{-2\theta p}{p-1}}\int_{\frac{1}{2}R^\theta}^{R^\theta}\xi^{\ell-\frac{2p}{p-1}}(R^{-\theta}t)\,dt \\ &\le CR^{\theta\left(1-\frac{2p}{p-1}\right)}. \end{aligned} \tag{30}$$

Moreover, we have

$$\begin{aligned} I_2^{(2)}(\varphi_2) &= \int_0^L x^{\frac{-\sigma}{p-1}}\varphi_2(x)\,dx \\ &= \int_{\frac{1}{2}R^{-1}}^L x^{\frac{-\sigma}{p-1}}(L-x)\mu^\ell(Rx)\,dx \\ &\le C\int_{\frac{1}{2}R^{-1}}^L x^{\frac{-\sigma}{p-1}}\,dx. \end{aligned}$$

On the other hand, by (11), we have $\sigma < p-1$, thus we deduce that

$$I_2^{(2)}(\varphi_2) \le C. \tag{31}$$

Combining (29)–(31), there holds

$$I_2(\varphi) \le CR^{\theta\left(1-\frac{2p}{p-1}\right)}. \tag{32}$$

Now, let us estimate $I_3(\varphi)$. This term can be written as

$$I_3(\varphi) = \left(\int_0^\infty \varphi_1^{\frac{-1}{p-1}}(t)|\varphi_1'(t)|^{\frac{p}{p-1}}\,dt\right)\left(\int_0^L x^{\frac{-\sigma}{p-1}}\varphi_2(x)\,dx\right) := I_3^{(1)}(\varphi_1)I_3^{(2)}(\varphi_2). \tag{33}$$

A similar calculation as above yields

$$I_3^{(1)}(\varphi_1) \le CR^{\theta\left(1-\frac{p}{p-1}\right)}. \tag{34}$$

Observe that $I_3^{(2)}(\varphi_2) = I_2^{(2)}(\varphi_2)$. Thus, by (31), (33), and (34), we obtain

$$I_3(\varphi) \le CR^{\theta\left(1-\frac{p}{p-1}\right)}. \tag{35}$$

Next, combining (28), (32), and (35), we obtain

$$\sum_{j=1}^{3} I_j(\varphi) \le C\left(R^{\theta+\frac{p+1+\sigma}{p-1}} + R^{\theta\left(1-\frac{p}{p-1}\right)}\right). \tag{36}$$

Let θ be such that

$$\theta + \frac{p+1+\sigma}{p-1} = \theta\left(1-\frac{p}{p-1}\right),$$

that is,

$$\theta = \frac{-(p+1)-\sigma}{p}.$$

Notice that by (11), we have $\theta > 0$. Then, (36) reduces to

$$\sum_{j=1}^{3} I_j(\varphi) \le CR^{\theta\left(1-\frac{p}{p-1}\right)}. \tag{37}$$

Next, let us estimate the terms from the right side of (22). Observe that by the definition of the function φ, and the properties of the cut-off function μ, we have

$$\frac{\partial\varphi}{\partial x}(t,0) = 0, \quad t > 0.$$

Moreover, since $g \equiv 0$, there holds

$$\int_0^\infty \left(f(t)\frac{\partial\varphi}{\partial x}(t,0) - g(t)\frac{\partial\varphi}{\partial x}(t,L)\right) dt = 0. \tag{38}$$

By the properties of the cut-off function ξ, we have

$$\varphi(0,x) = \varphi_2(x), \quad \frac{\partial\varphi}{\partial t}(0,x) = 0, \quad x \in (0,L).$$

Thus, we obtain

$$\begin{aligned}
&\int_0^L \left(u_1(x)\varphi(0,x) - u_0(x)\frac{\partial\varphi}{\partial t}(0,x) + u_0(x)\varphi(0,x)\right) dx \\
&= \int_0^L (u_0(x)+u_1(x))\varphi(0,x)\,dx \\
&= \int_0^L (u_0(x)+u_1(x))\varphi_2(x)\,dx \\
&= \int_0^L (u_0(x)+u_1(x))(L-x)\mu^\ell(Rx)\,dx.
\end{aligned}$$

Then, taking into consideration that $u_0, u_1 \in L^1([0,L])$, by the dominated convergence theorem, we obtain

$$\begin{aligned} &\lim_{R\to\infty} \int_0^L \left(u_1(x)\varphi(0,x) - u_0(x)\frac{\partial \varphi}{\partial t}(0,x) + u_0(x)\varphi(0,x) \right) dx \\ &= \int_0^L (u_0(x)+u_1(x))(L-x)\,dx. \end{aligned} \tag{39}$$

Hence, by (10), for sufficiently large R, there holds

$$\int_0^L \left(u_1(x)\varphi(0,x) - u_0(x)\frac{\partial \varphi}{\partial t}(0,x) + u_0(x)\varphi(0,x) \right) dx \geq \frac{1}{2}\int_0^L (u_0(x)+u_1(x))(L-x)\,dx. \tag{40}$$

Next, combining (22), (37), (38), and (40), we obtain

$$\frac{1}{2}\int_0^L (u_0(x)+u_1(x))(L-x)\,dx \leq CR^{\theta\left(1-\frac{p}{p-1}\right)}.$$

Passing to the limit as $R \to \infty$ in the above inequality, we obtain

$$\frac{1}{2}\int_0^L (u_0(x)+u_1(x))(L-x)\,dx \leq 0,$$

which contradicts (10). Consequently, (1) admits no global weak solution. The proof is completed. □

4.2. Proof of Theorem 2

Proof. As was performed previously, suppose that u is a global weak solution to (1). From the proof of Theorem 1, for sufficiently large R, there holds

$$\begin{aligned} &-\int_0^\infty g(t)\frac{\partial \varphi}{\partial x}(t,L)\,dt \\ &+\int_0^L \left(u_1(x)\varphi(0,x) - u_0(x)\frac{\partial \varphi}{\partial t}(0,x) + u_0(x)\varphi(0,x) \right) dx \\ &\leq C\left(R^{\theta+\frac{p+1+\sigma}{p-1}} + R^{\theta\left(1-\frac{p}{p-1}\right)} \int_{\frac{1}{2}R^{-1}}^L x^{\frac{-\sigma}{p-1}}\,dx \right), \end{aligned} \tag{41}$$

where $\theta > 0$ and φ is the function defined by (24). On the other hand, by the definition of the function φ, for sufficiently large R, there holds

$$\frac{\partial \varphi}{\partial x}(t,L) = -\varphi_1(t), \quad t > 0,$$

which yields

$$\begin{aligned} -\int_0^\infty g(t)\frac{\partial \varphi}{\partial x}(t,L)\,dt &= \int_0^\infty g(t)\varphi_1(t)\,dt \\ &= C\int_0^\infty t^\gamma \xi^\ell(R^{-\theta}t)\,dt \\ &\geq C\int_0^{\frac{1}{2}R^\theta} t^\gamma\,dt \\ &= CR^{\theta(\gamma+1)}. \end{aligned}$$

Then, by (41), we deduce that

$$
\begin{aligned}
&C+R^{-\theta(\gamma+1)}\int_0^L\left(u_1(x)\varphi(0,x)-u_0(x)\frac{\partial\varphi}{\partial t}(0,x)+u_0(x)\varphi(0,x)\right)dx\\
&\leq C\left(R^{-\theta\gamma+\frac{p+1+\sigma}{p-1}}+R^{-\theta\left(\gamma+\frac{p}{p-1}\right)}\int_{\frac{1}{2}R^{-1}}^{L}x^{\frac{-\sigma}{p-1}}\,dx\right).
\end{aligned}
\tag{42}
$$

Let $\sigma<-(p+1)$. In this case, (42) reduces to

$$
\begin{aligned}
&C+R^{-\theta(\gamma+1)}\int_0^L\left(u_1(x)\varphi(0,x)-u_0(x)\frac{\partial\varphi}{\partial t}(0,x)+u_0(x)\varphi(0,x)\right)dx\\
&\leq C\left(R^{-\theta\gamma+\frac{p+1+\sigma}{p-1}}+R^{-\theta\left(\gamma+\frac{p}{p-1}\right)}\right).
\end{aligned}
\tag{43}
$$

Taking $\theta>0$ so that

$$
\theta\gamma>\frac{p+1+\sigma}{p-1},
\tag{44}
$$

passing to the limit as $R\to\infty$ in (43), and using (39), we obtain a contradiction with $C>0$. This proves part (i) of Theorem 2.

Let $\sigma\geq-(p+1)$ and $\gamma>0$.

If $-(p+1)\leq\sigma<p-1$, then (43) holds. Since $\gamma>0$, there exists $\theta>0$ such that (44) holds. Thus, passing to the limit as $R\to\infty$ in (43), we obtain a contradiction.
If $\sigma=p-1$, then (42) yields

$$
\begin{aligned}
&C+R^{-\theta(\gamma+1)}\int_0^L\left(u_1(x)\varphi(0,x)-u_0(x)\frac{\partial\varphi}{\partial t}(0,x)+u_0(x)\varphi(0,x)\right)dx\\
&\leq C\left(R^{-\theta\gamma+\frac{p+1+\sigma}{p-1}}+R^{-\theta\left(\gamma+\frac{p}{p-1}\right)}\ln R\right).
\end{aligned}
$$

As in the previous case, since $\gamma>0$, there exists $\theta>0$ such that (44) holds. Thus, passing to the limit as $R\to\infty$ in the above inequality, we obtain a contradiction.
If $\sigma>p-1$, then (42) yields

$$
\begin{aligned}
&C+R^{-\theta(\gamma+1)}\int_0^L\left(u_1(x)\varphi(0,x)-u_0(x)\frac{\partial\varphi}{\partial t}(0,x)+u_0(x)\varphi(0,x)\right)dx\\
&\leq C\left(R^{-\theta\gamma+\frac{p+1+\sigma}{p-1}}+R^{-\theta\left(\gamma+\frac{p}{p-1}\right)+\frac{\sigma}{p-1}-1}\right).
\end{aligned}
$$

Taking θ such that (44) is satisfied, and passing to the limit as $R\to\infty$ in the above inequality, a contradiction follows. Thus, part (ii) of Theorem 2 is proved. □

4.3. *Proof of Theorem 3*

Proof. Suppose that u is a global weak solution to (2). Then, by (13), for every $T>0$ and $\varphi\in\Phi_T$, there holds

$$
\begin{aligned}
&\int_{Q_T}x^{\sigma}|u|^p\varphi\,dx\,dt+\int_0^T\left(f(t)\frac{\partial\varphi}{\partial x}(t,0)-g(t)\frac{\partial\varphi}{\partial x}(t,L)\right)dt\\
&+\int_0^L\left(u_1(x)(I_T^{2-\alpha}\varphi)(0,x)-u_0(x)\frac{\partial(I_T^{2-\alpha}\varphi)}{\partial t}(0,x)+u_0(x)(I_T^{1-\beta}\varphi)(0,x)\right)dx\\
&\leq\int_{Q_T}|u|\left|\frac{\partial^2\varphi}{\partial x^2}\right|dx\,dt+\int_{Q_T}|u|\left|\frac{\partial^2(I_T^{2-\alpha}\varphi)}{\partial t^2}\right|dx\,dt+\int_{Q_T}|u|\left|\frac{\partial(I_T^{1-\beta}\varphi)}{\partial t}\right|dx\,dt.
\end{aligned}
\tag{45}
$$

On the other hand, using Lemma 3 with $\varepsilon = \frac{1}{3}$ and adequate choices of a and b, we obtain

$$\begin{aligned} &\int_{Q_T} |u| \left| \frac{\partial^2 \varphi}{\partial x^2} \right| dx\,dt \\ &\leq \frac{1}{3} \int_{Q_T} x^{\sigma} |u|^p \varphi \, dx\,dt + C \int_{Q_T} x^{\frac{-\sigma}{p-1}} \varphi^{\frac{-1}{p-1}} \left| \frac{\partial^2 \varphi}{\partial x^2} \right|^{\frac{p}{p-1}} dx\,dt, \end{aligned} \tag{46}$$

$$\begin{aligned} &\int_{Q_T} |u| \left| \frac{\partial^2 (I_T^{2-\alpha} \varphi)}{\partial t^2} \right| dx\,dt \\ &\leq \frac{1}{3} \int_{Q_T} x^{\sigma} |u|^p \varphi \, dx\,dt + C \int_{Q_T} x^{\frac{-\sigma}{p-1}} \varphi^{\frac{-1}{p-1}} \left| \frac{\partial^2 (I_T^{2-\alpha} \varphi)}{\partial t^2} \right|^{\frac{p}{p-1}} dx\,dt, \end{aligned} \tag{47}$$

and

$$\begin{aligned} &\int_{Q_T} |u| \left| \frac{\partial (I_T^{1-\beta} \varphi)}{\partial t} \right| dx\,dt \\ &\leq \frac{1}{3} \int_{Q_T} x^{\sigma} |u|^p \varphi \, dx\,dt + C \int_{Q_T} x^{\frac{-\sigma}{p-1}} \varphi^{\frac{-1}{p-1}} \left| \frac{\partial (I_T^{1-\beta} \varphi)}{\partial t} \right|^{\frac{p}{p-1}} dx\,dt. \end{aligned} \tag{48}$$

Using (45)–(48), we obtain

$$\begin{aligned} &\int_0^T \left(f(t) \frac{\partial \varphi}{\partial x}(t,0) - g(t) \frac{\partial \varphi}{\partial x}(t,L) \right) dt \\ &+ \int_0^L \left(u_1(x)(I_T^{2-\alpha}\varphi)(0,x) - u_0(x) \frac{\partial (I_T^{2-\alpha}\varphi)}{\partial t}(0,x) + u_0(x)(I_T^{1-\beta}\varphi)(0,x) \right) dx \\ &\leq \sum_{j=1}^{3} J_j(\varphi), \end{aligned} \tag{49}$$

where

$$\begin{aligned} J_1(\varphi) &= \int_{Q_T} x^{\frac{-\sigma}{p-1}} \varphi^{\frac{-1}{p-1}} \left| \frac{\partial^2 \varphi}{\partial x^2} \right|^{\frac{p}{p-1}} dx\,dt, \\ J_2(\varphi) &= \int_{Q_T} x^{\frac{-\sigma}{p-1}} \varphi^{\frac{-1}{p-1}} \left| \frac{\partial^2 (I_T^{2-\alpha} \varphi)}{\partial t^2} \right|^{\frac{p}{p-1}} dx\,dt, \\ J_3(\varphi) &= \int_{Q_T} x^{\frac{-\sigma}{p-1}} \varphi^{\frac{-1}{p-1}} \left| \frac{\partial (I_T^{1-\beta} \varphi)}{\partial t} \right|^{\frac{p}{p-1}} dx\,dt. \end{aligned}$$

For sufficiently large T, λ, ℓ, and R, let

$$\varphi(t,x) = \eta(t)\varphi_2(x), \quad t \geq 0,\ x \in [0,L], \tag{50}$$

where η is the function defined by (4), and φ_2 is the function given by (23). Using Lemma 2 and the properties of the cut-off function μ, it can be easily seen that the function φ defined by (50), belongs to Φ_T. Thus, (49) holds for this function.

Let us estimate the terms $J_j(\varphi)$, $j = 1,2,3$. For $j = 1$, by (50), we have

$$J_1(\varphi) = \left(\int_0^T \eta(t)\,dt \right) \left(\int_0^L x^{\frac{-\sigma}{p-1}} \varphi_2^{\frac{-1}{p-1}}(x) |\varphi_2''(x)|^{\frac{p}{p-1}} dx \right). \tag{51}$$

An elementary calculation shows that

$$\int_0^T \eta(t)\,dt = \frac{T}{\lambda+1}. \tag{52}$$

Hence, using (27), (51), and (52), we obtain

$$J_1(\varphi) \le CTR^{\frac{\sigma+2p}{p-1}-1}. \tag{53}$$

For $j=2$, we have

$$J_2(\varphi) = \left(\int_0^T \eta^{\frac{-1}{p-1}}(t)|(I_T^{2-\alpha}\eta)''(t)|^{\frac{p}{p-1}}\,dt\right)\left(\int_0^L x^{\frac{-\sigma}{p-1}}\varphi_2(x)\,dx\right). \tag{54}$$

Moreover, by Lemma 2, we obtain

$$\eta^{\frac{-1}{p-1}}(t)|(I_T^{2-\alpha}\eta)''(t)|^{\frac{p}{p-1}} = \left[\frac{\Gamma(\lambda+1)}{\Gamma(1-\alpha+\lambda)}\right]^{\frac{p}{p-1}} T^{-\lambda}(T-t)^{\lambda-\frac{\alpha p}{p-1}}.$$

Integrating over $(0,T)$, there holds

$$\int_0^T \eta^{\frac{-1}{p-1}}(t)|(I_T^{2-\alpha}\eta)''(t)|^{\frac{p}{p-1}}\,dt = CT^{\frac{-\alpha p}{p-1}+1}. \tag{55}$$

Next, taking into consideration that $\sigma < -(p+1)$ (so $\sigma < p-1$), it follows from (31), (54), and (55) that

$$J_2(\varphi) \le CT^{1-\frac{\alpha p}{p-1}}. \tag{56}$$

Proceeding as above, we obtain

$$J_3(\varphi) \le CT^{1-\frac{\beta p}{p-1}}. \tag{57}$$

Hence, by (53), (56), and (57), we obtain

$$\sum_{j=1}^{3} J_j(\varphi) \le C\left(TR^{\frac{\sigma+2p}{p-1}-1} + T^{1-\frac{\beta p}{p-1}}\right). \tag{58}$$

Consider now the terms from the right side of (49). By (50) and the properties of the cut-off function μ, since $g \equiv 0$, there holds

$$\int_0^T \left(f(t)\frac{\partial\varphi}{\partial x}(t,0) - g(t)\frac{\partial\varphi}{\partial x}(t,L)\right)dt = 0. \tag{59}$$

On the other hand, using (50) and Lemma 2, for all $x \in [0,L]$, we obtain

$$\begin{aligned}
(I_T^{2-\alpha}\varphi)(0,x) &= \frac{\Gamma(\lambda+1)}{\Gamma(3-\alpha+\lambda)}T^{2-\alpha}\varphi_2(x) &:= C_1T^{2-\alpha}\varphi_2(x),\\
\frac{\partial(I_T^{2-\alpha}\varphi)}{\partial t}(0,x) &= -\frac{\Gamma(\lambda+1)}{\Gamma(2-\alpha+\lambda)}T^{1-\alpha}\varphi_2(x) &:= -C_2T^{1-\alpha}\varphi_2(x),\\
(I_T^{1-\beta}\varphi)(0,x) &= \frac{\Gamma(\lambda+1)}{\Gamma(2-\beta+\lambda)}T^{1-\beta}\varphi_2(x) &:= C_3T^{1-\beta}\varphi_2(x).
\end{aligned}$$

Consequently, we obtain

$$\begin{aligned}
&\int_0^L \left(u_1(x)(I_T^{2-\alpha}\varphi)(0,x) - u_0(x)\frac{\partial(I_T^{2-\alpha}\varphi)}{\partial t}(0,x) + u_0(x)(I_T^{1-\beta}\varphi)(0,x) \right) dx \\
&= \int_0^L \left(C_1 T^{2-\alpha} u_1(x) + C_2 T^{1-\alpha} u_0(x) + C_3 T^{1-\beta} u_0(x) \right) \varphi_2(x)\, dx \\
&= \int_0^L \left(C_1 T^{2-\alpha} u_1(x) + C_2 T^{1-\alpha} u_0(x) + C_3 T^{1-\beta} u_0(x) \right) (L-x)\mu^\ell(Rx)\, dx.
\end{aligned} \tag{60}$$

Thus, combining (49), (58)–(60), we obtain

$$\begin{aligned}
&\int_0^L \left(C_1 T^{2-\alpha} u_1(x) + C_2 T^{1-\alpha} u_0(x) + C_3 T^{1-\beta} u_0(x) \right) (L-x)\mu^\ell(Rx)\, dx \\
&\le C\left(TR^{\frac{\sigma+2p}{p-1}-1} + T^{1-\frac{\beta p}{p-1}} \right).
\end{aligned}$$

Next, taking $T = R^\theta$, where $\theta > 0$ is a constant that will be determined later, the above inequality reduces to

$$\begin{aligned}
&\int_0^L \left(C_1 R^{\theta(2-\alpha)} u_1(x) + C_2 R^{\theta(1-\alpha)} u_0(x) + C_3 R^{\theta(1-\beta)} u_0(x) \right) (L-x)\mu^\ell(Rx)\, dx \\
&\le C\left(R^{\theta+\frac{\sigma+2p}{p-1}-1} + R^{\theta\left(1-\frac{\beta p}{p-1}\right)} \right).
\end{aligned} \tag{61}$$

Suppose that (14) holds. In this case, we obtain

$$\begin{aligned}
&\lim_{R\to\infty} R^{-\theta(2-\alpha)} \int_0^L \left(C_1 R^{\theta(2-\alpha)} u_1(x) + C_2 R^{\theta(1-\alpha)} u_0(x) + C_3 R^{\theta(1-\beta)} u_0(x) \right) (L-x)\mu^\ell(Rx)\, dx \\
&= C_1 \int_0^L u_1(x)(L-x)\, dx \\
&> 0.
\end{aligned}$$

Hence, for sufficiently large R,

$$\int_0^L \left(C_1 R^{\theta(2-\alpha)} u_1(x) + C_2 R^{\theta(1-\alpha)} u_0(x) + C_3 R^{\theta(1-\beta)} u_0(x) \right) (L-x)\mu^\ell(Rx)\, dx \ge C R^{\theta(2-\alpha)}. \tag{62}$$

Combining (61) with (62), we obtain

$$C \le R^{\theta(\alpha-1)+\frac{\sigma+2p}{p-1}-1} + R^{\theta\left(\alpha-\frac{\beta p}{p-1}-1\right)}. \tag{63}$$

Observe that, since $\alpha < \beta + 1$, we have

$$\alpha - \frac{\beta p}{p-1} - 1 < 0.$$

Hence, taking into consideration that $\sigma < -(p+1)$, picking $\theta > 0$ so that

$$\theta < \frac{-(p+1)-\sigma}{(p-1)(\alpha-1)},$$

and passing to the limit as $R \to \infty$ in (63), we obtain a contradiction with $C > 0$.

Suppose that (15) holds. Then,

$$(I_T^{2-\alpha}\varphi)(0,x) = (I_T^{1-\beta}\varphi)(0,x).$$

Thus, (61) reduces to

$$\begin{aligned}&\int_0^L \Big(C_1 R^{\theta(2-\alpha)}(u_0(x)+u_1(x)) + C_2 R^{\theta(1-\alpha)} u_0(x)\Big)(L-x)\mu^\ell(Rx)\,dx\\&\leq C\bigg(R^{\theta+\frac{\sigma+2p}{p-1}-1} + R^{\theta\left(1-\frac{\beta p}{p-1}\right)}\bigg).\end{aligned} \tag{64}$$

Moreover, we have

$$\begin{aligned}&\lim_{R\to\infty} R^{-\theta(2-\alpha)}\int_0^L \Big(C_1 R^{\theta(2-\alpha)}(u_0(x)+u_1(x)) + C_2 R^{\theta(1-\alpha)} u_0(x)\Big)(L-x)\mu^\ell(Rx)\,dx\\&= C_1\int_0^L (u_0(x)+u_1(x))(L-x)\,dx\\&> 0,\end{aligned}$$

which yields

$$\int_0^L \Big(C_1 R^{\theta(2-\alpha)}(u_0(x)+u_1(x)) + C_2 R^{\theta(1-\alpha)} u_0(x)\Big)(L-x)\mu^\ell(Rx)\,dx \geq C R^{\theta(2-\alpha)},$$

for sufficiently large R. Hence, using (64), and following the same argument as above, a contradiction follows.

Finally, suppose that (16) holds. In this case, we obtain

$$\begin{aligned}&\lim_{R\to\infty} R^{-\theta(1-\beta)}\int_0^L \Big(C_1 R^{\theta(2-\alpha)}u_1(x) + C_2 R^{\theta(1-\alpha)} u_0(x) + C_3 R^{\theta(1-\beta)}u_0(x)\Big)(L-x)\mu^\ell(Rx)\,dx\\&= C_3\int_0^L u_0(x)(L-x)\,dx\\&> 0.\end{aligned}$$

Hence, for sufficiently large R,

$$\int_0^L \Big(C_1 R^{\theta(2-\alpha)}u_1(x) + C_2 R^{\theta(1-\alpha)} u_0(x) + C_3 R^{\theta(1-\beta)}u_0(x)\Big)(L-x)\mu^\ell(Rx)\,dx \geq C R^{\theta(1-\beta)}. \tag{65}$$

Combining (61) with (65), we obtain

$$C \leq R^{\theta\beta+\frac{\sigma+2p}{p-1}-1} + R^{\frac{-\theta\beta}{p-1}}. \tag{66}$$

Taking $\theta>0$ such that

$$\theta < \frac{-\sigma-(p+1)}{\beta(p-1)},$$

and passing to the limit as $R\to\infty$ in (66), a contradiction follows. This completes the proof of Theorem 3. □

4.4. *Proof of Theorem 4*

Proof. Suppose that u is a global weak solution to (2). From the proof of Theorem 3, for sufficiently large T and R, there holds

$$\begin{aligned}&-\int_0^T g(t)\frac{\partial\varphi}{\partial x}(t,L)\,dt\\&+\int_0^L \Big(C_1 T^{2-\alpha}u_1(x) + C_2 T^{1-\alpha}u_0(x) + C_3 T^{1-\beta}u_0(x)\Big)(L-x)\mu^\ell(Rx)\,dx\\&\leq C\bigg(TR^{\frac{\sigma+2p}{p-1}-1} + T^{1-\frac{\beta p}{p-1}}\int_{\frac{1}{2}R^{-1}}^L x^{\frac{-\sigma}{p-1}}\,dx\bigg),\end{aligned} \tag{67}$$

where φ is the function defined by (50). On the other hand, by (50) and the properties of the cut-off function μ, we have

$$\begin{aligned} -\int_0^T g(t)\frac{\partial \varphi}{\partial x}(t,L)\,dt &= \int_0^T g(t)\eta(t)\,dt \\ &= T^{-\lambda}\int_0^T t^\gamma (T-t)^\lambda\,dt \\ &= B(\gamma+1,\lambda+1)T^{\gamma+1} \\ &:= CT^{\gamma+1}, \end{aligned}$$

where B denotes the Beta function. Thus, by (67), we obtain

$$\begin{aligned} &C+\int_0^L \Big(C_1 T^{1-\alpha-\gamma}u_1(x)+C_2T^{-\gamma-\alpha}u_0(x)+C_3T^{-\beta-\gamma}u_0(x)\Big)(L-x)\mu^\ell(Rx)\,dx \\ &\le C\left(T^{-\gamma}R^{\frac{\sigma+2p}{p-1}-1}+T^{-\frac{\beta p}{p-1}-\gamma}\int_{\frac{1}{2}R^{-1}}^L x^{\frac{-\sigma}{p-1}}\,dx\right). \end{aligned}$$

Taking $T=R^\theta$, where $\theta>0$ is a constant that will be determined later, the above inequality reduces to

$$\begin{aligned} &C+\int_0^L \Big(C_1 R^{\theta(1-\alpha-\gamma)}u_1(x)+C_2R^{-\theta(\gamma+\alpha)}u_0(x)+C_3R^{-\theta(\beta+\gamma)}u_0(x)\Big)(L-x)\mu^\ell(Rx)\,dx \\ &\le C\left(R^{-\theta\gamma+\frac{\sigma+2p}{p-1}-1}+R^{-\theta\left(\frac{\beta p}{p-1}+\gamma\right)}\int_{\frac{1}{2}R^{-1}}^L x^{\frac{-\sigma}{p-1}}\,dx\right). \end{aligned} \tag{68}$$

Let $\sigma<-(p+1)$. In this case, for sufficiently large R, there holds

$$\int_{\frac{1}{2}R^{-1}}^L x^{\frac{-\sigma}{p-1}}\,dx \le C.$$

Hence, (68) yields

$$\begin{aligned} &C+\int_0^L \Big(C_1 R^{\theta(1-\alpha-\gamma)}u_1(x)+C_2R^{-\theta(\gamma+\alpha)}u_0(x)+C_3R^{-\theta(\beta+\gamma)}u_0(x)\Big)(L-x)\mu^\ell(Rx)\,dx \\ &\le C\left(R^{-\theta\gamma+\frac{\sigma+2p}{p-1}-1}+R^{-\theta\left(\frac{\beta p}{p-1}+\gamma\right)}\right). \end{aligned} \tag{69}$$

Since by (17), $\beta+\gamma>0$, there holds

$$\frac{\beta p}{p-1}+\gamma>0.$$

Thus, taking $\theta>0$ so that

$$\theta\gamma>\frac{\sigma+p+1}{p-1}, \tag{70}$$

using (17), and passing to the limit as $R\to\infty$ in (69), we obtain a contradiction with $C>0$. This proves part (i) of Theorem 4.

Let $\sigma\ge-(p+1)$ and $\gamma>0$.

If $-(p+1)\le\sigma<p-1$, then (69) holds. Since $\gamma>0$, there exists $\theta>0$ satisfying (70). Thus, passing to the limit as $R\to\infty$ in (69), a contradiction follows.
If $\sigma=p-1$, then (68) yields

$$\begin{aligned} &C+\int_0^L \Big(C_1 R^{\theta(1-\alpha-\gamma)}u_1(x)+C_2R^{-\theta(\gamma+\alpha)}u_0(x)+C_3R^{-\theta(\beta+\gamma)}u_0(x)\Big)(L-x)\mu^\ell(Rx)\,dx \\ &\le C\left(R^{-\theta\gamma+\frac{\sigma+2p}{p-1}-1}+R^{-\theta\left(\frac{\beta p}{p-1}+\gamma\right)}\ln R\right). \end{aligned} \tag{71}$$

As in the previous case, since $\gamma > 0$, there exists $\theta > 0$ satisfying (70). Thus, passing to the limit as $R \to \infty$ in (71), a contradiction follows.
If $\sigma > p-1$, then (68) yields

$$\begin{aligned} C &+ \int_0^L \left(C_1 R^{\theta(1-\alpha-\gamma)} u_1(x) + C_2 R^{-\theta(\gamma+\alpha)} u_0(x) + C_3 R^{-\theta(\beta+\gamma)} u_0(x) \right) (L-x) \mu^\ell(Rx)\, dx \\ &\leq C \left(R^{-\theta\gamma + \frac{\sigma+2p}{p-1} - 1} + R^{-\theta\left(\frac{\beta p}{p-1} + \gamma\right) + \frac{\sigma}{p-1} - 1} \right). \end{aligned} \tag{72}$$

So, taking $\theta > 0$ satisfying (70) and

$$\theta\left(\frac{\beta p}{p-1} + \gamma\right) > \frac{\sigma}{p-1} - 1,$$

and passing to the limit as $R \to \infty$ in (72), a contradiction follows. This proves part (ii) of Theorem 4. □

5. Conclusions

Using the test function method, sufficient conditions for the nonexistence of global weak solutions to problems (1) and (2) are obtained. For each problem, an adequate choice of a test function is made, taking into consideration the boundedness of the domain and the boundary conditions. Comparing with previous existing results in the literature, our results hold without assuming that the initial values are large with respect to a certain norm.

In this paper, we treated only the one dimensional case. It will be interesting to study problems (1) and (2) in a bounded domain $\Omega \subset \mathbb{R}^N$ under different types of boundary conditions, such as Dirichlet boundary conditions, Neumann boundary conditions, and Robin boundary conditions.

Author Contributions: Investigation, A.B.S.; Supervision M.J. and B.S. All authors have read and agreed to the published version of the manuscript.

Funding: The second author is supported by the Researchers Supporting Project number (RSP-2021/57), King Saud University, Riyadh, Saudi Arabia.

Institutional Review Board Statement: Not applicable.

Informed Consent Statement: Not applicable.

Data Availability Statement: Not applicable.

Conflicts of Interest: The authors declare no conflict of interest.

References

1. Tsutsumi, M. On solutions of semilinear differential equations in a Hilbert space. *Math. Japon.* **1972**, *17*, 173–193.
2. Levine, H.A. Some additional remarks on the nonexistence of global solutions to nonlinear wave equations. *SIAM J. Math. Anal.* **1974**, *5*, 138–146. [CrossRef]
3. Galaktionov, V.A.; Pohozaev, S.I. Blow-up and critical exponents for nonlinear hyperbolic equations. *Nonlinear Anal.* **2003**, *53*, 453–466. [CrossRef]
4. Erbay, H.A.; Erbay, S.; Erkip, A. Thresholds for global existence and blow-up in a general class of doubly dispersive nonlocal wave equations. *Nonlinear Anal.* **2014**, *95*, 313–322. [CrossRef]
5. Kalantarov, V.K.; Ladyzhenskaya, O.A. The occurrence of collapse for quasilinear equations of parabolic and hyperbolic type. *J. Soviet Math.* **1978**, *10*, 53–70. [CrossRef]
6. Li, F. Global existence and blow-up of solutions for a higher-order Kirchhoff-type equation with nonlinear dissipation. *Appl. Math. Lett.* **2004**, *17*, 1409–1414. [CrossRef]
7. Wang, X.; Chen, Y.; Yang, Y.; Li, J.; Xu, R. Kirchhoff-type system with linear weak damping and logarithmic nonlinearities. *Nonlinear Anal.* **2019**, *188*, 475–499. [CrossRef]
8. Guedda, M.; Labani, H. Nonexistence of global solutions to a class of nonlinear wave equations with dynamic boundary conditions. *Bull. Belg. Math. Soc. Simon Stevin.* **2002**, *9*, 39–46. [CrossRef]
9. Messaoudi, S.A. Blow-up of positive-initial-energy solutions of a nonlinear viscoelastic hyperbolic equation. *J. Math. Anal. Appl.* **2006**, *320*, 902–915. [CrossRef]

10. Kafini, M.; Messaoudi, S.A. blow-up result for a viscoelastic system in $\mathbb{R}^N$. *Electron. J. Differ. Equ.* **2007**, *113*, 1–7.
11. Kafini, M.; Messaoudi, S.A. On the decay and global nonexistence of solutions to a damped wave equation with variable-exponent nonlinearity and delay. *Ann. Pol. Math.* **2019**, *122*, 49–70. [CrossRef]
12. Freeborn, T.J. A survey of fractional-order circuit models for biology and biomedicine. *IEEE J. Emerg. Sel. Top. Circuits Syst.* **2013**, *3*, 416–423. [CrossRef]
13. Bagley, R.L.; Torvik, P.J. A theoretical basis for the application of fractional calculus to viscoelasticity. *J. Rheol.* **1983**, *27*, 201–210. [CrossRef]
14. Povstenko, Y.Z. Fractional heat conduction equation and associated thermal Stresses. *J. Therm. Stress.* **2005**, *28*, 83–102. [CrossRef]
15. Chen, W.; Sun, H.G.; Zhang, X.; Korosak, D. Anomalous diffusion modeling by fractal and fractional derivatives. *Comput. Math. Appl.* **2010**, *59*, 1754–1758. [CrossRef]
16. Zhao, Y.; Hou, Z. Two viscoelastic constitutive models of rubber materials using fractional derivations. *J. Tsinghua Univ.* **2013**, *53*, 378–383.
17. Samko, S.G.; Kilbas, A.A.; Marichev, O.I. *Fractional Integrals and Derivatives: Theory and Applications*; Gordon and Breach: Yverdon, Switzerland, 1993.
18. Agarwal, R.P.; Benchohra, M.; Hamani, S. A survey on existence results for boundary value problems of nonlinear fractional differential equations and inclusions. *Acta Appl. Math.* **2010**, *109*, 973–1033. [CrossRef]
19. Podlubny, I. *Fractional Differential Equations*; Academic Press: New York, NY, USA, 1999.
20. Kilbas, A.A.; Srivastava, H.M.; Trujillo, J.J. *Theory and Applications of Fractional Differential Equations*; Elsevier Science Limited: Amsterdam, The Netherlands, 2006.
21. Li C.; Zeng F.H. *Numerical Methods for Fractional Calculus*; Chapman and Hall/CRC: Boca Raton, FL, USA, 2015.
22. Kirane, M.; Tatar, N.-E. Exponential growth for a fractionally damped wave equation. *Z. Anal. Anwend.* **2003**, *22*, 167–177. [CrossRef]
23. Georgiev, V.; Todorova, G. Existence of a solution of the wave equation with nonlinear damping and source terms. *J. Differ. Equ.* **1994**, *109*, 295–308. [CrossRef]
24. Tatar, N.-E. A blow up result for a fractionally damped wave equation. *Nonlinear Differ. Equ. Appl.* **2005**, *12*, 215–226. [CrossRef]
25. Mitidieri, E.; Pohozaev, S. A priori estimates and blow-up of solutions to nonlinear partial differential equations and inequalities. *Proc. Steklov Inst. Math.* **2001**, *234*, 1–383.
26. Korpusov, M.O.; Lukyanenko, D.V.; Panin, A.A.; Shlyapugin, G.I. On the blow-up phenomena for a 1-dimensional equation of ion sound waves in a plasma: Analytical and numerical investigation. *Math. Methods Appl. Sci.* **2018**, *41*, 2906–2929. [CrossRef]
27. Pelinovsky, D.; Xu, C. On numerical modelling and the blow-up behavior of contact lines with a 180 degrees contact angle. *J. Eng. Math.* **2015**, *92*, 31–44. [CrossRef]
28. Cangiani, A.; Georgoulis, E.H.; Kyza, I.; Metcalfe, S. Adaptivity and blow-up detection for nonlinear evolution problems. *SIAM J. Sci. Comput.* **2016**, *38*, A3833–A3856. [CrossRef]
29. Carl, S.; Le, V.K.; Motreanu, D. *Nonsmooth Variational Problems and Their Inequalities*; Springer: New York, NY, USA, 2007.

fractal and fractional

Article

Boundary Value Problem for Fractional q-Difference Equations with Integral Conditions in Banach Spaces

Nadia Allouch [1], John R. Graef [2,*] and Samira Hamani [1]

1 Laboratoire des Mathematiques Appliqués et Pures, Université de Mostaganem, B.P. 227, Mostaganem 27000, Algeria; nadia.allouch.etu@univ-mosta.dz (N.A.); hamani_samira@yahoo.fr (S.H.)
2 Department of Mathematics, University of Tennessee at Chattanooga, Chattanooga, TN 37403, USA
* Correspondence: john-graef@utc.edu; Tel.: +1-423-425-4545

Abstract: The authors investigate the existence of solutions to a class of boundary value problems for fractional q-difference equations in a Banach space that involves a q-derivative of the Caputo type and nonlinear integral boundary conditions. Their result is based on Mönch's fixed point theorem and the technique of measures of noncompactness. This approach has proved to be an interesting and useful approach to studying such problems. Some basic concepts from the fractional q-calculus are introduced, including q-derivatives and q-integrals. An example of the main result is included as well as some suggestions for future research.

Keywords: boundary value problems; fractional q-difference equations; Caputo fractional q-difference derivative; measure of noncompactness; Mönch's fixed point theorem

MSC: 26A33; 34A37

Citation: Allouch, N.; Graef, J.R.; Hamani, S. Boundary Value Problem for Fractional q-Difference Equations with Integral Conditions in Banach Spaces. *Fractal Fract.* **2022**, *6*, 237. https://doi.org/10.3390/fractalfract6050237

Academic Editor: Rodica Luca

Received: 8 March 2022
Accepted: 23 April 2022
Published: 25 April 2022

1. Introduction

Fractional differential equations play an essential role when attempting to model phenomena in a number of areas and have recently been studied by researchers in engineering, physics, chemistry, biology, economics, and control theory. For additional details see, for example, the monographs of Hilfer [1], Kilbas et al. [2], Miller and Ross [3], Podlubny [4], Samko et al. [5], and Tarasov [6] as well as the references they contain. The existence of solutions to fractional boundary value problems is currently a very active area of research as can be seen, for example, from the recent papers of Ahmad et al. [7], Agarwal et al. [8], Benchohra et al. [9], Benhamida et al. [10], Hamini et al. [11], and Zahed et al. [12].

Considerable attention has been given to the problem of existence of solutions to boundary value problems for fractional differential equations in Banach spaces, and we refer the reader to the recent contributions in [13–15].

The q-difference calculus, or quantum calculus, was first introduced by Jackson in 1910 [16,17]. The basic definitions and properties of the q-difference calculus can be found in [18,19]. Later, Al-Salam [20] and Agarwal [21] proposed the study of the fractional q-difference calculus. Fractional q-difference calculus by itself and nonlinear fractional q-difference boundary value problems have appeared as the object of study for a number of researchers. Recent developments on the fractional q-difference calculus and boundary value problems for such can be found in [7,22–25] and the references therein.

In this paper, we study the existence of solutions to the boundary value problem (BVP for short) for fractional q-difference equations with nonlinear integral conditions

$$({}^{C}D_q^{\alpha}y)(t) = f(t, y(t)), \text{ for a.e. } t \in J = [0, T], \quad 1 < \alpha \leq 2, \tag{1}$$

$$y(0) - y'(0) = \int_0^T g(s, y(s))ds, \tag{2}$$

$$y(T) + y'(T) = \int_0^T h(s, y(s))ds, \quad (3)$$

where $T > 0$, $q \in (0,1)$, ${}^{C}D_q^{\alpha}$ is the Caputo fractional q-difference derivative of order $1 < \alpha \leq 2$, and $f, g, h : J \times E \to E$ are given functions and g and h are continuous.

In our investigation of the existence of solutions to the problem above, we utilize the method associated with the technique of measures of noncompactness and Mönch's fixed point theorem. This approach turns out to be very useful in proving the existence of solutions for several different types of equations. The method of using measures of noncompactness was mainly initiated in the monograph of Banas and Goebel [26], and subsequently developed and used in many papers; see, for example, Banas et al. [27], Guo et al. [28], Akhmerov et al. [29], Mönch [30], Mönch and Von Harten [31], and Szufla [32].

This paper is structured as follows. In Section 2, we introduce some preliminary concepts including basic definitions and properties from fractional q-calculus and some properties of the Kuratowski measure of noncompactness. In Section 3, the existence of solutions to problem (1)–(3) is proved by using Mönch's fixed point theorem. Section 4 contains an example to illustrate our main results. The final section contains some concluding remarks and suggestions for future research.

2. Materials and Methods

We begin by introducing definitions, notations, and some preliminary facts that are used in the remainder of this paper.

Let $J = [0, T]$, $T > 0$, and consider the Banach space $C(J, E)$ of continuous functions from J into E with the norm

$$\|y\|_\infty = \sup\{|y(t)| : t \in J\}.$$

We let $C^2(J, E)$ be the space of differentiable functions $y : J \to E$, whose first and second derivatives are continuous, and let $L^1(J, E)$ be the Banach space of measurable functions $y : J \to E$ that are Bochner integrable with the norm

$$\|y\|_{L^1} = \int_J |y(t)|dt.$$

Let $L^\infty(J, E)$ be the Banach space of bounded measurable functions $y : J \to E$ equipped with the norm

$$\|y\|_{L^\infty} = \inf\{c > 0 : \|y(t)\| \leq c, \ a.e\ t \in J\}.$$

We now recall some definitions and properties from the fractional q-calculus [18,19]. For $a \in \mathbb{R}$ and $0 < q < 1$, we set

$$[a]_q = \frac{1 - q^a}{1 - q}.$$

The q-analogue of the power $(a - b)^{(n)}$ is given by

$$(a - b)^{(0)} = 1, \ (a - b)^{(n)} = \prod_{k=0}^{n-1}(a - bq^k), \ a, b \in \mathbb{R}, \ n \in \mathbb{N}.$$

In general,

$$(a - b)^{(\alpha)} = a^\alpha \prod_{k=0}^{\infty}\left(\frac{a - bq^k}{a - bq^{k+\alpha}}\right), \ a, b, \alpha \in \mathbb{R}.$$

Note that if $b = 0$, then $a^{(\alpha)} = a^\alpha$.

Definition 1 ([19]). *The q-gamma function is defined by*

$$\Gamma_q(\alpha) = \frac{(1-q)^{(\alpha-1)}}{(1-q)^{\alpha-1}},\ \alpha \in \mathbb{R} - \{0, -1, -2, \ldots\}.$$

We wish to point out that the q-gamma function satisfies the relation $\Gamma_q(\alpha+1) = [\alpha]_q \Gamma_q(\alpha)$.

Definition 2 ([19]). *The q-derivative of order $n \in \mathbb{N}$ of a function $f : J \to \mathbb{R}$ is defined by* $(D_q^0 f)(t) = f(t)$,

$$(D_q f)(t) = (D_q^1 f)(t) = \frac{f(t) - f(qt)}{(1-q)t},\ t \neq 0,\ (D_q f)(0) = \lim_{t \to 0}(D_q f)(t),$$

and

$$(D_q^n f)(t) = (D_q^1 D_q^{n-1} f)(t),\ t \in J,\ n \in \{1, 2, \ldots\}.$$

Now set $J_t = \{tq^n : n \in \mathbb{N}\} \cup \{0\}$.

Definition 3 ([19]). *The q-integral of a function $f : J_t \to \mathbb{R}$ is defined by*

$$(I_q f)(t) = \int_0^t f(s) d_q s = \sum_{n=0}^{\infty} t(1-q)q^n f(tq^n),$$

provided that the series converges.

We note that $(D_q I_q f)(t) = f(t)$, while if f is continuous at 0, then

$$(I_q D_q f)(t) = f(t) - f(0).$$

Definition 4 ([21]). *The Riemann–Liouville fractional q-integral of order $\alpha \in \mathbb{R}_+$ of a function $f : J \to \mathbb{R}$ is defined by $(I_q^0 f)(t) = f(t)$, and*

$$(I_q^\alpha f)(t) = \int_0^t \frac{(t-qs)^{(\alpha-1)}}{\Gamma_q(\alpha)} f(s) d_q s,\ t \in J.$$

Note that for $\alpha = 1$, we have $(I_q^1 f)(t) = (I_q f)(t)$.

Lemma 1 ([33]). *For $\alpha \in \mathbb{R}_+$ and $\beta \in (-1, +\infty)$, we have*

$$(I_q^\alpha (t-a)^{(\beta)})(t) = \frac{\Gamma_q(\beta+1)}{\Gamma_q(\alpha+\beta+1)}(t-a)^{(\alpha+\beta)},\ 0 < a < t < T.$$

In particular,

$$(I_q^\alpha 1)(t) = \frac{1}{\Gamma_q(\alpha+1)} t^{(\alpha)}.$$

In what follows, we let $[\alpha]$ denote the integer part of α.

Definition 5 ([34]). *The Riemann–Liouville fractional q-derivative of order $\alpha \in \mathbb{R}_+$ of a function $f : J \to \mathbb{R}$ is defined by $(D_q^0 f)(t) = f(t)$, and*

$$(D_q^\alpha f)(t) = (D_q^{[\alpha]} I_q^{[\alpha]-\alpha} f)(t),\ t \in J.$$

Definition 6 ([34]). *The Caputo fractional q-derivative of order $\alpha \in \mathbb{R}_+$ of a function $f : J \to \mathbb{R}$ is defined by $(D_q^0 f)(t) = f(t)$, and*

$$({}^C D_q^\alpha f)(t) = (I_q^{[\alpha]-\alpha} D_q^{[\alpha]} f)(t),\ t \in J.$$

Lemma 2 ([34]). *Let $\alpha, \beta \in \mathbb{R}_+$ and let f be a function defined on J. Then:*

(1) $(I_q^\alpha I_q^\beta f)(t) = (I_q^{\alpha+\beta} f)(t)$;
(2) $(D_q^\alpha I_q^\alpha f)(t) = f(t)$.

Lemma 3 ([34]). *Let $\alpha \in \mathbb{R}_+$ and let f be a function defined on J. Then:*

$$(I_q^\alpha\, {}^C D_q^\alpha f)(t) = f(t) - \sum_{k=0}^{[\alpha]-1} \frac{t^k}{\Gamma_q(k+1)} (D_q^k f)(0).$$

In particular, if $\alpha \in (0,1)$, then

$$(I_q^\alpha\, {}^C D_q^\alpha f)(t) = f(t) - f(0).$$

Next, we recall the definition of the Kuratowski measure of noncompactness and summarize some of the main properties of this measure.

Definition 7 ([26]). *Let E be a Banach space and let Ω_E be the family of bounded subsets of E. The Kuratowski measure of noncompactness is the map $\mu : \Omega_E \to [0, \infty)$ defined by*

$$\mu(B) = \inf\{\epsilon > 0 : B \subset \cup_{i=1}^m B_i \text{ and } diam(B_i) \leq \epsilon\}, \text{ where } B \in \Omega_E.$$

Property 1 ([26]). *The Kuratowski measure of noncompactness satisfies:*

(1) $\mu(B) = 0$ *if and only if $\overline{B}$ is compact (B is relatively compact).*
(2) $\mu(B) = \mu(\overline{B})$.
(3) $A \subseteq B$ *implies* $\mu(A) \leq \mu(B)$.
(4) $\mu(A + B) \leq \mu(A) + \mu(B)$.
(5) $\mu(cB) = |c|\mu(B),\ c \in \mathbb{R}$.
(6) $\mu(conB) = \mu(B)$.
(7) $\mu(B + x_0) = \mu(B)$, *for all* $x_0 \in E$.

Here $\overline{B}$ and $conB$ denote the closure and the convex hull of the bounded set B, respectively.

Definition 8. *The map $f : J \times E \to E$ is Carathéodory if*

1. $t \to f(t, u)$ *is measurable for each* $u \in E$, *and*
2. $u \to f(t, u)$ *is continuous for almost each* $t \in J$.

For a given set V of functions $v : J \to E$, let

$$\begin{aligned} V(t) &= \{v(t) : v \in V\},\ t \in J, \\ V(J) &= \{v(t) : v \in V,\ t \in J\}. \end{aligned}$$

We next recall Mönch's fixed point theorem.

Theorem 1 ([30,35]). *Let D be a bounded, closed, and convex subset of a Banach space E such that $0 \in D$, and let N be a continuous mapping of D into itself. If the implication*

$$V = \overline{con}N(V) \text{ or } V = N(V) \cup \{0\} \text{ implies } \mu(V) = 0,$$

holds for every subset V of D, then N has a fixed point.

The next lemma is a useful result.

Lemma 4 ([28]). *If $V \subset C(J,E)$ is a bounded and equicontinuous set, then*

1. *The function $t \to \mu(V(t))$ is continuous on J.*
2. $\mu\left(\left\{\int_J y(t)dt \ : \ y \in V\right\}\right) \leq \int_J \mu(V(t))dt.$

3. Results

We now define what is meant by a solution of the problem (1)–(3).

Definition 9. *A function $y \in C^2(J,E)$ is said to be a solution of the problem (1)–(3) if y satisfies the equation $({}^C D_q^{\alpha} y)(t) = f(t, y(t))$ on J, and satisfies the boundary conditions (2) and (3).*

In order to prove the existence of solutions to the problem (1)–(3), we need the following lemma.

Lemma 5. *Let σ, ρ_1, $\rho_2 : J \to E$ be continuous functions. The solution of the boundary value problem*

$$({}^C D_q^{\alpha} y)(t) = \sigma(t),\ t \in J = [0,T], \quad 1 < \alpha \leq 2, \tag{4}$$

$$y(0) - y'(0) = \int_0^T \rho_1(s)ds, \tag{5}$$

$$y(T) + y'(T) = \int_0^T \rho_2(s)ds, \tag{6}$$

is given by

$$y(t) = K(t) + \int_0^T H(t,s)\sigma(s)d_qs, \tag{7}$$

where

$$K(t) = \frac{(1+T-t)}{(2+T)} \int_0^T \rho_1(s)ds + \frac{(1+t)}{(2+T)} \int_0^T \rho_2(s)ds, \tag{8}$$

and

$$H(t,s) = \begin{cases} \frac{(t-qs)^{(\alpha-1)}}{\Gamma_q(\alpha)} - \frac{(1+t)(T-qs)^{(\alpha-1)}}{(2+T)\Gamma_q(\alpha)} - \frac{(1+t)(T-qs)^{(\alpha-2)}}{(2+T)\Gamma_q(\alpha-1)}, & 0 \leq s < t, \\ -\frac{(1+t)(T-qs)^{(\alpha-1)}}{(2+T)\Gamma_q(\alpha)} - \frac{(1+t)(T-qs)^{(\alpha-2)}}{(2+T)\Gamma_q(\alpha-1)}, & t \leq s \leq T. \end{cases} \tag{9}$$

Proof. Applying the Riemann–Liouville fractional q-integral of order α to both sides of Equation (4), and by using Lemma 3, we have

$$y(t) = \int_0^t \frac{(t-qs)^{(\alpha-1)}}{\Gamma_q(\alpha)} \sigma(s)d_qs + c_0 + c_1 t. \tag{10}$$

Using the boundary conditions (5) and (6), we obtain

$$c_0 - c_1 = \int_0^T \rho_1(s)ds, \tag{11}$$

and

$$c_0 + (1+T)c_1 + \int_0^T \frac{(t-qs)^{(\alpha-1)}}{\Gamma_q(\alpha)}\sigma(s)d_qs + \int_0^T \frac{(t-qs)^{(\alpha-2)}}{\Gamma_q(\alpha-1)}\sigma(s)d_qs = \int_0^T \rho_2(s)ds. \quad (12)$$

Equations (11) and (12) give

$$c_1 = \frac{1}{(2+T)}\left(\int_0^T \rho_2(s)ds - \int_0^T \rho_1(s)ds - \int_0^T \frac{(t-qs)^{(\alpha-1)}}{\Gamma_q(\alpha)}\sigma(s)d_qs - \int_0^T \frac{(t-qs)^{(\alpha-2)}}{\Gamma_q(\alpha-1)}\sigma(s)d_qs\right), \quad (13)$$

and

$$c_0 = \frac{(1+T)}{(2+T)}\int_0^T \rho_1(s)ds + \frac{1}{(2+T)}\left(\int_0^T \rho_2(s)ds - \int_0^T \frac{(t-qs)^{(\alpha-1)}}{\Gamma_q(\alpha)}\sigma(s)d_qs - \int_0^T \frac{(t-qs)^{(\alpha-2)}}{\Gamma_q(\alpha-1)}\sigma(s)d_qs\right). \quad (14)$$

From (10), (13), and (14) and using the fact that $\int_0^T = \int_0^t + \int_t^T$, we have

$$y(t) = K(t) + \int_0^T H(t,s)\sigma(s)d_qs,$$

where

$$K(t) = \frac{(1+T-t)}{(2+T)}\int_0^T \rho_1(s)ds + \frac{(1+t)}{(2+T)}\int_0^T \rho_2(s)ds,$$

and

$$H(t,s) = \begin{cases} \frac{(t-qs)^{(\alpha-1)}}{\Gamma_q(\alpha)} - \frac{(1+t)(T-qs)^{(\alpha-1)}}{(2+T)\Gamma_q(\alpha)} - \frac{(1+t)(T-qs)^{(\alpha-2)}}{(2+T)\Gamma_q(\alpha-1)}, & 0 \le s < t, \\[2ex] -\frac{(1+t)(T-qs)^{(\alpha-1)}}{(2+T)\Gamma_q(\alpha)} - \frac{(1+t)(T-qs)^{(\alpha-2)}}{(2+T)\Gamma_q(\alpha-1)}, & t \le s \le T, \end{cases}$$

which is what we wanted to show. □

We now prove an existence result for the problem (1)–(3) by applying Mönch's fixed point theorem (Theorem 1 above).

Let

$$H^* = \sup_{(t,s)\in J\times J} |H(t,s)|.$$

Theorem 2. *Assume that the following conditions hold.*

(P1) The functions $f, g, h : J \times E \to E$ satisfy Carathéodory conditions.

(P2) There exists $p_f, p_g, p_h \in L^\infty(J, \mathbb{R}_+)$ such that

$$\|f(t,y)\| \le p_f(t)\|y\|, \text{ for a.e. } t \in J \text{ and all } y \in E,$$

$$\|g(t,y)\| \le p_g(t)\|y\|, \text{ for a.e. } t \in J \text{ and all } y \in E,$$

$$\|h(t,y)\| \le p_h(t)\|y\|, \text{ for a.e. } t \in J \text{ and all } y \in E.$$

(P3) For almost all $t \in J$ and each bounded set $B \subset E$, we have

$$\mu(f(t,B)) \leq p_f(t)\mu(B), \ for \ a.e. \ t \in J,$$

$$\mu(g(t,B)) \leq p_g(t)\mu(B), \ for \ a.e. \ t \in J,$$

$$\mu(h(t,B)) \leq p_h(t)\mu(B), \ for \ a.e. \ t \in J.$$

Then, the BVP (1)–(3) has at least one solution in $C^2(J,E)$, provided

$$\frac{T(1+T)}{(2+T)}(\|p_g\|_{L^\infty} + \|p_h\|_{L^\infty}) + H^*T\|p_f\|_{L^\infty} < 1. \tag{15}$$

Proof. In order to transform problem (1)–(3) into a fixed point type problem, consider the operator

$$N : C^2(J,E) \longrightarrow C^2(J,E)$$

defined by

$$(Ny)(t) = K(t) + \int_0^T H(t,s)f(s,y(s))d_qs, \tag{16}$$

where

$$K(t) = \frac{(1+T-t)}{(2+T)}\int_0^T g(s,y(s))ds + \frac{(1+t)}{(2+T)}\int_0^T h(s,y(s))ds,$$

and H(t,s) is given by (9). It is easy to see that the fixed points of N are solutions of (1)–(3).

Let $R > 0$ and consider

$$D_R = \{y \in C^2(J,E) : \|y\|_\infty \leq R\}. \tag{17}$$

Clearly, D_R is a closed, bounded, and convex subset of $C^2(J,E)$. We show that N satisfies the hypotheses of Mönch's fixed point theorem. We give the proof in three steps.

Step 1: *N is continuous.* Let $\{y_n\}_{n\in\mathbb{N}}$ be a sequence with $y_n \to y$ in $C^2(J,E)$. For each $t \in J$, we have

$$\begin{aligned} |(Ny_n)(t) - (Ny)(t)| \leq & \frac{(1+T-t)}{(2+T)}\int_0^T |g(s,y_n(s)) - g(s,y(s))|ds \\ & + \frac{(1+t)}{(2+T)}\int_0^T |h(s,y_n(s)) - h(s,y(s))|ds \\ & + \int_0^T |H(t,s)||f(s,y_n(s)) - f(s,y(s))|d_qs. \end{aligned}$$

Hence,

$$\begin{aligned} \|N(y_n) - N(y)\| \leq & \frac{T(1+T)}{(2+T)}\|g(s,y_n(s)) - g(s,y(s))\| \\ & + \frac{T(1+T)}{(2+T)}\|h(s,y_n(s)) - h(s,y(s))\| \\ & + H^*T\|f(s,y_n(s)) - f(s,y(s))\|. \end{aligned}$$

Let $\rho > 0$ be such that

$$\|y_n\|_\infty \leq \rho, \ \|y\|_\infty \leq \rho.$$

By (P2), we have

$$\|f(s,y_n(s)) - f(s,y(s))\| \leq 2\rho p_f(s) := \sigma_f(s),$$

$$\|g(s, y_n(s)) - g(s, y(s))\| \leq 2\rho p_g(s) := \sigma_g(s),$$
$$\|h(s, y_n(s)) - h(s, y(s))\| \leq 2\rho p_h(s) := \sigma_h(s),$$

and $\sigma_f(s), \sigma_g(s), \sigma_h(s) \in L^1(J, \mathbb{R}_+)$. Since the functions f, g, and h satisfy Carathéodory conditions, the Lebesgue-dominated convergence theorem implies that

$$\|N(y_n) - N(y)\|_\infty \to 0 \ as \ n \to \infty.$$

Consequently, N is continuous on $C^2(J, E)$.

Step 2: *N maps D_R into itself.* Now, for any $y \in D_R$, (P2) and (15) imply that for each $t \in J$,

$$\begin{aligned}
\|(Ny)(t)\| &\leq \frac{(1+T-t)}{(2+T)} \int_0^T \|g(s, y(s))\| ds + \frac{(1+t)}{(2+T)} \int_0^T \|h(s, y(s))\| \, ds \\
&+ \int_0^T |H(t,s)| \|f(s, y(s))\| d_q s, \\
&\leq \frac{(1+T-t)}{(2+T)} \int_0^T p_g(s) \|y\| ds + \frac{(1+t)}{(2+T)} \int_0^T p_h(s) \|y\| ds \\
&+ \int_0^T |H(t,s)| p_f(s) \|y\| d_q s, \\
&\leq R\left(\frac{T(1+T)}{(2+T)} \|p_g\|_{L^\infty} + \frac{T(1+T)}{(2+T)} \|p_h\|_{L^\infty} + H^* T \|p_f\|_{L^\infty} \right), \\
&\leq R.
\end{aligned}$$

Step 3: *$N(D_R)$ is bounded and equicontinuous.* In view of Step 2, it is clear that $N(D_R)$ is bounded. To show the equicontinuity of $N(D_R)$, let t_1, $t_2 \in J$, $t_1 < t_2$, and $y \in D_R$. Then,

$$\begin{aligned}
\|(Ny)(t_2) - (Ny)(t_1)\| &= \Bigg\| \frac{(t_1 - t_2)}{(2+T)} \int_0^T g(s, y(s)) ds + \frac{(t_2 - t_1)}{(2+T)} \int_0^T h(s, y(s)) ds \\
&+ \int_0^T (H(t_2, s) - H(t_1, s)) f(s, y(s)) d_q s \Bigg\|, \\
&\leq \frac{(t_1 - t_2)}{(2+T)} \int_0^T \|g(s, y(s))\| ds + \frac{(t_2 - t_1)}{(2+T)} \int_0^T \|h(s, y(s))\| \, ds \\
&+ \int_0^T |H(t_2, s) - H(t_1, s)| \|f(s, y(s))\| d_q s.
\end{aligned}$$

By (P2), we have

$$\begin{aligned}
\|(Ny)(t_2) - (Ny)(t_1)\| &\leq \frac{(t_1 - t_2)}{(2+T)} \int_0^T p_g(s) \|y\| ds + \frac{(t_2 - t_1)}{(2+T)} \int_0^T p_h(s) \|y\| \, ds \\
&+ \int_0^T |H(t_2, s) - H(t_1, s)| p_f(s) \|y\| d_q s, \\
&\leq RT \frac{(t_1 - t_2)}{(2+T)} \|p_g\|_{L^\infty} + RT \frac{(t_2 - t_1)}{(2+T)} \|p_h\|_{L^\infty} \\
&+ R \|p_f\|_{L^\infty} \int_0^T |H(t_2, s) - H(t_1, s)| \, d_q s.
\end{aligned}$$

As $t_1 \to t_2$, the right-hand side of the above inequality tends to zero, which shows the equicontinuity of $N(D_R)$.

Now, let $V \subset D_R$ be such that $V \subset \overline{con}(N(V) \cup \{0\})$. Since V is bounded and equicontinuous, the function $v \to v(t) = \mu(V(t))$ is continuous on J. Moreover, (P3), Lemma 4, and properties of the measure μ imply that for each $t \in J$,

$$\begin{aligned} v(t) &\leq \mu(N(V)(t) \cup \{0\}), \\ &\leq \mu(N(V)(t)), \\ &\leq \frac{(1+T-t)}{(2+T)} \int_0^T p_g(s)\mu(V(s))ds + \frac{(1+t)}{(2+T)} \int_0^T p_h(s)\mu(V(s))ds \\ &+ \int_0^T |H(t,s)| p_f(s)\mu(V(s))d_q s, \\ &\leq \|v\|_\infty \left[\frac{T(1+T)}{(2+T)} (\|p_g\|_{L^\infty} + \|p_h\|_{L^\infty}) + H^* T \|p_f\|_{L^\infty} \right]. \end{aligned}$$

This means that

$$\|v\|_\infty \left(1 - \left[\frac{T(1+T)}{(2+T)} (\|p_g\|_{L^\infty} + \|p_h\|_{L^\infty}) + H^* T \|p_f\|_{L^\infty} \right] \right) \leq 0.$$

From (15), we see that $\|v\|_\infty = 0$, so $v(t) = 0$ for $t \in J$, and hence, $V(t)$ is relatively compact in E. The Ascoli–Arzelà theorem yields that V is relatively compact in D_R. Applying Theorem 1, we see that N has a fixed point that in turn is a solution of (1)–(3). □

4. Example

Let

$$E = l^1 = \{(y_1, y_2, \cdots, y_n, \cdots) : \sum_{n=1}^{\infty} y_n < \infty\},$$

be our Banach space with the norm

$$\|y\|_E = \sum_{n=1}^{\infty} |y_n|.$$

Consider the boundary value problem for fractional $\frac{1}{4}$-difference equations given by

$$({}^C D_{\frac{1}{4}}^{\frac{3}{2}} y)(t) = \frac{1}{(e^t+5)} y_n(t), \quad for\ a.e.\ t \in J = [0,1],\ 1 < \alpha \leq 2, \tag{18}$$

$$y(0) - y'(0) = \int_0^1 \frac{s^3-1}{9} y_n(s)ds, \tag{19}$$

$$y(1) + y'(1) = \int_0^1 \frac{s^3+1}{6} y_n(s)ds. \tag{20}$$

Here, $\alpha = \frac{3}{2}$, $q = \frac{1}{4}$, $T = 1$, and

$$f_n(t,y) = \frac{1}{e^t+5} y_n,\ (t,y) \in J \times E,$$

$$g_n(t,y) = \frac{t^3-1}{9} y_n,\ (t,y) \in J \times E,$$

and

$$h_n(t,y) = \frac{t^3+1}{6} y_n,\ (t,y) \in J \times E,$$

where

$$\begin{aligned} y &= (y_1, y_2, \ldots, y_n, \ldots), \\ f &= (f_1, f_2, \ldots, f_n, \ldots), \end{aligned}$$

$$g = (g_1, g_2, \ldots, g_n, \ldots),$$

and

$$h = (h_1, h_2, \ldots, h_n, \ldots).$$

Clearly, conditions (P1) and (P2) hold with

$$p_f(t) = \frac{1}{e^t + 5}, \quad p_g(t) = \frac{t^3}{9}, \quad p_h(t) = \frac{t^3}{6}.$$

From (9), we have

$$H^* = \sup_{(t,s)\in J\times J} |H(t,s)| = \frac{5}{3\Gamma_{\frac{1}{4}}(\frac{3}{2})} + \frac{2}{3\Gamma_{\frac{1}{4}}(\frac{1}{2})}.$$

To see that condition (15) is satisfied with $T = 1$, notice that

$$\frac{T(1+T)}{(2+T)}(\|p_g\|_{L^\infty} + \|p_h\|_{L^\infty}) + H^*T\|p_f\|_{L^\infty}$$

$$= \frac{2}{3}\left(\frac{1}{9} + \frac{1}{6}\right) + \left(\frac{5}{3\Gamma_{\frac{1}{4}}(\frac{3}{2})} + \frac{2}{3\Gamma_{\frac{1}{4}}(\frac{1}{2})}\right)\frac{1}{6} \simeq 0.5564 < 1.$$

Then, by Theorem 2, the problem (18)–(20) has a solution on $[0,1]$.

5. Discussion

In this work, we proved the existence of solutions to a fractional q-difference equation with nonlinear integral type boundary conditions in Banach spaces using a method involving the Kuratowski measure of noncompactness and Mönch's fixed point theorem. An example was presented to illustrate the effectiveness of the results.

An interesting direction for future research of course would be to consider fractional q-difference equations of order $0 < \alpha \leq 1$ and orders greater than the $1 < \alpha \leq 2$ considered here. Another direction would be to consider Riemann–Stieltjes integral-type boundary conditions. Adding impulsive effects to the problem would expand the ares of possible applications as well.

Author Contributions: Conceptualization, N.A., J.R.G. and S.H.; methodology, N.A., J.R.G. and S.H.; formal analysis, N.A., J.R.G. and S.H.; investigation, N.A., J.R.G. and S.H.; writing—original draft preparation, N.A. and S.H.; writing—review and editing, J.R.G. All authors have read and agreed to the published version of the manuscript.

Funding: This research received no external funding.

Institutional Review Board Statement: Not applicable.

Data Availability Statement: Not applicable.

Conflicts of Interest: The authors declare no conflict of interest.

References

1. Hilfer, R. *Applications of Fractional Calculus in Physics*; World Scientific: Singapore, 2000.
2. Kilbas, A.A.; Srivastava, H.M.; Trujillo, J.J. *Theory and Applications of Fractional Differential Equations*; North-Holland Mathematical Studies; Elsevier: Amsterdam, The Netherlands, 2006; Volume 204.
3. Miller, K.S.; Ross, B. *An Introduction to the Fractional Calculus and Differential Equations*; Wiley: New York, NY, USA, 1993.
4. Podlubny, I. *Fractional Differential Equations*; Academic Press: San Diego, CA, USA, 1998.
5. Samko, S.G.; Kilbas, A.A.; Marichev, O.I. *Fractional Integrals and Derivatives. Theory and Applications*; Gordon and Breach: Yverdon, Switzerland, 1993.
6. Tarasov, V.E. *Fractional Dynamics: Application of Fractional Calculus to Dynamics of Particles, Fields, and Media*; Springer: Berlin/Heidelberg, Germany, 2010.
7. Ahmad, B.; Ntouyas, S.K.; Purnaras, I.K. Existence results for nonlocal boundary value problems of nonlinear fractional q-difference equations. *Adv. Differ. Equ.* **2012**, *2012*, 140. [CrossRef]

8. Agarwal, R.P.; Benchohra, M.; Hamani, S. A survey on existence results for boundary value problems for nonlinear fractional differential equations and inclusions. *Acta Appl. Math.* **2010**, *109*, 973–1033. [CrossRef]
9. Benchohra, M.; Hamani, S.; Ntouyas, S.K. Boundary value problems for differential equations with fractional order. *Surv. Math. Appl.* **2008**, *3*, 1–12.
10. Benhamida, W.; Hamani, S.; Henderson, J. Boundary value problems for Caputo-Hadamard fractional differential equations. *Adv. Theor. Nonlinear Anal. Appl.* **2018**, *2*, 138–145.
11. Hamani, S.; Benchohra, M.; Graef, J.R. Existence results for boundary-value problems with nonlinear fractional differential inclusion and integral conditions. *Electron. J. Differ. Equ.* **2010**, *2010*, 1–16.
12. Zahed, A.; Hamani, S.; Henderson, J. Boundary value problems for Caputo-Hadamard fractional differential inclusions with integral conditions. *Moroc. J. Pure Appl. Anal.* **2020**, *6*, 62–75. [CrossRef]
13. Agarwal, R.P.; Benchohra, M.; Seba, D. On the application of measure of noncompactness to the existence of solutions for fractional differential equations. *Results Math.* **2009**, *55*, 221–230. [CrossRef]
14. Benchohra, M.; Cabada, A.; Seba, D. An existence result for nonlinear fractional differential equations on Banach spaces. *Bound. Value. Probl.* **2009**, *2009*, 628916. [CrossRef]
15. Hamani, S.; Henderson, J. Boundary value problems for fractional differential equations and inclusions in Banach spaces. *Malaya J. Mat.* **2017**, *5*, 346–366.
16. Jackson, F. On q-definite integrals. *Quart. J. Pure Appl. Math.* **1910**, *41*, 193–203.
17. Jackson, F. On q-functions and a certain difference operator. *Trans. R. Soc. Edinb.* **1908**, *46*, 253–281. [CrossRef]
18. Gasper, G.; Rahman, M. *Basic Hypergeometric Series*; Cambridge Univ. Press: Cambridge, UK, 1990.
19. Kac, V.; Cheung, P. *Quantum Calculus*; Springer: New York, NY, USA, 2002.
20. Al-Salam, W. Some fractional q-integrals and q-derivatives. *Proc. Edinb. Math. Soc.* **1966**, *15*, 135–140. [CrossRef]
21. Agarwal, R. Certain fractional q-integrals and q-derivatives. *Proc. Camb. Philos. Soc.* **1969**, *66*, 365–370. [CrossRef]
22. Salahshour, S.; Ahmadian, A.; Chan, C.S. Successive approximation method for Caputo q-fractional IVPs. *Commun. Nonlinear Sci. Numer. Simul.* **2015**, *24*, 153–158. [CrossRef]
23. Zhou, W.X.; Liu, H.Z. Existence solutions for boundary value problem of nonlinear fractional q-difference equations. *Adv. Differ. Equ.* **2013**, *2013*, 113. [CrossRef]
24. Abbas, S.; Benchohra, M.; Laledj, N.; Zhou, Y. Existence and Ulam stability for implicit fractional q-difference equation. *Adv. Differ. Equ.* **2019**, *2019*, 480. [CrossRef]
25. Ahmad, B. Boundary value problem for nonlinear third order q-difference equations. *Electron. J. Differ. Equ.* **2011**, *94*, 1–7. [CrossRef]
26. Banas, J.; Goebel, K. *Measure of Noncompactness in Banach Spaces*; Lecture Notes in Pure and Applied Mathematics; Dekker: New York, NY, USA, 1980; Volume 60.
27. Banas, J.; Sadarangani, K. On some measures of noncompactness in the space of continuous functions. *Nonlinear Anal.* **2008**, *68*, 377–383. [CrossRef]
28. Guo, D.; Lakshmikantham, V.; Liu, X. *Nonlinear Integral Equations in Abstract Spaces*; Math. and Its Applications; Kluwer: Dordrecht, The Netherlands, 1996; Volume 373.
29. Akhmerov, R.R.; Kamenskii, M.I.; Patapov, A.S.; Rodkina, A.E.; Sadovskii, B.N. *Measures of Noncompactness and Condensing Operators*; Iacob, A., Ed.; Operator Theory: Advances and Applications; Birkhäuser: Boston, MA, USA, 1992; Volume 55. (In Russian)
30. Mönch, H. Boundary value problem for nonlinear ordinary differential equations of second order in Banach spaces. *Nonlinear Anal.* **1980**, *4*, 985–999. [CrossRef]
31. Mönch, H.; Harten, G.F.V. On the Cauchy problem for ordinary differential equations in Banach spaces. *Arch. Math.* **1982**, *39*, 153–160. [CrossRef]
32. Szufla, S. On the application of measure of noncompactness to existence theorems. *Rend. Semin. Mat. Univ. Padova* **1986**, *75*, 1–14.
33. Rajkovic, P.M.; Marinkovic, S.D.; Stankovic, M.S. Fractional integrals and derivatives in q-calculus. *Appl. Anal. Discrete Math.* **2007**, *1*, 311–323.
34. Rajkovic, P.M.; Marinkovic, S.D.; Stankovic, M.S. On q-analogues of Caputo derivative and Mittag-Leffler function. *Fract. Calc. Appl. Anal.* **2007**, *10*, 359–373.
35. Agarwal, R.P.; Meehan, M.; O'Regan, D. *Fixed Point Theory and Applications*; Cambridge Tracts in Mathematics: Cambridge, UK, 2001; p. 141.

fractal and fractional

Article

Solvability Criterion for Fractional q-Integro-Difference System with Riemann-Stieltjes Integrals Conditions

Changlong Yu [1,2,*], Si Wang [2], Jufang Wang [2] and Jing Li [1,*]

[1] Interdisciplinary Research Institute, Faculty of Science, Beijing University of Technology, Beijing 100124, China
[2] College of Sciences, Hebei University of Science and Technology, Shijiazhuang 050018, China
* Correspondence: yuchanglong@emails.bjut.edu.cn (C.Y.); leejing@bjut.edu.cn (J.L.)

Abstract: Due to the great application potential of fractional q-difference system in physics, mechanics and aerodynamics, it is very necessary to study fractional q-difference system. The main purpose of this paper is to investigate the solvability of nonlinear fractional q-integro-difference system with the nonlocal boundary conditions involving diverse fractional q-derivatives and Riemann-Stieltjes q-integrals. We acquire the existence results of solutions for the systems by applying Schauder fixed point theorem, Krasnoselskii's fixed point theorem, Schaefer's fixed point theorem and nonlinear alternative for single-valued maps, and a uniqueness result is obtained through the Banach contraction mapping principle. Finally, we give some examples to illustrate the main results.

Keywords: q-calculus; fractional q-integro-difference system; solvability; Riemann-Stieltjes q-integrals; fixed point theorems

Citation: Yu, C.; Wang, S.; Wang, J.; Li, J. Solvability Criterion for Fractional q-Integro-Difference System with Riemann-Stieltjes Integrals Conditions. *Fractal Fract.* **2022**, *6*, 554. https://doi.org/10.3390/fractalfract6100554

Academic Editor: Rodica Luca

Received: 23 August 2022
Accepted: 27 September 2022
Published: 29 September 2022

1. Introduction

In the early twentieth century, Jackson [1] proposed a new mathematical direction of q-calculus, and it plays an indispensable role in the fields of nuclear, conformal quantum mechanics and dynamics. In the 1960s, Agarwal [2] and Al-Salam [3] put forward a novel concept of fractional q-calculus, its relevant application and development can be seen in the literature [4–6]. Compared with classical q-calculus, fractional q-calculus can more accurately describe some phenomena in nature, and many practical problems can be abstracted into fractional q-difference equations or a system of fractional q-difference equations by mathematical modeling. In recent years, abundant theoretical achievements have been made in the research of boundary value problems (BVPs) for fractional q-difference equations, according to the literature [7–16] and the references therein.

Riemann-Stieltjes integral is a generalization of Riemann integral. As well as we known, the classical Riemann-Stieltjes integral can be widely applied in several areas of analysis, such as probability theory, stochastic processes, physics, econometrics, biometrics and informetrics and so on. BVPs with Riemann-Stieltjes integral boundary condition (BC) have been considered as both multi-point and integral type BCs are treated in a single framework. In recent years, some interesting results about the existence of solutions for nonlinear fractional differential equations with the Riemann-Stieltjes integral BC have been researched, see [17,18] and the references therein.

Nowadays, the system of nonlinear fractional differential equations has important applications in engineering, economy and other fields. This is mainly because the effect of using fractional calculus to solve problems is more practical and efficient than that of classical calculus. Over the years, the BVPs for a system of fractional differential equations have developed rapidly, and numerous mature conclusions have been obtained, which can be referred to the literature [19–25].

In [24], Tudorache, A. and Luca, R. applied the Guo-Krasnoselskii fixed point theorem to study the existence of solutions for a system of fractional differential equations with p-Laplacian operators

$$\begin{cases} D_{0+}^{\alpha_1}(\varphi_{\varrho_1}(D_{0+}^{\beta_1}x(t))) + \lambda f(t, x(t), y(t)) = 0, & t \in (0,1), \\ D_{0+}^{\alpha_2}(\varphi_{\varrho_2}(D_{0+}^{\beta_2}y(t))) + \mu g(t, x(t), y(t)) = 0, & t \in (0,1), \end{cases}$$

with the nonlocal BCs

$$\begin{cases} x^{(j)}(0) = 0,\ j = 0, \dots, n-2;\ D_{0+}^{\beta_1}x(0) = 0, \\ D_{0+}^{\gamma_0}x(1) = \sum_{i=1}^{p} \int_0^1 D_{0+}^{\gamma_i}y(t)dH_i t, \\ y^{(j)}(0) = 0,\ j = 0, \dots, m-2;\ D_{0+}^{\beta_2}y(0) = 0, \\ D_{0+}^{\delta_0}y(1) = \sum_{i=1}^{q} \int_0^1 D_{0+}^{\delta_i}x(t)dK_i t. \end{cases}$$

In [25], Luca, R. considered the existence of solutions of the nonlinear system of fractional differential equations by using a variety of fixed point theorems

$$\begin{cases} D_{0+}^{\alpha}x(t) + f(t, x(t), y(t), I_{0+}^{\theta_1}x(t), I_{0+}^{\sigma_1}y(t)) = 0, & t \in (0,1), \\ D_{0+}^{\beta}y(t) + g(t, x(t), y(t), I_{0+}^{\theta_2}x(t), I_{0+}^{\sigma_2}y(t)) = 0, & t \in (0,1), \end{cases}$$

with the nonlocal BCs

$$\begin{cases} x(0) = x'(0) = \cdots = x^{(n-2)}(0) = 0,\ D_{0+}^{\gamma_0}x(1) = \sum_{i=1}^{p} \int_0^1 D_{0+}^{\gamma_i}y(t)dH_i(t), \\ y(0) = y'(0) = \cdots = y^{(m-2)}(0) = 0,\ D_{0+}^{\delta_0}y(1) = \sum_{i=1}^{q} \int_0^1 D_{0+}^{\delta_i}x(t)dK_i(t). \end{cases}$$

Despite quite a number of contributions dealing with the solvability for the system of classical fractional difference equations. However, as the generalization of the above system, limited work has been done in the nonlinear system of fractional q-difference equations. In particular, there is little research on the existence and uniqueness of solutions for the system of fractional q-difference equations with Riemann-Stieltjes integral BC. To fill this gap, we investigate the system of nonlinear fractional q-difference equations

$$\begin{cases} (D_q^{\alpha}u)(t) + P(t, u(t), v(t), I_q^{\omega_1}u(t), I_q^{\delta_1}v(t)) = 0, \\ (D_q^{\beta}v)(t) + Q(t, u(t), v(t), I_q^{\omega_2}u(t), I_q^{\delta_2}v(t)) = 0, \end{cases} \tag{1}$$

with the nonlocal BCs

$$\begin{cases} u(0) = D_q u(0) = \cdots = D_q^{n-2}u(0) = 0,\ D_q^{\zeta_0}u(1) = \int_0^1 D_q^{\zeta}v(t)d_qH(t), \\ v(0) = D_q v(0) = \cdots = D_q^{m-2}v(0) = 0,\ D_q^{\xi_0}v(1) = \int_0^1 D_q^{\xi}u(t)d_qK(t), \end{cases} \tag{2}$$

where $t \in (0,1)$, $0 < q < 1$, $\alpha \in (n-1, n]$, $\beta \in (z-1, z]$, $n, z \in \mathbb{N}$, $n \geq 2$ and $z \geq 2$, $\omega_1, \omega_2, \delta_1, \delta_2 > 0$, $0 \leq \zeta < \beta - 1$, $0 \leq \xi < \alpha - 1$, $\zeta_0 \in [0, \alpha - 1)$, $\xi_0 \in [0, \beta - 1)$, D_q^i denotes the Riemann-Liouville q-derivative of order i ($i = \alpha, \beta, \zeta_0, \zeta, \xi_0, \xi$), I_q^{ϖ} is the Riemann-Liouville q-integral of order ϖ ($\varpi = \omega_1, \omega_2, \delta_1, \delta_2$), P and Q are nonlinear functions. The BCs include Riemann-Stieltjes integrals, where $H(t)$, $K(t)$ are the bounded variation functions. In the case where $H(t) = K(t) = t$, the Riemann–Stieltjes integrals in (2) reduce to the classical q-integral.

The present paper is bulit up as follows. The second part offers the necessary definitions, lemmas and theorems needed in the following. The third part obtains the important conclusions by applying various fixed point theorems, including nine theorems or corollaries. In the final part, four examples are provided to verify our main results.

2. Preliminaries

In this section, we present some definitions, lemmas and theorems.

Definition 1 ([11])**.** *Let $\beta \geq 0$ and f be a function defined on $[0,1]$. The fractional q-integral of the Riemann-Liouville type is*

$$(I_q^{\beta} f)(s) = \frac{1}{\Gamma_q(\beta)} \int_0^s (s-qt)^{(\beta-1)} f(t) d_q t, \;\; \beta > 0, \, s \in [0,1].$$

Obviously, $(I_q^{\beta} f)(s) = (I_q f)(s)$, when $\beta = 1$.

Definition 2 ([11])**.** *The fractional q-derivative of the Riemann-Liouville type of order $\beta \geq 0$ is defined by $(D_q^0 f)(s) = f(s)$ and*

$$(D_q^{\beta} f)(s) = (D_q^l I_q^{l-\beta} f)(s), \quad \beta > 0, \quad s \in [0,1],$$

where l is the smallest integer greater than or equal to β.

Lemma 1 ([11])**.** *Let $\alpha, \beta \geq 0$ and f be a function defined on $[0,1]$. Then, the following formulas hold:*

1. $(I_q^{\beta} I_q^{\alpha} f)(x) = (I_q^{\alpha+\beta} f)(x)$,
2. $(D_q^{\alpha} I_q^{\alpha} f)(x) = f(x)$.

Lemma 2 ([11])**.** *Let $\alpha > 0$ and p be a positive integer. Then, the following equality holds:*

$$(I_q^{\alpha} D_q^{p} f)(x) = (D_q^{p} I_q^{\alpha} f)(x) - \sum_{k=0}^{p-1} \frac{x^{\alpha-p+k}}{\Gamma_q(\alpha+k-p+1)} (D_q^k f)(0).$$

Lemma 3. *If $x \in C[0,1]$, then for $\kappa > 0$, we get*

$$|I_q^{\kappa} x(t)| \leq \frac{\| x \|}{\Gamma_q(\kappa)},$$

where $\| x \| = \sup_{t \in [0,1]} |x(t)|$.

Proof. According to Definition 1, this lemma clearly holds. □

Definition 3 ([15])**.** *The function $f : I \times \mathbb{R}^4 \to \mathbb{R}$ is called an S-Carathéodory function if and only if*

(i) *for each $(u,v,x,y) \in \mathbb{R}^4$, $t \to f(t,u,v,x,y)$ is measurable on I;*
(ii) *for a.e. $t \in I$, $(u,v,x,y) \to f(t,u,v,x,y)$ is continuous on $\mathbb{R}^4$;*
(iii) *for each $r > 0$, there exists $\psi_r(t) \in L^1(I,\mathbb{R}^+)$ with $t\psi_r(t) \in L^1(I,\mathbb{R}^+)$ on I such that $\max\{|u|,|v|,|x|,|y|\} \leq r$ implies $|f(t,u,v,x,y)| \leq \psi_r(t)$, for a.e.$I$, where $L^1(I,\mathbb{R}^+) = \{u \in X : \int_0^1 u(t) d_q t \text{ exists}\}$, and normed $\| u \|_{L^1} = \int_0^1 |u(t)| d_q t$ for all $u \in L^1(I,\mathbb{R}^+)$.*

Theorem 1 ([26])**.** *(Schauder fixed point theorem) Let D be a bounded closed convex set in E (D does not necessarily have an interior point), and $A : D \to D$ is completely continuous, then A must have a fixed point in D.*

Theorem 2 ([12])**.** *(Krasnoselskii's fixed point theorem) Let K be a closed convex and nonempty subset of a Banach space X. Let T, S be the operators such that*

(i) *$Tu + Sv \in K$ whenever $u, v \in K$;*
(ii) *T is compact and continuous;*
(iii) *S is a contraction mapping.*

Then, there exists $z \in K$ such that $z = Tz + Sz$.

Theorem 3 **([16]).** *(Schaefer's fixed point theorem) Let T be a continuous and compact mapping of a Banach space X into itself, such that the set $E = \{x | x \in X : x = \lambda Tx, 0 \leq \lambda \leq 1\}$ is bounded. Then T has a fixed point.*

Theorem 4 **([15]).** *(Nonlinear alternative for single-valued maps) Let E be a Banach space, let C be a closed and convex subset of E, and let U be an open subset of C and $0 \in U$. Suppose that $F : \overline{U} \to C$ is a continuous, compact (that is, $F(\overline{U})$ is a relatively compact subset of C) map. Then either*

(i) *F has a fixed point in $\overline{U}$, or*
(ii) *there is a $u \in \partial U$ (the boundary of U in C) and $\lambda \in (0,1)$ with $u = \lambda Fu$.*

Throughout this paper, we adopt the following assumptions:

$(\mathcal{H}_1)$ The functions $P, Q \in C([0,1] \times \mathbb{R}^4, \mathbb{R})$ and for $x_i, y_i \in \mathbb{R}$, there exist $L_i(t),\ l_i(t) \in C([0,1], [0,+\infty)),\ i = 1,2,3,4$, such that

$$\big|P(t,x_1,x_2,x_3,x_4) - P(t,y_1,y_2,y_3,y_4)\big| \leq \sum_{i=1}^{4} L_i(t)|x_i - y_i|,$$
$$\big|Q(t,x_1,x_2,x_3,x_4) - Q(t,y_1,y_2,y_3,y_4)\big| \leq \sum_{i=1}^{4} l_i(t)|x_i - y_i|.$$

$(\mathcal{H}_1')$ The functions $P, Q \in C([0,1] \times \mathbb{R}^4, \mathbb{R})$ and for $x_i, y_i \in \mathbb{R}$, there exist real constants $L_i,\ l_i > 0,\ i = 1,2,3,4$, such that

$$\big|P(t,x_1,x_2,x_3,x_4) - P(t,y_1,y_2,y_3,y_4)\big| \leq \sum_{i=1}^{4} L_i|x_i - y_i|,$$
$$\big|Q(t,x_1,x_2,x_3,x_4) - Q(t,y_1,y_2,y_3,y_4)\big| \leq \sum_{i=1}^{4} l_i|x_i - y_i|.$$

$(\mathcal{H}_1'')$ The functions $P, Q \in C([0,1] \times \mathbb{R}^4, \mathbb{R})$ and for $x_i, y_i \in \mathbb{R}$, there exist real functions $\rho_i(t),\ \varrho_i(t) \in C([0,1], \mathbb{R}^+),\ i = 1,2,3,4$, such that

$$|P(t,x_1,x_2,x_3,x_4) - P(t,y_1,y_2,y_3,y_4)| \leq \sum_{i=1}^{4} \rho_i(t)|x_i - y_i|,$$
$$|Q(t,x_1,x_2,x_3,x_4) - Q(t,y_1,y_2,y_3,y_4)| \leq \sum_{i=1}^{4} \varrho_i(t)|x_i - y_i|.$$

$(\mathcal{H}_2)$ The functions $P, Q \in C([0,1] \times \mathbb{R}^4, \mathbb{R})$, and for $x_i \in \mathbb{R}$, there exist functions $c_i(t),\ d_i(t) \in C([0,1], \mathbb{R}^+)$, and $h_i, m_i \in (0,1),\ i = 1,2,3,4$, such that

$$|P(t,x_1,x_2,x_3,x_4)| \leq c_0(t) + \sum_{i=1}^{4} c_i(t)|x_i|^{h_i},$$
$$|Q(t,x_1,x_2,x_3,x_4)| \leq d_0(t) + \sum_{i=1}^{4} d_i(t)|x_i|^{m_i}.$$

$(\mathcal{H}_3)$ The functions $P, Q \in C([0,1] \times \mathbb{R}^4, \mathbb{R})$, and for $x_i \in \mathbb{R},\ i = 1,2,3,4$, there exist functions $\sigma_1(t),\ \sigma_2(t) \in C([0,1], \mathbb{R}^+)$ such that

$$|P(t,x_1,x_2,x_3,x_4)| \leq \sigma_1(t),$$
$$|Q(t,x_1,x_2,x_3,x_4)| \leq \sigma_2(t).$$

$(\mathcal{H}_4)$ The functions $P, Q : [0,1] \times \mathbb{R}^4 \to \mathbb{R}$ and for a.e. $t \in [0,1]$, $x_i \in \mathbb{R}$, there exist $r_1(t), r_2(t), L_i(t), l_i(t) \in C([0,1], \mathbb{R}^+),\ i = 1,2,3,4$, such that

$$|P(t,x_1,x_2,x_3,x_4)| \le \sum_{i=1}^{4} L_i(t)|x_i| + r_1(t),$$
$$|Q(t,x_1,x_2,x_3,x_4)| \le \sum_{i=1}^{4} l_i(t)|x_i| + r_2(t).$$

$(\mathcal{H}_4')$ The functions $P, Q : [0,1] \times \mathbb{R}^4 \to \mathbb{R}$ and for a.e. $t \in [0,1]$, $x_i \in \mathbb{R}$, there exist non-negative real numbers L_i, l_i $(i = 1,2,3,4)$, and r_1, r_2, where at least one of r_1 and r_2 is positive, such that

$$\big|P(t,x_1,x_2,x_3,x_4)\big| \le \sum_{i=1}^{4} L_i|x_i| + r_1,$$
$$\big|Q(t,x_1,x_2,x_3,x_4)\big| \le \sum_{i=1}^{4} l_i|x_i| + r_2.$$

$(\mathcal{H}_5)$ The functions $P, Q : [0,1] \times \mathbb{R}^4 \to \mathbb{R}$ and for a.e. $t \in [0,1]$, $x_i \in \mathbb{R}$, there exist functions $p_i(t)$, $q_i(t) \in C([0,1],\mathbb{R}^+)$, where $p_i(t)$, $q_i(t)$ have at least one non-zero function, and there exist nondecreasing functions $\varphi_i, \eta_i \in C([0,\infty),\mathbb{R}^+)$, $i = 1,2,3,4$, such that

$$\big|P(t,x_1,x_2,x_3,x_4)\big| \le \sum_{i=1}^{4} p_i(t)\varphi_i(|x_i|) + p_0(t),$$
$$\big|Q(t,x_1,x_2,x_3,x_4)\big| \le \sum_{i=1}^{4} q_i(t)\eta_i(|x_i|) + q_0(t).$$

For convenience, we denote

$$\begin{aligned}
C_1 =& 1 + \frac{1}{\Gamma_q(\omega_1)}, \quad C_2 = 1 + \frac{1}{\Gamma_q(\delta_1)}, \quad C_3 = \max\{C_1, C_2\},\\
C_4 =& 1 + \frac{1}{\Gamma_q(\omega_2)}, \quad C_5 = 1 + \frac{1}{\Gamma_q(\delta_2)}, \quad C_6 = \max\{C_4, C_5\},\\
C_7 =& \frac{1}{\Gamma_q(\alpha)} + \frac{\Gamma_q(\beta)}{|\Omega|\Gamma_q(\alpha-\zeta_0)\Gamma_q(\beta-\xi_0)}\\
&+ \frac{\Gamma_q(\beta)}{|\Omega|\Gamma_q(\alpha-\xi)\Gamma_q(\beta-\zeta)}\left|\int_0^1 s^{\beta-\zeta-1} d_qH(s)\right| \cdot \left|\int_0^1 d_qK(s)\right|,\\
C_8 =& \frac{1}{\Gamma_q(\beta)} + \frac{\Gamma_q(\alpha)}{|\Omega|\Gamma_q(\alpha-\zeta_0)\Gamma_q(\beta-\xi_0)}\\
&+ \frac{\Gamma_q(\alpha)}{|\Omega|\Gamma_q(\alpha-\xi)\Gamma_q(\beta-\zeta)}\left|\int_0^1 s^{\alpha-\xi-1} d_qK(s)\right| \cdot \left|\int_0^1 d_qH(s)\right|,\\
C_9 =& \frac{\Gamma_q(\alpha)}{|\Omega|\Gamma_q(\alpha-\zeta_0)\Gamma_q(\alpha-\xi)}\left|\int_0^1 s^{\alpha-\xi-1} d_qK(s)\right|\\
&+ \frac{\Gamma_q(\alpha)}{|\Omega|\Gamma_q(\alpha-\zeta_0)\Gamma_q(\alpha-\xi)}\left|\int_0^1 d_qK(s)\right|,\\
C_{10} =& \frac{\Gamma_q(\beta)}{|\Omega|\Gamma_q(\beta-\xi_0)\Gamma_q(\beta-\zeta)}\left|\int_0^1 s^{\beta-\zeta-1} d_qH(s)\right|\\
&+ \frac{\Gamma_q(\beta)}{|\Omega|\Gamma_q(\beta-\xi_0)\Gamma_q(\beta-\zeta)}\left|\int_0^1 d_qH(s)\right|,\\
C_{11} =& C_7 - \frac{1}{\Gamma_q(\alpha)}, \quad C_{12} = C_8 - \frac{1}{\Gamma_q(\beta)}.\\
\Omega_1 =& \frac{\Gamma_q(\beta)}{\Gamma_q(\beta-\zeta)}\int_0^1 s^{\beta-\zeta-1} d_qH(s), \quad \Omega_2 = \frac{\Gamma_q(\alpha)}{\Gamma_q(\alpha-\xi)}\int_0^1 s^{\alpha-\xi-1} d_qK(s),\\
\Omega =& \frac{\Gamma_q(\alpha)\Gamma_q(\beta)}{\Gamma_q(\alpha-\zeta_0)\Gamma_q(\beta-\xi_0)} - \Omega_1\Omega_2.
\end{aligned} \tag{3}$$

3. Criterion of Uniqueness and Existence

In this section, we show some existence and uniqueness results for the Systems (1)–(2).

Lemma 4. *Let $h, k \in C(0,1) \cap L^1(0,1)$ and $\Omega \neq 0$, then the system of fractional q-difference equations*

$$\begin{cases} D_q^{\alpha} u(t) + h(t) = 0, & t \in (0,1), \\ D_q^{\beta} v(t) + k(t) = 0, & t \in (0,1), \end{cases} \tag{4}$$

with the coupled BCs (2) has a unique solution $(u(t), v(t))$, namely

$$\begin{aligned} u(t) = & -\frac{1}{\Gamma_q(\alpha)} \int_0^t (t-qs)^{(\alpha-1)} h(s) d_q s + \frac{t^{\alpha-1}}{\Omega} \left[\frac{\Omega_1}{\Gamma_q(\beta-\xi_0)} \int_0^1 (1-qs)^{(\beta-\xi_0-1)} k(s) d_q s \right. \\ & - \frac{\Omega_1}{\Gamma_q(\alpha-\xi)} \int_0^1 \left[\int_0^s (s-q\tau)^{(\alpha-\xi-1)} h(\tau) d_q\tau \right] d_q K(s) \\ & + \frac{\Gamma_q(\beta)}{\Gamma_q(\alpha-\zeta_0)\Gamma_q(\beta-\xi_0)} \int_0^1 (1-qs)^{(\alpha-\zeta_0-1)} h(s) d_q s \\ & \left. - \frac{\Gamma_q(\beta)}{\Gamma_q(\beta-\zeta)\Gamma_q(\beta-\xi_0)} \int_0^1 \left[\int_0^s (s-q\tau)^{(\beta-\zeta-1)} k(\tau) d_q\tau \right] d_q H(s) \right], \\ v(t) = & -\frac{1}{\Gamma_q(\beta)} \int_0^t (t-qs)^{(\beta-1)} k(s) d_q s + \frac{t^{\beta-1}}{\Omega} \left[\frac{\Omega_2}{\Gamma_q(\alpha-\zeta_0)} \int_0^1 (1-qs)^{(\alpha-\zeta_0-1)} h(s) d_q s \right. \\ & - \frac{\Omega_2}{\Gamma_q(\beta-\zeta)} \int_0^1 \left[\int_0^s (s-q\tau)^{(\beta-\zeta-1)} k(\tau) d_q\tau \right] d_q H(s) \\ & + \frac{\Gamma_q(\alpha)}{\Gamma_q(\beta-\xi_0)\Gamma_q(\alpha-\zeta_0)} \int_0^1 (1-qs)^{(\beta-\xi_0-1)} k(s) d_q s \\ & \left. - \frac{\Gamma_q(\alpha)}{\Gamma_q(\alpha-\xi)\Gamma_q(\alpha-\zeta_0)} \int_0^1 \left[\int_0^s (s-q\tau)^{(\alpha-\xi-1)} h(\tau) d_q\tau \right] d_q K(s) \right], \quad t \in [0,1]. \end{aligned}$$

Proof. The proof is similar to the Lemma 2.1 in [24]. □

Let $U = C[0,1]$ and $V = U \times U$ be the Banach spaces with the norms $\| u \| = \sup_{t \in [0,1]} |u(t)|$ and $\| (u,v) \|_V = \| u \| + \| v \|$, respectively. Nowdays, we introduce the operator $\mathcal{T} : V \to V$, where $\mathcal{T}(x,y) = (\mathcal{T}_1(x,y), \mathcal{T}_2(x,y))$ for $(x,y) \in V$, and $\mathcal{T}_1, \mathcal{T}_2 : V \to U$ are defined by

$$\begin{aligned} \mathcal{T}_1(u,v)(t) = & -\frac{1}{\Gamma_q(\alpha)} \int_0^t (t-qs)^{(\alpha-1)} F_{uv}(s) d_q s + \frac{\Omega_1 t^{\alpha-1}}{\Omega \Gamma_q(\beta-\xi_0)} \int_0^1 (1-qs)^{(\beta-\xi_0-1)} \\ & \cdot G_{uv}(s) d_q s - \frac{\Omega_1 t^{\alpha-1}}{\Omega \Gamma_q(\alpha-\xi)} \int_0^1 \left[\int_0^s (s-q\tau)^{(\alpha-\xi-1)} F_{uv}(\tau) d_q\tau \right] d_q K(s) \\ & + \frac{\Gamma_q(\beta) t^{\alpha-1}}{\Omega \Gamma_q(\alpha-\zeta_0)\Gamma_q(\beta-\xi_0)} \int_0^1 (1-qs)^{(\alpha-\zeta_0-1)} F_{uv}(s) d_q s \\ & - \frac{\Gamma_q(\beta) t^{\alpha-1}}{\Omega \Gamma_q(\beta-\zeta)\Gamma_q(\beta-\xi_0)} \int_0^1 \left[\int_0^s (s-q\tau)^{(\beta-\zeta-1)} G_{uv}(\tau) d_q\tau \right] d_q H(s), \end{aligned}$$

and

$$
\begin{aligned}
\mathcal{T}_2(u,v)(t) = & -\frac{1}{\Gamma_q(\beta)}\int_0^t (t-qs)^{(\beta-1)}G_{uv}(s)d_qs + \frac{\Omega_2 t^{\beta-1}}{\Omega\Gamma_q(\alpha-\zeta_0)}\int_0^1 (1-qs)^{(\alpha-\zeta_0-1)} \\
& \cdot F_{uv}(s)d_qs - \frac{\Omega_2 t^{\beta-1}}{\Omega\Gamma_q(\beta-\zeta)}\int_0^1 \left[\int_0^s (s-q\tau)^{(\beta-\zeta-1)}G_{uv}(\tau)d_q\tau\right]d_qH(s) \\
& + \frac{\Gamma_q(\alpha)t^{\beta-1}}{\Omega\Gamma_q(\beta-\xi_0)\Gamma_q(\alpha-\zeta_0)}\int_0^1 (1-qs)^{(\beta-\xi_0-1)}G_{uv}(s)d_qs \\
& - \frac{\Gamma_q(\alpha)t^{\beta-1}}{\Omega\Gamma_q(\alpha-\xi)\Gamma_q(\alpha-\zeta_0)}\int_0^1 \left[\int_0^s (s-q\tau)^{(\alpha-\xi-1)}F_{uv}(\tau)d_q\tau\right]d_qK(s),
\end{aligned}
$$

for $t \in [0,1]$ and $(u,v) \in V$, where

$$
F_{uv}(s) = P(s,u(s),v(s),I_q^{\omega_1}u(s),I_q^{\delta_1}v(s)),\ G_{uv}(s) = Q(s,u(s),v(s),I_q^{\omega_2}u(s),I_q^{\delta_2}v(s)).
$$

According to Lemma 4, it is easy to see that $(u(t),v(t))$ is a solution of the Systems (1)–(2) if and only if $(u(t),v(t))$ is a fixed point of operator $\mathcal{T}$.

At first, we prove the existence and uniqueness theorem of the Systems (1)–(2) by Banach contraction mapping principle.

Theorem 5. *Suppose that* $(\mathcal{H}_1)$ *holds. If* $\Omega \neq 0$, *and*

$$
\Lambda = \Lambda_1 C_3(C_7 + C_9) + \Lambda_2 C_6(C_8 + C_{10}) < 1,
$$

where $\Lambda_1 = \max_{t\in[0,1]}\left\{\sum_{i=1}^4 L_i(t)\right\}$, $\Lambda_2 = \max_{t\in[0,1]}\left\{\sum_{i=1}^4 l_i(t)\right\}$. *Then the Systems (1)–(2) has a unique solution.*

Proof. Let $r > 0$ such that

$$
r = \frac{C_0(C_7+C_9) + \widetilde{C}_0(C_8+C_{10})}{1 - \Lambda_1 C_3(C_7+C_9) - \Lambda_2 C_6(C_8+C_{10})},
$$

where $C_0 = \sup_{t\in[0,1]}|P(t,0,0,0,0)|$, $\widetilde{C}_0 = \sup_{t\in[0,1]}|Q(t,0,0,0,0)|$.

We divide two steps to prove the theorem.

(i) Our first task is to show that $\mathcal{T}$ maps bounded sets into bounded sets in V.

Let $B_r = \{(u,v) \in V, \| (u,v) \|_V \leq r\}$ be a bounded set in V and $(u,v) \in B_r$. Then we show that $\mathcal{T}(B_r) \subset B_r$. By $(\mathcal{H}_1)$ and Lemma 3, we get

$$
\begin{aligned}
|F_{uv}(t)| \leq & |P(t,u(t),v(t),I_q^{\omega_1}u(t),I_q^{\delta_1}v(t)) - P(t,0,0,0,0)| + |P(t,0,0,0,0)| \\
\leq & \left[L_1(t)|u(t)| + L_2(t)|v(t)| + L_3(t)|I_q^{\omega_1}u(t)| + L_4(t)|I_q^{\delta_1}v(t)|\right] + C_0 \\
\leq & \Lambda_1\left[\| u \| + \| v \| + \frac{\| u \|}{\Gamma_q(\omega_1)} + \frac{\| v \|}{\Gamma_q(\delta_1)}\right] + C_0 \\
= & \Lambda_1(C_1 \| u \| + C_2 \| v \|) + C_0 \\
\leq & \Lambda_1 C_3 \| (u,v) \|_V + C_0 \leq \Lambda_1 C_3 r + C_0,
\end{aligned}
$$

similarly,

$$
|G_{uv}(t)| \leq \Lambda_2 C_6 r + \widetilde{C}_0.
$$

According to the expression of operators $\mathcal{T}_1$ and $\mathcal{T}_2$, we obtain

$$
\begin{aligned}
|\mathcal{T}_1(u,v)(t)| \leq & \frac{1}{\Gamma_q(\alpha)} \int_0^t (t-qs)^{(\alpha-1)} |F_{uv}(s)| d_q s \\
& + \frac{\Gamma_q(\beta) t^{\alpha-1}}{|\Omega| \Gamma_q(\beta-\xi_0)\Gamma_q(\beta-\zeta)} \int_0^1 (1-qs)^{(\beta-\xi_0-1)} |G_{uv}(s)| d_q s \\
& \cdot \left| \int_0^1 s^{\beta-\zeta-1} d_q H(s) \right| + \frac{\Gamma_q(\beta) t^{\alpha-1}}{|\Omega| \Gamma_q(\alpha-\xi)\Gamma_q(\beta-\zeta)} \\
& \cdot \left| \int_0^1 \left[\int_0^s (s-q\tau)^{(\alpha-\xi-1)} |F_{uv}(\tau)| d_q \tau \right] d_q K(s) \right| \cdot \left| \int_0^1 s^{\beta-\zeta-1} d_q H(s) \right| \\
& + \frac{\Gamma_q(\beta) t^{\alpha-1}}{|\Omega| \Gamma_q(\alpha-\zeta_0)\Gamma_q(\beta-\xi_0)} \int_0^1 (1-qs)^{(\alpha-\zeta_0-1)} |F_{uv}(s)| d_q s \\
& + \frac{\Gamma_q(\beta) t^{\alpha-1}}{|\Omega| \Gamma_q(\beta-\xi_0)\Gamma_q(\beta-\zeta)} \left| \int_0^1 \left[\int_0^s (s-q\tau)^{(\beta-\zeta-1)} |G_{uv}(\tau)| d_q \tau \right] d_q H(s) \right| \\
\leq & \left[\frac{1}{\Gamma_q(\alpha)} + \frac{\Gamma_q(\beta)}{|\Omega| \Gamma_q(\alpha-\zeta_0)\Gamma_q(\beta-\xi_0)} + \frac{\Gamma_q(\beta)}{|\Omega| \Gamma_q(\alpha-\xi)\Gamma_q(\beta-\zeta)} \right. \\
& \left. \cdot \left| \int_0^1 s^{\beta-\zeta-1} d_q H(s) \right| \cdot \left| \int_0^1 d_q K(s) \right| \right] \int_0^1 |F_{uv}(s)| d_q s \\
& + \left[\frac{\Gamma_q(\beta)}{|\Omega| \Gamma_q(\beta-\xi_0)\Gamma_q(\beta-\zeta)} \cdot \left| \int_0^1 s^{\beta-\zeta-1} d_q H(s) \right| \right. \\
& \left. + \frac{\Gamma_q(\beta)}{|\Omega| \Gamma_q(\beta-\xi_0)\Gamma_q(\beta-\zeta)} \left| \int_0^1 d_q H(s) \right| \right] \int_0^1 |G_{uv}(s)| d_q s,
\end{aligned}
$$

thus, we have

$$\| \mathcal{T}_1(u,v) \| \leq C_7(\Lambda_1 C_3 r + C_0) + C_{10}(\Lambda_2 C_6 r + \widetilde{C}_0), \tag{5}$$

in like wise,

$$\| \mathcal{T}_2(u,v) \| \leq C_9(\Lambda_1 C_3 r + C_0) + C_8(\Lambda_2 C_6 r + \widetilde{C}_0). \tag{6}$$

Using (5) and (6), we obtain that for $\forall (u,v) \in B_r$,

$$
\begin{aligned}
\| \mathcal{T}(u,v) \|_V = & \| \mathcal{T}_1(u,v) \| + \| \mathcal{T}_2(u,v) \| \\
& \leq (\Lambda_1 C_3 r + C_0)(C_7 + C_9) + (\Lambda_2 C_6 r + \widetilde{C}_0)(C_8 + C_{10}) = r,
\end{aligned}
$$

that is $\mathcal{T}(B_r) \subset B_r$.

(ii) The next step is to prove that operator $\mathcal{T}$ is a contraction.

For $(u_i, v_i) \in B_r (i = 1, 2)$, $t \in [0,1]$, we get

$$
\begin{aligned}
&\left|\mathcal{T}_1(u_1,v_1)(t)-\mathcal{T}_1(u_2,v_2)(t)\right| \\
\leq&\frac{1}{\Gamma_q(\alpha)}\int_0^t (t-qs)^{(\alpha-1)}\left|F_{u_1v_1}(s)-F_{u_2v_2}(s)\right|d_qs \\
&+\frac{\Gamma_q(\beta)t^{\alpha-1}}{|\Omega|\Gamma_q(\beta-\xi_0)\Gamma_q(\beta-\zeta)}\int_0^1(1-qs)^{(\beta-\xi_0-1)}\left|G_{u_1v_1}(s)-G_{u_2v_2}(s)\right|d_qs \\
&\cdot\left|\int_0^1 s^{\beta-\zeta-1}d_qH(s)\right| \\
&+\frac{\Gamma_q(\beta)t^{\alpha-1}}{|\Omega|\Gamma_q(\alpha-\xi)\Gamma_q(\beta-\zeta)}\left|\int_0^1\left[\int_0^s(s-q\tau)^{(\alpha-\xi-1)}\left|F_{u_1v_1}(\tau)-F_{u_2v_2}(\tau)\right|d_q\tau\right]d_qK(s)\right| \\
&\cdot\left|\int_0^1 s^{\beta-\zeta-1}d_qH(s)\right|+\frac{\Gamma_q(\beta)t^{\alpha-1}}{|\Omega|\Gamma_q(\alpha-\zeta_0)\Gamma_q(\beta-\xi_0)}\int_0^1(1-qs)^{(\alpha-\zeta_0-1)} \\
&\cdot\left|F_{u_1v_1}(s)-F_{u_2v_2}(s)\right|d_qs+\frac{\Gamma_q(\beta)t^{\alpha-1}}{|\Omega|\Gamma_q(\beta-\xi_0)\Gamma_q(\beta-\zeta)} \\
&\cdot\left|\int_0^1\left[\int_0^s(s-q\tau)^{(\beta-\zeta-1)}\left|G_{u_1v_1}(\tau)-G_{u_2v_2}(\tau)\right|d_q\tau\right]d_qH(s)\right|.
\end{aligned}
\tag{7}
$$

Since

$$
\begin{aligned}
\left|F_{u_1v_1}(s)-F_{u_2v_2}(s)\right| \leq&\Big[L_1(s)\left|u_1(s)-u_2(s)\right|+L_2(s)\left|v_1(s)-v_2(s)\right| \\
&+L_3(s)\left|I_q^{\omega_1}u_1(s)-I_q^{\omega_1}u_2(s)\right|+L_4(s)\left|I_q^{\delta_1}v_1(s)-I_q^{\delta_1}v_2(s)\right|\Big] \\
\leq&\Lambda_1(C_1\parallel u_1-u_2\parallel+C_2\parallel v_1-v_2\parallel) \\
\leq&\Lambda_1C_3\parallel(u_1,v_1)-(u_2,v_2)\parallel_V,
\end{aligned}
$$

and

$$
\left|G_{u_1v_1}(s)-G_{u_2v_2}(s)\right|\leq\Lambda_2C_6\parallel(u_1,v_1)-(u_2,v_2)\parallel_V.
$$

By (7), we have

$$
\begin{aligned}
&\left|\mathcal{T}_1(u_1,v_1)(t)-\mathcal{T}_1(u_2,v_2)(t)\right| \\
\leq&\frac{1}{\Gamma_q(\alpha)}\int_0^1\left|F_{u_1v_1}(s)-F_{u_2v_2}(s)\right|d_qs+\frac{\Gamma_q(\beta)}{|\Omega|\Gamma_q(\alpha-\zeta_0)\Gamma_q(\beta-\xi_0)}\int_0^1\left|F_{u_1v_1}(s)-F_{u_2v_2}(s)\right|d_qs \\
&+\frac{\Gamma_q(\beta)}{|\Omega|\Gamma_q(\beta-\xi_0)\Gamma_q(\beta-\zeta)}\int_0^1\left|G_{u_1v_1}(s)-G_{u_2v_2}(s)\right|d_qs\cdot\left|\int_0^1 s^{\beta-\zeta-1}d_qH(s)\right| \\
&+\frac{\Gamma_q(\beta)}{|\Omega|\Gamma_q(\alpha-\xi)\Gamma_q(\beta-\zeta)}\left|\int_0^1\left[\int_0^1\left|F_{u_1v_1}(\tau)-F_{u_2v_2}(\tau)\right|d_q\tau\right]d_qK(s)\right| \\
&\cdot\left|\int_0^1 s^{\beta-\zeta-1}d_qH(s)\right|+\frac{\Gamma_q(\beta)}{|\Omega|\Gamma_q(\beta-\xi_0)\Gamma_q(\beta-\zeta)} \\
&\cdot\left|\int_0^1\left[\int_0^1\left|G_{u_1v_1}(\tau)-G_{u_2v_2}(\tau)\right|d_q(\tau)\right]d_qH(s)\right| \\
\leq&\Lambda_1C_3\parallel(u_1,v_1)-(u_2,v_2)\parallel_V\left[\frac{1}{\Gamma_q(\alpha)}+\frac{\Gamma_q(\beta)}{|\Omega|\Gamma_q(\alpha-\zeta_0)\Gamma_q(\beta-\xi_0)}\right. \\
&\left.+\frac{\Gamma_q(\beta)}{|\Omega|\Gamma_q(\alpha-\xi)\Gamma_q(\beta-\zeta)}\left|\int_0^1 d_qH(s)\right|\left|\int_0^1 s^{\beta-\zeta-1}d_qH(s)\right|\right] \\
&+\Lambda_2C_6\parallel(u_1,v_1)-(u_2,v_2)\parallel_V\left[\frac{\Gamma_q(\beta)}{|\Omega|\Gamma_q(\beta-\xi_0)\Gamma_q(\beta-\zeta)}\left|\int_0^1 s^{\beta-\zeta-1}d_qH(s)\right|\right. \\
&\left.+\frac{\Gamma_q(\beta)}{|\Omega|\Gamma_q(\beta-\xi_0)\Gamma_q(\beta-\zeta)}\left|\int_0^1 d_qH(s)\right|\right],
\end{aligned}
$$

hence, we deduce

$$\| \mathcal{T}_1(u_1,v_1) - \mathcal{T}_1(u_2,v_2) \| \leq (\Lambda_1 C_3 C_7 + \Lambda_2 C_6 C_{10}) \| (u_1,v_1) - (u_2,v_2) \|_V . \tag{8}$$

For the same way, we can obtain

$$\| \mathcal{T}_2(u_1,v_1) - \mathcal{T}_2(u_2,v_2) \| \leq (\Lambda_1 C_3 C_9 + \Lambda_2 C_6 C_8) \| (u_1,v_1) - (u_2,v_2) \|_V . \tag{9}$$

From (8) and (9), we have

$$\begin{aligned} &\| \mathcal{T}(u_1,v_1) - \mathcal{T}(u_2,v_2) \|_V \\ =&\| \mathcal{T}_1(u_1,v_1) - \mathcal{T}_1(u_2,v_2) \| + \| \mathcal{T}_2(u_1,v_1) - \mathcal{T}_2(u_2,v_2) \| \\ \leq&\Big[\Lambda_1 C_3(C_7 + C_9) + \Lambda_2 C_6(C_8 + C_{10})\Big] \| (u_1,v_1) - (u_2,v_2) \|_V \\ =&\Lambda \| (u_1,v_1) - (u_2,v_2) \|_V . \end{aligned}$$

Due to $\Lambda < 1$, it follows that $\| \mathcal{T}(u_1,v_1) - \mathcal{T}(u_2,v_2) \|_V < \| (u_1,v_1) - (u_2,v_2) \|_V$, so operator $\mathcal{T}$ is a contraction. Hence, we obtain that the Systems (1)–(2) has a unique solution $(u,v) \in B_r$ by using Banach contraction mapping principle. The proof is completed. □

Corollary 1. *Suppose that $(\mathcal{H}_1')$ holds. If $\Omega \neq 0$, and*

$$\Lambda^* = \Lambda_3 C_3(C_7 + C_9) + \Lambda_4 C_6(C_8 + C_{10}) < 1,$$

where $\Lambda_3 = \sum_{i=1}^4 L_i$, $\Lambda_4 = \sum_{i=1}^4 l_i$. Then the Systems (1)–(2) has a unique solution.

Corollary 2. *Suppose that $(\mathcal{H}_1'')$ holds. If $\Omega \neq 0$, and*

$$\widetilde{\Lambda} = \Lambda_5 C_3(C_7 + C_9) + \Lambda_6 C_6(C_8 + C_{10}) < 1,$$

where $\Lambda_5 = \sup_{t\in[0,1]}\{\sum_{i=1}^4 \rho_i(t)\}$, $\Lambda_6 = \sup_{t\in[0,1]}\{\sum_{i=1}^4 \varrho_i(t)\}$. Then the Systems (1)–(2) has a unique solution.

Next, we apply several kinds of fixed point theorems to achieve the existence results of solutions for the Systems (1)–(2).

Theorem 6. *Suppose that $(\mathcal{H}_2)$ and $\Omega \neq 0$ hold. Then the System (1)–(2) has at least one solution.*

Proof. Let $B_R = \{(u,v) \in V, \ \| (u,v) \|_V \leq R\}$, and we denote

$$\begin{aligned} R_1 = \max\Bigg\{&\Bigg[\| c_0 \| + \| c_1 \| (\mathcal{N}_1)^{h_1} + \| c_2 \| (\mathcal{N}_2)^{h_2} + \| c_3 \| \left(\frac{\mathcal{N}_1}{\Gamma_q(\omega_1)}\right)^{h_3} \\ &+ \| c_4 \| \left(\frac{\mathcal{N}_2}{\Gamma_q(\delta_1)}\right)^{h_4}\Bigg] C_7, \Bigg[\| d_0 \| + \| d_1 \| (\mathcal{N}_1)^{m_1} + \| d_2 \| (\mathcal{N}_2)^{m_2} \\ &+ \| d_3 \| \left(\frac{\mathcal{N}_1}{\Gamma_q(\omega_2)}\right)^{m_3} + \| d_4 \| \left(\frac{\mathcal{N}_2}{\Gamma_q(\delta_2)}\right)^{m_4}\Bigg] C_{10}\Bigg\}, \\ R_2 = \max\Bigg\{&\Bigg[\| c_0 \| + \| c_1 \| (\mathcal{N}_1)^{h_1} + \| c_2 \| (\mathcal{N}_2)^{h_2} + \| c_3 \| \left(\frac{\mathcal{N}_1}{\Gamma_q(\omega_1)}\right)^{h_3} \\ &+ \| c_4 \| \left(\frac{\mathcal{N}_2}{\Gamma_q(\delta_1)}\right)^{h_4}\Bigg] C_9, \Bigg[\| d_0 \| + \| d_1 \| (\mathcal{N}_1)^{m_1} + \| d_2 \| (\mathcal{N}_2)^{m_2} \\ &+ \| d_3 \| \left(\frac{\mathcal{N}_1}{\Gamma_q(\omega_2)}\right)^{m_3} + \| d_4 \| \left(\frac{\mathcal{N}_2}{\Gamma_q(\delta_2)}\right)^{m_4}\Bigg] C_8\Bigg\}, \\ R = 2\max&\{R_1, R_2\}. \end{aligned}$$

where there exist $\mathcal{N}_1, \mathcal{N}_2 \in \mathbb{R}$ such that $|u(t)| \leq \mathcal{N}_1$, $|v(t)| \leq \mathcal{N}_2$.

Firstly, we show that $\mathcal{T}$ maps bounded sets into bounded sets in V. For $(u,v) \in B_R$, we obtain

$$\begin{aligned}\| \mathcal{T}_1(u,v) \| \leq & \left[\| c_0 \| + \| c_1 \| (\mathcal{N}_1)^{h_1} + \| c_2 \| (\mathcal{N}_2)^{h_2} + \| c_3 \| \left(\frac{\mathcal{N}_1}{\Gamma_q(\omega_1)} \right)^{h_3} \right.\\ & \left. + \| c_4 \| \left(\frac{\mathcal{N}_2}{\Gamma_q(\delta_1)} \right)^{h_4} \right] C_7 + \left[\| d_0 \| + \| d_1 \| (\mathcal{N}_1)^{m_1} + \| d_2 \| (\mathcal{N}_2)^{m_2} \right.\\ & \left. + \| d_3 \| \left(\frac{\mathcal{N}_1}{\Gamma_q(\omega_2)} \right)^{m_3} + \| d_4 \| \left(\frac{\mathcal{N}_2}{\Gamma_q(\delta_2)} \right)^{m_4} \right] C_{10} \leq 2R_1,\end{aligned}$$

similarly, $\| \mathcal{T}_2(u,v) \| \leq 2R_2$, then

$$\| \mathcal{T}(u,v) \|_V = \| \mathcal{T}_1(u,v) \| + \| \mathcal{T}_2(u,v) \| \leq R, \ \ (u,v) \in B_R,$$

as above, we obtain $\mathcal{T}(B_R) \subset B_R$.

Secondly, we prove that $\mathcal{T}$ maps bounded sets into equicontinuous sets of V. Let $\mathcal{N} = \max\{\mathcal{N}_1, \mathcal{N}_2\}$, for simplicity of presentation, we denote that

$$\begin{aligned}\Psi_{\mathcal{N}} &= \sup_{t \in [0,1]} \left\{ |P(t,u,v,x,y)|, \ |u| \leq \mathcal{N}, \ |v| \leq \mathcal{N}, \ |x| \leq \frac{\mathcal{N}}{\Gamma_q(\omega_1)}, \ |y| \leq \frac{\mathcal{N}}{\Gamma_q(\delta_1)} \right\},\\ \Theta_{\mathcal{N}} &= \sup_{t \in [0,1]} \left\{ |Q(t,u,v,x,y)|, \ |u| \leq \mathcal{N}, \ |v| \leq \mathcal{N}, \ |x| \leq \frac{\mathcal{N}}{\Gamma_q(\omega_2)}, \ |y| \leq \frac{\mathcal{N}}{\Gamma_q(\delta_2)} \right\},\end{aligned}$$

then for $(u,v) \in B_R$ and $t_1, t_2 \in [0,1]$ with $t_1 < t_2$, we have

$$\begin{aligned}& \left| \mathcal{T}_1(u,v)(t_2) - \mathcal{T}_1(u,v)(t_1) \right| \\ \leq & \frac{\Psi_{\mathcal{N}}}{\Gamma_q(\alpha+1)} (t_2^{\alpha} - t_1^{\alpha}) + \Psi_{\mathcal{N}} (t_2^{\alpha-1} - t_1^{\alpha-1}) \left[\frac{\Gamma_q(\beta)}{|\Omega| \Gamma_q(\alpha-\xi) \Gamma_q(\beta-\zeta)} \left| \int_0^1 s^{\beta-\zeta-1} d_q H(s) \right| \right.\\ & \left. \cdot \left| \int_0^1 d_q K(s) \right| + \frac{\Gamma_q(\beta)}{|\Omega| \Gamma_q(\alpha-\zeta_0) \Gamma_q(\beta-\xi_0)} \right] + \Theta_{\mathcal{N}} (t_2^{\alpha-1} - t_1^{\alpha-1}) \left[\frac{\Gamma_q(\beta)}{|\Omega| \Gamma_q(\beta-\xi_0) \Gamma_q(\beta-\zeta)} \right.\\ & \left. \cdot \left| \int_0^1 s^{\beta-\zeta-1} d_q H(s) \right| + \frac{\Gamma_q(\beta)}{|\Omega| \Gamma_q(\beta-\xi_0) \Gamma_q(\beta-\zeta)} \left| \int_0^1 d_q H(s) \right| \right] \\ = & \frac{\Psi_{\mathcal{N}}}{\Gamma_q(\alpha+1)} (t_2^{\alpha} - t_1^{\alpha}) + (\Psi_{\mathcal{N}} C_{11} + \Theta_{\mathcal{N}} C_{10}) (t_2^{\alpha-1} - t_1^{\alpha-1}).\end{aligned}$$

The same can be proved that

$$\left| \mathcal{T}_2(u,v)(t_2) - \mathcal{T}_2(u,v)(t_1) \right| \leq \frac{\Theta_{\mathcal{N}}}{\Gamma_q(\beta+1)} (t_2^{\beta} - t_1^{\beta}) + (\Psi_{\mathcal{N}} C_9 + \Theta_{\mathcal{N}} C_{12}) (t_2^{\beta-1} - t_1^{\beta-1}).$$

Hence, we conclude

$$\left| \mathcal{T}_1(u,v)(t_2) - \mathcal{T}_1(u,v)(t_1) \right| \to 0, \quad \left| \mathcal{T}_2(u,v)(t_2) - \mathcal{T}_2(u,v)(t_1) \right| \to 0,$$

as $t_2 \to t_1$, $(u,v) \in B_R$. Thus, $\mathcal{T}(B_R)$ is equicontinuous. According to the Arzela-Ascoli theorem, it follows that the set $\mathcal{T}(B_R)$ is relatively compact. Therefore, $\mathcal{T}$ is compact on B_R. By Theorem 1, we get that the System (1)–(2) has at least one solution. The proof is completed. □

Theorem 7. *Suppose that* $(\mathcal{H}_1')$ *and* $(\mathcal{H}_3)$ *hold. If* $\Omega \neq 0$*, and*

$$\overline{\Lambda} = \Lambda_3 C_3 \frac{1}{\Gamma_q(\alpha)} + \Lambda_4 C_6 \frac{1}{\Gamma_q(\beta)} < 1.$$

Then the System (1)–(2) has at least one solution.

Proof. Take $r_0 > 0$ such that

$$r_0 \geq (C_7 + C_9) \parallel \sigma_1 \parallel + (C_8 + C_{10}) \parallel \sigma_2 \parallel .$$

Let $B_{r_0} = \{(u,v) \in V, \parallel (u,v) \parallel_V \leq r_0\}$, and let the operators be $\mathcal{X} = (\mathcal{X}_1, \mathcal{X}_2) : B_{r_0} \to V$ and $\mathcal{Y} = (\mathcal{Y}_1, \mathcal{Y}_2) : B_{r_0} \to V$, where $\mathcal{X}_1, \mathcal{X}_2, \mathcal{Y}_1, \mathcal{Y}_2 : B_{r_0} \to U$ are denoted by

$$\begin{aligned}
\mathcal{X}_1(u,v)(t) =& -\frac{1}{\Gamma_q(\alpha)} \int_0^t (t-qs)^{(\alpha-1)} F_{uv}(s) d_q s, \\
\mathcal{Y}_1(u,v)(t) =& \frac{\Omega_1 t^{\alpha-1}}{\Omega \Gamma_q(\beta-\xi_0)} \int_0^1 (1-qs)^{(\beta-\xi_0-1)} G_{uv}(s) d_q s \\
& - \frac{\Omega_1 t^{\alpha-1}}{\Omega \Gamma_q(\alpha-\xi)} \int_0^1 \left[\int_0^s (s-q\tau)^{(\alpha-\xi-1)} F_{uv}(\tau) d_q \tau \right] d_q K(s) \\
& + \frac{\Gamma_q(\beta) t^{\alpha-1}}{\Omega \Gamma_q(\alpha-\zeta_0) \Gamma_q(\beta-\xi_0)} \int_0^1 (1-qs)^{(\alpha-\zeta_0-1)} F_{uv}(s) d_q s \\
& - \frac{\Gamma_q(\beta) t^{\alpha-1}}{\Omega \Gamma_q(\beta-\zeta) \Gamma_q(\beta-\xi_0)} \int_0^1 \left[\int_0^s (s-q\tau)^{(\beta-\zeta-1)} G_{uv}(\tau) d_q \tau \right] d_q H(s), \\
\mathcal{X}_2(u,v)(t) =& -\frac{1}{\Gamma_q(\beta)} \int_0^t (t-qs)^{(\beta-1)} G_{uv}(s) d_q s, \\
\mathcal{Y}_2(u,v)(t) =& \frac{\Omega_2 t^{\beta-1}}{\Omega \Gamma_q(\alpha-\zeta_0)} \int_0^1 (1-qs)^{(\alpha-\zeta_0-1)} F_{uv}(s) d_q s \\
& - \frac{\Omega_2 t^{\beta-1}}{\Omega \Gamma_q(\beta-\zeta)} \int_0^1 \left[\int_0^s (s-q\tau)^{(\beta-\zeta-1)} G_{uv}(\tau) d_q \tau \right] d_q H(s) \\
& + \frac{\Gamma_q(\alpha) t^{\beta-1}}{\Omega \Gamma_q(\alpha-\zeta_0) \Gamma_q(\beta-\xi_0)} \int_0^1 (1-qs)^{(\beta-\xi_0-1)} G_{uv}(s) d_q s \\
& - \frac{\Gamma_q(\alpha) t^{\beta-1}}{\Omega \Gamma_q(\alpha-\xi) \Gamma_q(\alpha-\zeta_0)} \int_0^1 \left[\int_0^s (s-q\tau)^{(\alpha-\xi-1)} F_{uv}(\tau) d_q \tau \right] d_q K(s),
\end{aligned}$$

where $t \in [0,1]$, $(u,v) \in B_{r_0}$. Thus, $\mathcal{T}_1 = \mathcal{X}_1 + \mathcal{Y}_1$, $\mathcal{T}_2 = \mathcal{X}_2 + \mathcal{Y}_2$ and $\mathcal{T} = \mathcal{X} + \mathcal{Y}$.

By $(\mathcal{H}_3)$, we know that $\forall (u_1, v_1), (u_2, v_2) \in B_{r_0}$,

$$\begin{aligned}
&\| \mathcal{X}(u_1,v_1)+\mathcal{Y}(u_2,v_2) \|_V \\
\leq &\| \mathcal{X}(u_1,v_1) \|_V + \| \mathcal{Y}(u_2,v_2) \|_V \\
= &\| \mathcal{X}_1(u_1,v_1) \| + \| \mathcal{X}_2(u_1,v_1) \| + \| \mathcal{Y}_1(u_2,v_2) \| + \| \mathcal{Y}_2(u_2,v_2) \| \\
\leq &\frac{1}{\Gamma_q(\alpha)} \| \sigma_1 \| + \frac{1}{\Gamma_q(\beta)} \| \sigma_2 \| + \| \sigma_1 \| \left[\frac{\Gamma_q(\beta)}{|\Omega|\Gamma_q(\alpha-\xi)\Gamma_q(\beta-\zeta)} \left| \int_0^1 d_qK(s) \right| \right. \\
&\cdot \left| \int_0^1 s^{\beta-\zeta-1} d_qH(s) \right| + \left. \frac{\Gamma_q(\beta)}{|\Omega|\Gamma_q(\alpha-\zeta_0)\Gamma_q(\beta-\xi_0)} \right] + \| \sigma_2 \| \left[\frac{\Gamma_q(\beta)}{|\Omega|\Gamma_q(\beta-\xi_0)\Gamma_q(\beta-\zeta)} \right. \\
&\cdot \left| \int_0^1 s^{\beta-\zeta-1} d_qH(s) \right| + \left. \frac{\Gamma_q(\beta)}{|\Omega|\Gamma_q(\beta-\xi_0)\Gamma_q(\beta-\zeta)} \left| \int_0^1 d_qH(s) \right| \right] + \| \sigma_1 \| \\
&\cdot \left[\frac{\Gamma_q(\alpha)}{|\Omega|\Gamma_q(\alpha-\zeta_0)\Gamma_q(\alpha-\xi)} \left| \int_0^1 s^{\alpha-\xi-1} d_qK(s) \right| + \frac{\Gamma_q(\alpha)}{|\Omega|\Gamma_q(\alpha-\xi)\Gamma_q(\alpha-\zeta_0)} \left| \int_0^1 d_qK(s) \right| \right] \\
&+ \| \sigma_2 \| \left[\frac{\Gamma_q(\alpha)}{|\Omega|\Gamma_q(\alpha-\xi)\Gamma_q(\beta-\zeta)} \left| \int_0^1 d_qH(s) \right| + \frac{\Gamma_q(\alpha)}{|\Omega|\Gamma_q(\alpha-\zeta_0)\Gamma_q(\beta-\xi_0)} \right] \\
= &(C_7+C_9) \| \sigma_1 \| + (C_8+C_{10}) \| \sigma_2 \| \leq r_0.
\end{aligned}$$

For $\forall (u_1,v_1),(u_2,v_2) \in B_{r_0}$, and $\overline{\Lambda} < 1$, we have

$$\begin{aligned}
&\| \mathcal{X}(u_1,v_1) - \mathcal{X}(u_2,v_2) \|_V \\
= &\| \mathcal{X}_1(u_1,v_1) - \mathcal{X}_1(u_2,v_2) \| + \| \mathcal{X}_2(u_1,v_1) - \mathcal{X}_2(u_2,v_2) \| \\
\leq &(\Lambda_3 C_3 \frac{1}{\Gamma_q(\alpha)} + \Lambda_4 C_6 \frac{1}{\Gamma_q(\beta)})(\| u_1 - u_2 \| + \| v_1 - v_2 \|) \\
= &\overline{\Lambda} \| (u_1,v_1) - (u_2,v_2) \|_V \\
< &\| (u_1,v_1) - (u_2,v_2) \|_V .
\end{aligned}$$

Hence, the operator $\mathcal{X}$ is a contraction.

Owing to the continuity of P and Q, $\mathcal{Y}$ is continuous. Next, we need to verify that $\mathcal{Y}$ is a compact operator. Due to $\forall (u,v) \in B_{r_0}$,

$$\| \mathcal{Y}(u,v) \|_V = \| \mathcal{Y}_1(u,v) \| + \| \mathcal{Y}_2(u,v) \| \leq (C_9 + C_{11}) \| \sigma_1 \| + (C_{10} + C_{12}) \| \sigma_2 \|,$$

we have derived that the functions from $\mathcal{Y}$ are uniformly bounded.

We can show the equicontinuous of the functions from $\mathcal{Y}(B_{r_0})$. We denote that

$$\Psi_{r_0} = \sup_{t\in[0,1]} \left\{ |P(t,u,v,x,y)|,\ |u| \leq r_0,\ |v| \leq r_0,\ |x| \leq \frac{r_0}{\Gamma_q(\omega_1)},\ |y| \leq \frac{r_0}{\Gamma_q(\delta_1)} \right\},$$

$$\Theta_{r_0} = \sup_{t\in[0,1]} \left\{ |Q(t,u,v,x,y)|,\ |u| \leq r_0,\ |v| \leq r_0,\ |x| \leq \frac{r_0}{\Gamma_q(\omega_2)},\ |y| \leq \frac{r_0}{\Gamma_q(\delta_2)} \right\},$$

for $(u,v) \in B_{r_0}$ and $t_1, t_2 \in [0,1]$ with $t_1 < t_2$. An argument similar to the one used in the proof of Theorem 6 shows that

$$|\mathcal{Y}_1(u,v)(t_2) - \mathcal{Y}_1(u,v)(t_1)| \to 0, \quad |\mathcal{Y}_2(u,v)(t_2) - \mathcal{Y}_2(u,v)(t_1)| \to 0,$$

as $t_2 \to t_1$, $(u,v) \in B_{r_0}$. Therefore, $\mathcal{Y}(B_{r_0})$ is equicontinuous. Then, we can see that $\mathcal{Y}(B_{r_0})$ is relatively compact. Hence, $\mathcal{Y}$ is compact on B_{r_0}. Using Theorem 2, we know that the System (1)–(2) has at least one solution. The proof is completed. □

Remark 1. *Evidently, we prove that the operator $\mathcal{X}$ is a contraction, the operator $\mathcal{Y}$ is compact and continuous in Theorem 7. An alternative method of proof is to show that $\mathcal{X}$ is compact and continuous, $\mathcal{Y}$ is a contraction, that is Theorem 8.*

Theorem 8. *Suppose that* $(\mathcal{H}_1')$ *and* $(\mathcal{H}_3)$ *hold. If* $\Omega \neq 0$, *and*

$$\widehat{\Lambda} = \Lambda_3 C_3 (C_9 + C_{11}) + \Lambda_4 C_6 (C_8 + C_{10}) < 1.$$

Then the Systems (1)–(2) has at least one solution.

Proof. On the basis of Remark 1, this theorem can be proved by the same method as employed in Theorem 7. □

Theorem 9. *Suppose that* P, Q *are S-Carathéodory functions and* $(\mathcal{H}_4)$ *hold. If* $\Omega \neq 0$, *and*

$$\Xi = \max\{C_{13}, C_{14}\} < 1,$$

where $C_{13} = (j_1 + \frac{j_3}{\Gamma_q(\omega_1)})(C_7 + C_9) + (k_1 + \frac{k_3}{\Gamma_q(\omega_2)})(C_8 + C_{10})$, $C_{14} = (j_2 + \frac{j_4}{\Gamma_q(\delta_1)})(C_7 + C_9) + (k_2 + \frac{k_4}{\Gamma_1(\delta_2)})(C_8 + C_{10})$, *and there exist* A_1, A_2, j_i, $k_i > 0$ *such that* $|r_1(t)| \leq A_1$, $|r_2(t)| \leq A_2$, $|L_i(t)| \leq j_i$ *and* $|l_i(t)| \leq k_i$ $(i = 1, 2, 3, 4)$. *Then, the System (1)–(2) has at least one solution.*

Proof. The main point of Theorem 9 is to prove $\mathcal{T}$ is completely continuous. Firstly, for the continuity of functions P and Q, we obtain that the operator $\mathcal{T}$ is continuous. Secondly, we show that $\mathcal{T}$ is compact.

Let the set $\Phi \subset V$ be bounded. Then, there exist integrable functions $M_1(t)$ and $M_2(t) \in L^1([0,1], \mathbb{R}^+)$ such that for $\forall t \in [0,1]$, $(u,v) \in \Phi$, we have

$$\begin{aligned} &\left|P(t, u(t), v(t), I_q^{\omega_1} u(t), I_q^{\delta_1} v(t))\right| \leq M_1(t), \\ &\left|Q(t, u(t), v(t), I_q^{\omega_2} u(t), I_q^{\delta_2} v(t))\right| \leq M_2(t). \end{aligned}$$

According to the Theorem 5, we get

$$\begin{aligned} |F_{uv}(t)| &= \left|P(t, u(t), v(t), I_q^{\omega_1} u(t), I_q^{\delta_1} v(t))\right| \leq \| M_1 \|_{L^1}, \\ |G_{uv}(t)| &= \left|Q(t, u(t), v(t), I_q^{\omega_2} u(t), I_q^{\delta_2} v(t))\right| \leq \| M_2 \|_{L^1}, \end{aligned}$$

where $\| u \|_{L^1} = \int_0^1 |u(t)| d_q t$.

Then

$$\begin{aligned} \| \mathcal{T}_1(u,v) \| \leq & \| M_1 \|_{L^1} \left[\frac{1}{\Gamma_q(\alpha)} + \frac{\Gamma_q(\beta)}{|\Omega| \Gamma_q(\alpha - \zeta_0) \Gamma_q(\beta - \xi_0)} \right. \\ & \left. + \frac{\Gamma_q(\beta)}{|\Omega| \Gamma_q(\alpha - \xi) \Gamma_q(\beta - \zeta)} \left| \int_0^1 s^{\beta - \zeta - 1} d_q H(s) \right| \cdot \left| \int_0^1 d_q K(s) \right| \right] \\ & + \| M_2 \|_{L^1} \left[\frac{\Gamma_q(\beta)}{|\Omega| \Gamma_q(\beta - \xi_0) \Gamma_q(\beta - \zeta)} \left| \int_0^1 s^{\beta - \zeta - 1} d_q H(s) \right| \right. \\ & \left. + \frac{\Gamma_q(\beta)}{|\Omega| \Gamma_q(\beta - \xi_0) \Gamma_q(\beta - \zeta)} \left| \int_0^1 d_q H(s) \right| \right] \\ = & \| M_1 \|_{L^1} C_7 + \| M_2 \|_{L^1} C_{10}, \end{aligned}$$

in a similar manner, we have

$$\| \mathcal{T}_2(u,v) \| \leq \| M_1 \|_{L^1} C_9 + \| M_2 \|_{L^1} C_8,$$

so $\forall (u,v) \in \Phi$,

$$\| \mathcal{T}(u,v) \|_V = \| \mathcal{T}_1(u,v) \| + \| \mathcal{T}_2(u,v) \| \leq \| M_1 \|_{L^1} (C_7 + C_9) + \| M_2 \|_{L^1} (C_{10} + C_8),$$

therefore, $\mathcal{T}(\Phi)$ is uniformly bounded.

Another step is to show that $\mathcal{T}(\Phi)$ is equicontinuous. Proceeding as in the proof of Theorem 6, we obtain $|\mathcal{T}_1(u,v)(t_2) - \mathcal{T}_1(u,v)(t_1)| \to 0$ and $|\mathcal{T}_2(u,v)(t_2) - \mathcal{T}_2(u,v)(t_1)| \to 0$, as $t_2 \to t_1$, $(u,v) \in \Phi$. Thus, $\mathcal{T}(\Phi)$ is equicontinuous. At the same time, we can also obtain that $\mathcal{T}$ is completely continuous.

Finally, we illustrate that $\mathcal{S} = \{(u,v) \in V,\ (u,v) = \lambda\mathcal{T}(u,v),\ 0 \leq \lambda \leq 1\}$ is bounded. Let $(u,v) \in \mathcal{S}$, then $\forall t \in [0,1]$, we have $u(t) = \lambda\mathcal{T}_1(u,v)(t)$, $v(t) = \lambda\mathcal{T}_2(u,v)(t)$. For simplicity, we denote that

$$\begin{aligned}\hat{F}_{uv}(s) &= r_1(s) + L_1(s)|u(s)| + L_2(s)|v(s)| + L_3(s)|I_q^{\omega_1}u(s)| + L_4(s)|I_q^{\delta_1}v(s)|,\\ \hat{G}_{uv}(s) &= r_2(s) + l_1(s)|u(s)| + l_2(s)|v(s)| + l_3(s)|I_q^{\omega_2}u(s)| + l_4(s)|I_q^{\delta_2}v(s)|,\end{aligned}$$

so,

$$\begin{aligned}\hat{F}_{uv}(s) &\leq A_1 + j_1|u(s)| + j_2|v(s)| + j_3|I_q^{\omega_1}u(s)| + j_4|I_q^{\delta_1}v(s)|,\\ \hat{G}_{uv}(s) &\leq A_2 + k_1|u(s)| + k_2|v(s)| + k_3|I_q^{\omega_2}u(s)| + k_4|I_q^{\delta_2}v(s)|,\end{aligned}$$

then

$$\begin{aligned}|u(t)| \leq& |\mathcal{T}_1(u,v)(t)|\\ \leq& \frac{1}{\Gamma_q(\alpha)}\int_0^t (t-qs)^{(\alpha-1)}\hat{F}_{uv}(s)d_qs + \frac{\Gamma_q(\beta)t^{\alpha-1}}{|\Omega|\Gamma_q(\alpha-\zeta_0)\Gamma_q(\beta-\xi_0)}\int_0^1 (1-qs)^{(\alpha-\zeta_0-1)}\\ &\cdot \hat{F}_{uv}(s)d_qs + \frac{\Gamma_q(\beta)t^{\alpha-1}}{|\Omega|\Gamma_q(\beta-\xi_0)\Gamma_q(\beta-\zeta)}\left|\int_0^1 s^{\beta-\zeta-1}d_qH(s)\right|\int_0^1 (1-qs)^{(\beta-\xi_0-1)}\\ &\cdot \hat{G}_{uv}(s)d_qs + \frac{\Gamma_q(\beta)t^{\alpha-1}}{|\Omega|\Gamma_q(\alpha-\xi)\Gamma_q(\beta-\zeta)}\left|\int_0^1 s^{\beta-\zeta-1}d_qH(s)\right|\left|\int_0^1\left[\int_0^s (s-q\tau)^{(\alpha-\xi-1)}\right.\right.\\ &\left.\left.\cdot \hat{F}_{uv}(\tau)d_q\tau\right]d_qK(s)\right| + \frac{\Gamma_q(\beta)t^{\alpha-1}}{|\Omega|\Gamma_q(\beta-\xi_0)\Gamma_q(\beta-\zeta)}\left|\int_0^1\left[\int_0^s (s-q\tau)^{(\beta-\zeta-1)}\right.\right.\\ &\left.\left.\cdot \hat{G}_{uv}(\tau)d_q\tau\right]d_qH(s)\right|,\end{aligned}$$

hence,

$$\begin{aligned}\| u \| \leq& \int_0^1 |\hat{F}_{uv}(s)|d_qs\left[\frac{1}{\Gamma_q(\alpha)} + \frac{\Gamma_q(\beta)}{|\Omega|\Gamma_q(\alpha-\xi)\Gamma_q(\beta-\zeta)}\left|\int_0^1 s^{\beta-\zeta-1}d_qH(s)\right|\right.\\ &\left.\cdot\left|\int_0^1 d_qK(s)\right| + \frac{\Gamma_a(\beta)}{|\Omega|\Gamma_q(\alpha-\zeta_0)\Gamma_q(\beta-\xi_0)}\right] + \int_0^1 |\hat{G}_{uv}(s)|d_qs\\ &\cdot\left[\frac{\Gamma_q(\beta)}{|\Omega|\Gamma_q(\beta-\xi_0)\Gamma_q(\beta-\zeta)}\cdot\left|\int_0^1 s^{\beta-\zeta-1}d_qH(s)\right|\right.\\ &\left.+\frac{\Gamma_q(\beta)}{|\Omega|\Gamma_q(\beta-\xi_0)\Gamma_q(\beta-\zeta)}\left|\int_0^1 d_qH(s)\right|\right]\\ =&(A_1 + j_1 \| u \| + j_2 \| v \| + \frac{j_3}{\Gamma_q(\omega_1)} \| u \| + \frac{j_4}{\Gamma_q(\delta_1)} \| v \|)C_7\\ &+ (A_2 + k_1 \| u \| + k_2 \| v \| + \frac{k_3}{\Gamma_q(\omega_2)} \| u \| + \frac{k_4}{\Gamma_q(\delta_2)} \| v \|)C_{10}.\end{aligned} \tag{10}$$

Similarly,

$$\begin{aligned}\| v \| \leq& (A_1 + j_1 \| u \| + j_2 \| v \| + \frac{j_3}{\Gamma_q(\omega_1)} \| u \| + \frac{j_4}{\Gamma_q(\delta_1)} \| v \|)C_9\\ &+ (A_2 + k_1 \| u \| + k_2 \| v \| + \frac{k_3}{\Gamma_q(\omega_2)} \| u \| + \frac{k_4}{\Gamma_q(\delta_2)} \| v \|)C_8,\end{aligned} \tag{11}$$

by means of (11) and (12), we have

$$\begin{aligned}\| (u,v) \|_V =& \| u \| + \| v \| \\ &\le A_1(C_7 + C_9) + A_2(C_8 + C_{10}) + C_{13} \| u \| + C_{14} \| v \| \\ &\le A_1(C_7 + C_9) + A_2(C_8 + C_{10}) + \Xi \| (u,v) \|_V .\end{aligned}$$

Due to $\Xi < 1$, we get

$$\| (u,v) \|_V \le \big[A_1(C_7 + C_9) + A_2(C_8 + C_{10})\big](1 - \Xi)^{-1}, \ (u,v) \in \mathcal{S},$$

thus, $\mathcal{S}$ is bounded.

By Theorem 3, it is time to say that the Systems (1)–(2) has at least one solution. Hence, the statements in Theorem 9 are proved. □

Corollary 3. *Suppose that P, Q are S-Carathéodory functions and $(\mathcal{H}_4')$ hold. If $\Omega \neq 0$, and*

$$\hat{\Xi} = \max\{C_{15}, C_{16}\} < 1,$$

where $C_{15} = L_1(C_7 + C_9) + \frac{L_3}{\Gamma_q(\omega_1)}(C_7 + C_9) + l_1(C_8 + C_{10}) + \frac{l_3}{\Gamma_q(\omega_2)}(C_8 + C_{10})$, $C_{16} = L_2(C_7 + C_9) + \frac{L_4}{\Gamma_q(\delta_1)}(C_7 + C_9) + l_2(C_8 + C_{10}) + \frac{l_4}{\Gamma_q(\delta_2)}(C_8 + C_{10})$. *Then the Systems (1)–(2) has at least one solution.*

Theorem 10. *Suppose that P, Q are S-Carathéodory functions and $(\mathcal{H}_5)$ hold. If $\Omega \neq 0$ and there exists $\Pi > 0$ such that*

$$\begin{aligned}&\Big[\| p_0 \| + \| p_1 \| \varphi_1(\Pi) + \| p_2 \| \varphi_2(\Pi) + \| p_3 \| \varphi_3\Big(\frac{\Pi}{\Gamma_q(\omega_1)}\Big) \\ &+ \| p_4 \| \varphi_4\Big(\frac{\Pi}{\Gamma_q(\delta_1)}\Big)\Big](C_7 + C_9) + \Big[\| q_0 \| + \| q_1 \| \eta_1(\Pi) \\ &+ \| q_2 \| \eta_2(\Pi) + \| q_3 \| \eta_3\Big(\frac{\Pi}{\Gamma_q(\omega_2)}\Big) + \| q_4 \| \eta_4\Big(\frac{\Pi}{\Gamma_q(\delta_2)}\Big)\Big](C_8 + C_{10}) < \Pi.\end{aligned}$$

Then the Systems (1)–(2) has at least one solution.

Proof. Let $B_\Pi = \{(u,v) \in V, \| (u,v) \|_V \le \Pi\}$. Firstly, we prove that $\mathcal{T} : B_\Pi \to B_\Pi$. For $(u,v) \in B_\Pi$ and $t \in [0,1]$, we have

$$\begin{aligned}\| \mathcal{T}_1(u,v) \| \le& C_7\Big[\| p_0 \| + \| p_1 \| \varphi_1(\Pi) + \| p_2 \| \varphi_2(\Pi) + \| p_3 \| \varphi_3\Big(\frac{\Pi}{\Gamma_q(\omega_1)}\Big) \\ &+ \| p_4 \| \varphi_4\Big(\frac{\Pi}{\Gamma_q(\delta_1)}\Big)\Big] + C_{10}\Big[\| q_0 \| + \| q_1 \| \eta_1(\Pi) + \| q_2 \| \eta_2(\Pi) \\ &+ \| q_3 \| \eta_3\Big(\frac{\Pi}{\Gamma_q(\omega_2)}\Big) + \| q_4 \| \eta_4\Big(\frac{\Pi}{\Gamma_q(\delta_2)}\Big)\Big],\end{aligned}$$

and

$$\begin{aligned}\| \mathcal{T}_2(u,v) \| \le& C_9\Big[\| p_0 \| + \| p_1 \| \varphi_1(\Pi) + \| p_2 \| \varphi_2(\Pi) + \| p_3 \| \varphi_3\Big(\frac{\Pi}{\Gamma_q(\omega_1)}\Big) \\ &+ \| p_4 \| \varphi_4\Big(\frac{\Pi}{\Gamma_q(\delta_1)}\Big)\Big] + C_8\Big[\| q_0 \| + \| q_1 \| \eta_1(\Pi) + \| q_2 \| \eta_2(\Pi) \\ &+ \| q_3 \| \eta_3\Big(\frac{\Pi}{\Gamma_q(\omega_2)}\Big) + \| q_4 \| \eta_4\Big(\frac{\Pi}{\Gamma_q(\delta_2)}\Big)\Big].\end{aligned}$$

For $(u,v)\in B_\Pi$, we have

$$\begin{aligned}\| \mathcal{T}(u,v) \|_{\mathcal{V}} =& \| \mathcal{T}_1(u,v) \| + \| \mathcal{T}_2(u,v) \| \\ \leq& (C_7+C_9)\Big[\| p_0 \| + \| p_1 \| \varphi_1(\Pi) + \| p_2 \| \varphi_2(\Pi) + \| p_3 \| \varphi_3\Big(\frac{\Pi}{\Gamma_q(\omega_1)}\Big) \\ &+ \| p_4 \| \varphi_4\Big(\frac{\Pi}{\Gamma_q(\delta_1)}\Big)\Big] + (C_{10}+C_8)\Big[\| q_0 \| + \| q_1 \| \eta_1(\Pi) + \| q_2 \| \eta_2(\Pi) \\ &+ \| q_3 \| \eta_3\Big(\frac{\Pi}{\Gamma_q(\omega_2)}\Big) + \| q_4 \| \eta_4\Big(\frac{\Pi}{\Gamma_q(\delta_2)}\Big)\Big] < \Pi.\end{aligned}$$

Consequently, $\mathcal{T}(B_\Pi)\subset B_\Pi$. At the same time, it is easy to see that $\mathcal{T}$ is completely continuous, which can be derived in the same way as employed in Theorem 6.

Furthermore, assume that there exists $(u,v)\in\partial B_\Pi$ such that $(u,v)=\lambda\mathcal{T}(u,v)$ for $\lambda\in(0,1)$, it is simple to get $\| (u,v) \|_{\mathcal{V}} \leq \| \mathcal{T}(u,v) \|_{\mathcal{V}} < \Pi$, this leads to a contradiction for $(u,v)\in\partial B_\Pi$. Therefore, by applying Theorem 4, we deduce that $\mathcal{T}$ has a fixed point $(u,v)\in B_\Pi$, which is a solution of the Systems (1)–(2). The proof is completed. □

4. Application Examples

In this section, for the system with the different nonlinearity terms, some examples are appreciated to illustrate our main results.

We consider the following system of fractional q-difference equations:

$$\begin{cases} (D_q^{\frac{3}{2}}u)(t) + P(t,u(t),v(t),I_q^{\frac{1}{4}}u(t),I_q^{\frac{4}{3}}v(t)) = 0, & t\in(0,1), \\ (D_q^{\frac{5}{2}}v)(t) + Q(t,u(t),v(t),I_q^{\frac{9}{4}}u(t),I_q^{\frac{2}{3}}v(t)) = 0, & t\in(0,1), \end{cases} \tag{12}$$

with the nonlocal BCs

$$\begin{cases} u(0)=0, \quad D_q^{\frac{1}{5}}u(1) = \int_0^1 D_q^{\frac{5}{4}}v(t)d_q(-t^2), \\ v(0)=D_qv(0)=0, \quad D_q^{\frac{7}{5}}v(1) = \int_0^1 D_q^{\frac{1}{6}}u(t)d_qt, \end{cases} \tag{13}$$

where $\alpha=\frac{3}{2}$, $\beta=\frac{5}{2}$, $\omega_1=\frac{1}{4}$, $\delta_1=\frac{4}{3}$, $\omega_2=\frac{9}{4}$, $\delta_2=\frac{2}{3}$, $\zeta_0=\frac{1}{5}$, $\xi_0=\frac{7}{5}$, $\zeta=\frac{5}{4}$, $\xi=\frac{1}{6}$, $q=\frac{1}{2}$, $H(t)=-t^2$, $K(t)=t$.

After a simple caculation, we obtain $\Omega=2.58954375\neq0$, $C_1=1.34100597$, $C_2=2.08201688$, $C_3=C_2$, $C_4=1.92455621$, $C_5=1.79251862$, $C_6=C_4$, $C_7=2.29230629$, $C_8=1.75022309$, $C_9=0.7590784$, $C_{10}=1.42695841$, $C_{11}=1.20641206$, $C_{12}=0.91031044$.

Example 1. *Consider the nonlinear terms of the system*

$$P(t,x_1,x_2,x_3,x_4) = e^t + \frac{t}{36}\cos x_1 - \frac{t}{54}\sin x_2 + \frac{1}{63+t}\arctan x_3 - \frac{x_4}{(t+9)^2},$$

$$Q(t,x_1,x_2,x_3,x_4) = \frac{1}{\sqrt{5+t^2}} - \frac{t}{48}\sin x_1 + \frac{t}{64}\cos x_2 - \frac{1}{36+t}\arctan x_3 + \frac{x_4}{t^2+56},$$

where $t\in[0,1]$, $x_i\in\mathbb{R}$ $(i=1,2,3,4)$. *For* $x_i,y_i\in\mathbb{R}$ $(i=1,2,3,4)$, *we obtain*

$$
\begin{aligned}
&\left|P(t,x_1,x_2,x_3,x_4)-P(t,y_1,y_2,y_3,y_4)\right|\\
&\leq\frac{t}{36}|x_1-y_1|+\frac{t}{54}|x_2-y_2|+\frac{1}{t+63}|x_3-y_3|+\frac{1}{(t+9)^2}|x_4-y_4|\leq\Lambda_1\sum_{i=1}^{4}|x_i-y_i|,\\
&\left|Q(t,x_1,x_2,x_3,x_4)-Q(t,y_1,y_2,y_3,y_4)\right|\\
&\leq\frac{t}{48}|x_1-y_1|+\frac{t}{64}|x_2-y_2|+\frac{1}{t+36}|x_3-y_3|+\frac{1}{56+t^2}|x_4-y_4|\leq\Lambda_2\sum_{i=1}^{4}|x_i-y_i|.
\end{aligned}
$$

It is obvious that $L_1(t)=\frac{t}{36}$, $L_2(t)=\frac{t}{54}$, $L_3(t)=\frac{1}{63+t}$, $L_4(t)=\frac{1}{(t+9)^2}$ and $l_1(t)=\frac{t}{48}$, $l_2(t)=\frac{t}{64}$, $l_3(t)=\frac{1}{36+t}$, $l_4(t)=\frac{1}{t^2+56}$. By a simple computation, we obtain $\Lambda_1=0.07451499$, $\Lambda_2=0.08209325$ and $\Lambda=0.97536897<1$, respectively. By Theorem 5, the Systems (12)–(13) has a unique solution.

Example 2. *Consider the nonlinear terms of the system*

$$
\begin{aligned}
P(t,x_1,x_2,x_3,x_4)=&(3t+5)^2+\frac{t}{30}|x_1|^{\frac{1}{3}}+\frac{t}{t^2+9}\arctan|x_2|^{\frac{1}{2}}+\frac{1}{5+8t}\sin|x_3|^{\frac{3}{4}}\\
&-\frac{1}{(4t+9)^2}|x_4|^{\frac{1}{5}},\\
Q(t,x_1,x_2,x_3,x_4)=&e^t+\frac{1}{46(t+1)}|x_1|^{\frac{3}{5}}+\frac{t}{37}|x_2|^{\frac{1}{6}}+\frac{1}{t+29}\sin|x_3|^{\frac{2}{3}}-8t\arctan|x_4|^{\frac{5}{6}},
\end{aligned}
$$

where $t\in[0,1]$, $x_i\in\mathbb{R}$ $(i=1,2,3,4)$. *It is clear that*

$$
\begin{aligned}
&\left|P(t,x_1,x_2,x_3,x_4)\right|\leq(3t+5)^2+\frac{t}{30}|x_1|^{\frac{1}{3}}+\frac{t}{t^2+9}|x_2|^{\frac{1}{2}}+\frac{1}{8t+5}|x_3|^{\frac{3}{4}}+\frac{1}{(4t+9)^2}|x_4|^{\frac{1}{5}},\\
&\left|Q(t,x_1,x_2,x_3,x_4)\right|\leq e^t+\frac{1}{46(t+1)}|x_1|^{\frac{3}{5}}+\frac{t}{37}|x_2|^{\frac{1}{6}}+\frac{1}{t+29}|x_3|^{\frac{2}{3}}+8t|x_4|^{\frac{5}{6}}.
\end{aligned}
$$

Therefore, the assumption $(\mathcal{H}_2)$ is satisfied with $c_0(t)=(3t+5)^2$, $c_1(t)=\frac{t}{30}$, $c_2(t)=\frac{t}{t^2+9}$, $c_3(t)=\frac{1}{8t+5}$, $c_4(t)=\frac{1}{(4t+9)^2}$, $d_0(t)=e^t$, $d_1(t)=\frac{1}{46(t+1)}$, $d_2(t)=\frac{t}{37}$, $d_3(t)=\frac{1}{t+29}$, and $d_4(t)=8t$. By Theorem 6, the Systems (12)–(13) has at least one solution.

Example 3. *Consider the nonlinear terms of the system*

$$
\begin{aligned}
P(t,x_1,x_2,x_3,x_4)&=e^t+\frac{t}{40}\arctan x_1-\frac{1}{(t+6)^2}\sin x_2+\frac{1}{4(t+9)}\sin x_3-\frac{t}{32}\cos x_4,\\
Q(t,x_1,x_2,x_3,x_4)&=\frac{5t}{6+t^2}-\frac{3t}{56}\cos x_1+\frac{1}{t+28}\sin x_2-\frac{t}{72}\sin^2 x_3+\frac{t}{18}\arctan x_4,
\end{aligned}
$$

where $t\in[0,1]$, $x_i\in\mathbb{R}$ $(i=1,2,3,4)$. *For* $\forall t\in[0,1]$, $x_i,y_i\in\mathbb{R}$ $(i=1,2,3,4)$, *We obtain*

$$
\begin{aligned}
\left|P(t,x_1,x_2,x_3,x_4)-P(t,y_1,y_2,y_3,y_4)\right|\leq&\frac{1}{40}|x_1-y_1|+\frac{1}{36}|x_2-y_2|+\frac{1}{36}|x_3-y_3|\\
&+\frac{1}{32}|x_4-y_4|,\\
\left|Q(t,x_1,x_2,x_3,x_4)-Q(t,y_1,y_2,y_3,y_4)\right|\leq&\frac{3}{56}|x_1-y_1|+\frac{1}{28}|x_2-y_2|+\frac{1}{36}|x_3-y_3|\\
&+\frac{1}{18}|x_4-y_4|,
\end{aligned}
$$

and

$$|P(t,x_1,x_2,x_3,x_4)| \leq e^t + \frac{\pi t}{80} + \frac{1}{(t+6)^2} + \frac{1}{4(t+9)} + \frac{t}{32},$$
$$|Q(t,x_1,x_2,x_3,x_4)| \leq \frac{5t}{6+t^2} + \frac{3t}{56} + \frac{1}{t+28} + \frac{t}{72} + \frac{\pi t}{36},$$

It is obvious that $L_1 = \frac{1}{40}$, $L_2 = \frac{1}{36}, L_3 = \frac{1}{36}$, $L_4 = \frac{1}{32}$, $l_1 = \frac{3}{56}$, $l_2 = \frac{1}{28}$, $l_3 = \frac{1}{36}$, $l_4 = \frac{1}{18}$. By a simple computation, we have $\Lambda_3 = 0.11180556$, $\Lambda_4 = 0.17261905$, and $\overline{\Lambda} = 0.53180725 < 1$, respectively. Therefore, the assumptions $(\mathcal{H}_1')$, and $(\mathcal{H}_3)$ are satisfied, by Theorem 7, the Systems (12)–(13) has at least one solution.

Example 4. *Consider the nonlinear terms of the system*

$$P(t,x_1,x_2,x_3,x_4) = \frac{t}{20} + \frac{6t}{35}\sin x_1 - \frac{1}{4t+9\sqrt{6}}\sin 2x_2,$$
$$Q(t,x_1,x_2,x_3,x_4) = \frac{2t}{3} + \frac{5t}{56}\sin x_1 - \frac{3}{2(7\sqrt{5}+t)}\sin 2x_2,$$

where $t \in [0,1]$, $x_i \in \mathbb{R}$ $(i = 1,2,3,4)$. *It is clear that*

$$|P(t,x_1,x_2,x_3,x_4)| \leq \frac{1}{20} + \frac{6}{35}|x_1| + \frac{2}{9\sqrt{6}}|x_2|,$$

$$|Q(t,x_1,x_2,x_3,x_4)| \leq \frac{2}{3} + \frac{5}{56}|x_1| + \frac{3}{7\sqrt{5}}|x_2|.$$

Hence, $L_1 = \frac{6}{35}$, $L_2 = \frac{2}{9\sqrt{6}}$, $L_3 = L_4 = 0, r_1 = \frac{1}{20}$, $l_1 = \frac{5}{56}$, $l_2 = \frac{3}{7\sqrt{5}}$, $l_3 = l_4 = 0$, $r_2 = \frac{2}{3}$. By a simple computation, we obtain $C_{15} = 0.80677144$, $C_{16} = 0.88577528$, and $\hat{\Xi} = 0.88577528 < 1$, respectively. By Corollary 3, the Systems (12)–(13) has at least one solution.

5. Discussion

The system of fractional q-difference equations plays an extremely crucial role in many fields, such as quantum mechanics, dynamical systems, black holes, mathematical physics equations and so on, see [2,3,5,6,27–30] and the references therein. In this article, we are concerned with the solvability of a system of fractional q-difference equations with Riemann-Stieltjes integrals conditions based on some classical fixed point theorems. We obtain the multiple existence and uniqueness conclusions for the Systems (1)–(2). As a matter of fact, in the limit $q \to 1^-$, the system studied in this paper reduces to the classical system of fractional differential equations. It follows that the results we have discussed are the generalization of the classical analysis, they can extend classical theory in order to expand the range of the possible applications. In the future, we will devote ourselves to finding new inspirations and outstanding methods to overcome the more complex practical problems associated with the system of fractional q-difference equations. Moreover, we will investigate numerical methods for this kind of system.

Author Contributions: Conceptualization, C.Y. and J.W.; methodology, C.Y. and S.W.; validation, C.Y., J.W. and J.L.; formal analysis, J.W.; resources, S.W.; data curation, C.Y.; writing—original draft preparation, S.W.; writing—review and editing, C.Y., J.W. and J.L.; supervision, C.Y. and J.L.; funding acquisition, C.Y., J.W. and J.L. All authors have read and agreed to the published version of the manuscript.

Funding: The research project is supported by National Natural Science Foundation of China (12272011, 11772007), Beijing Natural Science Foundation (Z180005, 1172002), Natural Science Foundation of Hebei Province (A2015208114) and the Foundation of Hebei Education Department (QN2017063).

Data Availability Statement: Not applicable.

Acknowledgments: The authors would like to thank referees for their extraordinary comments, which help to enrich the content of this paper.

Conflicts of Interest: The authors declare no conflict of interest.

References

1. Jackson, F.H. On q-functions and a certain difference operator. *Trans. Roy. Soc. Edin.* **1909**, *46*, 253–281. [CrossRef]
2. Agarwal, R.P. Certain fractional q-integrals and q-derivatives. *Proc. Camb. Philol. Soc.* **1969**, *66*, 365–370. [CrossRef]
3. Al-Salam, W.A. Some fractional q-integrals and q-derivatives. *Proc. Edinburgh. Math. Soc.* **1966**, *15*, 135–140. [CrossRef]
4. Koornwinder, T.H.; Swarttow, R.F. On q-analogues of the Fourier and Hankel transforms. *Proc. Trans. Am. Math. Soc.* **1992**, *333*, 445–461. [CrossRef]
5. Atici, F.M.; Eloe, P.W. Fractional q-calculus on a time scale. *J. Nonlinear Math. Phys.* **2007**, *14*, 341–352. [CrossRef]
6. Rajković, P.M.; Marinković, S.D.; Stanković, M.S. Fractional integrals and derivatives in q-calculus. *Appl. Anal. Discret. Math.* **2007**, *1*, 311–323.
7. Ahmad, B. Boundary-value problems for nonlinear third-order q-difference equations. *Proc. Electron. J. Differ. Equ.* **2011**, *2011*, 107384. [CrossRef]
8. Ahmad, B.; Ntouyas, S.K. Boundary value problems for q-difference inclusions. *Abstr. Appl. Anal.* **2011**, *2011*, 292860. [CrossRef]
9. Ahmad, B.; Alsaedi, A.; Ntouyas, S.K. A study of second-order q-difference equations with boundary conditions. *Adv. Differ. Equ.* **2012**, *2012*, 35. [CrossRef]
10. Ferreira, R.A.C. Nontrivial solutions for fractional q-difference boundary value problems. *Electron. J. Qual. Theory Differ. Equ.* **2010**, *70*, 1–10. [CrossRef]
11. Ferreira, R.A.C. Positive solutions for a class of boundary value problems with fractional q-differences. *Comput. Math. Appl.* **2011**, *61*, 367–373. [CrossRef]
12. Ma, J.; Yang, J. Existence of solutions for multi-point boundary value problem of fractional q-difference equation. *Electron. J. Qual. Theory* **2011**, *92*, 1–10. [CrossRef]
13. Yu, C.; Wang, J. Positive solutions of nonlocal boundary value problem for high-order nonlinear fractional q-difference equations. *Abstr. Appl. Anal.* **2013**, *2013*, 928147. [CrossRef]
14. Liang, S.; Zhang, J. Existence and uniqueness of positive solutions for three-point boundary value problem with fractional q-differences. *J. Appl. Math. Comput.* **2012**, *40*, 277–288. [CrossRef]
15. Yu, C.; Wang, J. Existence of solutions for nonlinear second-order q-difference equations with first-order q-derivatives. *Adv. Differ. Equ.* **2013**, *2013*, 124. [CrossRef]
16. Yu, C.; Li, J.; Wang, J. Existence and uniqueness criteria for nonlinear quantum difference equations with p-Laplacian. *AIMS Math.* **2022**, *7*, 10439–10453. [CrossRef]
17. Wang, Y. Positive solutions for fractional differential equation involving the Riemann-Stieltjes integral conditions with two parameters. *J. Nonlinear Sci. Appl.* **2016**, *9*, 5733–5740. [CrossRef]
18. Ahmad, B.; Alsaedi, A.; Alruwaily, Y. On Riemann-Stieltjes integral boundary value problems of Caputo-Riemann-Liouville type fractional integro-differential. *Filomat* **2020**, *34*, 2723–2738. [CrossRef]
19. Hu, Z.; Liu, W.; Liu, J. Existence of solutions for a coupled system of fractional p-Laplacian equations at resonance. *Adv. Differ. Equ.* **2013**, *2013*, 312. [CrossRef]
20. Zhao, X.; Kang, S.; Gao, Y. Existence and uniqueness of solution to a coupled system of fractional difference equations with nonlocal conditions. *J. Biomath.* **2013**, *28*, 302–306.
21. Hu, L.; Zhang, S. Existence and uniqueness of solutions for a higher-order coupled fractional differential equations at resonance. *Adv. Differ. Equ.* **2015**, *2015*, 202. [CrossRef]
22. Lyu, P.; Vong, S. A linearized and second-order unconditionally convergent scheme for coupled time fractional Klein-Gordon-Schrodinger equation. *Numer. Meth. Part Differ. Equ.* **2018**, *34*, 2153–2179. [CrossRef]
23. Nouara, A.; Amara, A.; Kaslik, E.; Etemad, S.; Rezapour, S.; Martinez, F.; Kaabar, M.K. A study on multiterm hybrid multi-order fractional boundary value problem coupled with its stability analysis of Ulam-Hyers type. *Adv. Differ. Equ.* **2021**, *2021*, 343. [CrossRef]
24. Tudorache, A.; Luca, R. Positive solutions for a system of Riemann-Liouville fractional boundary value problems with p-Laplacian operators. *Adv. Differ. Equ.* **2020**, *2020*, 292. [CrossRef]
25. Luca, R. On a system of Riemann-Liouville fractional differential equations with coupled nonlocal boundary conditions. *Adv. Differ. Equ.* **2021**, *2021*, 134. [CrossRef]
26. Guo, D. *Nonlinear Functional Analysis*; Shandong Science and Technology Press: Jinan, China, 2001; pp. 1–559.

27. Page, D.N. Information in black hole radiation. *Phys. Rev. Lett.* **1993**, *71*, 3743–3746. [CrossRef]
28. Youm, D. *Q*-deformed conformal quantum mechanics. *Phys. Rev. D* **2000**, *62*, 276–284. [CrossRef]
29. Lavagno, A.; Swamy, P.N. *Q*-deformed structures and nonextensive statistics: A comparative study. *Physica A* **2002**, *305*, 310–315. [CrossRef]
30. Annaby, M.H.; Mansour, Z.S. *Q*-Fractional Calculus and Equations. In *Lecture Notes in Mathematics 2056*; Springer: Berlin, Germany, 2012; pp. 1–318.

MDPI
St. Alban-Anlage 66
4052 Basel
Switzerland
Tel. +41 61 683 77 34
Fax +41 61 302 89 18
www.mdpi.com

Fractal and Fractional Editorial Office
E-mail: fractalfract@mdpi.com
www.mdpi.com/journal/fractalfract

MDPI

www.ingramcontent.com/pod-product-compliance
Lightning Source LLC
LaVergne TN
LVHW070142100526
838202LV00015B/1874